PERIOD DETAILS

KT-173-224

*Wallpapers used on the endpapers
and on pages 1, 3, 4 & 5 are from
The Temple Newsam Collection
from Zoffany.*

JUDITH AND MARTIN MILLER

PERIOD DETAILS

MITCHELL BEAZLEY

PERIOD DETAILS
A SOURCEBOOK FOR HOUSE RESTORATION
JUDITH AND MARTIN MILLER
Chief Contributor **Margaret Crowther**
Consultant in America **Fayal Greene**
Kitchens chapter **Robin Murrell**

Edited and designed by Mitchell Beazley International Ltd,
Michelin House
81 Fulham Road
London SW3 6RB

Project Manager and Senior Executive Art Editor
Jacqui Small
Executive Editor **Robert Saxton**
Assistant Art Editor **Prue Bucknall**
Production **Philip Collyer**

Copyright © Mitchell Beazley International Ltd 1987
Text and illustrations © MJM Publishing Projects Ltd 1987
No part of this work may be reproduced or utilized in any form by
any means, electronic or mechanical, including photocopying,
recording or by any information storage and retrieval system, without
the prior written permission of the publishers.
Reprinted 1987, 1988 twice, 1989, 1990
Paperback edition 1993

BRITISH LIBRARY CATALOGUING IN PUBLICATION DATA

Miller, Judith H.
        Period details: a sourcebook for house restoration.
        I. Dwellings --- Conservation and restoration
        I. Title II. Miller, Martin, 1946-
        728.3'028'8 NA7125

        ISBN 1-85732-043-3

The publishers have made every effort to ensure that all instructions
given in this book are accurate and safe, but they cannot accept
liability for any resulting injury, damage or loss to either person or
property whether direct or consequential and howsoever arising.
The authors and publishers will be grateful for any information
which will assist them in keeping future editions up to date.

Typeset by *Bookworm Typesetting, Manchester*
Colour reproduction by *Novacolour Ltd, Birmingham*
Printed in Hong Kong

Cover photograph by James Merrell

Code letters in picture captions refer to the photographic
sources listed on page 191.

CONTENTS

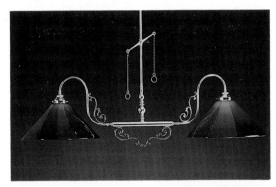

The past decade has seen a remarkable and accelerating interest in period houses – in the idea of living in a home with traditional character. Property advertisements with their emphasis on "authentically restored" – rather than "completely modernized" – show that estate agents are more alive to this fundamental change of taste than are many architects and interior designers.

In Britain, the post-war impulse to replace the old with the new destroyed many good period houses, especially in the inner cities, and replaced them with characterless blocks of flats. But we are fortunate still to have about 6 million buildings built before 1920. This book deals with the restoration of a very wide range of such buildings from 16th-century farm cottages to Georgian terraces and Victorian mews. We made a decision to concentrate not on the grand houses which are well documented in other books but on the kind of old houses that are on the market.

As our principal aim is to convey a sense of what looks right in terms of period style, the book is highly visual, with nearly a thousand photographs dealing with everything from skirting boards to panelling, from door knobs to kitchens.

Successful restoration begins with understanding your house as a total entity. To do this, you have to read, to look and to listen. There are excellent books on old houses, many wonderful museums and individual experts in various periods who can help with dating and explaining how houses were used – an important aspect of understanding the house. Was the original drawing room in your house on the first floor? Was the kitchen in the basement? Where were the original fireplaces? Which was the master bedroom?

All questions to be answered before rushing to the nearest salvage yard. It is also important to educate your eye. Buy magazines; build up files of images; ask to see your neighbour's cornicing; approach a local historical society for visual reference. All of this will build up an idea of what is right historically but also what is pleasing to you. You, after all, have to live in the house. You have to like it.

With tradition goes responsibility. Luckily, people now realize we have as much duty to preserve and restore a terrace of houses built in 1870 as we do to maintain a Queen Anne manor house. Both contribute to the heritage of our country. On a more personal note, creating a period feel, finding out what should be in a house, what colour the walls would have been, is, quite simply, fun. It can, of course, also be profitable, as shown by the steadily rising values of well-restored houses. One of the most important things to realize is that houses evolve over the centuries. Sometimes the purist can be wrong. The Georgians sometimes adapted Elizabethan houses and the much-maligned Victorians often created interesting additions to Adam-inspired houses (as at Newby Hall). Such developments and variations, additions and oddities, can give the house the acceptable fallibility of an old friend.

Not many of us want to live in a museum. We want our house to reflect our life style. It is important that it should look as though it has been lived in by successive generations. One of our own restorations, which is featured in this book, is Chilston Park at Lenham in Kent. It is basically an Elizabethan house built round a central courtyard. It was thought old-fashioned in the 1720s when the then owner had it re-facaded with a classical Georgian facade but interestingly reused the old bricks. Many other improvements were made through the years and in 1880 the owners introduced a grand staircase hall which filled in the central courtyard. Though a purist would abhor the result, the house has a pleasing feel with its combination of wonderful details from both the Georgian and Victorian periods. This is why I prefer restoration to strict period replacement where possible. Old plaster and woodwork have slight imperfections, and too perfect a finish can be cold, even inhuman. Our affection for an old house should involve a respect for its past. It is important to understand the way it has evolved and to accept the authenticity of this evolution even if it means that the house is not an example of one particular period.

We hope this book goes some way to showing the diversity and delight of period details. The joy of owning an old house and restoring it can become a positive obsession. We have ourselves converted houses as diverse as a 15th-century manor house in Kent which has a 19th-century Pugin-designed concert hall attached, a mid 17th-century stone house in West Sussex, a 19th-century farm labourer's cottage in the Scottish borders, an Arts and Crafts country house in Kent and an Art Deco flat in London. All had their distinctive attractions and we learned a great deal from each one. A period house does not have to be large or grand to be interesting but it does need to have a sense of overall cohesion. If you know how to see and understand their essential character, houses themselves dictate their individual styles. The joy of seeing one's own research reflected in the overall detail of a house is reward enough for all the hard work of restoration.

JUDITH MILLER

When we think of the domestic architecture of the past, we think first and foremost of grand country houses and town mansions – buildings that are rightly famous thanks to their distinguished history and in many cases to their association with a particular architect, such as Inigo Jones or Robert Adam. Of course, few of us can afford to live in homes of such grandeur and esteem. Even if our houses have a long history, they were mostly built not as conscious works of art but principally as homes, in which any one of a thousand daily routines may take place.

Nevertheless, most smaller period houses owe something to the taste of their age, and in this the great architects and patrons were the innovators. Fashions gradually filtered down the social scale. Classical ornamentation and Neo-Gothic detailing – to take just two examples – enjoyed their various waves of popularity not only in the homes of the fashionably rich but also in thousands of proud but unpretentious dwellings built for the prosperous middle classes. The middling professional man, building a home for his family, wished to convey something of his standing in the community by aping what was smart in aristocratic circles. A display of wealth was a good advertisement for his business. But at the same time a careful economy would be observed: display was all very well, in moderation. These feelings, or something like them, have been prevalent for centuries. Despite financial restraints there remains today a great reserve of fine period homes, well constructed, simply and appropriately ornamented, in which it was – and still is – a pleasure to live.

If modest houses reflect the buildings put up by the great, they usually do so after a time-lag, and often in curious ways. Style begins either with a new solution to a practical problem or, more usually from 1550 to the end of the 19th century, with a fashion. The staying power of a fashion generally depends on how compatible it is with practical requirements. This is why classical features, based on the architecture of the ancient Greeks or Romans, appear over such a long period: they were so well adapted to so many different buildings. A practical equation which could be applied to anything from a palace to a potting shed, classical design remains a constant. However, this consistency should not be exaggerated. As constants go, it is a very variable one. Classicism has meant many different things to different generations, departing far from the original intentions in Greece or Rome.

In the absence of documentary evidence, dating a house depends on careful detective work based on materials, layout and architectural and stylistic features. Sometimes the house will incorporate a date-stone, but this should be treated with suspicion. It may denote a date of repair or refurbishment, or even commemorate a marriage. Occasionally, such date-stones have been imported from another building altogether.

Architectural style is more reliable as a dating guide, but you should always bear in mind that the pace of change varied in different regions. Generally, fashions started in the towns and spread out slowly to the countryside. However, the grander rural homes usually flaunted the latest fashions some time before smaller rural houses caught up with the trends. The picture is complicated further by regional variations. If the dating of an old house proves difficult, your local history society will usually help.

Many period homes have evolved by a process of gradual "improvement" and accretion. Modern extensions are generally thought to be unfortunate unless they are built in a style that makes some concessions to history. However, an early house that has been modified over the centuries so that it manifests a wide range of historic styles, different but compatible, may be regarded as no less "authentic" than a house that remains as it was originally conceived. This is largely a matter of personal taste. Some people prefer the charm of the piecemeal. Others like their homes to be homogeneous. Even the recent trend towards "facadism" – preserving or restoring the facade while leaving the remainder of the building out of period – is not without its supporters.

Period features will sometimes be found during the course of refurbishment – perhaps a door or window opening that comes to light after you have removed plaster from a wall. In such cases, you might consider halting the work in progress and changing your plans to incorporate the newly discovered feature.

Decoration, furnishings and interior layout cannot easily be separated in period homes. Each aspect of an interior emerged in association with all other aspects of the house – all of which need to be taken into account when refurbishing in period style. For example, it is not enough to ensure that you have the furniture of the appropriate period. Plasterwork, doorcases, chimneypieces and doors are equally important as indexes of style, and the taste of a period can be obliterated from a room simply by a mistake in the choice of one or more of these elements. On the other hand, certain compromises are inevitable.

Few people would want to sacrifice every modern convenience for the sake of total historic authenticity. However passionately you feel about your period home, there is no reason to go back to unhealthy sanitation, inconvenient cooking facilities, primitive bathrooms or icy-cold draughts. Fortunately, up-to-date fittings are often available either in traditional styles or in low-key modern styles that will not clash with a historic interior. This need for sensible compromise is highlighted most clearly in the case of working buildings that have been converted for living in. Barns, schoolhouses, toll houses, chapels, churches, windmills and railway buildings that have been adapted as homes have all required radical alteration, with decisions taken at every turn as to what to change and what to leave intact. Similar compromises have to be made by those of us who live in large houses that have been divided up into separate units, with the addition of new internal walls. In such circumstances the attempt to create a period feel has to be judged with

2

1 This modest but very fine example of early 19thC architecture is in Islington, north London. In its symmetry, and its ornamental detailing on the fanlight and lower windows, it exhibits the characteristic features of the era.

2 Detail is all-important in period homes: the fireback is no less interesting or significant than the front door. This particular example is a modern reproduction of a 16thC original.

page 7: An example of true conservation in Roslyn, Long Island, New York, this house built in 1836 has been painstakingly restored with absolute attention to detail both outside and inside.

especial care: authentic features such as mouldings, friezes and fireplaces may be out of proportion in rooms that have been reduced in size.

Until the 17th century most houses in Britain were made of wood. It was the holocaust of the Great Fire of London in 1666, more than any other influence, that encouraged the use of non-flammable materials. However, wood remained cheap, easily accessible, and economic to work. Carpenters could build more quickly than stone masons; and in wooded areas without suitable building stone, wood was in any case the obvious choice. The timber-framed house thus remained a familiar feature of domestic architecture.

In Britain the typical all-timber or infill house of around 1200 had a central hall rising through two stories, flanked by parlour and solar on one side and servants' quarters on the other. The parlour was the sitting room for the master of the house; the solar was the family's private bedroom.

The timber-frame house developed from that functionally simple structure, the barn. As in a cathedral, the principle was to provide a framework that through its members carries the weight of the roof to the ground. The walls of these houses are infill only; they bear no direct load. At its simplest, the system consists of two wooden members forming together a gable frame, which is linked by a ridge beam to another, similar frame. Together the frames support the skin of roof and wall. This type of house, in some regions known as the "cruck" house, existed by 1300.

By the middle of the 14th century the disposition of rooms and people in the house was well established. The centre of the structure, the heart of community life, was the hall. Here all ate together, whether it was the lord of the manor and his servants or the yeoman farmer and his farmhands. The staff quarters lay to one side of the hall, and on the other side a single room at

ground and first-floor level gave privacy to the master and mistress. The fireplace, its smoke rising to a hole in the hall roof, was a symbol of the communal, cheek-by-jowl way of living. Interestingly, the open fire persisted in ordinary dwelling places long after the technology of chimneys and fireplaces had been introduced. Loyalty to the open fire as a gathering point in life preserved it in Britain into the 15th century, serving to illustrate an important aspect of the way in which houses developed over the centuries. Technological advances, at least initially, are not always potent enough to overcome the emotional and psychological needs answered by an earlier arrangement. Thus, in an age of central heating, the hearth – even if it throws out no heat – serves an important function as a focal point and symbol of family warmth. And indeed, the pleasure of living in a period home surrounded by period details is similarly based on evocations of traditionalism, community and historical continuity.

The frame house was not without possibilities for decoration. Within the main rectangle of the wooden frame, uprights of wood might be placed close together, between which would be set the infill of wattle and daub or plaster – or brick in the 15th century. This sort of essentially decorative infill (known as "close stud-work") is typical of the south and eastern regions of England. The quantity of wood used was an index of the town's prosperity. Brick too, replacing the plaster, was a sign of wealth, which could be indicated additionally by carving on the wooden frame.

The structural evolution of the house from shelter to home was reflected in the parallel evolution of interior furnishings and fittings. Floors that had previously been laid with mud or rushes were now paved with stone, tiles or brick. The comfort of a wealthy

15th-century home was further improved by replacing the central hearth by a wall fireplace which provided an effective means of warming the solar. In towns, where land was at a premium, the fireplaces and chimneys were arranged in such a way that the maximum number of people would receive heat efficiently – a feature that looks forward to the modern expectations we have of a house and how it should work.

Painted designs on interior walls were a popular type of decoration. In the houses of the great, from the 14th century on, tapestries were used as wallcoverings – usually over just the upper part of walls. The lower half would sometimes be wainscoted with overlapping vertical timbers, a style which developed into the characteristic linenfold panelling of the Tudor period – ribbed woodwork giving the impression of pleated cloth. Heraldic tapestries, hung on pegs, frequently decorated the wall behind the high table. Owners of more modest dwellings contented themselves with painted linen hangings.

Stone, of course, had been used for castles, palaces and cathedrals in Britain throughout the 14th and 15th centuries. It resisted fire, as well as assault. However, it was expensive to work, even in areas where stone was plentiful – such as the Cotswolds. There were some stone houses in England as early as the 13th century, but only in the late 15th century did stone come into general use, largely as an expression of national prosperity at that period. The overall planning of a stone house was not very different from that of a frame house – except when the building served a defensive role. However, stone offered greater scope for design. Projecting structures known as "oriels" are sometimes found nestling in the angle between the main hall and a private wing. Later the term "oriel" came to be applied to a projecting window, which developed with the passage of time into the bay window.

1 *An infill of wattle-and-daub was common in timber-frame houses. The traditional thin laths of mud and plaster can be either painted or left natural. Brick infill was more common in grander houses.*

2 *The Van Nostrand Starkins house in Roslyn, Long Island, shows the functional quality of building of the late 17thC.*

3 *A 19thC reconstruction porch added to a 15thC house. The timber framing is in this case purely ornamental.*

4 *This 15thC weaver's house is a good example of timber framing. It is not surprising that many such houses have undergone alteration over the* years. Here, the introduction of oriel windows, copied from stones houses of the period, has augmented the basic dwelling.

CG

5

8

5-7 Timber-framed construction was a popular method of building well into the 17thC, and brick with timber infill was again used in the 19th and 20thC. These pictures of a 17thC house belie the fact that much of the building is Edwardian.

8, *9* These garden features from the same house sustain the nostalgic mood outdoors.

10 Smallhythe Place in Kent, now owned by The National Trust and opened as the Ellen Terry Museum, is an early 16thC half-timbered house, with the typical overhanging (jetted) upper storey.

9

6

7

10

1

2

In this early period houses tended to grow haphazardly, rather than following a fixed and conscious design. But with the turn of the 16th century we find new ideas and design forces penetrating Britain from France and Italy. This was the first wave of influence from the great European Renaissance, whose heartland was Italy. During the early 15th century, centred on Florence, there was a tremendous revival of interest in the art, literature and design of the ancient Romans, and this had an important effect on the work of Italian architects – initially just in public architecture but later in the grander sorts of houses. Classical columns, pilasters (shallow columns applied to wall surfaces) and rounded arches were incorporated in buildings notable for their symmetry and harmonious proportion. The columns, and the distinctive decorative entablatures which they supported, were categorized according to the ancient system of classical "Orders", depending on the precise decorative arrangement. Columns could be solid-looking Doric, fluted Ionic or delicate Corinthian, with its acanthus-leaved capital. Composite combined Ionic volutes (scrolls) with Corinthian acanthus leaves.

Tudor England, in its anti-papal isolation, was initially not well-placed to be influenced by Renaissance architecture. By the early 16th century a few aristocratic houses had acquired Italianate flourishes, but in a superficial manner only, without radically affecting native English styles. However, the

1, 2, 3 The influence of classical architecture from the 16thC onwards cannot be overemphasized. These examples of the proud use of

classical features are a magnificent classical porch of a Carolean house in Kent (1) and a Port Washington (New York) house of 1735.

impact of Renaissance architecture was precipitated by the appearance in 1563 of the first English architectural treatise, John Shute's *The First and Chief Groundes of Architecture*, inspired by an architectural study tour of Italy. Before long, the classical Orders which Shute describes were being used as decoration, and as badges of high fashion, on the facades of English country houses such as Longleat in Wiltshire (1546–80) and Burghley House in Northamptonshire.

The significance of these developments for the future of architecture in Britain and America cannot be overestimated. Every column, architrave and frieze on the simplest terraced house of the 18th or 19th centuries has come to be there, indirectly, as a result of the Renaissance passion to recover the glory of Rome in its heyday.

By the mid-16th century many small manor houses were being built entirely of brick, rather than of timber with a brick infill. The wonder of the age was Hampton Court Palace, expensively built in brick and enriched with terracotta ornament and towering chimneystacks, and setting a fashion which persisted through the century. Even in relatively modest houses a complex skyline of spiralling chimneypots may be found, loudly proclaiming the owner's taste and discernment. Tudor brickwork, together with a complex silhouette of stacks and gables and a garden full of topiary, were to become a powerful archetype, an "ideal home", copied in the earlier 20th century not only in new country houses but also in the unlikely setting of suburbia.

The first decades of the 17th century saw a more thorough-going classicism emerge. This was the achievement of one man, Inigo Jones (1573–1652), who was the first architect to bring back to England the purer forms of classical architecture which designers like Robert Smythson had handled half-comprehendingly a generation before.

3

4

Jones was entirely at home in the world of classical allusions, and unlike most of his fellow designers actually went to Italy. There he encountered the work of Andrea Palladio. The greatest Italian architect of the 16th century, Palladio had revived and revised the architectural theory of the Roman writer Vitruvius, whose *Five Books of Architecture* describes various building types which Palladio adapted – notably the villa. The Roman villa was a spreading country house with attendant farm buildings. Palladio turned it into a classical pavilion – compact, elegant and well-suited to life in the country estates of the Veneto, the area around Venice where Palladio chiefly worked. It was these buildings which Inigo Jones saw and copied on his return to England – with the help of Palladio's own publication, *The Four Books of Architecture*.

In London, the Queen's House, Greenwich, built as a small-scale retreat for Queen Anne of Denmark, is the single pre-eminent domestic building which we know for certain that Jones designed. Incorporating many innovative features derived from Italy, this is the first classical English villa, ancestor of so many other villas, large and small, designed for daily life. The ground floor is rusticated – finished with cut stone resembling monumental blocks. Each window is marked by a dropped keystone, which lends weight and individuality to the composition. The upper storey is contrastingly lighter, its smooth wall surface broken by windows beneath which there are blind balustrades – that is, balustrades applied to the wall. These prepare the eye for the central loggia taken from Palladio's designs and intended originally for warmer southern climates. The groundplan is simple, effective and adapted to the purposes of the house. The whole is a very modern building in many ways: perhaps the first English house in which a 20th-century spectator can sense the contact between his own world and that of the original occupants.

4 Despite the infiltration of classical influence, many English houses retained a particularly English style. There is nothing Italianate about this stone manor house built in 1640 and substantially enlarged in the mid 19thC. S&P

5 Melton Constable Hall in Norfolk, designed by Sir Christopher Wren and built between 1644 and 1670, shows an impressive English interpretation of classical styles, with its great central pediment echoed by the pedimented doorway, and its hipped roof. The house is reminiscent of the work of Sir Roger Pratt, a follower of Inigo Jones. S&P

6 This house near Hampton Court Palace illustrates the continuing appeal of classicism in the late 19thC, when pilasters, balconies and classical swags were added.

7 The delight in the classical facade was to last in England well into the 18thC. Chilston Park, Kent, was built in the 16thC with a central three-storey porch-turret and a central courtyard. In 1728 the owners refaced the house in refined classical taste.

6

5

7

first floor indicated the main living level – the *piano nobile*, raised above the noise and dirt of the street and inaccessible to thieves or enemies. This idea too was derived from Italian practice – in 16th-century Italy the ground floor of a house or palace was heavily defended against the street, with small dark windows.

Covent Garden points forward to modern city design. From the late 17th to the early 20th century grand private houses, and their more modest urban neighbours, conform to the same basic principles of planning, the grand facade suggesting a single splendid building but concealing behind it practical housing for the upper or middle classes.

This innovative concept of housing took root gradually. For some time houses continued to be built in brick, and followed designs closer to those prevalent in Holland than those in Italy. Culturally, England and Holland had much in common in the 17th century. Both were Protestant mercantile countries, opposed to the Catholic might of Spain and the Holy Roman Empire. Trade links were close. Later in the century there was to be rivalry ending in open war. Before this crisis, however, there was considerable enthusiasm in England for the Dutch style of building – the redbrick steep-gabled style favoured by the burghers of Amsterdam and Antwerp. Via England, the Dutch style also travelled to colonial America where it emerged in a modified form.

The successor upon whom Jones's mantle fell was Sir Roger Pratt, a gentleman dilettante architect who built some of the most graceful and lovely houses of the 17th century. Notable among his achievements was the great house of Coleshill in Oxfordshire (now destroyed), where he successfully adapted Palladian designs to the

Many 18th- and 19th-century houses are arranged around a square – an aspect of city planning that originated in the 17th century. In this too Inigo Jones was involved. The first fully worked out and planned piazza in Britain is that of Covent Garden, for which Jones designed the church, St Paul's. This square reveals a new approach to urban living. It follows the principles of Italian city design by allowing light and air to reach individual houses. Designed to look like a series of grand palaces set around the central space, it in fact provided behind its great facades a number of houses of more modest scale. The tall windows on the

4 Regional variations should always be taken into account by anyone restoring a period house. This English street of the Georgian age is characterized by knapped flintwork, some of which hides earlier timber-framed dwellings.

5,6 These beautifully restored houses in Roslyn, Long Island, New York, were built in the mid-1830s but owe much to the previous century. The interest in vernacular architecture is an interesting trend in conservation today.

1 In small English country towns such as Mayfield, Sussex, houses and cottages from the 15th to the 19thC present a delightfully varied picture. Many early houses have been refaced – particularly with weatherboarding in the mid-18thC.

2 This William and Mary red brick house is actually timber-framed. This is unusual at this date: the explanation is that the owner was a timber merchant.

3 Another timber-framed house – a 17thC example, hung with tiles.

British climate and way of life. Here he used for the first time the double-pile plan, in which two series of rooms run in parallel through the house, linked by a transverse corridor. This system had the distinct advantage of supplying each room with fine windows and therefore good lighting. A similar house, built twenty years later, is Belton in Lincolnshire, where the plan is H-shaped. Both these houses are grand, but they served, well into the 18th century, as models for many smaller and simpler buildings. The steep roof lined with dormer windows, the regular facade around a simple centrepiece, the use of classical detailing in a facade unenriched by columns – all were elements easily adaptable to modest gentlemen's houses.

The archetypal English house at the close of the 17th century (exemplified by Fenton House, Hampstead) is built of brick dressed with stone – that is, stone was used for the doorcase and other architectural details. The windows were quite tall and narrow, with a lean elegant line encouraged by the innovation of the sash window. The roof was high-pitched – perhaps with a wooden balustrade replacing the stone balustrade of grander homes. Of course, this pattern was not followed rigidly. More sophisticated houses (such as Mompesson House in the Cathedral Close at Salisbury) might have a richly carved broken pediment and coat of arms above the door, with stonework and other fine details on the facade adding a sense of density and brilliance to the house. Elegant gate piers and railings might also play their part, strengthening the effect of gracious formality. Such houses, belonging to doctors, lawyers, men of property and gentlemen, were to be found in both city and country. In a townhouse of this period, however grand or simple the facade, the general disposition of rooms and the style of life within them would tend to conform to a certain pattern. The standard format for the single-fronted row house was developed in the early 18th century and held sway in modified form until the early 20th. It featured a front door and hallway at one side and two rooms, one behind the other, at the other side. This kind of house, which ranged over three or four floors with a basement, became known as the "universal plan". Variations on the theme ranged from the simple to the relatively grand.

In double-fronted houses the prevalent plan was based on a square block divided into four rooms, arranged two deep in pairs either side of a central hall or reception area. Front and back rooms were linked by interconnecting doors. The hall led directly to the staircase, which would often be flanked by columns or pilasters to emphasize its importance. Stairs became increasingly gracious, but were still in wood, except in the grander houses, where wrought-iron balustrades in swirling patterns might be found.

5

6

In complete contrast to such practical developments in the planning of townhouses, the early years of the 18th century also saw the fashion for Baroque design at its height. The importance of this theatrical style for the average house is limited. The hallmarks of Baroque are grandeur of scale and a rich strangeness of effect – characteristics that appear mainly in the grand country mansions of the era. However, without an understanding of the Baroque style at its most extreme the curious design elements that appear in quite ordinary houses – boldly modelled garlands, volutes, mouldings and scroll work – can hardly be explained.

The Baroque style takes the formal elements of classical architecture and lends them scale, dynamic movement and singularity. When the style is transposed to England, drama is still the leading impression. It can be found in the detailing of domestic interiors, and in fine deepcut plasterwork and elaborate woodcarving – even in quite small houses. This was the era of Grinling Gibbons, the master woodcarver, whose rich naturalistic carvings set a style that was emulated in numerous houses until naturalism was in due course superseded by the more formal decorations of the Palladian style.

1

1 *It is sometimes believed that all building in England in the early 18thC was influenced by the Palladian style, but this is far from the truth. This is a fairly typical early 18thC red brick house of the kind found in villages and towns all over southern England.*

2 *This classical English doorway exhibits an open-bed entablature with associated pilasters. Such features were influenced by the designs of Kent, Burlington and Campbell and other 18thC innovators, which filtered down from grand houses to more modest homes.*

2

The varieties of taste in smaller houses can seem confusing, because several styles often seem to be asserting themselves at once. The classicism introduced by Inigo Jones was still percolating down to provincial houses when the brief tide of Baroque washed over the architectural scene. Neither had ceased to influence the average country house or small town square when Palladianism began its powerful rule.

The "Queen Anne" house was popular enough not to be easily displaced by the Palladian style. The most distinctive aspects of a typical Queen Anne house of around 1720 were its happy and agreeable proportions and its suitability for daily life. Often there would be an instinctive balance in the placing of windows and doors. The staircase, broad and shallow, would have a fine balustrade. The parlour on the ground floor might be lined with good panelling, but there would be nothing ostentatious in its decoration.

Palladianism introduced a new and dominant note in English, and American, architecture. Chief among the prime movers in this new rule of taste was the young Lord Burlington. Inspired by a book by the designer Colen Campbell, *Vitruvius Britannicus*, Burlington travelled to Italy and there absorbed the same lessons that Inigo Jones had learned a hundred years before – the same lessons, but with subtly different effects. He took with him William Kent, a brilliant designer who was to be his main ally in introducing Palladian taste in England. Their idea was to resuscitate the classicism begun by Inigo Jones, but following a new set of rules by which all builders and architects should be guided. Burlington's plan was ambitious: the transformation of the face of English architecture. This dream was very nearly realized, for in one form or another the format adopted by Campbell, Burlington and Kent was to influence the building of all grand houses, and many modest ones, for sixty years.

Among the most interesting of all Palladian building are the villas built by Campbell and Burlington in imitation of Palladio's Villa Rotonda at Vicenza, with its central domed space and portico on each of the four facades. The original is a folly, essentially a banqueting house, and suitable only for a warm climate. Campbell's Mereworth Castle followed this model closely, adapting the plan as much as possible (but with only limited success) to the needs of a small country house. Burlington's own exercise on the same theme, the Chiswick Villa, was designed as an addition to the

3

7

8

4

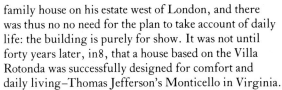

5

9

family house on his estate west of London, and there was thus no no need for the plan to take account of daily life: the building is purely for show. It was not until forty years later, in8, that a house based on the Villa Rotonda was successfully designed for comfort and daily living–Thomas Jefferson's Monticello in Virginia.

One of the great virtues of Palladian design was the simple and pleasing relation of room to room in the the overall plan, and this too had a major impact: planning becomes particularly important when working in a limited space. Individual elements of Palladianism were also taken over. For example, the Palladian portico, although perhaps serving a more practical purpose in the hot south than in northern zones, was widely copied as an imposing style of entranceway. Another characteristic feature is the "Palladian window" – an arched central opening flanked by two rectangles, with columns in between.

6

3 *This somewhat later house, in the Queen Anne style, shows fine Georgian proportions and symmetry with a good classical portico. The combination of glorious brickwork with stone corners and other details help to give the building its impact.*

4, 5 *Simple Georgian cottages such as these tell us as much about the 18thC as do the grand manor houses and stately homes. Restoration of such buildings will benefit from thorough research into their origins.* CG

6 *This shallow internal arch in a reconstructed 1760 house in New York shows subdued classical influence, especially in its keystone. This is a fine example of Colonial architecture.*

7, 8 *The Palladian pediment is sometimes seen in combination with a small circular window and often with dentils – small square or rectangular blocks evenly spaced in ornamental series.*

9 *A detailed view of stone dentils on a brick townhouse of the 18thC.*

The development of classical proportions in the 18th century shows a marked tendency towards increasing slenderness and attenuation. Height and refinement were the keynotes, perhaps expressed (as in Bath's Royal Crescent) by giant Orders of columns rising through all floors. Even the window bars became more and more slim as the century progressed. The Wood family's designs at Bath reflect a new archaeological spirit of accuracy, based on careful study of ancient Roman originals. For many people the characteristic style of the 18th century is "the Adam style" – especially in room decoration. The design ideas introduced by Robert and James Adam in the late 1750s and through the 60s and 70s were new and sophisticated variations on the traditional classical motifs. The secret of the Adam style was the cumulative effect of many finely wrought elements. The genius behind the style was the way in which so

2

3

1

1-4 These interiors (in No. 1, Royal Crescent, Bath, designed by the Wood family) show a delicacy and liveliness indebted to the designs of Robert Adam, whose work became influential from the middle of the 18thC. Adam treated classical motifs with an unprecedented lightness and simplicity, and subordinated every detail – including the bell-pushes – to an overall conception. RC, SC

4

much variety was subordinated to a greater plan. Furniture, carpets, curtains, door handles – all fitted in harmoniously with the grand scheme. This was the definitive statement of Roman opulence toward which English architecture had been tending for fifty years.

Running counter to the classical influence, an entirely new strain in building styles emerged after the mid-18th century, looking back to the Middle Ages. This was the taste for Gothick – the final K is used of the 18th-century style to differentiate it from the medieval architecture it aped and from the Victorian revival which would succeed it. The vogue for pointed Gothick arches and other mock-medieval features, in

5, 6, 7 *The crescent – a curving row of homes – was an architectural form devised by John Wood the Younger at Bath in 1761-65. Note the giant columns which unify the facade.*

5

6

7

8

9

8, 9 *These two fireplaces from a Georgian house in Bristol show the late 18thC fondness for exquisite decorative details. Such* *fireplaces were always intended to be painted white to add to the overall effect of airy grace.*

both houses and garden buildings, grew through the 1750s and 60s

The Adam brothers and their followers increasingly worked in houses which were remodelled or rebuilt in the newly fashionable castellated romantic style. The interiors themselves remain classical but within a Gothick shell. The overall profile of the house could be fashionably Picturesque. Such exercises need not, however, be Gothick or castellated: they could equally well be Italian in style, and in the latter years of the 18th century and in the early 19th century this was a frequent choice. Just as important for houses of moderate scale was the revival of Greek architecture (led by James Wyatt), which was extremely fashionable in the 1780s and 90s.

Externally, the Georgian house, whether large or small, had a plain dignity and elegance, owed in part to the balance between a handsome door and generously proportioned sash windows, symmetrically arranged. The sense of proportion and order, immediately recognizable on the facade, was also reflected within. In the grander homes, the plain dignified exteriors encompassed interiors that were highly ornamental, full of exquisite detailing, yet controlled by good proportion. A reception room was treated as an architectural composition in its own right, with classically inspired features echoing each other to create an integrated effect. For example, a moulded architrave over the door might complement a pediment above a fireplace. Doric pilasters in a doorcase might be echoed in the uprights of the wall panelling, which in turn might reflect the ceiling pattern. Ornamentation could include swags, scrolls, fruit and flower festoons, gryphons and arabesques, or urns and vases – or relief work in strict geometrical patterns. More modest Georgian houses are not architecturally articulated inside, ornament being confined in most cases to skirting boards, dado rails and doorcases.

Georgian townhouses are characterized by unity, balance and elegance, not only when viewed as a whole but also in individual details such as doors, windows and ironwork.

A distinctive feature of early 19th-century houses is the use, on exteriors, of stucco – a type of hard, fine plaster that was coated onto brickwork to counterfeit stone. In the long run, stucco turned out to be an uneconomical finish requiring constant upkeep, without which it deteriorated rapidly. Many owners of period homes will have discovered this to their cost. Frequently stucco is found in combination with the cast-iron verandas, balconies and porches that we associate with the typical Regency house. Cast iron was used for mass-produced fanlights. These could have an impressive filigree delicacy, although the best Regency cast iron is extremely austere.

Among the experiments unleashed by the Picturesque movement, with its fondness for eccentric versions of other times and other places, was the mock country cottage, complete with thatched roof. The Regency idea of a cottage was highly fanciful, bearing little relation to the realities of rural life. However, this cosy ideal, the *cottage ornée* (ornamental cottage), initiates on a modest scale a whole century of romantically revived styles of housing.

The Victorians adapted past styles to their own purposes instead of following them strictly. Middle-class homes were often overcharged with furnishings, creating an atmosphere of exaggerated comfort and affluence, but ornament was frequently restrained, although rich. Externally, a richer Italianate treatment succeeded the Neo-classicism of 1800–1835. However, the stuccoed terrace was still part of a restrained, albeit splendid, unit. The architectural vocabulary was extended: Gothic and "Tudor" detailing could be used as alternatives to classical.

The terrace gradually became less smart, except in certain exclusive areas such as London's Belgravia, Bayswater or Holland Park. The fashionable thing for the aspiring middle classes was to have a detached "villa" in the newly expanded suburbs – or, alternatively, a semi-detached house. The scale of life that could be lived in a semi-detached home was relatively modest. Living-in servants of necessity would be kept to a minimum, although there would be servant accommodation in the attic. The privacy of individual plots, with gardens front and back, reflects a new desire for independence from one's neighbour – a trend that remained prevalent into the 20th century.

The plan of the semi-detached house does not admit of much variation. Clearly, the reception rooms have to abut onto the party wall or there is wasteful repetition of flues and chimney stacks. In the absence of a basement, the kitchen must lie behind the house to preserve the proprieties of the master-servant relationship. Bedrooms and owners' bathrooms were on the first floor. In the typical 1870s house, an attic storey served whatever staff purposes were necessary.

1-5 These grand English townhouses capture the mood of the late Regency/early Victorian period. Highly influential at this time were Sir John Nash's Regent's Park Terraces in London and contemporary developments at Bath. Stucco was favoured on facades, while balconies and canopies added touches of individuality.

6, 7 This New York house built in 1864 has one of the earliest mansard roofs in America. Note the decoratively exuberant brackets and cornices.

1 **2** **3** **4** **5** **6** **7**

8

9

10

11

12

13

8-12 The Victorian terrace gave plenty of scope for design variations. The diversity of styles drew on centuries of local, national and international traditions. Such eclecticism adds greatly to the visual interest of our towns and cities.

13 These San Francisco houses of around 1880 are typical in their diversity of decoration. The well-maintained paintwork is an all-important aspect of their period charm.

Purpose-built blocks of flats were a feature of the late Victorian period. However, apartment blocks never found in England the favour they enjoyed in France and America – probably for the same reasons that the garden suburb remained the English ideal.

Most Victorians lived in very simple terraces if they occupied a house at all. From the "universal plan" developers created a row house with two reception rooms, kitchen and scullery, four bedrooms, bathroom and attic. The detail varies but the plan does not. The facade has a two-storey bay, its mullions tricked out with a very debased form of Gothic decoration – for example, formalized flowers. The keystone of the arch of the porch often had a grotesque head for ornament. Above the front door, a single window marked the small bedroom.

In some metropolitan areas, gentility and raffish unrespectability fought endless battles over speculative housing. The ever-expanding terraces might fall into multiple occupation almost before they were finished. It is a mistake to think that the decay of the Victorian terrace and its division into flats is a purely 20th-century phenomenon.

In England, Victorian houses make up a small group of standardized types. Variations upon these types were possible, but rare. It is therefore rewarding to turn to parallel developments in 19th-century America. For example, in San Francisco in the 1880s there was a rich diversity of experiments on the basic single-fronted format. This developed as a detached house, but the surprise is in the carpentry. For the debased ornament so repetitively applied in the London type, California substitutes the inventiveness of the individual carpenter. The painted clapboard and the exuberant detail indicate how individual a simple building may become.

While such developments were taking place in towns, the vernacular tradition continued largely unchanged, except where fashion in the form of a landowner and his metropolitan architect had descended upon a village. The important factors in vernacular building have always been practical innovations. For the average farm worker the sash window had more appeal than the Greek Revival simply because it was more useful.

In the Victorian age aspects of this sensible, vernacular tradition were reclaimed for fashion by architects and critics. For example, windows might be placed where they are needed in rooms rather to present a pattern from outside. By taking elements from the vernacular, architects such as A.W.N. Pugin (chief promoter of the Gothic Revival) were able to create a pseudo-vernacular house, irregular for practical reasons rather than simply because irregularity was all the rage.

1

2

3

From the 1870s onwards the Arts and Crafts Movement led a reaction away from the mediocrity of mass-produced Victorian design. The guru of the movement was William Morris, who argued for dignified simplicity and honesty of materials. Morris's ideas were shared by the major Arts and Crafts architects Philip Webb and Richard Norman Shaw. But despite their commitment to better standards for all, Webb and Shaw were most often employed to provide fine large houses for a small wealthy sector of the middle classes. Both were inspired in part by the age in which English architecture had produced the most habitable house: the 17th century. The historic elements – for example, the combination of warm red brick and white woodwork – were transfused by a freshness and originality in the detailing. Windows might be elongated to admit more light, in the process creating a sense of airy delicacy. This was architecture well adapted to reduction for use in a suburb. It did not rely on scale for effect. Shaw provided a number of influential models for domestic architecture – both detached and semi-detached – over the years. They are forerunners of much that we expect in the modern suburban house. The half-timbering of houses such as Cragside in Northumbria initiated a taste that leads directly to the 20th-century popularity of "stockbroker" Tudor.

The characteristic swirling forms of Art Nouveau, which first appeared after 1890, made a modest impact on British furniture, tiles and light fittings, and to a lesser extent on decorative windows and wooden

4

5

panelling. Equally admired today is the Art Deco style of the 1920s and 30s, whose plain lines (sometimes combined with geometric ornament) accorded well with mass-production techniques and the need for economy. Art Deco-inspired homes sprouted sporadically in suburbia, alongside an entrenched loyalty to the false timbers that evoked the Golden Age of English architecture. The obstacle to a more widespread acceptance of modernism in domestic architecture was simply that it was associated with factories and office blocks. As in the 19th-century, dwellers in the suburbs wanted their homes to be homely, and stylistically as far removed as possible from any associations with work.

1, 2 The interior of Leighton House, London, may seem eccentric, but it encapsulates all the self-confidence of the late 19thC, as well as reflecting the taste for travel and collecting. The 15thC tiles are Persian. The whole feel of this room is quite unEnglish. Such opulent strangeness seldom fails to delight visitors. 1.11

3, 4, 5 In the late Victorian/ early Edwardian era, houses that may seem rather anonymous to the unaccustomed eye reveal interesting decorative flourishes. Any historic style might be borrowed, from classical pillars and porticos (5) to brick gables of the English Renaissance and mock-Tudor oriel windows (3). Tragically, such buildings are often given unsympathetic extensions (4).

6, 7, 8 *This house dating from 1890 is in a Neo-Renaissance style. The hipped tile roof and projecting bays with gabled pediments are typical of large country houses of this period. Some such houses were designed to be light* *and airy inside, as here; others have a deliberately dark and cloistered feel. The marble fireplaces and other interior details would fit easily into a house of about 100 years earlier.* S&P

Monarch chronology

DATES	MONARCHS	PERIOD
1558-1603	Elizabeth I	Elizabethan
1603-1625	James I	Jacobean
1625-1649	Charles I	Carolean
1649-1660	Commonwealth	Cromwellian
1660-1685	Charles II	Restoration
1685-1689	James II	Restoration
1689-1694	William & Mary	William & Mary
1694-1702	William III	William III
1702-1714	Anne	Queen Anne
1714-1727	George I	Early Georgian
1727-1760	George II	Georgian
1760-1812	George III	Late Georgian
1812-1820	George III	Regency
1820-1830	George IV	Late Regency
1830-1837	William IV	William IV
1837-1860	Victoria	Early Victorian
1860-1901	Victoria	Late Victorian
1901-1910	Edwardian VII	Edwardian

The front door is usually the most eye-catching feature of the house, and altering or replacing it without due forethought is all too often disastrous. The mock Georgian door with built-in fanlight is painfully unauthentic, and will look wrong everywhere. Interior doors also need to be looked at carefully in relation to the style of their surroundings. Cheap modern doors in a baldly utilitarian style will look totally out of place if the rest of the interior has well-judged period details. A solid plank door, however well-made, will be intrusive in an elegant townhouse. And an 18th-century-style door, despite its good proportions (or because of them), will look ill at ease in a setting of homely rusticity.

Other common pitfalls include using knobs and knockers of the wrong type (such as wrought iron on painted panelled doors) and the insensitive insertion of glass. On no account should bull's eyes be inserted. Such lapses can spoil not only the door but the house itself.

1 An original wrought-iron spur knocker for a six-panel front door. BH

2 This original 1680s door was enlarged in the 18thC. The hinges are old replacements which fit exactly the marks found on the door. This attention to detail makes all the difference when authentic restoration is the aim. VNS

3 A reproduction of a mid-16thC Gothic arched door and frame. This is an elaborate example for the period, with deep chamfered framing and small panels. SI

4 A classical Italianate front door and porch on a London terrace house of 1868-74. It is important to research suitable colours for different periods. Here the white-painted stucco dressings and two shades of green on the door are authentic, but the steps are no longer whitened every day by a maid! LSH

5 The brass door furniture of the late-Victorian era was highly refined in comparison with 16thC wrought-iron examples. The contrast is graphically illustrated in the four examples below. Both wrought-iron pieces are modern reproductions. LSH,SI

6 A genuine early-mid 16thC door with linenfold panels. These doors can be tracked down, but not easily. Frequently they do not fit the space intended. It would be a tragedy to cut down such a piece, so you should always take dimensions into account before buying. AH

7 The six-panel door came into vogue at the end of the 17thC. This is a late 19thC example.

8

8 *A massive oak door of the type standard in England from the 15thC until it was overtaken by the framed door with inset panels in the 17thC. It's worth remembering that oak was not always dark. When these houses were built, the oak was a glorious honey colour. Reproduction oak doors are "aged" to suit modern tastes. Imagine a 15thC house with bleached floor boards, honey-coloured beams, doors and skirting boards.*

9 *An oak plank door hung on sturdy iron hinges of the strap and pin type. Note the enormous strap or iron arm which stretches across two-thirds of the door – this drops into a pin set into the door post. The leaded side lights bordering the door and matching the windows are typical of the 15th and 16thC.*

10 *An interior view of the same door, showing the original fittings.*

THE OAK STUDDED DOOR

In Tudor England doors were built to last. Amply wide, they were almost invariably of oak. The simplest were rows of planks, laid vertically, edge to edge, joined and strengthened by oak pegs or iron nails driven through to similar planks (the ledges), usually four in number, set across the back. For simpler houses this type of door continued to be made, in softwood versions, well into the 20th century in Europe and America. Sometimes there were diagonally set braces between the horizontals.

This type of door is known as the batten door. Variations on the theme include doors with narrower boards, or tongued and grooved, or with moulding on the face, or joined like overlapping clapboard; also doors whose ledges are let into the thickness of the wood. Broader planks might be grooved to make them look narrower. Double-thick doors had edge-to-edge

9

10

planks across their width at the back. On external doors the vertical joins were usually protected from the weather by thin strips of oak.

In timber-framed buildings inside and outside doors were mostly square-headed, but when set in stone they were often low-arched, like the windows of the period Square-headed doors might be set against an arched head under the lintel or moulded to give the appearance of an arch.

Linenfold moulding was developed and refined in England during the Tudor period and applied to doors as well as panelling. On both sides of the Atlantic it later became a hallmark of the mock-Tudor style.

1

2

3

1 Iron butterfly hinges like these have frequently been replaced.

2 Handmade ironwork lends a more authentic "feel" to a reproduction.

3 A plain oak door (right) consisting of vertical planks with oak pegs or iron nails driven into horizontal ledges on the back. On external doors the smooth "right" side faced outward, while on internal doors it faced into the room.

4 A 17thC Spanish or Portuguese door with fielded panels.

5 An early panelled door. Rather crude panelled doors were produced in the 16thC but the style really came into its own in the 17thC.

6 An original door with double bead moulding – note the carving on the door posts.

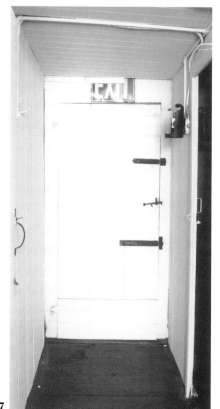

4

5

6

7

7 *These basic three-plank doors were used from the early 17thC well into the 18th.* BH

8 *This three plank door in the same New York house is divided and has slightly more intricate wrought ironwork hinges and locks. Note the differing shape and size of the handmade hinges — uniformity was not called for: function was more important than form.* BH

9 *Double entrance doors to a late 19thC house with leaded side lights have as their inspiration the plank doors of the 15thC and 16thC.*

10 *The exterior of this restored New York house of 1680 shows the original placement of the doors. The tall upstairs door is for loading as the staircase was too narrow.* VNS

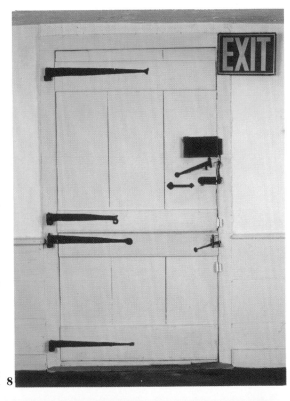

8

9

10

1

2

4

3

1 *The porchway and plank door of a house dating from the 16thC. The much later stained-glass panels harmonize and, perhaps because of the rather amateurish cutting of the "windows", lend their own charm to the house.*

2,3 *These oak plank doors were introduced into a 17thC house in the early years of the 20thC. The importance of using properly aged wood, traditional methods and wrought-iron work cannot be overemphasized.*

4 *This wrought-iron boot scraper is an early 20thC copy of a 17thC design.*

Door cases

The early, simple method of hanging a door was to attach it to timber posts that formed part of the structure of the building. But later, doors came to be hung on doorposts set against the wall. The join between the post and the face of the wall was concealed by an architrave, which made a surround or case for the door. During the later 17th century, such surrounds were given increasingly decorative treatment in the grander houses. They were ornamented with classically inspired swags and medallions and headed with bold pediments. Inside the house, pediments were often broken: that is, they terminated in an open curve instead of a completed triangle, thus creating a lighter effect. Some pediments incorporated panels designed to contain pictures.

The treatment of door surrounds reflected that of mantelpieces (or chimneypieces as they were then called). Similarly, the style of moulding or carving on the doors themselves was echoed in the panel work on the walls.

5 *An 18thC door typically enhanced by decorative architraves and door surrounds. The addition of panelling elegantly solved the problem of unusually thick walls.*

6,7,8 *These early 19thC architraves show the classic Greek Revival style in both ornate and simple forms.* OMH

9 *By the late 19thC stepped moulding was the most popular form of architrave: sometimes simple and narrow, other times elaborate and deep.*

10 *This chestnut and walnut door with fielded panels is in a New York house dating from 1875. The details of the door and architrave are echoed by the chair rail and panelling.*

6

7

8

5

9

10

PANELLED DOORS

Doors constructed as two panels set within a frame began to appear in the great English houses late in the 16th century, and soon became the norm, taking over from the solid plank door. Until late in the 17th century panelled doors were elaborately moulded and more and more exuberantly carved, painted and gilded to satisfy increasingly Baroque taste.

At the beginning of the 17th century the two-panel form remained the most common, with the heavy panels fielded – that is, raised in profile. Panels were given applied moulding in geometric patterns, and the broad door cases were treated to match. By mid-century, as classical proportions began to govern the design, six, eight or ten panels were inset; and by 1700 the six-panelled door was settling in for its long period of popularity. This was the favourite front door of the entire Georgian period and of the classical style in America. Interior doors had six, four or sometimes only two panels. The panelled door ceased to belong only in the houses of the wealthiest, and was repeated in less expensive wood, often with remarkable craftsmanship, for over a hundred years across the social scale.

In the smallest 18th-century townhouses, where a six-panel front door would be out of proportion, four panels were more usual. Both inside and out, the hand-sawn, increasingly slim panels were set into a rebate into the frame, with applied moulding around their edge. This moulding was absent in humbler houses and on the backs of cupboard doors.

At the beginning of the 18th century, door panels were raised or fielded. However, on external doors, the lower two panels were often flush with the frame. This helped rainwater to run off – as did the outward-curving rails at the bottom of the door. By the end of the century sunk door panels are more frequently found.

1 This light oak reproduction linenfold door blends perfectly with an early house. The simplicity of the wrought-iron hinges and door catch maintains the period character.

2 These 17thC oak double doors were introduced into a 15thC house in Kent in the 1950s. It is important to remember that all is not always what it seems. Early houses have often had many adaptations through the centuries.

3 An interesting mid-17thC divided door showing the influence of both English and Dutch vernacular architecture on a New York house built in 1661. BH

4 By the middle of the 17thC, oak panelled doors had six, eight or ten panels. These doors were frequently used as replacements for the earlier plank doors, particularly internally.

5 *Eight-panelled solid mahogany doors were much favoured by the first half of the 18thC and often replaced earlier examples.* CP

6 *This double or split door is made to resemble a panelled one by a simple frame around a board and batten body. The plank edges are beaded, a typical form of primitive ornamentation.* VNS

7 *From the late 17thC on, the six-panel door became the most popular form, particularly for front doors, and this was to be the most fashionable during the whole Georgian period.*

8 *This early 19thC four-panelled door in its original door frame remained standard in both Britain and America throughout the 19thC. The white paint work is totally authentic.*

9 *Today you will often find pine doors stripped of generations of paint – a simple treatment which works successfully in many cases. However, the original owners would probably be horrified to see so humble a wood being given such importance.*

6

8

5

7

9

1 *A classic six-panel Georgian door from the late 1760s. The paint on this door simulates the slightly streaked effect produced by the thinner paints used in the 18thC. You can achieve this by dragging a faintly tinted coat of scumble glaze over a surface coat of oil-based paint.* RC

2 *These sturdy iron hinges work as well today as they did in the late 18thC.* MJ

3 *The rectangular fanlight over this six-panel internal door with simple door frame and architrave reflects the understated proportion of late 18thC and early 19thC design. Such features tended to be used in secondary positions or in lesser houses.* MJ

4 *The same door has plain but sturdy brass door furniture with a well-concealed lock on the underside.* MJ

5 *The front porch and doorway of a classic Greek Revival house built in New York c.1835.*

6 *Behind a later louvre door is a mahogany one of 1835 with its original brass fittings. These doors cope well with most weather conditions, apart from strong sunlight, and need virtually no maintenance.*

6

5

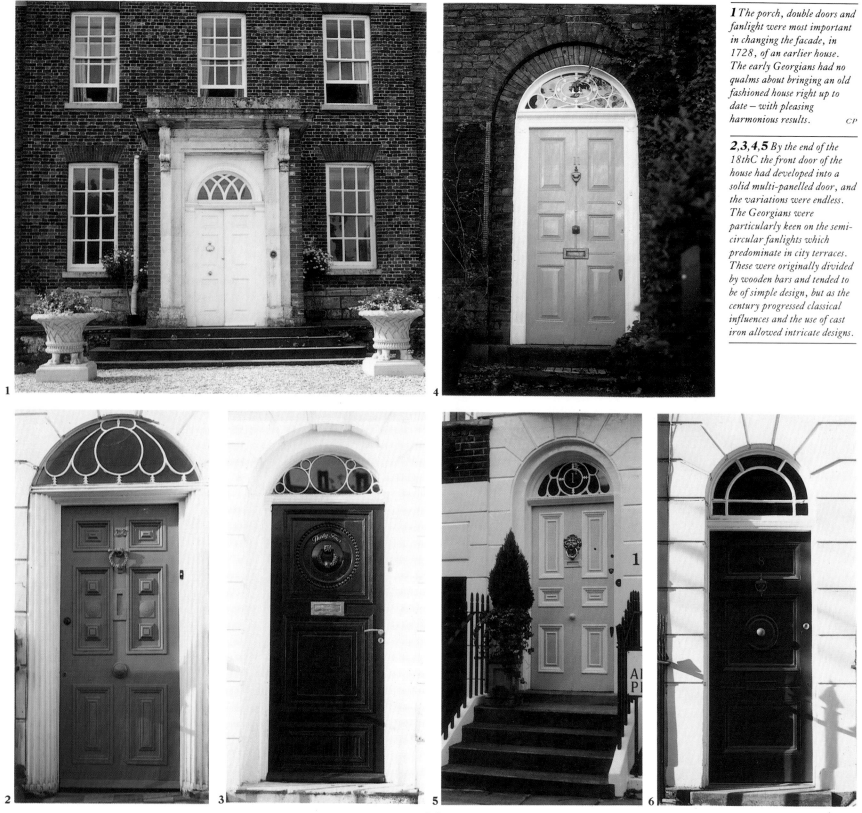

1 *The porch, double doors and fanlight were most important in changing the facade, in 1728, of an earlier house. The early Georgians had no qualms about bringing an old fashioned house right up to date – with pleasing harmonious results.* CP

2,3,4,5 *By the end of the 18thC the front door of the house had developed into a solid multi-panelled door, and the variations were endless. The Georgians were particularly keen on the semi-circular fanlights which predominate in city terraces. These were originally divided by wooden bars and tended to be of simple design, but as the century progressed classical influences and the use of cast iron allowed intricate designs.*

6,7,8 *Both late 18thC and early 19thC houses gave greater prominence to the front door, by use of pillars, brick arches or white painted stone. If a house is in a terrace it is important to view the street as a whole. It is also sensible to get advice on door furniture from a brass specialist.*

9,10 *In the 19thC front doors continued to mirror the changing faces of architecture. The square fanlight which had appeared in the 18thC gained popularity.*

11 *This wonderful example of a Victorian Gothic Revival door and fanlight is in a square in North London.*

12 *An attractive Edwardian door has replacement etched glass in its panels, side windows and rectangular light above despite the arched opening.* LDC

The colour of front doors

One of the most important decisions to be made is what colour to paint the front door. Experts, museums and societies often disagree. Therefore, all that can be suggested is what the authors have found works in practice. On Georgian houses:- white, black, dark green, dark blue, burgundy. On Victorian houses:- brighter colours are acceptable, as is a two-toned effect. If the house is in a terrace consider the whole ensemble, avoiding jarring colours. Brickwork should also be considered. For example, red doors can often compete with the brick colour if the shades are mismatched. You should remember that the colour of the front door is something we inflict on the outside world more than on ourselves: great care should therefore be taken.

FANLIGHTS

From about 1700 the glass fanlight over the front door was developed as an elegant solution to the problem of letting light into the hall and passageway. With glazing bars first of wood, and later of lead or wrought iron, the fanlight window offered scope for endless pattern variations. The influence of the Adam brothers encouraged increasing use of cast iron for delicate patterning. By the end of the century fanlights were being mass produced in a wide range of increasingly informal designs. Loops and spider's webs took over from fans and scallops, and elaborate heart and honeysuckle motifs were popular in the early 1800s.

No one nowadays would want to remove one of these lovely features. However, many were unfeelingly ripped out earlier in the present century. Fortunately, it is possible to find craft workers who will provide new fanlights following designs contemporary with the house.

3

1

2

1 This classical Georgian six-panelled front door has an equally classical fanlight. Such features should, of course, be restored and retained. They are functional, adding to the light in the hallway, and delightful, adding to the overall splendour of the façade.

2 The proportion and feel of this hallway owe much to the American Empire style in this New York house built in 1765 and refurbished, after the owners' trip to France, in 1826. The fanlight and side panels, which are original to the house, are copies of early Colonial glass.　MJ

3 This house is a reconstruction of the best colonial architecture from Maine to Charleston, South Carolina. It was built in 1929-30 by the architect Richard Henry Dana as a replica of a 1760 house. Some elements are original, salvaged from old houses being demolished, many more are copies – but perfect and sensitively made. This entrance door of stone is in the formal pedimented Greek Revival style.　HH

4 The divided front door (sometimes called a Dutch door) from the inside. The sophisticated panelling reflects that of the chair rail in the hall. By the mid-18thC in this quality of house far more attention was being paid to detail; ornamentation was taking over from pure functional design.　HH

5

8

5 *This fanlight from an 1830s house in New York shows all the exuberance of the period. The front door was an important statement of wealth and position. Such a fanlight and associated decoration were intended to portray an owner of gentility. Restoration of such a detail requires a skilled craftsman, and even repainting should be done with great care.* OMH

6

9

6,7,8,9 *These typical 18thC fanlights were still popular in the 19thC. The intricacy of design was at its height in the mid-18thC and tended, in modest homes, to become less delicate as the century progressed. Standard shapes, such as circles, loops and spiderwebs, were mass produced and used in terraces in cities and towns in both Britain and America.*

10

10,11 *Many Victorian houses had simple square fanlights, which should be retained, especially when they mirror other houses of the same design.*

7

11

HOODS

When not placed within an entrance porch or under a projecting upper storey, outside doors were initially set beneath a moulded projecting lintel which helped to keep off the rain. Alternatively, stone houses had drip mouldings across the tops of doors. In the 1650s decoratively carved wooden hoods began to appear at the head of the door case to afford protection from the weather and add a superb ornamental flourish to the flat front of the house. Supported visually by carved brackets (though often with further concealed support), these hoods are still frequently found, as an unaltered feature, in houses dating from this time onward. Until the 1720s, English examples were often carved in a florid Baroque manner. However, the vigour of the curving acanthus leaves, cherubs and lions' heads, fruits and flowers, was curbed by the influence of stricter Palladian classicism, and hoods went out of fashion.

The brackets and hoods were made of well-seasoned softwood, which was quite deeply carved. Successive applications of white paint has often blurred the details, in which case the old paint should be carefully stripped or burnt off and fresh white paint applied. In shape, hoods of the later period might be arching, coved or modelled to suggest shells. The smaller townhouses had simple, flat, moulded projections which nevertheless had elaborate scrolled brackets. In 19th-century terraced houses hoods often provided a touch of individuality to enliven a relatively plain exterior, as shown by the examples opposite (9).

1

1 This interesting thatched house in the Bushey Park Estate in London has an equally eccentric porch. Porches frequently mirrored the style of the house and the Victorians, in particular, liked to add interest to a plain facade.

2,3 Pillars were frequently employed to give a classical feel to the entrance. These are common features in the 18thC but were also used by the Victorians as a classical revival.

4 In this example the functional use of the porch – to give shelter from inclement weather – finds a natural expression.

2

3

4

5 *A successful modern porch added to a 16thC farmhouse using old timbers and a classic vernacular design.*

6 *The influence of chinoiserie is to be found in the design of porches and furniture at the end of the 18thC and beginning of the 19thC. The pagoda-style top is typical of the Regency period.*

7,8 *Porches were often thought inappropriate, and by the late 18thC the style had reverted to the hood.*

9 *This late Victorian terrace is an example of hoods used purely as decorative features. That such detail was added to quite plain doors shows the Victorians' concern to beautify.*

5

6

7

8

9

ENTABLATURES

From the mid-1700s a classical door surround was preferred, with columns or pilasters on each side of the door and a horizontal entablature over the top, with or without a triangular or segmental (curved) pediment. This type of surround, christened the tabernacle frame, was much loved by the Adam brothers. Both inside and out the tabernacle frame persisted throughout the rest of the century, first with Roman orders, then Greek, and with console brackets later replacing the columns.

Above interior doors, broken pediments were often used in the style first adopted some hundred years before. However, towards the end of the 19th century, pediments had fallen out of favour. Inside the home, the areas above the doors now had stucco panels – in parallel with the increasing use of stucco on exteriors.

1

1 This door and frame of the early 19thC exhibit all the style of the Egyptian Revival popular at the time. The sphinxes and tall pillars are actually the entrance to the house. The front door is in a small external hallway.

2 This spectacular Georgian door and surround epitomize the classical influences of the later part of the 18thC. Such doors were usually painted white. As with internal cornices, the decoration at the head of the columns can be greatly improved by careful cleaning and repainting.

2

3 This wonderful broken pediment above classical columns develops a style popular in architecture and furniture from the mid-18thC on. The beautifully proportioned front door reflects the Georgian love of symmetry.

4,5 On less grand houses, entablatures were often much simpler but still had the effect of increasing the elaboration of the door. This was also the case in later Georgian houses. If your entablature is in a bad state of repair or has been removed, a specialist carpentry firm can copy a similar design.

6, 7 In the late 18thC the classical columns could be either freestanding or incorporated into the door frame. These columns developed into a mainly decorative feature rather than a structural one. White painted stucco was a common treatment for a door surround. Pilasters were also favoured, as in picture 7.

CHANGES IN STYLE

With the arrival of Gothic, Greek and Picturesque influences in the early 19th century, there was less stylistic conformity. Decorative details varied immensely according to individual taste. However, certain broad trends can be identified.

A feature of the period was the door with two vertical panels side by side, sometimes narrowing toward the top like doric columns. Sometimes a door would be ornamented with a rectangular frieze and a central circular motif or a reeded lower half. The surround was more and more played down. Front doors became less significant decoratively, the principal decorative element being the fanlight. Treatments ranged from the classic radiating bars like the spokes of a wheel to loops and swirls and spiderwebs. In humbler houses, right until the early 20th century, plainer rectangular fanlights were to be seen in abundance.

Mahogany almost completely replaced oak for doors in grand houses, although for greater economy there was considerable use of Baltic fir, well seasoned and of good quality. More ordinary houses had doors of "dry yellow" deal or American pine. For front doors in stone surrounds, white was the preferred colour, but black, dark green or brown was also considered suitable.

1 *A Federal-style entrance built in 1832 with coffered stone sides and columns. Note that the outer fanlight is heavier than the inner one and the doors echo but do not duplicate each other. This is one of only two surviving examples of the hundreds of similar houses built in New York in the first half of the 19thC.* OMH

2 *The outer door and fan seen through the inner doorway. The regular panelling owes more to the Greek Revival than the Federal style.* OMH

3 *The parlour door frame. On more unusual door frames like this, you may have to take moulds to copy the detail.* OMH

4 *The classic division of a 19thC American house – pocket doors in a double Greek Revival doorway between twin parlours.* OMH

5 **6** **7**

5,6,7 *Three examples of Greek Revival door frames from a New York Neoclassical stone mansion built between 1837 and 1846. The first with understated elegance; the second and third, with their wonderful carving, demonstrating the true opulence of the period.* BP

8 *A six-panel door in the upstairs' reception room has a simple classical frame.* BP

9 *Another Greek Revival door frame from the same house, similar to the one in picture 6, but with a different motif.* BP

10 *The frame of these large mahogany pocket doors is moulded as Corinthian columns.* BP

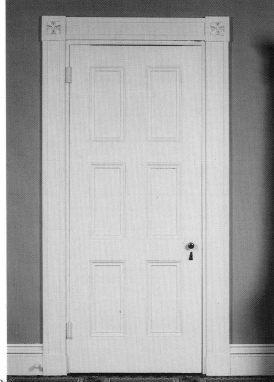

8

9

10

THE LATER 19TH CENTURY

The narrow Georgian terraced house demanded a narrow entranceway, and a front door proportioned accordingly. However, when the villa was introduced to towns, its wider entrance hall allowed a more generous entrance area, which permitted the introduction of side windows beside a wider front door, often set within a porch. This set the style for Victorian houses.

By the time of the building boom in the middle of the 19th century, mechanization had taken over from hand labour. Hand-sawn door panels had been around five-eighths of an inch thick. The later machine sawn panels were thicker, making the doors sturdier (and also more fireproof). The rules of 18th-century proportion had required the height of a door to be twice (or a little more than twice) its width. Now, though they were still panelled, doors were more various in their ratio of dimensions.

Basement storeys, where they existed, were not so deep as before. The raised ground-floor storey replaced the Georgian *piano nobile*, and the front door set into it was reached by a longer flight of steps.

The Gothic style that was favoured for public architecture also affected domestic buildings profoundly. In doors and window surrounds, coloured brick or carved stone were used – or a stone substitute of moulded papier mâché or powdered wood, frequently painted. Woodwork was grained artificially to look like oak.

With the mushrooming of suburbs from the mid-century onwards, and the spread of simpler terraced houses, the door position was variable. The rhythm of door/window, door/window down the street gave way to window/door, door/window, window/door. To provide privacy, a wooden partition might be added between the two neighbouring doors. Flats were being built to look like terraced houses, with double doors, one for downstairs and one for upstairs.

By the end of the century even the smaller houses had tiled paths leading to the stone steps and front door.

1 This original doorway to the west wing of a 1735 Port Washington house has simple pilasters and sidelights. SWH

2 By 1845, when the east wing porch was added, the taste was for something a little more ornate. The classical Doric columns and the porte-cochère are typical Victorian details. SWH

3 Etched glass panels like these are a feature of houses throughout the Victorian period. Fortunately, there are craftsmen who can reproduce the traditional designs. LSH

4 These narrower front doors were common in Georgian terraced houses. The square fanlight is typical of the early 19thC.

5

6

5 *Heavily ornamented brass door furniture vies for attention with the decorative paint treatment. Note the vase motif on the finger plates echoing that on the panel (although in different style).* LSH

6 *Another view of the same door showing more of the painted panels. This house is a unique example of its type. The owner was the chief political cartoonist of* Punch *and the interior has been kept the same since his death in 1910.* LSH

7 *This heavily moulded architrave repeats the design of the single door panel. The whole is given greater importance by the classical pediment and sombre, marble-like effect of black gloss paint.*

7

8

9

8 *A wide internal door and frame of the late 19thC with a series of formalized carved decorations emphasizing the proportions. 18thC proportion required doors to have a height of a little over twice their width. By 1870, however, many were higher or, as here, wider.* LH

9 *The motto incised over this dining room door salutes the guests and wishes them "good luck". The gilded scroll design repeats that around the door frame.* LH

sheltered within a porch (often with a curved or pointed arch) supported on thin columns. Sometimes now quite brightly painted, doors were four-panelled, with a rectangular light (high window) above. Stained glass became more and more popular, the familiar narrow blue or red framing panels with white stars at their corners later giving way to a more Arts and Crafts treatment, with subtle colours in leaded lights or the curvilinear Art Nouveau patterns which took over at the end of the century.

It is perfectly possible to have leaded panes restored and re-inserted in a front door, or to have a new panel made in the original style. However, such a panel does offer easy entry to burglars and should be backed with toughened burglar-proof translucent plastic .

1 A heavy, patterned velvet curtain trimmed with a deep fringe and thick cord drapes a painted door. Before restoring a Victorian house to this degree of authenticity, it is as well to consider whether you could live in such a claustrophobic atmosphere. It is possible to be true to the character of a house and still live in the 20thC. LSH

2 Another glorious example of Victorian self-confidence! The painted upper panels of the door pick up the motif of the walls, the lower panels are ornamented with coats of arms and the brass door furniture is highly elaborate. The door is swamped, and the whole area given new proportions and greater importance by the heavily trimmed curtains and a matching massive pelmet filling the space between cornice and picture rail. LSH

1

2

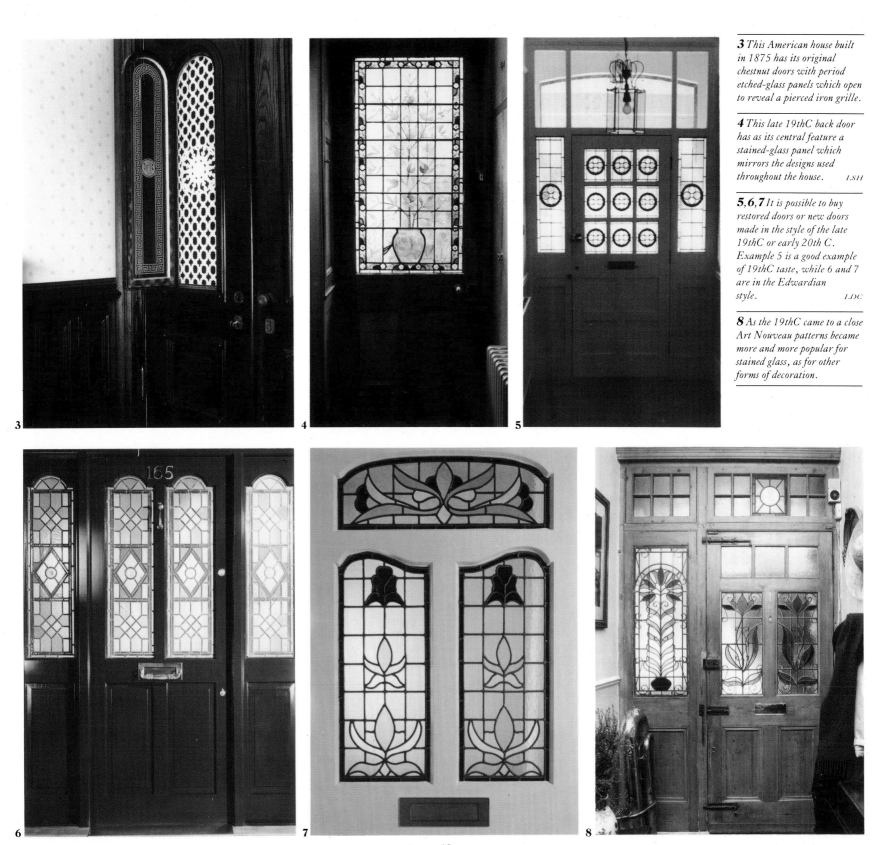

3

4

5

6

7

8

3 This American house built in 1875 has its original chestnut doors with period etched-glass panels which open to reveal a pierced iron grille.

4 This late 19thC back door has as its central feature a stained-glass panel which mirrors the designs used throughout the house.   *LSH*

5,6,7 It is possible to buy restored doors or new doors made in the style of the late 19thC or early 20th C. Example 5 is a good example of 19thC taste, while 6 and 7 are in the Edwardian style.   *LDC*

8 As the 19thC came to a close Art Nouveau patterns became more and more popular for stained glass, as for other forms of decoration.

Door Furniture

Until about 1700 latches, hinges and door handles were usually of wrought iron, and although simple in their conception they could be beautifuly ornamented. The simplest hinges, used on batten doors, are those of the strap and pin type, with a long strap attached to the door dropping on to a sturdy pin fixed to the door post.

The H hinge was also frequently used on batten doors. This has two "legs" which interlock by means of a bar across the middle: one leg is screwed to the door and the other to the post. The legs were given fancy, double S-shaped sides, the terminals of which were often embellished with cockspurs in true Gothic mannner.

Early external doors had no handles, being closed only at night and barred with wood on the inside. The simplest latches then became common: the iron latch, catch and guide were operated by a large wrought-iron ring on the plain side of the door. These fittings, or simple versions of them all remain in keeping with cottage doors.

Brass rim locks were introduced in the late 1660s. The knob and working parts were set into a metal box mounted on the door, and the latch closed into a metal catch mounted on the door frame. These devices were much more finely ornamented and were fitted to fine panelled doors. Elegant little brass handles were introduced instead of knobs for internal doors, and if there is a key hole it should be accompanied by elaborate escutcheons. Finger panels protected the door from finger marks and provided further scope for decoration. The basic design stayed in fashion, in porcelain, pressed metal and finally bakelite, until the 1940s.

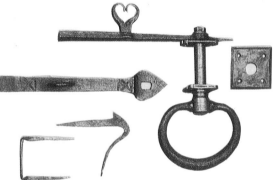

1

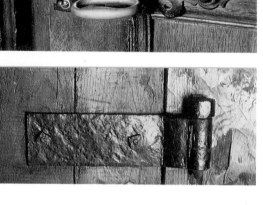

4

5

6

1 *A side door of a mid 18thC New York house showing the iron hardware.*

2 *Thorough research into old types of hardware found in the house gave the actual designs for these replacements. The doors are put together with clenched nails – soft wrought iron nails that are almost impossible to loosen. Contrary to popular belief, board and batten doors were always nailed.* VNS

3 *It is essential to use wrought-iron hinges to give an authentic feel to early doors.* SI

4 *By the 17thC internal door latches had become more decorative and more ingenious than formerly, and made use of brass as well as iron.*

5 *A strap-and-pin hinge on a lightweight plank door.*

6 *These authentic reproductions are readily available from such firms as Stuart Interiors.*

7 *The original iron hinge on an internal stripped and polished pine door.* HH

2

3

7

8

9 **10** **11** **13**

By the beginning of the 18th century door knockers were widely used on front doors. These were made of iron and lent themselves to all sorts of designs, usually based on animal heads. To complement these knockers, plain, bold doorknobs, also of iron, were set at waist height. Later brass knobs and knockers were more showy, but remained modest compared with 19th-century equivalents.

Brass was much less used before the 19th century than we seem to think now. Cast iron was by far the favourite material for door furniture in the Regency period. Ostentatious use of brass became commonplace later in the 19th century, when bells with pulls replaced knockers, until the introduction of porcelain pushes for electric bells.

Art Nouveau lent itself particularly well to door furniture. Its sinuous patterns can be found on large finger plates and bold letter boxes.

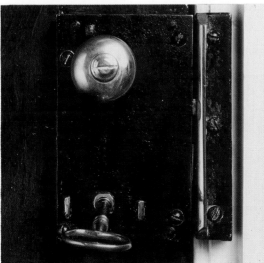

12

8 *It is possible to find excellent reproduction brass door furniture. These examples are perfect for doors from the early 19thC on.* Be

9 *This large solid early 19thC iron hinge supports triple doors. It should be noted that such hinges are brittle and can snap if attacked with a chisel or hammer. They were frequently covered with the stain used for the wood and were meant to blend with their surroundings rather than dominate.*

10 *Substantial brass hinges like this were used on both solid and glazed mahogany doors.* CP

11 *This beautifully-made late 19thC brass door catch is both functional and attractive.* LSH

12 *The original door lock and key of an early 19thC house. These should always be repaired and restored if possible.*

13 *Brass had become the main material for fittings in most houses of stature by the beginning of the 19thC.* CP

1 *A late 19thC example of useful information conveyed by means of a revolving brass plaque.* LSH

2,3 *Two examples of brass door furniture of the late 18thC.* RC

4 *This plain brass reproduction door furniture is perfectly suitable for doors of the late 18th and 19thC.* Be

5 *This wonderful late 19thC brass letter box is original although reproductions abound.*

6 *The choice of reproduction door furniture to suit a late 18th/early 19thC door is vast. The more ornate tends to suit a later house.* Br, Be

7 *As well as brass door furniture, the Victorians used china. These modern examples are available in many paint finishes.* Be

8,9,10,11,12,13,14 *Original brass Victorian door furniture is well worth seeking out as it has the added patina of wear, although there are good reproductions copied from old designs. All these examples are originals.*

15 *A lock imported from England to New York in the 1830s; the knob is 1890s'.*

16 *You can see how successive generations have renewed the door furniture here from the marks on the wood. The house was built in 1765 but this polished wooden door knob was made in the 1890s.* MJ

17 *This 19thC brass and glass door knob has a matching keyhole and escutcheon.*

18,19 *This original polished brass door furniture gives an elegant look to late 18th/early 19thC mahogany doors.*

1

4

2

3

5

6

7

8

9

10

11

12

13

14

15

16

17

18

19

Britain had its own glass industry from the 13th century but it was very rare for windows to be glazed until Tudor times. Even then it was only the nobility and wealthy new classes who could afford to use glass.

Windows were "wind-holes" or "wind-eyes" – necessary to let out the smoke and let in light and air. They were unglazed and tiny, and this tradition continued in smaller houses and in remoter areas well into the 16th century and beyond. A few houses from the Elizabethan period even survived into the 20th century with their windows still unglazed.

Where buildings were of stone, vertical stone posts, or mullions, helped to support the lintel of the window opening. They also served to deter intruders; and timber mullions were fitted in timber-framed houses for the same purpose, even though they were not structurally necessary.

1 *Vertical mullions were fitted into the windows of timber-framed houses as well as in stone ones, even though they were not structurally necessary. Setting the square mullions diagonally into the frame admitted more light than square-set posts.*

2 *The delicate glazing bars between the solid timber mullions would have been added at a much later date.*

3, 4 *The gable of a 16thC timber-framed house which has square leaded quarries. These are not original but 19thC replacements which harmonize with the building.*

5 *Diamond-shaped quarries are quite correct for a 15th or 16thC house. Never replace such windows with double-glazed imitation leaded lights, which give a most unsuitable flat look.*

3

1

2

5

Mullions, whether stone or wood, were usually square in section and set diagonally into the frame, splay fashion, admitting more light than square-set posts. Splayed reveals might be provided around the openings, both outside and in, to let in more light.

Before the introduction of glass, other materials were used – for example, oiled or waxed paper or linen cloth stretched across a lattice frame. Better still was parchment, also on a lattice frame and often decorated with figurative patterns or coats of arms before being brushed with oil. The frames (known as *fenestrals*), made of wicker or fine strips of oak, were still used in remoter places well into the 17th century, and later still in the poorest houses, where sheepskin or sacking would take the place of parchment. Their criss-cross pattern was echoed in the lead strips (*cames*) which held in place the small diamonds (*quarries*) of glass in the first glazed windows.

DEVELOPMENT OF MULLIONS AND TRANSOMS

The simple mullions of smaller Tudor houses were used to decorative effect in grander dwellings. Taller windows were made, with their lights (the divisions created by the mullions) divided horizontally by transoms. These windows were elegantly proportioned, usually with the dividing line of the transoms being halfway up the window plus the width of the transom.

In houses of timber construction the transoms and mullions were carved as if they were stone, and wood lent itself to a blossoming of ornamental work. The tallest windows would be topped with tracery, usually set within the shallow late medieval depressed arch or the Tudor arch. Such windows often had glazing in their upper parts and a complex arrangement of shutters and fenestrals opening below.

THE CASEMENT WINDOW

The early glass was blown. The ends of the bubbles were cut off and the cylindrical bubble itself was flattened before being cut out into "quarries", to be fitted into a lattice work of lead "cames". At first quarries were diamond or lozenge shaped but roundels of stained glass bearing coats of arms were made by European craftsmen for English houses. There was soon a multitude of quarry shapes, all of them small, because of the limitations of the lead "cames". And while grand new houses were being built with what must have looked like walls of glass, the smaller houses were having casements fitted into their existing window openings. Stone jambs and mullions were hung with iron casements while timber-framed houses had casements made of wood. The whole casement, rather than the pieces of glass within it, was known as the window pane.

By the 17th century, glass was quite readily available. Designs for quarry shapes had proliferated

6 A substantial late 19thC family house has a huge bay in the drawing room with five windows of four panes. This was the late Victorians idea of a Tudor "cottage"!

7 This six-paned arched window is a later addition to a timber-framed house. It is worth pointing out that, even in the interest of historical accuracy, it is not always possible to replace an external feature if the house is a listed building.

8 Casement windows became popular in the 16thC. By the 17thC, glass was readily available and larger, rectangular quarries began to be seen. The bull's eye was a feature of Crown or spun glass. Often this section was remelted, although it might be used in the windows of poorer homes. When its use is as regular as here one would assume it to be a later placement.

6

7

8

Cleaning old windows
To clean old glass, gently scrub with a soft brush and warm water, which will remove grime and lichen. Make sure that any lintels or drip mouldings round the windows are in good condition, as rainwater can damage antique glass. If lime has built up on a lattice window, cleaning is a job for the specialist, who will need to remove all the quarries (panes). Before doing so he will take a rubbing of the lattice work to use as a model when the glass is replaced. If you need new leading for lattice work, be sure to use milled lead.

in glass manufacture, and the industry in Britain moved to Lancashire and Newcastle, where sand was plentiful and coal could be used. Larger rectangular quarries of various proportions began to appear, and in the latter part of the century casement windows consisting of wooden mullions and transoms set in a wooden frame were able to hold larger pieces of glass.

Crown or spun glass, blown and spun out into a flat disc, was introduced during this period. The best parts of the disc were used in the wooden frames which were replacing the recently installed leaded lights. Those parts of the discs not suitable for use in replacement windows were usually remelted. However, these "bull's eyes" might be used in the casement windows of the poorer homes – although they were certainly never used in houses of quality.

Despite the fact that windows continued to be subject to renovation over the years, much 17th- and 18th-century spun glass has survived. It is glossy, often marked by tiny air bubbles and recognizable by the fine curving lines of the spinning and its slightly curved surface. As a clue to the age of the house, early glass deserves respect and care when old houses are being restored.

3,4 These 19thC windows in a 17thC house blend well with the early surroundings. Old stained glass was used for the decorative roundels, probably taken from an old church. Our predecessors frequently reused old features and materials.

5 In this 19thC extension to the same house, leaded lights and oak frames were used to blend the extension perfectly with the 17thC core. From the facade it is difficult to distinguish the modern wing.

1 This window in a 16thC house has diamond-shaped quarries. As well as the usual lead cames there are lead bracing bars and decorative catches, both fairly typical on a house of this age.

2 A decorative window catch in the same house. In areas such as this (south-east England) where many houses have leaded lights, it is relatively easy to find a glazier to undertake restoration work. The lead used today is softer and holds the glass more firmly.

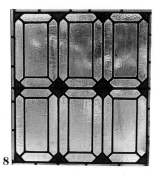

6 This stained and painted 19thC glass is in the medieval mood. Notice the return to lead cames and square quarries. *I.SH*

7 More 19thC glass – delicate tracery makes a background for a central monogram in jewel colours; the whole window is bordered with a design of formalized flowers. *I.SH*

8 A small 19thC stained glass window.

9 This early stained glass window is a 17thC addition to a 15thC house. Glass like this was reproduced in the late 19thC as part of the Arts and Crafts Movement.

10 A beautiful Arts and Crafts roundel, with lilies. *W&W*

11 Another example of the medieval theme in 19thC decorative glass. *G&G*

12 The designs on these brass catches pick up the motifs from nature on the windows. *I.SH*

13 An inset painted glass panel of Ariel from the side window of a Victorian bay. It shows the influence of the Arts and Crafts Movement in England. *I.SH*

1 This west wing of a house in Port Washington was built in 1735. The windows are of the sash type and on this bay are dominated by a massive stone chimney. SWH

2 By the time this house was renovated early in the 18thC, sashes were the order of the day. In existing houses casements were often removed and new sash windows installed; the proportions of later casements – 2½ to 1 – made such conversions fairly easy. CP

3, 4 An 18thC sash window of elegant proportion dominates a small room. With the introduction of pine window frames in the 18thC, painted woodwork became normal. White lead paint was universally used and so it is quite legitimate to use white paint in houses of this period. The authentic catch design completes the effect. CP

SASH WINDOWS

Toward the end of the 17th century, sash windows were introduced and began to displace casement windows. The English may have heard about them from the Dutch, but the French regarded them as characteristically English; whatever their origin, they were certainly a feature of British and North American dwellings until well into the 20th century. Well suited to classically inspired architecture, the sash was to appear in every main street and town development throughout the Georgian period.

In the simplest and earliest sashes the panes were propped in position on pegs while open or held in place by a pivoted iron quadrant which fitted into notches in the beading strip. The upper pane was often fixed, in the Dutch manner. The earliest weighted sash windows had solid wood frames flush with the wall, with grooves for the weights. Soon these constructions were replaced by boxed frames in which the pulleys were set and the weights hung – a system which was hardly to change over a period of two hundred years.

The weighted sash was not universal. In some areas casement windows were superseded by sideways-sliding sashes. These too were built into the 20th century. Despite their name, "Yorkshire windows", they are in fact found in numerous English counties. The sliding sash was suitable for smaller windows and could be used in smaller houses and upper storeys where rooms were low.

THE 18TH CENTURY

Until the early 18th century in England, the most popular wood for window frames was oak or other locally available hardwood. Glazing bars were very broad (roughly two inches (5cm) across) and never painted. Although oak continued to be the principal

wood for important work, occasionally imported mahogany was substituted. By the 1720s cheaper Baltic fir had been introduced.

The softwoods fir and pine acquired immense popularity. As neither of these woods weather as well as oak, exposed woodwork required a protective coat of paint. White lead paint, primed with red lead, was universally used until the Victorian period. These softwoods were also common on the East coast of America, where painted windows were the norm from an early date.

From 1709, window frames in London had to retreat to a minimum of four inches (10cm) behind the outer surface of the wall to reduce the risk of fire. This created a reveal in the exterior brickwork which was usually plastered and painted white. Elsewhere, houses

5

6

5 *It was customary for Georgian houses to have grand reception rooms of noble proportions at first-floor level – the* piano nobile. *This one has large floor-to-ceiling sash windows, with three pairs of panelled shutters.*

6 *Tall windows are a feature of Georgian architecture which give a sense of spaciousness. This window on a half-landing has panelled shutters housed in the deep reveal with panelling repeated around the arch.* GH

still had their window frames flush with the wall or only slightly set in. London houses after 1709 have flat gauged brick arches above the reveals instead of a timber lintel, although white pine lintels were still to be found inside. The new recessed windows were usually furnished with shutters inside the house. These folded back above the window board into splayed or recessed reveals and were fastened with pivoted iron locking bars. Although glazing bars were becoming thinner and thinner in towns, they remained relatively thick in country regions. In grand houses wide oak bars would be carved inside to match the carved mouldings of the panelled shutters.

By 1820 most glazing bars had been reduced in width to half an inch (1cm) or less, and twelve-pane windows (known as six-over-six windows in America)

had become standard. In another wave of window replacement, earlier sashes were removed and twelve-pane windows fitted. The rule of classicism, made fashionable by the Palladians early in the 18th century, was applied to buildings of all sizes in Britain and North America.

GEORGIAN VARIATIONS

During the 18th century the treatment of window surrounds and frames varied widely. Plain windows were commonly embellished with misunderstood classical details taken from the many "copy books" which served as textbooks to the British building trade at this time.

The Venetian or Palladian window, with three

sections, the side ones narrower than the round-arched central one, had been used by Inigo Jones early in the 17th century. A century later, when classical architectural features were commonplace, this style of window was in evidence even in quite modest houses. In various proportions and with different decorative details, the Palladian window enhanced many a facade at (usually) first-floor level for two thirds of the century. More simply, rectangular windows were divided into three with fixed side lights and a central sash.

The bay or bow typical of Georgian or Regency terraced houses in many towns was very popular from the middle of the 18th century. The word "oriel", once applied indiscriminately to any projecting window, now denoted a window supported by brackets and

1 Twelve-over-twelve sash windows are characteristic of virtually any house of the period in the East Coast of America. The gargoyle carvings in this example appear over the front windows only. VC

2 A dining room window of the 1830s. By 1850 most woodwork was painted white. OMH

3 This imposing bay of a house dating from 1875 is flanked by pilasters and defined by the cornicing and ceiling details. The bay is composed of five sash windows, each with just two panes. The ready availability by this time of large sheets of plate glass made it possible to dispense with glazing bars.

projecting from an upper floor, as distinct from the built-in angled bay or curved bow which often extended almost the entire height of the external wall. Bays were practical, especially in towns, as they admitted more light and cunningly extended the front room without increasing the width of the house. In the 1770s, elliptical and canted bays became popular, stopping complaints about buildings advancing into the street.

At the same time, in British town houses, the *piano nobile*, providing rooms of greater height at first-floor level, was being developed. Georgian architects began to focus their creativity on this storey, by adding entablatures above the windows and pilaster strips which ran between them vertically to the cornice, and by increasing the height of the windows themselves. Some grand American houses, particularly in the South, emulated this fashion.

By the end of the 18th century, even modest builder-designed terraced houses in Britain had a *piano nobile* of increased height, sometimes with small projecting balconies, and often with windows decreasing in proportion.

Windows of this period were more likely to have square than arched heads and tended to be set closer to the face of the wall. Attic rooms were lit by dormer windows which could be square-, round- or segmental-headed. Crowned with their own little roofs, they projected in varying degrees from the house roof and were concealed behind the parapet if one existed.

4 A finely detailed brass opener from the sashes shown in picture 3.

5 A built-in seat is a pleasant feature of this 18thC window. CP

9 This detail of stripped-back glazing bars shows the Georgian mitre. When replacing such bars it is essential to duplicate this design. Many mass-produced examples have flattened bars.

THE 19TH CENTURY

Plate glass was first introduced in 1773, cast and ground to remove flaws. However, it was not widely used until after 1838 when polished sheet glass became commercially available. Already Gothic influences had begun to make their mark on classical facades. The new age was prepared to sacrifice proportion altogether in pursuit of maximum light and air. Glazing bars could be dispensed with now that large sheets of glass were available.

In the mid-1800s, many older multi-paned windows were replaced with six- and soon four-paned windows. In houses that were reglazed at this time, windows on upper floors were often left undisturbed and many can now be found with four-paned sashes at ground level, Georgian twelve-paned sashes above, and even Stuart casements on the top floor. In America, however, the entire house was often reglazed.

THE 20TH CENTURY

By the turn of the century, in England and America, houses were being built with large sash windows, each half consisting of one huge pane. Shutters which could be closed from inside to keep out the light were now more or less abandoned and replaced by exterior blinds. Despite a growing demand for old-fashioned cosiness, the plate glass sash survived, developing into the modern "picture window". A frequent compromise is the sash in which the lower part is one sheet of glass, with smaller panes in the upper part.

There was also a medievalist strain – dating back to William Morris in the second half of the 19th century – which manifested itself in the reintroduction of casements and leaded lights. Mock lattices of applied lead strips appeared in the 1930s and are now common features in "pseudo-Tudor" houses and flats, despite the horror with which they were once viewed and their glaring inappropriateness in older buildings. Equally popular are the metal-framed, smaller-paned windows of the mid-20th century, which today have a period look of their own.

6, 7 Two examples of shutters from Regency villas, one showing the original brown varnish, the other painted white. It is a matter of personal taste whether to paint or revarnish; however there is no doubt that shutters should be restored and used. They are a form of double glazing and provide extra security.

8 This view shows the shutters in picture 7 open and folded back. Even with curtains these are useful additions. The windows, in an early 19thC house, have the interesting addition of small side panes.

SHUTTERS

Window openings could be shuttered to give substantial protection from intruders and the elements. In Britain, shutters were almost always on the inside, which is why the European-style external shutters unwisely added nowadays look so out of keeping in houses following British styles. Shutters were made strongly of wooden boards, sometimes hinged and folding and sometimes sliding horizontally or up and down, and fastened with wooden bars or iron fastenings. Those which opened horizontally were often housed in the reveals of the inside walls. Shutters and their hinges were usually constructed in a similar way to the doors of the house, and the two developed together.

1 The late 19thC fascination with Oriental styles shows here – red and gold wallpaper, rich green curtains trimmed with gold, shining brass curtain pole. The painting of the woodwork, including the shutters, adds to the sombre grandeur.

Although the window area is large it has the same heavy "feel" as the rest of the room. The tall concertina shutters were a common security feature. Each shutter is made up of four tall narrow sections; these fold into a small wall niche. I.H

2 The artist who had this London house built in 1877 travelled extensively and was fascinated by Eastern art, and the decoration of this room reflects this taste. The bay is almost a half circle with floor-to-ceiling sash windows taking up most of it. The circular form is defined by the ceiling decoration and emphasized by the unusual curved brass curtain pole. The shutters work on a brass pulley system and are housed in reveals in the wall. I.H

3, 4 The panelling below this window in an 18thC room matches that on the two pairs of shutters. The back of the shutter is typically plain while the front has intricate moulding.

5 The unusual cutout over the bed in this room in an American house was probably intended to hold fabric. It dates from 1720, when the room was added to an earlier house, and still has its original studs and shingle lath. VNS

6 Two pairs of bi-fold shutters are still in good working order in this 18thC house in New York. The radiator "box" is panelled to match. VC

7 *This small 18thC window in a New York house has a pair of triple-fold shutters. In this upstairs room the normal six-by-six panels have been adapted to three panes over six.* MJ

8 *Houses evolve over the centuries and thus may show a variety of window styles. Early 19thC shutters blend well with 17thC features on this New York house.* BH

9 *Triple-fold shutters in this dining room of a New York mansion built in 1765 are panelled only on the section which is seen when they are housed in the reveal. The colour of the woodwork is correct for the Federal Period and exactly the same paint formula was used; hence the streaked effect. The wallpaper is a reproduction of one of the era.* MJ

10 *The narrow proportions of this 1860s floor-to-ceiling sash window in a New York house are changed dramatically when the adjustable shutters are open – the width is doubled.* WW

11 *This house was built in 1929-30 – a replica of a mid-18thC one; the aim of the architect was to represent the best of colonial architecture between Maine and Charleston, South Carolina. For instance, this Palladian window in the ballroom was copied from a New England mansion.* HH

12 *The New York mansion featured in picture 9 also shows the influence of later tastes. The hall was designed in American Empire style c.1800 and you will notice that the tall narrow windows with their plain bi-fold shutters are a foil for the rather flamboyant decoration.* MJ

1,2 *It is important to have the correct accessories. The silvered glass and pewter tieback and the Empire style brass knob are both suitable for the curtain treatments in this 1830s house.* BP

3 *These parlour windows have Victorian curtains and rods from 1867; the mirror too is Victorian. To gain the full effect it is important to study the whole "look": curtains in particular can give a Georgian or Victorian feel.* OMH

4 *The "Volunteer" chintz by Tissunique Ltd hanging in the Brown Study at Castletown House, Celbridge, County Kildare. It is an exact reproduction of an 18thC Irish chintz showing the review of the Irish Volunteers, Phoenix Park, Dublin, in 1782.* T

1

3

2

4

5

5 *A fairly elaborate example of the Greek Revival style, this window has a carved pediment over the top and Corinthian columns on either side. The draperies are a copy of originals of 1826.* BP

6 *This is an excellent example of curtaining a Victorian bay. The machine made lace inner curtains are absolutely in period.* LSH

7, 8, 9 *It is important to drape period windows in an appropriate style. Many firms produce copies of historic designs which blend well with a period room. These are some oustanding examples.*

O & L, C & F, O & L

Sash windows

The lower rail of sash windows may have rotted if rainwater has been trapped around it. It can be professionally repaired by "scarfing" in new wood after the rotten wood has been cut out. The new wood should be well primed before you repaint the frame.

It is a fairly simple job to replace a broken sash cord yourself. However, if the glass is heavy, two people working together will cope better. Upstairs windows should not be tackled by the inexperienced.

1 *Remove the guard beads.* 2 *With the lower sash raised, cut through the unbroken cords at the pulleys.* 3 *Remove the lower window.* 4 *Take off the parting beads.* 5 *Push up the upper window and cut through the unbroken cords.* 6 *Remove the upper window.* 7 *Take out the cover of the weight boxes in the boxed frame (at bottom of sides). (To make this easier, remove old paint with chemical paint stripper.)* 8 *Note how the old cords are tied to the weights. Replace them with new cords cut to the same length: thread the cords through the pulleys and allow to drop down the hollow inside of the frame. Tie to the weights at the bottom. Fix the other ends of the cords to the grooves in the sides of the sash, by nailing.* 9 *Replace the weight box covers and reassemble the window by following instructions 1-6 in reverse order.*

FLOORS

The basement or ground floor is one of the most vulnerable parts of the house. Although most materials used for floors are hardwearing, they may still have suffered from damp and rot. Many have been concreted or adulterated by stick-on tiles; more have to be lifted to insert a damp-proof course. Irrespective of the type of floor or the cause of its deterioration, careful consideration should be given to replacement. A simple regime of maintenance should then make your floor last for centuries yet.

TIMBER FLOORS

These were first used for upper rooms as lofty houses were divided by the insertion of a ceiling. Sometimes they even served as ceiling, floor and joists in one; alternate boards were extra thick, giving them the strength of joists, and the thinner boards in between rested in angular grooves cut along the length of the thicker ones. The underside of the floor was limewashed to make a light ceiling downstairs.

Although oak is by tradition the finest building timber, elm has often been preferred for floorboards since their earliest use, and with good reason. Old elm floors, in cottages as well as larger houses, have developed a beautiful colour and sheen and have a hardness and grain which even oak cannot match.

Early boards were of course sawn by hand, and this was done with a carefree disregard for standardization. As a result the generous boards of older floors, all at least a foot (30cm) wide, are often of different widths and depths, with the supporting joists packed out as necessary to make the boards lie evenly.

As early as the 17th century, imported firs (referred to as deal when imported in ready-cut planks) came into use as a cheap and ready alternative to solid oak or elm. Red fir was reckoned to be almost

1 These yew floorboards are new replacements in a late 18thC house. It is well worth considering bleached boards when replacing a floor, particularly in a basement or kitchen area. RC

2 A floor with 16thC wooden floorboards. These were covered with oil cloth in the later 19thC and hence do not have the deep colour of wood floors polished in the Victorian taste.

3 17thC boards with wooden dowels are more regular and even than those of a century earlier. It is a pity to cover period boards but leaving them exposed causes problems in itself: the floors are frequently uneven, and stiletto heels inflict permanent damage.

4 There is some hesitancy about leaving boards bleached when combining them with period mahogany furniture. However, No. 1 Royal Crescent in Bath shows that this can produce very pleasing results. RC

5 The deep, glorious colour of these oak boards is totally unoriginal. An American visitor to England in 1772 commented that the floors were "washed and rubbed almost daily" and "have a whitish appearance". This pallor did not appeal to the Victorians, who polished the boards.

6 It is possible to buy salvaged floorboards. This early 19thC French oak flooring has good colour and patination. LAS

7 By the late 19thC floorboards were really intended to be covered – our fashion for leaving them naked, as here, would have shocked the Victorians. A favourite method of covering such floors was Persian or scatter rugs. These have to be treated with care on polished floors.

equal in quality to oak and less subject to woodworm than white fir. At least an inch (2.5cm) thick, the hardwood or good fir boards of the time gave worms a lot to tunnel through, and so have often survived in good condition despite attack.

In Stuart England the nobility had their floors inlaid with woods in different colours, a treatment known as parquetage. By the early 18th century, wooden block floors were being introduced into all the best houses of the gentry, but at the same time deal boards had become the norm for most floors.

Floorboards which had not usually been fixed, and like casements and locks could be removed if the house was vacated, were now fixed to the joists and the boards themselves began to be narrower. Perhaps partly because of the increasing development of a basement level, ground floors, which had rarely been boarded at the beginning of the 17th century, were now of wood.

8 Parquetage had been used in the grandest houses from the Stuart period; it lost popularity but was reintroduced in the 19thC. The Victorian use of parquet flooring gave an interesting new look to wooden floors; it often replaced the plain oak boards and was covered in places by Persian carpets.

9 To polish wooden floors, use a dry polish and polisher – a cloth impregnated with paraffin and malt vinegar gets rid of dust whilst leaving the boards shiny.

10 In this late 19thC American house, the boards are totally regular due to mass production. If the colour of the boards offends or the dust becomes unbearable they can be sealed. Try a test area first – seals seep into the boards and too often give a very yellow colour.

11 For the purist these Victorian pine floorboards give an authentic look to a 19thC floor. LAS

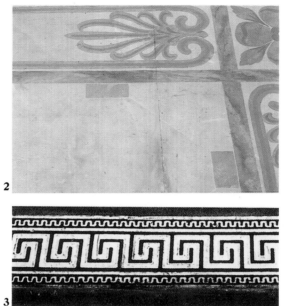

DECORATION AND COVERINGS

Until the 17th century, wooden floors were strewn with rushes for warmth and to keep down the dust. Sometimes instead of boards, lathes or rushes were laid to make the floor itself and smoothly coated with lime or gypsum plaster. Mats of rush or straw became more usual in the 16th century either on their own or as underlay for rare imported carpets. In the 17th century carpets began to be introduced more widely, especially in London; but they were generally used as hangings or table covers and it was not until at least a hundred years later that they would become at all common for floors.

Throughout the 18th century, floor coverings other than rush, straw or grass mats were still unusual, but paler, knotted deal boards were painted to darken them and hide their imperfections (in Bath, a mixture of soot and beer was used for the purpose). Later in the century, although the smart new houses were often carpeted, even when their floors were of good quality deal or Dutch oak, other fashions were developing. Floor colouring and patterning and the use of patterned, oiled floor cloths were much more common than carpets going into the 19th century.

To make plaster floors suitable for elegant houses pigments were added to plaster of Paris, and different parts of the country had long had local ways of colouring and patterning solid floors. Painted floors were an extension of this tradition and became very popular. With the application of stencilled patterns as well as plain coloured floors, the simple technique developed in North America into a fine craft which is enjoying a revival today.

In England patterned cloths were used to hide the imperfections of a deal floor. When placed under the table they made cleaning easier, and their geometric patterns in strong colours provided a decorative alternative to simple woven mats before cheap home-manufactured carpets became available.

THE 19TH CENTURY

More carpets were to be found in the 19th century, but floor painting survived in plain-painted and glazed floors, and in the borders round the carpet, which were often painted in the same colour as the rest of the room's woodwork. Oil cloths were also still used, on their own or to provide a surround to a central carpet; these were floral patterned, with designs more and more like Turkish carpets, or any other covetable carpet pattern. They developed a *trompe l'oeil* quality for, like the linoleum flooring and modern vinyls of which they were ancestors, they were patterned to look like natural materials – stone, marble or wood, knots and all. Then, as now, these cloths were despised by persons of "good taste".

By the middle of the 19th century carpets were common in the main rooms of even small houses, and linoleum replaced oil cloths at the end of the century. Floor boards, still about an inch (2.5cm) thick, were only about four inches wide (10cm) in better houses, though up to nine inches (23cm) wide in poorer quality dwellings. Tongued and grooved boards, which had been introduced in the 1820s, were increasingly machine-prepared and hence of even width. The timber used was well seasoned and will not usually have shrunk.

1 *Floor cloths were a practical 19thC solution to floor covering, especially in entrance halls. Either home-made or commercially manufactured, they were usually of canvas covered with many layers of paint and varnish, and were the forerunners of modern linoleum. This example, with a marbled pattern and a border adapted from a carpentry design, is an exact copy, painted onto linoleum, of a design that might have been used originally in this New York mansion of 1840.* BP

2 *This floor covering from this mid-19thC house in Lancaster, Pennsylvania, is laid throughout first-floor front and rear halls. It is stencilled in a geometric pattern to imitate tiles. The backing is made of cork, the surface is oil cloth. This was an extremely popular method of floor covering in both Britain and America at this time.* JBF

3,4 *This late 19thC linoleum border interestingly mimics the key pattern dado.* LSH

5 *This bleached beech tongue-and-groove flooring is a good modern solution to the challenge of replacing a period floor.*

6, 7, 8 *In parallel with the current interest in polished floorboards, stencilled floors are now very popular, and can be found in many colours and designs.* LG

9 *This staircase is carpeted in "Higford", a design based on an early 19thC pattern and seen here in its original colouring, in an American house.* C & F

6

7

8

9

PROBLEMS AND SOLUTIONS

Timber had become standard for ground floors during the 19th century, though it was not until 1860 that such floors were required by law to have an air gap beneath them. From 1900, air bricks were also provided in order to keep the air circulating, but neglect together with dislike of draughts have meant that this ventilation has often been stopped and the timber floors may well now be rotten as a result. To prevent deterioration of floor boards at ground level it is important to restore good ventilation by clearing away any earth lying against the outside walls and reopening any blocked air bricks.

Worm tunnels in timber floors may be aesthetically displeasing but are not in themselves a problem. Badly damaged parts of otherwise sound boards can be sawn out and replaced, and the quality of the wood usually makes up for the signs of woodworms once at work. Treatment with one of the proprietary sprays kills any live woodworm and prevents further infestation for a limited period.

Dry rot, detected by its damp smell, as well as signs (such as wood distortion) of the damage it has caused, is a different problem and often affects poorly ventilated ground floors. It must be carefully checked for and dealt with immediately when found. The fungus can spread rapidly through sound timber, plaster and even brickwork causing untreatable decay in any conditions once it has a hold. It is essential to remove and burn every bit of rot-affected timber when renovating an older house.

SOLID FLOORS

From the earliest times and into the 20th century solid floors were widely made of baked, dampened and beaten earth, patched with clay. Superior beaten earth floors could be made by mixing clay with ox blood, which dried to make a hard, smooth and gleaming surface, not unlike the quarry tiles which later replaced them.

During the 17th and early 18th centuries in Britain, the earth floors of prosperous farmers' houses were replaced with brick or kiln-burnt paviors (shaped like bricks but only about an inch and a half (4cm) thick) or square quarry tiles just like those still being manufactured today (measuring roughly nine by nine inches (23×23cm)). These are unglazed, but technically non-porous and therefore practical.

If suitable stone was available locally, huge flags would be laid instead of tiles. The various English marbles: Purbeck, Sussex, Kent and Derbyshire, were used only when the finest materials could be afforded. Many of the freestones were not suitable for flooring; but Bristol houses had blue stone slab floors, and other areas had a suitable local stone for flagging. Smarter houses reserved both flagging and tiling for pantries or other service rooms. In Devon and South Wales "pitched" floors were made from small pieces of stone cut with wedged backs and laid like street cobblestones. These were arranged in patterns curiously like those of woven straw mats – a craft which survived into the 19th century. Local slate was successfully used for solid floors in parts of Wales and Cornwall, and this extremely waterproof material was transported to other parts of Britain in the 19th century.

Portland stone was used in big houses from the 17th century, often laid in diamond pattern rather than on the square, and with a small square of black marble at the intersection of the cut-off corners of every four meeting slabs. It was not until late in the 19th century that marble and other polished stones became available to the ordinary householder. Tessellated floors of white and black marble and coloured stone then became quite common, especially in entrance halls. From 1900 all sorts of stone, slate and ceramic tiles were used within the house to complement the tiled paths and porches which led in from outside.

1 A stone floor emulating a type made of Portland stone and marble popular from the 17thC. CP

2 *Basic stone flags have been a popular floor covering from the 17thC to the 20thC in more modest houses or servants' areas. They are serviceable but care should be taken not to leave the floor wet as salts can damage the surface. These particular huge blue stone slabs can be found in many Bristol houses of the late 18thC.*

3 *Lighter coloured stone flags are typical of many floors from the 17thC on. They varied according to the availability of local stone and were used extensively in the service areas of larger houses.*

4 *Warm coloured tiles make a solid floor less utilitarian. They look more inviting still when covered by rugs.* F.E.

PROBLEMS AND SOLUTIONS

All the materials used for non-wood solid floors are hard-wearing, but some damp is nearly always present, if only rising through the joints. Although this may partly be due to condensation, which can be tolerable, or poor drainage of the site, which can be remedied outside, it will nearly always be rising through the tired fabric of the floor itself as well. The remedy is to have a damp-proof course laid (for which a local authority grant may be available). This involves removing the floor and storing it while a new base is made of hard-core, a damp-proof membrane, concrete, and a sand and cement screed onto which the floor is relaid.

You should do this for yourself only if you are experienced at building work; otherwise you should find a reliable contractor, as skill is involved as well as spadework. Although new materials of good quality are available, the signs of age are usually very much part of an old floor's charm. Some of the money you would save by re-using original materials could well be spent on the contractor's skill in relaying them, but many people still prefer to do this in order to preserve the character of the house.

CLEANING AND POLISHING

All these floors can be cleaned by scrubbing with water to which two tablespoons of washing soda have been added. When old polish has built up excessively, a cup of detergent and a cup of soda should be mixed in a pail of water, and the floor should be kept wet with this for half an hour before being scrubbed and rinsed.

Caustic soda is very effective for cleaning dirty, grease-stained quarry tiles and stone floors, used (with care) in the proportions of one tablespoon (15ml) (a wooden spoon should be used) to a gallon of water (4.5l), and well rinsed afterwards. Marble should be dried with a leather, and stains in it can sometimes be lightened with bleach, although they may reappear in time. Slate is improved by being cleaned with a 1:4 mixture of linseed oil and white spirit.

These materials are all maintenance-free, and it is simply a matter of taste whether or not they are polished.

Slate should be re-cleaned every few months to keep its lustre. Quarry tiles, paviors and stone can be given a gleam, using a polishing machine (which can be hired by the day), with a wax polish or one of the proprietary multi-purpose floor polishes, which also give some protection against stains. Liquid wax polish, well-buffed, brings life to dulled marble and polished stone but it should be used very sparingly if the floor is not to become dangerously slippery.

3

4

1 Reproductions of square quarry tiles. Many realistic copies of tiles dating from the 17thC in different parts of Britain and North America are now manufactured.　FE

2 These original square quarry tiles have been relaid in a refurbished kitchen.　PC

3 Brick paviors replaced the beaten earth floors in rural areas from the 17thC. These were popular until the late 19thC and are often used as replacements in country kitchens today.

4,5 It is possible to buy original tiles to be relaid. The tiles shown here are taken from period houses and chateaux in France prior to their being demolished. These have the advantage of a certain charm due to their age although they would not be strictly correct outside France. However, it should always be borne in mind that throughout history, particularly from the 18thC, the rich have imported period details from Europe to houses in Britain and North America　PC

2

5

6

9

6, 7 *This mosaic floor was designed by George Aitchison, architect of Leighton House. It was executed by Italian craftsmen around 1879-80 and although it was probably of local English marble, the floor has proved a problem to restore.* 		*LH*

8 *Mosaic floors of white and black marble and coloured stones became very common in entrance halls in the late 19thC.*

9 *Geometric tiles were popular in entrance halls in the late 19thC. These were probably made by Maw of Coalbrookdale. The "welcome" mat is also in period.* 		*LSH*

10 *The mid-19thC "encaustic" tiles in the Minton residence in Torquay, Devon, are identical to those supplied by the Minton company to the Capitol, Washington D.C.*

11 *The tiles in the hall of the Minton residence are a form of early Victorian mosaic pavement. These tiles became increasingly popular during the 19thC especially in hallways and terraces. They added colour and interest while primarily being functional.* 		*C* **10**

7

8

11

Bare walls are like giant canvases, and the impulse to decorate them is almost as old as civilization itself. But the origin of most methods of treating internal walls was functional — to make houses less damp and draughty.

The thick stone walls of medieval houses absorbed some water from outside and were hard and cold, encouraging condensation on the inside in winter. To reduce this, and to cut down draughts in the large open halls, the rich hung imported tapestries on walls and across doors. Later, woollen or canvas hangings in imitation of tapestry became increasingly common in houses of all sizes, and these were among the ancestors of modern wallpapers. Panelling was also used to line walls and act as screens. By Tudor times, this was often exquisitely carved in grand houses; in more humble ones it was developed into the fitted furniture that we find so useful in small houses today. By the 17th and 18th centuries simple oak or softwood panelling was common in the houses

of the gentry, and wood was further employed to add the classical detailing so much in vogue at the time.

Plastering walls began in Britain as a method of reducing heat loss or fire risk and strengthening wattle-and-daub walls. Yet colour washes of yellow ochres, blues and umbers can be found in plaster layers of early Anglo-Saxon origin. From this basic decorative start there developed the art of stucco and the parget work of East Anglia, culminating in the decorative swags of the Adam brothers in the 18th century.

Narrative scenes, patterns or simple colour washes enriched nearly all these wall coverings. The range of pigments and techniques has of course widened greatly and continues to change in line with fashion. Machine-printed rolls of paper brought quick, inexpensive decoration to every householder in the 19th century, and it is probably behind layers of this that you will find the clue to the original scheme for your house.

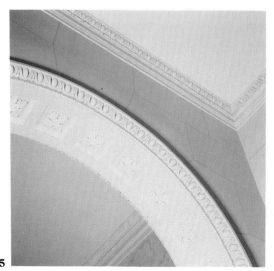

1 Many firms now produce wallpapers which use designs and colours to blend with a period house. Both 18th and 19thC designs are available. M. Armitage's hand-printed designs use traditional subjects in interesting new ways. MA

2 This wonderful wallscape in a house of the 1870s has, as a central feature, a bookshelf built in an unused doorway. Note too the olive green paint for skirting boards, dado and architrave. This all adds to the Victorian feel of the house. LSH

3 A faithful copy of a mid-18thC ballroom, reconstructed by careful study of original examples. IIII

4 Decorative ceramic tiles were features of many 19thC or early 20thC houses. Original examples have become expensive, but designers are now producing attractive examples such as this based on old patterns. MR

5 Plaster archways in this 18thC Bath house mirror the design of the cornice. The fake marbling on the walls is also in period. RC

PANELLING

In the 13th century Henry III imported wood from Norway and used it to line the rooms at Windsor Castle. These plain boards, unpanelled and unframed, were the first wainscots. They were intended to be painted, as were the plain plastered walls of the palaces. They were decorated with paintings of biblical stories, or stencilled (literally "starred") with gold, and whitewashed walls were "pointed" or patterned with a framework containing flowers. By Tudor times the fashion for panelling had spread in areas where timber was available. Oak panelling was used for screens, to line walls and as internal partitions to make more, and smaller, rooms within the large open walls. In these partitions, the narrow panelling boards were fixed into vertical studs, which were either split in half and fixed on each side of the boards or grooved to hold them. It was simpler to make narrow grooves, and accordingly the panels themselves were narrowed along their edges, creating the effect of raised surfaces. The middle of

such panels would be moulded with a rib as if to imitate stonework. The panels would usually also be set into a timber sill at the base and a frieze or moulded beam at the top, which gave the effect that was to develop into what is now known as linenfold.

The creation of linenfold, or "wavy woodwork" as it was called, had developed into a fine art by the early 16th century. Rectangular panels had fluted ribs placed close together, with realistic open folds at the tops, which were punched and carved to look like a needlework border. Sometimes the flowing ribs were opened out into honeycomb patterns or twined and interwoven and adorned with carved fruit and flower motifs.

By the middle of the 16th century a crude Renaissance classicism was taking over, as medallion heads and urns replaced linenfold. Sometimes, geometric patterns with an inner square or rectangle surrounded by "L" shapes of moulding echoed those on the two-panelled doors. In the best examples different woods were used instead of painting for pattern, and by the end of the century arcading was sometimes used to

6, 7 These panels of wainscot have had a fairly adventurous history. Carved in the mid-16thC for a chapel in Kent, they eventually found their way into a late 19thC staircase made to fill the courtyard of a 17thC house. CP

8 A Victorian reproduction of linenfold panelling in the same area of this house is an illustration of how elements from different periods can work together in harmony. CP

9 Detail of a carved pilaster which is part of a careful restoration of a 16thC house in Somerset. SI

separate the various panels, especially on the upper parts of the walls.

Applied pilasters began to appear on panelling in the grand houses of the 17th century. They were like those of the door cases, and were used for a similar reason – to provide an architrave which elegantly concealed the join between the stiles and the panels set into them. This device became prevalent in the big houses; like other classical borrowings it was often applied in a cheerfully unscholarly way, but sometimes the effect was very pleasing, with divisions in the length of the columns matching the divisions in the panelling itself. Applied pilasters – and columns – continued to be used in grand houses as classical architecture became a stricter discipline in the 18th century. As panelling went out of fashion pilaster strips and columns were applied to punctuate the wall surface or emphasize the window positions and give a flowing look to long rooms, as well as to divide the shelves in libraries.

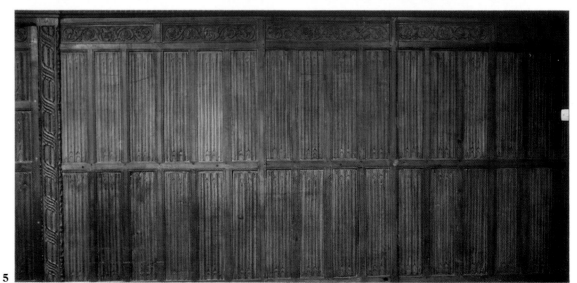

1, 2, 3, 4 Before decorative interior wall finishes became widely popular, it was not unusual for the boards that made up the fabric of the house to form the interior surface as well. VNS

5 Salvaged Tudor linenfold panelling with decorative pilasters and frieze has here been installed to create an authentic 16thC interior. CofSt.

6, 7, 8 *Simple panelling with sunk framed squares or rectangles was popular in the 16th and 17thC and is a particularly appropriate choice when restoring a country manor house. Such panelling is still made today using 17thC methods.* AS

9 *This room in a 17thC Oxfordshire manor had been robbed of all of its original features over the centuries, but recently it was completely restored – fireplace, panelling and ornate overmantel are all new but are faithful reproductions of the correct period of around 1640.* SI

10 *This panelling was put into a 17thC New York house about a hundred years after it was built, demonstrating how succeeding generations have always "improved" on their old houses. From the mid-17thC it was the fashion to paint not only softwood panelling, but also oak. So, if you have painted panelling in your house, do not feel you necessarily have to strip it.* BH

1, 2 The original panelling of this room of 1720 has been repainted in the style of the period, with marbled panels and authentic colours. At that period, paint for wood had a slightly glossy finish — oils, waxes or milk were included to achieve this effect. SI

3 Emulsion paint with a streaked effect gives the correct period flavour to the panelling of this 18thC room. RC

4 A George II panelled room, rescued complete from a house that was being demolished and reinstated in another house of the period. C of SL

5 An interior of the same period that has undergone the same happy fate. This time the panelling is waxed pine. The room has a dentilled cornice and door surrounds and a chimneypiece carved with masks flanked by drapery swags. C of SL

6

7

8

9

10

6 Simple but elegant painted panelling is featured in a house built in the Bronx in the second half of the 18thC. The colouring is authentic. VC

7 An elegantly carved pediment over this door is set off by fairly plain panelling and cornice. The room is a copy of a 1760s interior. The pine panelling, unpainted in the original, has mellowed to a marvellous honey.

8 A late 19thC answer to the problem of concealing the heating system. This cast-iron grille conceals a hot air duct. It neatly fills one whole panel, its formal decoration complementing the chestnut and walnut.

9, 10 Panelled rooms of the 18thC often featured ornate carving in the form of swags, fruit, leaves and classical motifs. These are by a follower of William Kent. CofSI.

EARLY FITTED FURNITURE

Wooden partitions and straightforward boarded or rectangular-panelled wainscotting were used increasingly in modest houses from the beginning of the Tudor period. From such features, the first fitted furniture developed. Lack of space meant that living rooms had to double as bedrooms. In the 16th century, many two-roomed dwellings consisted of two bed-sitting rooms, with the beds neatly boxed into an alcove and hidden by a curtain during the day – a tradition strong in Scotland.

During the 17th century this development was refined, with beds hidden completely behind wainscot-like panelling by sliding doors across the opening. Similarly, a fixed seat might run along the panelling, with the panelling itself acting as a settle back, perhaps decorated with a painted pattern, perhaps folding down to form a bed. Examples of this built-in furniture survive in parts of Wales, northern England and across the Channel in Brittany.

In vernacular buildings, where change was slow, the wooden partition dividing the rooms from the passage often contained seating or cupboards on the room side. Beside the fire, a built-in spice cupboard was worked in similar style, and sometimes a much larger cupboard was to be found in the same position. These handsome features, rather than filtering down from higher up the social scale, developed out of necessity and are rare examples of features which then ascended the social ladder. From early in the 18th century, the alcoves produced on either side of the fire by the chimney breast were put to use as cupboards in the new townhouses, in England and in North America, with panelled and well-proportioned doors and frames — the modern instinct to build cupboards or shelves in this position has a long history. The fireside alcoves were also adapted into niches, sometimes with covered tops of modelled plasterwork, in imitation of styles in grander houses.

1

2

3

1 Building furniture – particularly wardrobes – into a period house can all too easily spoil the period feel. It can be done, but the style must be chosen carefully. This wall of cupboards, drawers and glazed display cabinets, for example, would work well in a well-proportioned 18th or early 19thC bedroom. s

2 A Neo-classical room with finely moulded cornice and walls painted in one of the light shades favoured by the brothers Adam. GH

3 A cleverly faked and antiqued library in an 18thC building. The cornice (an elaborate reproduction) and also the bookcases were dragged in two shades of green. CP

4

7

4 *This panelled hall and staircase are a 19thC addition to an earlier house. This is a good example of the Victorians' habit of imposing their own taste on a building with little regard for its original character. However, it is here done with such confidence that somehow it works!* CP

5, 6 *A restored turn-of-the-century room with mahogany panelling and doors and Art Nouveau-style marquetry panels. Fortunately, there are still craftsmen able to carry out this type of work.* RDL

7, 8 *Built-in furniture is by no means a recent invention. This fitted dresser and chest-of-drawers in an 18thC house in Bath look quite surprisingly modern.* GH

5

6

8

PLASTER

The plasterer's art developed alongside the use of timber. Stucco or moulded plasterwork was much used in Palladian and Neoclassical houses of the 18th century, but it had first been used some 200 years earlier in Henry VIII's palace of Nonesuch. It appeared in friezework and panels in many of the great Tudor and Jacobean houses, modelled into stylized scenes, with countryside, forests, beasts and huntsmen, or scenes from mythology, and often painted.

Modelled stucco was a European, especially Italian tradition, but in the late 16th and early 17th centuries a native style developed in England. This was known as parget work. It was executed in the plaster mix of lime, sand, animal hair and dung with which the walls were usually lined. Parget work is particularly associated with East Anglia, though by no means confined to that area, and is found on both internal and external walls for friezes, overmantels and gable ends. The craft died out at the end of the 19th century as it became difficult to obtain plaster of the right quality.

This plaster was so strong that much parget work has survived. Its formal patterns are still familiar to us with their herringbone, basket work, strap work,

2 *This 18thC room had several "layers" of restoration. It was refurbished during the later 19thC, and recently the two doors were added. When creating new doorways, make sure that they balance with the existing architecture. Here the proportions of the doors are correct and their symmetrical positioning within the arch is in harmony with the room.* CP

3 *A niche in a Neo-classical interior may be painted a darker shade of the wall colour to give it more definition and set off objects placed against it. The choice of a marble pillar and bust is correct for the period.* BP

4 *Around the turn of the century there was something of a classical revival in both architectural detail and wall colouring. Creams, pinks and pale greens and greys are good choices for such interiors.*

1 *The wallpaper border in this American house shows clearly the way in which Empire decoration has been overlaid on earlier, Federal period architecture.* MJ

combed waves and charming and naive birds and human figures, myths and fables.

Hand-modelled plasterwork was originally applied to ceilings, cornices and friezes. It was the Palladian architects who, abandoning the use of panelling, introduced wall plasterwork and plaster wall panels based on a French pattern, and framed ornament with swagged surrounds were soon to become the fashion. Examples of such plaster modelling, with scenes from mythology set within panels of plaster architrave, with pediments and swags, can be seen in the houses built in Bath from 1727.

Later in the century the Adam brothers used plaster ornament widely for inside walls. Despite its classical appearance, their graceful decorative work was something of an innovation. They used a mixture known as Liardet's preparation, containing gypsum or fibre and glue, the exact composition of which is not known. Instead of being modelled *in situ* it was pressed when hot into metal moulds. The Adams painted their groundwork in light tints of pink, green or blue to relieve the ornament, and sometimes the ornament itself was painted. The mass-produced mouldings of the 19th century were merely a development of this approach and can themselves be reproduced by taking further moulds.

5

6

7

8

5, 6 A good alternative to distressing walls to resemble marbling, graining and so on is the paint-effect wallpapers currently on the market. Here such papers have been successfully used in a grand 18thC interior. The plaster columns followed the classical tradition of the early 19thC.　　　*CP*

7,8 The Victorians were great travellers and collectors. Lord Leighton, who lived in this grand house, travelled extensively in the Middle East and his wanderings greatly influenced the decoration. The columns in this case are marble. The screen was brought back from Damascus, and the room is hung with brocaded silk creating an opulent Arabian mood.　　*I.H*

PAINT AND PAPER

The most frequently used hand-mixed paints, for over six hundred years, were simple whitewash, colour washes with pigments added to the whitewash to give ochre yellow or red, blues and greens, or limewash, which had slaked lime as a main constituent and seems to have had disinfectant qualities. A more glossy finish came from paints which contained a proportion of oils, waxes, or even milk; these were the ancestors of our emulsion paints. They were used for wainscots and indoor woodwork from the mid-17th century, and we now know that all but the finest timbers were painted – our taste for stripped pine would have seemed very odd to our ancestors.

With the increasing variety of paint pigments available during the late 1600s, it became fashionable to completely hide the timber used for panelling by covering it with cloth, paper, or even leather. At the same time silks and papers were used to decorate plastered walls in expensive interiors, backed with linen and mounted on wooden frames that were nailed to the walls. Small pieces of patterned paper, publishers' rejects, had also been made available since the 15th century in an enterprising waste-not, want-not spirit and were glued by artistic householders to the insides of cupboards and chests.

As printing developed printed wallpapers were produced to replace more expensive cloth hangings.

But even wallpaper was quite a luxury. It was made by hand from shredded cloth, and as part of the manufacturing process involved draining it in flat sieves, it was available only in quite small pieces, based on the dimensions of the sieves. Nevertheless, it was common enough to be taxed from 1694.

Elizabethan wallpapers were patterned and coloured with stencilling or hand-painted designs, often with heraldic shields, vases and flowers very similar to the plasterwork of the time. Tiny flowers on bright backgrounds were popular in the 16th and 17th centuries. By the end of the period brocades were imitated and flocked papers replaced real hangings.

Increased Eastern trade late in the 17th century meant that luxurious papers could be imported from China. These came in large pieces decorated with scenes of flowers, birds, villages, mountains and clouds and were popular in the stylish Palladian houses of the 1700s. Towards the end of the 18th century, plasterwork was again imitated with delicate Neoclassical prints, while Georgian townhouses had another treatment for walls in which distemper backgrounds were "distressed" or "scumbled" with oil paints to produce the effect of marbling or graining.

3

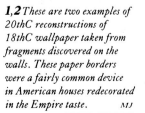

1

2

4

1,2 These are two examples of 20thC reconstructions of 18thC wallpaper taken from fragments discovered on the walls. These paper borders were a fairly common device in American houses redecorated in the Empire taste. MJ

3,4 Original hand-painted Chinese papers can be found both at auctions and in specialist shops. These papers were created by the Chinese for the European market and were used in English stately homes during the 18th and *early 19thC. Those shown here are the "bird and flower" type – a common design on the porcelain of the period. Such papers need expert hanging and often need some restoration once they are installed.* TC

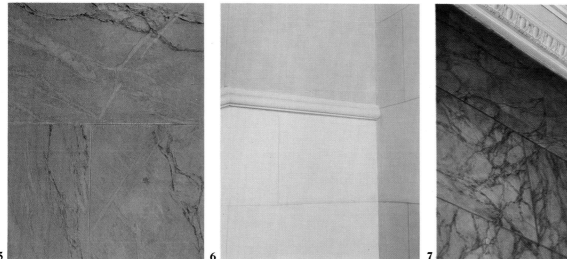

5 *Marbling walls became fashionable in the 18thC when imported marble was too costly for most people.* RC

6 *In this example, delicately marbled paper contrasts with simulated blocks.* RC

7 *Splendid marbling in an early 19thC New York house. The walls had been painted over but a protective coat of varnish saved the original marbling.* OMH

Simultaneously, cheaper "domino" prints with little geometric designs, of the type often found again today, were produced. Their use was generally restricted to the sitting room and the best bedroom; elsewhere, whitewash or tinted whitewash was still the rule, with stencilling providing any pattern. Stencilling was extremely popular in the USA from the late 1700s and survived well into the 19th century.

Printing methods improved, and early in the 19th century a method of producing continuous rolls was patented with the result that wallpapers became much more common, and tax on them eventually had to be dropped in 1861. Nevertheless plain tinted whitewash (or distemper) continued well into the 20th century and was given a further lease of life by the restrictions caused by the Second World War.

While other manufacturers were producing cheap substitutes for stone and wood, and casting moulded plaster by the yard, Victorian wallpaper makers developed imitation panelling and moulding in embossed papers which soon completely replaced wall plasterwork. By the end of the 1900s every house had this "Lincrusta" paper up to the dado rail and machine-printed patterned paper above. Very similar, but much lighter and more pliable embossed papers are available now to give the original look to Victorian

8,9 *These hand-printed wallpapers using traditional themes and colours would be ideally suited to 18th or 19thC rooms. It is worth remembering that the effect is often more dramatic if the paintwork is painted a complementary colour.* JO

10,11 *These papers give the right feel in a period room as the blocks are cut and the paper printed by hand. This method also gives a wider colour choice as the inks are individually mixed.* MA

houses, although the rich patterns and sombre colours of some of the printed papers may not be to everyone's decorative taste.

Since the practice of stripping off old wallpaper is a recent one, the layers of old papers can usually still be found in unrestored Victorian and later houses and this will give a clear idea of how the house was decorated. You are most likely to find machine-printed papers, which almost completely ousted hand-blocked prints by the middle of the 19th century. Woodblock printing was kept alive by designers such as William Morris, but their use was restricted to those discerning people who could afford to pay for hand-work. These deliberately two-dimensional prints have remained in production for over a hundred years, and are still available. Ironically perhaps, they are more often found in Victorian houses now than when they were first produced.

1 The decoration in this Georgian mansion, built in the Palladian style, is mainly in the French Empire manner.

The walls in the bedroom were papered and then finished with a paper border. The colour is authentic to the 18thC. MJ

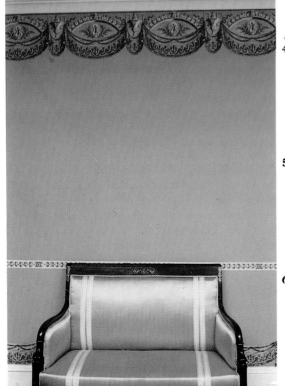

2-13 *A range of modern wallpapers based on original designs of the late 18th-early 19thC. The paper shown in picture 12 is derived from motifs chosen by Lady Hertford for the Chinese Room at Temple Newsam in the early 19thC. Number 13, though surprisingly modern-looking, is an exact copy of an 18thC paper.* Z, Z, Z, C&F, Z, Z, Z, C&F, HW, C&F, Z, C&F

14 *A fine example of an original wallpaper from Robespierre's apartment in the rue St Honoré, Paris, dating from 1793.* T

15 *This wallpaper is an accurate reproduction of a fragment found in a house in Bloomsbury Square, London, dating from c.1810.* HW

16 *A pomegranate design taken from a mid-18thC wallpaper found at Temple Newsam.* Z

17 *This paper is based on one illustrated in a pattern book of c.1840.* HW

18 *Wallpapers with a Chinese inspiration have been popular since the 18thC. This copy is another from the Temple Newsam collection.* Z

19 20 *These two copies of early 18thC papers would suit a house from that period through to the early 20thC.* Z

21 *A handprinted frieze by Louis W. Bowen Inc., N.Y., suitable as a replacement for a cornice.* TC

22 *A design by A.W.N. Pugin (1811-1852), rediscovered in 1975. This paper would fit well into Gothic Revival and Arts and Crafts interiors.* Wa

1 The Victorians had no hesitation about mixing pattern and surface decoration in their interiors. This late 19thC artist's house exemplifies how well such mixes can work. The whole interior is beautifully integrated. *LSH*

2 This wallpaper in the same house was made in Japan by an English firm, Rothman and Co. It is embossed and gilded to look like leather and was so expensive that it was used very sparingly: there is none behind the pictures or the Florentine mirrors! *LSH*

3 The dark colour under the dado rail and the darker skirting add to the enclosed feel of this Victorian interior. Note the stick rack. *LSH*

4,5 These Lincrusta papers are based on Art Nouveau and Edwardian originals *C*

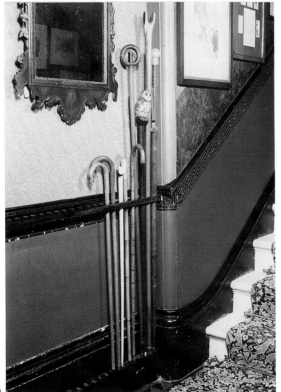

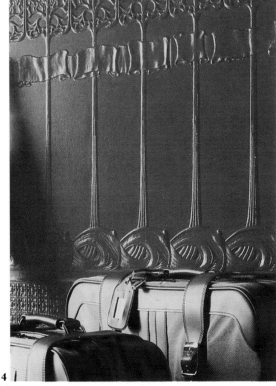

6

7

8

9

10

6 Murals, frieze paintings and trompe l'oeil *can be effectively introduced into most period houses. The decorative style of* trompe l'oeil *works best in 18th and 19thC houses.*   *CB*

7 *Figure painting was of special interest in the 18thC. It works well in period houses, but you should select the artist carefully.*   *TP*

8, 9 *The range of possibilities for* trompe l'oeil *is extensive. Paintings of vistas, windows and furniture are popular themes.*   *TP*

10 *Stencilling is an effective wall decoration and can be used in most periods of houses so long as the general feel of the room is taken into account. It has always been popular in America and has recently come into vogue in Britain.*

1 *These wonderful 15th and 16thC Persian tiles were brought back by a Victorian collector and now decorate a late 19thC London house.* I.H

2,3 *These allegorical tiles are based on a traditional 17thC design and made by the traditional method. This gives them the slight imperfections which blend with period settings.* PC

4 *Hand-painted tiles like these Spanish examples can be used as a panel or a border.* PC

5 *Blue and white is such a classic tile coloration that modern designs still retain a period feel.* BCS

6 *Hand-painted tiles made by traditional methods may be more expensive but successfully recreate the Dutch Delft originals. These tiles were designed by ceramic artist Doug Wilson.* PC

8

7,8 *Tiles can also create a trompe l'oeil effect and can give the impression of a niche in a wall. Geometric patterns and flowers are classic motifs here used in an innovative and interesting way.* SR

9 *By the end of the 19thC tiles were produced in strong colours. This modern tile has a similar inspiration and could be used to good effect in 19thC as well as 20thC homes.* MR

10 *Vases of flowers with simple borders have been used on tiles since the 18thC. These hand-painted tiles in strong colours provide excellent panels.* SR

11 *This blue and white panel successfully uses themes popular on tiles from the 18thC. As many original panels have been damaged, such hand-painted modern tiles are a useful alternative.* SR

12 *Tiles can also be used on exteriors and these highly glazed ochre, brown and deep blue tiles form an interesting archway to a late 19thC/early 20thC facade.* S of D

13 *As original 18thC English delft tiles become more expensive and difficult to find, replacements using sketchy designs can be found from firms specializing in modern reproductions.* FE

9

10

11

12

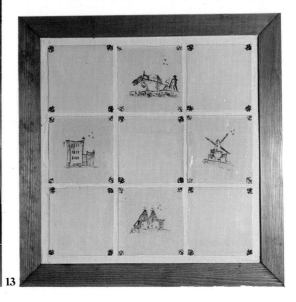

13

1 *Prints interestingly placed on a staircase wall lead the eye upwards. The plain walls in this example of a late 19thC hallway are brought to life by the prints in maple frames, some original and some reproduction.*

2,3,4 *These exuberant examples of Victorian wallscapes show great confidence in mixing dark colours, wallpapers, prints, mirrors and Chinese porcelain. The owner of this house was a noted cartoonist and obviously had a special interest in drawings, paintings, prints and photographs. But the general effect can be recreated by similar handling of masses of mostly monochromatic pictures. Used singly on such busy backgrounds the pictures would have been lost; but grouping them to almost cover the walls gives them unity and importance. In picture 3 it is interesting to note the combination of oil paintings, Japanese prints, silhouettes, mirrors and medallions.* I.SH

5 *Simply framed photographs (mainly of the house's owner Mr Linley Samborne) cover a bathroom wall. Again the whole effect is gained by the sheer quantity of pictures decorating most of the wall area.* I.SH

1

2

3

4

5

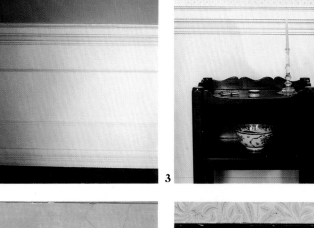

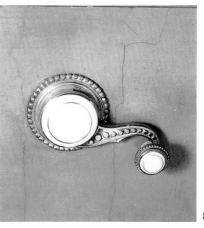

DADO RAILS

Dado rails complemented skirtings. Again they are a reminder of earlier wall treatments, being placed at the height of the middle rail in panelling. Visually pleasing but also practical, dado rails protected the wall where chairs were most likely to scrape, and thus may also be called "chair rails".

Often the dado rail was inversely related in outline to the skirting board; the greatest projection was at the upper part of the rail, whereas on skirtings it was nearest the floor. In the later 19th century, dado rails are found less frequently, except in entrance halls and on stairways, and mouldings became simpler.

When walls are being replastered to tackle damp, it is well worth keeping a record of the exact position and profile of the original skirting boards and dado rails, as even in the simplest houses these were often sensitively proportioned and deserve to be carefully replaced. Where the skirtings and rails are in plaster and you cannot match the mouldings in wood, make new ones from a mould taken from the originals: they will then blend in perfectly.

1 *In the very grandest rooms in 18thC houses, walls might be covered in fine fabrics such as silk damask. Here the joins have been covered in gilded beading which serves also to define the lines of the room. There are many companies today specializing in putting fabric on walls and advising on appropriate types to use. Braid would be an apt substitute for the beading. Note the deep moulding on this dado rail which reflects the deep skirting below.* RC

2 *An 18thC house can have walls simply painted in a suitable colour. Here, blue walls are set off by panelling and mouldings in white. The dado is part of the panelling – a common feature at this time.* RC

3 *From the 17thC small geometric wallpaper designs were being used in the houses of the gentry. This paper in the bedroom of a restored 18thC house is a copy of one of the period from Temple Newsam, Leeds. Wallpaper designs in country regions lagged dramatically behind those in capital cities. Laura Ashley's early mini-prints were based on fragments of wallpaper found in a 19thC cottage in Wales. As these would have been up to a hundred years out-of-date by London standards, her designs fit well into 18thC as well as 19thC interiors. The paper is given a more authentic look in this well-researched Georgian house by the plain colour from dado to skirting.* RC

4 *This Georgian room has paper of a much later period, but the design successfully picks up the detail from the panelling, giving the room the correct feel. The dado here is quite elaborate with the central motif picked out in gilding.* GH

5 *If you cannot afford to line the walls of your 18thC drawing room with fabric, a paper which simulates a fine fabric (such as moire) is a helpful possibility.* CP

6 *Strong colours can work in well-proportioned period rooms – provided that they are based on authentic colours of the period. The secret is to use them with conviction.* CP

7,8,9 *These three examples show the interesting variety in bell pulls. The Georgians often used sashes or decorative brass pulls. The Victorians also used these but added china pulls decorated with gilding or painted with flowers. An interesting feature of picture 8 is the revival of the classical key pattern frieze under the dado. Most homeowners today do not need bells to summon up legions of servants. However, if you are lucky enough to find pulls intact in your house, leave them in as a novel period feature.* LSH

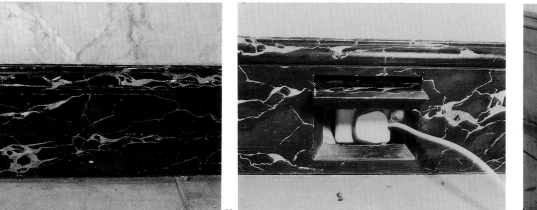

10   11   12

13   14   15

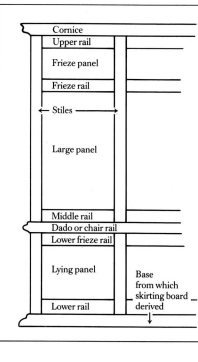

Panelling: THE NAMING OF PARTS
By the mid-17th century a pattern based on classical proportioning had been developed for the wainscot. A base, or *sill*, had a panel above it known as the *lying panel*. This was fixed at the top into the *middle rail*, *chair rail* or *dado rail*. The second level of panelling, known as the *large panel*, was fixed at the bottom to the middle rail and at the top to the *frieze rail*, above which ran a further panel, the *frieze panel*. In higher rooms the frieze panel would be surmounted by an upper rail and cornice, and extra rails would be placed above the base and above and below the middle rail. The diagram, which shows the typical arrangement for higher rooms, would make a suitable model from which to plan reconstruction work for wainscoting in 18th- or 19th-century houses.

Diagram labels:
Cornice
Upper rail
Frieze panel
Frieze rail
Stiles
Large panel
Middle rail
Dado or chair rail
Lower frieze rail
Lying panel
Lower rail
Base from which skirting board derived

10, *11* *These marbled skirtings in an 18thC house in Bath have been skilfully adapted to conceal the electric sockets essential to 20thC life.*   RC

12, *13*, *14* *Stripping woodwork of its painted surface is very much a modern fashion, but one which often works well in a period house. Painted woodwork is correct for most Victorian interiors, but bare wood is fine for an 18thC or early 20thC context, and is certainly easy to live with.*

15 *Sombre colours are typical of the Victorian period, although black woodwork like this can be a little too much to live with!*   I.II

The skirting board was a consequence of the 18th-century preference, in grand houses, for plastered walls rather than panelling. Marble floors had a marble skirting which protected the wall when the floor was being cleaned. However, 18th-century skirting boards were usually made of wood. Plaster was frequently found in 19th-century houses.

A reminder of the sill of old panelling, these deep skirtings were moulded and often intricately carved – in keeping with the architraves around windows and doors and with the shutters of the room. Palladian houses have rich but restrained and subtly varied carving: the "egg-and-tongue" type of moulding was especially popular. Deep but simply moulded skirting boards are characteristic of Victorian and Edwardian houses, becoming shallower and more austere as the 20th century wore on.

When houses were chiefly one high open space the only ceiling was the inside of the roof. Timber-framed houses were usually thatched and the underside of the thatch, increasingly blackened by soot, was all that could be seen from the room below. Even when pantiles were used (as in East Anglia) a layer of thatch was put beneath as lining and insulation.

The introduction of an upper floor naturally created a ceiling in the lower room. At first the term "ceiling", or "sealing", referred to the panelling which lined or sealed the walls of a room. However, when the underside of upper floors came to be treated in the same way, the word came to acquire its current usage.

As with so many architectural elements, the earliest treatments for the undersides of floors survived in vernacular buildings long after they had been superseded elsewhere. Thatch roofs were often sealed on both sides with lime plaster, partly to reduce fire risk and partly to make them longer-lasting and even warmer. Sometimes upper floors were simply plastered rushes laid between the narrowly spaced joists. Wooden floorboards laid over the joists were often sealed on the underside with plaster too, for insulation and cleanliness, leaving the joists themselves exposed. Ceilings like this continued to be made in country houses **1**

1 Many original beamed ceilings were painted, and any traces of this should be preserved. Complete restorations should follow appropriate period colours. In this example red, cream, blue and gilding give the room a mellow "aged" feel.

for hundreds of years and still look right today.

The bare undersides of floorboards made a simpler ceiling still. However, if the original wide floorboards of oak or elm have been replaced with narrower pine boards, the visual impact may be inferior, and it will be preferable to apply a coat of plaster between the joists for sound or heat insulation between lower and upper floors. When this practice was followed in the 17th century, the space between the boards and the plaster was filled with straw. The modern version of this is to use lengths of fibre-glass insulation between floorboards and plaster-board panels on the ceiling below.

As vernacular building skills were dying out early in the 20th century, there was a curious fashion for painting joists black to give an "olde worlde" country look. However, this has no foundation in history. Fine timber in better-quality houses was usually left untreated, but for centuries in cottages and farmhouses the joists and floorboards have been limewashed, occasionally with pigments added, or patterned with flowers and leaves. With great patience you can remove 20th-century black and restore the ceiling woodwork by sanding and treating with paint stripper. Often the dark staining has penetrated the wood, so that planing may even be necessary. An alternative is to paint white or off-white emulsion directly over the black to give an acceptable and hard-wearing period effect. Limewash, which needs to be reapplied more frequently, may be used by the purist restorer.

TUDOR ORNAMENT

Timber beams and joists were at first merely functional, but the Tudors saw decorative possibilities in them. Using the limited tools available then, they began to give them champfered corners and mouldings similar to those on stone ribs. Many handsome Tudor ceilings have survived, with oak beams chiselled and gouged into smoothly flowing ribs, like those in the linenfold panelling of the same period. The undersides of beams could be carved

2 Tudor beams were often painted. Such decoration should be preserved if possible. Restoration should only be undertaken by an expert, as colours have to be carefully matched.

3 Friezes are one of the great joys of Tudor interiors. The carving often reached great heights of grotesque ornamentation.

with Gothic ornament, and gaps between them further divided by mouldings.

The Tudors also became prolific plasterers. Like the wooden ceilings, the plaster ones were at first divided into compartments by moulded ribs with plaster bosses or pendants at their intersections, just as in stone vaulting. Gradually, ribs became flatter and developed into the characteristic strapwork, with lozenges and geometric shapes, scrolls and Tudor roses. Bosses and pendants punctuated the junctions where ribs intersected. Much of the repeated background ornament was made in moulds, while figures and other ornament in deep relief were hand-modelled *in situ*.

Early in the Tudor period wooden friezes were carved and moulded to match the heavy beams. Plaster ceilings also were soon accompanied by a modelled plaster frieze. Although coving was sometimes used at the conjunction of wall and ceiling, deep plaster friezes

5

7

4

6

8

were more often applied at the tops of walls. They had an even greater wealth of decoration than the ceilings themselves. There was no real precedent for the frieze, and its ornament developed freely. Dolphins and mermaids were much liked; secular and biblical narratives were told in high relief; scrolls, lozenges, acorns and flowers complemented identical motifs on the ceilings; and landscapes based on Flemish engravings unfolded around the top of the walls. Sometimes the ornament featured personifications of the Virtues or the senses. Such flourishes, naturally restricted to the greater houses, came to an end as purist classical influences were felt, although they were to enjoy a vernacular revival some hundred years later.

In lesser houses plastered ceilings also became more ornamental, though less spectacularly so. They spread over the beams and joists themselves, with ornamented

panels on the flat infilling and mouldings on the beams. Unplastered ceilings were frequently lined between the beams with tongued-and-grooved boarding, again divided into compartments by strips of moulding and sporting carved wooden bosses – when, that is, the owners could afford such embellishment. Plain timber boarding was often used for farmhouse and cottage ceilings in succeeding centuries, usually white-washed or painted and sometimes extending over the beams to form a flat ceiling.

4 *Some rot has to be expected in beams that have survived 300 years. Parts of beams can be replaced, and this may well be essential with structural beams. If possible, however, you should cut back to good wood and treat with a proprietary brand of woodworm killer. Over-restoration can be totally counterproductive.* CP

5 *The 18thC addition to this house saw little improvement in insulation. The ceiling is just the inside of the roof shingles.*

6 *It has recently been accepted that the natural honey colour of oak is in itself a delight and the practice of painting or staining black is totally unnecessary. If beams have been painted, sanding is the most effective solution. Protect your furnishings adequately against the dust.*

7 *This 17thC New York house has a perfect example of a beamed ceiling of the time. The beams were hewn from white oak close to the house and the ceiling is merely the underside of the floorboards above.*

8 *When taking a ceiling down to expose the beams underneath, one is usually left with lathe marks. You can remove these by sanding, although this gives the beams a very new look. Waxing with clearwax will often create a pleasing effect.*

1 *Note the fine cotton damask used in the first-floor drawing room of this late 18thC house. This was usually the most richly decorated room, as it was used principally for entertaining. The cornice and frieze are original.* RC

2 *This pierced cornice is typical of the late 18thC. Such cornices should be vacuumed at least once a year. If the moulding is finely carved, clean with a small brush.* RC

CLASSICISM

In his work for the Court in the 1620s and 30s Inigo Jones introduced smoothly plastered and often coved and painted ceilings decorated with mouldings and gilded ornament in a much more authentic classical tradition. After 1630 and as a result largely of Jones's influence, plaster dolphins, badges and pendants took over from compact fruit and flowers, ribbons and wreaths, musical instruments and suspended cherubs in many great houses. Perhaps to our eye plasterwork had lost some of its earlier verve but it remained highly decorative in Palladian houses in Britain into the 18th century and in North America up to the 1750s. By Regency times the divided ceilings of the Palladians with their heavily ornamented compartments and elaborate friezes and cornices were thought to be ponderous and ugly. The Adam brothers ridiculed them almost as much as they ridiculed the mid-century vogue for French Rococo ornament.

In Georgian houses right across the scale of wealth, relief plasterwork was very much in demand, often

3,4 *Two examples of cornices which show the refined classical taste so prevalent in the late 18th and early 19thC.* RC

5,6 *Classical swags on the frieze were a popular late 18th and early 19thC design. The first example here is a modern reproduction. The second, with a Greek key pattern cornice, is original.*

7

8

15

9

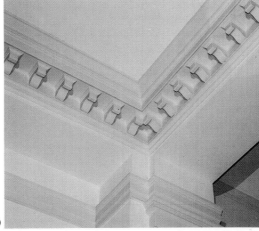

10

providing surprising contrasts to the rather plain exteriors of the houses. Italian plasterers from France took their art to Dublin and there you can find grand schemes in plaster relief with gods and clouds and birds in flight and borders of acanthus leaves. These feature even in relatively modest houses as the Italians' work was imitated and developed by local craftsmen during the 1740s.

The Adam brothers revolutionized all this with their chaste ornament in Grecian or Etruscan style for ceilings, friezes and walls. Meanwhile, owners of humbler contemporary houses contented themselves with a straightforward cornice. The very simplest houses either continued in the floorboards-and-joists tradition or, in towns, had plain plastered ceilings and nothing more.

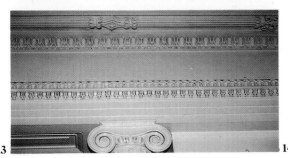

11

12

13

14

7,8 *Two cornices from a New York house built in 1765. The first picture shows some of the architectural wallpaper fashionable in the Federal period, used extensively in hallways in the 18th and 19thC. The second, in a bedroom, is a plain cornice in the style popular from the 18th to the 20thC.* MJ

9 *Often, plasterwork panels were inserted into beamed areas in an attempt to keep up with the new fashion.* CP

10 *Deep cornices such as this one are often found in high rooms. Owing to years of over-painting, such cornices may sometimes be left with no real detail. The most effective method of cleaning is by hand with a paint stripper. This often loosens pieces of plaster, and instant repairs may be necessary.*

11 *The fashion for white painted ceilings gave more light and started a new trend for a decorative plastered effect.* CP

12,13 *Two views of an elaborate cornice and pillar from the parlour of an early 19thC New York house. The cornice is accentuated by being painted in three tones.* OMH

14 *This early 18thC cornice would have been added to the house during remodelling in 1728. The leaf design is of particular interest: a new mould had to be made for each leaf. Today, we have the advantage of rubber, but such cornices are still expensive to restore.* CP

15 *In this reproduction of a mid-18thC American house the cornice decoration is in carved wood.* HH

1 *The Victorians often imitated a much earlier design, as this late 19thC ceiling shows. It is a good copy of the Chinese Chippendale style, although the cornice is slightly too ornate.* CP

THE 19TH CENTURY

The *nouveaux riches* of the turn of the century tended to opt for profuse decoration in their houses. Their ceilings were stuccoed and painted with landscapes and mythical scenes. Later in the century the many new houses being built also enjoyed the luxury of decoration. Cornices and friezes were cast in moulds, and a sort of *papier mâché* was often used for ornaments so that despite their elaborateness they were light enough to be fixed in place with screws.

Compared with earlier craftwork this moulded decoration, which remained in favour into the 20th century, certainly owes more to repetition than to inspiration. Nevertheless, acanthus-leaf cornices and heavy central ceiling roses in halls, and main rooms of 19th-century houses are very much part of their imitable style. They have often been made ugly by successive coatings of distemper which have blurred their relief, and will be much improved with careful cleaning. There are specialist restorers who undertake this work; however, it can done by anyone whose affection for the original is enough to inspire endless patience. A crisp relief will repay the careful work involved, giving a marked uplift to the room.

At the end of the 19th century there was a new emphasis on craftsmanship and individualism. Rather than conforming to a predetermined model, each room was treated as a unique problem with its own solution with regard to the size, angle and enrichment of cornice, ceiling bands and other decoration. Flower and leaf ornament and scrolls and loops were sometimes used very expressively in domestic public buildings. The pattern and depth of relief were scaled to suit the ceiling height. Schemes were determined by the shape of the room and the position of the windows. The acorn was a much-loved motif. Other themes included oak trees, squirrels, daisies and even fairies; sometimes these motifs were coloured while the plaster was still comparatively moist.

At the same time new methods of mass-producing plasterwork were being found, using clay models to make jelly (gelatine) moulds. Definition was lost in the process, so that castings from such moulds were indistinct. Today, however, the jelly mould comes into its own as a way of casting replacements for damaged work to match existing ornament.

2 *As the 19thC progressed, friezes were often incorporated into other features to augment the decorative effect.* CP

3, 4 *These simple but elegant Greek Revival cornices were used in both Britain and America from the late 18th to the end of the 19thC. Their very simplicity contributed to their longevity.* BP

5,6,7 *The simple classical cornice in the main reception room of a New York house built in 1875 is in direct contrast to the plaster columns and arches (pictures 6 and 7).*

12 *Cornices in bedrooms were usually simpler than those in the main rooms of the house. However, this elegant pattern would have been considered suitable for the living room in a lesser early 19thC house.*   OMH

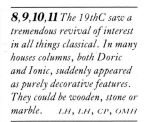

8, 9, 10, 11 *The 19thC saw a tremendous revival of interest in all things classical. In many houses columns, both Doric and Ionic, suddenly appeared as purely decorative features. They could be wooden, stone or marble.*   LH, LH, CP, OMH

In the 19thC the ceiling rose became an essential adjunct of a tastefully decorated room. The size and complexity of the rose was dictated by the room's importance. There are many different types, often needing careful cleaning to show the true magnificence of the plasterwork.

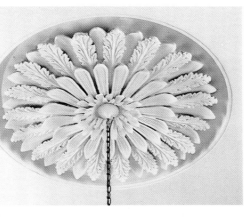

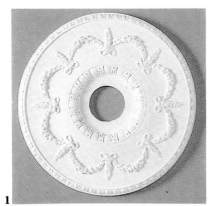

1

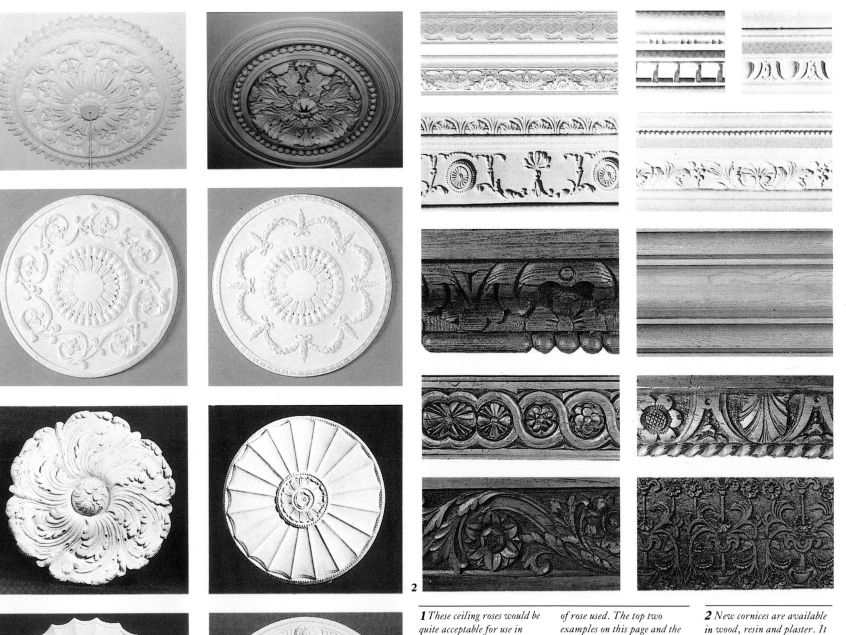

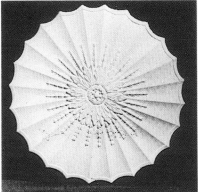

2

1 These ceiling roses would be quite acceptable for use in houses built between the later years of the 18thC and the end of the 19thC. You have to bear in mind the size and proportion of the room when adding a ceiling rose. It is also worth checking throughout the house or, if possible, in similar houses to see the style and size of rose used. The top two examples on this page and the top four opposite are original cornices from 19thC houses in America and Britain. The other roses shown are modern, designed to blend with 18th and 19thC styles; these particular examples are made by Hodkin and Jones.

2 New cornices are available in wood, resin and plaster. It should be noted that good plaster cornices which are moulded to a specific design can be expensive. However, the above are good examples of standard designs.

Cornice cleaning

Distemper paints are water-bound and can be removed with water. You can use water-soaked rags or sponges to wet the old distemper, but this is a messy job and cannot easily be done without also soaking the walls and floor. A steam spray (which can be hired), more often used for stripping wallpaper, does the job with less fuss.

When distemper is thoroughly damp you can scrub it out of crevices with a bottle brush or nail brush – and sometimes you can use a small spoon to gently clean out the hollows. For intricate work, you may need to use wood-carving tools bought from an art shop.

It is not advisable to paint distemper-laden plaster relief work with emulsion paint as a stopgap until you can find time for a proper cleaning job. First, the emulsion cannot get a proper "purchase" on top of the flaky distemper; and secondly it will ultimately make the distemper much more difficult to remove.

These views of an early 19thC cornice show a three-stage restoration process. The first shows the uncleaned cornice, with the detail totally obscured by layers of distemper. The second shows the same cornice after hours of painstaking cleaning, using a wood-carving tool. The result is really quite dramatic. The third example was produced by a specialist plaster firm who took a mould from a restored section. Each leaf is made up of two parts, as is each flower; the back is produced in lengths.

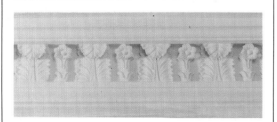

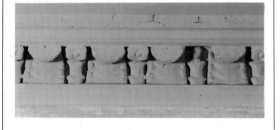

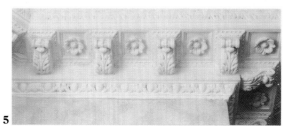

1,2 These friezes in a late 19thC house are reminiscent of earlier designs, in theme if not in execution. Period styles tend to be cyclical. LH

3 This ceiling offers an excellent example of early anaglypta wallpaper. The cornice is lincrusta, a pioneering material in the mass production of period detail. LSH

4 The authentic feel of this late Victorian cornice is achieved by using a classic period green with gold. LSH

5 This "wedding cake" ceiling was introduced into a Georgian drawing room by exuberant 1880s craftsmen. CP

6,7,8 Modern cornicing, readily available in standard lengths, can be used with reasonable success in period rooms from the end of the 18thC, especially if the rooms themselves are plain. Alternatively, if parts of the original cornice are intact, restoration is possible from a mould (picture 8).

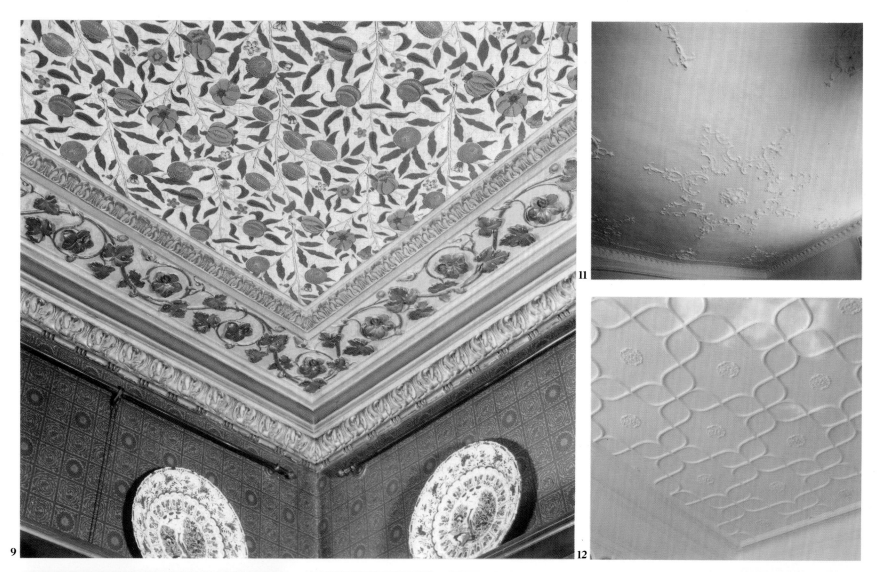

9,10, *As the 19thC progressed, the style changed from light classical to the heavy late Victorian. Wallpaper was often used on the ceiling, and numerous colours and textures added to the overall impression of confident vulgarity.* LSII

11 *The late Victorians did, on occasion, emulate 18thC motifs, as in this copy of a Chinese Chippendale style.* CP

12,13 *By the end of the 19thC, even grand ceilings could be wallpapered to give the impression of plasterwork.*

Early houses often had no stairs at all: the upper floor was reached by a ladder. Stone houses, however, were likely to have one or both of two simple stair types: a flight of stone steps ascending on the outside of the house, or a winding flight set into a wall inside. The former type persisted in vernacular buildings, especially in northern England and in Scotland, for over five hundred years. Sometimes it provided access to separate quarters for people employed by the house; sometimes, in the Norman tradition and especially on sloping sites, storage rooms were on the ground floor and the steps led to the living quarters above.

Wooden Stairs

The upstairs rooms that became a feature of late medieval halls were reached by ladders, even when the rooms were used for living rather than storage space: they were easy to move and took up very little space. When wooden stairs first appeared, early in the 16th century, they were little more than fixed, solid ladders made of oak blocks set against the wall and cased on the open side with bare, functional panelling.

As galleried show houses began to be built for courtiers and gentry during the course of the century, it was realized that stairs could be handsome features, although they remained simple compared to those of the following century. Gradually, they became broader. They were usually of oak, in keeping with the other parts of the house. Sometimes the steps were made of solid blocks instead of the separate treads and risers now normal. Running from floor to floor in a succession of straight flights, they had stout newel posts supporting a balustrade of sturdy balusters and a broad handrail, moulded like the beams. The newel posts had big carved terminals, or extended up to the ceiling and acted as structural supports for the floor above. Sometimes they were carved with strapwork designs that reflected the ornamental plasterwork of the ceiling. In less grand houses where solid, hand-carved balusters were inappropriate, craftsmen instead produced flat balusters with similar outlines but in two dimensions and often perforated to give a lighter effect.

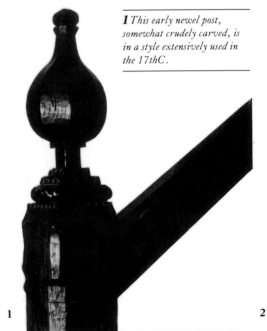

1 This early newel post, somewhat crudely carved, is in a style extensively used in the 17thC.

1

2 When the central chimney was removed from the heart of the house, it was normally replaced by a staircase or "pair of stairs". The dogleg stair first appeared in the mid-17thC and has remained a firm favourite, especially in terrace houses, to the present day.

2

17TH-CENTURY STAIRS

Beginning with the work at Knowle House, Kent, in 1605, the 17th century saw much more magnificent stairways in the great houses, and scaled-down grandeur in big farmhouses. At the same time smaller houses were moving more and more towards built-in and cased flights of stairs instead of ladders.

Long straight flights with right-angled dog-leg changes in direction gave way to shorter flights punctuated by landings – an arrangement which had a dramatic visual impact. Stairs could be articulated round to form a well or could lead in separate stages to a gallery above. The balustrade and the string running along the side of the stairs at its base were painted in complex colour schemes. Newel posts in the best houses terminated in carved heraldic beasts, symbols of the owner's family. Balusters were now often rectangular but highly carved, and the stair handrails were flatter. Sometimes balusters were replaced with ornamentally carved panels, casing in the stairs to handrail level. This panelling, of painted pine or oak, would be matched by panelling up to the dado rail on the wall.

Inigo Jones introduced many fine staircases in the Italian manner and stairs with marble steps and pretty iron balustrades – ironwork was often used for balustrading after the Restoration. Jones's stairs might be curved round in a sweep instead of rising in angular straight flights, but even so they could still occupy a confined space. However, by the end of the century the tendency was for stairs to occupy key positions as they rose up the two storeys of the hall, the grandest room of the house.

3

3 *This secondary staircase in a 16thC house is a good example of a simple form of stairs. It is often a mistake to use over-elaborate features in an early house.*

4,5 *Early stairs were often beautifully joinered, balustraded and enriched with carving. If a stick is missing, a local wood turner should be able to make a replacement.*

6 *Although the newel post on this 17thC stairway is highly decorative, the actual sticks are flat.*

4

5

6

THE 18TH CENTURY

The concept of the magnificent entrance hall in which the stairs had pride of place was fully developed by Palladian architects in the houses for the wealthy built from around the 1720s in Britain and the United States. Marble steps were flanked by exquisitely worked iron balustrades and the ceiling above the staircase was singled out for superlative treatment, such as *trompe l'oeil* coffering. The walls along the stairs were also treated grandly, perhaps painted with architectural subjects from classical antiquity. Many fine new town houses were built on a smaller scale, but still following the same principles, with the stairs designed to make a major impact on entrance .

In houses with wooden stairs the chunky look of earlier examples would now have been quite out of keeping and newel posts were much slimmed down. Balusters were made finer too, and were evenly spaced, two or three per stairs. Handrails were generally narrower, to team up with the lighter newel posts. The barleysugar twist, which had first appeared around 1690, came into vogue for balusters and long remained fashionable, even though there were many other imaginative designs by the middle of the century. In England classically fluted and vase-shaped balusters were applied to elegant mid-18th-century stairs, and, of course, wrought iron was used in grand houses with stone stairs; however, in the United States barleysugar continued in popularity until the end of the century.

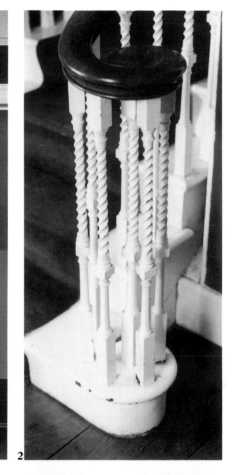

1,2 This type of turning on the sticks was extremely popular in England in the 18thC and was mirrored by a similar development in America. Often one or several sticks have been broken. If this involves complicated turning, a perfect stick may have to be removed and taken to a wood turner to be copied.

3,4 The panelling and decorative elements on this staircase are typical of grand houses of the mid-18thC. The use of three different patterns of turning on the balusters is common in America. IHI

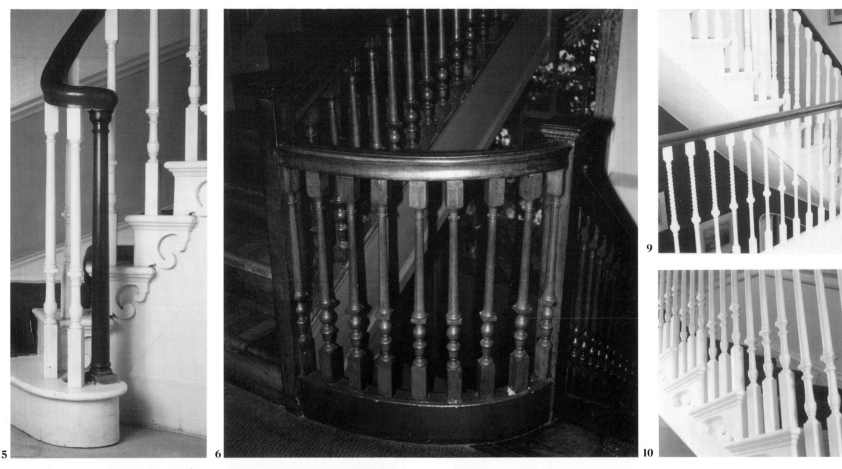

5

6

7

8

9

10

9,10 *Stair turning in the 18thC developed into a fine art form, with turners producing either intricate or plain designs. Many local forms developed, which makes it difficult to replace sticks with mass-produced items. It is also worth pointing out that much decoration on stairs is hidden by layers of paint. To reveal original carving, paint must be stripped back to bare wood.*

5 *Classic 18thC wooden stairs like these can be found in town houses in both Britain and America. Many have been vandalized or replaced by plain sticks, and thus need restoring to their original condition.* RC

6 *This mid-18thC stairway in a New York house is a fine example of simple but elegant balusters.* VC

7,8 *Many 18thC houses had quite plain staircases with straight sticks and a minimum of carved decoration.* MJ

1 *These cast-iron sticks were popular in the 18th and 19thC. They were frequently painted.* GH

2 *Stairs were often built in stone. Old stone steps which are beginning to break up are very dusty, and should be vacuumed regularly.* GH

3 *An interesting example of a secondary staircase added to a 17thC New York house in 1820.* BH

4 *A classic example of an early 19thC staircase in a terrace house. Note the plain square sticks.*

5 *The wooden newel post of this period had lost its 18thC flamboyancy. In less grand houses in the early 19thC it was a purely functional end to the handrail.*

6 *In an 1830s New York house, the hole left by the bolt that holds the post into the floor joist is capped with a mother-of-pearl coat button. The story is that, when the mortgage was paid off, the button would be replaced with a silver coin.*

7 *An interesting solution, in a 1830s New York House, to the problem of how to make a handsome staircase without expensive turned elements. The newel post is not turned, and the simple balusters are set at an angle in the plain round banister.*

8 *This interestingly carved mid-19thC newel post at the top of the cellar steps actually faces the front door.* BP

9,10 *This excellent staircase has been well restored in a Neo-classical stone mansion built between 1837 and 1846. The cluster of sticks forming the newel post is a common 19thC device.* BP

THE 19TH CENTURY

The fashion for balusters with complex shapes died out at the end of the 18th century, and square-sectioned wooden bars had become common. Panelling in place of balusters had disappeared, and so, in general, had the solid string. In the 19th century, balusters (three per step in good houses, but two in smaller ones) almost always rested directly on the stairs themselves, and in most houses of the period they were accompanied by smooth mahogany handrails, which were characteristically oval in section.

Many 19th-century houses had a two-storey rear extension, making the stairs even darker than they had been in the Georgian period: the half-landing at the first level now led to the back extension, so there was no possibility of a window. Sometimes such staircases would be lit by a skylight, with the light filtering down the well to the ground level.

4

5

6

7

8

9

10

1 *This 1830s New York staircase is a perfect example of the period.*

2 *A highly decorative newel post from the 1830s. The original builder of this New York house used many details from pattern books of the time. This design was probably meant to be executed in stone; but here it was made in oak.* OMH

3 *This first-floor landing newel post is much simpler than the previous ground-floor example.* OMH

4 *By the last quarter of the 19thC, although the staircase could often be quite small, the newel post was still a major feature.*

5 *These cast-iron staircases, with all their intricate detail, are very much a part of the late Victorian terrace. The greens and browns which predominate in this 1870s house accentuate the Victorian character.* LSH

6 *This Arts and Crafts house is a good example of the reintroduction in the late 19thC of the grand staircase.*

In the simplest Victorian houses, with front doors opening into the small front room, the staircase was a cased-in and extremely modest flight leading from the corner of the back room to a tiny landing between the two rooms on the upper floor. The large new terraced and semi-detached houses of the time still managed to give a flourish to the stairs, sometimes with a moulded nose extending along the exposed sides of the treads as well as along the front, and often with the bottom step broader from side to side than the rest and curving round at the ends. This feature, and the handrail sweeping round above it, were fashions developed from the grander houses of the preceding century. With them went ornate cast-iron balusters or balusters turned in soft wood on a square base; the latter became standard in smaller houses by the 20th century.

In comfortable private houses of the early 20th century, the traditional wooden staircase with turned balusters and broad moulded handrail enjoyed a final moment of glory before being ousted by the trend towards modernistic simplification.

7

8

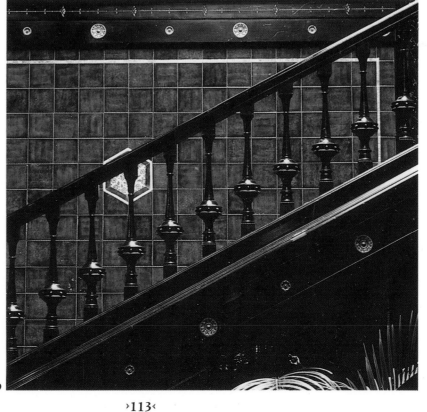

9

10

11

7 The central courtyard of this essentially Elizabethan house was filled with the staircase hall in the 1880s. Late Victorian taste demanded a spectacular stairway in a house of this importance. CP

8,9 This late 19thC staircase in Leighton House, London, was designed by George Aitchison. The balustrading is oak which has been stained and lacquered, the detailing in gold. The carpet is modern but woven from the original cards, based on the pattern "The Tree of Life" from a historic rug. LH

10 By the turn of the century, sticks were being mass-produced. If you are replacing damaged sticks, always have at least one extra turned.

11 Many firms produce new staircases with an acceptable period feel. This example is admirable. WB

A fireplace is one of the obvious things to install or replace when you set about restoring a period room. The right choice can bring the whole interior together; a mismatch, on the other hand, can absolutely destroy the whole carefully wrought effect.

However, distinctions between "right" and "wrong" are not always clear-cut. There is a bewildering range of original and reproduction fireplaces available but not so much guidance on where to use them.

It is relatively easy to replace a Victorian or even an 18th-century fireplace correctly, as such interiors are well-documented. More difficult, however, is the question of what you put into a 15th-century house – few of us really want a central hearth with a hole in the roof to let out the smoke! In such cases you have to accept a compromise, matching materials and styles that are as sympathetic as possible. Whatever type of house you are restoring, your choice will be governed by its position on the social scale and the particular room with which you are concerned.

The Saxon tradition of a central open fire was still the norm in most

houses until the beginning of the 16th century.

In the great houses of medieval times the fire was placed at the upper end of the large communal living hall and the burning wood was controlled by an iron fire-dog (an endiron or andiron) which also served as a spit. The basic fireplace was established when a hood was introduced to minimize smoke: this was most easily supported by a wall, so the fire was moved from a central to a lateral position. An indentation was made to accommodate the fire, and a chimney was provided, with flues that conducted smoke to holes in the wall or to a louvre in the roof. However, chimney building was inhibited by a tax imposed by Rome. Until the Reformation smoke still left many houses through a hole in the roof, whether the fire was against a wall or against a plaster-covered wooden reredos (usually of elm, which does not ignite easily) with a wattle-and-daub canopy and funnel.

From the 16th century a single central chimney normally heated the whole of the house. When a further room was added to the basic plan, this would be provided with its own fireplace and chimney on the end wall.

1 Even in the 16th and 17thC many fireplaces were imported from Italy, Spain, Portugal and France. These extended chimneypieces became very popular.

2 The typical 16thC inglenook fireplace which provided the family with heating and cooking facilities. It may take quite a bit of detective work to find an original fireplace, as many were filled in over the centuries. Note: the original fireplace may look out of place in a "Georgianized" room.

3 The inglenook (from the Scottish Gaelic aingeal, and nook meaning corner) may well need quite extensive renovation. Old bricks should be used where possible and care must be taken in choosing an acceptable colour. The main beam or mantel has sometimes been removed. It is possible to find old beams in most areas.

FIRE SURROUNDS

The simplest form of fire surround was a hood set in the wall over the fire, supported either by piers or by a stone lintel bracket. This survived through more than three centuries, while grander or more elegant chimneypieces were being developed. In Tudor houses the deeply recessed fireplace was given a Tudor arch of stone and otherwise treated as part of the panelled wall.

4

7

5

6

4,5,6 *The fire surround and overmantel provided the perfect surface for incorporating the decoration that was a measure of wealth and status in the 17thC. These beautifully made examples are modern reproductions.* SI

7 *A fine Continental carved marble overmantel of hybrid taste, 16thC, set over a more classically orthodox fire surround. Imports were sometimes of whole fireplaces, but often of finely carved panels to set into locally made surrounds.*

1

2

3

However, the mongrel classicism of European craftsmen soon influenced the decoration. Grander houses had a carved wooden ledge above the stone arch and richly carved panels above that.

In the Elizabethan great houses the fireplace, framed with columns and an entablature with highly ornamented carved wooden panels above, was the focal point of an already much decorated room. This type of surround was elaborately applied in showy Jacobean houses too, with the owner's coat of arms carved in the panel above the fire. Inigo Jones and his pupil John Webb were later to handle this same treatment with a better understanding of classicism and Italian Renaissance models. However, their work was confined to important buildings and was not taken up generally until the 18th century.

CHANGES IN THE 17TH-CENTURY

In some country districts twigs, peat, furze or even dung were still being burnt in the middle of the room in the old manner, with the occupants seated on low stools under the smoke. In more prosperous and forested areas the fuel was wood, and fireplaces were high and wide to accommodate it. When coal was introduced it produced still more smoke than timber; however, coal was not in common use until the 18th century in Britain and the 19th in North America.

To reduce smoke a chimney cloth was placed across the mantle and this soon became a decorative feature of

3 A wonderful example of a George II (1727-1760) Siena marble chimneypiece taken from a substantial English house in Wiltshire. These fire surrounds are extremely rare and have *frequently cost a great deal to restore. It is worth noting that such a fireplace demands a prestigious setting and would look out of place in anything but a grand room. As always, scale is crucial.* cofsi.

1 A 17thC Baroque chimneypiece in Verona marble, originally intended for a grand Italian house. Many such fireplaces were imported into England from Italy and many more were made in England by Italian craftsmen.

2 When considering the fireplace, one of the most important decisions is whether you are going to have a modern reproduction, put in a genuine period fireplace which is not original to the house or try to restore what is there. This example is authentic, but an import: a 17thC Italian chimneypiece in pale yellow Verona marble, beautiful and rare. cofsi.

4

8

6

9

the fireplace. It continued to appear in Victorian homes, even though by this time fires had supposedly been cured of smoking.

With the introduction of coal came a narrower grate placed in the wide hearth. In new buildings the fireplace itself was now set further back. This meant that in thinner-walled brick buildings the chimneystack formed a projection on the outside wall. Fireplaces in older homes tend to have been modified over the years and have often been made narrower, but if building work is being done on houses with chimneys like this, it will almost certainly reveal that the house originally had a wide fireplace.

Another feature dating back to the 17th century which may still be found in country houses, even of very modest size, is the clay bread oven, an early ancestor of the kitchen range. This was a British invention, found especially in Devon and Cornwall, but exported to North America soon after the Pilgrim Fathers. And you still may find in country kitchens the built-in box in which salt was kept to dry beside the fire, and the lockable fireside spice cupboard.

7 A detail of the mantel in 6, right, showing the intricate carving and classical ornamentation that was becoming popular in both Britain and America in the late 18thC. VC

7

4 This example is from a mid-18thC New York house. The fireplaces in the servants' quarters or, as in this case, the children's nursery, were usually simple in style. VC

5 A simple fireplace with no mantel and surrounded by panelling – typical of mid-18thC New York. The paint is modern but an authentic colour. VC

6 In the same house, a splendid fireplace of late 18thC style. It would have been added around 1780. VC

8,9 This mid-18thC fireplace is set into the panelling with Delft tiles surrounding the opening. Tiles like these have frequently been damaged either by heat or over-zealous workmen. It is interesting to discover if the tiles in such fireplaces are English or Dutch and also their date: the glaze and colour can be quite different depending on origin. VC

FIREPLACE FURNITURE

Where wood was the fuel, fire dogs continued to be necessary as a means of propping up logs and keeping them in place. The early fire dogs had been permanently joined together at the base by a low bar which went across the front of the fire. By the 17th century the two dogs stood separately, one at each side of the fire.

A detachable spit was still placed between them at the front, often with a tray beneath to catch the hot fat and juices from roasting meat.

To solve the problem of damage to brickwork, a cast-iron fireback was produced with designs which range from simple to immoderate. Stout bellows and cast-iron tongs, sometimes with a shovel for heaping up the wood ash, completed the furniture of the fireplace. Today it is possible to obtain authentic cast-iron reproductions of fire dogs and backs, bellows and tongs from specialist founders.

THE 18TH CENTURY

In the bigger Tudor and Jacobean houses the fireplaces were all placed centrally, so that the smoke left the building through one chimneystack. But when classically inspired houses became the only acceptable fashion the central chimneystack was a problem in the design: it looked ungainly. One solution was to place fireplaces at the four corners of the house, and to hide the chimneytops as much as possible behind the parapet. These corner fireplaces were given very lavish treatment in early 18th-century stately homes, while simpler corner fireplaces are found in smaller houses of the time. Even when fireplaces were not set in the corners of the rooms, chimneys at the gable ends of the house became standard.

At the beginning of the century many town houses simply had a stone or brick hearth and fireback. The hearth was often given a daily whitening. But with the growth of streets of fashionable new houses, fireplaces become more sophisticated, reflecting those of the great houses. Inigo Jones's designs were at this time being circulated, along with many pattern books showing classical details. Accordingly, fireplaces were given classical frames, with columns or pilasters, and consoles supporting an entablature topped by a picture panel, the whole planned to echo the door case of the room.

In simpler houses the frames were at first in wood. Soon they were lined or made completely with marble or stone. The picture panel above the fire was widely copied in houses for the well off, while grander people were beginning to prefer mirrors.

As coal was increasingly used for fuel, the fireplace opening was made smaller. The fire basket came into being for holding the coals in the old wide hearths, while in new houses the trend was to install a cast-iron coal-burning hob grate with urn-shaped sides – this is the familiar grate of Georgian interiors. Unlike the earlier free-standing grates and contemporary fire baskets, Georgian cast-iron grates were fixed and took up the whole width of the new narrow fireplace, in the manner which persisted into the present century.

This type of grate, its front patterned with classical motifs, its curved sides developing into the double-U shape, suits Georgian and Regency rooms perfectly. Old grates can be restored, and new or restored replacements can be obtained. Even if central heating is more appealing than the thought of carrying coals up and down narrow Georgian stairs, a fireplace in the original style can be cherished for its looks. Unused chimneys need ventilation to keep them dry and should never be sealed without the provision of air vents.

Because the new grates raised the height of the fire, a fender became necessary to catch any falling coals. A poker was also essential. Both fenders and pokers were made in brass, with matching tongs and shovel.

1 *After James Gibbs published his* Rules for drawing the several parts of Architecture *in 1732 his designs were copied and embellished in both England and America. In this example the picture frame has been replaced by a mirror.* CP

2 *From the mid-18thC white marble was considered the most prestigious material for the fireplace in the drawing room – not only in the grand houses but increasingly in smaller houses. This fireplace in a first-floor drawing room is in fact a Victorian copy.* CP

3 *An 18thC fireplace with a classical broken pediment and additional 19thC embellishments.* CP

2

Restoring marble fireplaces

Before attempting to restore a marble fireplace, ensure that you allow yourself plenty of time. It is certainly not a job to be done in a hurry. A point to remember before you begin cleaning is not to use any acids, dyes or alcohol: marble is a porous substance, and fluids such as these will soak into it and stain, or eventually cause the marble to rot.

There are three main problems to be overcome when restoring marble. First, it is likely to be broken or chipped; secondly, it may have been painted; and lastly it may be heavily stained. If you are unlucky you may have to deal with all three!

If the fireplace has been badly damaged, and is in pieces, you will have to break it open and reassemble it from scratch. To do this you will need a special marble glue and extra pieces of marble to make good the breakages. Often a fireplace will be only slightly chipped, in which case it is only necessary to mix up a coloured marble glue to blend with the surrounding marble. Apply this to the damaged area, allow to set and then rub down in turn with a fine wet and dry sandpaper until the surface takes on the same decorative form as the original marble.

You can quite easily remove paint from marble using "Nitromors" stripper. Working on only a few square inches at a time, take off excess stripper with acetone on small swabs of cotton wool. Repeat this until the paint disappears. It is essential to wear rubber gloves to protect your own skin and clothing. If you are very careful, you can also do this using a paint scraper: but bear in mind that marble is easily scratched.

Staining, due to years of neglect, is the most common problem in restoring a marble fireplace. The best way to tackle it is to use a substance called Sepiolite mixed with de-ionized water to a paste of custard-like consistency. This should be applied in a ½in/1cm thickness and left for 12 hours or so, depending on the humidity of the room. When it begins to dry and crack (a process known as *craquelure*), remove the covering and wipe over the marble with de-ionized water on small swabs of cotton wool. This process should remove all stains.

When polishing marble, use a white hard polish: any colouring in the polish will stain. Rub the polish hard into the marble using a soft white cloth. (Any dye in the cloth, again, could seep into the marble.) For a matt finish use a softer polish.

After a long and laborious restoration, it is important to look after the marble. For day-to-day upkeep use a white polish such as "Pledge" to keep it clean. Remember that marble is porous, and careless placement of plantpots and glasses will cause staining.

3

4

4 This very pleasing marble fireplace has been introduced into an early 19thC house. The marble had been painted, but a professional firm stripped the paint before installation. Putting in a marble fireplace is a heavy, dirty, skilled job, not to be undertaken lightly.

1

4

5

2

6

1 This simple French design from the 18thC was intended to be used in lesser rooms. 11

2 By the late 18thC, cameos of fine ceramics were often applied to chimneypieces. Such fireplaces were intended to be painted.

3 This popular mid-18thC design in the William Kent style is suitable for a grand room. Such fireplaces could be used in houses dating from the 1740s through to the turn of the century. 11

4,5 Modern reproduction fireplaces are available in marble. It is interesting to remember that, in the 18thC, fireplaces were often made in marble workshops which the 18thC architect or home owner visited to choose from the many designs available — just as he would today. MII

6 Consideration of proportion is essential when choosing a mantelpiece. This classic Georgian design with square fluted frieze and jambs is ideal for a smaller room where a more ornate, heavily carved example would look totally out of place. 11

7 An inlaid marble chimneypiece decorated with Wedgwood plaques. These fireplaces became very popular after 1778, when Josiah Wedgwood produced them from designs by John Flaxman. The jambs are typically in the form of architectural pilasters. COFSI

3

7

8

9

12

10

13

11

14

ADAM-INSPIRED DEVELOPMENTS

A visually lighter fire surround deprived of pediments was preferred in the later 18th century and was ornamented to perfection by the Adam brothers. From then on, the simple albeit enriched form of pilasters and consoles supporting an entablature with a ledge or shelf above the fire continued as the model fire surround for most of the 19th century.

8 *This carved statuary marble and Blue John (Derbyshire Spa) chimneypiece was made in the 1780s. The delicately carved overmantel is in the manner of Grinling Gibbons (1648-1721).* COfSI.

9-14 *As the 18thC advanced there were two main developments in fireplace design: first, a dominant taste for classical architecture encouraged by the Adam brothers; and secondly, chimneypieces became smaller in standard town houses. These reproduction fireplaces are all eminently suitable for houses built from the later 18thC until well into the 19thC.*
AB,AB,PF,PF,COfSI.,AB

1-14 The range of classically inspired fireplaces on the market from the 1760s on was enormous, with almost every conceivable classical motif applied somewhere or other. Swags, urns and foliage have never really gone out of style since. *Poor modern reproductions are frequently discernible by the hesitant application of undersized motifs. 1-5 are original fireplaces in 18thC houses, and 6-14 are modern reproductions.*

GH,RC,RC,RC,HH,H,MH,
H,H,MH,H,PF,MH,MH

1

2

3

4

5

1 *A humble fireplace was a common feature of many servants' rooms in the late 18thC. This housekeeper's room in the semi-basement is typically plain but very functional.* GH

2 *This early 19thC marble chimneypiece depends for its effect on contrasting marble. Fireplaces of this style demand a grand room.* CofSL

3 *A Regency period statuary marble chimney displaying a more exuberant classical motif. The frieze is carved with Bacchanalian figures at play, the jambs in the form of Antonio Canova's dancing girls.* CofSL

4 *A Scottish white marble fireplace which shows more austere decoration, from the early 19thC.* CofSL

1

3

2

4

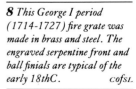

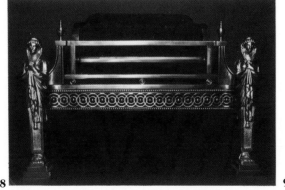

5 *A simple 19thC white marble fireplace imported from France.* MB

6 *By the mid-19thC in minor rooms cast-iron fireplaces like this were often used, often painted white to emulate marble examples.* BH

7 *This marble fireplace is actually French but would equally enhance a drawing room in America or Britain. It has the advantages of small size and not excessive decoration.* MH

8 *This George I period (1714-1727) fire grate was made in brass and steel. The engraved serpentine front and ball finials are typical of the early 18thC.* CofSL

9 *This Regency period, c.1810, brass and steel dog grate could be used to good effect in fireplaces of the late 18th and early 19thC.* CofSL

1

2

3

1 A marble fireplace in a New York house illustrating early 19thC trends. The slightly raised hearth is typically American. MJ

2 French influence is apparent in this fireplace in a front drawing room. White marble was universally thought to be a statement of wealth and taste. MJ

3 This fireplace with its recessed hearth is made from English fossilized marble, but is original to the New York house in which it remains. MJ

4,5 In this 1830s New York house the Greek Revival style is still very much in evidence but both these wooden fireplaces are restrained examples.

6 A wooden fireplace in a mid-1830s house. This is a reconstruction from "paint ghosts" – the traces left on the wall after a fire destroyed it completely. The more ornate surround was used in the front parlour where guests were received.

7 A much plainer wooden surround. The Franklin stove is of the period, around 1836, and would have been in the back parlour where the family spent most if its time.

4

5

6

7

8

9

8, 9 The 19thC saw a wide diversity of styles and materials. This Greek Revival Belgian black marble fireplace dominates the room when placed in an earlier New York house in the 1860s. The grate is original. The capital on the fireplace matches the capitals on the pocket doors. In this period of nostalgia, people were very aware of proportion and symmetry. OMH

10 By around 1840, the American taste for intricately carved chimneypieces was waning. Marble was often used in slab form and surrounds tended to be geometric – a simplification which had happened slightly earlier in Britain. This high coal grate of brass and iron is an English import. It would have been permanently fitted to the fireplace opening with masonry. It was more efficient than andirons. BP

11 This black marble fireplace in the same house is in the upstairs reception room. The fact that the more impressive fireplaces are downstairs would tend to suggest that this upstairs room would be for family, rather than for entertaining on a grand scale. BP

12 A classic Greek Revival white fireplace, very common in houses in New York in the 1830s. OMH

10

11

12

VICTORIAN AND EDWARDIAN DEVELOPMENTS

In Britain experiments towards more efficient burning eventually led to "register grates", with dampers to control the supply of air to the fire, and additional dampers in the chimney throat. These grates were cast in one piece as part of the inner frame and back of the hearth, and set as an insert within the marble surround.

Fire regulations strictly controlled chimney construction in the 19th century, and the risk of fire was further reduced by the almost exclusive use of marble or cast iron in the massive and mass-produced fire surrounds of *piano nobile* rooms in Victorian houses and in the minor fireplaces provided in most of their other rooms. Now that plate glass was readily available, the huge ornamental mirror descended the social scale and replaced the picture or stucco panel over the fireplace. This was a forerunner of the overmantel with side mirrors and shelves around a mahogany-framed central mirror.

Gothic and Picturesque influences affected fireplace design later in the century, and the Arts and Crafts movement's nostalgic yearnings led to a taste for wide hooded hearths, with stone frames and wood surrounds, in which to burn wood again. Most fireplaces, however, became smaller, with surrounds in painted pine or slate – marble was becoming too expensive. At the same time ornament became heavier from the 1860s on. Painted and glazed tiles were fixed into the sides of the cast-iron insert, and tiled hoods became an integral part of the construction. At the turn of the century Art Nouveau brought opulent curving motifs to the tiles, which until now had been patterned rather formally.

With the introduction of gas and electric fires, the outer surround became less and less imposing, simply serving as a frame for a wide area of plain coloured tiles. By easy transitions this became the very modest "modern" fireplace, with free-standing grate and brick back and a surround entirely composed of tilework in mottled buff or beige.

Luckily, when central heating or portable electric fires and 1950s taste conspired to banish older fireplaces, they were as frequently boxed in as removed. You may be surprised how easy it is either to restore the original or put in a replacement to create an authentic focal point in your home.

Before having a new fireplace installed, have the chimney swept and light a fire to make sure that the chimney is sound. Before doing anything in a downstairs room check that the chimney breast has not been removed upstairs – an obvious precaution, but one which the enthusiast may overlook with distressing results!

1,2,3,4,5 By the late 19thC there were as many fireplace designs as there were designers. In the reception areas they tended to be quite grand, while in the servants' areas they were simple and usually small. The size of the fireplace was scaled to that of the room and the degree of ornament was in strict proportion to the room's social importance. CP

6 *While the actual surrounds were frequently simple, much decoration was added to the wrought-iron grates in the later 19thC.* CP

7 *Early 19thC tiles like these should be retained if at all possible. Some damage is totally acceptable and can often add to the period feel, whereas new tiles frequently detract.*

8,9 *In small rooms, cast-iron surrounds were common. These were frequently painted white, as were carved timber or plaster fireplaces. The Victorians would have found our love for stripped pine very amusing: it was a cheap timber which was always concealed.* CP

6

7

8

9

1 *This small fireplace in the hallway of an 1870s terraced house is given prominence by a gilt and mirrored overmantel. The 17thC chimney cloth reappeared at this period: it may have helped to reduce the smoke but was mainly a decorative feature.* LSH

2 *The late Victorians used marble for their most prestigious fireplaces. While the fireplace itself could be quite understated, the brass fire accessories were quite the opposite.* LSH

3 The actual fireplace here is quite small but the overall impression is of a massive, extended chimneypiece. *I.SH*

4 Many of these simple Victorian cast-iron grates still survive. The tiles are often earlier than the grate.

5 To recreate a Victorian fireplace you need to attend to more than merely the fabric. The colours, clutter and general confusion are all necessary parts of the Victorian mood. *I.SH*

6 A detail of a small cast-iron grate with brass hood. These fireplaces were both efficient and highly decorative. *I.SH*

1 *This type of wooden surround with all its classical inspiration fits quite easily into the larger rooms of most substantial 19thC houses. LSH*

2 *A small simple stripped pine fireplace which was standard in many small homes or in secondary rooms in grander houses from the mid-19thC. The English delft tiles assist with the rustic feel, as does the original mass-produced cast-iron grate.* FE

3 *Late 19thC cast-iron fireplaces were frequently painted white. These functional items were also highly decorative. Note the ash drawer at the base – enhanced with a painted tile.*

4 *In America, as in Britain, the decorative qualities of materials such as matt black slate were fully utilized. This example had been painted white in the 20thC and had to be painstakingly stripped.*

5 *Toward the end of the 19thC it became increasingly popular to break up the solid mass of black slate or marble with inset panels – tiles, ceramics and marble were ideally suited.*

6 *This black slate fireplace in the same 1875 house has inserted Minton tiles.*

7 *This squat white marble fireplace is strangely positioned under a window. The situation is attributable to Lord Leighton, who placed it there as a joke. Note the mirrored shutters – is the window a mirror or not? and where does the smoke go?* LH

1

2

3

4

6

5

7

2 *The whole feel of a Victorian fireplace must be enhanced by the surroundings as a whole, as in this evocative ensemble. Although the fireplace is classically Victorian, the real impact is derived from the collection of old glass, treen, porcelain and dried flowers.*

3 *This reproduction sand-blasted fireplace, cast from an old mould, is ideal for a house built at the end of the 19thC or the beginning of the 20thC.* AF

4 *By the end of the 19thC, fire surrounds could be marble, wood (painted and unpainted) or metal. They were sometimes simple and elegant — sometimes highly decorated and charmingly vulgar. Tiles were used to good effect. The actual grate by this period had become small, and the fire was thus more efficient. This reproduction fireplace used in a Victorian or Edwardian house would add considerable character to a room.* AF

1 *The permutations of decorated cast fireplaces and multi-coloured tiles are innumerable. Such features have frequently been despised and are only now receiving due attention.* MH

5,6 *These chimneypieces are in an Arts and Crafts house, but have a light, classical feel. The Victorians did not feel the need to rely simply on one style. This philosophy created some interesting interiors along with some very incongruous designs.*

7 *The solidity of Victorian design is often mistaken for lack of taste. This grand but simple fireplace has stature and elegance.*

8 *This Arts and Crafts house entrance hall fireplace depends much on the Renaissance revival.*

9 *These solid carved wood late Victorian fireplaces have sometimes been most inappropriately sited. Their quality is undeniable but they require careful consideration of their environment to be in keeping.*   I.H

STOVES

Stoves in glazed earthenware or cast iron were much more common in the United States and Europe than in Britain, perhaps because the winters are more consistently extreme outside the British Isles and because wood was widely available for fuel. The completely closed European stove was adapted in Pennsylvania by Dr Benjamin Franklin, whose designs for an open-fronted box stove were imported to England. These extremely functional objects were available from the 1750s to the end of the century, but stoves were never widely adopted in Britain.

1,2,3,4,5 In the 19thC, stoves were more popular in America and Europe than in Victorian England. These reproductions can be used to good effect in any 19th or early 20thC house. They combine the decorative elegance of their Victorian and Edwardian predecessors with modern heating technology. They not only heat the room and provide a hot plate, but they also provide a focal point without the mess associated with an open fire.
S&W,CF,CF,H&S,H&S

6 *Radiators can always be concealed. This screen with a marble top was a late-Victorian way of hiding the massive, ugly but useful heating contraption. The grilles could be either painted or brass.* CP

7,8 *These original 19thC cast-iron radiators look more in keeping with a period house than modern slimmer versions.*

9 *This squat radiator is unusually low and long. This type of radiator, although not authentic, does not look out of place in a large period room.*

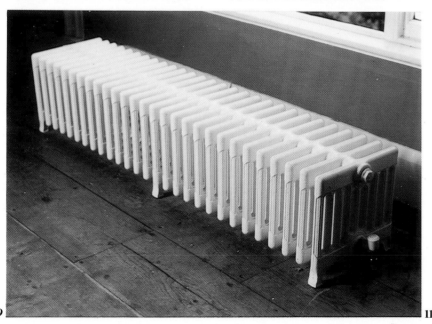

10 *This black-painted radiator is actually inset into the wall. The loss in heating efficiency is balanced by a gain in aesthetic appeal.* I.H

11 *There are firms now producing efficient and modern look-alikes of the original cast-iron Victorian radiators which are fast disappearing from architectural scrap yards.* B

It was not until the 1880s that bathrooms existed as we know them. Anyone restoring an older house therefore has the choice of simple modern sanitary ware, which need not jar whatever the surroundings, or a Victorian or Edwardian style bathroom which will have a "period" look, even though the period may be different from that of the house.

Cleanliness, of course, was valued long before the 19th century. Soap was made in England from the 14th century, and the highest classes in the Middle Ages had decorated jugs and basins in gold or silver, with brass and pewter for the slightly less well-placed. Obvious ancestors of the washstand existed as gilt and copper ornamented lavers, which had a top for the metal wash bowl, a little water vessel and tap above the bowl, a shelf for soap below, and a fixed towel rail.

Bathing in a tub was a sociable activity for nobles and their ladies. Although the tub was usually round like a barrel, longer versions more like the baths of today were also known. Medieval palaces even had precursors of the modern bathroom, with tiled floors and plumbed-in baths supplied with water from a lead tank. Queen Elizabeth I possessed vast bathing rooms lined with wainscotting and mirrors. These early models may serve as fanciful inspiration, but only the jugs and bowls, and perhaps the lavers, can really be borrowed as practical ideas for houses today, when pools and jacuzzis supply the modern equivalent of social bathing.

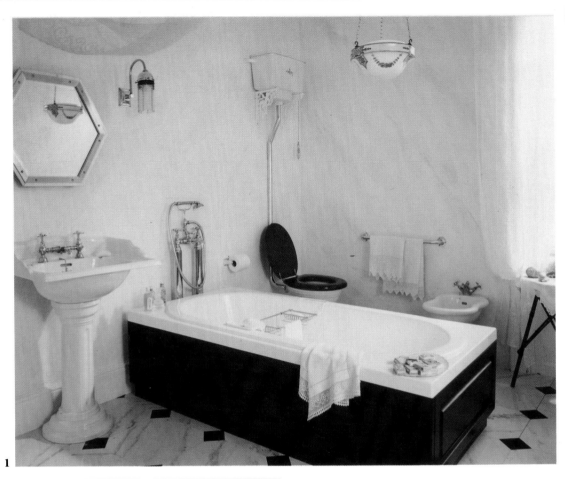

1

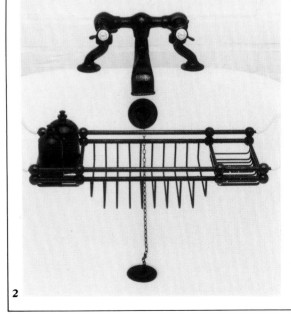

2

1 *This reproduction Victorian bathroom ware has as its central feature a roll-top bath set in a mahogany panel surround. The pedestal basin, the cistern on brackets and the bidet all have a Victorian or Edwardian feel. This effect is accentuated by the lighting, marbled walls and hanging antique lace.* BCS

2 *It is worth remembering that there are alternatives to brass finishes when you are considering bathroom fittings: nickel, chrome, antique copper, antique bronze and, as here, black chrome are some of the many available. This bath filler and rack are part of the Edwardian range.* CS

3 *The roll-top bath which was so spurned in the middle years of this century has made a dramatic comeback. Its design causes a slight plumbing problem but here the brass pipework plays a decorative role.* SP

3

THE BATH

By 1730 communal pumps and aqueducts supplied water to the towns, while some large country houses had their own water supply. Very occasionally, a grand house could also boast a marble-walled bathroom with a large sunken marble bath and piped water. Portable metal baths were quite widely in use by this time – made of tin, flat-bottomed, roll-topped, and filled and emptied by hand. They were not unlike the simpler tin baths, with a handle to carry and suspend them by, which were filled with hot water from the kitchen range in many houses until relatively recently.

Baths as we know them could not become widespread until water tanks were installed in lofts and enamelling and cast-iron techniques had been developed. In France, the wealthiest few had huge "theme" bathrooms with plumbed-in baths, rather like sofas in design, draped with fine cloth in a most unfunctional way. Usually, baths were still portable tubs, painted outside and in.

It was from the 1850s that sheet-metal baths were plumbed in and a small bedroom given over to their use. The style was decorative, with flower-sprigged wallpaper and gathered curtains. The outside of the bath would be stencilled or painted to look like wood. No attempt was made to conceal the plumbing – a blessing to anyone who wishes to recreate a bathroom of this period.

Even in the 1880s flowery wallpaper was still

4

7

5

8

6

4 Few people living in an 16thC beamed house would want to live with bathroom furniture of the period – you can carry authenticity too far! Victorian fittings, either original or reproduction, will give a period feel combined with modern comfort. OR

5 Sponged and marbled walls with classical-motif stencils are a good choice for an 18thC or early 19thC house with large high-ceilinged rooms. The design of the pedestal basin and lavatory is from the first half of the present century, but their simple lines suit the formality of the setting. SI

6 This room successfully recreates the feeling of the late Victorian taste for opulence and elaborate decoration. The bath is enclosed in a lavish mahogany surround and is further decorated with insets of decorated tiles. The basin too is set into a washstand-type unit. VN

7 A Victorian-style roll-top bath is a much more convenient choice than the portable metal ones more usually found at the time. OB

8 The elegant proportions and drag-painted finish on these built-in bathroom units sympathize with the proportions and style of the Georgian house. SI

1,2 These are faithful reproductions of late 19thC fittings. The roomy high-sided basin has a shape that is practical as well as decorative. Often such basins were made in even more elaborate forms of crouching lions or dolphins. Attention to detail is reflected here in the brass and porcelain lavatory chain and ornamental brackets holding the basin and cistern.

TB, AS

4 Following a practice begun around the 1850s, a bedroom in this Victorian house has been turned into a bathroom. The lavatory and pedestal basin are of modern design but echo the rounded line of the roll-top bath. As the room is spacious enough, the owners have added some original Victorian furniture – the mahogany mirror and the chest of drawers with its old lace cloth.

TB

3 This house built in the 1870s still has its original fittings and decoration. Flushing lavatories were well-established by this time and the embossed pedestal is typical of the period. The deep tub made from slabs of marble would have been cold-fill only: cold baths were a normal part of life until well into the 20thC.

LSH

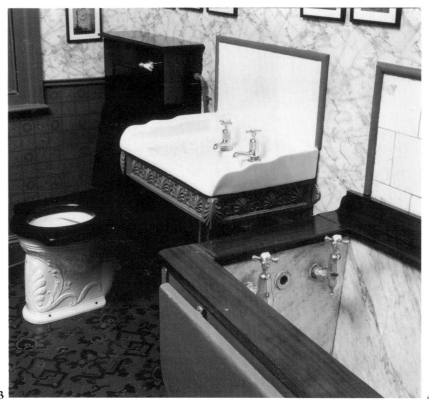

thought suitable, but by now separate bathrooms were included in the planning of new houses, and tiled walls and floors set a new style. Often, the baths themselves were hidden behind solid mahogany panelling, with tiled splash panels around the top. More and more ambitious effects were available, including mahogany hoods and a battery of brass and porcelain taps and buttons to operate all the different types of douche and spray which came gushing forth. In humbler homes, plain cast-iron baths with roll tops and claw feet paved the way for more modest 20th-century bathrooms.

5,6,7 *Three bathrooms which follow the mid-19thC fashion of decorating the outside of the bath. They also reflect the fashion then and later on in the century of adopting a bedroom style of decoration – flowery wallpaper and gathered curtains. This style of bath was produced well into this century, and works with a variety of styles of basin and lavatory.* BCS, CPH, TD

8 *Classic square pedestal basins like this were still being made thirty or so years ago, and work especially well in houses built between the wars. A black and white colour scheme has a particularly good feel of the period.* OB

9 *Whether you are renovating a cottage or a Victorian townhouse, painted fittings like these are a good choice. Their fresh blue and white colouring works well against stronger designs or with beams, low ceilings and white-painted walls.* TB

10 *The choice of tiles is important. The colours here – dark green with cream – are typical of the late 19thC and early 20thC. So are the border designs used at skirting, dado and cornice level and the design of patterned tiles arranged in a diagonal trellis.* TB

1 *A reproduction roll-top bath which gives an excellent period feel without the discomfort. No attempt has been made to hide the pipework which, with the taps and shower mixer, is an attractive as well as authentic feature.* BCS

2 *A Spanish portable bath of the 18thC with carrying handles on either side. It was not until the 1850s that plumbed-in baths began to appear in any other than very grand houses. In humbler homes portable baths were still in use until quite recently. However, this solid marble bath is quite a grand affair. A bath like this can be plumbed-in and would look splendid in a large room, perhaps with marbled walls with a stencilled Greek key border and fittings housed in mahogany cabinets.*

3 *This roll-top bath with brass feet as well as fittings solves the plumbing problem in an interesting way. The shower fitting and porcelain taps are all that are visible, the pipework being hidden by panelling.* SP

4 *By contrast, this roll-top bath displays the brass furniture as part of its decorative appeal. Note also the towel rail and bath rack, which all add to the nostalgic feel. The marble floor and painted brick walls also add to the general mood but could make the bathroom rather cold.* CS

5 *An ordinary shower curtain would strike a jarring note in a period-style bathroom. An etched-glass screen like this one is a more appropriate choice.* BCS

6

9

7

8

10

WASHSTANDS AND BASINS

Tripod washstands made of wrought iron with pewter basins appeared in the 1750s. From the 1770s superior dressing-room furniture included elegant mahogany or rosewood washstands designed by Sheraton or Hepplewhite or their imitators. Set in a quarter circle, so that they could stand in a corner, they had raised, shaped backs, circular bowls and round indentations for the soap. Very soon, even washstands and gentlemen's shaving tables were disguised to look like other furniture, with tops and shelves which opened out, as if their inner workings were slightly indecent. The bidet, also for the dressing room, was introduced from France and was even more convincingly concealed in cabinetwork, while the bedroom chamber pot was hidden away in a beautifully made bedside table or cabinet.

In the 1830s washstands became larger and rectangular, with marble tops which had round openings for deep bowls, and slop pails on a low shelf. They developed into the late Victorian stands which could readily be found in junk shops until quite recently. These had patterned tiled tops and splash-

6 *Even when piped water became fairly common, basins were still set in dark mahogany cabinets with marble tops like washstands. If you are thinking of installing a basin in the bedroom of a Victorian house, copying this idea is an authentic solution.* LSH

7 *Setting deep bowls into marble surrounds was a practice which continued into the 20thC. The classic simplicity of this one on chrome legs, dating from the 1920s or 30s, works well in a Georgian house.* CP

8 *A fascinating example of Victorian ingenuity. This sink, still in its original marble surround, does not look particularly unusual – until you notice that it has no waste outlet. The basin is pivoted: after use you simply swing it over to empty the water into a bucket below – which is then emptied by a menial!* LSH

9 *From the late 18thC, elegant washstands were made in the shape of a quarter-circle to fit in a corner. Here is a Victorian plumbed-in extension of the same idea. Notice how well the marble splashback surround has kept its original good looks.* LSH

10 *The interior of this Neo-classical mid-19thC stone mansion is in the Greek Revival style. This pedestal washbasin with its pedestal in the shape of a column mirrors the overall design. The mirror surround is also classically inspired.* BP

backs with cupboards underneath. A variety of prettily decorated jugs and bowls, perforated soap dishes and false-teeth holders went with them.

As piped water became more common, plumbed-in wash basins were still given surrounds in dark mahogany. Bathrooms sported extravagantly patterned ceramic basins which complemented the water closets and cisterns and opulent gleaming brass taps. By the end of the century, however, plain white ceramic ware was beginning to take precedence over patterns, and by the time the pedestal wash basin was developed in the early 1900s hygenic white was universal.

1 *From the early 20thC pedestals which hid the pipework began to be fashionable. It is therefore quite allowable to use reproductions such as this.* BCS

2,3,4 *Late Victorian inventiveness produced all sorts of elaborate systems for douches and sprays, whose style is reflected in these brass and porcelain reproductions.*
TB, WA, CS

5 *Attention to small details is important when putting in a bathroom. If you can find original taps like these, so much the better.*

6 *An unfussy traditional shape like this works well in a variety of settings from the 18thC to the 1940s* CPH

7 *A modern pine reproduction of a Victorian washstand intended to be plumbed in.* TB

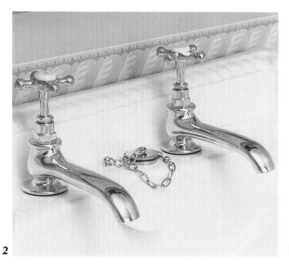

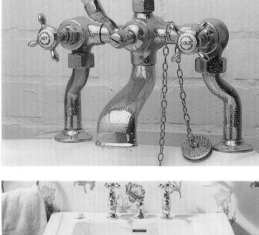

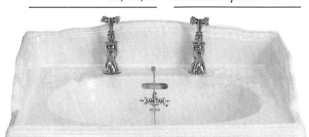

LAVATORIES

A version of the flushing lavatory was invented in 1596 by Sir John Harington, and supplied to Queen Elizabeth herself. After a long and insanitary delay, water was piped to Georgian town houses, and brick drains and public sewers were built. Closets were supplied in the gardens, sometimes flushing and sometimes connected to the main drain, but more often emptying into a cesspit. Proper water closets with traps and valves were introduced in the late 1700s. By the 1840s substantial country houses, at least, were usually well supplied with flushing pans.

Glazed clay pipes made by Doulton were replacing the London brick sewers at the same time. Lavatories too were increasingly made of various kinds of glazed earthenware, and the early types were surrounded by substantial wooden framing. The inside of the bowl was treated as an opportunity for decoration, and was florally adorned in all but the very cheapest models. The outside of the new pedestal lavatory was also decorated. Doultons and Twyfords led the field, and throughout the rest of the century, in Britain and the United States, an astonishing variety of designs and decorative treatments became available.

Pedestals could take the form of crouching lions or dolphins, or were embossed with classical fluting on the outside. Both outside and inside, the bowls might be painted or printed with fruit, flower or willow-pattern designs before being glazed. Blues, reds and pinks were commonly used, and gilding was not unknown. Several reproductions of these designs, with matching basins, bidets and cisterns, are now available.

Seats were usually of polished mahogany or other wood. Porcelain handles, paper-holders (often set into the back of the lavatory itself) and matching porcelain cisterns added to the decorative effect. Cisterns were also made in cast iron, mahogany or other wood (lined with lead or copper) to match the bath panelling. Push-button flushes became available at the end of the 19th century, and surprisingly, low-level suites were first made as early as 1825.

8,9,10 Three modern reproductions suitable for period bathrooms. The first shows that with a simple rounded shape plus a natural wood seat you can achieve an attractive period effect; the second has a certain Edwardian feel; the third is a versatile classic shape.
CS, BCS, CPH

11 From the 1840s lavatories were made of glazed earthenware and were usually set in handsome wooden framing, as in this example. Here the pull for the flush is also housed in the surround.
LSH

8

11

9

10

12   13

12,13 The Victorians had many different types of lavatories, and modern reproductions are thus available in many styles. The first of these examples shows the classic high cistern supported by decorative brackets; the second is a copy of the highly ornate painted style.
BCS, BCS

Kitchens in old houses worked well because they had to. Perhaps the standards of ventilation, light to work by and even hygiene would not satisfy us today, but as domestic workshops old kitchens simply had to be efficient in terms of layout and furnishings because of the almost total lack of labour-saving devices.

The ways in which old kitchens were planned, furnished and equipped are of interest for two reasons. If you are restoring a period property, a kitchen which looks as if it belongs to the appropriate era is likely to be more visually compatible with the remainder of the building than wall-to-wall plastics. But many people are also realizing that in planning today's multi-user family kitchens there are many practical lessons to be learned from the kitchens of a century or more ago.

Consider sinks, for example. Thirty years ago everyone wanted to get rid of their Butler sinks and get the latest stainless steel models instead. Then came the Germans with small round coloured bowls. Today the practical advantages of the old Butler sink are being appreciated anew and there is a trend towards big sinks in cast iron, plastics, stone or terrazzo, or even towards reusing old china sinks in good condition.

Period kitchens, designed around a large central working table, contained a large walk-in larder for food storage. Dresser shelves and racks were used for items in constant use. Function dictated the form of the furniture, which was always plain and easy to keep clean.

Floors and shelves were scrubbable and walls and ceilings were generally lime-washed until Victorian times.

1

1 *It is quite practical to restore an inglenook fireplace for cooking, as this example in an Elizabethan house in Kent illustrates. This "down hearth" was recreated with a mixture of antiques and reproduction ironwork hand-forged from old iron with hand tools. Attention to detail is the key to success. For instance, the ropes for the spit drive were traditionally spun at Hawes in Wensleydale.* ST

2

2 *The National Trust of Scotland have completely restored this magnificent Georgian kitchen at No. 7 Charlotte Sq, Edinburgh, and it contains a host of reference details which are very useful to the student of period kitchen restoration. The kitchen range is typical of models which were produced in many Scottish iron foundries at this time and can still be found in kitchens all over Britain.*

3 *In the classic domestic kitchen, such as this delightful Victorian example which is preserved by the National Trust at Uppark, West Sussex, everything revolved around the central working table. This was served by dressers and cooking areas, larders, still rooms, pantries and a scullery for dishwashing and wet food preparation. Note how simple and functional the furniture is and how it is the kitchenwares which create such decoration as there is. The basic table top was of ash but pine planks were fitted at a later date as it wore away and these would have been replaced from time to time.* ST

4 *When this kitchen was restored it was decided to keep as many authentic details as possible, such as the brick floor and rough plastered walls and ceiling. The table was made of English oak with a top of elm and the rack above is a copy of a Yorkshire "bacon flake". The walk-in larder was created from a disused entrance porch. A dishwasher and microwave oven are completely hidden in cupboards when not in use.* ST

5 *The swing towards "unfitted" kitchens is noticeable in the market generally but it started among people refurbishing kitchens for old houses. Here a "gamekeeper" sink has been pressed back into service, together with a mixture of real kitchen antiques and objets trouvés. The snag with old sinks is that they do not accept waste disposers or basket strainer fittings but new versions which do are now available.* ST

6 *In this kitchen for a rebuilt barn in Suffolk, elements of traditional thinking were used to create an attractive but practical sink area. As a dishwasher is used for all washing up, the rack above the sink is mainly used to store and display chinaware in regular use. The china sink by Imperial with brass taps from Czech & Speake are set in an oiled solid maple worktop.* ST

The fascination of old kitchens is that, compared with main living areas, no effort was made in most cases to dress them up for appearance's sake. So what you will find, unless someone has done a thorough job of "renovation", is an inbuilt record of all the ideas and changes which have come and gone since the kitchen was first built. That record can provide the clues you need to plan your restoration.

Every lump in the walls, every odd stump of iron and every piece of joinery has a tale to tell. For example, if in the Georgian period the cook needed a new shelf, the local joiner took the first piece of wood of about the right size that came to hand and pressed it into service: it may have been part of some Queen Anne or Jacobean wall panelling stripped out of another part of the house a few years before. Authentic old kitchens often present a patchwork appearance of this kind.

In our heritage of remaining period kitchens we have the purest examples of vernacular design, influenced to a far greater degree by local traditions of craftsmanship and style passed down from one generation to the next than by any awareness of passing fashion. Details of moulding in old pieces of kitchen furniture, the materials used in floors and for working surfaces and the design of incidental items such as hanging racks and fireplace ironwork vary from one county or state to the next and sometimes even from town to town. Sadly, the trade in antiques and kitchenalia has displaced much valuable evidence of local traditions in the half-century or more of modernization following the advent of factory-made kitchen furniture between the wars. In trying to reconstruct how the kitchen originally looked, a little detective work will be necessary. The original may be

still there, walled up in a hidden inglenook. A big open chimney is probably evidence of a "down hearth" for a wood fire. Look for signs of an old "chimney crane" or marks to indicate where a weight-driven "spit engine" may have been mounted. Iron stumps in the sidewalls may indicate a later coal-burning roasting hearth.

Try to work out how the kitchen was laid out in earlier times. Clues may be offered by blocked-up doorways, changes in floor levels or materials or apparently pointless notches and breaks in beams. Consider the facilities such as pantries and sculleries needed in the days before fridges and dishwashers.

It is worth checking any sheds or barns you have where old wood is stored. Old cupboards, shelves and other joinery may have been stripped out of the backstairs areas many years before. With care such fittings can be restored to use.

KITCHENS BEFORE THE 18TH CENTURY

The kitchen as we understand it today was born in the Georgian era with the arrival of early cooking ranges in many homes. Before that, most cooking took place at various types of open fires and hearths, and water was obtained from a pump in the back yard or from a communal source.

From the 15th and 16th centuries onwards, inglenook fireplaces (or whatever they are called in the part of the country where you live) were being added to existing houses and incorporated in new buildings. At about the same time we begin to see early sculleries, initially little more than a roofed-over space to make access to the water pump more convenient.

Until Georgian times, most inglenooks were entirely woodburning. They had huge chimneys which worked well enough because the fire was never let out between the end of the summer and the middle of spring. The warmth of that fireplace meant that this room was the centre of all family life.

Unless you are exceptionally fortunate, no indications will now be left of how such a kitchen was originally furnished because any furniture there was (and it did not amount to much in most cases) would

1 *The kitchen is frequently the area of a house which remains virtually unaltered. This mid-18thC house was much modernized in the 19thC but as the kitchen was below stairs it was left with its original features.* MJ

2 *This mid-18thC open hearth fireplace in a New York house is filled with the many kitchen implements in use during this period.* VC

3 *Kitchens were frequently below ground level and were often dark and gloomy places. These oak beams were whitewashed to add some light.* VC

4 *This 17thC open hearth in a New York house is backed by a beehive oven. These provide a multitude of cooking possibilities along with the main source of heat and light.* BH

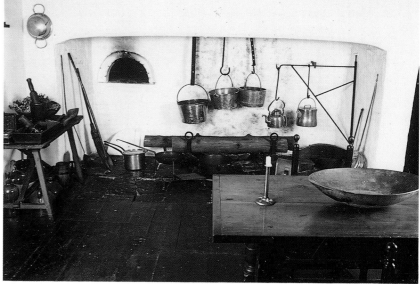

have been freestanding. The one essential piece was a big central table, but there might also have been a sideboard and later a dresser. People sat on benches mainly, with perhaps two "back stools" for the husband and wife.

The key to restoring such a kitchen today is simplicity. Closed cupboards are completely out of place, though for practical reasons most people will nonetheless consider them essential below the sink. A walk-in larder solves most food storage problems but you must disguise any modern equipment or hide it away when not in use or the effect will be spoiled.

GEORGIAN AND VICTORIAN KITCHENS

The arrival of coal as fuel for cooking led initially to raised roasting hearths. At first these still used spits and many of the other familiar fittings of the woodburning down hearth, but later they began to evolve into enclosed cooking ranges. In the Georgian period we also begin to see sinks and indoor plumbing: it is thus quite realistic to consider restoring such a kitchen to something like its original appearance and layout.

The first built-in kitchen furniture dates from this period as the increasing range of kitchenwares and utensils created a need for much more storage space. Most such furniture was very simply made from softwood using traditional joinery methods. All was painted for ease of cleaning, apart from working surfaces which were regularly scrubbed or sanded and had to be replaced periodically.

The main items of furniture would still have been the centre table and dresser (or dressers), but tall cupboards for dried goods, preserves and the storage of reserve china and kitchenwares became commonplace. Usually such items were styled to match the wood wall panelling which gradually took over from lime-washed plastered walls. The design and construction of panelling and built-in furniture varied greatly from one part of the country to another and also at different dates. It is thus invaluable as an accurate dating guide.

In practice it is almost impossible to remove such furniture from the room in which it was made without considerable damage. That means that much of it has been destroyed during subsequent "improvements", and that much of what we are now offered as kitchen furniture of Georgian times is nothing of the sort.

5 *This "tin" kitchen sink was actually made of soapstone and was part of the 1850 update of this 1830 house.* OMII

6 *This fireplace of c.1790 was discovered behind a Victorian wall. The fittings are in period. In the late 18thC there would have been several small fires rather than one large fire.* VNS

7 *This kitchen range would have been the height of fashion when put in place in 1850. It was made by Abendroth Bros. in 1845. The fireplace crane was left in place.* OMII

A century later the Victorians were embarking on the hunt for labour-saving devices, and the number and sophistication of the cooking ranges which came onto the market in late Victorian and Edwardian times were quite remarkable. Many are still in excellent working order and can be incorporated in a restored kitchen.

Furniture styling depended very much upon whether the kitchen was also the parlour in a smaller one-family house; if so, its styling became gradually more complex, although plain painted finishes were still the norm. In larger establishments, the furnishings became ever more utilitarian as the importance of ease of cleaning increased.

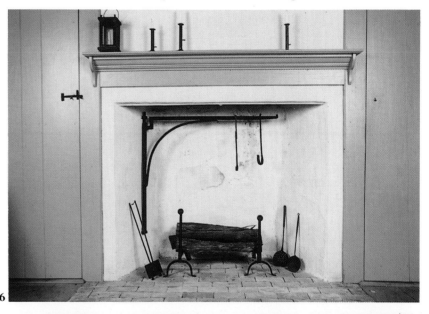

6

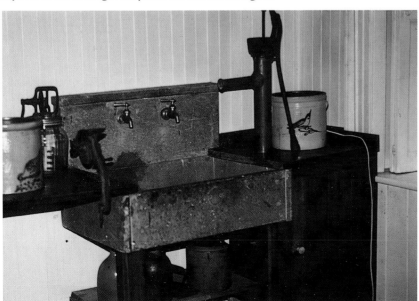

5

7

New Kitchens in the Traditional Idiom

Of course, the "traditional" kitchen furniture which is manufactured today is waywardly inauthentic. Generally, it is modern system unit furniture fitted with wood or painted fronts which ape certain elements of period style. Such ideas as "wall units" (which make things more difficult to get at, not easier) and working surfaces covered with tiles would have been laughed to scorn by any sane Victorian cook and the sheer impracticality of many of today's fanciful paint finishes would have been regarded in the same light. The essence of the traditional British kitchen in its heyday was the practical combination of certain key elements – a big centre table as the main working area; a carefully planned larder where most food was stored; dressers and hanging racks for those items most in use; deep drawers for other kitchenwares and utensils; and finally a really large sink surrounded by large scrubbable surfaces and a plate draining rack. When creating a kitchen which will be compatible with the style and atmosphere of a period house, always bear in mind that a real traditional kitchen was utterly practical and functional as well as warm, friendly and inviting.

It was the most important place in the house, even if normally used by servants. It is unrealistic to expect a modern housewife to dispense with her dishwasher, food mixer, microwave and refrigerator. However, these can be hidden away in period kitchen furniture.

1 Interest is increasing in "unfitted" kitchens involving little or no unit furniture at all and specialist companies such as John Lewis of Hungerford are making careful copies of old items of kitchen furniture which work well in such settings. This is their Bakers Table. JL

2, 3 Two views of a "high Victorian" kitchen with some later practical additions in a mansion at Duns near the Scottish border. Allowing for differences in scale, there are lessons to be learned from such kitchens in layout, constructional and practical details and even the materials used. Local hardwoods have been used almost throughout for cupboards and surfaces, though the working table shown here is of pine and of an earlier date.

4 *Some of today's specialist kitchen furniture workshops are very skilled at recapturing the spirit of past ages. This inset cupboard by Hathaway Country Kitchens will be appreciated by anyone with a taste for that type of Victorian furniture which mixed design ideas from a dozen sources with such abandon.* HA

5 *The alternative to restoring a kitchen with old furniture or with reproduction joinery styled to match the period and locality concerned is to use the traditionally-styled kitchen furniture which is now offered by a number of companies. This Smallbone dresser in bleached oak, for instance, would not look out of place in a kitchen dating anywhere from the 17th to the early 20thC.* S

6 *The atmosphere of a traditional British kitchen is recaptured in this apparently casual but in fact thoroughly practical dresser setting. A dishwasher lives behind one of the centre doors. Much of the woodwork here has been adapted from other uses, just as most "backstairs" joinery was a century or so ago.* ST

7 *This Continental Art Deco stove can indeed be used for decorative purposes, but it is just as practical and efficient for every day use as the modern day Aga.*

CUSTOM-BUILT AND READY-MADE KITCHENS

The traditional kitchen discussed above is the purist's answer to restoration. However, many people will find the prospect of working in an original kitchen distinctly uninviting. We have become accustomed to fitted units and work surfaces. Fortunately, many firms produce a wide range of kitchen furniture compatible with a period house. Many are styled after traditional patterns and some use old timber. There is a broad spectrum to choose from – innumerable colours and designs, textures and accessories. It is, however, vital to remember that country cottages demand a different style of kitchen from Georgian town houses.

1 This old pine kitchen has been carefully planned to give a modern design an old feel. The central Aga is a convenient modern day equivalent of the Victorian cooking range. The solid pine table imitates the central table which was the hub of the period kitchen. This pleasing modern design would not jar in a period house. S

2 A modern Aga can be given a period feel with suitable accessories. Note in particular the clock and the lighting. AR

3 Not everyone is an advocate of unpainted solid wood kitchens, especially as many kitchens are in dark areas. Smallbone of Devizes have a wide range of painted kitchens based on dresser designs. S

4, 5, 6 *There are many examples of solid wood kitchens, ranging from dark solid mahogany to light honey-coloured pine. Some kitchens use old wood, others are totally new although deriving from old designs. Plate racks, spice cupboards and traditional utensils give a pleasingly authentic look.*

M, S, PV

7 *An Art Deco house allows yet another design solution to kitchen planning. Note how the design on the doors is mirrored in the window glass. (Woodstock Furniture, Pakenham St, London WC1.)*

W

4

5

6

7

oday we are spoilt by the convenience and design possibilities offered by electric light in the home. This is a recent luxury. Despite the introduction of gas and electricity, candles and lamps were still widely employed at the beginning of the 20th century, especially in country regions.

Gas was first introduced in the 1780s. Electric light suitable for domestic purposes was not available until the late 1870s. Even oil lamps were not very useful until the invention in the 1780s of an improved reading lamp in which a current of air and a gravity feed made the wick burn ten times more brightly than before. Paraffin was not available until the middle of the 19th century. Few people restoring a period house are likely to want to return completely to the old laborious, dirty and inefficient methods, although a candlelit dinner will always hold its charms.

What you can do, however, is adapt the early fittings to electricity or use them as supplementary lighting.

2

3

1

4

5

1 *This free-standing iron candlestand is an accurate replica of early lighting. Candles can give out a surprising amount of heat and light.* SI

2 *By 1877 this house was illuminated by gaslight pendants (except in the dining room). The decorative ceiling rose served a useful purpose, the holes in the grille providing an outlet for noxious gas fumes.* LSH

3 *This brass three-tiered chandelier would be equally at home in an 18th or 19thC environment.*

4,5 *Accurate reproduction Art Deco lamps help to create an instant atmosphere of the cool, contrived style of the 1930s.* EDL

EARLY CANDLES AND RUSH LIGHTS

In the great halls of medieval tradition, a big central fire was supplemented by torches thrust onto iron spikes or by light from cressets – metal baskets high up on poles, in which oil or pitch were burnt. Cressets were much used in Elizabethan times. Piques (or spikes), used to impale the soft wax or tallow candles, either were small, holding a single candle, or stood four or five feet high with spikes for many candles. "Candle beams", usually of wood, with four stout bars to hold the candles (sometimes two per bar) radiating from a central bar suspended from the ceiling, were the handsome predecessors of elegant chandeliers. Brass candelabra were also used. Candles were also held aloft in staffs by servants or placed on spikes in wall sconces and on stands. Sometimes light was supplied by strips of rushes, dipped in oil and held in a simple iron stand and clip with a wooden base. Candles were much too expensive for ordinary cottagers, who used rush lights, sometimes dipped in mutton fat rather than less readily available oil.

The socket candlestick emerged in the 16th century, and sturdy brass candlesticks were made. During the 17th century candleholders of all kinds became objects for display. The idea of a six-or twelve- branched candelabrum in brass was borrowed from the Low Countries. Candelabra were also produced in carved and gilded wood and ornamental wrought iron. Snuffers were of brass and precious metals as well as iron. Silver sconces were now set against the wall to help increase the spread of light.

In areas where fish oil was available, the poor used small oil lamps from shallow vessels with rough wicks, perhaps of twisted rag.

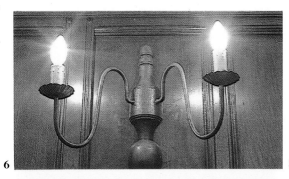

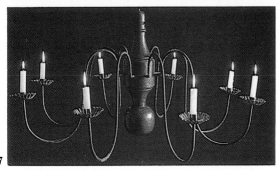

13 *There are many types of candlesticks and rush lights available. This is an original, but reproductions can easily be found.*

6 *This traditional-style wrought-iron and wood chandelier has a simplicity which is exactly right for a building of the 16th or 17thC. Such items can also be used in rustic or less sophisticated houses of a later date. They are ideal with candles but can be wired for candle-like bulbs. Wrought iron has a naturally rustic look and should never be over-polished or buffed.* SI

7,8,9 *There is a movement back to more authentic-looking fittings. Specialist companies make wall fittings that give the right feel to early houses while still using electricity. These examples are from Stuart Interiors.* SI

10,11 *These chandeliers, also from Stuart Interiors, are particularly well-matched to their period settings.* SI

12 *This reproduction 18thC chandelier would also be appropriate for a 19thC interior. To create a truly authentic 18thC atmosphere it would have to be lit by candles.*

14 *An original Regency lamp that has been restored and re-gilded. This would fit perfectly into any Egyptian Revival interior.*

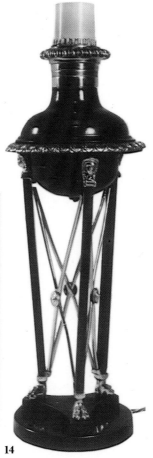

18TH-CENTURY STYLES

Fine, handsome candlesticks contributed to the character of Georgian interiors, even though they provided little light. At first sturdy holders were still created, in a variety of metals but especially in brass and bronze, to hold one or several candles. Slimmer, more elegant candlesticks were preferred by the middle of the 18th century, and although solid-looking ones later came back into fashion, these were plainer and often made of sheet iron or burnished steel.

This century saw more use of lanterns, which could be suspended or set against the wall (and, of course, carried). Their horn panels protected the flame from draughts. By the 1790s we find huge oil-burning lanterns, with a brass or iron frame housing six or eight glass panels, hung in halls and stairways and welcoming guests at the front of the house.

Pendant light fittings ranged from the relatively modest brass candelabrum, with a bowl-shaped body and six curved, branching candle holders, to the most exquisitely ornate chandeliers. The latter hung, huge, glittering and splendid, from the ceilings of ballrooms and drawing rooms, or with as few as six candles springing from a little shower of sparkling cut glass in less grand though still substantial surroundings. On the walls of these interiors, elaborately backed sconces held yet further candles: scores would be burnt in the course of an evening. In less wealthy homes tall, thin taper stands were common. These either had tripods, or round or square bases, and came complete with attached scissors for snuffing the rush tapers which were burnt in them.

5

1

1 Chandeliers occupy a lot of space and should only be used in a generously proportioned room. This example is a perfect copy of a Regency original.

6

2 Looking-glass lights between the windows of an early 19thC house would have shed a fine, even light.　OMH

3 A late 19thC wall light need not look incongruous in an 18thC house. As lighting developed, homeowners would install the most modern and practical form of lighting without necessarily changing the decorative aspects.

4 A wrought-iron outside lantern, made in the 1930s but a perfect replica of mid-18thC style.　HH

5 Hall lanterns give a warm and welcoming atmosphere to a hallway. This type would fit well into most late 18th and 19thC houses.　BP

6 Gas chandeliers were a common sight in the parlour of a 19thC house. This example, typically High Victorian, has a "water-slide" system enabling the apparatus to be lowered.　OMH

7 This 19thC hallway is devoid of the furniture and fabrics which would create the "upholstered" feel of a Victorian interior. However, 19thC lighting is enough to evoke the period.　OMH

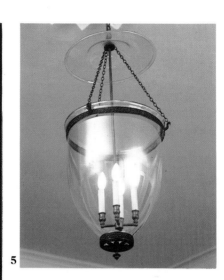

2

3

4

7

THE 19TH CENTURY

Plain steel candlesticks continued to be fashionable during the early 19th century, when the recently discovered wax-hardening process made the candles burn more steadily and with less mess. Spermaceti candles, a product of the whaling industry, gave an even better light; and oil lamps, not much used in the 18th century, were also improved.

During the 19th century, despite gas light and even individual gas plants for some country houses, oil lamps were the most common source of light. When mineral oils became available in the middle of the century, they represented a huge step forward. Many Victorian paraffin lamps are still gently illuminating dinner tables and sitting rooms. Wicks can still be obtained for them, and so too can replacement chimneys and shades, should the originals get broken. Despite the limitations imposed by their working methods, Victorian oil lamps, or excellent reproductions of them, are found in an apparently endless range of designs, in glass as well as brass and other metals.

Gas was widely used in upper-middle-class homes during the second part of the 19th century, until it was eclipsed by electricity. Gas light fittings took their form from oil lamps, but could of course dispense with the reservoir. Pendant oil lamps with three or four burners fed from a central container for the oil were produced contemporaneously with suspended gas lights of similar appearance. However, gas lamps could easily be fixed to the wall as well, and piped gas lent itself perfectly to the European *fin de siècle* look, with sweeping curves and sinuous ornamentation.

10

12 An Edwardian rise-and-fall hanging lamp with opaline glass lampshade. The great advantage of electricity was that light was thrown downwards where it was most needed. LSH

12

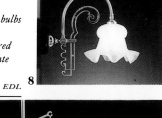

8 An electric bracket light in the style of a 19thC gas fitting. The glare of light bulbs can be hidden behind translucent frosted, coloured or engraved shades to create the mellow lighting of the era. EDL

8

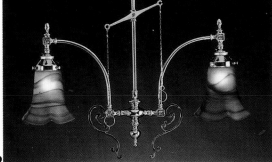

9

9 A good example of a reproduction 19thC ceiling pendant. The original would have been fitted for gas or oil; however, adaptation to electricity does not detract from the period feel. EDL

10 This Venetian chandelier does not look out of place in a 19thC house, but really belongs to the less cluttered, classical style of the 18thC. It requires a high room. LH

11 Gas fittings often remained in place even when electricity had largely superseded gas. Their hollow pipes made them easy to convert. LSH

11

13

13 A typical Victorian lamp, evocative of the clutter and cosiness of the period. LSH

ELECTRICITY

From the 1880s Edison lamps in the United States and Swan lamps in Britain brought the blessings of clean, controllable and odour-free electric light into the home. Electric light gave all possible scope to designers. Some stuck rigidly to the candle theme, and placed the light bulbs on candle-like stalks set in traditional candelabra or table-standing burners. The advantage (if it was one) provided by the new source of light was that the bulbs could now be dressed in little shades, whether plain or pleated and frilled.

Electric lights were also set in wrought-iron fittings of branches, leaves and flowers. They were equipped with shades in glass and metal, the glass fluted and shaped like bluebells and harebells, or in the form of simple globes and cones. European Art Nouveau contributed its characteristic curves and milkily opaque glass in subtle colours. Perhaps most spectacular of all were the American Tiffany lamps in their glowing stained-glass shades.

These and their coolly 20th-century Art Deco successors are now available in perfect reproductions from specialist manufacturers. Those whose purse cannot stretch to handmade reproductions will find that a search through antique and second-hand shops may still yield derivative period light fittings. An Edwardian mottled glass bowl suspended by a brass chain or an Expressionist faceted wall light in metal housing would complete a well-contrived interior.

1

6

2

3

4

5

1 *A selection of modern reproduction lighting switches which can look preferable in a period house to white plastic. However, some feel white fittings are less conspicuous.*

2 *A reproduction late 19thC three-light wall fitting, here fitted for electricity with candle-like bulbs. Such fittings would originally have held candles.* PH

3 *Wall lights of the 19thC characteristically had brackets with etched globe or upturned shades. Even when gas-fuelled, they still followed the styles of oil or candle power. These are now usually converted to electricity.*

4 *A Regency gilt metal hanging lantern, now fitted for electricity.*

5 *Hall lanterns were still being used to light the way for guests in the late 19thC, but they had become much more ornate.* PCA

6 *Standard rise-and-fall pendant lights of the late Victorian and Edwardian periods can still be found intact in their original settings.*

7,8,9,10 *Art Nouveau lamps have become highly desirable in recent years. Many of the best were made by the firm of Tiffany in New York, as illustrated by the examples here. These are originals. Similar lamps are to be found in auction rooms and antique shops.*

11,12,13,14,15 *Art Deco lamps can add greatly to the atmosphere of a 1920s or 30s flat or house. These examples are reproductions but follow the lines and colours of the originals.* EDL

The visual pleasure we derive from the outsides of period houses comes partly from the architectural elements – the doors, windows and so on – and the ways in which they are treated and related to each other. Enjoyment also comes from the materials – weathered limestone, shining granite, knapped flint or bricks of every type, size and arrangement, whether Elizabethan herringbone or 19th-century polychrome, perhaps dressed up in contrasting stone on the corners (quoins), pilaster strips and window surrounds. The hardened oak of half-timbering, the ornamental impact of plasterwork, the soft contours of clay daub: all have their own characteristic "feel". Additionally, the personality of a house is expressed in its immediate surroundings, the nature of the boundaries (walls, fences, railings, hedges), the materials and detailing of access points (gates, paths and steps), and features such as window boxes.

1 A stone pineapple offers a sign of welcome beside an entrance. Although such ornaments are always called pineapples, they are in fact pine cones, ancient symbols of fertility and wealth.

2 One of the interesting features of architecture is the recurrence of themes. These sphinxes and obelisks reflect the fascination with Ancient Egypt in the Regency period (1812-30).

3 This doorway combines many features from the late 18th and early 19thC. The classical pediment seems somehow to vye with the decorative ironwork on the door and holding the lantern.

4 Exterior lead pipework was formerly treated as part of the decoration of a house.

5 Decorative ironwork on balconies was popular in both the 18th and 19thC.

6 When designing this house in New York – a replica of one of 1760, built in the 1920s – the architect included some elements salvaged from old houses. However, most features here are faithful copies. The ornate carving over the entrance includes the beaver symbol of New York State. HH

SCROLLS, URNS AND STATUES

The Tudors elaborated doorways with terracotta panels and stucco coats-of-arms, roses and animals. Then the Jacobeans continued this tradition and developed it, sometimes covering whole facades of half-timbered houses with plaster ornament. Patterns could be simple scrolls set in large panels or, in East Anglia, swirling "parget work" decorated with clumsy but charming classical motifs such as swags.

With the Restoration came the fashion for classical facades, though usually without the parapets of later classical houses. Ornament was rather in the form of bold pediments partly concealing the sloping roofs and decorated with stone swags and emblems and stone pilasters with elaborate capitals. The niches of the Palladian mansions of the 18th century were occupied by stucco figures in contemporary dress, in place of the classical statues in stone that were favoured previously.

In the early 18th century, gardens of grand houses were still designed formally in the French manner, with broad avenues and *rond-points* (intersections). Main avenues were flanked with trees, but urns, vases and classical statuary along the paths also made an important contribution, and these features were continued in the facade niches, along the tops of walls and set into parapets. Stone garden urns were often encrusted with swags and cherubs, more ornamental than the plants themselves.

Later in the 18th century the Picturesque landscape superseded the formal garden, but niches were still provided for classical statues, for example in clipped yew hedges, and stone lions overlooked the parkland from the balustraded terrace next to the house.

7

9

Gardening and plants had become a passion at all levels of society from the middle classes upward. In an age when pattern books were disseminating details of classical design among builders, gardening manuals were also widely distributed, with advice on all subjects, including ideas for tubs and window boxes for houses without gardens.

In the 19th century many of the older features were revived. The parget work and stucco of the period have a vigour which makes them hard to distinguish them from their 17th-century models, while houses built in the same spirit as the Palladian mansions have classical statuary in the same manner, with the niches inhabited by figures such as Venus and Apollo.

6

8

10

7 This Victorian house has ornamental balustrading which dominates the roof and is mirrored by that around the top of the bay window. Note also the popular scroll design.

8 Classically inspired eagles are often later additions.

9 Many 17thC buildings have the timbers, particularly under the eaves, carved with scrolls, leaves or flowers.

10 It is still possible to buy garden ornaments made from old moulds or based on 18th and 19thC patterns. CS

BOUNDARIES

Small country houses may be bounded with picket fences – simple wooden slats placed quite closely together and driven into the ground or fixed to supporting posts with wire, or often nailed to wooden horizontal bars themselves fixed to posts.

Larger country houses with roots still in the vernacular tradition consort well with low walls of local brick or stone in front of dense box or yew hedges – which may be clipped into extraordinary shapes.

RAILINGS AND GATES

Ironwork was introduced to Britain by William and Mary when they brought the French Huguenot smith Tijou to work under their patronage in 1689. He made beautiful gates, balustrades and garden screens in sheet iron embossed into scrolls, gilded flower and acanthus leaves in a way not seen in England before. Subsequently ironwork became enormously popular, and with good reason. The gates might be set within stone piers, perhaps with niches and topped with eagles or covered urns, or fluted and bearing proud gryphons. Charming pastoral figures in lead were found on gate piers by the end of the 17th century and were in vogue during the 18th. Wrought iron might also be used for the piers themselves and for delicate overthrows across the top of wide gateways.

With the passage of time, upper-class styles in ironwork filtered down to the less privileged social strata. Wrought, *repoussé* (hammered) and eventually cheaper cast iron were used for plain and decorative railings, gateways and other features right up to the 20th century. In the 18th century simple, well-proportioned cast-iron work was as much favoured as more elaborate wrought-iron scrolls and curves. Even simple town houses had plain cast-iron railings round

their areas (that is, the enclosed spaces between the street and the drop to the basement) and up the steps to the front door. In the Regency period wrought iron flourished in England in the form of elaborate balconies, verandas and porches. Door hoods were revived, but now made in curving sheets of lead like the veranda canopies of the same period. All such flourishes, however decorative, were still accompanied by plain boundary railings at the front of the house.

Throughout the 19th century similar plain cast-iron railings continued to be provided at the front of countless new houses, and sometimes also for little balconies above the porch. By the turn of the century even the smallest houses had such railings at the front. Often they still stand, set into a low wall in front of the privet hedge which the builder planted as part of the complete package.

Towards the end of the 19th century, grand houses in the Queen Anne style, though so different in appearance from these terraced rows, also had iron-work boundary fences. In keeping with their attachment to old traditions, these were usually wrought, not cast. Fortunately the art of the smith is still flourishing today, and there are many architectural metalworkers who can restore wrought- and cast-iron work to make replacements in keeping with the style of the house.

1 Ornate wrought-iron balustrades, terminating in lantern-shaped newel posts, flank the stone steps at the entrance to this Federal-style American house. OMH

2,3 Two views of the fence and gate of an 1830s house in Roslyn, New York. The white painted picket fence has elaborate spear tops and the supporting posts of the gateway with their vase decoration have the importance of columns. The close-up shows the original iron hinges and shutting mechanism.

4, 5 Wrought-iron railings are a delightful and interesting adjunct to houses of the 18th and 19thC. On smaller houses they were often quite plain but in grander houses they used many classical themes such as the pineapple or pine cone.

6-14 *Wrought-iron and, later, cast iron balconies and railings were common in both grand and simple houses. It is essential to the look of our streets that terraces retain a feeling of continuity. Blacksmiths can reproduce perfect copies, and these do improve the overall* appearance of the exteriors of period houses. Your local historical or architectural society should be able to advise on the style of balcony or railing which would have been original to the house. Otherwise, copies of neighbouring styles will suffice.

15 *On a Neo-classical stone mansion built between 1837 and 1846 the wrought ironwork sweeps down on either side of the steps to curve around the newel posts.* BP

1 Plain railings were not always mirrored in the treatment of balconies and ironwork around windows. Houses develop piecemeal, as owners decide to introduce more up-to-date features.

2 The entrance porch of a late 19thC house is given greater importance with pillars, arches and a balcony above.

3, 4 Whether in a simple terrace or grander entranceway the Georgians had a feeling for proportion and the continuity of classical themes.

5 Wrought and plain ironwork provide a useful security device for this basement of an early 19thC house.

STEPS AND STAIRS

The great Palladian houses had magnificent double staircases curving or angling up to a terrace along the house. On a smaller scale, the front doors of town houses (however close to the street) were from the late 17th century almost universally approached by stone steps the breadth of the doorcase. No fine house, however handsome, would be quite so imposing without the steps leading up to its front door.

When the entrance was at a sufficiently high level, the flight of steps could be longer. However, until well into the 19th century often as few as two or three treads were needed. The builder's or architect's skill in judging proportions came fully into play: it is surprising how harmonious two steps can be. The lower step in 18th-century houses may rise only slightly above the street; sometimes it is wider than the step above and curved at the sides; and often a moulded nose finishes the edge of each step.

Railings round the basement area usually continued up the sides of the steps to the porch or front door. In smarter houses, the railings included lamp holders and conical link extinguishers, which may still survive .

Houses of the 19th century may have lacked the finely judged proportions of their predecessors but their broader entranceways, set higher up from street level and farther back, enabled them to have impressive flights of stone steps. These might have simply moulded noses, continuing round the rounded-off corners, or be flanked by wide stone flat-topped or solidly balustraded ramps, in keeping with the solid, comfortable houses. Later Victorian houses with semi-basements and set close to the road have ended up with an awkwardly steep flight of inelegant steps, compensated for, perhaps, by the lofty rooms inside. Edwardian family houses, their main rooms and entrance halls at ground level, may lack this lofty spaciousness, but their prettily tiled paths leading up to timbered porches are friendly and inviting.

6

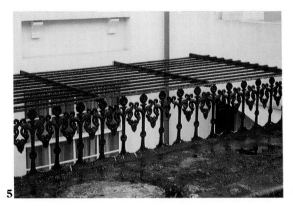

5

7

8

6 A long flight of steps leads up to the side door of a 1748 Bronx mansion. The lattice work under the steps is to facilitate a good flow of air.

VC

7 A Victorian house in London where cast-iron railings and gate are matched by low rails in front of the bay windows. The areas too have simple railings cutting them off from the approach to the house. The front door is reached by a flight of stone steps, flanked by flat-topped balustraded ramps terminating in pillars and flower urns. LSH

8 Steps to the front door were standard even in the simple terrace. These steps are tiled. Note also the highly decorative ironwork on the upper floor.

We generally think of the conservatory as a Victorian invention, and indeed it had its heyday in the 19th century. However, it was first popular in the 18th, in the form of the elegant orangery. The advantages of a conservatory, not only as a place for growing plants but also as a living area with a summery atmosphere, remain undiminished today.

The orangery was a gracious extra room in the Palladian mansion. Its transitional role between house and garden satisfied the Georgian passion for the pastoral – a terrace would often run along the outside, adjoining the garden – and as the name implies it was a place where exotic fruits could be grown. These would be raised in tubs so that they could be set out or even planted in the summer. Orangeries were designed and built in the same manner as the rest of the house. Although the walls consisted of glazed windows on three sides (the fourth often being joined to the house), the parapets usually concealed a conventional slate or tiled roof. After cast iron began to be used in the 1770s, the orangery retained its noble, restrained form. It was at this period a carefully proportioned, unobtrusive building, very different from its showy Victorian relative, which bristled with cast-iron ornament and flaunted huge sheets of polished glass.

By the end of the 18th century the metamorphosis had begun. Robert Adam designed orangeries with slighter glazing bars and coved ceilings. Some wooden-framed glass roofs were also to be found at this time.

However, it was Joseph Paxton and his contemporaries in the 1830s who completed the

1

2

3

1,2 These two large conservatories are essentially glass houses in the tradition of Paxton and his followers. It is a modern convention to paint conservatories white: Victorian examples would more often have been green. Green canvas awnings give excellent shade while retaining a period feel. ML

3 A conservatory that joins two sections of a house in the form of a corridor with roof and frontage aligned. ML

4

5

8

6

7

4 In townhouses where there is no space to put a conservatory in the garden, one answer is to add one at first floor level over a protruding downstairs room. ML

5 An original Victorian "window-box" type of conservatory. These are close relations to the "Wardian cases" in which travellers transported ferns and other exotics from foreign places. LSH

6,7 A Victorian-style conservatory that completely fills the space between an L-shaped house and an adjacent outbuilding. Notice how the transitional feel between indoors and out is accentuated by using the same tiling on the conservatory floor and the terrace: if you do this, make sure the tiles will stand up to the weather. ML

8 A conservatory must harmonize with the building to which it is attached. Here, the stone and brick base blend with the main dwelling. MJ

transformation. Paxton's passion was as much for plants as it was for the new technology of glass and iron. The vogue for collecting and displaying new exotic varieties spread rapidly. In 1851, the year of the Great Exhibition in London, window tax was finally abolished; the duty on glass, which had made heavier glass prohibitively expensive, was removed in 1857. The Crystal Palace, built by Paxton for the Exhibition, thrilled thousands of visitors and helped to create a craze for glasshouses and conservatories. The demand was quickly met by prefabricated glass-and-iron structures. These provided long, high rooms with underfloor heating for tropical trees, or glazed extensions to the sitting room in which to cultivate ferns.

The new ornamented conservatories, perfect for mid-19th-century houses whose design was free from classical constraints, remained in fashion until the First World War. In larger terraced houses they sometimes provided all the garden there was, and in the smallest they were little more than exotic lean-tos. Edwardian examples were less ornate, and the simple lines of the Edwardian style might well be preferable if you are adding a conservatory onto a small house.

Although they can make the rooms from which they extend darker, conservatories are wonderfully light in themselves and remove the need for double glazing. However, they do need their own heating and shading systems to avoid extremes of climate hostile to sensitive plants. In the northern hemisphere, a south-west wall is the safest choice of situation.

If you are adding a conservatory to a pre-19th-century house, a building modelled on the orangery would be more authentic, with large windows in the same style as the house rather than a prominent all-glass room which would strike an anachronistic note. For Victorian and later houses glass and metal styles are perfectly acceptable.

Very satisfactory reproduction period conservatories are available today. They are expensive but they add a whole new living area, and provided that they are carefully integrated in style and scale they give a special atmosphere of elegance to both house and garden.

ANDIRON (OR ENDIRON): *a metal bar, supported on feet, to hold burning logs above hearth level (also called FIRE-DOG).*

ARCADING: *a series of arches on columns or PIERS which can be freestanding or attached to a wall.*

ARCHITRAVE: *the moulded frame around a window or door; or, more properly, the lowest portion of an ENTABLATURE.*

BACON FLAKE: *traditional Yorkshire Dales name for a wood rack hung from the kitchen ceiling on extended iron hooks. It was used to store cured hams and smoked bacon sides during the winter. "Bread flakes", to a somewhat different design, were used in a similar way to store loaves and the large biscuits which were traditionally cooked on iron plates over open fires.*

BALUSTER: *a banister, typically turned and undulating in form (which is why the term baluster is given to coffee pots, glass stems and so on of this shape).*

BALUSTRADE: *a series of BALUSTERS supporting a handrail or coping.*

BAROQUE: *rather heavy, flamboyant style which originated in Italy in the 17th century and appeared in England late in the same century.*

BATTEN DOOR: *a door made from rows of vertical planks, nailed or pegged to supporting horizontal planks.*

BOSS: *an ornamental knob at the intersection of ribs in a ceiling or a vault.*

BULL'S EYE: *see CROWN GLASS.*

BUTLER SINK: *a large, oblong proprietary sink of all-white or white and beige porcelain on fireclay. The name is now commonly used for all sinks of this type, though most of those offered as Butler sinks are later and much deeper laboratory sinks. The true Butler sinks were rarely more than 6in deep.*

CAMES: *the strip of metal used for leaded lights.*

CAPITAL: *the crowning feature of a column.*

CASEMENT WINDOW: *a window with the sash hung vertically and which opens inwards or outwards by means of a hinge.*

CHAMFER: *to cut or grind off bevel-wise the edge of a piece of wood or stone originally right-angled.*

CHIMNEYPIECE (OR MANTELPIECE): *the frame around a fireplace which may be made from brick, stone, marble or wood.*

CONSOLE BRACKET: *ornamental bracket, often of S-form and usually having more height than projection.*

CORNICE *a decorative projecting moulding around the top of a wall or arch (in an interior it usually disguises the join between walls and ceilings); the projecting top section of an ENTABLATURE.*

CROWN GLASS: *a sheet of glass made by blowing a bubble and spinning it rapidly on the rod; a BULL'S EYE is formed where the rod is attached.*

DAMP-PROOF COURSE: *a layer of impervious material laid in a wall to stop rising damp.*

DEPRESSED ARCH: *a shallow slightly pointed arch.*

DOG-LEG STAIRCASE: *two parallel flights of stairs with a half-landing between.*

DOORCASE: *the ARCHITRAVE enclosing a door.*

DOWN HEARTH: *Southern English name for an open fireplace in which a log fire was formed directly on the floor of the inglenook. Often used for cooking as well, using turnspits, pots and griddle plates hung over the fire from bars or cranes and three-legged gunmetal pots pushed into the edge of the fire.*

ENTABLATURE: *in classical architecture, the top part of a column made up of ARCHITRAVE, FRIEZE and CORNICE; a decoration made up in this way popular from the mid-18th century.*

FANLIGHT: *a window over a door, often semi-circular with radiating glazing bars.*

FENDER: *a low metal screen which prevents burning coals or logs from rolling into the room.*

FENESTRAL: *a lattice frame across which oiled or waxed paper or linen was stretched to keep out draughts while letting in the light.*

FIELDED PANEL: *panel with the centre raised in profile.*

FIREBACK: *a thick cast-iron panel put at the back of a hearth to protect the wall and to reflect heat into the room.*

FIRE-DOG: *see ANDIRON.*

FLAG: *stone slab used for flooring.*

FREESTONE: *stone that cuts well in any direction, notably fine-grained sandstone or limestone.*

FRIEZE: *the middle section of an ENTABLATURE: the upper part of a wall directly below the cornice.*

GRATE: *a framework of bars to hold a fire.*

INGLENOOK: *a recess for a seat beside a fireplace, often covered by the chimney breast.*

KNAPPED FLINT: *flints split and laid so that the smooth black split surfaces form the facing of the wall.*

LIGHT: *vertical opening between MULLIONS of a window.*

LIMEWASH: *a mixture of slaked lime and water used for painting walls.*

LINENFOLD: *a panelling decorated with design representing vertical folds of linen.*

LINK: *a torch.*

LINTEL: *a horizontal beam or stone across an opening.*

MANTELPIECE: *see CHIMNEYPIECE.*

MULLION: *upright dividing a window into two or more LIGHTS.*

NEWEL POST: *the upright post at the end, or at the corner, of the handrail of a staircase; on a circular staircase, the column around which the stairs wind.*

OVERMANTEL: *an ornamental structure placed over a MANTELPIECE.*

PALLADIAN: *a style of architecture taken from the designs of the 16th-century Italian architect Palladio. Inigo Jones brought the style to England in the 17th century but the great revival of Palladianism was brought about by Lord Burlington and Colen Campbell in the first quarter of the 18th century.*

PANELLED DOOR: *a door constructed of panels set within a frame.*

PANTILE: *a roofing tile with a curved S-shaped section.*

PARGET WORK: *a style of moulded plaster decoration particularly associated with East Anglia.*

PARQUETAGE: *thin hardwood laid in patterns on a wood sub-floor.*

PAVIORS: *thin "bricks" used for flooring.*

PEDIMENT: *a low-pitched gable above a portico, door or window which may be either straight-sided or curbed; a broken pediment is one which is open at the top.*

PIANO NOBILE: *the principal storey of a house – more lofty than the others – containing the reception rooms; there is a basement or ground floor below and shallower floors above.*

PIER: *a solid vertical masonry support; the solid section of wall between openings – windows, doors etc – in a building.*

PILASTER: *a shallow column or PIER set against a wall and projecting only slightly from it.*

PITCH FLOORS: *floors made from small pieces of stone laid like cobblestones and arranged in patterns.*

PLATE GLASS: *glass used for mirrors and windows, originally made by pouring moulten glass onto an iron plate.*

QUARRY (OR QUARREL): *a small pane of glass, most often diamond-shaped, used for medieval leaded windows.*

REBATE (OR RABBET): *a rectangular recess along an edge of a piece of wood or stone to receive a tongue of another piece.*

REEDED: *decorated with parallel convex mouldings which touch one another.*

REREDOS: *a screen. The term is more commonly used for the decorative wall or screen behind an altar.*

RESTORATION: *the time of the reinstatement of the monarchy in England in 1660.*

REVEAL: *the side surface of a recess or of the opening for a door or window between the frame and outer surface of the wall. If the reveal is cut diagonally it is called a splay (or splayed) reveal.*

ROASTING HEARTH: *Georgian and later cooking hearth in which coal was burned in a grate of variable width raised well above the floor of an inglenook on horizontal bars. These hearths were the predecessors of early cooking ranges.*

ROCOCO: *the delicate and elegant style which followed the BAROQUE, characterized by S-curves, naturalistic motifs and a tendency towards asymmetry.*

SASH WINDOW: *a window composed of sliding glazed frames (sashes) running in vertical grooves.*

STENCIL: *originally "to spangle", from the Old French estinceller: now describes a method of decoration where paint is brushed over a cut-out design usually in varnished manilla paper.*

STILES: *the vertical parts of a door, window, or other frame.*

STRAPWORK: *decoration consisting of interlaced bands and shapes like fretwork.*

STRINGS: *the sloping sides of a staircase which hold the treads and risers.*

STUCCO: *smooth or modelled plasterwork.*

STUDS: *secondary vertical wall timbers.*

TABERNACLE FRAME: *a style of door surround composed of columns or pilasters surmounted by an ENTABLATURE.*

TESSELLATED FLOOR: *a floor composed of small cubes of marble, stone or glass embedded in cement.*

TRANSOM: *a bar dividing a window opening horizontally.*

TROMPE L'OEIL: *something which gives the appearance of reality by means of paint, architecture etc; literally "something that deceives the eye".*

TUDOR ARCH: *a very flattened arch coming to a definite point.*

WAINSCOT: *wood panelling on an internal wall.*

WATTLE AND DAUB: *a type of wall construction whereby laths are plastered over with mud.*

Addy, Sidney Oldall, **The Evolution of the English House.** *London:* The Macmillan Co; *New York:* Swan Sonnenschein & Co., 1898.

Airs, Malcolm, **The Buildings of Britain: Tudor and Jacobean.** *London:* Barrie & Jenkins, 1982.

Amery, Colin, **Three Centuries of Architectural Craftsmanship.** *London:* The Architectural Press, 1977; paperback edition, 1978.

Artley, Alexandra, **Putting Back the Style.** *London:* Evans Brothers, 1982.

Aslet, Clive & Powers, Alan, **National Trust Book of the English House.** *London:* Penguin Books, 1986.

Ayres, James, **The Shell Book of the House in Britain.** *London* and *Boston:* Faber & Faber, 1981.

Bankart, George, **The Art of the Plasterer: An account of the decorative development of the craft.** *London:* Batsford, 1908.

Barley, M.W., **The House and Home: a review of 900 years of house planning and furnishing in Britain.** *London:* Studio Vista, 1963.

Beard, Geoffrey, **Craftsmen and Interior Decoration in England 1660-1820.** *Edinburgh:* John Bartholomew & Sons, 1981.

Bowyer, Jack, **Vernacular Building Conservation.** *London:* The Architectural Press, 1980.

Clifton-Taylor, Alec, **The Pattern of English Building.** *London:* Faber & Faber, 1962.
— **Six English Towns.** *London.* British Broadcasting Corporation, 1982.
— **Another Six English Towns.** *London:* British Broadcasting Corporation, 1984.
— **English Stone Building.** *London:* Victor Gollancz, 1983.

Cook, Olive, **The English House through Seven Centuries.** *London:* Thomas Nelson, 1968; paperback edition: Penguin Books, 1984; *New York:* Overlook Press, 1983.

Cooper, Nicholas, **The Opulent Eye: Late Victorian and Edwardian taste in interior design.** *London:* The Architectural Press, 1976.

Cornforth, John, **English Interiors 1790-1848: the quest for comfort.** *London:* Barrie & Jenkins, 1978.

Cruikshank, Den & Wyld, Peter, **The Art of Georgian Building.** *London:* The Architectural Press; *New York:* Architectural Book Publishing Co, 1975.

Curl, James Stephens, **Victorian Architecture: its practical aspects.** *Newton Abbot:* David & Charles, 1973.

Dixon, Roger & Muthesius, Stefan, **Victorian Architecture.** *New York* and *Toronto:* Oxford University Press, 1978.

Dutton, Ralph, **The English Country House.** *London:* Batsford, 1935.
— **The English Interior, 1500-1900.** *London:* Batsford, 1948.

Edmunds, R.C., **Your Country Cottage: a guide to purchase and restoration.** *Newton Abbot:* David & Charles, 1970.

Fletcher, Banister F. & Fletcher, H. Phillips, **The English Home.** *London:* Methuen & Co, 1910.

Girouard, Mark, **Sweetness and Light: the 'Queen Anne' movement 1860-1900.** *Oxford:* Oxford University Press, 1977.

Good Housekeeping Institute, **Good Housekeeping Quick Home Repairs.** *London:* Ebury Press, 1982.

Gotch, J. Alfred, **The English House from Charles I to George IV: its architecture decoration and garden design.** *London:* Batsford, 1918.

The Guild of Master Craftsmen, **Guide to Restoration Experts.**

Hanna, Max & Binney, Marcus, **Preserve and Prosper: Save Britain's Heritage.**

Hemming, Charles, **Paint Finishes.** *London:* Macdonald.

Hill, Oliver & Cornforth, John, **English Country House: 'Caroline' 1625-1685.** *Suffolk:* Antique Collector's Club, 1985.

Hills, Nicholas, **The English Fireplace.** *London:* Quiller Press 1983, 1985.

The Historic Buildings Co, **Period Property Register.** Published 11 times a year.

Jackson-Stops, Gervase & Pipkin, James, **The English Country House – A Grand Tour.** *London:* Weidenfeld & Nicholson.

Johnson, Lorraine, **New Decorator's Directory.** *London:* Michael Joseph/Design Council; paperback edition: Mermaid Books, 1986.

Keltel, Russell Hawes, **Early American Rooms.** *New York:* Dover, 1967.

Lambourne, Lionel, **Utopian Craftsmen: The arts and crafts movement from the Cotswolds to Chicago.** *London:* Astragal Books, 1980.

Lasdun, Susan, **Victorians at Home.** *London:* Weidenfeld & Nicholson.

Le Grice, Lyn, **Lyn Le Grice's Art of Stencilling:** Viking Press, 1986.

Lloyd, Nathanial, **A History of the English House.** *London:* The Architectural Press, 1931, 1949, 1975; paperback edition, 1975.

McCorquodale, Charles, **The History of Interior Decoration.** Phaidon Press, 1983.

McDonald, Roxana, **The Fireplace Book.** *London:* The Architectural Press, 1984.

McGown, John & Du Ben, Roger, **The Book of Home Restoration.** *London:* Ebury Press, 1985

Moore, Derry & Pick, Michael, **The English Room.** *London:* Weidenfeld & Nicholson.

Muthesius, Stefan, **The English Terraced House.** *New Haven and London:* Yale University Press, 1982.

Paint Research Association, **Paint and Pretreatment Products Directory.** Second edition March 1983.
— **Evaluation of Biocidal Masonry Coatings and Guide to Paint Film Biocides.** March 1986.

Palmer, Roy, **The Water Closet: a new history.** *Newton Abbot:* David & Charles, 1973.

The Penguin Dictionary of Architecture, John Fleming, Hugh Honour and Nikolaus Pevsner, Penguin Books, London.

The Penguin Dictionary of Decorative Arts, John Fleming and Hugh Honour, Penguin Books, London.

Pilcher, Donald, **The Regency Style 1800 to 1830.** *London:* Batsford, 1947.

Plumb, J.H., **Georgian Delights.** *London:* Weidenfeld & Nicholson, 1980.

Quennel, Marjorie & C.H.B., **A History of Everyday Things in England, Vol III, 1733-1851.** *London:* Batsford, 1961.

Radford, Penny, **Surfaces and Finishes.** *London:* Macmillan, 1984.

Reid, Richard, **The Shell Book of Cottages.** *London:* Michael Joseph, 1977, 1986.

Scott, John S., **A Dictionary of Building.** *London and New York:* Penguin Books, 1964; revised edition, 1974.

Seymour Lindsay, J., **Iron and Brass Implements of the English House.** *London:* Alec Tiranti, 1970.

Summerson, John, **Georgian London.** *London:* Pleiades Books, 1945; revised paperback edition: Penguin Books 1978.
— **The Architecture of the 18th C.** *London:* Thames & Hudson, 1986.

Watkin, David, **The Buildings of Britain: Regency** (Series editor, Alastair Service). *London:* Barrie & Jenkins, 1982.

Williams, Constance, **A Continuing Tradition . . . the development of wallpaper manufacture.** Good Housekeeping, 1976.

Wilson, Everett B, **Fifty Early American Towns.** *South Brunswick, N.J.:* A.S. Barnes & Company; *London:* Thomas Yoseloff, 1966.

Wood, Margaret, **The English Medieval House.** Ferndale Editions, 1981.

Wright, Lawrence, **Clean and Decent: the fascinating history of the bathroom and the WC.** *London:* Routledge & Kegan Paul, 1960.

Doors (front and interior)

A. & H. Brass
201-203 Edgware Road
London W2 1ES
Supply brass door and window fittings, electrical accessories, chandeliers, lights and bathroom fittings.

Architectural Components Ltd
(Locks and Handles)
4-10 Exhibition Road
London SW7 2HF
Three showrooms, near the South Kensington museums and Underground station, supply a large range of period fittings used in the renovation and furnishing of property. Over 6,000 different items in stock door and cabinet fittings, bathroom accessories, all types of locks, window fittings, hinges, curtain hardware, door closers, grilles and vents, electrical switch plates, fireplace furniture.

Artisan Period and Victorian Joinery
Grange Farm
Buxshalls Hill
Lindfield
Sussex
See WINDOWS

Bailey's Architectural Antiques
The Engine Shed
Ashburton Industrial Estate
Ross-on-Wye
Herefordshire HE9 7BW
Large stock of traditional fixtures and fittings, including their own range of recycled lead planters and fountains, brass and aluminium brackets and blacksmith-made door knockers. Also an ever-changing range of garden furniture, fireplaces, unfitted kitchens, bathrooms, mirrors, tiles, taps etc.

Beardmore Architectural Ironmongery
3-5 Percy Street
London W1P 0EJ
Ornamental period-style brassware, from electrical accessories to door furniture.

Philip Bradbury Glass
83 Blackstock Road
London N4 2JW
See WINDOWS

N. T. Brassart Ltd
Atwood Street
Lye
Stourbridge
West Midlands DY9 8RY
Period, Georgian, Art Deco and Constable solid brass door and window fittings and electrical accessories. Catalogue available.

Brass Tacks Hardware Ltd
177 Bilton Road
Perivale
Greenford
Middlesex UB6 7HJ
Manufacturers and distributors of decorative brass door fittings and accessories. The range of products includes locks, hinges and furniture, electrical accessories and bathroom fittings. The company also produces special items and decorative grilles for covering radiators etc. Catalogue available.

Bridgwater Reclamation Ltd
Monmouth Street
Bridgwater
Somerset
See FIREPLACES AND STOVES

British Gates and Timber Ltd
Castletons Oak Sawmills
Biddenden
Nr Ashford
Kent TN27 8DD
A range of traditional interior oak-ledged and boarded doors with original details and authentic hand finishes. Also other ranges of traditional interior and exterior doors. Catalogue available.

Bromley Demolition Co Ltd
75 Siward Road
Bromley
Kent
Items such as bricks, doors and floorboards for demolition.

Classic Designs
Unit 15
Biltyon Industrial Estate
Humber Avenue
Coventry CV3 1JL

Clayton-Munroe Ltd
Kingston
Staverton
Totnes
Devon TQ9 6AR
Manufacturers of 17th-century hand-forged door hardware and fittings.

Comyn Ching (Sheffield) Ltd
296 Penistone Road
Sheffield S6 2FT
Specialists in door furniture, locks, hinges, door closers, sliding door gear – wholesale and export. A large range of black antique ironmongery. Catalogue available.

Conservation Building Products Ltd
Forge Works
Forge Lane
Cradley Heath
Warley
West Midlands B64 5AL
See EXTERIORS

Cotswood Door Specialists (Kew) Ltd
63A Park Road
Kingston-upon-Thames
Surrey KT2 6DE
Suppliers of high-quality hardwood joinery, and an emphasis on doors and entrances, with the associated mouldings, architraves, skirtings etc. A range of standard designs is available in mahogany. A design and installation service is also offered and doors and joinery can be made to customers' own designs, or to match any existing pattern, particularly in period and/or listed properties. Also matching garage doors.

Counterparts Demolition Ltd
Station Yard
Topsham
Exeter
Devon
See EXTERIORS

Crittall Windows Ltd
Springwood Drive
Braintree
Essex CM7 7YN
See WINDOWS

Domus Doorbells Ltd
Somers House
Linkfield Corner
Redhill
Surrey RH7 7BB
Design, manufacture and renovation of traditional doorbells.

Door Controls Ltd
19-21 The Broadway
Herne Bay
Kent CT6 8LG
Specialists in door operating equipment.

The Empire & Colonial Knocker Co
PO Box 1876
Tamworth
Staffordshire B77 4RY
Manufacturers of period-style door knockers using moulds from originals.

Grandisson Doors
The Old Hall
West Hill Road
West Hill
Ottery St Mary
Devon EX11 1TP
Exclusive hand-carved doors in traditional and period styles. Standard and non-standard sizes available. Brochure on request.

The Great Northern Architectural Antiques Co Ltd
New Russia House
Chester Road
Tattenhall
Chester CH3 9AH
Suppliers of period doors, fire surrounds, pews, panelling, brassware, pub fittings, sanitaryware, stained glass, spindles, newel posts, handrails and reclaimed timber. Also restorers of architectural woodwork, which can be carried out in their own workshops and on site.

Charles Harden
14 Chiltern Street
London W1
Specialists in brass, glass and china door furniture, bathroom fittings in brass, chrome and gold-plated finishes, also brass Regency-pattern Espagnolette bolts. The firm has been in existence for 65 years and is a one-man business.

T. J. Hardwood & Co Ltd
Ellenshaw Works
Kay Street
Darwen
Lancashire BB3 3EW
Georgian, Victorian and other period styles of reproduction door hardware in brass, porcelain and cast-iron. Brochure available.

Havenplan's Architectural Emporium
1 The Old Station
Station Road
Killamarsh
Sheffield S31 8EN
See FIREPLACES AND STOVES

Heritage Oak Ltd
Unit V1
Dean Clough Industrial Park
Halifax HX3 5AX
West Yorkshire
Restoration work carried out exclusively in English oak. Doors nailed and pegged, waxing and ageing. Staircases reproduced from original patterns using traditional craft methods. Panelling and flooring as well as decorative panels, wainscots, screens and traditional/period-style floors.

E. A. Higginson & Co Ltd
Unit 1
Carlisle Road
London NW9 0HD
See STAIRCASES

The House Hospital
68 Battersea High Street
Battersea
London SW11
Specialists in second-hand period fireplaces, doors, basins, baths, WCs, cisterns, garden fencing and gates, brass door handles, brass taps and many other items of architectural salvage.

"In" Doors Ltd
Invicta Works
Mill Street
East Malling
Kent ME19 6BP
Suppliers of original solid pine doors as well as glazed doors with plain and stained glass and kitchen cupboard doors.

J. S. R. Joinery Ltd
Poole Street
Great Yeldham
Halstead
Essex CO9 4HN
Specialist joinery manufacturers of all types of doors, new and replacements, including panelled and framed, ledged and braced and ledged and boarded. Produced to customers' requirements.

Knobs and Knockers
Head Office:
36 York Way
Camden Town
London N1 9AB
Leading retailers of architectural ironmongery with over 50 branches throughout the United Kingdom, also providing a full scheduling and estimating service. Brochure available.

Langham Architectural Materials
Langham Farm
East Nynehead
Wellington
Somerset TA21 0DD
See FIREPLACES AND STOVES

W. & R. Leggott Ltd
East Parade
Bradford
West Yorkshire BD1 5HA
Brass founders and manufacturers of period door furniture and specialist fittings.

B. Lilly & Sons Ltd
Baltimore Road
Birmingham B42 1DJ
Craftsmen in brass including the Sadler architectural hardware.

The London Architectural Salvage and Supply Co
St Michael's Church
Mark Street
Shoreditch
London EC2A 4ER
Providers of a full range of good quality interior and exterior materials, fixtures and fittings for the refurbishment and decoration of commercial and domestic period buildings, including chimneypieces, panelling for rooms, fencing and gates, flooring in oak, ash, pine and marble, bathroom fittings, kitchen furniture, doors and joinery, shop and bar fittings, lamposts and lanterns, carved stonework, York flagstones, garden furniture and statuary.

The London Door Co
165 St John's Hill
London SW11 1TQ

A wide range of doors including hardwood front doors, security doors, carved and traditional doors. Doors also made-to-measure for people requiring non-standard or unusual size doors. Also in stock are stained-glass panels for leaded lights. A complete fitting service is available. Brochure also available on request.

Mackinnon & Bailey
72 Floodgate Street
Birmingham B5 5SL
Manufacturers of architectural hardware including fittings for doors, windows and cupboards in polished brass, chromium plate and satin chromium plate. Other items include door stops, finger plates, footrail brackets, coat and hat hooks and ventilator panels. Brochure available on request.

Malvern Studios
56 Cowleigh Road
Malvern
Worcestershire WR14 1QD
See LIGHTING

Manorhouse Stone
Pinehouse
Oaks Industrial Estate
Ravenstone Road
Coalville
Leicestershire LE6 2MB
See FIREPLACES AND STOVES

Meer End Woodturners
Torrington Avenue
Coventry CV4 9AP
See WINDOWS

Midland Veneers Ltd
Hayseech Road
Halesowen
West Midlands B63 3PE
Manufacturers of veneered panels and flush doors to specification. Manufacturers of preformed plywood curved components for the furniture and construction industry.

Mounts Hill Woodcraft Ltd
Paynetts Lane
Cranbrook Road
Goudhurst
Kent TN17 1DY
A small well-established business situated in the Weald of Kent. Only manufacture to order: exact reproduction period joinery such as doors, windows, staircases and fitted furniture. They are able to reproduce most mouldings and turnings with a degree of precision. The firm also manufactures from and supplies a large range of quality hardwoods from locally grown oak to selected imported timbers.

Newman Tonks Consumer Products Ltd
71 Allesley Street
Birmingham B6 4ND

Oakcraft Sawmills & Joinery Ltd
Hammer Pond Road
Plummers Plain
West Sussex RH13 6PE

Specializing in English oak, suppliers of fine quality oak and oak products. Handmade doors and door frames. Floors, skirting and architraves. Other hardwoods available are maple, beech and ash.

One Off Joinery
13 Holmes Road
Earley,
Reading
Berkshire RG6 2BH
See STAIRCASES

The Original Choice
1340 Stratford Road
Hall Green
Birmingham B28 9EH
See FIREPLACES AND STOVES

Original Door Specialist
298 Brockley Road
London SE4 2RA
A large stock of original doors, original front doors many with stained glass. All types and sizes of interior doors also available.

Peco of Hampton
72 Station Road
Hampton
Middlesex
Original period doors, over 2,000 in stock in all types, including stained glass and sandblasted glass front doors. Over 150 original and reproduction cast-iron and pine fireplaces on display. They are also designers, manufacturers and repairers of stained and sandblasted glass.

Perkins & Powell
(A subsidiary of Samuel Heath & Sons plc)
Leopold Street
Birmingham B21 0UJ
Manufacturers of marine brassware as well as producers of a wide range of brass door and window fittings.

Posterity Architectural Effects
Baldwins Farm
Dymock Road
Newent
Gloucestershire
Stockists of architectural salvage items, doors, windows, fire surrounds flooring etc.

A. L. Rattray
Craighall
Blairgowrie
Perthshire PH10 7JB
Scotland
See BATHROOMS

Relay Windows
by Glass Relay Ltd
211 London Road
Kent DA9 9DQ
See WINDOWS

John Sambrook
Park House
Northiam
East Sussex TN31 6PA
Makes fanlights.

Solopark Ltd
The Old Railway Station
Station Road
Nr Pampisford
Cambridge CB2 4HB
Specialist suppliers of traditional building materials and other architectural items including bricks, roofing tiles, slates, oak beams, floor pammets, staircases, window frames, panelling, mouldings, internal and external doors.

Stuart Interiors
Barrington Court
Barrington
Ilminster
Somerset TA19 0NQ
Stuart Interiors are leading specialists in all aspects of recreating 16th- and 17th-century English homes. They offer a total interior design package for clients with period homes or those looking for a period style. This includes antique and reproduced furniture, lighting, panelling, doors, staircases, stonework and a vast range of accessories. Stuart Renaissance Textiles design and weave accurate copies of English and European fabrics from the Byzantine period to the 19th century. At Barrington Court, a beautiful Elizabethan manor in Somerset, Stuart have created a national centre for all aspects of early English interior design for private and commercial clients and the academic world. Brochure available on request.

Robert Thompson's Craftsmen Ltd
Kilburn
York YO6 4AH
Manufacturers of individual items executed in seasoned English oak, including staircases, panelling and doors.

A Touch of Brass Ltd
210 Fulham Road
London SW10 9PJ
and: 61 Fulham High Street
London SW6 3JJ
Suppliers of high-quality brass products, with many different ranges to suit every period of architecture beginning from the 16th century. Over 2,000 items in stock at each branch. Brochure available.

Verdigris Art Metalwork Restorers
Arch 290
Crown Street
London SE5 0UR
Repairs, fine patinas, french gilding, metal colouring and lacquering expertly carried out on antique and modern metalwork in brass, bronze, copper and pewter.

Verine Products & Co
Folly Faunts House
Goldhanger
Maldon
Essex CM9 8AP
See FIREPLACES AND STOVES

Walcot Reclamation
108 Walcot Street
Bath
Avon BA1 5BG
See FIREPLACES AND STOVES

Whiteway Waldron Ltd
305 Munster Road
London SW6
See WINDOWS

Winther Browne & Co Ltd
Eley's Industrial Estate
Nobel Road
Edmonton
London N18 3DX
Suppliers and manufacturers of period home products including authentic styled beams, available in dark oak, light oak, grey or unstained finishes. Doors, staircases, windows and mouldings. Catalogue available on request.

C. H. Wood (Security) Ltd
221 Wakefield Road
Bradford BD4 7PE
Manufacturers, restorers and repairers of locks, also key cutting.

WINDOWS

Architectural Components Ltd
(Locks and Handles)
4-10 Exhibition Road
London SW7 2HF
See DOORS

Architectural Heritage Ltd
Taddington Manor
Taddington
Nr Cutsdean
Cheltenham
Gloucestershire GL54 5RY
See WALLS

Artisan Period and Victorian Joinery
Grange Farm
Buxshalls Hill
Lindfield
Sussex
Traditional handmade joinery including windows, doors, panelling and kitchens. Catalogue available.

Bailey's Architectural Antiques
The Engine Shed
Ashburton Industrial Estate
Ross-on-Wye
Herefordshire HE9 7BW
See DOORS

Philip Bradbury Glass
83 Blackstock Road
Highbury
London N4 2JW
Etched windows reproduced with authentic 19th-century patterns on new glass. Also restorers of doors, sashes and fanlights.

Bridgwater Reclamation Ltd
Monmouth Street
Bridgwater
Somerset
See FIREPLACES AND STOVES

Brighton Architectural Salvage
33 Gloucester Road
Brighton
Sussex
See FIREPLACES AND STOVES

Cantabrian Antiques
16 Park Street
Lynton
North Devon
See FIREPLACES AND STOVES

Peter Chapman Antiques
10 Theberton Street
Islington
London N1 0QX
See FIREPLACES AND STOVES

The Cotswold Casement Co Ltd
Moreton in Marsh
Gloucestershire GL56 OHH
Specialists in period-style windows in steel and aluminium. Window repairs and refurbishment.

Crittall Windows Ltd
Springwood Drive
Braintree
Essex CM7 7YN
Steel, aluminium and UPVC windows and doors. For refurbishment of period buildings, steel windows in traditional styles with hinged or pivoted opening casements supplied with the glazing bars sub-dividing the lights as required, including the classical Georgian" proportion of panes. Catalogues available.

Goddard & Gibbs Studios
41 & 49 Kingsland Road
Shoreditch
London E2 8AD
Installation of stained and decorative glass, ranging from windows, interior panels and murals to domes and rooflights using techniques of dalles-de-verre, acid-etching and sandblasting. A design service is also available.

Grandisson Doors
The Old Hall
West Hill Road
West Hill
Ottery St Mary
Devon EX11 1TP
See DOORS

The Great Northern Architectural Antiques Co Ltd
New Russia House
Chester Road
Tattenhall
Chester CH3 9AH
See DOORS

Hartley Wood & Co Ltd
Portobello Glass Works
Portobello Lane
Monkwearmouth
Sunderland
Tyne & Wear SR6 0DN
Manufacturers of stained glass also hand-blown and rolled glass.

Haywards
73 Holland Pines
Bracknell
Berkshire
Specialists in box sash window renovation and repair. Any style of window reproduced.

James Hetley & Co Ltd
School House Lane
Glasshouse Fields
Stepney
London E1 9JA
Stockists, distributors and exporters of antique glass including a full range of Pilkington, laminated and silvered float glass, hand-blown and reproduction bullions, glass lampshades in Art Nouveau, Art Deco and Tiffany styles, also antique and rolled glass.

E. A. Higginson & Co Ltd
Unit 1
Carlisle Road
London NW9 0HD
See STAIRCASES

Illumin Glass Studio
82 Bond Street
Macclesfield
Cheshire SK11 6QS
See LIGHTING

The London Shutter Co
Windsor Road
Ascot
Berkshire SL5 7AF
Interior shutters in pine with movable louvres. Can be produced to any design, style or colour. On-site surveys and a professional fitting service carried out.

Manorhouse Stone
Pinehouse
Oaks Industrial Estate
Ravenstone Road
Coalville
Leicestershire LE6 2MB
See FIREPLACES AND STOVES

Meer End Woodturners
Torrington Avenue
Coventry CV4 9AP
Architectural and industrial joinery manufacturers specializing in reproducing joinery such as sliding sash windows, Georgian windows, doors and staircases.

Mounts Hill Woodcraft Ltd
Paynetts Lane
Cranbrook Road
Goudhurst
Kent TN17 1DY
See DOORS

M. S. Glass Decorators
336 Aldridge Road
Streetley
Sutton Coldfield
West Midlands
Specialists in all kinds of glass decorating including sand-blasting, engraving, acid-etching, stained glass, gilding and screen printing.

Mumford & Wood Ltd
Hallsford Bridge Industrial Estate
Ongar
Essex CM5 9RB
Manufacturers of ovolo moulded double-hung sash windows, doors and French doors with many frame options in period Georgian, Victorian and Regency styles. Offer technical advice on individual projects requiring special items such as casements, bullseye or shaped windows to complement their standard sash window and door products. Single and double glazing ranges. Brochure available on request.

One Off Joinery
13 Homes Road
Earley
Reading
Berkshire RG6 2BH
See STAIRCASES

The Original Box Sash Window Company
The Joinery
Unit 10
Bridgwater Way
Windsor
Berkshire SL4 1RD
Manufacturers of box sash windows in traditional designs made with pulleys and sash cords also casement windows, with single or double glazing. Finishes include wax, stain or white paint.

The Original Choice
1340 Stratford Road
Hall Green
Birmingham B29 9EH
See FIREPLACES AND STOVES

A . & H. Pemberton Ltd
63 Shaw Street
Liverpool L6 1HN
Specialist designers of mirrors, (acid-etched, sand-blasted, or both), glass, gilding and painted designs or lettering. Stained glass or leaded lights manufactured to order.

Posterity Architectural Effects
Baldwins Farm
Dymock Road
Newent
Gloucestershire
See DOORS

Relay Windows
by Glass Relay Ltd
211 London Road
Nr Dartford
Kent DA9 9DQ
Manufacturers of quality windows, doors and conservatories in a choice of mahogany, oak or pine. Brochure available.

Sashy and Sashy
5 Phoenix Lane
Ashurst Wood
Forest Row
East Sussex RH19 3RA
Specialists in sash window restoration and replacement.

Solopark Ltd
The Old Railway Station
Station Road
Nr Pampisford
Cambridge CB2 4HB
See DOORS

Stained Glass Period Glazing
Warryfield Barn
Walford
Ross-on-Wye
Herefordshire
Producers of wrought iron opening casements, oak mullion window frames and leaded crown glass windows.

Andy Thornton Architectural Antiques Ltd
Victoria Mills
Stainland Road
Greetland
Halifax
West Yorkshire HX4 8AD
A large range of reproduction architectural antiques.

Tomkinson Stained Glass
129 Pancras Road
London NW1 1UN
Specialists in restoration and manufacture of stained glass windows and Georgian leaded lights. Stockists of antique windows, doors and architectural items.

Townsends (Hallmore Trading Ltd)
108 Boundary Road
London NW8 0RH
Specialists in the design, fabrication, restoration and supply of leaded stained glass windows. Supplier of etched, sandblasted, bevelled, brilliant-cut glass made to order. Many antique windows and glazed doors in stock.

M. Tuckey Joinery
20 Cherry Street
Warwick CV34 4LR
See KITCHENS

Walcot Reclamation
108 Walcot Street
Bath
Avon BA1 5BG
See FIREPLACES AND STOVES

West Country Workshops
Kingstone
Herefordshire HR2 9HY
Custom-made solid oak windows.

Whiteway Waldron Ltd
305 Munster Road
Fulham
London SW6 6BJ
Stained glass and architectural fittings, including doors and fire surrounds.

Winther Browne & Co Ltd
Eley's Industrial Estate
Nobel Road
Edmonton
London N18 3DX
See DOORS

Floors

Eleanor Allit
Thickthorn Cottage
108 Leamington Road
Kenilworth
Warwickshire CV8 2AA
See WALLS

The Art Tile Co Ltd
Heathfield
Newton Abbot
Devon TQ12 6RF
See WALLS

Bridgwater Reclamation Ltd
Monmouth Street
Bridgwater
Somerset
See FIREPLACES AND STOVES

Bromley Demolition Co Ltd
75 Siward Road
Bromley
Kent
See DOORS

Campbell Marson & Co Ltd
Unit 34
Wimbledon Stadium Business Centre
Riverside Road
London SW17 0BA
Specialists in supplying and laying hardwood flooring, eg strip, strip overlay, tongued and grooved, mosaic panels, wood block, parquet and cork tiles.

Candy Tiles Ltd
Heathfield
Newton Abbot
Devon TQ12 6RF
Ceramic wall tiles, frost-proof vitrified floor tiles of Swiss origin, terracotta floor tiles suitable for period-style kitchens of French origin.

Capitol Tile Supplies
Designer Studio
PO Box 80
Albion Works
Endemere Road
Coventry CV6 5SE
Suppliers of a wide range of wall and floor tiles, including a specialized service for designers, architects and specifiers. Catalogue available.

Carvall Group
Ceramics and Flooring
Unit 1, Lawrence Trading Estate
Blackwall Lane
London SE10 0AR
Importers of Italian ceramic tiles, Cisa and Cerdisa. Catalogue available.

Castelnau Tiles
175 Church Road
Barnes
London SW13 9HR
Suppliers of marble, terracotta and Mexican floor tiles. A wide choice of Italian and French tiles for walls and floors.

Ceramique Internationale Ltd
386 Kings Road
London SW3 5UZ
Stockists of a wide range of handmade ceramic wall and floor tiles. Advice on special installations, eg swimming pools, patios, external claddings, restaurants and other commercial uses.

Conservation Building Products Ltd
Forge Works
Forge Lane
Cradley Heath
Warley
West Midlands B64 5AL
See EXTERIORS

Criterion Tiles Ltd
196 Wandsworth Bridge Road
Fulham
London SW6 2UF
Also: 2A England's Lane
Hampstead
London NW3 4TG
A range of English and Continental ceramic tiles with a variety of finishes and effects, including hand-applied transfer and stencilling, relief moulding, in-glaze hand-painting, screen-printing in special colours for floors, fine terracotta, slate and large quarries both glazed and unglazed. Creative advice given. Catalogue available.

Domus Tiles Ltd
33 Parkgate Road
London SW11 4NP
Suppliers of glazed and unglazed floor and wall ceramic tiles, plain and patterned, refined porcelain stoneware, frostproof heavy-duty tiles, including relief finishes, polished finishes, anti-slips, step treads and skirtings, natural rustic terracotta tiles, patterned resin-bonded marble tiles.

Elon
166 Fulham Road
South Kensington
London SW3 6HH
A range of terracotta, slate and glazed floor and wall tiles. Catalogue available.

Fired Earth
Head Office and Warehouse:
Middle Aston
Oxford
Oxfordshire OX5 3PX
Oxford Showroom: Arena
Thomas Yard
6 Rectory Road
St Clements
Oxford
London Showroom: 102 Portland Road
London W11
Designers and manufacturers of ceramic tiles made by craftsmen using centuries-old methods and techniques. Over 35 different types of terracotta tiles in stock. Suitable for kitchens, dining rooms, halls, conservatories, patios etc. Also reproduction early English delft tiles.

Forbo-Nairn Ltd
Leet Court
14 King Street
Watford
Hertfordshire WD1 8BZ
Linoleum and contract vinyl floorcovering and carpet tiles available in sheets and in tiles. Catalogue available on request.

Froyle Tiles Ltd
Lower Froyle
Nr Alton
Hampshire GU34 4LL
Producers of handmade stone tiles suitable for interior and exterior areas ie floors and walls in a wide variety of colours. Catalogue available.

Galerie Seven
7 Church Road
Wimbledon Village
London SW19 5DW
Producers of handmade tiles in materials ranging from terracotta to mosaics. Ideal to create unique designs for interior and exterior wall and floor areas. Also an expanding range of handmade and painted ceramic tiles and borders. Can also produce to customers' individual specifications, colour and design. Brochure available on request.

David Gunton
Grange Lane
Whitegate
Nr Winsford
Cheshire CW7 2PJ
Manufacturers of hardwood floors.

Diana Hall
1 Thatched Cottage
Ilford
Lewes
Sussex BN7 3EW
Mediaeval and Victorian encaustic tiles for floor restoration.

Heritage Oak Ltd
Unit V1
Dean Clough Industrial Park
Halifax HX3 5AX
See DOORS

Heritage Woodcraft
14 Carlyon Road
Carlyon Road Industrial Estate
Atherstone
Warwickshire CV9 1JE
Manufacturers and suppliers of all types of hardwood flooring, a large stock of reclaimed woodblock flooring, strip flooring and planking. Hardwood flooring is machined to customers' requirements.

H. & R. Johnson Tiles Ltd
Highgate Tile Works
Tunstall
Stoke-on-Trent
Staffordshire ST6 4JX
Manufacturers of encaustic and geometric tiles for the restoration of 19th-century floors and the Minton Hollins Victorian range of wall tiles.

John Burgess Tiles
Unit B25
Maws Craft Centre
Jackfield
Shropshire TF8 7LS
Reproduction Victorian and Art Nouveau ceramic wall and floor tiles.

Kibblewhite & Blackmur Ltd
Long Reach Road
Barking
Essex IG11 0JN
See EXTERIORS

Lambeth Dixon
Eric Lambeth
84 South Hill Road
Bromley
Kent BR2 0RT
Also: Mike Dixon
Horseshoes
Little Yeldham
Halstead
Essex CO9 4LB
Hardwood flooring consultants and suppliers offering a full range of traditional flooring materials including wood blocks, strip flooring and mosaic panels as well as the popular pre-finished materials such as Kahrs, Junckers, Tarkett, Panaget and Wicanders, together with a full range of accessories. Specialists in matching wood blocks, strip flooring and mosaic panels for repair and renovation work. As consultants they offer advice and carry out surveys on site, screed testing and assist in the drawing up of suitable specifications – fees for this are quoted on request.

The London Architectural Salvage and Supply Co
St Michael's Church
Mark Street
Shoreditch
London EC2A 4ER
See DOORS

Francis N. Lowe Ltd
The Marble Works
New Road
Middleton-by-Wirksworth
Derbyshire DE4 4NB
Specialist designers and manufacturers in natural marble, granite and slate.

Naturestone
1 Kings Ride Park
Ascot
Berkshire SL5 8AR
Stone flooring.

Oakcraft Sawmills & Joinery Ltd
Hammer Pond Road
Plummers Plain
West Sussex RH13 6PE
See DOORS

Paris Ceramics
543 Battersea Park Road
Battersea
London SW11 3BL

Specialists in restoration and installation of antique terracotta and stone floors from France. Also suppliers of new Spanish terracotta floor tiles, Blue English limestone and unglazed decorated floor tiles in a variety of styles. Several wall tiles from Spain, Holland and France, some reproduced from antique patterns. Colour brochure available.

Petit Roque Ltd
5a New Road
Croxley Green
Hertfordshire WD3 3EJ
See FIREPLACES AND STOVES

Daniel Platt & Sons Ltd
Brownhills Tileries
Tunstall
Stoke-on-Trent ST6 4NG
Staffordshire
Manufacturers and exporters of quarry floor tiles.

Posterity Architectural Effects
Baldwins Farm
Dymock Road
Newent
Gloucestershire
See DOORS

Ramus Tile Co Ltd
Palace Road
Southgate
London N11 2PX
Manufacturers and suppliers of ceramic wall and floor tiles for all situations and decors. Distributors of Colourmatch tiles.

The Real Stone Company
The Forge
Penthouse Hill
Bath
Avon BA1 7EL
Traditional Bath stone flooring and staircases. Individually designed Bath stone summer houses and garden furniture.

Realstone Ltd
Wingerworth
Chesterfield
Derbyshire S42 6RG
Natural stone tiles in various colours, textures and finishes.

Reclaimed Materials
Northgate
White Lund Industrial Estate
Morecambe
Lancashire
See EXTERIORS

The Reject Tile Shop
178 Wandsworth Bridge Road
Wandsworth
London SW6 2UQ
Specializes in second-hand quality discontinued tiles, particularly those from the Edwardian and Victorian periods. Many of the tiles in the shop cannot be found anywhere else as they only find their way on to the domestic market as rejects.

Robus Pottery & Tiles
Evington Park
Hastingleigh
Ashford
Kent
See WALLS

Rogers Demolition and Dismantling Service Ltd
Belgrave Road
Portswood
Southampton
See EXTERIORS

Royal Dutch Sphinx Ltd
Untis 1 & 2
Pipers Court
Thatcham
Newbury
Berkshire RG13 4ER
Manufacturers and suppliers of ceramic wall and floor tiles in many colours and designs.

Dennis Ruabon Ltd
Hafod Tileries
Ruabon
Wrexham
Clwyd LL14 6ET
North Wales
Manufacturers of unglazed floor quarry tiles, for refurbishment and renovation.

Rye Tiles
The Old Brewery
Wishward
Rye
Sussex TN31 7DH
Hand-decorated wall and floor tiles made to order. Export orders also welcome. Contract and hotel work as well as decorators and private customers. Catalogue available on request.

H. & E. Smith Ltd
Van Delft
Britannic Works
Broom Street
Hanley
Stoke-on-Trent
Staffordshire ST1 2ER
Manufacturers of reproduction Victorian, Edwardian and Art Nouveau tiles for walls and floors, suitable for internal and external areas. Also hand-painted and embossed Victorian tiles for fireplace surrounds. Catalogue available.

Solopark Ltd
The Old Railway Station
Station Road
Nr Pampisford
Cambridge CB2 4HB
See DOORS

Stone Age
67 Dendy Street
Balham
London SW12 8DA
Real stone floor tiles. Perfect for conservatories, halls, kitchens and bathrooms.

Stuart Interiors
Barrington Court
Barrington
Ilminster
Somerset TA19 0NQ
See DOORS

Sussex Terracotta
Nye Road
Burgess Hill
Sussex RH15 0LZ
Handmade terracotta floor tiles.

Tiles of Newport and London
Head Office: Dumfries Place Estate
Lower Dock Street
Newport
Gwent
Also: Unit 9
23a Bagleys Lane
London SW6 2BW
See BATHROOMS

Treework Flooring
Treework Services Ltd
Cheston Combe
Backwell
Nr Bristol BS19 3JO
Hardwood floors. Solid boards machined from oak, ash, elm and other timbers. For restoration and new build.

Verity Tiles
Unit 7
101 Farm Lane
London SW6
Suppliers of a range of hand-glazed ceramic floor and wall tiles, with over 16 standard tile sizes and shapes, supplied in about 500 different glaze colours and designs. To complement the tiles, there is a special range of hand-formed ceramic pieces for use as dado rails, arch surrounds, mouldings and covings, available in any glaze colour.

Walcot Reclamation
108 Walcot Street
Bath
Avon BA1 5BG
See FIREPLACES AND STOVES

Wellington Tile Co
Milverton Road
Wellington
Somerset
A wide range of terracotta floor tiles.

Wicanders (GB) Ltd
Stoner House
Kilnmead
Crawley
West Sussex
Suppliers of a wide range of cork-based materials to the specialist flooring trade, working with interior designers and other specifiers.

Angus Williams
10 Worthington Road
Surbiton
Surrey KT6 7RX

Handwoven linen floorcoverings. Hand dyed to any colour. They are reversible, the obverse side having the alternate colour scheme.

Anna Wyner
2 Ferry Road
Barnes
London SW13 9RX
Specialist designer of mosaics, either pre-cast or fixed on site. Materials used are mainly Italian Smalti, with an almost limitless range of colours. Fees for designing, supplying and fixing are relative to the size, design and materials involved.

WALLS

David Ackroyd Ltd
Henley Farm
Henley Common
Church Stretton
Shropshire SY6 6RS
Repairs and replacements of existing woodwork, from re-polishing veneered and inlaid rosewood doors to making oak window frames, skirting and panelling. Also turning, inlaying, carving and a complete range of specialist paint finishes including ragging, rolling, stippling, marbling and woodgraining.

Eleanor Allit
Thickthorn Cottage
108 Leamington Road
Kenilworth
Warwickshire CV8 2AA
Stencil designers offering a range of standard designs to choose from or specially designed to customers' requirements. A variety of textural grounds provided such as sponging and colour-washing. Stencilling can be used on almost any surface: walls, ceilings, floors, furniture etc.

Sally Anderson (Ceramics) Ltd
Parndon Mill
Harlow
Essex CM20 2HP
Ceramic tiles, hand decorated to order. Range begins with 40 plain colours and then combinations of up to five of these are used to create modular designs and system murals.

Architectural Heritage Ltd
Taddington Manor
Taddington
Nr Cutsdean
Cheltenham
Gloucestershire GL54 5RY
Purveyors of antique and reproduction garden statuary, antique wall panelling, fire surrounds, stained glass plus other items.

Aristocast Originals Ltd
Bold Street
Sheffield
South Yorkshire S9 2LR
Georgian-style feature plasterwork: mouldings, niches, ceiling centres, fire surrounds, door surrounds and canopies, columns and beams.

The Art Tile Co Ltd
Heathfield
Newton Abbot
Devon TQ12 6RF
Floor and wall tiles in original designs, including Victorian. Brochure available.

Bailey's Architectural Antiques
The Engine Shed
Ashburton Industrial Estate
Ross-on-Wye
Herefordshire HE9 7BW
See DOORS

Jacqueline Bateman
7 Rylett Crescent
London W12 9RP
Murals, trompe l'oeil, stencils, friezes and pastiche for hotels, companies, swimming pools, restaurants and private houses. Interior and exterior work undertaken. Sample work available.

Andrew Bradley
1 St Saviour's Terrace
Larkhall
Bath
Avon BA1 6RL
Decorative finishes, marbling, stippling, rag-rolling, dragging, design and cutting of stencils for specific interior finishes. Designs and paints murals to individual requirements.

Bridgwater Reclamation Ltd
Monmouth Street
Bridgwater
Somerset
See FIREPLACES AND STOVES

Brighton Architectural Salvage
33 Gloucester Road
Brighton
East Sussex
See FIREPLACES AND STOVES

Cantabrian Antiques
16 Park Street
Lynton
North Devon
See FIREPLACES AND STOVES

Capital Ceramics
Priors House
5 Beaumont Road
Plaistow
London E13 8RJ
Importers and distributors of ceramic tiles from Italy, Holland, France and Japan. Suppliers to retail outlets, architects, designers as well as direct to the public also offering a technical information service. Catalogue available.

Carlton Smith Joinery
Harewell Lane
Besford
Worcestershire WR8 9AP
Purpose-made joinery manufacturers, specializing in joinery for renovation and refurbishment of period buildings.

Carvers & Gilders
9 Charterhouse Works
Eltringham Street
Wandsworth
London SW18 1TD
Decorative carving to commission, original and period designs. Catalogue available.

Castelnau Tiles
175 Church Road
Barnes
London SW13 9HR
See FLOORS

Ceramique Internationale Ltd
386 Kings Road
Chelsea
London SW3 5UZ
See FLOORS

A. W. Champion Ltd
Champion House
Burlington Road
New Malden
Surrey KT3 4NB
Suppliers of a large range of period mouldings including skirtings, architraves, dados, picture rails, beads and sash materials. Can also produce custom mouldings to match any existing style.

Conservation Building Products Ltd
Forge Works
Forge Lane
Cradley Heath
Warley
West Midlands B64 5AL
See EXTERIORS

Copley Decor Ltd
Leyburn
North Yorkshire DL8 5QA
Suppliers of architectural mouldings in solid oak and pine. Range includes cornices, picture rails, panel mouldings, dado rails, architraves and skirtings. Full colour catalogue available.

W. G. Crotch Ltd
10 Tuddenham Avenue
Ipswich
Suffolk IP4 2HE
Manufacturers of fibrous plaster mouldings, overmantels, console brackets, ceiling roses etc. Catalogue available on request.

Crown Berger Europe Ltd
PO Box 37
Crown House
Hollins Road
Darwen
Lancashire BB3 0BG
Anaglypta wallcoverings.

Crowther of Syon Lodge
Busch Corner
London Road
Isleworth
Middlesex TW7 5BH
See EXTERIORS

Davies Keeling Trowbridge Ltd
3 Charterhouse Works
Eltringham Street
Petergate
London SW18 1TD
Specialist decoration including marbling, stippling, graining, stone blocking, plaster effects, trompe l'oeil, murals and stencilling.

Decorative Tile Works
Jackfield Tile Museum
Ironbridge
Telford
Shropshire TF8 7AW
Specialists in reproduction 19th-century English tiles.

Elon
166 Fulham Road
South Kensington
London SW3 6HH
See FLOORS

Farlow & Boulter
22 Grand Union Centre
Kensal Road
London W10 5AS
Decorative artists and muralists. All aspects of interior design undertaken.

Fine Art Mouldings
Unit 2, Heath Works
Grove Road
Chadwell Heath
Romford
Essex RM6 4UR
Producers of decorative plasterwork for classical interiors.

Fireplaces of Yesteryears
Office: The Granary
Church Lane
Bilton-in-Ainsty
York YO5 8LG
Showroom: Railway Station Platform
3 Crosley Street
Wetherby
West Yorkshire
See FIREPLACES AND STOVES

Froyle Tiles Ltd
Froyle Pottery
Lower Froyle
Nr Alton
Hampshire GU34 4LL
See FLOORS

Gallerie Seven
7 Church Road
Wimbledon Village
London SW19 5DW
See FLOORS

Gillespie UK Ltd
Alma House
38 Crimea Road
Aldershot
Hants GU11 1UD
See CEILINGS

The Great Northern Architectural Antiques Co Ltd
New Russia Hall
Chester Road
Tattenhall
Chester CH3 9AH
See DOORS

Eleanor Greeves
12 Newton Grove
Bedford Park
London W4 1LB
Designers using hand-printing method to decorate their range of ceramic wall tiles. Specialists in repeating foliage patterns, supplied direct from workshop in any of ten alternative colours. Special designs and other colours can be produced to order.

Hales & Howe
Picton House
25 Picton Street
Montpelier
Bristol
Avon BS6 5PZ
Showroom:
6 Perry Road
Park Row
Bristol
Avon BS1 5BQ
See CEILINGS

Hallidays
The Old College
Dorchester-on-Thames
Wallingford
Oxfordshire OX10 7HL
See FIREPLACES AND STOVES

Havenplan's Architectural Emporium
The Old Station
Station Road
Killamarsh
Sheffield S31 8EN
South Yorkshire
See FIREPLACES AND STOVES

Hereford Tiles
Whitestone
Hereford HR1 3SF
Manufacturers of period-style hand decorated ceramic tiles. Suitable for use on fireplace surrounds, in hallways, conservatories etc.

Heritage Oak Ltd
Unit V1
Dean Clough Industrial Park
Halifax
West Yorkshire HX3 5AX
See DOORS

Hinchcliffe & Barber
5 Town Farm Workshops
Dean Lane
Sixpenny Handley
Salisbury
Wiltshire SP5 5A
Hand decorated wall tiles. Brochure available on request.

H. & R. Johnson Tiles Ltd
Highgate Tile Works
Tunstall
Stoke-on-Trent ST6 4JX
Staffordshire
Encaustic and geometric tiles for restoration purposes.

John Burgess Tiles
Unit B25
Maws Craft Centre
Jackfield
Shropshire TF8 7LS
See FLOORS

Kenneth Clark Ceramics
The North Wing
Southover Grange
Southover Road
Lewes
Sussex BN7 1TP
Many ceramic wall tiles and murals of unique design, both those in stock and those individually designed and decorated. Notable are reproductions of Victorian tiles.

Catherine Lalau-Keraly MCSD
104 Hereford Road
Bayswater
London W2 5AL
A geometric approach to murals also sculptures and relief, Art Deco and interior decoration.

The London Architectural Salvage & Supply Co
St Michael's Church
Mark Street
Shoreditch
London EC2A 4ER
See DOORS

Malvern Studios
56 Cowleigh Road
Malvern
Worcestershire WR14 1QD
See LIGHTING

Sally Miles
37 Englewood Road
Clapham
London SW12 9PA
Painted murals and trompe l'oeil for hotels, stately homes, luxury homes and restaurants.

Oakleaf Reproductions Ltd
Ling Bob
Main Street
Wilsden
Bradford BD15 0JP
Reproduction timber in traditional and period styles, including simulated oak ceiling beams, panelling and embellishments, all manufactured in rigid polyurethane foam, moulded and hand-stained. Design service offered. Catalogue available.

The Original Choice
1340 Stratford Road
Hall Green
Birmingham B28 9EH
See FIREPLACES AND STOVES

Original Style
(A member of the Stovax group)
Stovax Ltd
Falcon Road
Sowton Industrial Estate
Exeter
Devon EX2 7LF
Fine quality reproduction ceramic wall tiles for kitchens and bathrooms, c.1750-1902.

Orleton Manor
Ludlow
Shropshire SY8 4HR
Ceramic decorated wall tiles.

Paintability Ltd
Paintability by Post
c/o Hillbury Press Ltd
Cranbourne Industrial Estate
Potters Bar
Hertfordshire EN6 3JN
An extensive range of pre-cut plastic stencil designs and painted furniture patterns inspired by ancient ornaments, decorative stucco and plasterwork, trompe l'oeil and grisaille painted decoration. Designs include William Morris, Classic Greek and floral. Catalogue available.

Paris Ceramics
543 Battersea Park Road
Battersea
London SW11 3BL
Specializing in different ranges of floor and wall tiles, including old French tiles retrieved from period houses and restored; hand-crafted delft tiles made to traditional 17th-century designs, and others. View by appointment only.

Petit Roque Ltd
5a New Road
Croxley Green
Hertfordshire WD3 3EJ
See FIREPLACES AND STOVES

Timothy Plant
7 Bramham Gardens
London SW5
Mural painter working in private homes and gardens, and commercial premises. All types of commission undertaken. Trompe l'oeil a speciality.

D. S. & A. G. Prigmore
Mill Cottage
Mill Road
Colmworth
Bedford
See EXTERIORS

Ramus Tile Co Ltd
Palace Road
London N11 2PX
See FLOORS

A. L. Rattray
Craighall
Blairgowrie
Perthshire PH10 7JB
Scotland
See BATHROOMS

R. C. D. Ltd
Crest
91 Ducks Hill Road
Northwood
Middlesex HA6 2SQ
A team of master decorators skilled in all types of renovation and refurbishment work including specialist paint finishes, joinery, plumbing, electrics, tiling and plastering.

Riva Design Ltd
The Ryecroft
Fanavon Buildings
Warrington Street
Stalybridge
Cheshire SK15 2LB
See KITCHENS

Robus Pottery and Tiles
Evington Park
Hastingleigh
Ashford
Kent
Tin-glazed wall tiles in traditional designs, floor tiles and a range of garden statuary.

Rogers Demolition and Dismantling
Service Ltd
Belgrave Road
Portswood
Southampton
See EXTERIORS

Maria Rosenthal, Hand Made Tiles
Unit 33
Kingsgate Workshops
110-116 Kingsgate Road
London NW6 2JG
A range of original, hand-made wall tiles with raised designs, individually dipped in glazes derived from Victorian recipes resulting in rich colours and a deep gloss finish. Can be used in entrance halls and porches, conservatories, around a fireplace and in kitchens and bathrooms. A variety of colours available, plain and border tiles available to match. New designs produced periodically. Tiles made mostly to order.

Royal Dutch Sphinx Ltd
Units 1 & 2 Pipers Court
Thatcham
Newbury
Berkshire RG13 4ER
See FLOORS

Rye Tiles Ltd
The Old Brewery
Wishward
Rye
Sussex TN31 7DH
See FLOORS

Shaws of Darwen
Waterside
Darwen
Lancashire BB3 3NX
Manufacturers of architectural terracotta and glazed faience for both refurbishment work and new projects. Also glazed bricks, fireclay and sanitaryware.

Shelston (Construction) Ltd
(St Giles Joinery Ltd)
Nine Yews
Wimborne St Giles
Dorset BH21 5PW
Suppliers of individual joinery to the building industry, ie special items such as cupolas and also specialist decorative finishing such as marbling, graining and mahoganizing.

H. & E. Smith Ltd
Van Delft
Britannic Works
Broom Street
Hanley
Stoke-on-Trent
Staffordshire ST1 2ER
See FLOORS

Solopark Ltd
The Old Railway Station
Near Pampisford
Cambridge
Cambridgeshire CB2 4HB
See DOORS

Stuart Interiors
Barrington Court
Barrington
Ilminster
Somerset TA19 0NQ
See DOORS

Toynbee-Clarke Interiors Ltd
95 Mount Street
London W1
See WALLPAPERS AND FABRICS

Verity Tiles
Unit 7
101 Farm Lane
Fulham
London SW6
See FLOORS

Wansdown Joinery Works (Southern) Ltd
327 Lillie Road
Fulham
London SW6 7NR
See STAIRCASES

WALLPAPERS AND FABRICS

Bentley & Spens
Studio 25
90 Lots Road
Chelsea
London SW10 0QD
Specialize in hand-printed fabrics for fashion and interiors with a good choice of grounds including silks, linens and cottons. A wide range of designs or artwork can be commissioned to individual requirements and advice is given on suitable fabrics, patterns and colourways. Customers are welcome to visit the showroom. Brochure on request.

Brunschwig & Fils
Chelsea Harbour Drive
Chelsea Harbour
London SW10
The French fabric house is well-known for the superb craftsmanship of its over 2,000 fabrics and wallpapers. Collections range from traditional flowered chintzes to contemporary designs.

Jane Churchill
135 Sloane Street
London SW1X 9B2
Also: Liberty
Regent Street
London W1R 6AH
and: 13 Christopher Place
St Albans
Hertfordshire AL3 5DQ
and: 13 Fitzroy Street
Cambridge
CB1 1EN
Known for the contemporary approach to classic designs, Jane Churchill offer, at a realistic price, a wide selection of fabrics and wallpapers which range in mood from fresh and simple to strong and decorative.

Colefax & Fowler
39 Brook Street
London W1Y 2JE
Also: 151 Sloane Street
London SW1X 9BX
and: 110 Fulham Road
London SW3 6RL
Well-known for their exclusive chintzes, several other wide ranging collections also include damasks, linens, woven fabrics and epingles as well as a varied choice of wallpapers.

Designers Guild
27½ 277 Kings Road
London SW3 5EN
Designers and manufacturers of fabrics and wallpapers including woven upholstery fabrics. Also a highly successful children's range.

Elizabeth Eaton
30 Elizabeth Street
Belgravia
London SW1W 9RB
*Renowned for work on period property from joinery and cabinet making to drawings. Advice on painting and decorating, preferably executed by their own team of workmen and services of a qualified architect. Sole UK agents for the following American companies specializing in period wallpapers and fabrics:
Schumacher – The Williamsburg Collection; A. Diament, Philadelphia; Clarence House – French Collection; Waterhouse – Boston; Katzenbach & Warren. Catalogue available.*

Guy Evans
51a Cleveland Street
London W1P 5PQ
Furnishing fabrics and wallpapers.

Christian Fischbacher (London) Ltd
913 Fulham Road
London SW6 5HU

Markets the fine cottons and voiles of Switzerland and are famous for their printed cotton furnishing fabrics produced in Britain and the USA.

Mary Fox Linton Ltd
Hewlett House
Havelock Terrace
London SW8 4AS
Distributors of silk fabrics and printed and woven fabrics. Specializing in designing interior spaces. Also produce their own range of furniture.

Anna French Ltd
343 Kings Road
London SW3 5ES
Printed and woven fabrics for curtains and upholstery together with related lace and wallpaper. Fabrics range from decorative woollen fabrics to delicate cotton laces.

Hamilton Weston Wallpapers
18 St Mary's Grove
Richmond
Surrey TW9 1UY
Specialists in documentary reproductions of wallpapers of the 18th and 19th centuries with designs taken from recently discovered fragments dating from c.1760-1840 found in London houses. Printing to order in special colours.

Geraldine St Aubyn Hubbard
Rosebrook
Farm Lane
Nutbourne
Chichester
West Sussex
Handwoven and blockprinted textiles. Cloth is handwoven from silk, cashmere and wool yarns and hand-dyed in the workshop from natural or synthetic dyes.

Intermura Furniture
27 Chalk Farm Road
Camden Town
London NW1 8AG
Extensive range of fabrics for curtains, blinds and furniture.

K. & K .Designs
Unit 1D
Reydon Business Park
Lowestoft Road
Reydon
Suffolk IP18 6SZ
Distributors and manufacturers of wallpapers, vinyls and borders.

Laura Ashley
71/73 Lower Sloane Street
London SW1W 8DA
The Decorator Collection offers a collection of fabric and wallpaper designs based on the prints of the 18th century wallpaper printer Jean-Baptiste Reveillon.

Lyn Le Grice Stencil Design Ltd
The Stencilled House
53 Chapel Street
Penzance
Cornwall TR18 4AF
Stencilling and designing fabrics and wallpapers.

Ian Mankin
109 Regents Park Road
Primrose Hill
London NW1 8UR
Natural fabrics.

Manuel Canovas
2 North Terrace
Brompton Road
London SW3 2BA
Manufacturers of period-style woven damasks.

Jean Monro Design
53 Moreton Street
London SW1
Established in 1926, specialists in reproducing period furnishings.

John S. Oliver Ltd
33 Pembridge Road
London W11 3HG
Reproduce wallpapers from client's own sample or design and, if required, in colourways of their own choice.

Osborne & Little plc
Showroom: 304-308 Kings Road
London SW3 5UH
Offices: 49 Temperley Road
London SW12 8QE
Designers and manufacturers of a wide range of furnishing fabrics, wallpapers and borders.

H. A. Percheron Ltd
97 Cleveland Street
London W1P 5PN
Exclusive importers of furnishing fabrics and trimmings. A fine range of traditional damasks, brocades, velours and plain fabrics available, fabrics can be made to order for special requirements. Trimmings also available.

Ramm, Son & Crocker Ltd
Chiltern House
Knares Beech Business Centre
Loudwater
High Wycombe
Buckinghamshire HP10 9QY
Producers of exclusive fabrics and wallcoverings reproduced from 19th-century documents in archive.

George Spencer
4 West Halkin Street
London SW1
Designers and manufacturers of high-quality traditional fabrics. Also a collection of wallpapers to complement.

Nicki Spice Designs
76 Chelsea Manor Street
London SE3 5QE
A comprehensive range of fabrics and accessories.

John Stefanidis & Associates Ltd
Unit 7
Chelsea Wharf
Lots Road
Chelsea
London SW10 0QJ
Collections of fabrics and co-ordinating wallpapers. Catalogue available.

Stuart Interiors
Barrington Court
Barrington
Ilminster
Somerset TA19 0NQ
See DOORS

Bernard Thorpe & Co Ltd
6 Burnsall Street
London SW3 3SR
Producers of hand screen-printed fabrics and wallpapers. Over 200 different designs in a million different combinations of colour, also many ground cloths to choose from. Wallpapers to match prints.

Tissunique Ltd
58 Berners Street
London W1P 3AE
Wholesalers and importers of high-class furnishing fabrics and wallpapers, braids and trimmings. Specialists in historic house reproduction work, Lyon silks, producers of the National Trust Collection of Traditional Chintzes and the Historic Print Collection.

Today Interiors
Head office:
Hollis Road
Grantham
Lincolnshire NG31 7QH
Showroom:
122 Fulham Road
London SW3 6HU
Fabrics, wallpapers and borders.

Top Layer Ltd
5 Egerton Terrace
London SW3 2BX
Suppliers of wallpapers and fabrics, from any age or period.

Toynbee-Clarke Interiors Ltd
95 Mount Street
London W1
Specialists in the restoration and installation of antique wallpapers, including 18th- and 19th-century hand-painted Chinese papers and French hand block-printed wallpapers, products of manufacturers such as Reveillon, Dufour, Zubert etc in stock.

Watts & Co Ltd
7 Tufton Street
London SW1P 3QE
Offering a collection of genuine Victorian wallcoverings and damasks. Elaborate 19th century scrolled floral designs, stylized leafwork and Gothic-inspired trellis patterns. The papers, to be seen in the Houses of Parliament and the National Portrait Gallery, can be hand-blocked or screen-printed and all orders are coloured as desired by the individual customer. Catalogue available.

Zimmer & Rohde UK Ltd
103 Cleveland Street
London W1P 5PL
Furnishing fabrics.

Zoffany Ltd
63 South Audley Street
London W1Y 5FB

Manufacturers of Document wallpapers, including the hand-printed Temple Newsam Collection. Reproductions of original papers can be hand-printed to commission. The Red Book of Paperhangings and The Temple Newsam Collection are available in the USA, Schumacher.

CEILINGS

Allied Guilds
Unit 19 Reddicap Trading Estate
Coleshill Road
Sutton Coldfield
West Midlands B75 7BU
Specializing in the manufacture, fixing and restoration of ornamental plasterwork, from Mediaeval designs to classical Georgian and Adam style, Louis XIV and Victorian.

Architectural and Industrial GRP
400 Ewell Road
Tolworth
Surrey KT6 7HF
Manufacturers of replacement building cornices and exterior stonework.

H. & F. Badcock (Fibrous & Solid Plastering) Ltd
Unit 9
Sandgate Street
Peckham
London SE15 1LE
Manufacturers of fibrous plaster mouldings and enrichments, ie cornices, ceiling centres, columns, pilasters etc. Repairers and renovators of existing damaged cornices, enrichments etc.

Bridgwater Reclamation Ltd
Monmouth Street
Bridgwater
Somerset
See FIREPLACES AND STOVES

Butcher Plastering Specialists Ltd
8 Fitzroy Road
Primrose Hill
London NW1 8TX
Fibrous plastering specialists, all aspects of ornamental plastering.

Clark & Fenn Ltd
(Incorporating G. Jackson & Sons)
Unit 19
Mitcham Industrial Estate
Streatham Road
Mitcham
Surrey CR4 2AJ
Specialists in ceilings, installation of fibrous plasterwork, suspended and integrated ceilings, design and decorating service. Catalogue available.

Classicana Ltd
"The Oak Tree Unit"
West Hoathly
Sussex RH19 4QF
See LIGHTING

Copley Decor Ltd
Leyburn
North Yorkshire DL8 5QA
Manufacturers of decor moulding in cellular resin. Range includes cornices, covings, ceiling roses, corbels, dado rails, panel mouldings etc. Colour catalogue available.

Gillespie UK Ltd
Alma House
38 Crimea Road
Aldershot
Hants GU11 1UD
Specialists in suspended and decorative ceilings, screens and space-dividers, sculptures, murals, crests and emblems, domes, Islamic decoration, architectural features and textured cladding. Catalogue available.

Hales & Howe
Picton House
25 Picton Street
Montpelier
Bristol
Avon BS6 5PZ
Showroom:
6 Perry Road
Park Row
Bristol
Avon BS1 5BQ
An independant company of ornamental plasterers providing a specialist service. A comprehensive range of traditional mouldings. Will also supply and install new mouldings for the restoration and conservation of period plasterwork. Specialists in the art of scagliola. Pendants, swags, tassles, ropes and cornices can also be modelled in fibrous plaster. Catalogue and brochure available on request.

Charles Hammond Design Services Ltd
Pepys Court
84 The Chase
Clapham
London SW4 0NF
Interior decorators and designers supplying interior furnishings, cornices and ceiling roses.

David J. Handley
Milton Laithe
Gargrave
Skipton
North Yorkshire BD23 3NN
Stockists of old oak beams, purlins, spars, scantlins, panelling, doors, floorboards and carvings. Inglenook pieces a speciality.

Jonathan James Ltd
17 New Road
Rainham
Essex RM13 8DJ
Plastering specialists including solid and fibrous plastering, dry lining, granolithic paving, suspended ceilings and decorative finishes. Servicing contracts throughout the UK and abroad. Catalogue available.

Malvern Studios
56 Cowleigh Road
Malvern
Worcestershire WR14 1QD
See LIGHTING

Oakleaf Reproductions Ltd
Ling Bob
Main Street
Wilsden
Bradford BD15 0JP
See WALLS

T. & O. Plaster Castings
7 Collier Row Road
Collier Row
Romford
Essex RM5 3NP
Fibrous plasterers, ornamental plasterwork, exterior refurbishing. Contractors to the Historical Society, Grade I and II Listed Buildings.

Simply Elegant
Callywhite Lane
Dronfield
Nr Sheffield F18 6XP
Manufacturers of fibrous plaster including cornices, ceiling roses, fire surrounds etc. Catalogue available.

Stevensons of Norwich Ltd
Rountree Way
Norwich
Norfolk NR7 8SQ
Producers of a wide range of traditional mouldings in fibrous plaster and GRP purpose made to any design. Any existing moulding can be matched or new ones produced in fibrous plaster, GRG, sand and cement or GRP. High quality of renovation and refurbishment work carried out. Specialist manufacturing, site fixing, designing and technical advice offered. Catalogue available.

W. Thompson & Sons Ltd
Nobel Road
Eley's Estate
Edmonton
London N18 3BH
Wood machining and turning including mouldings, cornices, dado rails, architraves, skirting, picture rails etc.

Wheatley Ornamental Plasterers Ltd
Avonvale Studio Workshops
Avonvale Place
Batheaston
Bath
Avon BA1 7RF
Full range of cornices, ceiling centres, niches, panel mouldings, corbels etc. Reproduction of existing cornices, also reinforcement and restoration of ornamental ceilings. Catalogue available.

W. J. Wilson & Son
Elm Tree Street
Mansfield
Nottinghamshire NG18 2HD
Manufacturers and fixers of fibrous plaster, moulded and ornamental cornices, ceiling centres, panel mouldings, niches, fire surrounds, arches and decorative plasterwork.

Winther Browne & Co Ltd
Eley's Industrial Estate
Nobel Road
Edmonton
London N18 3DX
See DOORS

STAIRCASES

Albion Design
12 Flitcroft Street
London WC2H 2DJ
Manufacturers of cast-iron spiral and straight staircases. Catalogue available.

Ballantine Bo'ness Iron Co
Links Road
Bo'ness
West Lothian
Scotland EH51 9PW
Manufacturer and fitter of ornamental cast-iron panels for railings, balconies, gates and stairways. Brochure available.

R. Bleasdale & Co Ltd
394 Caledonian Road
Islington
London N1 1DN
Reproduction Victorian spiral staircases, cast railings, balconies, straight staircases and balustrading.

Brittania
8 Normandy Street
Alton
Hampshire GU34 1DD
Large range of Victorian cast-iron work for balconies, spiral and straight staircases and the like. Also restoration and repair work and custom-made designs from original castings.

Cantabrian Antiques
16 Park Street
Lynton
North Devon
See FIREPLACES AND STOVES

Cottage Craft Spirals
Pear Tree Farm
Srubbins Lane
Chinley
Stockport
Cheshire SK12 6AE
Spiral staircases.

C. S. L. Davey & Jordan
3 Jennings Road
Kernick Industrial Estate
Penryn
Cornwall TR10 9DQ
Makers of hand-made ornamental ironwork.

Elite Stairs
Unit C, Wolston Business Park
Wolston
Coventry
Manufacturers of cast spiral staircases for interiors and exteriors in traditional designs. Brochure available.

The English Street Furniture Co
Pastures Drive
Caxton
Cambridge CB3 8PF
See FIREPLACES AND STOVES

Grandisson Doors
The Old Hall
West Hill Road
West Hill
Ottery St Mary
Devon EX11 1TP
See DOORS

The Great Northern Architectural Co Ltd
New Russia House
Chester Road
Tattenhall
Chester CH3 9AH
See DOORS

Havenplan's Architectural Emporium
The Old Station
Station Road
Killamarsh
Sheffield S31 8EN
See FIREPLACES AND STOVES

Heritage Oak Ltd
Unit V1
Dean Clough Industrial Park
Halifax
West Yorkshire HX3 5AX
See DOORS

E. A. Higginson & Co Ltd
Unit 1
Carlisle Road
London NW9 0HD
An architectural joinery company specializing in the manufacture and installation of staircases, balustrades, windows, doors and mouldings to customers' specifications. A range of standard-sized panelled and glazed doors in oak/sapele with or without a lacquer finish are available. Also supplied are Italian timber or steel spiral staircases.

House of Steel Antiques
400 Caledonian Road
Islington
London N1 1DN
See FIREPLACES AND STOVES

J. A. K. Products
Glebe Cottage
Hunsingore
Nr Wetherby
North Yorkshire LS22 5HY
Wood turnings for balusters, newels, columns and furniture posts.

J. S. R. Joinery Ltd
Poole Street
Great Yeldham
Halstead
Essex CO9 4HN
Specialist joiners manufacturing straight, winder or curved staircases including handrails (straight or continuous) and balusters if required.

Meer End Woodturners
Torrington Avenue
Coventry CV4 9AP

Manufacturers and designers of high-quality staircase furniture. Offers finishes and designs for a wide range of spindles, newel posts and staircase accessories. Current range of spindles encompasses 18 stylish designs but are able to offer a design and production service for customers' special requirements. Designs are based on classic period staircase architecture. Kiln-dried hardwoods used such as Brazilian mahogany, American cherry, German beech and a variety of American oaks. Other species can also be offered subject to suitability for turning.

Monarch Stairways
Unit 9
Westfield Road
Kineton Industrial Estate
Southam
Warwicks CV33 0JH
Manufacturers of cast-iron spiral staircases. Brochure available.

Mounts Hill Woodcraft Ltd
Paynetts Lane
Cranbrook Road
Goudhurst
Kent TN17 1DY
See DOORS

One Off Joinery Ltd
13 Holmes Road
Earley
Reading
Berkshire RG6 2BH
Handcrafters of staircases, windows and doors in softwood, hardwood, MDF, veneer and laminates.

A. L. Rattray
Craighall
Blairgowrie
Perthshire PH10 7JB
Scotland
See BATHROOMS

The Real Stone Co
The Forge
Penthouse Hill
Bath
Avon BA1 7EL
See FLOORS

Robert Coles Furniture and Architectural Joinery
Church House
Broad Street
Congresbury
Avon BS19 5DG
Fine, custom-designed and built period staircases with hand-carved traditional handrail work and turned hardwood or cast-iron balustrades.

Safety Stairways Ltd
141 Field Road
Bloxwich
Walsall
West Midlands
Cast-iron reproduction staircases in several styles including Tudor, Georgian, Regency and Victorian. Brochure available.

Solopark Ltd
The Old Railway Station
Station Road
Nr Pampisford
Cambridge CB2 4HB
See DOORS

Spiral Staircase Systems
The Mill
Glynde
Lewes
Sussex BN7 8SS
Manufacturers of spiral staircases. Design service available.

Staircraft
Unit 7
Boston Place
Coventry CV6 5NN
Custom-made joinery, staircases a speciality.

Stair Spindles & Newel Posts of Distinction
Tynwold Woodcrafts
The Workshop
Patrick Street
Peel
Isle of Man
Hand-sanded high quality stair spindles and newel posts. Brochure available.

Stuart Interiors
Barrington Court
Barrington
Ilminster
Somerset TA19 0NQ
See DOORS

Robert Thompson's Craftsmen Ltd
Kilburn
York YO6 4AH
See DOORS

Wansdown Joinery Works (Southern) Ltd
327 Lillie Road
Fulham
London SW6 7NR
Specialists in period staircases, panelled rooms in old pine, limed oak, mahogany and all types of period joinery. Catalogue available.

Weller Patents Development
1 Grand Parade Mews, rear of 96
Upper Richmond Road
London SW15 2RF
Specialist fabricators of internal and external architectural metalwork, including balustrading, gates, balconies and staircases, to clients' requirements either original designs or copies of existing designs, highlighting/matching period details.

Winther Browne & Co Ltd
Eley's Industrial Estate
Nobel Road
Edmonton
London N18 3DX
See DOORS

FIREPLACES AND STOVES

Robert Aagaard Ltd
Frogmire House
Stockwell Road
Knaresborough
North Yorkshire HG5 0JP
Antique mantels, marble interiors, hand-carved mantels, fireplace restoration, design and installation. Catalogue available.

Acquisitions (Fireplaces) Ltd
269 Camden High Street
London NW1 7BX
Also:
4 Jamestown Road
London NW1 7BY
Reproduction fireplaces using traditional materials. Wood and cast-iron mantels, cast-iron inserts, some incorporating hand-painted tiles from a wide range of designs.

Agaheat Appliances
PO Box 30
Ketley
Telford
Shropshire TF1 4DD

Amazing Grates
61-63 High Road
East Finchley
London N2 8AB
Manufacturers of fireplaces in period styles, also individual items such as mantels, marble surrounds, cast-iron grates and a wide range of accessories. Catalogue available.

A. Andrews & Sons (Marbles and Tiles) Ltd
324-330 Meanwood Road
Leeds
Yorkshire LS7 2JE
Contractors in marble, mosaic, terrazzo and ceramic tiling. Specialists in restoration and renovation of period marble fireplaces and associated work.

Antique Fireplace Warehouse (Buckingham Antiques)
194 Battersea Park Road
Battersea
London SW8
Specialists in cast-iron fireplaces, pine surrounds and marble chimneypieces. Restoration and installation service available.

Architectural Antiques Ltd
351 King Street
Hammersmith
London W6 9NH
Specialists in architectural antiques such as fireplace surrounds in wood, cast-iron and marble, cast-iron tiled fire inserts, fireplace accessories, tiles, doors in pine, oak and mahogany, with stained-glass or cut and etched panels, leaded lights, railings, gates, wrought ironwork, statuary, bathroom fittings and plasterwork. Restoration and repair service available.

Architectural Components Ltd
(Locks and Handles)
4-10 Exhibition Road
London SW7 2HF
See DOORS

Architectural Heritage Ltd
Taddington Manor
Taddington
Nr Cutsdean
Cheltenham
Gloucestershire GL54 5RY
See WALLS

Ashburton Fireplaces
West Street
Ashburton
Devonshire TQ13 7DU
Marble, timber and cast-iron restored fireplaces dating from c.1790-1910. Also in stock are antique fireplace accessories including fenders, fire irons and overmantels.

Bailey's Architectural Antiques
The Engine Shed
Ashburton Industrial Estate
Ross-on-Wye
Herefordshire HE9 7BW
See DOORS

Nigel Bartlett
67 St Thomas Street
London SE1
Dealers in fine antique chimneypieces in marble, stone and wood.

Baxi Heating
Brownedge Road
Bamber Bridge
Preston
Lancashire PR5 6SN
Manufacturer of gas and solid fuel domestic heating appliances.

A. Bell & Co Ltd
Kingsthorpe Road
Kingsthorpe
Northampton NN2 6LT
Designers and manufacturers of fine fireplaces, stoves and accessories since 1899, using a wide range of materials: brick, marble, slate, stone, steel, copper, bronze, brass and wood. Catalogue available.

La Belle Cheminee Ltd
81 Albany Street
London NW1 4BT
Specializing in the installation of antique marble chimneypieces, with a range of brass and steel fire-grates, fenders, screens, fire-dogs and other accessories.

Bridgwater Reclamation Ltd
Monmouth Street
Bridgwater
Somerset
Architectural salvage items including architraves, moulding, marble and cast-iron fire surrounds, panelling, sinks, doors and door furniture, windows, sanitaryware, skirtings, wood block flooring, structural and decorative ridges and finials.

Brighton Architectural Salvage
33 Gloucester Road
Brighton
East Sussex
Architectural antiques, including fireplaces and surrounds, stained glass, panelling, decorative ironwork, light fittings and garden ornaments.

T. F. Buckle (London) Ltd
427 King's Road
Chelsea
London SW10 0LR
Specializing in antique mantelpieces in pine, marble and stone; reproduction mantelpieces in old and new pine; reproduction grates and Victorian spiral staircases in cast-iron. World-wide shipping arranged. Catalogue available.

Cantabrian Antiques
16 Park Street
Lynton
North Devon
Specializing in pre 19th-century vernacular architectural antiques, particularly early oak items such as fireplaces, screens, plank doors, moulded timbers etc.

Peter Chapman Antiques
10 Theberton Street
Islington
London N1 0QX
Suppliers of period furniture and light fittings including some fireplaces and stained glass. Restoration and repair service offered on most items.

Chimney Pieces
227 Westbourne Grove
London W11 2SE
Specializing in period-style fireplaces, Victorian and French marble and stone chimneypieces, carved marble fireplaces, cast-iron grates and stone reproduction surrounds. Commissions undertaken. Full shipping and export services. Installation service. Brochures available on request.

The Chiswick Fireplace Co
68 Southfield Road
Chiswick
London W4 1BD
Victorian and Edwardian cast-iron fireplaces and original tiles. Also grates, fenders and fire-irons. Hearths and surrounds made to measure. Restoration and repair service, also installation service.

Classic Furniture Group plc
Audley Avenue
Newport
Shropshire
Manufacturers of reproduction Victorian ornamental cast-iron furniture including garden furniture, doorsteps and footscrapers, fire-backs, fire-grates, stoves and lamposts.

Counterparts Demolition Ltd
Station Yard
Topsham
Exeter
Devon
See EXTERIORS

Creda Ltd
Creda Works
PO Box 5
Blythe Bridge
Stoke-on-Trent ST11 9LJ
Manufacturers of domestic electrical appliances.

C. S. L. Davey & Jordan
3 Jennings Road
Kernick Industrial Estate
Penryn
Cornwall TR10 9DQ
See STAIRCASES

Distinctive Fireplaces
29a Walmgate
York YO1 2TX
Offering a comprehensive range of quality hand-crafted surrounds. Can also design to customer's specifications.

Dovre Castings Ltd
Weston Works
Weston Lane
Birmingham B11 3RP
Cast-iron fireplace inserts. A choice of three sizes with ceramic glass or cast-iron doors and decorative or plain back panels.

Dowding Metalcraft Ltd
Mulberry Road
Canvey Island
Essex SS8 0PR
Manufacturers of reproduction fire grates and fenders for wood, coal, gas and electric fires.

Dunedin Antiques Ltd
4 North West Circus Place
Edinburgh EH3 6ST
Scotland
A large stock of period chimneypieces and architectural items.

Emsworth Fireplaces Ltd
Unit 3
Station Approach
North Street
Emsworth
Hampshire PO10 7PN
Marble importers and manufacturers of fireplaces, supplying a range of ready-made and bespoke fireplaces from period to modern designs. Also cut to size marble granite and conglomerates. Marble tiles, vanity tops, worktops and wooden mantels. Installation service available in certain areas.

The English Street Furniture Co
Pastures Drive
Caxton
Cambridge CB3 8PF
Suppliers of architectural metalware, cast-iron fireplace installations, balustrading and balcony metalwork, interior and exterior staircase supports, together with a range of cast-iron gates, all of which are contemporary to the period 1800-1914. Most products are maintained on an ex-stock basis enabling rapid response to the requirements of architects and other specifiers engaged in conservation work. Agents in the USA, Australia and the majority of European countries.

Feature Fires Ltd
32 High Street
Northwood
Middlesex HA6 1BN
*Designers of fireplaces to customers' requirements
installation also carried out. Suppliers of fireplace
brassware, fire-guards, fenders, buckets etc. Gas, log/coal
effect fires.*

Fireplaces of Yesteryears
Office: The Granary
Church Lane
Bilton-in-Ainsty
York YO5 8LG
Showroom: Railway Station Platform
3 Crosley Street
Wetherby
West Yorkshire
*Distributors of fine period mantelpieces and Victorian
dado tiles plus hand-decorated tiles featuring floral,
classical and bird designs, ideal for conservation work or in
character properties as wall or fireplace tiles. Also border
tiles in single, double and multi-colours.
Brochure available.*

Firestyle Chimneypieces
158 Upminster Road
Upminster
Essex RM14 2RB
*Hand-crafted marble chimneypieces in several classical
period designs, also fireplace inserts and a fitting service
available.*

Fireworld (UK) Ltd
31 Welford Road
Leicester LE2 7AD
Fireplace builders merchants.

Galleon Claygate Ltd
216-230 Red Lion Road
Tolworth
Surbiton
Surrey KT6 7RB
*Fireplace manufacturers. 100 designs on display in every style
and material. Adam-style surrounds, brick and stone
fireplaces, marble fireplaces, Victorian fireplaces, gas/coal
effect fires, solid fuel baskets and grates and fireside
accessories. Air vents and colt top cowls. Installation service
available. Brochure on request.*

Godin
Morley Marketing
PO Box 38
Ware
Hertfordshire SG12 7JP
*These coal and woodburning stoves have been made in
France since the end of the last century and are finished in
antique colours. Suitable for Victorian and Edwardian
settings and conservatories.*

Grahamstone Iron Co
PO Box 5
Gowan Avenue
Falkirk
Stirlingshire FK2 7HH
*Iron founders and enamellers founded in 1868.
Manufacturers of fires, stoves and cookers including a range
of open fires and accessories. Catalogue available.*

Grandisson Doors
The Old Hall
West Hill Road
West Hill
Ottery St Mary
Devon EX11 1TP
See DOORS

James Gray & Son Ltd
89 George Street
Edinburgh EH2 3EZ
Scotland
*Specialists in the design and supply of period fireplaces,
Georgian, Regency and Victorian reproduction and original
fireplace mantelpieces, cast-iron Victorian fireplace interiors
with hand-painted ceramic tile inserts, reproductions and
originals, specially selected marble and fine-rubbed slate
hearths, jambs, lintels and interiors, a wide selection of dog
grates and basket grates together with purpose-made chain
mail screens.*

The Great Northern Architectural
Antiques Co Ltd
New Russia House
Chester Road
Tattenhall
Chester CH3 9AH
See DOORS

Hallidays
The Old College
Dorchester-on-Thames
Wallingford
Oxfordshire OX10 7HL
Also: 28 Beauchamp Place
Knightsbridge
London SW3 1NJ
*Specialists in Georgian panelling and fireplaces, particularly
carved pine mantelpieces.*

Havenplan's Architectural Emporium
The Old Station
Station Road
Killamarsh
Sheffield S31 8EN
*A large range of period doors, fire surrounds, bathroom
fittings, spindles, newels, handrails, reclaimed timber and
stone troughs.*

Samuel Heath & Sons plc
Cobden Works
Leopold Street
Birmingham B12 0UJ
*Specialists in the hand-crafting of hearthside furniture in
brass and copper, including companion sets, fire screens,
fenders, hods and log holders, etc. Catalogue available.*

Hereford Tiles
Whitestone
Hereford HR1 3SF
See WALLS

The Hotspot
53-55 High Street
Uttoxeter
Staffordshire ST14 7JQ
*Distributors of cast-iron wood and coal burning stoves, some
in period styles.*

The House Hospital
68 Battersea High Street
London SW11 3HX
See DOORS

House of Steel Antiques
400 Caledonian Road
Islington
London N1 1DN
*Stockists of antique architectural and ornamental metalwork,
300-400 Victorian and Edwardian cast-iron fireplaces,
original garden furniture, urns and statuary, spiral
staircases, railings, balconies and gates. Restoration and
polishing of metalware and fireplaces. Sand-blasting.
Castings in iron, brass and aluminium.*

Interoven Ltd
70-72 Fearnley Street
Watford
Hertfordshire WD1 7DE
*Manufacturers and purveyors of solid fuel heating appliances
and equipment. Main products Goodwood wood-burning
stoves, Homerette back boilers, with Virgil and Cokeglo all-
night burning fires.*

Inwood Stoves
1a London Road
Liphook
Hampshire
Retailers of gas, wood and multi-fuel stoves.

Langham Architectural Materials
Foxes Mill
Tonedale
Wellington
Somerset
*A wide range of period fixtures and fittings including
beams, hobs, grates, fire surrounds in stone, marble, cast
iron and pine, also doors, stained glass, railings and
metalwork.*

The London Stove Centre Ltd
49 Chiltern Street
London W1M 1HQ
*Suppliers of cast-iron wood-burning and gas stoves; central
heating cookers. Full range of accessories and fuel systems.
Installation service available.*

Malvern Studios
56 Cowleigh Road
Malvern
Worcestershire WR14 1QD
See LIGHTING

Manorhouse Stone
Pinehouse
Oaks Industrial Estate
Ravenstone Road
Coalville
Leicestershire LE6 2MB
*A specialized range of reconstructed architectural stonework.
Traditional style fireplaces, stone mullioned windows, door
surrounds and copings etc.*

Marble Hill Fireplaces Ltd
70-72 Richmond Road
Twickenham
Middlesex TW1 9AP
*Manufacturers of fine hand-carved Adam-style mantels
available in pine, mahogany and a range of decorative
finishes. We stock a fine selection of French antique marble
mantels and quality fireside accessories and custom-built
cupboards, radiator covers and panelling. Installation
service. Colour brochure available.*

Bertram Noller (Reigate)
14A London Road
Reigate
Surrey RH2 9HY
*Adam-style pine and marble mantelpieces, antique and
modern marble-work. Restoration and supply of decorative
metalwork.*

Nostalgia
61 Shaw Heath
Stockport
Cheshire SK3 8BH
*Architectural antique retailers. Specialists in fully restored
Victorian, Georgian and Edwardian fireplaces, in cast-
iron, mahogany, oak, pine, marble and stone. Over 1,000
items in stock. Also a range of Edwardian bathroom
fittings: basins, WCs, brass taps, shower fittings, towel
rails etc, all original and fully restored. Catalogue
available.*

The Original Choice
56 The Tything
Worcester WR1 1JT
Also: Castle Farm
Gaydon
Warwickshire CV35 0HE
*Specialists in expertly restored antique fireplaces.
100 fireplaces on display, mostly originals in marble,
pine, mahogany, oak and cast-iron. Complete design
and installation service, mantelpieces made to measure,
stained glass sold, restored and made. Mirrors, doors,
overmantels, lamps, tiles, fenders, firestools and much
more.*

Pageant Antiques
122 Dawes Road
London SW6
See EXTERIORS

Peco of Hampton
72 Station Road
Hampton
Middlesex
See DOORS

Period Reclamation and Restoration Services
205 Salisbury Road
Burton
Christchurch
Dorset BH23 7JT
Suppliers of restoration fireplace surrounds.

Petit Roque Ltd
5a New Road
Croxley Green
Hertfordshire WD3 3EJ
*Designers and installers of individual fireplaces. Also
produce period Adam-style fireplaces, vanity units,
worktops, marble flooring, marble wall tiles, gas, log/coal
fires and all fireplace accessories. Brochure available.*

Phoenix Fireplaces
51 Lark Lane
Sefton Park
Liverpool 17
Suppliers of cast-iron grates, decorated tiles, timber surrounds, living flame gas fires, hearths and replacement parts. Installations and restoratons carried out.

M. A. Pope (Fireplaces) Ltd
14 Western Parade
Barnet
Hertfordshire
Manufacturers of marble fireplaces. Installation service available.

H. W. Poulter & Son
279 Fulham Road
London SW10 9PZ
Specialists in English and French antique marble chimneypieces, grates, fenders, fire-irons etc, also chandeliers. Restoration and repair service.

D. A. & A. G. Prigmore
Mill Cottage
Mill Road
Colmworth
Bedford
See EXTERIORS

A. L. Rattray
Craighall
Blairgowrie
Perthshire PH10 7JB
Scotland
See BATHROOMS

Reclaimed Materials
Northgate
White Lund Industrial Estate
Morecambe
Lancashire
See EXTERIORS

Robeys Heating
"Old School House"
Green Lane
Belper
Derbyshire DE5 1BY
A large range of multi-fuel stoves, cookers and boilers.

Simply Elegant
Callywhite Lane
Dronfield
Nr Sheffield F18 6XP
See CEILINGS

Smith & Wellstood Est (1984) Ltd
Bonnybridge
Stirlingshire FK4 2AP
Specialists in vitreous enamelled castings. Dragon and Dolphin Heaters based on original Victorian designs.

Stuart Interiors
Barrington Court
Barrington
Ilminster
Somerset TA19 0NQ
See DOORS

Townsends (Hallmore Trading Ltd)
81 Abbey Road
London NW8 0AE
Specialists in the supply, salvage, restoration and installation of antique fireplaces. Suppliers of gas/coal effect fires to fit any fire basket. Over 100 antique fireplaces in stock. Marble and slate hearths cut and made to order. Design service.

Trianco Redfyre Ltd
Thorncliffe
Chapeltown
Sheffield S30 4PZ
South Yorkshire
Manufacturers of central heating, domestic and industrial boilers.

Verine Ltd
Goldhanger
Maldon
Essex CM9 8AP
Manufacturers of gas/coal effect radiant and convector fires, LPG stoves and reproductions of classical mantelpieces columns and porticos.

Walcot Reclamation
108 Walcot Street
Bath
Avon BA1 5BG
Architectural antiques with a wide range of fireplaces and accessories from all periods; also stained glass, panelled doors, flooring, roofing, beams, architectural joinery and bathrooms in stock.

Mr Wandle's Workshop
200-202 Garratt Lane
Wandsworth
London SW18 4ED
Suppliers and restorers of authentic Victorian cast-iron fireplaces, grates and accessories. Also Victorian kitchen ranges and stoves.

A. J. Wells & Son
Westminster Lane
Newport
Isle of Wight PO30 5DP
Manufacturers of multi-fuel, coal and wood-burning stoves.

Whiteway Waldron Ltd
305 Munster Road
Fulham
London SW6
See WINDOWS

W. J. Wilson & Son
Elm Tree Street
Mansfield
Nottinghamshire NG18 2HD
See CEILINGS

Wye Valley Stoves and Fireplaces
Palma Court
Brookend Street
Ross-on-Wye
Herefordshire
Specialists in cast-iron, enamelled, soapstone and multi-tiered stoves. Also cast-iron firebacks and accessories.

BATHROOMS

Adamsez Bathrooms Ltd
Dukesway
Team Valley Trading Estate
Gateshead
Tyne & Wear NE11 0SW
Manufacturers of contemporary and Victorian period sanitaryware available in hand-painted styles in white and other colours. Fittings in chrome, plate, brass and 22-carat gold.

W. Adams & Sons Ltd
Unit 6
Credenda Road
Bromford Road Industrial Estate
West Bromwich B70 7JE
Manufacturers of bathroom taps and mixers in period Georgian patterns with accessories to match. Brochure available.

A. & H. Brass
201-203 Edgware Road
London W2 1ES
See DOORS

Architectural Antiques Ltd
351 King Street
London W6 9NH
See FIREPLACES AND STOVES

Architectural Components Ltd
(Locks and Handles)
4-10 Exhibition Road
London SW7 2HF
See DOORS

Armitage Shanks Bathrooms
Armitage
Rugeley
Staffordshire WS15 4BT
Manufacturers of sanitaryware producing baths, bidets, washbasins, WCs, vanity units, plumbing products, showers and brassware. Catalogue available.

Arnull of London
13 Queen Street
Mayfair
London W1X 7PL
Importers and distributors of bathroom fittings and sanitaryware, also ceramic floor and wall tiles. Brochure available.

Aston Mathews Ltd
143-147 Essex Road
Islington
London N1
From traditional roll-top cast-iron baths to the latest continental suites.

Bailey's Architectural Antiques
The Engine Shed
Ashburton Industrial Estate
Ross-on-Wye
Herefordshire HE9 7BW
See DOORS

Balterley Bathrooms Ltd
PO Box 154
Stoke-on-Trent
Staffordshire ST1 2PT
Suppliers of sanitaryware, baths, bidets, WCs and washbasins. Also, Edwardian-style bathroom products. Catalogue available.

Barwill Traditional Taps
Barber Wilsons & Co Ltd
Crawley Road
Wood Green
London N22 6AH
Well-established manufacturers of traditional bathroom and kitchen fittings in non-tarnish brass, unplated polished brass, nickel plate and conventional chrome. Brochure available on request.

Birds Baths of Hainault, Builders Merchants
13 Hainault Street
Ilford
Essex IG1 4EN
Bathroom showroom specializing in reproduction bathroom products and accessories heated towel rails, tiles, furniture, linen boxes to co-ordinate. Also selling whirlpool systems, steam showers, hand-decorated tiles to match chosen fabrics. Fitted bathroom furniture from France, Germany and Italy.

Bonsack Baths (London) Ltd
14 Mount Street
Mayfair
London W1Y 5RA
Suppliers of sanitaryware, taps, tiles, marbles and wallcoverings. Classical, Art Deco and contemporary styles. Catalogue available.

Bridgwater Reclamation Ltd
Monmouth Street
Bridgwater
Somerset
See FIREPLACES AND STOVES

British Bathroom Centre
3 Portman Square
London W1H 0JB
Suppliers of bathroom products including baths, showers, whirlpools, tiles, sanitaryware, accessories etc. A design service available.

Cantabrian Antiques
16 Park Street
Lynton
North Devon
See FIREPLACES AND STOVES

Caradon Bathrooms Ltd
Lawton Road
Alsager
Stoke-on-Trent
Staffordshire ST7 2DF
Manufacturers and exporters of a full range of bathroom products from complete bathroom suites to individual items such as washbasins, cloakroom basins, WCs and bidets made from vitreous china; acrylic and steel baths, also many bathroom fittings and accessories including taps, screens and shower trays. Catalogue available.

Peter Chapman Antiques
10 Theberton Street
Islington
London N1
See FIREPLACES AND STOVES

The Complete Bathroom
61-63 Ber Street
Norwich
Norfolk NR1 3AD
Designers, suppliers and restorers of solid wood bathrooms; bathroom furniture made to customers' requirements.

Czech & Speake Ltd
39c Jermyn Street
London SW1Y 6DN
Also: 244 Cambridge Heath Road
London E2 9DA
Manufacturers of bathroom fittings, Edwardian range includes sink mixers and accessories in solid brass with porcelain fittings available in polished brass, lacquered brass, nickel and chrome. Also in other styles including Victorian with a complementary range of accessories, towel rings, grab rails, robe hooks, soap dishes etc. Catalogue available.

Doulton Bathroom Products
Lawton Road
Alsager
Stoke-on-Trent
Staffordshire ST7 2DF
Company head office is in Paris. Manufacturers of bathroom products: acrylic baths, washbasins, WCs, bidets in vitreous china, shower trays and complete suites. Also kitchen sinks.

Drummond's of Bramley
Birtley Farm
Horsham Road
Bramley
Guildford
Surrey
Period bathrooms, architectural antiques and garden statuary.

The Great Northern Architectural Antiques Co Ltd
New Russia House
Chester Road
Tattenhall
Chester CH3 9AH
See DOORS

C. P. Hart & Sons Ltd
Newnham Terrace
Hercules Road
Lambeth
London SE1 7DR
Suppliers of bathroom products offering a wide range of styles. Traditional cast-iron baths and also whirlpool baths in a variety of shades. Shower screens and doors, bidets, basins, WCs etc. Taps and shower mixers also in several ranges all have solid brass bodies. The plated finishes include chrome, "new-brass" and "aqualux gold". Accessories are also available. Brochure available on request.
See KITCHENS

Hathaway
Clifford Mill
Clifford Chambers
Nr Stratford-upon-Avon
Warwickshire CV37 8HW
Fitted bathrooms and bedrooms. Fitted kitchens in English hardwoods and pine. Painted finishes based on elegant 18th-century classical designs. Full interior design service available.

Havenplan's Architectural Emporium
The Old Station
Station Road
Killamarsh
Sheffield S31 8EN
See FIREPLACES AND STOVES

Heaton's Bathrooms Ltd
Denby Way
Hellaby
Rotherham S66 8HR
Manufacturers of acrylic baths, panels, shower trays and vanity basins. Catalogue available.

Heritage Bathrooms
Spring Street
Bristol
Avon
Victorian and Edwardian reproduction bathrooms: baths, washbasins, water closets, bidets and cabinets in pine and mahogany.

The House Hospital
68 Battersea High Street
London SW11 3HX
See DOORS

Ideal Standard Limited
PO Box 60
National Avenue
Kingston upon Hull
HU5 4JE
Designers and manufacturers of bathroom products. Complete suites, individual baths and basins, taps and mixers, showers, furniture and accessories.

Lefroy Brooks
Treasure Hill House
Treasure Hill
Newbury
Berkshire RG15 9EH
Producers of traditional bathroom taps, cistern lever handles, waste kits, mixers and shower mixers. Finishes and special finishes include chromium plate, natural brass, nickel plate, Inca brass and Inca black.

The London Architectural Salvage & Supply Co
St Michael's Church
Mark Street
Shoreditch
London EC2A 4ER
See DOORS

Miscellanea
Churt
Farnham
Surrey

A large selection of bathroom products. All major British and Continental manufacturers represented. Every shade and style, plus period reproductions, rare or discontinued colours unavailable elsewhere.

Newcastle Furniture Co
Unit 4
Green Lane Buildings
Pelaw
Tyne & Wear ME10 0UW
See KITCHENS

Nostalgia
61 Shaw Heath
Stockport
Cheshire Sk3 8BH
See FIREPLACES AND STOVES

Old Fashioned Bathrooms
Village End
Little London Hill
Debenham
Stowmarket
Suffolk IP14 6PW
Specialists in original bathroom fittings.

Only Bathrooms
27 London Road
Kingston-upon-Thames
Surrey KT2 6ND
One of London's largest showrooms for bathrooms.

Original Bathrooms Ltd
143-145 Kew Road
Richmond-upon-Thames
Surrey TW9 2PN

Original Style
Stovax Ltd
Falcon Road
Sowton Industrial Estate
Exeter
Devon EX2 7LF
See WALLS

Personal Bathrooms
Phoenix House
Lingfield Road
East Grinstead
West Sussex RH19 2EU
Distributors of reproduction period-style and contemporary bathroom products.

Pipe Dreams
70 Gloucester Road
London SW7 4QT
Suppliers of exclusive period-style bathroom products.

A. L. Rattray
Craighall
Blairgowrie
Perthshire PH10 7JB
Scotland
Architectural re-cyclers of Victorian bathroom fittings, doors, mantelpieces, panelling, iron and wood staircases, balconies, balustrades and stained, etched and cut-glass also building materials such as flagstones, stone balustrading and garden furniture. By appointment only.

Richwood Design
Chorley Road
Mowbray Drive Industrial Estate
Blackpool
Lancashire FY3 7XQ
Fitted bathrooms in antique pine, mahogany and oak.

Riva Design Ltd
"The Ryecroft"
Fanavon Buildings
Warrington Street
Stalybridge
Cheshire SK15 2LB
See KITCHENS

Robinson and Cornish
The Old Tannery
Swimbridge
Devon
See KITCHENS

Rufflette Ltd
Sharston Road
Manchester M22 4TH
A full range of bathroom accessories in solid brass and chrome. Powder-coated for a tarnish-free finish.

B. C. Sanitan
Unit 12
Nimrod Way
Elgar Road
Reading
Berkshire RG2 0EB
Period-style bathroom products in plain white or patterned in traditional Victorian designs. The range includes cast-iron rolled-top baths, mahogany panels and a range of traditional taps and accessories to match. Catalogue available.

Scottwood of Nottingham
Dabell Avenue
Blenheim Industrial Estate
Bulwell
Nottingham NG6 8WA
Manufacturers of fitted bathrooms, kitchens and bedrooms in pine and other hardwoods in a variety of finishes. Catalogue available.

Sitting Pretty Bathrooms
131 Dawes Road
Fulham
London SW6 7EA
Suppliers of classic and traditional bathrooms.

Stone Age
67 Dendy Street
Balham
London SW12 8DA
See FLOORS

Swadling Brassware
Victorian Bathrooms
53A Jubilee Road
Waterlooville
Portsmouth
Hampshire PO7 7RE
Solid brass period bathroom fittings in a variety of finishes.

Tiles of Newport and London
Head Office: Dumfries Place Estate
Lower Dock Street
Newport
Gwent
Also: Unit 9
23a Bagley's Lane
London SW6 2BW
Importers, retailers and distributors of bathroom equipment, baths, showers, shower doors, gold, silver and brass taps etc, shower curtains and wallpaper. Designers and manufacturers of hand-painted tiles. Importers of marble and designers of marble floors.

Vernon Tutbury
Department CBI
Bushton Works
Wetmore Lane
Burton-on-Trent DE14 1RH
Manufacturers of a full range of bathroom products. Hand-moulded basins, mahogany cabinets, baths, WCs and a whole range of brassware and ceramic tiling.

The Warehouse Antiques
17 Wilton Street
Holderness Road
Hull
Specialists in antique bathroom products.

The Water Monopoly
Showroom: 16/18 Lonsdale Road
London NW6 6RD
A fine range of English and French antique sanitaryware. View by appointment only.

B. & P. Wynn & Co
Unit 39
Metropolitan Centre
Halifax Road
Greenford
Middlesex
Importers and distributors for the Maurice Herbeau handmade hand-basins which are individually decorated for the cloakroom by Maurice Herbeau of Lille. The range also includes many accessories. Additionally, importers and distributors for the Julia Eloise range of luxury kitchen and bathroom products.

KITCHENS

Aga-Rayburn
PO Box 30
Ketley
Telford
Shropshire TF1 4OD
Kitchen ranges.

Allmilmo Ltd
48 The Broadway
Thatcham
Nr Newbury
Berkshire RG13 4HP
Door fronts available in 83 finishes as well as front finishes in high gloss. Solid wooden fronts are available in pine, oak and mahogany. A further 19 front finishes are offered in our "Modern Art" range.

Alno (UK) Ltd
Unit 10
Hampton Farm Industrial Estate
Hampton Road West
Hanworth
Middlesex TW13 6DB
Manufacturers of built-in kitchens, 33 ranges including traditional rustic, period and classical styles in red-brown oak with solid oak fronts, natural oak, light oak and brown oak; also in grey-white pigmented effect with pewter knobs. Catalogue available.

Artisan Period and Victorian Joinery
Grange Farm
Buxshalls Hill
Lindfield
Sussex
See WINDOWS

Rick Baker
13 Palace Road
Hornsey
London N8
Specializing in custom designing, anything from moulding to a complete panelled room. Also, character shop fronts and Victorian kitchens in a vast range of finishes such as French polish, lacquer, gilding and rag-rolling.

Barwill Traditional Taps
Barber Wilsons & Co Ltd
Crawley Road
Wood Green
London N22 6AH
See BATHROOMS

Garry Blanch
Mounts Farm
Benenden
Kent
Individually handmade kitchens in all types of solid woods.

Bordercraft
Old Forge
Peterchurch
Herefordshire HR2 0SD
Handmade fitted or freestanding hardwood kitchens including period and country styles. Catalogue available on request.

Brass and Traditional Sinks
Devauden Green
Nr Chepstow
Gwent NP6 6PL
A comprehensive range of high-quality solid brass kitchen taps in non-tarnish brass and antique nickel finishes. Many taps are fitted with ceramic discs and porcelain handles. Also brass sinks manufactured from solid naval brass handmade in the traditional manner and hand-polished. Catalogue available.

Bulthaup
38 Wigmore Street
London W1H 9LD
German manufacturers of kitchen furniture systems including fitted units in lacquers, laminate , oak, maple and cherry veneers, and stainless steel kitchenwork benches.

Bygone Ltd
Fieldside Farm
Quainton
Aylesbury
Buckinghamshire HP22 4DQ
Antique pine and painted kitchens in several styles. Catalogue available.

Chalon Originals
Chalon UK Ltd
Hambridge
Somerset TA10 0BP
Handmade kitchens in traditional and period styles of 18th and 19th centuries. Antique pine hand-painted to create the effects of ageing, painted in any twelve period colours or left natural in waxed pine. Catalogue available.

Chefco Products
10 Grove Market Place
Eltham
London SE9 5PU
Agents for Bauformat fitted kitchens.

Commodore Kitchens
West Horndon Industrial Park
West Horndon
Essex CM13 3HP
A selection of modern and antique kitchens including a comprehensive selection of kitchen appliances. Catalogue available.

Crabtree Kitchens
The Twickenham Centre
Norcutt Road
Twickenham
Middlesex TW2 6SR
Handmade, solid wood kitchens in pine, oak and ash, finished with lacquer and wax polish, or painted in styles inspired by Biedermeier faux bois, trompe l'oeil and faux marbling.

Crosby Kitchens Ltd
Orgreave Drive
Handsworth
Sheffield
South Yorkshire S13 9NS
Manufacturers of traditional-style ranges of self-assembly kitchen furniture.

Cuisines Bonnet UK Ltd
10-12 Bromley Road
Beckenham
Kent BR3 2GE
Suppliers of French fitted kitchens in several styles. Catalogue available.

Curtis Kitchens and Interiors
No. 4 Greatbridge Business Park
Budds Lane
Romsey
Hampshire SO51 0HA
Specialist designers and manufacturers of kitchens in the traditional idiom since 1979. Each kitchen is designed to customers' individual requirements. Fitting and installation is carried out by highly-skilled teams also wall tiling and floor covering if desired. Catalogue available.

Dennis and Robinson Ltd
Blenheim Road
Churchill Industrial Estate
Lancing
West Sussex BN15 8UH
Manufacturers and suppliers of kitchens to the building industry.

Foreson Partners Ltd
Longbridge Way
Cowley Mill Road
Uxbridge
Middlesex
Kitchen manufacturers: Panama Kitchens. General woodworkers and fabricators. The units range from melamine laminates, veneered oak, solid oak, mahogany and acacia. Catalogue available.

Gallery Interiors
12 East Cross
Tenterden
Kent
Design and installation specialists of fitted and free-standing period and modern furniture for kitchens, bedrooms and bathrooms. Hand-crafted styles in antique pine, oak, hand-painted and personalized finishes, reflecting English, European and American designs. Suppliers of high-quality kitchen equipment and accessories such as Miele, Gaggenau, Neff, Bosch, DeDietrich and other leading brand names. Also suppliers of the more unusual ceramic and quarry terracotta tiles. Design and fixing service available. Catalogue also available.

Geba UK Ltd (Kitchens)
Abbey House
Wellington Road
London Colney
Hertfordshire AL2 1EY
Suppliers of fitted kitchens, over 80 dealers in Britain. 60 high-quality ranges, from solid oak to high-tech laminates. Also bathroom furniture.

Grafham Woodcraft
6 Church Farm Workshops
Hetley St George
Sandy
Bedfordshire SG19 3HP
Unique unfitted kitchen furniture handmade from ash with polished granite worktops.

C. P. Hart & Sons Ltd
Newnham Terrace
Hercules Road
London SE1 7DR
Manufacturers of handmade kitchens in traditional and country styles. Also bedroom cupboards. Every item of furniture is designed, built and fitted precisely to customers' individual requirments. Woods used include solid teak and maple. Also many finishes to choose from. Catalogue available.

Hathaway
Clifford Mill
Clifford Chambers
Nr Stratford-upon-Avon
Warwickshire CV37 8HW
See BATHROOMS

Henslow and Fox
Horndon Industrial Park
West Horndon
Brentwood
Essex CM13 3HP
Builders of fitted kitchens developed from traditional period designs in limed oak. Also available by special order in natural, honey and white painted, as well as in a pigmented glaze in five different broken paint finishes typical of many 18th-century interiors.

Hygrove Kitchens
152-154 Merton Road
Wimbledon
London SW19 1EH
Custom-built wooden kitchens in both antique and traditional finishes and a variety of painted designs. Also a selection of fitted bathroom and bedroom furniture.

Jamesway Kitchen Centre
9 Masons Avenue
Wealdstone
Harrow
Middlesex HA3 5AH
Modern and period-style kitchens.

John Lewis of Hungerford
Unit 2
Limborough Road
Wantage
Oxfordshire OX12 9AJ

Kingswood Kitchen Systems
Allied Manufacturing Co Ltd
Serena House
Grove Park
London NW9
Manufacturers, suppliers and installers of kitchens in countryside oak, solid mahogany and several "designer" colourways. Also components and accessories. Catalogue available.

Kitchen Art
5-6 The Centre
The Broadway
Beaconsfield Road
Farnham Common
Buckinghamshire
Fitted and freestanding kitchens, both standard and custom-built. The original range is a traditional, all-timber design.

The Kitchen People
348 Kensington High Street
Kensington
London W14 8NS
Specialists in fitted kitchens and solid granite worktops. A range of 5,000 tiles in stock. Also design and installation of bathrooms. Export and fixing service available. Brochure on request.

Lanzet (UK) Ltd
Unit 20
Headley Park – 10
Headley Road East
Woodley
Reading
Berkshire RG5 4SW

Manufacturers of individually tailored kitchens, bedrooms and bathrooms offering more than 200 door styles ranging from traditional and classic to modern designer ranges. Hand-painted finishes are a speciality. Design and installation service available. Catalogue available.

Leicht Furniture Ltd
Leicht House
Lagoon Road
Orpington
Kent BR5 3QG

Lockhurst Kitchen Design
8-12 Lockhurst Lane
Coventry CV6 5PD
Manufacturers of kitchen furniture. Full installation service available.

The London Architectural Salvage & Supply Co
St Michael's Church
Mark Street
Shoreditch
London EC2A 4ER
See DOORS

Magnet Southerns plc
(Retail Division)
Alington Way
Darlington
Co Durham DL1 4XT
One of the largest home improvement companies in the country, manufacturing and selling kitchens and bedroom furniture.

Malvern Studios
56 Cowleigh Road
Malvern
Worcestershire WR14 1QD
See LIGHTING

Martin Moore
28 Church Street
Altrincham
Cheshire
Manufacturers of high-quality handmade kitchens in traditional styles. Woods such as beech, maple, mahogany, oak, pitch pine and yellow pine used for work surfaces or alternatively in stone, granite or corian. To complete the kitchens, tables, dressers, chairs and built-in seating are all available.

John Mead Country Kitchens Ltd
Roadside Farm
Pewsey
Wiltshire SN9 5NB
Designers, manufacturers and installers of solid wood kitchens in quarter sawn English oak, ash, cherry, maple or lacquered hardwoods. Also freestanding furniture and other built-in items such as concealed offices to extend the use of a room. Showroom at Roadside Farm, brochure available.

Mobens Kitchens Ltd
Bringley Road
Old Trafford
Manchester M16 9HQ

Reproduction period-style kitchens. Many different styles to choose from including Victorian and Country style. Catalogue available.

Newcastle Furniture Co
Unit 4
Green Lane Buildings
Pelaw
Tyne & Wear NE10 0UW
Fine hand-crafted furniture for all areas of the home. Woods used include oak, mahogany, maple and old pine. Each piece of furniture is handmade to customers' individual requirements. The kitchen furniture can be supplied either in its natural state or hand-painted in a variety of decorative finishes.

Original Style
Stovax Ltd
Falcon Road
Sowton Industrial Estate
Exeter
Devon EX2 7LF
See WALLS

Pinewood Custombuilt Kitchens
4 Harcourt Road
Redland
Bristol
Avon BS6 7RG
Traditional kitchens, with a variety of finishes antique pine, hand-painted surfaces and a choice of coloured stains. Fitting service and catalogue available.

Prior Unit Design
Woodbury
Exeter
Devon EX5 1LP
Kitchen planners, cabinet makers and joinery specialists. In-house design and drawing office.

Riva Design Ltd
"The Rycroft"
Fanavon Buildings
Warrington Street
Stalybridge
Cheshire SK15 2LB
Projects range from complete kitchens and bathrooms to panelling and architectural joinery. Interior design and installation service also available.

Robinson and Cornish
The Old Tannery
Swimbridge
Devon
Specialist designers and manufacturers of handmade fitted and free-standing traditional kitchens and bathroom furniture. Kitchens in antique pine and limed oak with solid ash and corian worktops. Each piece is finished in heat and water resistant varnish. Offer advice on additional furniture, floors, wall coverings, tiles and fabrics. Catalogue available.

Scottwood of Nottingham
Dabell Avenue
Blenheim Industrial Estate
Bulwell
Nottingham NG6 8WA
See BATHROOMS

Siematic Kitchen Furniture (UK) Ltd
Osprey House
Rookery Court
Primett Road
Stevenage
Hertfordshire SG1 3EE
Kitchen interior designers providing an extensive range from the ultra modern to the more traditional styles of Baroque Flemish and solid oak kitchens.

Smallbone of Devizes
The Hopton Workshop
London Road
Devizes
Wiltshire SN10 2EU
Hand-crafted fitted kitchens in old pine and English oak. Also a range of hand-painted kitchens which are finished with different paint techniques such as dragging, rag-rolling, stippling and sponging.

Solent Furniture Ltd
Pymore Mills
Bridport
Dorset DT6 5PJ
Specialists in rigid ready-made kitchens in pine, mahogany and oak. Catalogue available.

Stately Homes Kitchens Ltd
Coronation Parade
54 Cannon Lane
Pinner
Middlesex HA5 1HW
Manufacturers of kitchens in all types of hardwoods. Suppliers of all makes of kitchen appliances.

Stone Age
67 Dendy Street
London SW12 8DA
See FLOORS

Styles Kitchens Ltd
2 Rowhedge Close
Wollaston Industrial Centre
Basildon
Essex SS13 1QQ
Fully fitted kitchens, the country-colour range painted in any colour or shade, with two other similarly styled ranges – Country Pine and Country Oak, both in natural solid wood. A stippled, sponged, rolled or dragged effect can be added if required.

Sutton Kitchens
30 Beacon Grove
High Street
Carshalton
Surrey SM5 3BA
Small family business who design and refurbish kitchens in period houses dating back to the 16th century. Doors are hand-crafted in 200- or 400-year old reclaimed oak or reclaimed pine. Specialist paint finishes including marbling and stencilling.

Tielsa Kitchens
Wakefield Road
Gildersome
Leeds LS27 0QW
Manufacturers of hand-crafted kitchens exported world-wide.

M. Tuckey Joinery
20 Cherry Street
Warwick
Warwickshire CV34 4LR
*Specialists in handmade fitted kitchens and handmade
windows as copies of originals.*

Mr Wandle's Workshop
200-202 Garratt Lane
Wandsworth
London SW18 4ED
See FIREPLACES AND STOVES

Wellmann UK Ltd
Wakefield Road
Gildersome
Leeds LS27 7JZ
*Kitchen manufacturers with over 200 different finishes to
choose from, including a range of accessories to match. Wide
range of built-in appliances available as well as full
installation service. Catalogue available.*

Woodgoods
Unit 40
Woolmer Trading Estate
Bordon
Hampshire GU35 9QZ
*Country and period-style kitchens handmade from reclaimed
antique pine, oak, ash and many other hardwoods and hand-
painted finishes. All kitchens are handmade in their own
workshops.*

Wood Workshop
21 Canterbury Grove
Dulwich
London SE27 0NT
*Builders of fitted kitchens in many hardwoods and several
styles, including some of the Victorian period. Catalogue
available.*

LIGHTING

A. & H. Brass
201-203 Edgware Road
London W2 1ES
See DOORS

Albert Bartram
177 Hivings Hill
Chesham
Buckinghamshire HP5 2PN
*Reproduction pewter 17th-century chandeliers and wall
sconces, they are suplied to take candles but may be wired for
electricity.*

Bella Figura
Decoy Farm
Old Church Road
Melton
Nr Woodbridge
Suffolk IP13 6DH
*Specialists in distressed Florentine chandeliers and
sconces in painted metal finishes. Designs range from fairly
simple to extravagantly floral, and can either hold candles
or be adapted to electricity. Brochure available
on request.*

Best & Lloyd Ltd
William Street West
Smethwick
Warley
West Midlands B66 2NX
*Producers of brass light fittings including traditional
candlestick wall sconces after Adam and Hepplewhite, and
Victorian pendants.*

Beta Lighting Ltd
383-387 Leeds Road
Bradford BD3 9LZ
*Commercial and architectural lighting manufacturers
specializing in energy-saving and low-voltage lighting.*

The Birmingham Glass Studios Ltd
Unit 5
100-102 Edward Road
Balsall Heath
Birmingham B11 3SA
*Suppliers of all stained-glass materials, coloured and antique
glass, manufacturers of leaded lights, Tiffany lampshades
and terrariums.*

The Bradley Collection
The Granary
Flowton Brook
Flowton
Suffolk IP8 4LJ
*A range of iron candelabra and candle chandeliers. Wall-
fixed or floor-standing candle lighting. Traditional style
candles also available.*

Brighton Architectural Salvage
33 Gloucester Road
Brighton
East Sussex
See FIREPLACES AND STOVES

Chelsea Lighting Design Ltd
Unit 1
23a Smith Street
Chelsea
London SW3 4EJ
*Independent lighting design service. Suppliers of fittings,
including their own range.*

Chelsom Ltd
Heritage House
Clifton Road
Blackpool
Lancashire FY4 4QA
*Specialists in period reproduction lighting, Flemish,
Georgian, Regency, Adam, Louis XV, Victorian and
Edwardian light fittings, many available in a choice of 13
finishes including polished brass, silver, pewter, weathered
bronze and English antique. Fittings range from single-light
wall brackets through to a forty light chandelier from the
standard range. An additional collection includes period US,
Art Nouveau, Art Deco and Mackintosh. Stockists
nationwide.*

Clare House Ltd
35 Elizabeth Street
London SW1W 9RP
*Specialists in producing fine lampshades in silk, also
repair and rewire light fittings. A range of antique lamps
stocked.*

Classicana Ltd
"The Oak Tree Unit"
West Hoathly
Sussex RH19 4QF
*Period-style range of light switches and ceiling pendant roses
mounted on solid oak they are finished by hand in polished
brass, silver plate or antique bronze.*

Mrs M. E. Crick Chandeliers
166 Kensington Church Street
Kensington
London W8 4BN
*Specializes in 18th- to 20th-century lighting: chandeliers,
wall lights and candelabra in cut glass and ormolu.*

Decor
125 Kensington Church Street
London W8 7LP
*An extensive range of antique chandeliers and other light
fittings. Installation service available.*

Delomosne & Son Ltd
4 Campden Hill Road
London W8 7DU
*Antique dealers specializing in 18th- and 19th-century
English glass chandeliers and candelabra.*

Dernier & Hamlyn
47/48 Berners Street
London W1P 3AD
*Manufacturers of decorative light fittings of the 18th and
19th centuries. More than 200 different fittings, all
available in eight different finishes. Also specialize in the
restoration of light fittings. Catalogue available.*

End of the Day Lighting Co Ltd
54 Parkway
London NW1 7AH
*Specializes in Victorian, Edwardian and Deco lighting:
over 40 designs available, including ceiling pendants, wall
brackets, table and desk lamps. Most are made of solid brass
from original castings and vary in style from the simple to
the ornate. Catalogue available.*

The Facade
196 Westbourne Grove
London W11 2RM
Suppliers of lighting c.1880-1920.

David Fileman Antiques
Squirrels
Bayards
Horsham Road
Steyning
West Sussex BN4 3AA
*Period lighting including chandeliers, candelabra and wall
lights bought and sold. Restoration undertaken.*

Forbes and Lomax Ltd
205B St John's Hill
London SW11 1TH
*Suppliers of electric light switches and sockets for period
houses. Also antique bronze satin chrome switches.*

Fritz Fryer Decorative Antique Lighting
12 Brookend Street
Ross-on-Wye
Herefordshire HR9 7EG
*Specialists in all forms of decorative antique lighting from
Georgian to Art Deco. Main period 1850-1920. Advisory,
planning and fitting services available.*

Hoffmeister Lighting Ltd
Unit 4
Preston Road
Reading
Berkshire RG2 0BE
*Manufacturers of a wide range of lighting. Catalogue
available.*

Homelight
110 Goodmayes Road
Ilford
Essex
Stockists of a large range of light fittings.

Hooper & Purchase
303 King's Road
Chelsea
London SW3 5EP
*Selling 18th- and early 19th-century English and
Continental antique chandeliers and wall lights.*

David Hunt Lighting Ltd
Tilemans Lane
Shipston-on-Stour
Warwickshire CV36 4HP
*Manufacture light fittings for domestic and contractual use.
Also restoration and conversion of period lighting and
manufacture of one-off projects.*

Illumin Glass Studio
82 Bond Street
Macclesfield
Cheshire SK11 6QS
*Producers of stained-glass lighting and windows. Renovation
of antique light fittings including a selection of original
fittings and shades in stock.*

The Incandescent Lighting Co
36 Regent Street
Leamington Spa
Warwickshire CV32 5EG
Specialists in original and period-style lighting.

Jardine Leisure Furniture
Rosemount Tower
Wallington Square
Wallington
Surrey SM6 8RR
*Manufacturers and distributors of Italian marble, cut to any
size, architectural fittings, friezes and panels, cast
aluminium garden lighting, including lamposts, also ceiling
fittings.*

Jones Antique Lighting
194 Westbourne Grove
Bayswater
London W11
*The largest selection of original lighting from 1860-1960 in
Europe. No reproductions.*

Kalmar Lighting (UK) Ltd
Dacre House
Dacre Street
London SW1H 0DJ

Specialize in a wide range of lighting products and fittings, including traditional chandeliers. Catalogue available on request.

The Last Detail
341 Kings Road
Chelsea
London SW3 5ES
Specialists in lighting.

The Light Brigade
18 Regent Street
Cheltenham
Gloucestershire GL50 1HE
Wall lights, candle sconces and candle shades handmade and hand-painted. Colour brochure available.

Lights on Broadway
Showrooms: 17 Jerdan Place
Fulham Broadway
London SW1 1BE
and: 1c Camden Lock
Chalk Farm Road
London NW1
and: 6a Greenwich Market
Greenwich
London SE10
Manufacturing retailers. Specialists in authentic period brass lighting for walls, ceilings and tables.

Malvern Studios
56 Cowleigh Road
Malvern
Worcestershire WR14 1QD
Interior designers. Also stockists of period-style reproduction lighting, plaster mouldings, alcoves, niches, fireplaces and pliable wooden mouldings and wallpapers.

Millet Lighting Ltd
197-201 Baker Street
London NW1 6UY
A fine range of traditional and modern lighting, including table lamps, wall brackets and centre pieces.

Montrose International Ltd
47-48 Berners Street
London W1P 3AD
Designers and manufacturers of light fittings and architectural metalwork. Catalogue available.

Moorlite Electrical Ltd
Burlington Street
Ashton-under-Lyne
Lancashire OL7 0AX
Manufacturers of both standard and special luminaires for domestic and commercial environments.

Olivers Lighting Co
6 The Broadway
Crockenhill
Swanley
Kent BR8 8JH
Electric light switches in period styles.

Planet Shades Ltd
PO Box 118
Lampard Grove
London N16 6XB

Manufacturers of silk and fabric lampshades, hand-polished antique brass chandeliers and wall brackets, glass shades and single pendants, Strass chandeliers and wall brackets.

Poole Lighting Ltd
Cabot Lane
Creekmoore
Poole
Dorset BH17 7BY
Designers and manufacturers of a comprehensive range of traditional based and modern light fittings.

R. & S. Robertson Ltd
Unit 13
36 Bankhead Drive
Sighthill Industrial Estate
Edinburgh EH11 4EQ
Scotland
Manufacturers of an extensive range of period lighting and fittings made to customers' specific requirements.

Roger of London
344 Richmond Road
East Twickenham
Middlesex
Specialists in antique, oriental, classical and modern lamps, handmade shades, vases and statues converted into lamps, also chandelier restoration.

W. Sitch & Co Ltd
48 Berwick Street
London W1V 4JD
Dealers in 19th-century chandeliers, wall brackets, floor standards and other lighting fixtures. Repairers, bronzers, gilders and lacquerers to the trade. Also art metal workers and manufacturers.

Smithbrook Ltd
Smithbrook
Nr Cranleigh
Surrey GU6 8LH
Traditional wrought-iron lighting.

Somerset Country Furniture Ltd
The Old Chapel
Church Street
Ilchester
Somerset BA22 8LN
Designers and manufacturers of country-style furniture and hand-forged ironwork lighting.

Stair & Co Ltd
120 Mount Street
London W1Y 5HB
Antique glass chandeliers and wall lights, restoration and advice on decoration.

Starlite Chandeliers Ltd
127 Harris Way
Windmill Road
Sunbury-on-Thames TW16 7EL
Manufacture crystal light fittings, including chandeliers and wall brackets in Empire, Louis XV, Regency, Edwardian, Middle Eastern and contemporary styles. Fittings are available in a choice of Austrian Swarovski Strass crystal or Czechoslovakian Strass crystal. Frame finishes include 24ct gold plating.

Sugg Lighting Ltd
Sussex Manor Business Park
Gatwick Road
Crawley
West Sussex RH10 2GD
Specialist manufacturers of gas and electric lighting for exteriors and interiors in traditional Victorian and Edwardian styles. Manufacturers of replica lamp columns and specialist lighting fittings. Refurbishment of light fittings and mountings. Producers of specially designed light fittings. Light fittings also offered with modern conveniences such as remote control, electronic timing and photocell operation.

N. T. Sussex Brassware
Napier Road
Castleham Industrial Estate
St Leonards-on-Sea
East Sussex TN38 9NY
Full range of brass electrical accessories in four traditional designs: Georgian, Victorian, Regency and Adam gilt. Finishes available are wrought-iron, satin brass, polished chrome, gold- and silver-plated.

Wilchester County
Stable Cottage
Vicarage Lane
Steeple Ashton
Nr. Trowbridge
Wiltshire BA14 6HH
Manufacturers of primitive lighting copied from original American designs, available in candle or electrified form.

Woolpit Interiors
Woolpit
Bury St Edmunds
Suffolk
Manufacturers of English decorative lighting.

Christopher Wray's Lighting Emporium
600 King's Road
London SW6 2DX
Lighting Specialists. Catalogue available.

CONSERVATORIES

Abbeydale Conservatories
Hewell Road
Redditch
Worcester B97 6AR
Individually designed hardwood conservatories, manufactured and constructed by skilled craftsmen. Finished in polished mahogany or white.

Amdega
Faverdale
Darlington
Co Durham DL3 0PW
Manufacturers and designers of period-style conservatories. Several designs to choose from, will also produce conservatories to customers' designs. Also build porches and produce doors. Catalogue available.

Bartholomew Conservatories
277 Putney Bridge Road
London SW15 2PT

Charterhouse Conservatories
42A High Street
Walton-on-Thames
Surrey KT12 1BZ
Manufacturers of double-glazed conservatories in Victorian, Edwardian and other traditional styles.

Churchill Conservatories
Churchill Ltd
Unit 17
Park Street Industrial Estate
Aylesbury
Buckinghamshire HP20 1EB

Classical Conservatories
16c Chalwyn Industrial Estate
St Clements Road
Poole
Dorset BH15 3PE
Designers and builders of conservatories. Materials and styles used to complement those already in situ.

Cortical Ltd
Eastlands Court
Rugby
Warwickshire CV21 3QP
Bespoke conservatories, garden rooms, and swimming pool enclosures. Designed to customer's specifications.

Durabuild Conservatories Ltd
Wheler Road
Coventry CV3 4LB

Eclipse Conservatories
1 Cranfield Road
Lostock Industrial Estate
Lostock
Bolton BL6 4QP

Finch Conservatories Ltd
2-4 Parham Drive
Eastleigh
Hampshire SO5 4NU
Manufacturers of conservatories in UPVC or Brazilian mahogany, with polycarbonate or glass roofs.

First Country Classics
Dept C7
Charlwoods Road
East Grinstead
Sussex RH19 2HG
Purpose-built mahogany conservatories.

Haus Traditional Conservatories
Halls Homes & Gardens
1-3 Revenge Road
Lordswood
Chatham
Kent ME5 8VD
A range of traditional conservatories and complementary interior furnishings and accessories.

Imperial Conservatories Ltd
Watling Road
Bishop Auckland
Co Durham DL14 9AU
Custom-designed and modular conservatory systems in traditional styles.

The Kent Conservatory Co
Woodford Coach House
Maidstone Road
Staplehurst
Kent TN12 0RH

Machin Conservatories
Faverdale
Darlington
Co Durham DL3 0PW
*Leading company manufacturing conservatories.
Architects and designers of Machin are experienced in the
construction and application of conservatories. They offer
a comprehensive service ranging from planning
and design to technical data and quotations. Brochure
available on request.*

Marston and Langinger Ltd
Showroom & design studio:
192 Ebury Street
London SW1W 8UP
*Supply one-off conservatories and swimming pool
enclosures to complement the style of the house. Also offer a
complete interior design service. Showroom display has their
own range of willow and metal furniture, plants and
a range of accessories. Brochure available on
request.*

Mundy Conservatories
Brookend Works
Kempsey
Worcester WR5 3LF

Relay Windows
by Glass Relay Ltd
211 London Road
Nr Dartford
Kent DA9 9DQ
See WINDOWS

Robinsons of Winchester Ltd
Chilcombe Lane
Chilcombe
Winchester
Hampshire SO21 1HU

Rooks-Mist Conservatories
PO Box 6
Huntingdon
Cambridgeshire PE17 2DN
*Conservatories manufactured in cedar hardwoods or
metal to individual requirements. Traditional building
and ground work undertaken. Brochure available on
request.*

Room Outside Ltd
Goodwood Gardens
Goodwood
Chichester
West Sussex PO18 0QB
*Specialists in design and supply of conservatories and garden
accessories.*

Stone Age
67 Dendy Street
Balham
London SW12 8DA
See FLOORS

Summer House Conservatories
1b Parklands Avenue
Cleveland
Tyne & Wear TS23 1DZ
*Victorian and traditional conservatories manufactured to
individual specifications from cedar wood.*

Town and Country Conservatories
Thumb Lane
Horningtroft
Dereham
Norfolk NR20 5DY

Walton Conservatories
Unit 5
Rusham Industrial Estate
Rusham Road
Egham
Surrey TW20 9SL

Westbury Conservatories
Martels
High Easter Road
Barnston
Essex CM6 1NA

EXTERIORS

Alitex Ltd
Station Road
Alton
Hampshire GU34 2PZ
*Specialists in designing and building greenhouses for over
25 years. The Victorian style greenhouse is built with
modern materials with a combination of wood and powder-
coated aluminium. Free-standing or lean-to structures
incorporating special staging, heating, ventilation, shading
and irrigation.*

Architectural Antiques Ltd
351 King Street
Hammersmith
London W6 9NH
See FIREPLACES AND STOVES

Architectural Heritage Ltd
Taddington Manor
Taddington
Nr Cutsdean
Cheltenham
Gloucestershire GL54 5RY
See WALLS

Attracta Products Ltd
2nd Floor, Hyde House
The Hyde
London NW9 6LH
*Manufacturers and distributors of garden equipment and
DIY materials.*

Bailey's Architectural Antiques
The Engine Shed
Ashburton Industrial Estate
Ross-on-Wye
Herefordshire HE9 7BW
See DOORS

Bridgwater Reclamation Ltd
Monmouth Street
Bridgwater
Somerset
See FIREPLACES AND STOVES

Brighton Architectural Salvage
33 Gloucester Road
Brighton
East Sussex
See FIREPLACES AND STOVES

**Brittania Architectural Metalwork &
Restoration**
5 Normandy Street
Alton
Hampshire GU34 1DD
*Stockists of a wide range of standard traditional railings,
balusters, brackets, gratings etc, including Victorian and
Georgian patterns. Restoration and repair work, pattern-
making and design services. Deliveries in the UK and
abroad. Catalogue available.*

Bromley Demolition Co Ltd
75 Siward Road
Bromley
Kent
See DOORS

Capps & Capps Ltd
Llowes Court
Llowes
Hay-on-Wye
Herefordshire HR3 5JA
*Engaged in the repair of old buildings, masonry repairs a
speciality.*

Capricorn Architectural Ironwork Ltd
Tasso Forge
25 North End Parade
North End Road
London W14
*Specialists in hand-forged ironwork, ie railings,
balconies etc in traditional and avant garde styles. Garden
furniture, arbours, gates, railings and pergolas. Full design
service.*

Chilstone
Sprivers Estate
Horsmonden
Kent TN12 8DR
*Specialists in reproducing antique ornaments and
architectural items including Doric and Ionic columns,
architraves, cornices, balustrades, mullions, temples etc, as
well as a standard range of over 350 classical garden
ornaments. Catalogue available.*

Classic Furniture Group plc
Audley Avenue
Newport
Shropshire
See FIREPLACES AND STOVES

Clifton Little Venice
3 Warwick Place
Maida Vale
London W9 2PX
Garden and architectural antiques.

Conservation Building Products Ltd
Forge Works
Forge Lane
Cradley Heath
Warley
West Midlands B64 5AL
*Stockists of period roofing tiles, fittings, finials, bricks, oak
beams, joists, quarry floor tiles, paving, pine doors,
panelling and architectural ironwork.*

Counterparts Demolition Ltd
Station Yard
Topsham
Exeter
Devon
*Stock timbers, slates, doors and occasionally fire
surrounds.*

Crowther of Syon Lodge Ltd
Busch Corner
London Road
Isleworth
Middlesex TW7 5BH
*A world-renowned, family-run antiques business,
established over 100 years ago, which operates from the
tranquil Georgian setting of Syon Lodge, a Robert
Adam-built house. The company specializes in
period architectural features, dating from the
17th, 18th and 19th centuries, such as oak and pinewood
panelling, carved wood and marble mantelpieces, grates and
andirons. The extensive stock of antique garden ornaments
and statuary may all be viewed in the two acres of formal
garden which surround the Lodge, and include such items
as sundials, fountains, classical statues, animal
figures, temples, urns and vases, seats, benches,
wrought-iron gates and columns. The company offers a
complete room panelling service, from drawings through
manufacture and adaptation, all of which is handled in the
joinery workshops at Syon Lodge, to finally fixing on site if
required.*

C. S. L. Davey & Jordan
3 Jennings Road
Kernick Industrial Estate
Penryn
Cornwall TR10 9DQ
See STAIRCASES

Drummond's of Bramley
Birtley Farm
Horsham Road
Bramley
Guildford
Surrey
See BATHROOMS

Elite Stairs
Unit C
Wolston Business Park
Wolston
Coventry
See STAIRCASES

The English Street Furniture Co
Pastures Drive
Caxton
Cambridge CB3 8PF
See FIREPLACES AND STOVES

Froyle Tiles Ltd
Froyle Pottery
Lower Froyle
Nr Alton
Hampshire GU34 4LL
See FLOORS

Galerie Seven
7 Church Road
Wimbledon Village
London SW19 5DW
See FLOORS

Haddonstone Ltd
The Forge House
East Haddon
Northampton NN6 8DB
Designers and suppliers of reconstructed stoneware for
gardens, interiors and architectural decoration, including
balustrades, temples and pavilions, porticos, columns and
pilasters, pier caps and finials, as well as an extensive range
of garden urns and ornaments. Services include contract
work, interiors, restoration and special commissions.
Catalogue available.

Havenplan's Architectural Emporium
The Old Station
Station Road
Killamarsh
Sheffield S31 8EN
See FIREPLACES AND STOVES

James Horrobin
Doverhay Forge Studios
Doverhay
Porlock
Minehead
Somerset TA24 8QB
Architectural, ecclesiastical and domestic ironwork.

The House Hospital
68 Battersea High Street
Battersea
London SW11 3HX
See DOORS

House of Steel Antiques
400 Caledonian Road
Islington
London N1
See FIREPLACES AND STOVES

H. R .Contractors Ltd
Fairwater Yard
Staplegrove Road
Taunton
Somerset
Suppliers of second-hand building materials, including
slates, roof tiles, timber, basins, WCs, chimney pots and
flagstones.

Jardine International Ltd
Rosemount Tower
Wallington Square
Wallington
Surrey SM6 8RR
Manufacturers and distributors of cast aluminium and
traditional wooden garden furniture.

Kentish Ironcraft Ltd
Bethersden
Ashford
Kent TN26 3AT
Manufacturers of wrought-iron gates. Specialists in the
restoration and reproduction of period ironwork. Catalogue
available.

Kestner Building Products Ltd
Station Road
Greenhithe
Kent DA9 9NG
Manufacturers of reproduction period-style rainwater
fittings in glass and reinforced plastic. Catalogue
available.

Kibblewhite & Blackmur Ltd
Long Reach Road
Barking
Essex IG11 0JN
Suppliers of sawn timber, hardwood and softwood, also
hardwood and softwood mouldings, specialist milling
services, fencing materials, plywood, chipboard and
blockboard importers.

Langham Architectural Materials
Foxes Mill
Tonedale
Wellington
Somerset
See FIREPLACES AND STOVES

**The London Architectural Salvage &
Supply Co**
St Michael's Church
Mark Street
Shoreditch
London EC2A 4ER
See DOORS

J. & W. Lowry Ltd
64 Bath Lane
Newcastle-upon-Tyne
Tyne & Wear NE4 5TT
General builders and contractors, special stonemasonry
contractors, stonework restoration and repair. Also specialist
joinery makers.

Mounts Hill Woodcraft Ltd
Paynetts Lane
Cranbrook Road
Goudhurst
Kent TN17 1DY
See DOORS

Pageant Antiques
122 Dawes Road
Fulham
London SW6 7EG
Dealers in 18th- and 19th-century garden furniture and fine
chimneypieces in marble and wood.

B. L. Pattern & Foundry Co
37 Churton Street
Pimlico
London SW1V 2LT
Designers, manufacturers and restorers of cast- and wrought-
iron work.

Plantation Group Ltd
Temple Gardens
Holloway Lane
Harmondsworth
West Drayton
Middlesex UB7 0AD
Water features and fountains, garden design and landscape
gardening. Interior and exterior landscaping.

T. & O. Plaster Castings
7 Collier Row Road
Collier Row
Romford
Essex RM5 3NP
See CEILINGS

D. S. & A. G. Prigmore
Mill Cottage
Mill Road
Colmworth
Bedford MK44 2NU
A wide range of bricks, slates, ridge tiles, timber panelling,
fireplaces and wood blocks.

Richard Quinnell Ltd
Rowhurst Forge
Oxshott Road
Leatherhead
Surrey KT22 0EN
Architectural metalworkers and wrought-ironworkers,
working in all types of metal. Specialist restorers of antique
wrought- and cast-ironwork.

Rattee & Kett Ltd
(A Division of John Mowlem Construction
plc)
Purbeck Road
Cambridge
Cambridgeshire CB2 2PG
Specialists in all aspects of conservation and repair of
historic buildings, stonemasonry, joinery, carving, cast stone
and repair service, leadwork, specialized painting and
gilding.

The Real Stone Co
The Forge
Penthouse Hill
Bath
Avon BA1 7EL
See FLOORS

Reclaimed Materials
Northgate
White Lund Industrial Estate
Morecambe
Lancashire
A good selection of slates, flagstones, yellow pine timber,
timber flooring and fire surrounds.

Renzland Forge
London Road
Copford
Colchester
Essex CO6 1LG
Craftsmen in metal, manufacturing gates, railings, street
lamps, lanterns, posts, arches, corner tops, nameplates,
weather vanes, door grilles and bootscrapers. Catalogue
available.

Robus Pottery & Tiles
Evington Park
Hastingleigh
Ashford
Kent
See WALLS

**Rogers Demolition & Dismantling
Service Ltd**
Belgrave Road
Portswood
Southampton
Salvage material including bricks, panelling, flagstones,
skirting boards, coloured glass, peg tiles, pan tiles, door
handles, strip parquet flooring and even complete period
rooms.

Seagro
22 Pimlico Road
London SW1W 8LJ
Period garden statuary, ornament and exterior design.

Solopark Ltd
The Old Railway Station
Station Road
Nr Pampisford
Cambridge CB2 4HB
See DOORS

Southwell (Stockwell) Ltd
The Ironworks
3-9 Holly Grove
London SE15
Specialize in the casting, fabrication, restoration and site
fixing of cast-iron work with a vast range of pattern
equipment and original mouldings of street railings,
balustrades, window guards, boot scrapers, spiral and
straight staircases, balconies, gates etc from which cast-iron
reproductions are produced. Catalogue available.

Stuart Interiors
Barrington Court
Barrington
Ilminster
Somerset TA19 0NQ
See DOORS

**R. G. Trade Supplies and Engineering
Ltd**
Taurus Ornamental Design
Foley Street
Fenton
Stoke-on-Trent
Staffordshire ST4 3DR
Ornamental gate and railing specialists.

Walcot Reclamation
108 Walcot Street
Bath
Avon BA1 5BG
See FIREPLACES AND STOVES

Weller Patents Development
1 Grand Parade Mews, rear of 96
Upper Richmond Road
Barnes
London SW15 2RF
See STAIRCASES

OTHER USEFUL ADDRESSES

Acanthus
Associated Architectural Practices Ltd
Voysey House
Barley Mow Passage
Chiswick
London W4 4PN
Consultancy on listed buildings and conservation areas; historic building surveys and analysis; feasibility studies on uses for old buildings; quinquennial reports and programmes of maintenance and repair; conservation of sculpture and murals. Also offer expertise on landscape architecture and interior design undertaken for private or public clients. Brochure available.

Architectural Salvage
Netley House
Gomshall
Surrey GU5 9QA
Maintains an index of all kinds of architectural items, for a registration fee will put buyers in touch with appropriate sellers.

Art Workers Guild
6 Queen Square
London WC1N 3AR
Guild of artists, architects, craftsmen and others engaged in the design and practice of the arts.

British Ceramic Tile Council
Federation House
Station Road
Stoke-on-Trent
Staffordshire ST4 2RU

British Decorators Association
6 Haywra Street
Harrogate
North Yorkshire HG1 5BL
Over 1,000 members who specialize in the decoration of period homes.

British Institute of Interior Design
1c Devonshire Avenue
Beeston
Nottingham NG9 1BS
Established in 1899 and now a leading organization in the interior design industry. Its objectives are to encourage a better understanding, care and improvement of interior design. Has over 223 registered practices and about 1,500 members. A recommended short-list is available.

British Wood Preserving Association
Building No. 6
The Office Village
4 Romford Road
Stratford
London E15 4EA
A free and impartial advisory service on all problems concerning timber preservation and damp-proofing. Produces publications on dealing with practical problems and the latest developments in research. Leaflets and other information available.

Building Conservation Trust
Apartment 39
Hampton Court Palace
East Molesey
Surrey KT8 9BS
An independent educational charity established to promote the better care of buildings of all types and ages, with a permanent exhibition at Hampton Court Palace on house maintenance and home improvement. Provides advice, particularly to house holders on the technical aspects of building. Also runs short courses on basic building construction and maintenance problems. Technical library available for consulation.

Cadu Welsh Historic Monuments
9th Floor, Brunnel House
Fitzalan Road
Cardiff CF2 1UY
Wales
Awards grants for repairing historic buildings throughout Wales.

Chartered Institution of Building Services Engineers (C.I.B.S.E.)
Delta House
222 Balham High Road
London SW12 9BS
Advice on plumbing, heating, ventilation etc.

Church Farm House Museum
Greyhound Hill
London NW4 4JR
A collection consisting mainly of 19th-century domestic material. Two period furnished rooms – the kitchen set at c.1820 and the dining room at c.1850.

Civic Trust
17 Carlton House Terrace
London SW1Y 5AW
Encourages the protection and improvement of the environment.

Conservatory Association
2nd Floor Godwin House
George Street
Huntingdon
Cambridgeshire PE18 6BO

Design Council
28 Haymarket
London SW1Y 4SU

English Heritage
23 Savile Row
London W1X 1AB
Largest independent organization responsible for heritage conservation. Provides technical advice on conservation and repairs to historic buildings. Provides the major source of public funds for repairs to historic buildings throughout England. Also responsible for the preservation and presentation of some 700 historic properties in England.

The Georgian Group
37 Spital Square
London E1 6DY
Gives advice on repair and restoration to owners of Georgian buildings.

The Guild of Master Craftsmen
166 High Street
Lewes
East Sussex BN7 1XU
Trade association helping to put prospective clients in touch with experienced craftsmen and craftswomen able to carry out restoration and other work.

C. M. Hemming
Thrashers Barn
Norchard
Crossway Green
Stourport
Worcestershire
Timber-framed barn and house restoration.

The Historic Buildings Company
PO Box 150
Chobham
Surrey GU24 8JD
Publishers of the Period Property Register, *a publication devoted solely to the marketing, maintenance and improvement of period properties.*

Historic Houses Association
2 Chester Street
London SW1X 7BB

National Federation of Building Trades Employers
82 New Cavendish Street
London W1M 8AD
Recommends stonemasons, painters, plasterers, decorators etc.

National Fireplace Association
8th Floor
Bridge House
Smallbrook Queensway
Birmingham B5 4JP
Trade association.

The National Trust
36 Queen Anne's Gate
London SW1

The National Trust for Scotland
5 Charlotte Square
Edinburgh EH2 4DU
Scotland

McCurdy & Co Ltd
Manor Farm
Stanford Dingley
Reading
Berkshire RG7 6LS
Craftsmen and consultants. Specialists in the repair and conservation of historic framed buildings.

Royal Commission on the Ancient and Historic Monuments of Wales
Crown Building
Plas Crug
Aberystwyth
Dyfed SY23 2HP
Wales
Answers queries from the general public concerning the age, type and function of buildings.

Royal Commission on Historic Monuments
Fortress House
23 Savile Row
London W1X 1AB

Royal Incorporation of Architects in Scotland
15 Rutland Square
Edinburgh EH1 2BE
Scotland

Royal Institute of British Architects (R.I.B.A.)
66 Portland Place
London W1N 4AD

Royal Institute of Chartered Surveyors (R.I.C.S.)
12 Great George Street
Parliament Square
London SW1P 3AD

The Scottish Civic Trust
24 George Square
Glasgow G2 1EF
Scotland

Scottish Development Department of Historic Buildings and Ancient Monuments
3-11 Melville Street
Edinburgh EH3 7QD
Scotland
Awards grants for repairing historic buildings throughout Scotland.

The Society for the Protection of Ancient Buildings
37 Spital Square
London E1 6DY
Can supply names of specialist architects and other professionals on request. Issues technical publications and information on the repair and maintenance of historic buildings. Advises against conjectural restoration of period details.

The Victor Farrar Partnership
57 St Peter's Street
Bedford
Bedfordshire
Established in 1962, architects and surveyors specializing in the repair, conservation, alteration and extension of all forms of historic buildings from timber framed cottages and period houses to large ancient monuments. Also offers a full and comprehensive range of architectural services to suit clients' individual needs. Illustrated brochure available on request.

The Victorian Society
1 Priory Gardens
Bedford Park
London W4 1TT
The national amenity society responsible for preserving Victorian and Edwardian architecture. Publishes advice leaflets on Victorian house restoration, available on request.

Martin Miller, Geoff Dann, John Helfrick and Caroline Brown were specially commissioned to take photographs for this book. Thanks are also due to the *The World of Interiors* for Clive Frost's photograph on page 69, no. 9, and to David C. Golby for the photographs on page 73, nos. 10 and 11.

The following people allowed photography in specific houses or gave generously of their time or expertise: Jacqui and Colin Small, Alan and Smokey Parsons, Jeremy and Annie Parker, Christopher and Frances Everill, Ian and Jill Pooley, Doug and Pam Stewart, Paul and Angie Marsh, Gaby Tubbs, Liz and John Denning.
In America: Dr and Mrs Roger Gerry (Roslyn Landmark Society), Dr Stanley Fischer, Joe and Carolyn Roberto, Mrs Jean Bartlett.

For individual photographs and access to interiors the authors are also grateful to the sources named in the credits list below. The code letters are those used in picture captions throughout the book.

PICTURE CREDITS: ABBREVIATIONS

A Amdega, Faverdale, Darlington, County Durham.

AB A. Bell, Kingsthorpe Road, Kingsthorpe, Northampton.

AF Acquisitions (Fireplaces) Ltd, 269 Camden High Street, London NW1.

AH Architectural Heritage, Boddington Manor, Boddington, Nr Cheltenham, Gloucestershire.

AR Aga-Rayburn (Coalbrookdale) Glynwed Consumer & Building Products Ltd, PO Box 30, Ketley, Telford, Shropshire TF1 1BR.

AS Armitage Shanks, Armitage, Rugeley, Staffordshire.

AS&S Architectural Salvage and Supply Co., St Michael's Church, Mark St off Paul St, London EC2.

B Bisque, The Radiator Shop, 244 Belsize Road, London NW6.

Be Beardmore Ltd, 3-5 Percy St, London W1P 0EJ.

BCS B.C. Sanitan, 12 Nimrod Way, Reading, Berks.

BH Bowne House, 37-01 Bowne Street, Flushing, New York, NY 11354.

BP Bartow Pell Mansion, Shore Road, Pelham Bay Park, Bronx, NY 10464.

Br Brass Art Craft Birmingham Ltd (Brassart) 76 Atwood St, Lye, Stourbridge, West Midlands.

C Crown Decorative Products Ltd, PO Box 22, Queen's Mill, Hollins Rd, Darwen, Lancashire BB3 0BD.

CB Christopher Boulter, 43 Goodrich Rd, London SE22.

CF Classic Furniture Group, Audley Avenue, Newport, Shropshire.

C&F Colefax and Fowler, 39 Brook St, London W1.

CG County Group, 102 High St, Tenterden, Kent CN30 6HU.

CP Chilston Park, Sandway, Nr Maidstone, Kent.

CPH C.P. Hart, Newham Terrace, Hercules Road, London SE1.

CS Czech and Speake, 39c Jermyn Street, London SW1.

C of SL Crowther of Syon Lodge, London Road, Isleworth, Middlesex.

EDL End of Day Lighting, 44 Parkway, London NW1.

EW Erme Wood Forge, Woodlands, Ivybridge, Devon PL21 9HF.

FE Fired Earth Country Floors, Middle Aston, Oxfordshire.

G&G Goddard & Gibbs Studios, 41-49 Kingsland Road, London E2.

GH The Georgian House, 7 Great George Street, Bristol, Avon.

GJ G. Jackson & Sons Ltd, Rathbone Works, Rainville Road, London W6.

H Hallidays, 28 Beauchamp Place, Knightsbridge, London SW3.

Ha Hathaway Country Kitchens, Clifford Mill, Clifford Chambers, Stratford-upon-Avon.

HH Headquarters House, 215 East 71st Street, NYC 10021.

H&H Herschel House, 19 New King's Street, Bath.

HJ Hodkin & Jones (Sheffield) Ltd, 515 Queen's Road, Sheffield S2 4DS.

HPS Hand Painted Stencils, 6 Polstead Rd, Oxford OX2 6TW.

HW Hamilton-Weston Wallpapers, 11 Townsend Rd, Richmond, Surrey TW9 1YH.

H&S Hunter & Son (Mells) Ltd, Frome, Somerset BA11 3PA.

JBF The James Buchanan Foundation for the Preservation of Wheatland, 1120 Marietta Ave, Lancaster, Pennsylvania 17603.

JL John Lewis of Hungerford, 13 High Street, Hungerford, Berkshire.

JO John S. Oliver Ltd, 33 Pembridge Rd, London W11 3HG.

LAS London Architectural Salvage and Supply Co. Ltd, Mark Street, London EC2 4ER.

LG Lyn Le Grice, Alsia Mill Street, Buryon, Cornwall TR19 6HG.

LH Leighton House, 12 Holland Park Road, London W14.

LSH Linley Sambourne House, 18 Stafford Terrace, London W8.

MA Marthe Armitage, 1 Strand-on-the-Green, Chiswick, London W4 3PQ.

M Moben Kitchens Ltd, 100 Washway Road, Sale, Cheshire M33 1RE.

MH Marble Hill Fireplaces Ltd, 72 Richmond Road, Twickenham, Middlesex.

MJ Morris Jumel Mansion, West 160th and Edgecombe Avenue, New York, NY 10032.

ML Marston and Langinger, Hall Staithe, Fakenham, Norfolk.

MR Maria Rosenthal, Kingsgate Workshops, 110-116 Kingsgate Road, London NW6 2JD.

OB Original Bathrooms, 143-145 Kew Road, Richmond, Surrey TW9 2PN.

O&L Osborne & Little, 304 King's Road, London SW3.

OMH Old Merchants House, 29 East 4th Street, New York, NY 10003.

PC Paris Ceramics, 543 Battersea Park Road, London SW11.

PCA Peter Chapman Antiques, 10 Theberton Street, Islington, London, N1.

PF Patrick Fireplaces, Guildford Road, Farnham, Surrey GU9 9QA.

PH Phillip Henderson Co., 27 John Adam Street, London WC2.

PV Pine Village, 42-43 Peascod Street, Windsor, Berks.

RC No. 1 Royal Crescent, Bath, Avon.

S Smallbone of Devizes, Unit 10-11, Nimrod Way, Elgar Road, Reading, Berks.

SG Sekon Glassworks Ltd, Essian Street, London E1 4QE.

SI Stuart Interiors, Barrington Court, Barrington, Nr Ilminster, Somerset TA19 0NQ.

S of D Shaws of Darwen, Waterside, Darwen, Lancashire BB3 3NX.

S&P Strutt & Parker 13 Hill St, London SW1.

SP S. Polliack, Norton Industrial Estate, Norton, Malton, North Yorkshire YO17 9HQ.

SR Sylvia Robinson, Clarence House, Winchester Hill, Romsey, Hampshire SO51 7NJ.

ST Studio Two, 3d Town Street, Thaxted, Essex CM6 2LD.

S&W Smith & Wellstood Esse (1984) Ltd, Bonnybridge, Stirlingshire FK4 2AP.

SWH Sands Willet House, The Cow Neck Peninsula Historical Society, 336 Port Washington Boulevard, Port Washington, New York, NY 11050.

T Tissunique, 10 Princes St, Hanover Sq, London W1.

TB Traditional Bathrooms, 105 Regents Park Road, London NW1 8UR.

TP Tim Plant, 7 Bramham Gardens, London SW5.

TC Toynbee-Clarke Interiors Ltd., 95 Mount Street, London W1.

V Verdigris, Clerkenwell, Unit B.18, 31 Clerkenwell Close, London EC1.

VB Victoriana Bathrooms Ltd, 439 Leethorpe Road, Grimsby DN31 3BU.

VC Van Cortlandt Mansion, W.242nd Street and Broadway, Bronx, NY 10471.

VNS Van Nostrand Strakins House, 221 Main Street, Roslyn, New York.

W Woodstock Furniture, Pakenham Street, Mount Pleasant, London WC1.

Wa Watts & Co, 7 Tufton Street, Westminster, London SW1.

WA W. Adams & Sons Ltd, Westfield Works, Spon Lane, West Bromwich, West Midlands B70 6RH.

WB Winther Brown & Co. Ltd, Nobel Road, Eley's Estate, Edmonton, London N18 3DX.

WW Warren Wilkey, 741 Main St, Roslyn, New York.

W&W Whiteway & Waldron Ltd, 305 Munster Road, London SW6.

Z Zoffany Ltd, 27a Motcomb St, London SW1.

INDEX

Contents

Contents

AQA introduction

Nelson Thornes and AQA

Nelson Thornes has worked in collaboration with AQA to ensure that this book offers you the best support for your AS or A level course and helps you to prepare for your exams. The partnership means that you can be confident that the range of learning, teaching and assessment practice materials has been checked by the senior examining team at AQA before formal approval, and is closely matched to the requirements of your specification.

Blended learning

Printed and electronic resources are blended: this means that links between topics and activities between the book and the electronic resources help you to work in the way that best suits you, and enable extra support to be provided online. For example, you can test yourself online and feedback from the test will direct you back to the relevant parts of the book.

Electronic resources are available in a simple-to-use online platform called Nelson Thornes learning space. If your school or college has a licence to use the service, you will be given a password through which you can access the materials through any internet connection.

Icons in this book indicate where there is material online related to that topic. The following icons are used:

💡 Learning activity

These resources include a variety of interactive and non-interactive activities to support your learning. These include online presentations of concepts from the student book, worksheets and interactive activities.

☑ Progress tracking

These resources include a variety of tests that you can use to check and expand your knowledge on particular topics (Test yourself) and a range of resources that enable you to analyse and understand examination questions (On your marks . . .).

🔎 Research support

These resources include WebQuests, in which you are assigned a task and provided with a range of web links to use as source material for research.

🗐 Case studies

These resources provide detailed coverage of business scenarios, some of which extend material from this textbook and some of which are exclusively online.

When you see an icon, go to Nelson Thornes learning space at www.nelsonthornes.com/aqagce, enter your access details and select your course. The materials are arranged in the same order as the topics in the book, so you can easily find the resources you need.

How to use this book

This book covers the specification for your course and is arranged in a sequence approved by AQA.

The book content is divided into chapters matched to the sections of the AQA Business Studies specification for Units 1 and 2. Sections 1.1 and 1.2 cover Unit 1 (Planning and Financing a Business) and Sections 2.1 – 2.4 cover Unit 2 (Managing a Business). The chapters within each section provide full coverage of the AQA specification.

The features in this book include:

In this chapter you will learn to:

At the beginning of each chapter you will find a list of learning objectives that contain targets linked to the requirements of the specification.

Case study

The first case study in each chapter (Setting the scene) provides a real-life context for the theories which are to be discussed in the chapter. The concluding case study in each chapter focuses on testing the theories covered in the chapter. It will have five questions attached, each testing knowledge, application, analysis, evaluation and research.

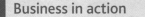

Key terms

Terms that you will need to be able to define and understand.

Links

Highlighting any areas where topics relate to one another.

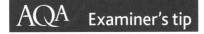

Activity

Suggestions for practical activities that you can carry out.

Business in action

A real life business example which demonstrates theory being put in to practice.

AQA Examiner's tip

Hints from AQA examiners to help you with your study and to prepare for your exam.

Summary questions

Questions that will test your knowledge of the preceding chapters.

AQA examination questions are reproduced by permission of the Assessment and Qualifications Alliance.

In this chapter you will heave learned to:

A bulleted list of learning outcomes at the end of each chapter summarising core points of knowledge.

■ Web links in the book

Because Nelson Thornes is not responsible for third party content online, there may be some changes to this material that are beyond our control. In order for us to ensure that the links referred to in the book are as up-to-date and stable as possible, the web sites provided are usually homepages with supporting instructions on how to reach the relevant pages if necessary.

Please let us know at **webadmin@nelsonthornes.com** if you find a link that doesn't work and we will do our best to correct this at reprint, or to list an alternative site.

Introduction to AS Business Studies

This book is the only textbook you will need if you are a student following the AQA Business Studies AS level course. It is different from all of the other books available for the following combination of reasons:

▪ It is written by senior examiners who are experienced teachers of Business Studies

▪ It follows exactly the AQA specification content and sequence of topics

▪ The material it contains not only explains the exact requirements of the specification but also defines what can and cannot be covered by the final AQA examinations

▪ It is the only text fully approved and endorsed by the AQA for use by students following this course and for teachers preparing students for it.

Each chapter covers one specification topic and takes the reader logically through each important issue. The key features of this book ensure that:

▪ All definitions required by the specification are clearly explained

▪ Text is clearly laid out to aid understanding

▪ Constant reference is made to actual business situations to allow application of understanding to the real world

▪ Practice at appropriate questions, testing examination skills, is gained at each important stage.

In addition, after every inter-related set of chapters, there are Summary Questions to test understanding of the material and skills covered in these sections. These offer invaluable preparation for the examination-style questions that feature on the interactive website.

The final chapter on examination skills is very important indeed. The main purpose of this chapter is to illustrate and reinforce the key skills that students will need to demonstrate in their examination answers if they are to gain that elusive grade A! The chapter makes clear that knowledge of appropriate Business Studies material is essential to gain any marks at all – but it is not sufficient to gain full marks. This is because Business Studies students are not just expected to be able to memorise facts, definitions and formulae but also show real understanding of how to apply them to a business problem. This means that content knowledge needs to be applied to a case study scenario, the problems and possible solutions need to be analysed and the final recommendation must be evaluated. Don't worry if this seems very complicated to start with – the secrets of how to show these skills are all explained in Chapter 35!

The authors believe that the:

▪ huge variety and number of presentational methods used in the book,

▪ range and diverse style of exercises and examination questions and

▪ accessibility of the text

will give students who work through it thoroughly, the best possible awareness of what Business Studies is about and what AQA examiners expect from grade A answers.

Starting a business

Introduction

Chapters in this section:

Why start a business?

In Unit 1 of *AS Business Studies* you will study many of the issues involved in starting up a business, including the research and planning needed to successfully start a business, and the factors that determine success. So the focus throughout this unit is on small to medium-sized businesses operating in national markets. Case studies of real businesses are used in each chapter to illustrate the main points.

Chapter 1: Enterprise You will study the role, importance and characteristics of entrepreneurs. You will discover why and how entrepreneurs start new businesses. You will also look at the importance of entrepreneurs and small businesses to the UK economy, and how the UK Government supports the creation and survival of small businesses.

Chapter 2: Generating and protecting business ideas Here we look at the way new business ideas are created and protected. You will study how new business ideas arise and the ways that the entrepreneur can carry out small-scale research to investigate the likely success of the product or service and the market in which it will be sold.

Chapter 3: Transforming resources into goods and services This chapter looks at the way businesses transform inputs into finished goods and services. You will look at primary, secondary and tertiary activity, as well as the process of adding value. You will consider the different ways that value can be added in the different sectors of business activity.

Chapter 4: Developing business plans This chapter is concerned with business planning. You will study the benefits of a business plan, its contents and some of the problems a small business would encounter when constructing and using a business plan. You will consider the sources of help and advice available to small businesses in constructing business plans.

Chapter 5: Conducing start-up market research Start-up research is explained and follows logically from the chapter on business planning. This chapter considers the sources of secondary and primary data available to small business start-ups, the sampling methods that can be used and the difference between qualitative and quantitative data.

Chapter 6: Understanding markets Here, we focus on numerical techniques to understand the markets in which small businesses tend to operate. In this chapter you will study the nature of markets and market segmentation. There is a section on numerical techniques and calculations of proportions of totals and percentage changes. These techniques will be applied to calculations of market size, market growth and market share.

Chapter 7: Choosing the right legal structure for the business This chapter is concerned with the key decision of choosing the right legal structure for a new business. You will learn about the benefits and drawbacks of sole traders, partnerships and private and public limited companies, as well as gain an appreciation of the importance of limited and unlimited liability status.

Chapter 8: Raising finance In this chapter you will consider the various sources of finance available to a new business, including internal and external sources. You will assess the advantages and disadvantages of different sources of finance and apply them to a number of different business situations.

Chapter 9: Locating the business This chapter concerns the location decision and considers the factors affecting the decision of where to locate a business. You will consider technology, costs, infrastructure and the market and you will apply your understanding to business case studies to make decisions about the best location in different circumstances.

Chapter 10: Employing people This chapter completes this section of Unit 1 with a look at employing people. You will consider the benefits and drawbacks of full and part time employees, as well as considering the role temporary employees might play alongside permanent staff. You will also analyse data relating to the changing nature of the UK labour market.

In this chapter you will learn to:

- understand and explain the terms enterprise and entrepreneurs

- use examples to illustrate your understanding of enterprise and entrepreneurs

- understand the importance of risk, reward and opportunity cost in starting a business

- understand and explain why entrepreneurs start up small businesses

- describe the help entrepreneurs can get from the Government and other sources

- evaluate the potential benefits to the UK economy of entrepreneurial activity and small businesses.

Fig. 1.1 *Martha Lane Fox started Lastminute.com in 1998, an online travel and gift business*

Setting the scene

Geared Up

Ian and Karen finished A levels with very different ideas about their future. Ian always knew he would go to University, and he chose to study Business and Accounting at a University close to his home town. Karen went to work for a large retailer after Sixth Form College to 'learn the ropes' before setting up her own company. She came from a family of business people; her mother and father ran a successful chain of hotels. The friends kept in touch and regularly talked about running a business together. Karen was unhappy with her current job and suggested they stopped talking about setting up a business and actually did it.

They got on well as friends despite the fact they were very different personalities. Ian was well organised, good with figures and naturally cautious. Karen was outgoing and confident, easily bored and had lots of energy. She liked extreme sports and was a keen cyclist. Karen's interest in cycling convinced her that they could successfully run a business selling top of the range bikes both online and from a shop. She immediately began investigating prices of a number of mountain and racing bikes, accessories and clothing. She asked a friend to build a website for the business so they could sell online. Many of her friends were keen cyclists and agreed with her that the business was certain to succeed. They started their own club, organising rides each weekend and social events.

Ian thought she was rushing things and tried to slow her down. He agreed the idea had potential, and investigated likely locations for the shop and looked around for possible sources of advice and help for small business start-ups. He remembered a unit on his Business course about Government help for small businesses and used his lecture notes to make some enquiries.

Discussion points

1   Describe the key personal characteristics that both Ian and Karen possess that might make them good entrepreneurs.

2   Assess whether Ian or Karen would be the most successful entrepreneur.

3   What do you think are the motives for Karen for starting Geared Up?

4   Karen wants to buy stock, get the website going and expand the cycling club. Ian wants to find a good shop location and get some financial help. Draw up a timeline of activities that Karen and Ian should do in the months leading up to starting the business.

What is enterprise?

Consider your own personality and the experiences you have had so far in your life, including jobs, or positions of responsibility. Make a list of how you could show that you have been enterprising.

Fig. 1.2 *Deborah Meadon*

Enterprise is something that many people possess, but they don't all decide to run their own businesses. It is the ability to come up with and carry out new ideas and new ways of doing things. It often involves making judgements about the risks and rewards of a situation and acting on them. So what is an **entrepreneur** and how does it differ from enterprise?

💡 What is an entrepreneur?

In the BBC television series *Dragons' Den*, the Dragons were all asked what it took to be an entrepreneur. They all had different ideas, proving there's no single definition, but they had some interesting ideas on what makes a successful entrepreneur.

To be a successful entrepreneur, personality counts. Here's what the Dragons have to say about personal qualities:

> First impressions count; in the first few minutes you get a pretty good idea about how you're going to click with someone. I'm looking for dedication, honesty and commitment.
>
> *Richard Farleigh*

> You need drive, an understanding of the product and tenacity.
>
> *Deborah Meaden*

It isn't as easy as just having the right personal qualities however. Successful entrepreneurs need to understand their product.

> The product needs to be original, not a 'me too' business.
>
> *Richard Farleigh*

> There's no need to be original, just do it differently and better. The riskiest investment is in a brand new untried and untested product. I like it when someone spots an opportunity and says 'you know, I can do that better'.
>
> *Deborah Meaden*

They need also to know their market.

> The biggest mistake people can make is to think they've got a great idea and not bother to find out if there's a market.
>
> *Deborah Meaden*

> I'm amazed how many don't get the yellow pages out to see the competition.
>
> *Duncan Bannatyne*

There's one more skill the Dragons think you need to be a successful entrepreneur. It's equally valuable if you want to be successful in your A Level Business Studies.

> I'm astonished at people's shaky grasp of numbers. The number of people who know their turnover but not their profit. I would know them even if I wasn't good at numbers.
>
> *Duncan Bannatyne*

> You have to understand the numbers and what they mean to the business.
>
> *Deborah Meaden*

www.bbc.co.uk/dragonsden

■ Key terms

Enterprise: the ability to handle uncertainty and deal effectively with change.

Entrepreneur: someone who starts and runs a business and has responsibility for the risks involved. In order to do this, an entrepreneur has to be able to manage the 4 factors of production effectively. They are:

- land or natural resources
- labour
- capital, which is any kind of equipment used in production
- enterprise.

AQA Examiner's tip

You'll need to understand the numbers involved in setting up, financing and running a business. You're going to come across a few numbers during the course. Make sure you take the time to understand them. You don't need to be a mathematical genius, but if you're not confident with numbers spend *more* time not less trying to understand them.

We've established what enterprise is and what an entrepreneur is. How important is enterprise and entrepreneurial activity to the UK economy? Think of the most well-known businesses in the UK today; however large and successful they are, they almost all started as small businesses run by the kind of entrepreneurs featured in *Dragons' Den*.

How important are entrepreneurs to the UK economy?

Entrepreneurs starting up their own business, usually start small. So small businesses are important to the UK economy for the simple reason that they are the origins of the large successful businesses of the future.

A small business has been defined in many ways:

- The EU defines a small business as having fewer than 50 employees.
- The Companies Act 1985 defines a business as small as long as it meets at least 2 of these criteria:
    - The value of sales is less than £2.8 million.
    - The value of the balance sheet is less than £1.4 million.
    - There are fewer than 50 employees.

These definitions are not perfect. A business with very few employees and low sales could still be relatively large if the overall market is small; a 'big fish in a small pond'. Also, different industries typically have different sized businesses in them. A firm of 100 accountants would be viewed as large, whereas a manufacturing business with 100 employees is seen as small.

Activity

Large or small?

1. Look at the list of businesses below and decide which of the three possible measures of size provided might be the best one to use. There's no single right answer. Provide a justification for each choice of measure.

Table 1.1

Accountant	Country hotel
Electrical goods manufacturer	Website designer
National chain of newsagents	Doctor's surgery
Chain of fitness clubs	Plumber
Jewellery shop	Mobile hairdresser

The possible measures of success you could use are:

- Number of employees
- Value of sales
- Market share

2. For each business, describe another possible measure of size, other than those suggested above. Evaluate the best possible measure, or combination of measures, in each case.

AQA Examiner's tip

As with all measurements, think about the context. What's 'small' in one context, could be 'big' in another. Is a business with 15 employees and a £300,000 turnover big or small? It's a pretty big dental surgery, but a tiny manufacturing business.

What are the motives for becoming an entrepreneur?

There are a number of reasons why people start their own business:

- to escape an uninteresting job
- to pursue an interest or a hobby

■ Key terms

Opportunity cost: the cost of an activity expressed in terms of the next best alternative, which has to be given up when making a choice. For example, what could an entrepreneur do with their time, expertise and money if they didn't start a business?

Government grants: sums of money given to a business for a specific purpose or project. They often contribute to the costs of a project rather than fund the whole thing. Grants do not usually have to be paid back.

AQA Examiner's tip

It's worth spending time in the early stages of your course familiarising yourself with the small businesses in your area. The focus of Unit 1 of the AS is on small businesses. The more you can apply your learning to small businesses the better you will perform in the AS exams.

■ Activity

Research a small local business and consider the risks involved in setting up. What do you think are the rewards enjoyed by the owner of that business if it is successful? Consider the risks the owner is taking. How likely, in your view, is it that the business will be a success?

■ Activity

The Prince's Trust

Research The Prince's Trust and investigate the help that the Prince's Trust can give to young people wanting to start their own business. Produce a summary of the help available.

■ to exploit a gap in the market

■ to market a new or innovative product

■ to be innovative in terms of the process of making a product

■ to be their own boss, be creative and make decisions

■ to work from home and reduce travelling time

■ to have a second career

■ to provide a service or product not for profit

■ to have a big business one day!

Risk and reward and opportunity cost

If you ask a successful business person why they started in the first place, they will often quote some of the above reasons, but the most frequently quoted reason is the ability to make your own decisions. Entrepreneurs take risks, often using their own money. In return they expect a reward. That reward is likely to be partly financial, but it is also likely to include the non financial reward of the satisfaction of meeting customer needs and doing a good job. **Opportunity cost** is the cost of the next best alternative. What would an entrepreneur do with their time, expertise and money if they didn't start a business?

💡 Government support for enterprise and entrepreneurs

Small businesses are vulnerable in the early stages, and many fail. However, there are lots of sources of help and guidance for entrepreneurs from the Government and other sources.

Government grants come from a variety of sources, including central and local government, the European Union and organisations that specialise in encouraging business growth in particular areas of the country such as Regional Development Agencies in England, Scottish Enterprise, the Welsh Development Agency and Invest Northern Ireland. There are also some charitable organisations. Grants are often linked to a particular business sector or geographical area. They are usually awarded for one of the following purposes:

■ Innovation, Research and Development

■ Training

■ Economic regeneration

■ Encouraging young people to start their own business

In addition, entrepreneurs can get advice from a wide range of sources. Try typing 'help for small businesses' into your search engine and see how much information you get! Local Business Link websites provide lists of support for small businesses. Put 'Business Link' in your search engine for more information.

■ Case study

Small businesses in the UK

Small businesses, however you define them, play an important role in the UK economy. In 2006 it was estimated that there were over 2 million businesses in the UK. Look at the data below and answer the questions that follow.

Table 1.2 *The numbers of businesses of different sizes in various sectors*

Type of industry	Number of businesses				Total number of businesses in industry
	0–4 employees	5–9 employees	10–19 employees	20–49 employees	
Construction	159,925	21,635	10,970	6,595	202,625
Retail	166,430	62,450	28,835	13,180	278,040
Hotels and catering	75,570	32,295	22,790	13,510	151,625
Total all industries	1,391,960	317,745	178,820	120,870	
Total all businesses					2,084,495

www.statistics.gov.uk

Questions

1 What do you understand by the term 'small business'?

2 Calculate the percentage of construction businesses that could be classified as small.

3 From the data above, assess the importance of small businesses in the three sectors.

4 To what extent does the above data show that small businesses are the most important part of the UK economy?

Case study

Why small businesses are vital to the UK

The late Sir John Harvey-Jones, when he was Chairman of ICI, was convinced that new businesses are vital to the success of the UK.

The decline in manufacturing and the rise of the 'knowledge economy' means the UK must capitalise on its innovative, entrepreneurial economic history to build prosperity, according to Harvey-Jones. He believed successful small businesses represent the future for British industry.

'The need for new small businesses has never been higher, and they have every advantage over large ones. By operating in niche markets, often with little or no competition, they do not have to play catch up with foreign firms and are free to focus on a changing business climate. They can react immediately to new competitors and they know their customers and their employees in detail, and are in a better position to move quickly and decisively.'

'If you have a unique product, for example, you may only have a dozen sales a year, so it's not worth their development time and money. The advantage is that a small business person is close to customers and can continually develop the product.'

'A latecomer who sets up as a competitor will only be able to copy what is already in the market. Whereas you will have been working on development of the next version of your product. You will be the market leader.'

AQA Examiner's tip

Understanding numbers is crucial. Percentages are one of the most misunderstood aspects of business data. It's worth spending time making sure you understand how to calculate and how to understand percentages.

'Start-up companies tend to use other start-ups as suppliers – there is an understanding and shared experience. It is in both their interests that they are successful and this helps expand the start-up economy'.

'Considering the importance of finance, it is essential that you are mean when it comes to spending your money. Avoid employing people full-time in the early days and watch your overheads – don't rent premises, work from your spare room or garage. The golden rule is 'don't spend it until you've got it'.'

'You will never work so hard in your life – your business will take priority over everything, so you must enjoy what you are doing. The good news, is that there are few satisfactions in life better than running a successful business.'

www.startups.co.uk

Questions

1. What do you understand by the term 'knowledge economy'?

2. Research a real small business in your local area and explain the main advantages small businesses have over large ones.

3. Analyse the possible benefits to the UK economy of the small business sector.

4. To what extent do you agree with Sir John's claim that 'there are few satisfactions in life better than running a successful business.'

5. Research a successful small business in your area. Interview the owner to establish the reasons for starting up, the factors leading to success and the major threats. Assess the likely ultimate success of the business in a presentation to the class.

☑ *In this chapter you will have learned to:*

- distinguish between enterprise and entrepreneurs, and be able to provide examples of actual entrepreneurs. You might also be able to recognise examples of enterprising behaviour from your own life

- explain the main motives for becoming an entrepreneur, including notions of risk, reward and opportunity cost. Entrepreneurs are willing to take risks in return for a financial reward

- understand that most entrepreneurs gain much more than just a financial reward from running their own business

- understand the important role that small businesses play in the UK economy, in terms of employment and output. You will also understand that there are different measures of the size of a business

- describe the help that entrepreneurs can get from the Government and other agencies

- evaluate the potential benefits to the UK economy of the small business sector.

2 Generating and protecting business ideas

Setting the scene

The Pure Package

In 2003 Jennifer Irvine had a brilliant idea, but she felt she was the least likely person in the world to make it happen. 'I'm actually a shy, nervous person. I was too scared to approach banks.' But she felt the idea was too good not to have a go. 'I found the idea exciting, and spotted a gap in the market.'

Her brilliant idea was to provide healthy meals, designed specifically for each customer, direct to the home. It's been called a 'healthy meals on wheels' or a 'diet brought to your door.'

The Pure Package establishes the exact diet a customer wants based on information provided in an interview. A profile is built up about the customer based on height, weight, fitness, lifestyle and goals. The Pure Package then makes and delivers all the meals and snacks directly to the customer.

'It's a unique concept, but quite a basic concept, but not something that was ever done in this country before.'

Jennifer had very little money to start with, but she knew she had to find out whether her 'brilliant idea' had a chance of succeeding. She researched existing businesses such as Patak's, who also started small in their own kitchens to find out some of the problems associated with starting that way. She also went on basic Health and Safety courses because she knew she needed to know about Health and Safety when dealing with food.

Jennifer asked friends about the idea, and all of them were very positive about it, but she knew she couldn't just rely on their opinions. She needed other evidence, but she had very little money to spend on market research. It was then she had her next brilliant idea.

She contacted food writers and journalists, asking them to sample some of her food and give her feedback. With the samples she sent out detailed questions. She received lots of useful feedback and amended her recipes. An unexpected outcome of this was that some of the journalists began to write articles about her product in the newspapers, giving her lots of free publicity. As a consequence, orders began to come in, including some from celebrities and supermodels.

Discussion points

1. Explain the main reasons why Jennifer decided to start her business.

2. Discuss the strengths and weaknesses of her early decisions when starting up.

💡 Sources of business ideas

In Chapter 1 we considered the reasons for setting up a business. But how does the entrepreneur go about deciding what product or service to offer? An entrepreneur will often base the decision on his/her own experience, that is on a product or service he/she is familiar with either through a previous job or through a hobby or interest. Alternatively, the decision might be generated by a realisation that there is an unmet need in the market – a gap in the market. This second approach might occur after a brain storming session where possible ideas are considered. Both approaches have advantages and disadvantages.

Table 2.1 *Ways to identify a business opportunity*

Advantage	Benefits	Disadvantages
Knowing the product or service	Entrepreneur will have a good knowledge of the features of the product	Is there room for another competitor?
	Entrepreneur may have a passion or interest in the product so will be motivated to do well	The entrepreneur's passion for the product might not be shared by anyone else
	Good contacts in an established market	The entrepreneur's passion may overestimate the size of the potential market
	Entrepreneur may already have a good reputation in the market that he/she can use	Knowledge of the product or service is not the only skill needed – the person may not possess the other skills needed for successful entrepreneurship
Spotting a gap in the market	Entrepreneur is basing idea on the customer's needs rather than their own, which might improve the chances of success	Entrepreneur will have little or no expertise in the product/service or market – prone to mistakes
	More likely to enjoy 'first mover advantage' – the benefits of being first in the market	Is the gap real? Has someone tried to exploit it before and discovered why it can't be done?
	Little or no competition in the early stages when a business start-up is most vulnerable	Competition may enter quickly and capture market share – how long can 'first mover advantage' last?
	Easier to market a new idea than to persuade people to buy an established idea from one business rather than another?	

A combination of the above approaches is often successful, where an entrepreneur starts a business in a market with which he/she is familiar, but in a unique way that has not been done before. This has the benefit of combining good knowledge with a differentiated approach.

Whichever way an entrepreneur decides upon the initial idea, he/she will need to carry out some initial small budget research. The main ways to do this are:

- Use business directories such as the Yellow Pages, Thomsons Local and the telephone directory.
- Use local maps to locate existing competition and identify gaps in provision.
- Use local and national demographic data to establish potential market features.
- Use small-scale research such as questionnaires or interviews.
- Use market mapping to identify market segments.

AQA Examiner's tip

When considering ways an entrepreneur might come up with an initial idea, always remember the limited resources s/he is likely to have, both in terms of money and time. Most base their initial ideas on something they already know. Often, s/he may still be working full time whilst initially researching the business idea.

Case study

The Pure Package idea

Jennifer Irvine's idea was a combination of her own interest and passion for healthy food and a realisation that no one was providing this service in quite this way. In an interview she gave to the smallbizpod website in August 2007 she admitted that at the start she did not have any money for market research, but tried to make the most of what little information she had about the market.

'I tried to find out about what competition, if any, there was out there, but I didn't know how to do it. Also, I couldn't afford to spend money researching customer tastes, so I used my friends. I cooked lots of recipes and asked them what they thought about the meals. They all gave very positive feedback, so I decided to go for it.'

Jennifer quickly realised that she needed more accurate market information when initial sales were disappointing. A friend suggested she contacted journalists and asked them for feedback. 'I wrote to loads of journalists and offered them free food. In return, they agreed to fill in a detailed questionnaire from which I got really useful feedback, not all positive! As a result I was able to change the product before launching it again. In addition, a few journalists wrote newspaper or magazine articles about the company, which gave us lots of free publicity. As a result, a few celebrities got in touch and wanted to try the product.'

www.smallbizpod.co.uk

Questions

1. Suggest additional ways Jennifer could have researched the existing competition before deciding whether the idea had potential to be a success.

2. Explain how Jennifer researched whether the idea might be a success in the early stages of the product.

3. Complete a spider diagram to illustrate the strengths and weaknesses of Jennifer's initial idea.

4. Discuss the limitations of small-scale research for Jennifer's business.

💡 Franchises

Some entrepreneurs start a business by buying a **franchise**. This is a a business structure in which the owner of a business idea (the franchisor) sells the right to use that idea to another person (the franchisee), usually in return for a fee and a share in any profit the franchisee makes.

■ Protecting business ideas

An entrepreneur will want to protect an idea in order to recover the costs of bringing that idea to the market. Businesses often protect their products, processes and images through **copyrights**, **patents** and **trademarks**. If a business has spent time building a brand, or money researching a product, then the entrepreneur will want to make sure there is a return on that investment. In fact, the existence of this kind of protection means that businesses are more willing to invest because they know their efforts will be protected long enough to recover some of the money invested.

AQA Examiner's tip

In Unit 1 the focus is on small businesses with limited resources. If you get asked a question about market research in the early stages of a business start-up remember to be realistic about the kind of research that can be afforded. Small scale research is not perfect, but it is better than none at all, and it is often all that an entrepreneur can afford in the early stages of a start-up.

Key terms

Franchise: a franchise is only one of a number of types of business structure.

Copyright: the protection given to books, plays, films and music.

Patent: an exclusive right to use a process or produce a product, usually for a fixed period of time, up to 20 years.

Trademark: a word, image, sound or smell that enables a business to differentiate itself from its competitors.

Table 2.2 *Advantages and disadvantages of a franchise to the franchisor*

Benefits to franchisor	Disadvantages to franchisor
Franchisor can expand business quickly	Potential loss of control over how the product/service is presented to the customers
Often, franchisor earns revenue from the franchisees' turnover rather than profit – so revenue is reasonably certain	May be difficult to control quality as franchise network expands
Risk is shared – much of the cost is met by the franchisee	Coordination and communication problems may increase as franchise network grows
Franchisee may have very good entrepreneurial skills, which will earn the franchisor revenue	Some franchisees become powerful as they acquire a number of franchises

Table 2.3 *Advantages and disadvantages of a franchise to the franchisee*

Benefits to franchisee	Disadvantages to franchisee
Able to sell an already recognised and successful product/service	Proportion of revenue is paid to franchisor
Take advantage of central services such as marketing, purchasing, training, stock control and accounting systems and administration provided by franchisor	Franchisee may not feel that business is his/her own, and may not benefit from the personal rewards of entrepreneurship
Franchisor may have experience in the market that the franchisee can benefit from	Right to operate the franchise could be withdrawn

■ Activity

Investigate how many well-known high street businesses are in fact franchise networks – you'll be surprised. Also, research the British Franchise Association on the internet for more information on franchises.

■ Case study

Dyson wins Hoover case

In 2000, the domestic appliance giant Hoover suffered a humiliating defeat by rival Dyson in the High Court.

The court ruled that Hoover copied Dyson's designs in the manufacture of its Vortex bagless cleaner range. Sales of the Vortex range could have been suspended as a result of the ruling and Hoover may have had to radically alter the design or cease production altogether. Commenting on the case, victorious company founder James Dyson, told BBC News 24: 'Why on earth don't they (Hoover) think of their own ideas instead of copying ours.'

Hoover has a history of bitter rivalry with Dyson, which has revolutionised the vacuum cleaner market with its 'dual cyclone' design.

In 1990, a quarter of all vacuum cleaners sold in the UK were made by Hoover, but in 2000 it had less than 10% of the market, according to industry estimates. More than half of the vacuum cleaners sold in the UK are made by Dyson.

www.news.bbc.co.uk

Questions

1 Consider the benefits to James Dyson of the protection that a patent gave his business.

2 To what extent does a patent give a business such as Dyson an unfair advantage over competition?

 Examiner's tip

Make sure you understand the difference between a patent, trademark and copyright. A patent protects a product or process; a trademark is an image or other representation of a commercial idea, whilst copyright protects a piece of creative work such as a song or book.

Case study

Domino's Pizza

Have you ever wondered why there are three dots in the Domino's Pizza logo? It's because when the company first started in the US, the original owner set himself the objective of owning three pizza delivery stores. Considering Domino's Pizza now has 8,000 stores in 50 countries, that seems a modest dream. Domino's has achieved rapid growth in the UK recently and predictions are this will continue. One reason for Domino's rapid growth is the fact that most of the branches are franchises. The right to set up a Domino's Pizza outlet in the UK is owned exclusively by Domino's Pizza UK and Ireland plc. This company sells franchises to individuals who operate Domino's outlets as separate businesses. There are about 400 Domino's Pizza franchises operating in the UK and the company has a target of 1,000 UK outlets by 2015.

Fig. 2.1 *Domino's Pizza logo*

In order to take advantage of market growth, Domino's needs more franchises. But it has to decide whether to allow existing franchisees to open up the new stores or invite new people to start them up. Existing franchisees are less risky, as they are already successful in selling the brand. They know the systems and are better able to maintain quality levels. New franchisees are more likely to fail, as they have to learn the systems and might struggle initially to achieve the efficiency and high quality of established franchises. However, they might generate a greater increase in profits if successful because they might be more entrepreneurial.

There are potential constraints on Domino's UK growth. There are concerns that a rapidly growing franchise network might be more difficult to control from the centre, especially as some of the franchises are themselves growing into large businesses.

Domino's is confident of its future growth potential. The UK pizza market as a whole grew by 60 per cent in the last five years and is set to double by 2010. With a 20 per cent market share Domino's position looks unbeatable, and the target of 1,000 outlets in the UK by 2015 looks achievable. 'We are confident that the company's growth is sustainable into the long-term. We're not even close to the end of the opportunities in this market', said Domino's Chief Executive Stephen Helmsley recently.

Questions

1. Describe the benefits to a franchisee of operating a Domino's Pizza franchise.

2. Calculate the percentage increase in Domino's Pizza outlets if the company is to meet its 2015 target.

3. Analyse the potential problems Domino's might face with managing its existing franchise network.

4. Discuss whether Domino's should expand its network by selling to existing or new franchisees.

☑ *In this chapter you will have learned to:*

- understand how entrepreneurs generate new business ideas, often relying on their own experience or brain storming in order to identify gaps in the market. Most entrepreneurs do not have much money at the start, so their options are limited

- understand how entrepreneurs identify and exploit a market niche through small-scale research

- appreciate how limited the resources of a small business are initially, and how difficult it is to spend large amounts of money on research

- analyse the role of patents, copyrights and trademarks in protecting new business ideas and understand the crucial role that these methods of protecting ideas are because they enable an entrepreneur to recover the money invested in the new product, service or process

- evaluate the benefits and disadvantages of franchises and be able to judge whether a franchise is the right structure for a given business situation.

3 Transforming resources into goods and services

Key terms

Input: something that contributes to the production of a product or service.

Output: something that occurs as a result of the transformation of business inputs.

AQA Examiner's tip

The idea of transforming inputs to produce an output is as relevant to services as it is to products. In the exam you may face a service sector business, but remember there is still a process of transforming inputs such as people's time, expertise, skills and experience to providing that service. Added value is as much a feature of a haircut as it is of a car.

Setting the scene

The Royal Oak

Pierre Cordin bought the Royal Oak pub to add to the three he already owned. He was the Managing Director of The Suffolk Pub Company, a business he started three years ago with the intention of providing a real alternative to the pubs owned by the larger breweries. He wanted to provide a restaurant quality menu in a pub environment. He researched each location carefully, choosing only those with a relatively high income earning local population.

Premium beers and lagers, good quality wine (including English wine which was growing in reputation) were on offer as well as food cooked by renowned chefs lured from London with the promise of high wages and a share in the profits. The first two had been very successful. He had learned that the more you add to the experience, beyond just the food, the more people wanted to visit, and the more they were willing to pay. When he trained as a chef, he had done a business course as well, and he had remembered the bit about adding value to his product.

Discussion points

1 Is a meal in a pub or restaurant a product or a service?

2 In what ways can you add value to a meal out?

Business inputs and outputs

In the chapters so far, you have looked at the ways in which entrepreneurs turn ideas into businesses. In this chapter you will learn how the various factors that go to make a product or service are combined successfully to add value and meet customer needs.

At its simplest, a business is a process whereby **inputs** are processed to produce **outputs**.

Business activity tends to be classified in terms of whether it is primary, secondary, tertiary or quaternary.

Primary production is the extraction of resources at the first stage of production, involving resources such as land and raw materials. Farming is the obvious example.

Secondary production is the transformation of resources to produce finished goods and components. Car manufacture is an example.

Tertiary production is the transformation of resources to provide a service, which is why it is sometimes referred to as the service sector. It includes retailing, which is the selling of products from the primary and secondary sectors.

Other examples of tertiary activity include the public services such as health care and education, transport, tourism and finance. It also includes those activities which recently have proven to be in such short supply such as plumbers, electricians and builders. The biggest growth

Fig. 3.1 *Car manufacture is an example of secondary production*

area in tertiary production is in business and financial services, where it is estimated that 1 in 5 people now work.

Quaternary production is the name given to industries whose main purpose is the transformation of information.

IT-based businesses are included in this definition, as are consultancy and Research and Development businesses. This sector continues to grow as the 'knowledge economy' becomes more important. The tertiary and quaternary sectors are sometimes referred to together, as they are both service based. They are by far the most important parts of the UK economy, accounting for about 75 per cent of total employment.

The changing importance of different sectors of business activity

It is tempting to assume that this process of transformation only takes place in the secondary sector of the economy, but as the primary and secondary sectors of advanced economies such as the UK decline, and tertiary and quaternary sectors expand, it is important to understand that the process of transformation of inputs to produce outputs is just as relevant for a service or an information based business as it is for a farm or a factory.

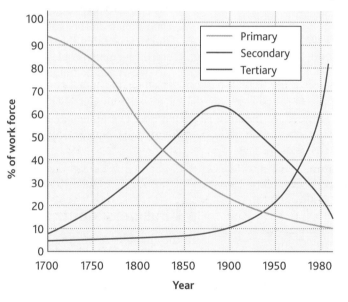

Fig. 3.2 *Primary, secondary and tertiary output adapted from www.bbc.co.uk*

Consider the data above, which shows clearly the change in significance of the various sectors.

It is becoming more difficult to provide precise definitions of each sector for two main reasons. Firstly, the significance of the sectors changes over time as economies evolve. Secondly, and more importantly, it is becoming increasingly difficult to classify individual businesses as they expand and innovate their product range to become successful. For example, it used to be easy to classify a farm as primary. But more and more farms have holiday accommodation or farm shops or activity centres attached. Some make local products such as wine or cider. Does that make them primary, secondary or tertiary, or a bit of all three! The innovation of entrepreneurs is making classifications such as this increasingly inaccurate.

Inputs include the raw materials, which are the basic 'ingredients' that go to make up a product or service. These will include component parts, semi assembled parts, energy, labour. But for service based businesses it will also include expertise, skills and information.

The processes are those activities that transform the raw materials. Some examples are included in the activity below.

The outputs are the finished product, service or other benefit to the customer. Other outputs that are becoming increasingly recognised are waste and pollution.

Adding value

Added value is the value of the process of transformation of inputs into outputs. It is measured by the difference in value between the price of the finished product or service and the cost of the raw materials. When a business adds value, the value of the finished product is greater than the sum of the values of all the inputs.

It can be represented with a diagram:

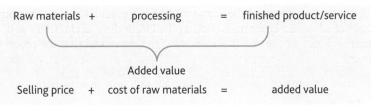

Fig. 3.3 *Adding value to a product*

Businesses add value in a number of ways: For example:

- Advertising – creates interest in a product or service and may convince a customer to pay a higher price, thereby increasing the added value.
- Branding – achieves a similar outcome because customers are often willing to pay more for a branded item than a non-branded one, even if the actual physical process of transformation is the same.
- Product features – often add value, particularly if the customer feels they improve the benefits. For example, the ability to take photos, play music and watch films on a mobile phone are not essential to its basic purpose, but they enable the business to charge a higher price for the phone or the network.
- Location – may enable a business to add value, for instance if the location is seen as particularly desirable.
- Personal service – allows a business to differentiate its product or service.

There are a number of benefits to businesses of adding value:

- Differentiation from the competition – customers might be more willing to choose a particular brand over its rivals.
- Charging a higher price.
- Reducing the sensitivity of demand to changes in price.
- Higher profit margins.
- Targeting product or service at a different market segment.

Case study

Penelope's

Penny and James hit on their idea for Penelope's after their daughter's prom night. They'd heard about limo services that take people to events and then bring them back again, but had been disappointed to find none existed in their area. Also, they had experienced a bad example of one themselves where they were made

Key terms

Added value: the difference in value between the price of the finished product and the cost of materials used.

Activity

Some examples of adding value

Consider the following businesses and try to identify the process of transformation of inputs that adds value to the finished product or service. Make a list of each raw material, then briefly describe the transformational process that takes place.

1. A themed hotel
2. A wedding cake manufacturer
3. A hand-built sports car manufacturer
4. A real ale brewery
5. A tax consultant
6. An author of children's books

AQA Examiner's tip

Consider the relationship between the changes in business sectors and added value. As the UK economy moves away from agriculture and low cost manufacturing and towards services and niche manufacturing, the ability to add value increases. In farming, it is often much easier to add value (and therefore make more profit) from selling holiday accommodation on the farm than farming the land.

to feel lucky to be in the car and that they should be grateful to ride in the back of a (not very well looked after) Rolls Royce.

Penny was convinced that a market existed for a genuinely top quality service involving a chauffeur-driven limousine. 'What we need to focus on is not the transport bit of the product, but everything else. A limo is just a posh taxi unless you do other things to make it special.' James was not convinced at first, worried that it wasn't possible to offer anything but a posh taxi ride.

'Think of all the things you could do to make that journey even more special!' said Penny. 'You mean like champagne on the way there?' said James. 'Obviously not if you're taking students to their Year 11 prom!' warned Penny, 'but if your customers are a couple celebrating a wedding anniversary then that would be a great idea'.

They sat down and tried to think of ways they could add to the value of the experience of a limo ride. At the same time, it became clear to James that their potential market could be broken down into different segments, so they first of all identified the potential segment, then tried to think of ways to add value for that type of customer.

1 Wedding anniversary/romantic occasion.

2 Young person's event such as a prom.

3 Business event.

Questions

1 Describe the small-scale research that Penny and James might have done to establish existing competition in the market.

2 Explain which sector of business activity Penelope's is in

3 Analyse three ways Penelope's could add value to each of the market segments.

4 Research other market segments to discover ways in which they could add value to their service.

5 To what extent is it always easier to add value to a product than a service? Use other real business examples to illustrate your answer.

☑ *In this chapter you will have learned to:*

■ understand how a business transforms inputs into outputs when making products or providing services, and appreciate that a service is as much a transformation of resources as a product

■ explain the primary/secondary/tertiary/quaternary classification of business activity and apply it to different businesses

■ understand also that these classifications evolve over time as the economy changes; with primary and secondary production declining and tertiary and quaternary production expanding

■ understand added value and how it arises in products and services and you'll begin to understand the relationship between added value and service sector activity

■ analyse the benefits of adding value in terms of a business's ability to differentiate itself from competition and its ability to generate profit.

Summary questions

Chapters 1–3

1   What do you understand by the term enterprise?   *(2 marks)*

2   List three likely characteristics of a successful entrepreneur.   *(3 marks)*

3   Analyse three possible benefits to the UK economy of a thriving small
    business sector.   *(8 marks)*

4   Describe three possible ways to measure the size of a business in the
    supermarket industry.   *(4 marks)*

5   Describe two possible sources of advice and help available to a young person
    starting a mobile catering business.   *(4 marks)*

6   What do you understand by the term opportunity cost?   *(3 marks)*

7   Distinguish between patents, trademarks and copyrights.   *(6 marks)*

8   Louise Murray imports jewellery from India and China and sells it in her West
    London shop and via her website. She has been in business for three years and
    has struggled to grow after an initial period of success. She decided to start this
    type of business because she was aware that a number of similar businesses in
    London had been successful and she was convinced there was room for more
    competition.
    a)   Evaluate the advantages and disadvantages of Louise starting a
            business in an existing market rather than attempting to meet the
            needs of a new market.   *(8 marks)*
    b)   Analyse three possible benefits to Louise who wishes to expand
            throughout the north of England, of franchising the business.   *(6 marks)*

9   Define the term 'value added'.   *(3 marks)*

10 Analyse three possible benefits of adding value to a restaurant specialising
    in sea food.   *(6 marks)*

11 Describe two ways that a restaurant specialising in sea food could increase
    its added value.   *(4 marks)*

12 Is a restaurant that specialises in sea food a primary, secondary or tertiary
    business? Explain your answer.   *(4 marks)*

13 Based near Chichester in West Sussex, East Head Ltd is a designer and
    manufacturer of a variety of safety helmets for surfers and windsurfers. The owner
    Paul Bradley said "I designed and made the first helmet for myself and when I
    asked around my friends who are also surfers, they all said they thought it was a
    great idea. I began selling initially just to friends, then word spread. Soon I couldn't

make them quick enough to meet demand. I didn't do any research to discover if there was a demand out there, I just got started and it grew.

I also was worried my design might be copied by other businesses, but I wasn't sure how to go about protecting my invention. I also needed to take on staff, which meant the company needed investment. An advisor from Business Link suggested I look for support from government or other agencies to help me in the first few months of trading.

My objective is to open up outlets in many of the main surfing and watersport areas in the UK within the next five years. I'm only 25 years old, and I expect to have a nationwide network of outlets before I'm thirty."

a)	Describe the main reasons why Paul decided to start his own business.	*(3 marks)*
b)	Is East Head Ltd in the primary, secondary or tertiary sector of business? Explain your answer.	*(3 marks)*
c)	Describe three possible sources of help and advice Paul could have sought in the early stages of the business.	*(6 marks)*
d)	Analyse the possible benefits to East Head Ltd of patenting its designs.	*(3 marks)*
e)	To what extent would Paul's future objectives be guaranteed by the franchising of East Head?	*(10 marks)*

4 Developing business plans

AQA Examiner's tip

Many people assume a business plan is something done for the bank manager or other lender. Whilst this is true sometimes, that is not the only purpose. If you are asked an exam question on business planning, remember the other benefits of planning, both at the start of the business, but also as the business is trading.

Setting the scene

AKC Home Support Services

Darren Jones launched his care business, AKC Home Support Services, in 1991 with his wife Sharron. Although writing their business plan was one of the first things the couple did, Darren admits he originally saw it as a bit of a chore. Now, he takes a different view, believing it has helped the business stay on track and true to its goals.

'When we started the firm I knew we needed a business plan but saw it more as a document for everyone else than something to help us. If I started another business tomorrow I would write one much more willingly as it brings a number of benefits – from helping you secure finance to keeping you focused on your goals. We got help from our local enterprise centre, looked at examples from other businesses and a template from the bank. We mixed and matched bits from these sources because not everything applied to us. For example, because we were going into a new market we couldn't write about our competitors but needed a lot of information about the market for care services.'

'We used our business plan to set out the financial and strategic goals we wanted to achieve in the short and long-term. We review it annually now unless there's a significant shift in our market and then we use it to immediately re-evaluate our goals. Our business plan has also helped us to avoid expanding too quickly. Early on, we were offered work in another county. This seemed great but when we looked at our business plan – and particularly our cashflow forecasts – we realised it was important to establish a firm base in one county before taking on work in another otherwise we would overstretch ourselves.'

'We purchased a residential unit four years ago and our business plan definitely helped us demonstrate why the bank should lend us the money. Without it being put down on paper I don't think it would have sounded like a very viable suggestion.'

'Our plan also helped us to get support from Shell LiveWire – the organisation that assists 16–30 year olds to start and develop businesses – as you must have a business plan to enter its competitions. We were awarded prizes twice – not only bringing in extra money but publicity too.'

www.businesslink.gov.uk

Discussion points

1 What appeared to be the main benefits to AKC of having a business plan at the start of the business?

2 What appear to be the main benefits of the business plan during the later stages of the business, as it grows?

■ Link

For more information on venture capitalists and business angels, see Chapter 8 – Raising finance, page 55.

Activity

Consider how much more successful most activities are when they are planned. The initial idea will probably be mapped out, and the plan might continue to be useful as you carry out your activity.

Often, the best way to decide whether you've been successful in something is to look back on what it was you initially set out to do. A business plan fulfils all these functions.

💡 What is a business plan?

A business plan is a document designed to allow a business to plan for the future, allocate resources, identify key decisions and prepare for problems and opportunities. It is particularly useful for business start-ups, but is also useful for applying for finance and for planning for growth.

A business plan has a number of purposes. It helps to plan for the future because it requires the entrepreneur to think carefully about the business, and commit all the main information and ideas to paper. The entrepreneur will therefore understand the business better and the market in which it operates. It will enable the entrepreneur to identify the main courses of action needed to start and run the business, and to set objectives against which the performance of the business can be measured.

A business plan allows an entrepreneur to present a request for extra funding. In the early stages of a business it is likely that money will be in short supply, so often entrepreneurs will need additional funding. A business plan will provide all the information a potential lender or investor will need to decide whether they wish to invest. Banks, venture capitalists and business angels all require detailed information before they make a decision.

Even after the business is up and running, a business plan continues to be an essential planning tool. It will provide a regular check on progress regarding things such as cash flow, objectives and financial forecasts.

The contents of a business plan

There is no single format for business plans, because they differ according to the type and size of business, the expertise of the entrepreneur and the precise purpose of the business plan, but a number of key elements are present in most business plans.

Executive summary: This is a summary of the main features of the business. It will be one or two pages in length and is often the most important part of your business plan. It is the first part that people see, and often it is the only part they will read! It should include highlights from each section of the rest of the plan and it is intended to explain the basics of the business in an interesting and informative way.

Business description: This is a description of the history of the business, its start-up plans, the type of business structure it has. It will tend to include:

■ start date (for new businesses) or how long the business has been trading, its history and any previous owners (for established businesses)
■ the type of business and sector of the market
■ the legal structure – is it a sole trader, partnership or limited company?
■ the entrepreneur's vision for the business.

Product or service: This is a description of the product or service being sold, its key features and how the customer will benefit. This will include:

■ what makes it different from the competition
■ what benefits the customers will gain

- plans for the further development of the product/service
- information on any copyrights, designs or trademarks.

Market analysis: This is an analysis of the market and competition. It also will include an analysis of the customers' needs, where they are, how to reach them and how the product or service meets the needs. This section will include:

- the market – data about the size and growth of the market as a whole
- the customer – the key features including who they are and where they are
- the competition – who they are, their strengths and weaknesses
- the future – how might the market change in the future and how can the business respond.

Strategy and implementation: This is an analysis of the key decisions and strategies that need to be carried out, together with who is responsible for carrying them out, when they have to do it by, and the money they have to do it with. The most important element here will be the marketing and sales strategies, which will include information on:

- pricing
- promotion
- sales strategies.

Production strategies might include:

- location – is it owned or rented, what are its advantages and disadvantages?
- production – are they owned or leased, how old are they, what is the capacity in relation to forecast demand?
- systems – stock control, quality control and financial management, IT.

Management team: This is a description of the key members of the business, together with their skills and experience. This section is also likely to include data on the number of employees, how the business is structured and salaries.

Financial plan: This will include a number of key financial documents such as the profit and loss account, cash flow forecast, balance sheet, break-even analysis. It might include some key financial ratios, as well any assumptions the business has made in putting its financial forecasts together.

Sources of help and guidance for business planning

Entrepreneurs can get a lot of help in the early stages of their business start-ups, particularly in writing a business plan. Some provide guidance on what to include, others provide templates that entrepreneurs can fill in with their own details.

Small business advisors

There is a wide range of help for small businesses. One example is Business Link, which provides detailed advice on the contents of a plan, templates, examples of completed business plans, as well as case studies of how small businesses have constructed and used business plans.

AQA Examiner's tip

Rather than try to memorise the precise contents of a business plan, have a look at a number of different ones and get an overall picture of the kinds of things that seem to appear. It's much better to understand **why** lenders and other interested parties would be interested in the information than it is to remember a precise format. If you understand the purpose and audience of business plans, you'll much more likely be able to recall the main contents.

Fig. 4.1 *Bytestart is one example of a source of help for business planning*

Accountants and bank managers

Most of the main high street banks offer a small business service, which includes advice about how to write and present a business plan. For example, Barclays Bank offer a small business advice service, a range of guides, in hard copy or on CD-ROM, a Local Business Manager, as well as a range of small business seminars.

Government agencies

The Government sees small business success as a key feature of a healthy economy. For example, the Department for Business, Enterprise and Regulatory Reform website describes its mission as being

> *to create the conditions for business success through competitive and flexible markets that create value for businesses, consumers and employees.*

www.businesslink.gov.uk

The Department offers a range of help and guidance, including a Business Plan competition, which provides the winners with £25,000 to help start-up a business.

There are Government grants available also to small businesses to help them set up and write their business plans.

Resources needed to create a business plan

It seems clear therefore, that a business plan is an essential planning tool for new business. So what does it take to draw up a good business plan?

Time – this is not an unlimited or free resource. Many entrepreneurs begin thinking about their new business venture while they are still in employment in their old jobs, or are still at home looking after their children. It is a time consuming activity, and the more time taken, the better the plan is likely to be.

Determination – an entrepreneur needs to remain determined to complete the plan accurately and fully, even if it proves difficult.

Vision – the entrepreneur needs a clear idea of the business and its USP.

Numbers – an entrepreneur cannot avoid financial information, and can't afford to be afraid of numbers.

Planning – this is a skill in itself, the ability to be organised and to plan a number of activities at once.

Problems for small business planning

Despite the benefits for a small business of a business plan, there are potential problems.

- Time – an entrepreneur may not feel he/she has the time to devote to putting together a business plan. This might be true if the entrepreneur wants to start trading as quickly as possible, perhaps because he/she is excited about the product, or just wants to get going.
- Money – although not expensive, a business plan costs some money, even if it is just in terms of the entrepreneur's own time. Any advice about planning might cost money.
- Expertise – an entrepreneur may not know enough about the product/ service or market initially to be able to construct a business plan

Link

For more information on Government support for enterprise and entrepreneurs, see Chapter 1 – Enterprise, page 4.

accurately. For instance, the financial elements of the plan require some forecasts about sales, which the entrepreneur may not know.

■ Opportunity cost – some people may feel that the time spent on a business plan is 'wasted' when it could be spent actually trading.

■ On balance, most people would agree that a business plan is worth the time and resources it takes to put it together. It might depend on the circumstances the entrepreneur is in. For instance, someone with a clear idea of the market and good existing knowledge of the product and no need of extra finance may decide a plan is less important than someone moving into a new area or needing financial support from a bank, venture capitalist or business angel.

■ Case study

The Old Railway Station Hotel

Six months ago Barry Morgan and his brother James bought the Old Railway Station Hotel near York from the previous owner who had spent large sums of money converting it from a dilapidated railway station on an abandoned line into a small, luxury hotel. The previous owner had converted the station building itself into the reception, restaurant and bar, whilst a number of carriages had been converted into hotel rooms. The conversion had taken six months, and expectations had been high that it would be a success. Indeed, the first three months trading had been healthy, but soon the bookings declined and the business struggled to meet its high costs.

The main problem seemed to be the very high costs of converting the property, which meant that the hotel needed a high level of sales to meet the loan repayments from the bank. James calculated that they needed an alternative source of finance that would not commit them to such high, regular interest payments. He estimated they needed £175,000 to reduce the debts of the business.

When the Morgans took over they were convinced that this could be a successful business if they could run it efficiently. Barry was convinced the concept was potentially attractive to customers, many of whom were foreign tourists drawn to the historical city of York.

James analysed the accounts for the first three months of trading under the previous owners and was shocked to find out that they had done very little investigation of the market. They had carried out no small budget research, and had set prices based on their previous experience of running a London hotel.

Questions

1 Suggest two possible types of small budget research that Barry and James might find useful in analysing the market.

2 Assess the benefits to Barry and James of approaching a business angel for the £175,000.

3 Analyse the likely information that Barry and James would need to include in their Business Plan.

4 To what extent would a business plan guarantee the success of The Old Railway Station Hotel?

✔️ *In this chapter you will have learned to:*

- understand the purposes of a business plan and its value to small businesses, both before trading, but also as a useful analytical tool as the business is trading

- appreciate that a plan allows an entrepreneur to decide where he or she wants to go with the business, and assess whether he/she is getting there

- explain the sources of information that are needed to construct a business plan, and the various sources of help and guidance that a small business can call upon. You'll understand that a range of government, bank and other agencies are willing to help business start-ups

- explain the time and skills needed to construct a business plan and appreciate why on occasion, entrepreneurs choose not to do a business plan. You'll understand that in the vast majority of cases, this is not a good idea

- evaluate the benefits of a business plan for small business start-ups in particular situations.

Conducting start-up market research

Link

For more information on how many entrepreneurs start up a business based on a hobby or interest, see Chapter 2 – Generating and protecting business ideas, page 10.

Key terms

Primary market research data: data collected by the entrepreneur, or paid to be collected, which does not already exist.

Secondary market research data: data already in existence that has not been collected specifically for the purposes of the entrepreneur.

Setting the scene

Star Financial Services

Jeremy and Jenny Bellinger had quit their well paid jobs in banking to start their own financial consultancy business. They were both convinced that their home town of Bedford could provide sufficient customers who needed advice on pensions, investments, savings and insurance. They had asked a number of friends and family and all had been very positive.

Jeremy had spent a useful morning looking through the phonebook for existing businesses in the same market and had only found a few. All of them were large, well-known high street names. Jeremy and Jenny believed there was a gap in the market for a small business giving personal financial advice.

Jenny agreed, but was nervous about going to the bank for a start-up loan without more evidence that their hunch was right. She had sat in too many meetings as a Small Business Adviser when she worked in a bank listening to poorly researched ideas. She knew the bank wanted evidence of a market, not a hunch there might be one.

Discussion points

1. What evidence could Jenny and Jeremy collect to support their request to the bank?

2. What limiting factors exist for Jenny and Jeremy preventing them from obtaining accurate information about the potential market?

Start-up market research

The benefits of setting up a business based on a hobby or interest include a passion for the product and knowledge of it. However, this can also be a disadvantage if the entrepreneur just assumes that his/her interest will automatically be shared by others. Entrepreneurs, and those looking carefully at the business plan to decide whether to invest in the new business start-up, will need evidence that there is likely to be a demand for the product or service. The problem that entrepreneurs face is that gathering this evidence can be costly, and money is often in very short supply at the start of the business. So the entrepreneur is often trying to balance the need to gather data about the market with the need to keep costs as low as possible. This chapter looks at the methods of market research that a small business start-up might reasonably hope to afford.

The first decision an entrepreneur faces is whether to use data that already exists – **secondary market research data** – or to collect data specifically for the purposes of the business start-up – **primary market research data**. Each has its own benefits and drawbacks. Often, the most successful strategy is to combine some secondary research, with a small amount of carefully collected primary research.

There is no perfect source of information or method of collecting data, but overall, some data is better than none at all.

AQA Examiner's tip

It is worth remembering that any question you get on this topic will be in the context of a small business start-up. The entrepreneur is likely to have very limited resources in terms of finance, time or skills. Be realistic in any suggestions you make about the kind of research an entrepreneur in that situation could carry out. Think small.

Fig. 5.1 *Yell.com is a useful source of secondary market research data*

Secondary market research data

An existing business may have lots of useful data internally that it could use, such as sales figures, stock records, geographical analysis of sales, financial records, reports from sales staff about customer opinions and even customer complaints! These can be very useful in analysing the performance of the business. However, the entrepreneur attempting a business start-up has no such data. There are many examples of sources of secondary market research that an entrepreneur might use for a small business start-up. Some will assist the entrepreneur to understand the market itself. These include:

- Many entrepreneurs forget to use the most obvious source of information about their local market: the listings of businesses in the BT phone book, Thomson Local or Yellow Pages.
- Trade Associations – most industries have an organisation which exists to advise and assist the businesses in it.
- The Chartered Institute of Marketing has a marketing library.
- Chambers of Commerce.
- Enterprise Agencies.
- Business link (government organisation providing advice and support to start, maintain and grow a business).
- The trade press – most industries have their own magazines and newspapers. These will include articles on the latest trends in the market, useful contacts and information about suppliers.
- Source reference materials such as surveys and directories. The Institute of Directors website at www.iod.com has a useful directory, as does www.is4profit.com/business-directory.html.
- Competition – competitors will issue brochures, price lists, special offers, product details. All of this is valuable information.

Other sources of secondary research to help understand the economy, and the demographics of the country or region include:

- Government publications such as the National Statistics online at www.statistics.gov.uk and the Department for Business Enterprise and Regulatory Reform at www.statistics.gov.uk. Also, there is information provided by the EU through Eurostat at www.epp.eurostat.cec.eu.int.
- If the entrepreneur is willing and able to spend some money purchasing secondary research, there are companies that specialise in collecting and analysing market information. Some well-known ones include Mintel (www.mintel.com), Dun and Bradstreet (www.dbuk.dnb.com) and Verdict (www.verdict.co.uk). These tend to be quite expensive, although they are detailed, so will tend only to be used by established businesses or entrepreneurs with money to spend (perhaps those that have a business angel or Dragon to invest in their business!)

Activity

Secondary research

There exists a lot of possible sources of market research data, and the internet has made this much more accessible. Included in this chapter is a range of possible sources. Use these, and any others you feel are appropriate to analyse a market of your choice in order to assess whether a new product or service could be successful. This could be done as part of a Young Enterprise company.

Primary market research data

If an entrepreneur wants detailed, precise information about the market, it is often necessary to collect it specifically for that purpose. This is primary market research data.

Business start-up entrepreneurs may not be able to afford to pay someone to collect primary research, so may have to do it themselves. A number of decisions need to be made by the entrepreneur when deciding on collecting primary research.

Sampling methods

Who shall I collect information from?

Ideally, the answer to this question is **everyone**. However, it is likely the entrepreneur does not have the resources or time or skills to research everyone so a choice has to be made to select a proportion of those that could be researched. This means sampling. The sample size is important, because the smaller the size of the sample the less confident, generally, an entrepreneur can be about its accuracy.

A **random sample** does not mean haphazard. It takes a lot of thought and care to get a truly random sample. Asking people in the street on a Thursday afternoon in a town centre is not going to get a random sample, because many people will not be able to be in town at that time. Computers are increasingly used to generate randomly chosen lists of people.

A **quota sample** is one in which the characteristics of the market as a whole are mirrored in the sample. For instance, a researcher might be given targets to ask 50 males between 20 and 29 years of age, 30 females between 30 and 39 years of age. Once the researcher has reached that number no more are asked. It can be cheaper to do however, and accurate if the entrepreneur knows about the key characteristics of the potential market. A quota sample can be collected on a street corner because the researcher just stays there until he/she has the required number of people with the key characteristics.

A **stratified sample** is one where a selection of people is randomly chosen from within a sub-group. For instance, a business might want to know the views of females aged between 17 and 24. People would be selected randomly from within that group.

Factors affecting choice of sampling methods

- Available finance – a small business start-up is unlikely to have large amounts of capital available, and the entrepreneur may be unwilling to spend money researching the market. So any market research in the initial stages is likely to be low cost, or free.

- The nature of the product – an existing product or service will already have created secondary data in the form of information about competitors, their location, sales, etc. New, innovative ideas are less likely to have data already in existence. Local products or services are easier to research than those with larger geographical markets. Many entrepreneurs find it easier to research customers' attitudes to a physical product than a service because there is something physical to see and try out.

- The level of risk – the newer the product the greater the risk (and the greater the potential rewards!). It is probably true that the greater the risk the more important the need for research.

- The target market – a clearly defined target market, whether in terms of age, income or some other factor, is easier to target in terms of sample.

Primary research methods

How shall I collect the information?

- Observation – sometimes, the most useful information is gathered by an entrepreneur just watching people walking through a shop, or past a particular location.

Key terms

Random sample: one in which each potential member of a group has an equal chance of being in the sample.

Quota sample: this is not random, as not everyone has an equal chance of being in it, and the results cannot be used to predict the behaviour of everyone.

Stratified sample: popular with researchers as it has the benefits of being random, thus reducing bias, and is not as expensive or as difficult as a full random sample.

Link

For more information on market segmentation, see Chapter 6 – Understanding markets, page 36.

Fig. 5.2 *Call centres can conduct primary market research with speed and efficiency*

- IT allows for far more detailed and accurate 'observation' through sales records on EPOS systems, loyalty card schemes, CCTV and interactive websites.

- Written questionnaire – the most obvious (and most over-used) method of primary research. The benefits are that a large number can be distributed quickly. However, badly designed questionnaires are worse than none at all. It is essential to avoid asking leading questions that encourage one answer more than others, and to be sure to use open and closed questions correctly. Written questionnaires are limited to collecting only the information from the questions; it isn't easy to respond on the spot to an answer with a follow up question.

- Face-to-face questionnaire – difficult and time consuming, but has the benefit of being able to respond to answers with follow up questions.

- Telephone surveys – have many of the same benefits of face-to-face contact, but are cheaper and quicker to do.

- Focus groups – people discussing a product can reveal information and opinions that might not be revealed by interviewing people individually. This method can reveal issues the business had not thought of. Focus groups can be useful in discovering the psychology of purchasing decisions, such as the importance of peer influences and image. The danger of this method is in drawing conclusions about the whole market based on a relatively small sample size.

- Test marketing – selling a product in a small segment of the market can generate useful data that can improve the product before a full launch. The small scale of many business start-ups means this may not be feasible.

Primary research has a number of disadvantages:

- It can be expensive, so it is often difficult for a small business to afford it.

- It is difficult to carry out accurately.

- It can be inaccurate, therefore the business might make inappropriate decisions.

- Entrepreneurs often lack the skills and time to carry out primary research.

AQA Examiner's tip

Market research is another area where numbers play a key part. Be sure you are confident in assessing simple numerical information such as the percentage of people who respond to a question in a certain way. Keep practising those numbers!

Case study

Market research at Bladonmore

Bladonmore is a financial training business, based in London. A customised service and a gritty, real-world approach to training have enabled the company to grow rapidly during its first two years. Director Richard Rivlin explains how effective use of market research has contributed to Bladonmore's development.

'Like most companies starting out, we needed to research our target market but didn't have limitless cash to pay someone to do it for us. Doing it yourself is cheap in money terms – but you have to invest your time if you expect to get anything useful out of it.'

'Over a period of three months, I went on a virtual fact-finding mission using the Internet. If you persevere, you can find an incredible amount of quality information for free, including market reports and expert analysis. Business consultants' websites, industry bodies and sector-leading companies are a good place to start.'

'I wanted to know the size of the market, to learn from competitors' successes and mistakes and to understand what potential clients want.'

'Research isn't just about reading the occasional market report. It should be an on-going process that keeps you up to date with your market, your rivals and your clients. I find newspapers one of the best research sources. There's something relevant to our business in the press almost every day.'

'I didn't wake up to the wonders of free expert research soon enough. If I had my time again, I'd head straight for the websites of top consultants like Ernst & Young and McKinsey. You may not be able to afford their research fees, but they publish enough in the public domain to meet the needs of many smaller businesses.'

'I now make it part of my daily routine to clip useful research out of newspapers. I even carry around a small pair of scissors for the purpose. It's yielded several business development ideas and I wish I'd got into the habit sooner.'

www.businesslink.gov.uk

Questions

1. Assess the benefits of secondary market research to Bladonmore.

2. Suggest three ways that Bladonmore could use primary market research data to add to the information provided by secondary techniques.

3. Discuss the most appropriate research method for Bladonmore. Justify your answer.

Quantitative and qualitative data

Some of the information will be in numerical form. For example, a business might discover that 70 per cent of its potential customers dislike the image of a product. This is **quantitative data** because it refers to numerical information. Quantitative data is good for establishing key information about a business and its market.

Techniques to collect quantitative data include:

- questionnaire
- telephone surveys
- online surveys.

Other types of research generate **qualitative data**, which is information about attitudes, feelings and opinions. This kind of data is often more revealing and useful, but it is more difficult and expensive to collect. This is probably especially true for the business start-up.

Techniques to collect qualitative data include:

- in-depth interviews
- group discussions.

It is often said that quantitative data reveals what is happening, whilst qualitative data explains why it is happening. To illustrate, it is often quoted that 'eight out of ten owners who expressed a preference said

Key terms

Quantitative data: data in numerical form. An example of this is '8 out of 10 owners who expressed a preference said their cats preferred Whiskers'. Quantitative data is usually collected from larger scale research in order to generate statistically reliable results.

Qualitative data: data about opinions, attitudes and feelings. It is usually expressed in terms of why people feel or behave the way they do.

THE HENLEY COLLEGE LIBRARY

their cats preferred Whiskers'. That piece of quantitative data is a good advertising slogan, but a more revealing piece of market research would be the qualitative data behind why 2 out of 10 didn't.

Case study

Market research plan: making the right decisions

For each of the scenarios below, discuss in groups and answer the questions in order to create a market research plan for each one.

- A dry cleaners is planning to open in a high street location in a small town. This is a franchise of a well-known national chain. The franchisee wants to know the size of the potential market, the price customers are willing to pay and the best location for the outlet.

- An employee of a large car manufacturer has been made redundant and is hoping to start up a business as a manufacturer of specialist parts for car engines. His customers are likely to be other car manufacturers in the UK and, eventually, other parts of the EU. He needs to know abut existing competitors in the UK, possible trends in car purchasing and likely changes in the economy.

- An entrepreneur is convinced there's a gap in the market for her theme hotel, which has a number of rooms decorated in themes such as 'Hollywood glamour', '1950's romance', 'space age', etc. She wants to know people's attitudes to themed hotels and whether they would be prepared to pay extra to stay in this type of room. She also wants to know how best to promote this product.

For each of the above scenarios, answer the following questions. **In each case, be prepared to justify your answer.**

Questions

1. What secondary data might the entrepreneur first use?
2. What sampling method should the entrepreneur use to decide who to collect primary data from?
3. What research method should be used to collect the primary data?
4. Discuss whether the entrepreneur should collect quantitative or qualitative data, or a combination of the two.
5. Research other small business case studies to establish how they investigated their market.

☑ *In this chapter you will have learned to:*

- explain the different methods of secondary and primary research available to a small business start-up and realise that the limited resources of a small business is likely to determine what data is collected and how it is collected

- understand the benefits of various methods of collecting market research information for small businesses, whilst also understanding that limited resources may mean a less than perfect picture of how the market is generated

■ explain the difference between qualitative and quantitative data and understand how each type of data is likely to be collected

■ analyse how sampling can be used effectively by an entrepreneur, and understand the factors behind sampling decisions

■ evaluate the usefulness of various research methods for small business start-ups and be able to make justified recommendations on the most appropriate market research strategy in a given situation.

Understanding markets

Setting the scene

New Horizons Travel

Kate and Anna had been operating their small travel business in Colchester for just two months. Business had been steady, but not as good as they had hoped. 'We need to promote certain kinds of destinations, the places people really want to go to' said Kate. 'But how do we find that out?' asked Anna. 'I looked at the National Statistics website and found this section' said Kate:

Visits abroad by UK residents increased by 1 per cent during the 12 months ending July 2007, from 68.3 million to 69.3 million. Over this period, visits to North America increased 3 per cent (to 4.8 million), visits to Europe remained broadly the same (at 54.5 million) and visits to other parts of the world rose by 9 per cent (to 10.0 million).

In the same 12-month period, visits by overseas residents to the UK rose by 6 per cent, from 31.2 million to 32.9 million. Visits from residents of Europe increased 7 per cent (to 23.7 million), North America remained broadly the same (at 4.6 million) and visits from other parts of the world rose 6 per cent (to 4.6 million).

During May to July 2007, the number of visits overseas by UK residents decreased by 4 per cent to 16.8 million when compared with the previous three months, while the associated spending decreased by 4 per cent to £8.8 billion.

Over the same period, there were 8.0 million visits to the UK by overseas residents, a decrease of 5 per cent when compared with the previous three months, while the associated spending decreased by 3 per cent to £3.9 billion.

'But you know I'm no good at numbers', said Anna. 'I need to see this in a different way'.

www.statistics.gov.uk

Link

For more information on how small business collect data about their product, market and competition, see Chapter 5 – Conducting start-up market research, page 27.

Discussion points

1. How could this information be presented differently so that Anna could make effective use of it to understand her market?

2. What other sources of information could Kate and Anna use to investigate their market?

Understanding the nature and type of markets

Market research data can help us to understand the market.

Table 6.1 *Features of local and national markets*

Type of market	Features
Is the market a **local market?**	Business may have a very good relationship with, and understanding of, the customers
	Communication with customers is likely to be easy, and relatively cheap
	Reputation will spread quickly and easily to customers and potential customers
	It is relatively easy to collect primary data from customers
	Changes in customer tastes are likely to be apparent quickly
	Market size may be small, or at least there is limited possibility for continuous growth
Is the market a **national market?**	More costly distribution of products/services to customers
	Slower communication with customers
	Competitors nearer to customers
	Slow spread of reputation – good or bad! – to customers
	Larger potential market

Key terms

Local market: customers are only a short distance away.

National market: a geographically dispersed market where customers are spread over a large area.

Electronic market: does not have a physical presence, but exists in terms of a virtual presence via the internet. Many businesses have gone from 'brick to click'. In fact there are businesses which exist to help other businesses create an online presence (e.g. Shopcreator. com).

Market segmentation: the technique where the market is broken down into smaller sections with similar characteristics.

In the above examples, the assumption is that there is a physical location for the business around which the customers are distributed. However, increasingly businesses do not have a physical presence in the market, but the market is an **electronic market**.

There is also open source software available that can build web pages, linked to a database, which a small business could use to create an online presence. Companies such as Pay Pal and World Pay can handle the financial transactions.

Factors affecting demand

Market research data can also be analysed to reveal the features of the demand for a product or service, as well the features of the market. The factors most likely to affect demand for a product or service include:

Price – some products/services have a demand which is very sensitive to price changes.

Competition – the actions of competition, particularly in relation to their prices, or the features of their products will affect demand.

Incomes – some products/services have a demand which is very sensitive to changes in people's income.

Marketing – there is a relationship between the amount of money spent on marketing and the demand for the product.

External factors such as seasonality will also affect demand and possibly price.

Market segmentation

One particularly useful technique that market research data analysis allows an entrepreneur to do is to assess how **market segmentation** might benefit the business.

AQA Examiner's tip

Too often in exams, candidates give the impression that only one factor affects price, when in fact it is likely to be a combination of factors that determine the price of a product. Consider the list of factors affecting demand and, choosing a number of different products and services, rank the factors in terms of the most influential for each product/service. See if you can draw conclusions about what types of products/ services feature which factor most prominently.

Table 6.2 *Advantages and disadvantages of a virtual presence*

The advantages of a virtual presence	The disadvantages of a virtual presence
All customers are equally near(or far) from the business, so distribution costs are reasonably constant	Price transparency, whilst good for the customer, means that any business that can't or won't keep its prices down will be found out
The world is the market	
A virtual presence is less expensive than a physical presence, both in terms of reaching customers with marketing information and distributing products	A website might get a lot of 'hits', but it doesn't mean people will buy. There are no sales staff to encourage and advise customers
24/7 opening. No need to close	A website crash is the equivalent of all the branches of a business having to close at the same time
No requirement for an expensive, highly visible high street location. An effective link to search engines will work just as well	Security issues can be a problem
Start-up and running costs are much lower than a physical presence	Some people like to go to a shop and browse – there are some purchases where the customer needs to see/hear/taste/smell the product
Business can react much more quickly to customer requests. Often products are distributed immediately upon payment which itself is often instant	Some people complain of a lack of help and support from online retailers if things go wrong
Real time information is gathered by the database as it operates, so the entrepreneur is constantly in touch with the performance of business	
We may be at the point now where customers expect businesses to have an online presence, so to not have one would be damaging to its reputation	

The most frequently used method is demographic segmentation which breaks the market down according to features of the customers such as age, gender, socio-economic group, income, family characteristics or ethnicity. Others include segmentation by lifestyle or personality and geography.

There are a number of benefits to segmentation:

■ A better understanding of the needs of a segment of the market and as a consequence a greater likelihood of being able to meet those needs.

■ It is generally less expensive to develop products or services that attempt to meet a more distinct need.

■ Less wasteful of resources than trying to sell a product to 'everyone'.

■ Segmentation is a way of differentiating a product or service from competition, thus enabling the business to charge a higher price.

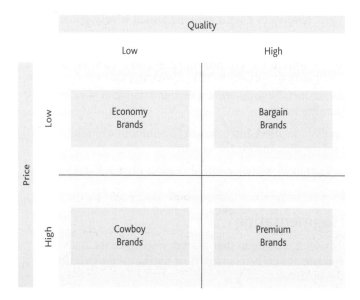

Fig. 6.1 *A positioning map is a useful visual way to represent segments of a market according to two variables adapted from www.tutor2u.net*

There are also limitations to segmentation:

■ Depends upon an entrepreneur's knowledge of the market – this may be limited in the case of a small business start-up.

■ Segmentation is an approximation of behaviour – not everyone behaves in the same way.

■ May not be appropriate for very small businesses with limited markets.

Case study

Activity on segmentation in TV and cinema

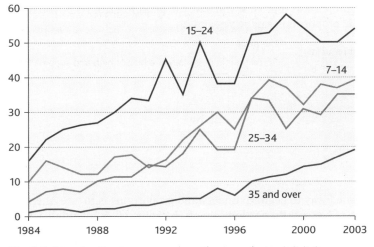

Fig. 6.2 *Attending the cinema once a month or more by age in Britain*

There were 171 million visits to UK cinemas in 2004, 2.4 per cent more than in 2003 and the second highest number for over 30 years.

Young people aged 15 to 24 are the most likely age group to go to the cinema. Just over half (54 per cent) of this age group reported attending the cinema once a month or more in Great Britain in 2003 compared with 19 per cent of those aged 35 and over.

In 2003 39 per cent of children aged 7 to 14 went to the cinema once a month or more. Almost all children (98 per cent) aged 4 to 9 are accompanied to the cinema by an adult. Children start to go to the cinema with friends aged 10 to 14. Over 7 in 10 children in this age group had been to the cinema with friends.

Of the top 20 films at the UK box office in 2004, 13 were US productions (including *Shrek 2*, *The Incredibles* and *Spider-Man 2*), two were joint UK/US productions (*Harry Potter and the Prisoner of Azkaban* and *Bridget Jones: The Edge of Reason*), and four were co-productions between the US and other countries (including *Troy* and *The Last Samurai*).

Questions

1 Assess the value of the above data to a business considering opening a cinema in a small town in the north of England.

2 How could the data be used to segment the products on offer at the cinema?

3 Discuss the value to the cinema of segmentation in maximising its market share?

AQA / Examiner's tip

It is important you understand basic numerical techniques. It is essential for this section, and there are a number of activities to help you develop your confidence. Don't avoid this section because it's got numbers in it, spend more time on it!

Using data to understand the market – numerical techniques

Proportions of a total – market share

One of the ways in which data can be analysed is in terms of how much a value is in relation to a total. Proportions can be expressed in many different ways, which is why they are often confusing. Many people find they understand proportions if they think of pieces of a cake or pizza.

If you were faced with a piece of data such as '47 out of 94 people interviewed said yes they liked the product' it might not be easy to see what proportion that is. If you saw the pizza in Figure 6.3, you'd instantly see the proportions saying yes and no.

Fig. 6.3

So a good way to begin to understand proportions is to 'see' them as pieces of a pizza. Proportions are often expressed as fractions. So in the above example, the proportion saying 'yes' is half, or ½. How do we arrive at ½? Well, we have *1 pizza, and we've split it in 2*. The number of pizzas we've got goes at the top, and the number of times it's divided up goes at the bottom.

Let's do another one. Suppose you went with 2 friends to a pizza restaurant and ordered the biggest pizza they had and wanted it divided so you each got a piece. The number of pizzas (1) goes at the top, and the number of pieces (3) goes at the bottom. So you'd each get 1/3rd of the pizza. Again it might be worth 'seeing' what that proportion looks like. See Figure 6.4.

Fig. 6.4

So, proportions might be expressed as pieces of a pizza or as fractions, but they also come in percentages. How does a fraction get turned into a percentage? Let's go back to our first example. In it we said a half is 1 over 2, or ½. Replace the number 1 at the top with 100. Then it becomes $\frac{100}{2}$, which is 50. So a half, or ½ is 50%. Try it with the pizza example. Each friend got ⅓ of the pizza. Replace the 1 at the top of the fraction with 100, and it becomes $\frac{100}{3}$, which is 33.3%.

So to turn a fraction into a percentage, replace the 1 at the top with 100.

Suppose 2 more friends arrived just as the pizza was brought to the table. What proportion of the pizza would each of you get? There's still only 1 pizza, so the number on the top is still 1, but there are now 5 of you, so the number on the bottom becomes 5. You'll get ¹/₅ of the pizza. What does that proportion look like? See Figure 6.5.

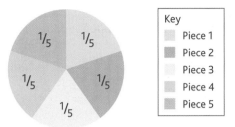

Fig. 6.5

Let's finally turn that piece of pizza into a percentage. Remember, to do this you replace the 1 at the top with 100. So now it's ¹⁰⁰/₅, which is 20%.

A pie chart looks just like a pizza, so that's why it's such a good way to display information such as proportions. One particularly useful way that pie charts are used is to calculate **market share**.

Case study

Calculating market share

Brian Henderson had been staring at the figures for what seemed like the whole of the day. 'I can't make sense of this' he said. 'Hendersons' sales last year were £125,000. I know that the total sales in the market were £625,000. So how do I work out our market share?'

'Let me show you . . . again' his wife Penny said patiently. 'How many times do our sales divide into the total sales of the market?' 'Er . . . 5' said Brian after he'd used the calculator. 'OK, so we have ¹/₅ of the market' said Penny. 'Can you remember how to turn ¹/₅ into a percentage?' she asked. 'Yes I do! You replace the 1 at the top with 100 then divide by 5' said Brian, rather pleased with himself. 'So, our market share is 100/5, which is 20%'.

Brian was getting confident now, so Penny said, 'look at the rest of the data and calculate the other companies' market shares'.

Questions

1 Calculate the market share for each competitor and display this information in a pie chart.

2 Using this information, assess the position of Hendersons in the market.

Changes in values – market size and growth

As well as looking at the way proportions of totals are calculated, market research data will often analyse how values are changing.

Suppose a business had sales last year of £300,000, and this year sales were £425,000. How do you calculate the size of the increase compared to what it was?

Key terms

Market share: the proportion of a total market accounted for by one product or company.

Table 6.3

Company	Sales
Hendersons	125,000
Williamson	250,000
Bryant	200,000
Topping	50,000
Total	**625,000**

AQA Examiner's tip

When completing calculations, it's often useful to do a check to see if your answer makes sense. In the above example, sales changed by £125,000 and they were originally £300,000.

Half of £300,000 is £150,000, which is quite close to £125,000, so you know that the correct answer is not going to be far from half – which you also know is 50%. 41% is close to 50%, so you can be quite sure you've probably got your calculation right.

First you have to calculate by how much sales in a market have changed. £425,000 – £300,000 is £125,000. Now we divide £125,000 by the original figure of £300,000 and finally multiply the answer by 100. The answer is 41.67%.

Let's go through that again.

$$\frac{\text{How much has the value changed?}}{\text{What was the original value?}} \times 100$$

In numbers this is:

$$\frac{£125,000}{£300,000} \times 100 = 41.67\%$$

Key terms

Market growth: the measurement of the change in market size, usually expressed as a percentage of its original size.

Market size: the measurement of the size of total sales for a whole market, either expressed in terms of the value of sales (in currency) or the volume of sales (in units).

This is a calculation of **market growth**, which is different from market share. In terms we used before, market share is a measure of how big your piece of pizza is. Market size is how big the pizza itself is. Market growth is how much the pizza has grown! Both **market size** and market growth are likely to be affected most by external factors such as economic growth. Market share is the most precise measure of the success of an individual business.

Case study

Hendersons' market calculations

Having correctly calculated Hendersons' current market share, Brian was feeling smug, so his wife decided to give him some more calculations to do. She put the following information in front of him:

Table 6.4

	Sales in 2007	Market share in 2007	Sales in 2008	Market share in 2008	% change in sales between 2007 and 2008
Hendersons	90,000		125,000		
Williamson	210,000		250,000		
Bryant	190,000		200,000		
Topping	60,000		50,000		
Total	550,000	100%	625,000	100%	

Penny asked Brian to answer the following questions:

Questions

1. Complete the table showing the market share for each business for 2007 and 2008 and calculate the % change in sales for each business and for the market as a whole.

2. Copy and complete Table 6.5 identifying which six of the following statements are true.

Table 6.5

Statement	Tick or cross to indicate true or false
Hendersons' sales have fallen.	
Hendersons' sales have risen.	
Hendersons' market share has fallen.	
Hendersons' market share has risen.	
The market as a whole has grown at a greater rate than Hendersons' sales.	
The market as a whole has grown at a slower rate than Hendersons' sales.	
Hendersons' market share has grown by 4 percentage points.	
Hendersons' market share has grown by 39%.	
Hendersons' and Williamson's sales have grown at a faster rate than the market as a whole.	
Hendersons' has the biggest market share in 2008.	
Bryant's sales have grown by 5%.	
Bryant's market share had risen by 3%.	

3 Analyse the relationship between the rate of growth of an individual business and the rate of growth of the market as a whole.

4 To what extent is it easier or harder for a business to increase its market share in a growing market compared to a static or shrinking market?

In this chapter you will have learned to:

- understand the key features of physical and virtual markets and be able to distinguish between local and national markets. You'll be able to explain the main benefits and drawbacks of each type of market

- explain the key factors affecting demand and be able to appreciate that it is likely that a combination of such factors will determine the price of a product or service. You'll understand that different products and services will have different priorities

- explain the features, benefits and limitations of market segmentation

- use accurately some of the numerical techniques to calculate proportions, percentages and changes and be able to use these techniques to analyse market size, growth and share and be able to distinguish between them.

Summary questions

Chapters 4–6

1   Define the term 'business angel'. *(3 marks)*

2   Describe three possible pieces of information that a venture capitalist might need before deciding whether to invest in a business that builds loft conversions. *(6 marks)*

3   Describe three possible problems that an entrepreneur might have when constructing a business plan for a window cleaning business. *(5 marks)*

4   Explain to an entrepreneur who is setting up a tanning salon the benefits of small business banking services. *(5 marks)*

5   Describe two sources of government help that an entrepreneur starting a business making organic sausages could use. *(4 marks)*

6   Explain two possible reasons why an entrepreneur might choose not to construct a business plan. *(4 marks)*

7   Clive Malcolm has had a window cleaning business for nearly 6 months, since he bought it from his brother, who decided to sell it because he couldn't make it a success. Clive has 150 customers who have their windows cleaned every 2 weeks. So far, Clive has not tried to get any new business, and in fact, he has lost 20 customers since he took the business over. He knows he needs to do something if he is to make the business a success.

   a)   Explain two benefits to Clive of conducting primary market research. *(4 marks)*

   b)   Distinguish between quantitative and qualitative market research data in the context of Clive's business. *(6 marks)*

   c)   Explain three problems Clive might have in selecting a random sample. *(6 marks)*

   d)   Evaluate the likely impact on Clive's business of a detailed market research strategy. *(10 marks)*

8   List three possible methods of primary research that an entrepreneur starting a hairdressers might use to find out about the likely demand for her service. *(3 marks)*

9   Analyse three possible difficulties to a clothes shop of seeking to expand from a local to a national market. *(6 marks)*

10   Analyse three likely factors affecting the demand for takeaway pizza. *(6 marks)*

11   Explain what you understand by the term 'market segmentation'. *(3 marks)*

12   Describe two benefits that a restaurant might enjoy from market segmentation. *(6 marks)*

13   Distinguish between market size, market growth and market share. Use the mobile phone market to illustrate your points. *(8 marks)*

14   Bill and Anne operated a smoothie bar – a business that sold healthy fruit and vegetable drinks and snacks. In the first 10 weeks of trading the business had attracted an average of only 350 customers per week and had yet to break even. Secondary market research had shown that the value of UK smoothie sales had risen from £6.3 million in 2001 to £34 million in 2006.

At the start they drew up a detailed business plan and carried out detailed primary market research in several towns. They borrowed £50,000 from the bank and funded the remaining £60,000 from the sale of their London house.

From the start, things went wrong. They opened late because of late delivery of supplies so missed the busy summer trading period. A competitor set up nearby and opened a month before them. Finally, they found it difficult to recruit good quality part time staff.

a)   What is meant by the term, 'entrepreneurs'?   *(2 marks)*

b)   State two non-financial items that the Bank Manager would have expected to see in the Business Plan for Just Juice Ltd before agreeing to the loan.   *(2 marks)*

c)   Explain one reason why Bill and Anne might have decided to use primary market research as part of their business planning.   *(3 marks)*

d)   Calculate the percentage growth in the UK market for smoothies between 2001 and 2006.   *(3 marks)*

e)   To what extent might the drawing up of a detailed business plan guarantee the success of Just Juice Ltd?   *(8 marks)*

7 Choosing the right legal structure for the business

Setting the scene

Compass Point counselling

Jane Howlett had been a manager at a counselling centre for 10 years before she set up her own sole trader business, specialising in counselling children and young adults in a range of areas such as depression, eating disorders and family problems. She was used to difficult situations, having to help people in distressing circumstances, but she wasn't ready for the enormous difference she found between being the manager and being the owner of a business.

Jane was happiest in her counselling room with her clients. She employed her husband John to deal with all the finance and administration, but inevitably wanted to get involved in all the decisions.

The business started small, with a bank loan and just the two of them, but quickly began to grow. Jane was very keen to make sure that all business decisions taken were for the benefit of the clients rather than with profit making in mind.

Discussion points

1. What do you think are the main differences between being the owner and manager of a business?

2. Which would you prefer and why?

3. Make a list of the main objectives that you think Jane might have had at the start of Compass Point.

Which is the right legal structure?

The decision about which legal structure a new business is to adopt is probably one of the earliest decisions to make, usually taken shortly after deciding on the product or service to be offered. This decision is important as it affects a number of things:

- How much tax and National Insurance the business pays.
- The records and accounts that have to be kept.
- The liability faced by the owner if the business fails.
- The sources of finance available to the business.
- The way decisions are made.

Sole traders

Features

This is the most common and simplest form of business organisation. At its very simplest, it is one person operating a business alone. There is very little procedure needed to start a sole trader business. It is usually just a matter of starting to trade. Once up and running, a sole trader is obliged to keep basic records for tax, National Insurance and VAT purposes.

Although sole traders are the most numerous of all types of business structure, they contribute less to total UK output than other types such as limited companies.

Table 7.1 *Benefits and drawbacks of sole trader status*

Benefits of a sole trader	Drawbacks of a sole trader
Simple and quick to set up – just the thing for the entrepreneur with the brilliant idea who can't wait to start trading	The most significant is that sole traders have **unlimited liability**, which means they are personally liable for all debts incurred by the business
Inexpensive to set up – the entrepreneur with only a little money may choose this structure	Difficult to raise additional finance, because sole traders often have limited funds of their own and very little security against which to raise more. Banks may be willing to help if there is a good business plan
Any profit made by the business is the owners to keep, or reinvest	
The owner has complete control of the business; all the decisions are hers/his	All the decisions rest with the owner, who may not possess all the necessary expertise. This is often the reason small businesses fail, because the owner knows everything about the product, but little about finance or insurance or other areas
Often a close relationship between business and customer can be built up because of the size and simplicity of the business structure	
Hours of work etc. can be tailored to suit the entrepreneur	The drive comes from the owner, so the business is vulnerable if the owner becomes ill, or interested or other things happen in her/his life

Key terms

Unlimited liability: a feature of unincorporated businesses where the owners are personally liable for all debts incurred by a business. All sole traders and most partnerships have unlimited liability.

Partnerships

Features

This is the simplest way that two or more people can be in business together. In a partnership, partners share the risks, costs, and responsibilities of the business. The partners take a share of the profits and share in the decision making. The partners are jointly and personally responsible for any debts that the business runs up.

A partnership does not have a legal existence of its own so if one of the partners resigns or dies, the partnership is dissolved. A new partnership must be formed with the remaining partners, or with new partners for the business to continue.

Although it is not a requirement, often partners draw up a Deed of Partnership. This specifies many of the key features of the partnership such as:

- How much of the finance each has contributed.
- How much control over decisions each partner has.
- How the profits will be shared.
- How the partnership can be ended.

AQA Examiner's tip

With business structures, the drawbacks are often the 'flipside' of the benefits. For example, although it's inexpensive to set up a sole trader, it's also difficult to raise extra money. Similarly, although there is very little bureaucracy associated with setting up, there's also very little protection if things go wrong.

So, in an exam, if you have trouble remembering any drawbacks, but can remember benefits, try to turn them around.

Table 7.2 *Benefits and drawbacks of partnership status*

Benefits of a partnership	Drawbacks of a partnership
As with sole traders, there are very few procedures to follow in order to set up a partnership	As with sole traders, the partners have unlimited liability. This is complicated by the fact that each partner is jointly liable for the debts incurred by the business. So a wrong decision by one of the partners can have consequences for all the partners
Unlike sole traders, the expertise of more than one person can be brought into the business for decision making and for sharing the work load	Profits are shared amongst the partners (according to the distribution agreed in the Deed of Partnership)
Often different partners specialise in different aspects of the business	The partners are legally bound to honour the decisions of the others
There are more sources of finance as each partner can contribute a share of the start-up funds	The partnership ends on the death or resignation of a partner
	A maximum of 20 people can join a partnership, thus limiting the size of the business and the sources of funds

AQA Examiner's tip

In the exam, you may have to justify a decision about which is the best form of legal structure for a particular business. Don't just restate all the various benefits and drawbacks itemised here. Apply your points by considering why the particular business in the question would benefit most from one form of legal structure rather than another.

Incorporated and unincorporated businesses

Before going on to talk about limited companies, it's worth pausing to consider the process of incorporation. Sole traders and partnerships are examples of unincorporated businesses, whilst private limited companies and public limited companies are incorporated. There is no requirement for you to understand the exact procedure, but it's worth knowing the basics. Incorporation basically creates a legal entity, something that exists as far as the law is concerned. This has a significant impact on the owners of a business. For example, if J. Smith is a sole trader and the business accumulates debts, or is sued by a customer, then it is J. Smith the person that is liable for the debts, or J. Smith the person who will appear in court. If the business is J. Smith Ltd, then the debts are the businesses, not the owners, and it is the business that appears in court. So with incorporated businesses, it is true to say that the business itself exists, whereas with an unincorporated business, the owner (or owners in the case of partnerships) **is** the business.

Business in action

Jennings Cycles Ltd

Adam Jennings spent ages thinking about whether to remain a sole trader or become a limited company. His bank manager (and cycling-mad friend) advised him. 'When considering the difference between unincorporated and incorporated businesses it's worth thinking abut risk. For a sole trader and partners, there's a lot of risk, but it's all yours. You put the money into the business, and you take the risks. But you're risking your own money, so there is very little you have to do in terms of a start-up process or documentation. For limited companies, both private and public, there may be less risk, but you're risking other peoples' money. The shareholders need to know that their investment is reasonably secure, and that if the business is unsuccessful, they won't lose all of their assets. Hence there is limited liability. They also need to be sure that the business is using their money appropriately, hence the need to produce detailed financial information. The limited liability and the need to provide detailed records are both because, essentially, limited companies use other people's money.'

'So if I want long-term growth and security, and I don't mind a more formal process to set up and a bit more paperwork, I should go for limited company status?' asked Adam.

Private limited companies

Features

The key feature of a private limited company is that the owners are the shareholders, and their ownership of the business is determined by the proportion of the total shares each person holds. So, for instance, if there are 100 shares in a business, and a particular shareholder owns 20, then he/she owns 20% of the shares. This is sometimes referred to as 20% of the equity in the business. The business must have Ltd in its name. A shareholder in a limited company has limited liability, which means that they are not liable for the debts the business might incur, beyond what they might have invested into the business. As a consequence of limited liability, limited companies are required by law to go through a much more complicated process when they are created, and are required to keep much more detailed records once they begin trading. The main reason for this is so that potential investors and lenders can make sure the company is being run properly. This form of business is the popular form for family businesses and for small, well established businesses. Shares can only be sold privately and with the consent of the shareholder.

■ Key terms

Limited liability: a feature of incorporated businesses such as private and public limited companies, which means that the owners' liability is limited to the amount they have invested in the business.

Benefits and drawbacks

Table 7.3 *Benefits and drawbacks of a limited company*

Benefits of a limited company	Drawbacks of a limited company
Access to funds through the issue of shares	Banks may see the business as a risk
Stable form of business structure	More complicated set up process than unincorporated business structures
Limited liability is a benefit for the shareholders, who may see the risk as more acceptable than if the business were unincorporated	Limited liability might be a benefit for shareholders, but lenders may see it as a risk
Incorporation means the business exists, and will continue to exist even if a shareholders resigns or dies	

Public limited companies

Features

The key feature that distinguishes a public limited company from a private limited company is that the shares are bought and sold publicly. Both types of structure are owned by shareholders, but whereas in a limited company the shares are only bought and sold privately between individuals, with a public limited company, shares are traded publicly, and anyone can buy them. This means they have a market value. On any given day, the shares in a plc can be bought and sold, and this affects the share price. The share price of a plc is important because it indicates how popular the business is, and it can influence how successful future issues of shares might be. The share price of a plc is also a crucial factor in determining how easy it would be to take it over by buying a proportion of the shares. The initial sale of shares to the public is known as flotation.

Many of the benefits and drawbacks of a plc are the same as for a limited company. There are additional things to bear in mind.

AQA Examiner's tip

There's a lot of confusion in students' minds about shares and share prices. Often students claim that a rising share price means the plc gets more money. But the Stock Exchange, which is where these shares are bought and sold, is just a second hand market. So share price movements are important to a plc, but a rising share price doesn't directly generate more funds, any more than a falling share price would mean the plc had to give money back.

Table 7.4 *Benefits and drawbacks of a public limited company*

Benefits of a public limited company	Drawbacks of a public limited company
The main benefit is the scale of the funds that can be raised from a flotation. A successful business that wants to grow may find many investors wanting to buy shares in the initial share offer, which means large sums of money can be raised. Future funds can be raised because banks and lenders see a plc as a very stable, secure type of business and they are willing to lend large sums of money.	The process of flotation is expensive. Documents have to be produced to advertise the company and explain its financial situation, there are legal fees, and shares have to be underwritten. What that means is that someone has to guarantee to buy any unwanted shares. The underwriters are paid a fee for this. In addition, the company must have a minimum of £50,000 in share capital, of which 25% must have been sold before the plc can trade. So, you can see, it's a very different process from starting a sole trader! It is not possible to control who owns the shares in a plc as the shares are traded publicly. This has a number of implications. Firstly, there's nothing stopping competitors, customers or suppliers buying shares. Secondly, a takeover cannot be prevented if someone is willing and able to buy enough shares. The plc must provide regular, detailed financial information. This is so that any investor, or potential investor can see how well, or badly, the company is doing. A drawback often quoted is the **separation of ownership and control**. A plc is owned by shareholders, but often run by managers. The two groups of stakeholders are different people, with different objectives. This can cause conflict and can make decision making difficult.

■ **Key terms**

Separation of ownership and control: describes a situation in which the owners (often the shareholders) are not the same people as those controlling the business on a day-to-day basis (often the managers).

Fig. 7.1 *The Eden Project in Cornwall is an example of a not-for-profit business*

Not-for-profit businesses – social enterprises

Features

So far, we've assumed that entrepreneurs are motivated to make a profit. Some, however, have other objectives. These not-for-profit businesses are growing in importance. The government estimates that there are now 55,000 social enterprises in the UK, employing more than 775,000 people and contributing £8.4bn each year to the economy. Examples include The Eden Project, Café Direct and Jamie Oliver's restaurant Fifteen.

One type of business that does not have profit as its main objective is a social enterprise organisation. This type of business mainly aims to provide a social benefit. It may make a profit, but often those profits are reinvested back into the business so that the social aims can be met, rather than paid out to the owners.

Table 7.5 *Benefits and drawbacks of a not-for-profit business*

Benefits of a not-for-profit structure	Drawbacks of a not-for-profit structure
Entrepreneurs can earn a living doing something valuable, which can be motivating	Profits and social aims may conflict, leading to difficult choices
The more successful the social enterprise the more society benefits	The entrepreneur will always have to accept a lower return than with a profit-making business because a proportion of the profits will go towards the social aim
Customers may be more willing to buy from a social enterprise	
It might be easier to recruit, motivate and retain employees in a social enterprise	
Grants or other forms of finance might be available from sources sharing the same social aim	

Compass Point Counselling – the way forward

When Jane Howlett looked back, it didn't feel like five years had passed since she started her own business, a not-for-profit counselling service for young people called Compass Point Counselling. In those five years Jane had seen her business grow from just her and her husband to a total staff of 10 people, including 8 full- or part-time counsellors, as well as Jane and her husband.

The business was a victim of its own success. Jane had started as a sole trader and employed John, to look after the finance while she counselled. This worked well initially, because they were able to begin operating quickly and the business was cheap to run. John's background in accountancy meant he could run the office side of things, but as the business grew, and took on more employees, it became clear that neither of them had experience in managing people. They'd taken out a second mortgage to turn their garage into an office and counselling room, and used the income from the business to pay it off. All employees including Jane and John were paid a salary, and any spare money they had was reinvested.

The business didn't struggle to pay its bills on a day-to-day basis, but the potential to expand remained limited. The couple had a derelict barn in the grounds of their house, and Jane had always felt this would make a perfect counselling centre. However, it would cost a lot to convert it, and there were probably legal issues to consider. Also, the possibility existed for other people to join the business. John's friend Sahir was keen to invest an inheritance in a business which made a contribution to the local community. He currently worked as a Human Resources Manager in the local council, but was looking for a different challenge.

Although Jane had put it off so far, she knew she had to sit down and make some decisions about the future of the business, but she didn't know when she was going to find the time or what she should do. One thing was certain, she couldn't carry on much longer as a sole trader.

Questions

1. Describe the main benefits to Jane of initially setting up as a sole trader.
2. Explain the benefits and drawbacks of Jane forming a partnership with John and Sahir.
3. Analyse the impact of Compass Point's not-for-profit objective on the likely type of business structure chosen.
4. To what extent would the future success of Compass Point be guaranteed by the formation of a limited company?

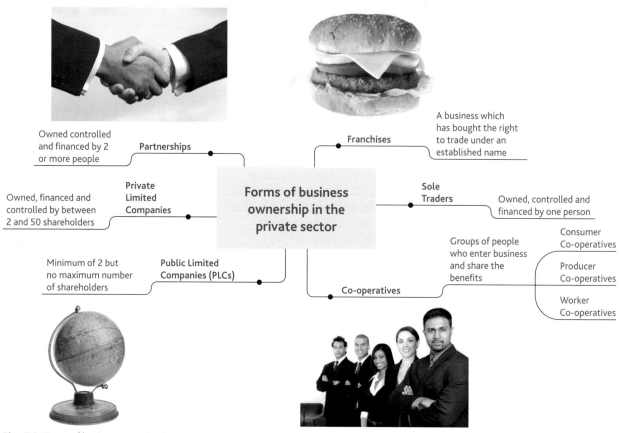

Owned controlled and financed by 2 or more people — **Partnerships**

Owned, financed and controlled by between 2 and 50 shareholders — **Private Limited Companies**

Minimum of 2 but no maximum number of shareholders — **Public Limited Companies (PLCs)**

Forms of business ownership in the private sector

Franchises — A business which has bought the right to trade under an established name

Sole Traders — Owned, controlled and financed by one person

Co-operatives — Groups of people who enter business and share the benefits — Consumer Co-operatives / Producer Co-operatives / Worker Co-operatives

Fig. 7.2 *Types of business organisation adapted from www.businesslink.co.uk*

☑ *In this chapter you will have learned to:*

- understand the main features of the different types of business structure, and their benefits and drawbacks

- understand the difference between unincorporated and incorporated business structures and in particular understand the significance of incorporation in terms of the liability of the owners of the business

- explain the process of starting different types of business structure

- evaluate the benefits and drawbacks of each type of business structure for specific situations and be able to make reasoned conclusions about the most appropriate.

8   Raising finance

In this chapter you will learn to:

- explain the difference between internal and external sources of finance

- understand the various sources of internal and external finance

- analyse the appropriateness of various sources of internal and external finance for different needs.

Setting the scene

Geared Up gets bigger

So far, Karen had been right. Her initial enthusiasm for the bike shop, and her absolute confidence that it could be a success had proved right. Ian's cautious words had not been necessary, as the business grew from one shop and a website, to three shops and an online business with an annual turnover of over £1,000,000.

'We're ready for the next big step,' said Karen one day and, although he felt scared and convinced it was too soon, Ian knew he'd go along with Karen's latest plan.

'We need to get bigger if we're going to be more successful,' she said. 'You and I are the biggest shareholders, and we've now got my dad and your mum as minority shareholders,' she added. 'Their investment was crucial at the time,' Ian reminded her, as they both remembered the time two years ago when the business nearly went under.

'But we need to think much bigger,' argued Karen, 'I want to supply a supermarket chain with a range of bikes endorsed by a professional cyclist and branded with the Geared Up brand, and that's only going to happen with a massive injection of capital.'

At the start of every new business, decisions have to be made about where to get money from. Usually, the entrepreneur has to put some of his/her own money into the business. Sometimes, friends and family contribute, but often the entrepreneur has to approach a lender for loan capital. If the new business is a limited company, then share capital is a possible source. It is usually the case that the new business start-up has a number of things it needs to spend money on before any revenue is earned from the sale of the product or service. Premises have to be rented or bought, machinery and equipment, stocks of raw materials and components and various professional service fees all need to be paid for. This is usually before a single item has been made or sold.

Discussion points

1. What factors should Karen and Ian take into account when deciding whether to expand further?

2. Draw up a list of factors to consider when choosing the source of finance should they decide to expand.

AQA Examiner's tip

Think back to the chapter on business planning – if you were the friend or relative of someone about to start a business and who wanted to borrow money from you, what would you need to know before you said yes. Most of the answers to your questions should be in the business plan.

💡 Internal sources of finance

Internal sources of finance are ones which come from the owners of the business. These include the owner's personal funds, retained profit and the income from a sale of the company's assets. There is some debate about whether share capital is internal or external. The best way to look at it is to say that the first issue of shares to new shareholders is an external source of finance, because until they become shareholders, they're not part of the business. Any subsequent issue of shares to those shareholders through rights issues for example, are internal sources.

Personal sources of finance

It's very rare that a small business start-up doesn't require some investment from the owner. So the most important source of finance is the owner's own money. Sometimes entrepreneurs will borrow from friends or family.

Table 8.1 *Advantages and disadvantages of personal sources of finance*

Advantages of personal sources of finance	Disadvantages of personal sources of finance
There's no cost to using this money, in terms of a rate of interest	It's not strictly true there's no cost to an owner using his/her own money. There's the opportunity cost in terms of the alternative uses to which the money could have been put
An entrepreneur putting his/her own money into a business start-up is a sign of confidence. If they're willing to put their own money at risk, maybe others will as well	
The entrepreneur doesn't have to worry about the money being withdrawn, which could happen if the money was borrowed	Most entrepreneurs have limited finance at the start, which limits what the business can purchase
There's no risk of interference in decision making by a lender	New business start-ups are risky, so the entrepreneur could lose everything
The entrepreneur does not have to pay out anything from profits if he/she does not want to, it's all available for reinvesting	Borrowing from friends or family can cause a strain on relationships if the business does not do well
Borrowing from friends or family rarely means interest has to be paid	
Friends and family may be more willing to lend than other lenders	

Case study

Neville Construction Group and Neville Funeral Service

Peter Henman was 15 when he joined his brother as the fourth generation in his family's Bedfordshire-based construction and funeral businesses. He worked his way up from teaboy to chairman and now both he and the businesses are reaping the benefits of the fifth generation to join the companies. His daughter Vicky is a director and company secretary of both.

'Vicky has brought in a new period of confidence for the future. In most companies you can do three- or five-year plans but now we talk about 10 or even 15 years ahead. With Vicky's arrival, shareholders could see we had the ability to make longer-term investment plans that she would bring to fruition and were happy the investment was made.'

'Now the ownership and leadership of the company is spread between the older and experienced family members and the enthusiastic younger generation, giving balance and stability and a mixture of ideas gained from different environments. It also gives confidence to the staff for the long-term future of the business.'

'It's almost inconceivable that a chairman of a family firm could ever walk out and shut the door on the business completely, but personally I am in favour of moving sideways. I've got the confidence to do that with Vicky there.'

'Vicky did a business administration course and she did her project work on IT related to the business. That was particularly useful because she's from a generation at home with IT. Because of my age we were behind with this technology before she joined but now it's spread throughout the business.'

www.businesslink.gov.uk

Questions

1 Assess the benefits to Neville's of including different members of the family in the management of the business.

2 Discuss the possible drawbacks of such a strategy, and suggest ways the company could reduce the impact of such drawbacks.

💡 External sources of finance

External sources of finance are ones which come from outside the business. These include the issue of new shares in a limited company, bank loans, overdrafts and venture capital.

Loan capital – overdraft

An **overdraft** is a very flexible source of finance, particularly useful for managing cash flow during periods when the money going out of a business is temporarily greater than the money coming in. The banks usually charge a fee for arranging an overdraft, and usually charge interest. Sometimes, there's an interest-free amount before interest is charged.

It is not a good source of finance for longer term uses, such as buying equipment or machinery because the interest rates tend to be high and the bank could remove the overdraft at any time.

Table 8.2 *Advantages and disadvantages of an overdraft*

Advantages of an overdraft	Disadvantages of an overdraft
It is a flexible source of finance, because it is only used when it is needed	It is expensive if used for a long period of time or for large amounts
It is quick and easy to arrange	Arrangement fees and fees for going over the overdraft limit can be high
	The overdraft can be removed at short notice
	The business has to have a bank account with that bank in order to get an overdraft

Loan capital – bank loan

A **loan** is a sum of money lent for a fixed period of time, repaid over an agreed schedule. The price of the loan is a rate of interest, which is a percentage of the loan amount and added to the repayments. The actual rate of interest will depend upon a range of factors including the size of the loan, the length of the repayment period and the level of risk.

Key terms

Overdraft: a temporary arrangement which allows the business to draw out more money than is in its account, up to an agreed limit.

Loan: a good source of finance for assets such as machinery and equipment and other start-up costs.

AQA Examiner's tip

Always try to match the period of need to the life of the loan. In other words, if the business needs money for a short period of time, only borrow the money for a short period of time. If the business is going to use the money for an asset it intends to keep and use for a long time, use a longer term source of finance.

Table 8.3 *Advantages and disadvantages of a loan*

Advantages of a loan	Disadvantages of a loan
The length of the loan can be matched to the length of the need for the loan. The business can then plan for the repayments	Interest is paid regardless of whether the business is making a profit or not
The interest is fixed for the period of the loan, so it is easier to budget for the loan	The loan may have to be secured against a personal asset or an asset of the business, placing it at risk if the business cannot keep up the payments
The loan is guaranteed for the period, so the business knows it has got the money	The length of the loan may turn out to be longer than the life of the asset purchased with it. This means a business is paying for something it no longer needs
There is no need to give the lender a proportion of the profits earned by the business	
The lender does not have any say in how the business is run	

■ **Business in action**

Advice about loan capital

There is a large range of sources of advice about loan capital for small business start-ups. Here are just a few:

Table 8.4

Source of advice		Features
The Princes Trust www.princes-trust.org.uk	 **Fig. 8.1** *Princes Trust*	Provides advice and support for young people starting up in business
The Prime Initiative www.primeinitiative.org.uk	 **prime** 50 + self-employment & enterprise www.primebusinessclub.com **Fig. 8.2** *Prime initiative*	Provides similar advice and support for older people
The Islamic Bank www.islamic-bank.com	 ✳IBB ISLAMIC BANK OF BRITAIN **Fig. 8.3** *Islamic bank*	Helps Muslim entrepreneurs with advice, guidance and financial support
Small Business Loan Guarantee Scheme www.berr.gov.uk	BERR | Department for Business Enterprise & Regulatory Reform **Fig. 8.4** *BERR*	Help for businesses that find it difficult to get a loan. This is operated by the Department for Business Enterprise and Regulatory Reform

Share capital

Another source of finance is to ask an investor to put money into a business in return for a share of the business. This is known as share capital or equity capital. It is called share capital because the people who provide it are entitled to a share of the profits earned by the business, and usually own a share of the business itself. It is sometimes known as equity because each share is an equal part of the business.

People who invest share capital in a business aren't entitled to regular interest payments, but are entitled to a proportion of any profit the business makes at the end of the year. The other big difference between share capital and loan capital is that share capital is never paid back. So it is best used for very long term purposes.

The selling of shares in a business represents the selling of parts of the ownership of the business. So an entrepreneur loses some control over a business as soon as he/she sells shares in it.

In many cases, small businesses grow by becoming **incorporated** so that friends, family or other private investors can buy shares in the business in return for a lump sum investment.

If a business has a lot of growth potential, or it is seeking to grow rapidly, it could look for investment from other, more formal, investors such as **venture capitalists** or **business angels**.

Business angels differ from venture capitalists in two main ways, they are often individuals rather than companies, and they tend to look for smaller investments of between £10,000 and £250,000. In return for a capital investment, a business angel would expect a share in the business. Sometimes angels group together to provide a larger investment. Business angels often work closely with the owners of the business.

Case study

Show me the money

Gavin Thomas had been at his work placement for just three weeks and already he felt he'd learnt more about business than in all the two years of his Business Studies degree. He'd managed to get a place at a large well-known investment bank in Manchester for the third year of his degree. Already he was looking forward to his final year when he could add his business theory and practice together. His manager had been showing him how the bank advised clients, particularly small businesses, on the various sources of finance available to them. Now his manager wanted to test him on what he'd picked up. 'I'm going to give you a project; I want you to advise a number of my clients on the most appropriate sources of finance for their various needs. I want to know why you choose each source'. Below is a summary of the clients and their needs.

AQA Examiner's tip

The vast majority of limited companies are private, so their shares are bought and sold privately, often between family members, employees or other individuals, and not on the Stock Exchange.

Key terms

Incorporated: the process of forming a limited liability company. The process involves creating a separate legal identity for the business, and the creation of shares, or equity.

Venture capitalist: usually a professional investor, often another company, interested in high growth, high risk businesses, who will invest an amount into a business in return for shares, and an expectation for a high return. Venture capitalists are usually interested in larger investments of around £250,000 or more.

Business angel: a wealthy, entrepreneurial individual willing to invest in a small, high risk business who expects a high return. The business is likely to have a high growth potential.

Table 8.5 *Client's finance needs*

Client and need	Suggested source of finance	Reasons for choice of source of finance
a A newsagent needs to cover expenditure over a short period of time. She is expecting high sales at the end of the month.		
b A new business in a high tech market is looking for £100,000 to fund expenditure on equipment. The business is looking for an innovative solution to house design which will reduce fuel consumption. The owner is willing to consider giving up some of the control of the company.		
c A dry cleaners needs to update its equipment following a series of breakdowns which have damaged its reputation. It expects the new equipment to cost approximately £30,000, and have a useful life of about 5 years.		
d A self-employed builder needs a new van.		
e An unemployed woman, aged 23, is hoping to set up a business designing and making greetings cards from her home. She has no finance of her own, and has been turned down by a number of High street banks.		
f A very successful, profitable business selling sports cars wants to expand and purchase a second showroom. The owner is unwilling to consider giving up any control of his business.		
g Two brothers operate a partnership which does loft conversions. They are looking to expand the business in order to do a wider range of construction work.		

Questions

1 Copy and complete the table above, explaining your choice of source of finance in each case.

2 Explain the potential benefits of becoming a Limited company and obtaining share capital to the partners in business g.

3 Imagine you are a business angel with £100,000 to invest. Analyse each business and draw up a list of questions you would ask before deciding on which to invest in.

4 Evaluate each business and decide on the most appropriate one for a business angel to invest in.

5 Research local small business help and advice on finance in your area.

In this chapter you will have learned to:

- distinguish between internal and external sources of finance for small business start-ups and be able to explain the various sources

- understand the importance of matching the period of the need for the finance to the length of the source

- understand the benefits and drawbacks of each source of finance and be able to analyse the appropriateness of various sources of finance in particular situations.

9

Locating the business

Setting the scene

Teleworking myth exploded

Flexible working from home creates a whole new set of stressful problems, according to research done by a business school in Nottingham.

Teleworkers face increased pressure from family, feelings of guilt unless they work long hours, and disruption of normal home life, the study shows.

Dr Susanne Tietze from the Nottingham Business School, who led the study, said: 'Many companies are becoming more and more flexible with working patterns – and for some people that can be a godsend. But for others it is having a dramatic effect on family life and often leaves partners with a kind of secretarial role keeping disruptions to a minimum.'

Dr Tietze said that many home workers put in far more hours than they would have done at the office to ensure colleagues do not think they are taking advantage of the flexible work arrangements.

Teleworkers, especially women, often find themselves becoming more and more involved with running the home because they are always available.

Men were more effective at separating work from home and found it easier to divide themselves off from the demands of young children while working.

A number of people said they are considering returning to their offices full time, not for practical reasons but because they wanted a more normal working day, despite the added pressures of commuting and finding suitable childcare.

'Despite the problems, working from home is a growing trend because people can avoid commuting, traffic and other urban hassles,' she said.

www.bbc.co.uk

Discussion points

1. Despite the obvious problems outlined above, why do many entrepreneurs decide to start up their new businesses from home?

2. Apart from the problems outlined above, what other difficulties might an entrepreneur face when working from home?

Factors affecting location decisions

There are various factors affecting the choice of location for a business start-up. With a small business start-up, there may be different priorities

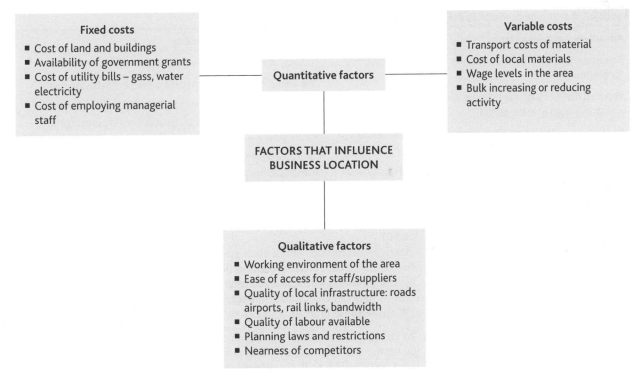

Fig. 9.1 *Location factors*

for different **stakeholders.** The most important factor for some businesses is to be close to customers. For retail outlets, being close to the customer, or at least in a location that the customer expects the business to be, is essential. Passing trade influences footfall, the number of people entering a premises in a given time period, and this can be crucial to the success of a new business because it is trying to establish itself. To an employee, transport to and from work is perhaps the most important factor, so proximity to transport links becomes important. Transport might be the most important factor in relation to suppliers, particularly if the products or parts are expensive to transport. The location of competitors might be a relevant factor, either in terms of avoiding being near them, or perhaps the opposite; in some cases, it pays to be located near to competition so that customers can easily visit all alternatives.

As IT influences business more, the physical location of companies becomes less important. Businesses are becoming more 'footloose' and less dependant on the traditional locational factors.

For some entrepreneurs, the chance to work from home is a key decision to go into business in the first place, so the location is determined by non-business factors.

Technology – teleworking

Undoubtedly technology is affecting location decisions for many small businesses. The most significant is the impact of the internet on the ability of entrepreneurs to work from home. This is sometimes referred to as teleworking. Improvements in communications mean that for many people, the home is either an extension of the office, or it is the office. There are a number of benefits and drawbacks in running a business from home.

Key terms

Stakeholder: an individual or group with an interest in a business. Stakeholders include employees, management, shareholders, customers, suppliers and competitors.

AQA Examiner's tip

In the exam, be prepared to justify why particular location factors are relevant to businesses in specific circumstances. The significance of a factor will vary according to the precise circumstances in which the business finds itself.

Table 9.1 *Advantages and disadvantages of teleworking*

Advantages of teleworking	Disadvantages of teleworking
Reduced costs, because the entrepreneur does not have to pay for premises	It is sometimes difficult to separate work from home life
Reduced risk, because the business does not have to commit to a lengthy rental or lease period	There may be initial set up costs, a house is rarely perfectly suitable as a workplace
Reduced travelling so that more time can be spent actually working as opposed to travelling to work	There may be a loss of social aspects of work, causing the entrepreneur to feel lonely
Allows some entrepreneurs to plan work around family and other commitments	There may be hidden costs such as the effect on house insurance, council tax or a tenancy agreement
Family are on hand to help if needed	It might not be possible to avoid distractions such as children, pets, etc

■ Link

For more information on costs (such as fixed and variable) see Chapter 11 – Calculating costs, revenues and profits, page 15.

Costs

Clearly, with finance being such an issue at the start of a business, the costs associated with location decisions are likely to be crucial. Techniques such as break-even analysis and investment appraisal can be used to help decide a location based on financial information, and you will study these later in your course.

An entrepreneur is likely to consider the costs associated with particular locations, and compare the revenues gained. There will be a number of fixed costs, which will not depend on the level of output, but will differ in different locations. These include the cost of purchasing or renting the building. A location that is cheap to buy may save money in the short term, but will the location maximise revenue? Also, its value as an asset for resale will be lower if it is an unattractive place. In addition, there might be costs associated with transforming the location into suitable premises. If the business needs staff who will be paid a fixed salary, then that fixed cost will need to be taken into account. In areas which are high cost, salaries tend to be high also to compensate, pushing up the fixed costs of the business start-up. If skilled staff are needed, this might push costs up even more if they are in short supply. Costs of utilities will also need to be considered.

Some of these fixed costs might be reduced if there are incentives to locate in particular areas. For example, the Department for Business, Enterprise and Regulatory Reform is responsible for the nine Regional Development Agencies, whose role it is to improve efficiency, employment and skill levels in particular areas of England. Scotland, Wales and Ireland have similar arrangements.

Variable costs may differ at different locations. Transport costs may differ because of the distances travelled, and the quality of the transport links. The impact of this will depend upon whether the product becomes more costly to transport as a finished product or as component parts. If labour is needed as a variable cost, this may also differ between locations. Some skilled labour costs can vary significantly in different parts of the country.

■ Case study

Boodles Beers

Karen Hodges opened Boodles in 2007 in a recently converted building in Chichester. She and her husband Tom had both worked for a large brewery running pubs throughout the South of England. When the possibility came up to buy their own pub and make the beer on the premises, they didn't have a moment's hesitation.

A key to locating in Chichester was proximity to the key ingredients of malt, yeast and Kent and Sussex hops. They use a brewing technique largely unchanged for decades and have begun to attract customers from throughout Sussex, Kent and Hampshire.

Questions

1 List the main factors other than raw materials likely to affect the location of a brewery such as Boodles.

2 Analyse whether a brewery such as Boodles is likely to locate near its raw materials or near its market.

3 To what extent is location likely to be the most significant factor affecting the price of Boodles' finished product?

Infrastructure

In the majority of cases, transport links will be a relevant factor in a company's choice of location, whether in terms of the distance from the raw materials or the customer. As the quality of service becomes more important as a way to add value, the speed, reliability and flexibility of delivery takes on greater significance. In these circumstances, being close to your customers or being easy to get to, is a selling point. Infrastructure also means local services such as waste disposal, entertainment, health, education and other public services.

The market

For many small business start-ups, being close to the customer is essential. It is often the reason the business started in the first place. What some entrepreneurs forget is that as they grow their customer base becomes more geographically dispersed, and what seemed like a good location, may quickly become a disadvantage. This factor is more significant for a product that gains weight in the production process as the cost of transporting the finished product is greater than the cost of transporting the raw materials.

The number of competitors in a given market may differ with changing locations. It might be better to locate a new business in a position away from a lot of competition.

Qualitative factors

So far, the factors considered have all been quantitative, but some factors cannot have numerical values attached to them.

For example, the decision to start a business is sometimes determined by a person's desire for a different kind of life. So the quality of life in a location might be a significant factor. The quality of local schools and hospitals, the weather, the local sports facilities or the nightlife, might all play a part in the location decision.

Other factors such as local planning laws, local regulations and the availability of land for expansion might be important. The quality of labour, and the ease with which workers can travel to work could be relevant.

In the end, an entrepreneur will have to take a number of quantitative and qualitative factors into account, and the relative importance of each one will depend upon:

■ The nature of the product – does it gain or lose weight in the production process.

■ Is it a service? – in which case its location is more likely to be influenced by the customers' location needs.

■ Business in action

Regus

Wouldn't it be great if you could locate your business anywhere? Move it temporarily to suit your needs? Never have to commit to long-term locations?

With Regus, you're free to run your business without the financial or management burden that comes with traditional office rental. That's because we take care of everything – your office is equipped and ready to go. All you need to do is choose the right location and move in. Offices can be chosen from over 950 locations, each supported by technology and a team of people to help with running the office, greeting visitors or taking calls. Offices can be rented for short periods of time, or for occasional use.

Fig. 9.2 *Regus*

■ Do costs, both fixed and variable differ in different locations?

■ How limited is the entrepreneur in her/his choice of locations?

■ What qualitative factors, if any, are important?

Case study

Xtreem

When Zachary Hardingham decided to start a business, there was only ever going to be one thing he would do, and that was to open a shop selling windsurfing and kitesurfing equipment. The other thing that was certain was the location. 'I've loved West Wittering in Sussex since I was a kid' he said. 'We went to Bognor Regis every year for our holidays, and I loved going to the beach at West Wittering and seeing the windsurfers'. So his decision to locate Xtreem was an easy one for him. It helped that local amenities were good and that the weather was better than most other parts of the UK. There were good business reasons for locating to the Sussex coast as well. For example, windsurfing, sailing and other water sports are very popular in the area, which is a very popular tourist destination in the summer, with tourists spending over £150m annually in the area. Suppliers were close by, and there was a steady supply of people able to teach the visitors the basics of windsurfing.

Zachary and his family had struggled to afford a house in the area, because house prices were 20 per cent above the national average, and he still hadn't managed to employ an office manager. It seemed that salaries for skilled professionals were high as well.

Still, as Zachary headed for the sea for his regular morning session out on the waves, he wasn't worried by this, or by the two other windsurfing shops that had opened nearby this summer.

Questions

1 Describe the main factors that influenced Zachary's location for Xtreem.

2 Assess whether Zachary was influenced more by qualitative or quantitative factors

3 Analyse the possible problems of the location chosen by Zachary

4 To what extent is the opening of two other windsurfng shops in the area an opportunity or a threat to the success of Xtreem?

💡📓✔ *In this chapter you will have learned to:*

■ describe the main quantitative and qualitative location factors affecting location decisions and appreciate that different factors will have varying importance to different businesses, depending on their particular circumstances

■ understand why some entrepreneurs start businesses from home, and understand some of the potential disadvantages of teleworking

■ use location factors to make and justify location decisions for particular businesses.

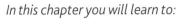

10 | Employing people

Setting the scene

The employment scene

In July 2007, there were just over 29 million people in employment. 21.7 million were in full-time employment, and 7.45 million were in part-time employment.

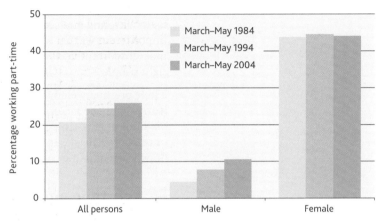

Fig. 10.1 *Percentage of people in employment working part-time: by sex, 1984, 1994, 2004*

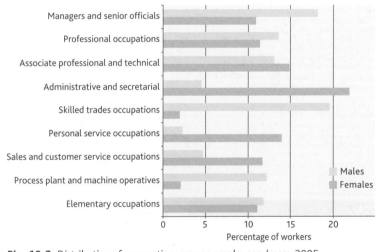

Fig. 10.2 *Distribution of occupations among employees: by sex 2005*

Labour Force Survey (Figures 10.1 and 2)

Men accounted for 14 million and women 7.7 million of full-time employees. There were 1.75 million male part-time and 5.7 million female part-time employees.

82 per cent of those in employment were employed in services, and 12 per cent in manufacturing.

Temporary workers account for approximately 1.5 million employees.

Discussion points

1 Using the information above, what do you think is the importance of part time and full-time employment in the UK labour market?

2 How has that importance changed over time?

So far, you have learned about many of the key decisions that an entrepreneur will need to take at the start of a business. Many business textbooks, and most successful business people will say that the most important asset that a business has is its staff. So that means that the most important decision that an entrepreneur can take is employing the right people.

There are many elements to this decision, and in this chapter you will learn about the factors relating to the decision whether to employ people on a full or part-time basis and whether to employ them on a permanent or temporary basis. In addition, you'll learn about the benefits and drawbacks of using consultants and advisors.

Full-time employees

As the figures above show, full-time employment is by far the most significant part of total employment in the UK. For the entrepreneur starting a business, there are a number of benefits to employing people on a full-time basis.

Benefits

- Higher output may be possible from employees who work full-time because they are able to commit to longer hours. Many people choose to work longer hours than they are contracted to because they want to do a good job.
- Full-time employees are available all the time to handle unexpected events.
- Full-time employees might be able to build up better working relationships with each other because they spend a lot of time together.
- Full-time employees might be able to build up good relationships with customers or suppliers. In a competitive market, good customer service may be a key differentiating factor.
- It might be easier for full-time employees to take advantage of training opportunities.

Drawbacks

- High cost of employing people full time, especially if the value of their output falls in times of less than full capacity.
- Full-time employees might not give the business flexibility in terms of an ability to increase capacity or improve the skills base of the business.

AQA Examiner's tip

Despite the benefits of employing people part time, and the trend towards more part-time employees, remember that most employees are full-time. Many businesses employ a combination of full- and part-time employees in order to combine the benefits of having a core of workers full time with the flexibility that a proportion of part-time employees give the business.

Part-time employees

Part-time employment is a relatively small part of the overall labour market in terms of numbers, but it is growing in significance. Examples of part-time arrangements include:

Term-time workers – some businesses employ people during term time and give unpaid leave during school and college holidays.

Zero hours contracts – this is an arrangement whereby there is no fixed number of hours that a person is expected to work, but the hours worked changes as the demand for the employee changes.

Benefits

Flexibility is the key benefit. A small business that wants to operate for longer, or increase output slightly will often do it by employing someone part time to cover the extra work.

Part-time employees can be used when there are busy periods of trade. For example, hotels, restaurants and supermarkets all use part-time employees to cover peak trading.

Part-time employees can also be used to extend trading or production periods. For example, a supermarket might employ part time staff to operate in the evening and at weekend, or a petrol station might extend its night time hours with part-time staff.

Part-time work allows some people to manage work alongside other commitments, such as family. This means that businesses have access to a wider pool of labour and can employ people who they would not otherwise be able to attract if all they offered was full-time work.

Some part-time staff job share, allowing a wider range of skills and talents to enter the business.

If someone cannot or does not want to continue working full-time, employing them on a part-time basis means the business retains valuable experienced staff.

Finally, as a small business just starting out, part-time staff represent a starting point, enabling the business to build itself slowly, as it becomes more established.

Drawbacks

There can be drawbacks to employing people on a part-time basis. However, it is important for an entrepreneur to realise that it is illegal to treat part-time staff less favourably than full-time staff. In particular, employers should be careful not to indirectly discriminate against female employees, many of whom work part-time.

Part-time staff may find it more difficult to be able to access training opportunities to the same extent as full-time staff and special arrangements may need to be made.

It may be more difficult to communicate with part-time employees.

Part-time employees may be less able to build close relationships with customers.

The costs of employing and managing people on a part-time basis may not be much lower than on a full- time basis. For example, it costs as much to administer a part-time salary as it does a full-time one.

Recent legislation has given many employees with children and other dependents the right to request to go from full-time to part-time work, and employers have a legal duty to consider these requests and can only reject them on business grounds.

AQA Examiner's tip

When considering the benefits of employing people part-time, don't forget that legislation brought in over the last few years gives part-time workers the same rights as full-time workers. This might act to reduce the flexibility enjoyed by small businesses.

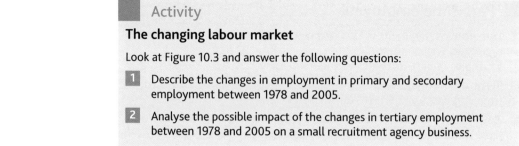

The changing labour market

Look at Figure 10.3 and answer the following questions:

1 Describe the changes in employment in primary and secondary employment between 1978 and 2005.

2 Analyse the possible impact of the changes in tertiary employment between 1978 and 2005 on a small recruitment agency business.

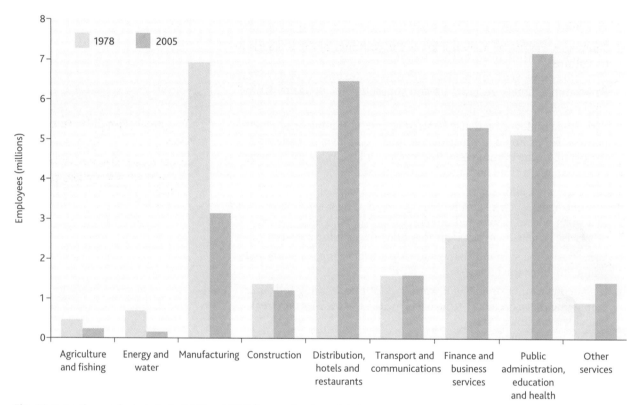

Fig. 10.3 *Employee jobs: by industry 1978 and 2005 (Source: Employee Jobs)*

Another choice that a business has is whether to employ people permanently or on a temporary basis. The majority of employees are permanent. This means that they are employed on an indefinite basis, and will end their employment either by resigning, retiring, by being made redundant or being sacked. An increasing number of businesses are using **temporary employees**.

■ Temporary employees

Benefits

■ If the volume of business may be uneven or uncertain the entrepreneur can keep the level of staffing flexible.

■ There may be specific tasks or jobs that need doing, which may have a finite time period. For instance, a small business might need an IT system designing and installing. This could mean a period of intense work, but only for a period of time.

■ Key terms

Temporary employee: one who is employed for a fixed period or periods of time. Often these workers are seasonal workers and may work full or part time. They rarely have the same benefits as permanent employees such as pensions or health insurance.

- The business may lack certain skills, which are only needed for specific periods of time. For example, a small business may need specialist HR advice as it goes through a period of recruitment or redundancy.

- A small business may wish to make or sell a product or service for a fixed period of time, and therefore has a need for a type of labour for a fixed time period.

- Temporary employees may help a business through a period of short term staff shortage or loss. A common example is maternity cover.

- Temporary workers who prove extremely valuable may eventually become permanent.

Drawbacks

- Temporary employees may not know the workings of the business or its culture.

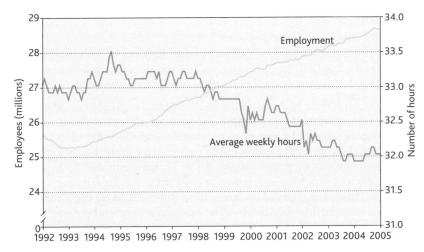

Fig. 10.4 *Average weekly hours of work and total number of people in employment 1992–2005 (Source: Labour Source Survey)*

Activity

Changes in the pattern of work

Look at Figure 10.4. What does it tell you about the changing pattern of employment?

- Temporary employees may not be as motivated as permanent employees.

- Constant changeover of employees may make communication more difficult.

- Customers may not like a constantly changing workforce, particularly if the business is a service business.

Consultants and advisors

Finally, some small businesses need very specific help and advice, often about the general running of the business, rather than about particular tasks that need carrying out. In these circumstances, small businesses will sometimes hire **consultants** or advisors.

Benefits

- Small businesses can gain the benefits of specialist skills without having the cost of employing people full-time.

- Entrepreneurs can add to their skills base as and when they need to.

- Business can adjust size of workforce up or down quickly.

Key terms

Consultants: businesses or individuals who provide professional advice or services for a fee. Often the advice is on how to make the small business more successful or to deal with a specific problem.

THE HENLEY COLLEGE LIBRARY

■ Avoids the need to search for and recruit staff, which can be risky if the wrong people are recruited.

■ Business start-ups can gain the advice of specialists in the early stages of the business. Often this is provided free or at a subsidised rate.

Drawbacks

■ Consultants will not know the business as well as employees.

■ Consultants may not be as motivated to work hard for the business as employees.

■ In some cases, consultants can be expensive.

Case study

Slivers-of-Time

Slivers-of-Time Working is for anyone with spare hours to sell to local employers.

This new way of working gives individuals immediate cash, all sorts of skills and a verified CV of successful short bookings. Employers get an ultra-flexible, motivated pool of top-up workers who can be booked at short notice. They can be economically trained.

Slivers-of-Time is the ultimate in flexibility. People able to offer small amounts of time flexibly and at short notice for a wide range of jobs are known as 'work seekers' and they offer their time via a website. They do this via an online diary of the hours each particular day they are available for work. For example: *'It's now 5.00 pm, I want to work between 6.00 and 9.00 this evening.'* They also define the types of bookings they will do, how far they'll travel and how their hourly rate is to be calculated for each booking. Businesses looking for workers input their needs, for example *'3 people for 2 hours at lunchtime today'*, they see everyone who wants to do that specific booking ranked by reliability and hourly rate. They can buy instantly.

Table 10.1 *Buyers and sellers of Slivers-of-Time*

Sellers of slivers-of-time	Buyers of slivers-of-time
Parents	Local authorities
Students	Caterers
Newly retired	Retailers
Carers	Manufacturers
Partially employed	Leisure industry
Medically restricted	Hospitality providers
Business starters	Promotions companies
Job-seekers	Logistics providers
Experience seekers	Service companies
Work returners	Care providers

There are a number of benefits to this flexible way of working, and it is clear there is a growing number of people who want to work more flexibly.

Fig. 10.5 *The Slivers-of-Time marketplace (sliversoftime.com)*

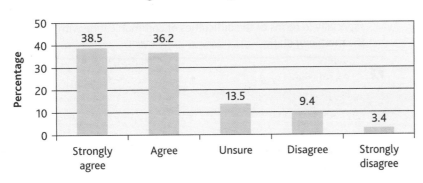

Fig. 10.6 *Changing attitudes to flexible working (continued overleaf)*

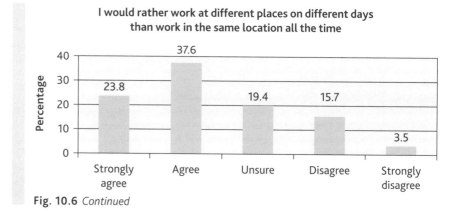

Fig. 10.6 *Continued*

Questions

1. Describe the possible benefits to the employee of the Slivers-of-Time system.

2. Explain the possible disadvantages of the system to a small printing business.

3. Analyse the importance of technology to the Slivers-of-Time system.

4. Evaluate the possible limitations of the Slivers-of-Time system.

In this chapter you have learned to:

- understand the benefits and drawbacks of employing workers on a full- and a part-time basis and understand some of the circumstances where part-time employment might be suitable for both employee and employer

- understand that many businesses employ a combination of full and part-time staff in order to enjoy both the benefits of a core of full-time workers with the flexibility that part-time employees give a business

- assess the benefits and drawbacks of temporary as opposed to permanent employment and appreciate the circumstances in which temporary employees might be useful to a business

- evaluate the limitations of part-time and temporary employment, especially in terms of the difficulties of communicating with or maintaining the morale of staff.

Summary questions

Chapters 7–10

1   Explain what is meant by the term 'sole trader'. *(2 marks)*

2   Describe two possible benefits of forming a partnership, to three school friends who are considering starting a business that designs and builds luxury houses. *(6 marks)*

3   Define the term 'stakeholders'. *(3 marks)*

4   What is the meaning of the term 'unlimited liability'? *(3 marks)*

5   Describe two differences between a private and a public limited company. *(4 marks)*

6   Analyse three factors a taxi service should consider before taking out a bank overdraft facility. *(6 marks)*

7   Evaluate three ways in which a not-for-profit business might differ from a business that has profit as its main objective. *(8 marks)*

8   Describe two disadvantages of using personal sources of finance to start up a bed and breakfast business. *(4 marks)*

9   Nick and Wendy Evans began their organic vegetable business three years ago and have slowly expanded the business by reinvesting profit. They started the business after moving to the Sussex countryside when they left their jobs in London. They now want to expand more quickly so they can supply to a large supermarket. The expansion will need to be financed from sources outside the business. Nick and Wendy are the only shareholders in the business, which is a limited company.

    a)   Describe three pieces of information that a bank is likely to need before making a decision whether to lend £20,000 to an organic vegetable grower. *(6 marks)*

    b)   Define the term 'venture capitalist' and explain the benefits to Nick and Wendy of this source of finance. *(8 marks)*

    c)   What is meant by the term 'qualitative location factors' and why might they be important to Nick and Wendy? *(6 marks)*

    d)   To what extent is it advisable for Nick and Wendy to grow slowly or more quickly? *(10 marks)*

10   Describe three possible location factors relevant to a decision about where to locate an accountant's business. *(6 marks)*

11   Analyse three possible drawbacks of an accountant operating her business from home. *(6 marks)*

12   Describe three possible benefits to a hotel of employing part time staff. *(6 marks)*

13   Analyse three possible difficulties a business growing and selling strawberries to supermarkets might encounter by employing temporary workers.   *(8 marks)*

14   Assess the likely problems a dry cleaning business might have when trying to decrease the proportion of part-time and increase the proportion of full-time staff working at its branches.   *(6 marks)*

15   Describe three ways a house builder might benefit from using a business consultant.   *(5 marks)*

16   Gemma Harcourt has run her sports-goods business, Finishing Line UK, as a sole-trading operation, a partnership and a limited company. She started the business in 2000 and the business is currently growing at a rate of over 25 per cent a year. The business grew quickly and soon she needed more space, more money, and some help. She formed a limited company in 2006.

The business still struggles financially, and is currently considering ways to raise finance for the purchase of a new shop in the centre of Manchester. She has looked at a number of possible locations in the city centre, but can't make up her mind as to the best location.

One of the most challenging and rewarding parts of running the business is dealing with staff. Each shop has a full time manager, and four part time sales staff, all of whom have been with the company for a few years now. She can't seem to get the number of staff right. At certain times of the week, staff struggle to find things to do, whilst at other times they are rushed off their feet. The problems are made worse when they suddenly get a large number of orders from the website, which they struggle to process quickly if they come in during a busy part of the week.

  a)   Describe three possible benefits to Finishing Line UK of incorporation into a limited company.   *(6 marks)*

  b)   Suggest two possible sources of external finance for the purchase of the new Manchester shop.   *(2 marks)*

  c)   Assess the possible factors likely to influence the location of the Manchester shop.   *(8 marks)*

  d)   To what extent would the use of temporary employees solve the problems experienced by Finishing Line UK?   *(10 marks)*

Introduction

Chapters in this section:

How would you try to calculate the profit made by this market stallholder?

It should be clear by now that setting up a new business is challenging but potentially rewarding. There are so many different issues to consider before a business idea can come to fruition. Yet there is still one vital aspect of entrepreneurship that has not yet been covered – PROFIT!

Most entrepreneurs will be setting up in business with the intention of 'making money'. This may not always be the primary goal, as we will see in Chapter 15 – Assessing business start-ups, page 105, but it is likely to be of some significance to all entrepreneurs. When some business owners say that 'I am not in it for the money' this does not mean that they do not care how much cash the business is creating or how much of a profit or loss it is making. It might suggest, though, that there are personal aims even more important than 'making money'.

However, no matter what these other aims might be, unless a lucky entrepreneur has bottomless pockets, it will be essential for anyone planning to start a business to have a clear idea of the importance of cash and profit to its future survival and success. This section provides a clear explanation of the financial issues and concepts that all budding business owners must be aware of. But the business owners will not be the only group interested in the financial forecasts for costs, revenue and profit (or loss). Investors and banks providing finance will be keenly aware of the need for entrepreneurs to forecast these financial data. They will also want to see records of what actually happens to sales, costs and profit when the business starts trading.

So, financial planning is an essential part of preparing to set up a new business. This section focuses on the key financial concepts that entrepreneurs must understand and apply to their new business plan.

These include business costs and revenue, profit, cash flow, the output level needed to break even and setting financial plans or budgets. Some essential calculations are carefully worked through and explained and the interpretation of these results is made clear.

The section is divided into five chapters.

Chapter 11: Calculating costs, revenue and profit What do we mean by profit and how is it calculated? What is the difference between profit and sales revenue? What are the most likely costs that have to be paid by a small business? If the aim of a new business is to make money for its owner, then understanding the factors that determine profit is essential.

Chapter 12: Using break-even analysis to make decisions How many customers will the business need before it covers all of its costs and starts to make a profit? How could the level of profit be increased by reducing the break-even number of customers? A new business will be required to 'break-even' as soon as possible so that the entrepreneur can start to make a return on the initial investment.

Chapter 13: Using cash flow forecasting What is meant by 'cash flow' and why is cash important to a business? Why is it important to plan for future cash needs and how is this done? What is the typical structure of a cash flow forecast? More small businesses fail due to lack of cash than for any other reason – cash flows must be planned for.

Chapter 14: Setting budgets Making financial plans and trying to keep to them. Which parts of the business need these plans and what are the advantages in setting them? What are the common problems often associated with setting budgets? Target setting is an important part of new business planning – budgets provide a direction for the business and a means of checking progress.

Chapter 15: Assessing business start-ups How can an entrepreneur judge whether the business is a success or not? What are the main risks that confront new business start-ups? What are the most common reasons for the failure of newly formed businesses? Despite the best laid plans of entrepreneurs there are still many risks that await every new business start-up – and these can overwhelm the unprepared.

11 Calculating costs, revenues and profits

Setting the scene

Rashid

Rashid was pleased with himself. In his first month of trading he had sold and fitted 10 car satellite navigation systems, two more than originally forecast in his Business Plan. Rashid's electrical skills and his friendly personality had impressed his customers.

He had purchased the first 50 satellite navigation kits from a website specialising in stock sell-offs from failed businesses. He had paid £100 each. This had swallowed up most of his start-up capital. He rented a small lock up garage for £120 a month. The large sign he fixed to the doors had cost him £120 but attracted lots of attention. Other advertising costs in his first month had been more than expected. The local newspaper had just increased its classified rates – £150 was £30 more than planned. He sold the kits for £275 fully fitted. Rashid could have just sold the kits themselves but he wanted to 'add value' to them by doing the fitting too. Each fitting kit cost Rashid £10. Other costs – such as business rates and fixed charges for electricity – had been paid and these totalled £200 per month, just as predicted. He had already paid an accountant for help with setting up the business and writing the business plan.

Rashid started to work out his profit for the first month. His only real worry was that two of his customers – whom he had known from school days – had asked for some time to pay him. He had agreed as he wanted to make the sale. But when would they pay? Should he include these two kits when working out his first monthly profits?

Discussion points

1 What evidence is there that Rashid had thought about the costs of running his business before he set it up?

2 Do you think he made a profit in his first month of trading? How would you try to work this out?

3 Why would profit be important to Rashid?

4 If you were Rashid, would you have offered the two customers 'credit', i.e. time to pay him back?

Key terms

Profit: what is left after costs have been deducted from revenue.

Profit = Total revenue – total costs.

The meaning and importance of profit

Profit is a surplus. It is the surplus of the value of sales made by a business over its total costs of production. It is very important to entrepreneurs and small businesses for a number of reasons:

1 Profit is used as a measure of success by the owners of a business who have invested capital into it.

2 Banks and other lenders will be unlikely or unwilling to lend to a business that does not either forecast a profit – or actually make one.

Key terms

Costs: these are expenditures made by a business as part of its trading operations.

Revenue: the value of sales made during a trading period.

> **Total revenue = selling price ×
> number of items sold.**

Fixed costs: costs that do not change with the level of output or sales.

Variable costs: costs that change directly with the level of output or sales

Total costs: fixed costs + variable costs.

3 It is the return or reward to entrepreneurs and business owners for taking risks with their capital. If no profit is made, this will discourage further investment and may lead to business closure.

4 As a surplus, profit provides a source of finance for further expansion of the business.

To understand profit it is essential to understand the relationship between profit, **revenue** and **costs**.

Measuring business costs

Consider Rashid's costs in the case study above. They were typical of the costs faced by most small businesses. Some of them had to be paid before he started trading such as the accountant's fees. These are start-up costs. Others did not vary with the number of kits he fitted. The garage rent and advertising costs would have to be paid even if Rashid did not sell a single kit. These are referred to as **fixed costs**. Even if Rashid sold a further ten kits the fixed costs of the business would not change. Finally, some costs were only incurred as he sold and fitted the kits. Clearly, the cost of the 'Satnav' kits themselves depended on the number of customers. These are called **variable costs**. Adding fixed and total costs together gives a firm's **total costs**.

AQA Examiner's tip

Total revenue includes products sold on credit as well as those sold for cash during the trading period.

Activity

1 In Rashid's case can you give ONE further example of:
   a a fixed cost, and
   b a variable cost?

2 Calculate the total monthly fixed and variable costs (ignoring set up costs) for Rashid if he sells and fits 12 units.

3 If Rashid had not made a profit in his first year of running his business,

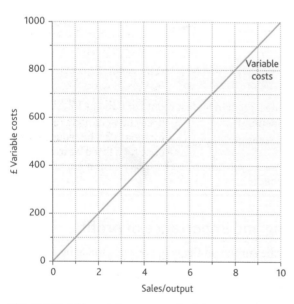

Fig. 11.1 *Variable costs increase as output rises*

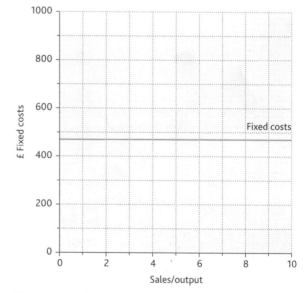

Fig. 11.2 *Fixed costs do not change as output rises*

Why calculate costs of production?

When planning to start a new business, entrepreneurs will need to forecast likely costs. These predictions will allow:

- A forecast of profit or loss to be made – will the business be a viable one?
- Forecasts of the likely break-even level of output – this is explained in the next chapter.
- Cash flow forecasts to be drawn up so that financial planning is undertaken.
- Pricing decisions to be made based on cost data.

Once a new business is up and running why should the owner need to know what costs are being incurred? There are several reasons for this:

- Keeping a check of actual costs against the forecasted costs that were part of the original business plan. Is the firm exceeding these costs and, if so, why?
- Using cost information to help in the pricing decision. In Rashid's case, any substantial increase in either variable or fixed costs may lead him to raising his price to customers.
- Calculating whether costs are greater or less than revenue – is the firm profitable at this level of sales or not?

Measuring sales revenue

Consider Rashid's sales in the case study above. Do you agree that his total revenue for the first month was £2,750? This figure is obtained by multiplying the price of each fitted kit (£275) by the number of kits sold (10). Remember: the sale of the two kits on credit is still included as revenue!

Rashid could try to increase his revenue in month 2 in two ways:

1 Try to sell and fit more than 10 kits this month – increase his sales.
2 Raise the selling price from £275.

If Rashid was absolutely confident that potential customers would pay more than £275 then his revenue would increase with a higher price. But how likely is this in reality? If he raised the price in month 2 to £300 for a fitted kit and customers fell to 8 his total revenue would fall to £2,400. So, entrepreneurs such as Rashid have to be cautious about price changes as they may have a negative impact on total revenue. The ability of any entrepreneur to increase price to gain extra revenue will depend on the level of competition the firm faces and how 'unique' the good or service is.

Making a profit?

Profit = total revenue – total costs

Rashid did indeed make a profit in his first month – this was a good start to his business. How could he try to increase this level of profit in later months?

The total profit of any business during a trading period depends on two main factors:

Business in action

Calculating costs and comparing these with revenue is important for all businesses. Southdown Infants School in Bath has been operating its own school catering service as a separate business for several years. Variable costs per meal are 90p and the meals are sold for £1.60. The fixed costs make up most of the difference – but that still leaves a healthy profit which is invested back into improving catering facilities.

AQA Examiner's tip

Students often confuse 'cost' with 'price' – the differences should now be clear. Don't think as a consumer all the time – think like an entrepreneur!

Activity

1 Can you suggest two ways Rashid could use to try to sell more kits **without** changing the price of them?

2 What might happen to the number of customers if he raised his selling price?

3 Recalculate Rashid's revenue for month 2 if he reduced the price for a fitted kit to £250 and sold 13 of them.

Link

The relationship between price and revenue is studied in more detail in Chapter 32 – Using the marketing mix: pricing, page 239.

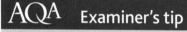

Activity

1 Calculate Rashid's profit (ignoring all other costs) from his first month of trading.

2 Ignoring all other costs, calculate Rashid's profit in month 2 if he sells 15 fitted kits at £275 each.

AQA Examiner's tip

Never confuse profit with cash. If products are sold on credit, a profit may be recorded but there is no cash to show for it yet!

Fig. 11.3 *Pricing decisions are very important in a competitive market such as pizza restaurants*

■ Profit on each item sold. Rashid makes £100 on each kit sold without fitting (price of £200 less the variable cost of each kit of £100). The profit margin of each fitted kit is

£165 (£275 – {£100 + £10 fitting kit})

■ The quantity sold in the trading period. If in month 2 he sells 15 fitted kits at the same price as month 1 his total profit will increase.

Case study

Pizza price dispute

It was the first time that the partners had disagreed since setting up Pizza Parlour four months ago. Sales revenue had exceeded forecasts but so had variable costs. Profit was therefore lower than planned. The cost of the 'quality ingredients' which were the original focus of the business had turned out to be much higher than expected.

Figures for the last month had been:

Sales: 1,000 pizzas @ £6 each

Fixed costs: £1,300

Variable costs: £4 per pizza (average)

'This profit is not enough to expand the business and I do not believe it pays us for the risks we are taking' said Markus, one of the two partners. 'I think we should buy cheaper ingredients – say £3 per unit – and cut the price by 50 pence. We would be cheaper than most local competitors and I estimate sales could rise to 1,200 per month'.

'This would hit the image we have worked hard to build up,' said Claire, the other partner. 'I think we should do the reverse. We should sell our pizzas at a 10% higher price and spend another £200 on advertising each month. Judging by our last adverts this could increase sales by 5% per month.'

Questions

1 Using examples from this case distinguish between the following:

   a Sales and sales revenue.

   b Fixed costs and variable costs.

2 Outline two reasons why profit is important to this newly formed business.

3 Analyse the possible drawbacks to this business of buying cheaper ingredients.

4 Which of the two suggestions for increasing profit would you recommend the partners to decide on? You should use calculations of profit before any price changes and forecasted profit after both price changes to support your recommendation.

5 Research topic: Assume that you are planning to open a restaurant in your town, find out in as much detail as you can the likely level of annual fixed costs for this business, assuming the property is to be rented and is to hold around 20 customers and the equipment is to be leased (a form of renting).

In this chapter you will have learned how to:

- understand why businesses need to make a profit
- explain the differences between variable and fixed costs
- calculate business costs at different output levels
- calculate revenue at different levels of output
- calculate profit or loss at different levels of output
- discuss different approaches that might be used to increase profit.

12 Using break-even analysis to make decisions

Setting the scene

Eat-your-fill

'We have been working flat out all month but I don't think we have made any profit yet,' complained Sara. 'I think we set our prices too low which is why we are so busy – but are we making any money, that's what I want to know?' Sara was the co-founder of 'Eat-your-fill' fast food restaurant. She and fellow entrepreneur, Jack, had been surprised by the huge demand from the public for their organic burgers and vegetarian menu options. However, the cost of their food supplies was proving to be higher than forecast due to seasonal shortages and yet the menus with fixed prices had been printed several weeks ago.

'We agreed on an average price of £10 yet the food costs per customer seem to have risen from the £3 forecasted when we drew up the business plan to about £4 now,' explained Jack. 'So we need to serve more customers each week just to cover our fixed weekly costs of £2,800'. 'Either we start looking for other, cheaper, food suppliers or we have to get the menus reprinted showing a 20% price rise – I am not going to exhaust myself for nothing,' warned Sara.

Discussion points

1. Would you classify the food costs as being a fixed or variable cost of this business?

2. Why does the increase in the cost of food supplies mean that the business 'needs to serve more customers each week just to cover fixed weekly costs of £2,800'?

3. What would be the advantages and disadvantages of each of the two proposals Sara made to increase the profitability of 'Eat-your-fill'?

Breaking-even

When a business is said to be 'breaking-even' it is just earning enough sales revenue to pay for all of its total costs. It is not yet making a profit but it is not recording a loss either. For an entrepreneur planning a new business this is a really important situation to aim for. If the business is able to break-even quickly then there should be opportunities to make progress to start earning a profit. Banks and other lenders to the business will be very interested to know whether the business is planned to break-even within one month or one year – the longer the period, the greater the business risk.

For existing businesses, just breaking-even will mean that business managers will need to take important decisions to turn 'breaking-even' into a profit.

How can the break-even level of production be calculated and how can decisions be made to reduce this level of output so that higher profits can be made? Answers to these crucial questions are the focus of this chapter.

■ Contribution and contribution per unit

■ **Key terms**

Contribution: this is the difference between sales revenue and variable costs of production.

Contribution is one of the most important financial concepts in Business Studies.

It is not the same as profit as in calculating contribution fixed costs are NOT subtracted. It is the surplus made after all variable costs have been paid for from sales revenue and this surplus goes towards paying for fixed costs. The following diagram helps to explain this relationship.

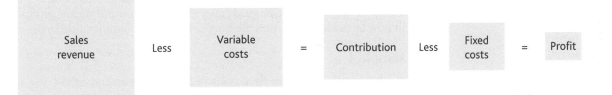

Fig. 12.1 *Contribution: how it is earned and what it is used for*

Contribution per unit of output is widely used by entrepreneurs and business managers to assist in taking important decisions. This figure can then be used to calculate the **total contribution**. Profit can then be calculated by using the formula: Total contribution - fixed costs.

■ **Key terms**

Contribution per unit: this is the difference between the selling price of one unit and the variable cost of producing one unit.

Total contribution: unit contribution × no. of units sold.

■ Case study

In the case study on page 80, Sara and Jack originally planned the contribution per customer to be £7 (£10 – £3). If they served 500 customers in one week then the total contribution would have been:

$$500 \times £7 = £3,500$$

This would be used to pay the restaurant's weekly fixed costs and any surplus is profit.

Questions

1. Using this total contribution figure, calculate the weekly profit from the restaurant if 500 customers were served each week?

2. What is the new contribution per unit following the increase in food costs?

3. What is the new total contribution per week if 500 customers are served each week?

4. Is the restaurant now making a weekly profit if 500 customers are served?

Some important points to remember about contribution per unit:

- It can be increased by raising the selling price
- It can be increased by reducing variable costs per unit
- It is not the same as profit per unit as fixed costs are not subtracted
- An increase in contribution per unit raises the potential profit that a business can make.

It is very useful in business decision making, such as in setting prices, and in calculating the break-even level of output.

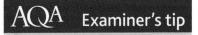

AQA **Examiner's tip**

Never make the mistake of describing 'contribution' as being profit – they really are different concepts.

■ Key terms

Break-even level of output: this is the level of output or the number of customers that earns enough revenue to cover total costs of production.

■ Calculating the break-even level of output

At the break-even level of output although revenue covers total costs there is no surplus so no profit is yet being earned. Obviously, if a business was **never** able to reach the **break-even level of output** it would never record a profit.

In the previous case study, should Sara and Jack have planned to achieve a high or a low number of customers in order to break-even?

There are obvious benefits from planning to reach a LOW break-even output. This means that all costs are being covered with a small number of customers. Any contribution made after this level of output means profits will now be made. But how is the break-even level of output calculated?

Example 1

If a printing business pays fixed costs of £500 per week and each customer earns the business a contribution of £250, how many customers each week are needed to pay for fixed costs – and therefore break-even? 2 is the answer – but what is the 'formula' used?

$$\text{Break-even output} = \frac{\text{Fixed costs of the business}}{\text{Contribution per unit}}$$

Example 2

A petrol station buys in petrol at 93p per litre. The selling price is 99p per litre. Weekly fixed costs are £1,200. How many litres of petrol does it have to sell to break-even?

$$\text{Break-even output} = \frac{\pounds1,200}{99p - 93p} = 20,000 \text{ litres}$$

Example 3

The petrol station owner has been able to negotiate lower annual electricity charges and weekly fixed costs fall to £1,140. How will this affect the break-even level of output?

$$\text{Break-even output} = \frac{\pounds1,140}{6p} = 19,000 \text{ litres}$$

The results from this activity are important. They show that, if nothing else changes, a **reduction** in contribution per customer or unit will RAISE the break-even level of output. If output does not increase then profits of the business will FALL. So, if one of Sara's two suggestions were put into effect, the increased contribution per customer would reduce the break-even level of output and increase profit – IF nothing else changes!

Calculating break-even output is an easy way of checking the viability of a new business proposal. It does not guarantee profitability or future success, of course, but it does give a really important indicator to the entrepreneur and the bank of the likely number of customers needed before the business can start to cover all of its costs. If this output level seems unreasonably high, then the entrepreneur may have to reconsider the original business plan and look at ways to either reduce fixed costs or raise contribution per unit of output.

Whilst these break-even calculations give a useful guide to the number of units of output or the number of customers needed to cover all costs they do not show how much profit the business could actually make. To be able to do this, we now need to turn to break-even charts.

■ Activity

1. Calculate the break-even number of customers needed by 'Eat-your-fill' restaurant at:

   a the original forecasted variable cost level and

   b the actual variable cost level. Comment on your results.

2. Even though Sara's suggestions will increase contribution per customer, why might they NOT lead to higher profits?

Table 12.1 *Cost and price data for 'Eat-your-fill' restaurant*

Information needed	'Eat-your-fill' data
Weekly fixed costs	£2,800
Variable costs per customer (original forecasted figure)	£3
Average revenue earned per customer	£10
Maximum weekly number of customers – the capacity of the restaurant	600

💡 Break-even charts

These are graphs that show the revenue and costs of a business at different levels of output. They can be drawn by following a number of stages. In our example we will be using the 'Eat-your-fill' data in the first case study of this chapter. Here is the essential information that we will need taken from that case study plus some other important data.

You are advised to follow these stages carefully by drawing the chart on graph paper.

Stage 1

Mark out the scales on graph paper. The vertical axis will record weekly costs and revenues in £. The scale will extend from zero at the origin to the maximum revenue that can be earned = 600 customers × £10 each = £6,000. Mark out the scale in squares of £1,000.

The horizontal axis records the number of customers (or units of output). This scale will extend from zero at the origin to a maximum capacity of 600. Mark out the scale in squares of 100.

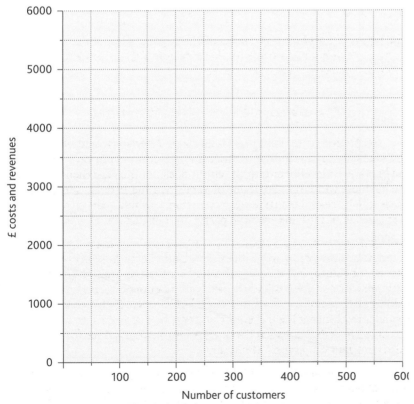

Fig. 12.2 *Mark out the scales as indicated*

Stage 2

Draw in the fixed cost line. Weekly fixed costs are £2,800 and – because they do not vary with the number of customers – this line can be drawn completely horizontal from the point £2,800 on the vertical scale.

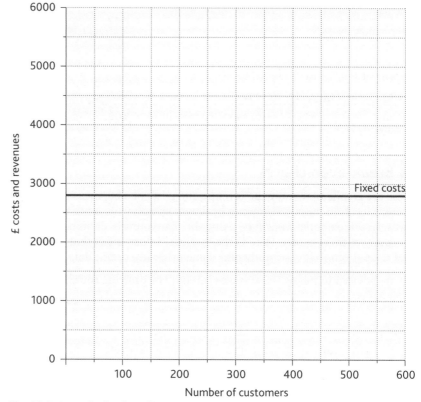

Fig. 12.3 *Draw the fixed cost line*

Stage 3

Draw in the variable cost line. Variable costs per customer were forecast to be £3. Start this line at zero – no customers means no variable costs are used in production. Just one more point is needed to complete the variable cost line. At 600 customers a week, total variable costs will be £1,800 – add this coordinate onto the graph and then join the two points with a straight line from zero to £1,800.

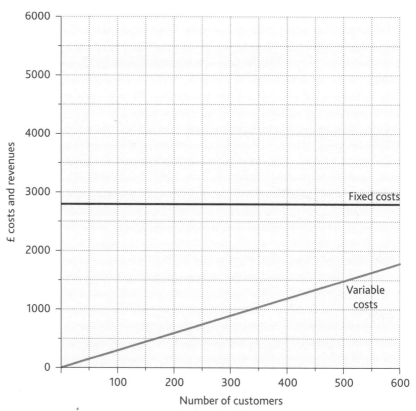

Fig. 12.4 *Draw in the variable cost line between zero and £1,800 (at 600 customers)*

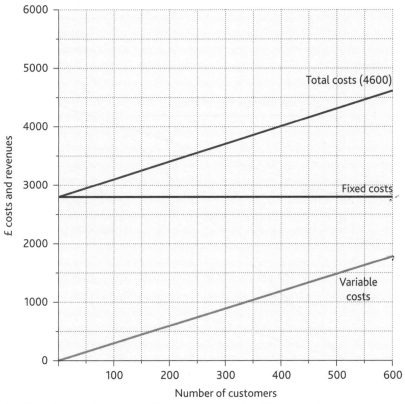

Fig. 12.5 *Total costs start at the fixed costs line and rise at the same rate as variable costs*

Stage 4

Add fixed and variable costs together at all levels of output to give the total weekly costs of the business. This line STARTS at £2,800 because even with no customers, there will be weekly fixed costs of £2,800. The fixed cost line is then drawn parallel to the variable cost line ending it at 600 customers. To check on this – the total costs at 600 customers will = £2,800 + (600 × £3) = £4,600. This coordinate will give you a total cost line parallel to variable costs.

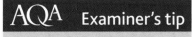

Examiner's tip

You only need two coordinates to draw a straight line – no need to plot more than two points.

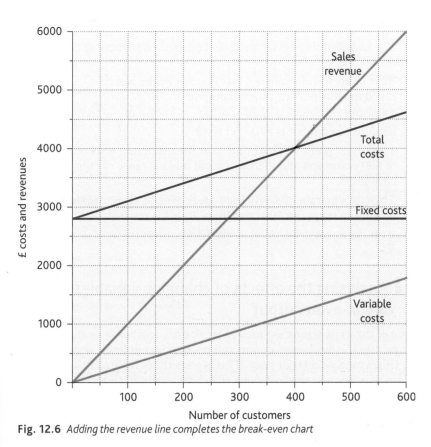

Fig. 12.6 *Adding the revenue line completes the break-even chart*

Stage 5

Add the revenue line to complete the break-even chart. The restaurant's revenue will be zero with no customers so this line starts at the origin. The other coordinate needed will be at maximum sales revenue – 600 customers × £10 = £6,000. Draw a straight line between zero and £6,000 (at 600 customers).

Stage 6

The level of output at which the firm just breaks even can now be shown by drawing a vertical line down to the horizontal axis from where total cost = total revenue.

At 500 customers per week, a profit of £700 is made.

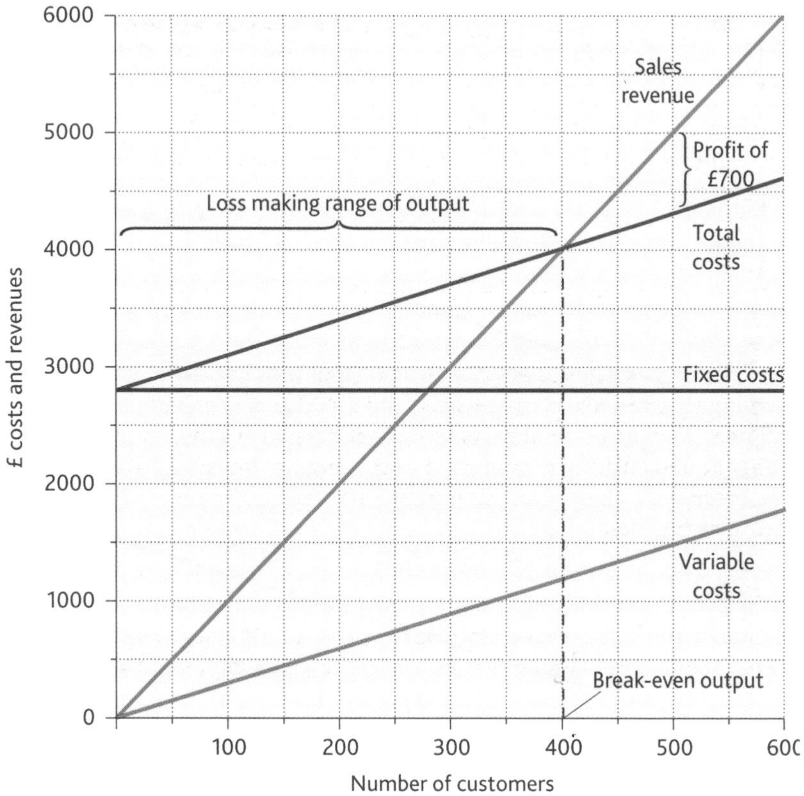

Fig. 12.7 *Draw a vertical line to the horizontal axis to show the break-even point*

AQA Examiner's tip

Good news! Examiners are MOST unlikely to ask you to draw a complete break-even chart. It is much more likely that you will be asked to add lines or change the position of existing ones.

Key terms

Margin of safety: this is the amount by which the existing level of output is greater than the break-even point.

Activity

1 Read off the forecasted level of profit if 550 customers were served in one week.

2 Calculate the margin of safety at 550 customers per week.

💡 Reading the break-even chart

What does the completed chart show us? Using the chart we are able to tell:

- The restaurant's original forecasted break-even number of customers = 400.
- That up to 400 customers a loss is made by the business – this is called the loss making range of output.
- After 400 customers a profit is made – for example, at 500 customers, the forecasted profit is £700 per week.
- The largest profit is, clearly, made at the maximum level of capacity of 600 customers and there is a profit making range of output of 200 customers.
- There is a **margin of safety** from break-even at 400 customers to maximum output at 600 customers, if this is reached.

Read off the forecasted level of profit if 550 customers were served in one week.

💡 Analysing the effects of changing variables on break-even output

One of the most significant uses of break-even analysis is to analyse the impact on the break-even output and potential profit levels of a change in either variable costs or price. This is sometimes referred to as 'what if analysis' because the technique allows managers to answer questions such as: 'What if the price increased, how would this affect the break-even point?' Both the break-even formula and break-even charts can be used for this analysis.

Example 1

Sara and Jack should have considered what would happen to their restaurant's break-even point and profitability if variable costs should rise – as food costs actually did. Using the break-even formula we can confirm the result you may have obtained earlier with variable costs now at £4 per customer:

$$\text{Break-even output} = \frac{\text{Fixed costs}}{\text{Contribution per unit}} = \frac{£2,800}{£6} = 467 \text{ customers}$$

Confirm the result in Example 1 by changing your break-even chart showing that variable costs now rise to £2,400 at 600 customers – you will need to increase total costs too. What happens to the restaurant's profits at 550 customers compared to the original forecast? Might this new break-even chart have discouraged Sara and Jack from setting up their new business?

Example 2

The following break-even chart was drawn by Bill Potter who planned to open a sports shoe shop. It was based on the following forecasted data.

Table 12.2 *Bill's cost and price data for the sports shoe shop*

Information needed	Bill Potter's forecasts
Annual fixed costs	£30,000
Variable costs per customer	£45
Selling price per pair of shoes	£105
Expected maximum sales level	2,000 pairs per year

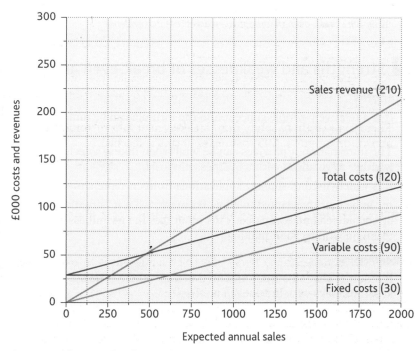

Fig. 12.8 *Bill Potter's break-even chart*

Bill included this break-even chart into his Business Plan. He was surprised when his bank's Business Development Manager queried the high forecasted selling price. She claimed that she knew the area that Bill was planning to set his shop up in better than he did and she didn't know anybody who would pay £105 for a pair of sports shoes! Bill agreed to revise the chart after he had done more market research.

Following visits to many sports shoe shops he decided that £85 was a more realistic selling price – but that this would mean buying cheaper styles with an average variable cost of £40. He also decided to rent a shop in a slightly better shopping centre costing an extra £20,000 a year. The new break-even chart now looked like this:

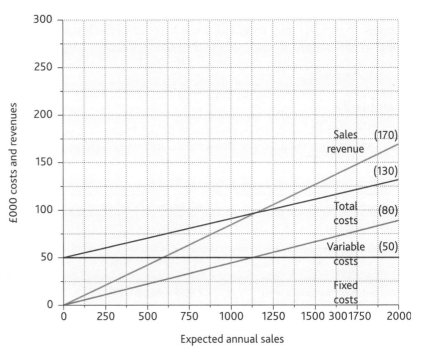

Fig. 12.9 *Bill's break-even chart based on market research evidence*

Activity

Compare Bill Potter's two break-even charts.

1 How has the expected break-even point changed?

2 What has happened to 'maximum' profit assuming 2,000 pairs sold a year?

3 Explain to Bill why his new business proposal is now less viable than with the original forecasts

💡 Strengths and weaknesses of break-even analysis

Strengths

■ It is a relatively simple concept and the formula can be understood and used by most entrepreneurs.

■ The information it provides can be vital when taking a decision whether to go ahead with a business proposal.

■ It is widely used to support applications from entrepreneurs for loans.

■ It can be quickly adapted to allow for many 'what if' situations to be considered and compared. This reinforces the usefulness of the technique for decision-making.

Weaknesses

■ It assumes that all output produced is sold – there is no scope for keeping stocks with break-even analysis.

■ It over simplifies business situations. For example, we have assumed above an 'average' customer revenue and 'average' variable cost and in reality there will be considerable variations.

- Many firms sell more than one product – e.g. a range of sports shoes not just one style! Break-even becomes much more difficult to apply in these cases.

- Fixed costs are rarely completely fixed over a wide range of output and variable costs could vary with bulk discounts as the business expands. Break-even analysis assumes 'steady and consistent' increases in variable costs.

- As we saw with Sara and Jack, misleading or inaccurate data leads to incorrect break-even forecasts.

- A break-even chart does not show what **will** definitely happen – it is a planning aid to help business managers consider the impact of various possible decisions.

Business in action

Cheet: Bags of Style

Setting up 'Cheet: Bags of Style' was always going to be a risky enterprise for fashion handbag designer Emily Cheetham. To cut start-up costs to a minimum she worked from a room in her flat and used her aunt's sewing machine. She used her wide circle of friends to help promote her products.

The business has recently had some success with made-to-order commissions and trade sales in two independent boutiques and this has increased sales to four bags per week. This means the business is just breaking even with a weekly sales turnover of £1,200.

Emily hopes to keep the business growing so that it becomes profitable but she is determined to continue to keep costs down. She has started to outsource production which gives her more time to design and sell. She is planning a ready-to-sell collection that should 'fly off the shelves' and help the business go beyond break-even and keep a healthy cash flow.

www.cheetlondon.com

Case study

Is it still worthwhile?

The meeting with the bank's Small Business Manager had not gone well. The manager had appreciated the work that Lena and Boris had put into their business plan but the assumptions behind the break-even analysis had been criticised as being too optimistic. The manager had redrawn the break-even chart with new assumptions about contribution per unit and the business seemed much less viable. 'Why should his figures be any more accurate than ours?' moaned Boris. 'That's not the point – he won't lend the money unless we make this business proposal seem more profitable,' explained Lena. 'What we need to do is rethink the figures behind the break-even and see if we can convince him that the business is worth the risk'.

The couple were planning to set up a home fitness business which offered specific, personalised get-fit courses for people who were not keen on traditional gyms. They both intended to keep their own gym jobs going but would employ others to provide the 'home service'. The main variable cost was going to be the employment of hourly paid well qualified fitness instructors. The main fixed costs were the leasing of vans and keep-fit equipment. The bank manager had doubted the low hourly wage rate included in the break-even calculation and the pricing levels forecast by Lena and Boris. 'You need to charge more than that if you expect to make much of a profit,' had been the manager's last comment.

Two weeks later the couple had revised their figures and had redrawn the break-even chart. They were prepared to do battle with the manager once more. The revised data used by Lena and Boris is in the table below – together with the manager's own estimates.

Table 12.3 Boris and Lena's financial data

	Bank Manager's estimates	Boris and Lena's revised data
Fixed costs – weekly	£2,100	£1,500
Variable cost per customer hour	£15	£12
Average price to customer	£45	£37
Expected number of customer hours per week	80	80

Boris and Lena had decided they could recruit less well-qualified fitness instructors and lease second-hand not new vans in drawing up their new revised figures.

Questions

1 What do you understand by the terms:
  a contribution per customer, and
  b break-even level of output?

2 Explain two benefits to Lena and Boris of undertaking break-even analysis in this case.

3 Analyse the viability of this business proposal by undertaking break-even analysis using either the formula or a chart. Compare the break-even points, the forecasted profit levels and the margins of safety (at assumed expected number of customers) using the data.

4 Using your results and any other information in the case, would you advise Lena and Boris to go ahead with this business proposal? Justify your answer.

5 Research topic: Use the BBC business website to research a company that is struggling to meet its break-even point. For example, search for the Airbus A380.

☑ In this chapter you have learned to:

- explain what contribution and contribution per unit mean
- explain what 'breaking-even' means and define break-even point
- use contribution per unit to calculate the break-even point

- draw a break-even chart and identify and explain its main features
- change any of the key variables – price, variable cost and fixed cost – and re-draw a break-even chart or recalculate the break-even level of output
- use the data provided by break-even charts to assist entrepreneurs in decisions about starting a business
- evaluate the usefulness of break-even analysis.

Summary questions

Chapters 11 & 12

1   Explain why profit is important to any business.   *(4 marks)*

2   Explain why the revenue of a business is unlikely to increase by 10% when it raises prices by 10%.   *(4 marks)*

3   Identify four costs that will have to be paid by a taxi business – and classify them into either variable or fixed costs.   *(8 marks)*

4   A friend of yours plans to set up a specialist online computer magazine. Customers would pay by subscription. Explain the importance to your friend of distinguishing between contribution and profit when starting up his business.   *(8 marks)*

5   Distinguish clearly between the break-even level of output and the margin of safety by sketching a typical break-even chart.   *(4 marks)*

6   Explain two reasons why a new entrepreneur might find break-even analysis useful.   *(4 marks)*

7   A garden maintenance business owner finds that she has to work four days a week just to 'break-even'. Analyse TWO steps she could take to reduce this break-even point of production.   *(8 marks)*

8   A jewellery retailer finds that its costs of new stock are rising due to increasing gold prices. Analyse TWO steps the business owner might take to maintain total levels of profit from the business.   *(8 marks)*

9   Analyse two possible reasons why a new business start-up might discover that the original break-even analysis in the Business Plan is very inaccurate.   *(8 marks)*

10   Analyse why the owner of a hotel in an area with considerable seasonal demand variations might find it useful to distinguish between the variable and fixed costs of the business.   *(8 marks)*

11   Evaluate the usefulness of break-even analysis to this same hotel business.

12   The break-even chart opposite shows the current position for a specialist manufacturer of executive computer desks or work stations. The current level of output is 3,000 per year, although capacity is 5,000 desks. The owner of the business is aiming to increase profitability and is considering the following change: Reducing the price to £450 but increasing output and (hopefully) sales to 4,000 desks.

a)   Mark the new expected sale revenue line on the chart.   *(2 marks)*

b)   Identify the new break-even level of output.   *(1 mark)*

c)   Compare the profitability of the business at 3,000 units @ £500 and at 4,000 units @ £450.   *(4 marks)*

d)   Do you think the business owner should make this change to a lower price? Explain your answer.   *(8 marks)*

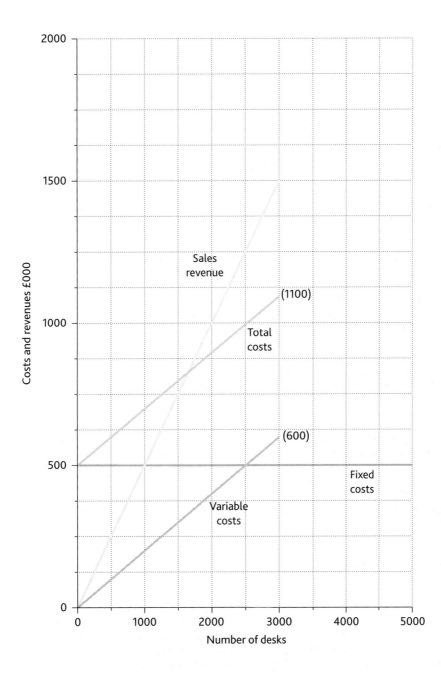

13   Using cash flow forecasting

Setting the scene

Sun Optical

Sun Optical had been making spectacles for years. The business was in a rut with no sales growth and low profits. The owners agreed to recruit a qualified Managing Director who could give a new direction. Geoff Harding did not take long to make changes. He suggested raising the annual sales revenue from £1 million to £4 million in two years by specialising in fashion sunglasses. New in-house designs were created. Geoff's links with the industry helped him gain big orders from some of the leading names – Dolland and Aitchison and John Lewis, for example. The sunglasses sold for high prices. These large orders were profitable but there was a big problem. The biggest firms were the slowest payers! The big retailers expected several months of credit and such high standards that some production had to be scrapped.

Geoff became concerned about the firm's cash flow. Suppliers were screaming for payment. The bank overdraft had reached record levels. Overtime working by staff to complete orders on time was leaking more cash out of the business. Then Geoff discovered that his bookkeeper had not included VAT or transport costs into the monthly cash flow forecast – they had even less money than they thought! He even asked long-serving staff for cash loans which many agreed to.

Friday the 13th was not lucky for Geoff. A department store buyer was visiting in the morning and the bank manager was due in the afternoon. Mid-way through the day, he learnt that the major 'finishing' machine had broken down and a major supplier had rejected the latest order for materials.

Within weeks, the assets of the business had been sold off and the people and firms owed money by Sun Optical received a fraction of what they were owed.

Discussion points

1. Why did this business fail to survive? Explain the problems the business faced in as much detail as you can.

2. Can you suggest ways in which the business could have overcome its major problems?

3. To what extent was lack of forward planning or forecasting a weakness of the business?

What do you think the term cash flow means?

Cash gives 'immediate spending power'. A firm's cash will be held in its tills and safes but also in current accounts with a bank. A business needs cash to pay bills and expenses such as:

- Rent
- Taxes

- Wages
- Suppliers
- Electricity

Without enough cash, as Sun Optical found out, bills cannot be paid and the firm will be forced out of business. The amount of cash held is never constant – it changes with the payments made and received. These are called **cash flows**.

In this chapter we discover why cash flow is important to all businesses and how cash flows can be forecasted to reduce – but not to eliminate – the risk of running out of cash.

The importance of cash flow

The Sun Optical case study allows us to see the importance of cash flow to all businesses – even those that claim to be making a profit! Profit does not pay the bills and expenses of running a business – but cash does. Of course profit is important – especially in the long term when investors expect rewards and the business needs additional finance for investment. Cash is always important – short- and long-term. Cash flow relates to the timing of payments **to** workers and suppliers and receipts **from** customers. If a business does not manage the timing of these payments and receipts carefully it may run out of cash even though it is operating profitably. If suppliers and creditors are not paid in time they can force the business into **liquidation** of the business's assets as it appears to be **insolvent**.

So, cash flow is certainly important – especially to small business start-ups. Why is cash flow planning so vital for entrepreneurs?

- New business start-ups are often offered much less time to pay suppliers than larger, well-established firms – they are given shorter credit periods.
- Banks and other lenders may not believe the promises of new business owners as they have no trading record. They will expect payment at the agreed time!
- Finance is often very tight at start-up so not planning accurately is of even more significance for new businesses.

How to forecast cash flow

This is one of the most challenging sections in a typical Business Plan. The entrepreneur will have to consider the sources and timing of **cash inflows** and **cash outflows** usually on a month by month basis. Let's take the case of Jim, an entrepreneur planning to open a car valeting service aiming to offer this service to individual customers and owners of car fleets such as taxi firms.

Forecasting cash inflows

Where to start? Jim will probably attempt to forecast cash inflow first. Some of these will be easier to forecast than others. Here are some example cash inflows and how they might be forecast:

- Owners own capital injection – easy to forecast as this is under the owner's direct control.
- Bank loans received – easy to forecast if it has been agreed with the bank in advance, both in terms of amount and timing.
- Customers cash purchases – difficult to forecast as it depends on sales. So, a sales forecast will be necessary – but how accurate might this be?

Key terms

Cash flow: the total cash payments (inflows) into a business minus the total cash payments (outflows).

Liquidation: this is turning assets into cash and may be insisted on by courts if suppliers have not been paid.

Insolvent: when a business cannot meet its short-term debts.

Cash inflows: payments in cash received by a business such as those from customers or from the bank e.g. receiving a loan.

Cash outflows: payments in cash made by a business such as those to suppliers and workers.

■ Key terms

Debtors: these are customers who have bought products on credit and will pay cash at an agreed date in the future.

Credit sales: value of goods sold to customers who do not pay cash immediately.

AQA Examiner's tip

Never fall in to the trap of referring to forecasts as ACTUAL accounts – they are financial planning estimates that are dealing with the future.

■ Link

For further explanation of overdrafts, see Chapter 8 – Raising finance, page 53.

■ Key terms

Cash flow forecast: an estimate of a firm's future cash inflows and outflows.

Net monthly cash flow: the estimated difference between monthly cash inflows and outflows.

Opening balance: cash held by the business at the start of the month.

Closing balance: cash held at the end of the month – becomes next month's opening balance.

■ Activity

Try to think of as many likely cash payments that could be received and made by a business as you can.

■ **Debtors** payments – difficult to forecast as these depend on two unknowns. Firstly, what is the likely level of **credit sales**? Secondly, when will debtors actually pay? One month's credit may have been agreed with them but payment after this period can never be guaranteed.

Forecasting cash outflows

Again, some of these will be much easier to forecast than others. Here are some example cash outflows and how they might be forecast:

■ Lease payment for premises – easy to forecast as this will be in the estate agents details of the property.

■ Annual rent payment – easy to forecast as this will be fixed and agreed for a certain time period. The landlord may increase the rent after this period, however.

■ Electricity, gas, water and telephone bills – difficult to forecast as these will vary with so many factors such as the number of customers, seasonal weather conditions and energy prices.

■ Labour cost payments – these forecasts will be based largely on demand forecasts and the hourly wage rate that is to be paid. These payments could vary from week to week if demand fluctuates and if staff are on flexible contracts.

■ Variable cost payments such as cleaning materials – the cost of these should vary consistently with demand so revenue forecasts could be used to assess variable costs too. How much credit will be offered by suppliers – the longer the period of credit offered the lower will be the start-up cash needs of the business.

When there appears to be so many uncertainties involved in cash flow forecasting you may start to wonder why firms bother! We will leave this argument to the final section of this chapter. Now we turn to the drawing up of a cash flow forecast.

💡 The structure of cash flow forecasts

A simplified **cash flow forecast** is shown in Table 13.1. It is based on Jim's car valeting service. Although there are different styles of presenting this information, all cash flow forecasts have three basic sections:

Section 1 – Cash inflows. This section records the cash payments to the business including cash sales, payments from debtors and capital inflows.

Section 2 – Cash outflows. This section records the cash payments made by the business including wages, materials, rent and other costs.

Section 3 – **Net monthly cash flow** and **opening** and **closing balance**. This shows the net cash flow for the period and the cash balances at the start and end of the period. It is common to assume that if the closing balance is negative (shown by a figure in brackets) then a bank overdraft will be necessary to finance this.

What does this tell Jim about the prospects for his business? In cash terms, the business appears to be in a good position at the end of four months. This is because:

■ In April the closing cash balance is positive so the bank overdraft has been fully repaid.

■ There was only one month – the first month of operation – in which the monthly net cash flow was negative.

■ The monthly net cash flow is positive from February onwards.

Table 13.1 *Jim's cash flow forecast for the first four months (figures in brackets are negative)*

Cash inflows	All figures in £000	JAN	FEB	MAR	APR
	Owner's capital injection	6	0	0	0
	Cash Sales	3	4	6	6
	Payments by debtors	0	2	2	3
	Total cash in	9	6	8	9
Cash outflows					
	Lease	8	0	0	0
	Rent	1	1	1	1
	Materials	0.5	1	3	2
	Labour	1	2	3	3
	Other costs	0.5	1	0.5	1.5
	Total cash out	11	5	7.5	7.5
Net cash flow	**Net monthly cash flow**	(2)	1	0.5	1.5
	Opening balance	0	(2)	(1)	(0.5)
	Closing balance	(2)	(1)	(0.5)	1

BUT – never forget that these are only forecasts and the accuracy of the cash flow forecast will depend greatly on how accurate Jim was in his demand, revenue and material cost forecasts.

Why businesses forecast cash flows

There are several important advantages to cash flow forecasting, especially for new businesses:

■ By indicating times of negative cash flow, plans can be put in place to provide additional finance, for example arranging a bank overdraft or preparing to inject more owner's capital.

■ If negative cash flows appear to be too great then plans can be made for reducing these for example, by cutting down on purchase of materials or machinery or by not making sales on credit, only for cash.

■ A new business proposal will never progress beyond the initial planning stage unless investors and bankers have access to a cash flow forecast – and the assumptions that lie behind it.

💡 Cash flow forecasting – what are the limitations?

Although an entrepreneur should take every reasonable step to increase the accuracy of the business cash flow forecast – by using relevant market research for example – it would be foolish indeed to assume that it will always be accurate. There are so many factors, either internal to the business or in the external environment, that can change to blow a cash flow forecast off course. This does not make them useless – but, as with any business forecast they must be used with caution and the ways in which the cash flows have been estimated should be understood. Here are the most common limitations of them:

■ Mistakes can be made in preparing the revenue and cost forecasts or they may be drawn up by inexperienced staff or entrepreneurs.

Activity

With reference to Table 13.1 draw up a revised cash flow forecast for April assuming:

1 Cash sales are forecast to be £1,000 higher.

2 Materials are forecast to be £500 higher.

3 Other costs were forecast to be £1,000 higher.

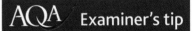

AQA Examiner's tip

In Unit 1 you will not be asked questions about how a business might improve its cash flow position – these questions might appear in Unit 2 though.

■ Business in action
Rendezvous

Cash flow forecasts are vital planning tools for all businesses, whatever their size. Peter Spivack, owner of Merseyside-based restaurant Rendezvous, prepared his first year's cash flow forecast as part of his original business plan. 'I decided early on that I would review the forecast monthly and I update the figures weekly to keep on top of things,' he explained. 'The forecast has enabled me to spot looming net cash outflows on three occasions. I didn't panic because I could see the problem was temporary; I used a pre-arranged overdraft facility from my bank to tide the business over.'

www.thebestof.co.uk

■ Unexpected cost increases can lead to major inaccuracies in forecasts. Fluctuations in oil prices lead to the cash flow forecasts of even major airlines being misleading.

■ Wrong assumptions can be made in estimating the sales of the business, perhaps based on poor market research, and this will make the cash inflow forecasts inaccurate.

Case study

Fashion shop forecasts look good

'I have stood outside of some of these fashion shops for hours counting the number of people coming out with their carrier bags and I am convinced my sales forecasts are OK,' announced Sayuri to her business partner, Korede. They were both putting the finishing touches to their business plan for an exclusive 'top brands only' fashion store in the city. Sayuri's primary research was not the only evidence they had used in arriving at the sales forecasts and the cash inflow forecasts. Some desk research on the internet had also revealed the rapid growth of high income consumers spending increasing amounts on expensive clothing.

Cash outflow forecasts had been based on estimates of electricity and telephone usage. Korede had found what he thought was a suitable shop so they knew how much the rent would be. They would pay themselves a salary of £2,000 a month each initially. Other labour costs were less certain. Should they employ full-time salaried staff or part-time hourly wage employees? The cost of buying the clothes was also uncertain. There would be no problem if they sold all the suits and dresses that they bought in – but how likely was that? And what would happen to cash flow forecasts if stock was left unsold and huge price reductions had to be advertised? Whatever the uncertainties, both Sayuri and Korede realised why they had to construct a cash flow forecast for their business plan. The almost completed forecast is shown opposite:

Questions

1. Complete the cash flow forecast shown in Table 13.2 by inserting values for x, y and z.

2. Analyse two problems of drawing up a cash flow forecast Sayuri and Korede may have experienced.

3. The first three months actual trading was poor and cash sales were 20% below forecast. Draw up a new cash flow forecast for July assuming 20% lower cash sales, 20% lower clothes purchases, an opening cash balance of £2,000 and all other factors remaining unchanged.

4. To what extent would drawing up a cash flow forecast increase the chances of this business being successful?

5. Research topic: Visit a bank branch and ask for a pack of information for starting up a new business. This pack will almost certainly contain a pro-forma cash flow forecast. Comment on any differences between this format and the one used in this chapter.

Table 13.2 *Sayuri's and Korede's cash flow forecast for the first four months of trading (all figures in £000)*

Cash inflows	All figures in £000	APRIL	MAY	JUNE	JULY
	Owners' capital injection	28	0	0	0
	Cash sales	6	8	12	9
	Payments by debtors (e.g. credit card companies)	0	2	2	3
	Total cash in	34	10	14	12
Cash outflows					
	Lease	18	0	0	0
	Rent	2	2	2	2
	Clothes purchases	6	4	3	4
	Labour	3	3	4	3
	Other costs	6.5	2	2.5	1.5
	Total cash out	35.5	11	11.5	*y*
Net cash flow	Net monthly cash flow	*x*	(1)	2.5	*z*
	Opening balance	0	(1.5)	(2.5)	0
	Closing balance	(1.5)	(2.5)	0	1.5

☑ *In this chapter you will have learned to:*

- explain the difference between cash and profit
- understand how a profitable business can run out of cash
- analyse the most likely sources of data for cash flow forecasts
- understand the structure of a typical cash flow forecast
- change a cash flow forecast on the basis of new information
- evaluate the usefulness of cash flow forecasts.

14　Setting budgets

Setting the scene

ChipRepair fails to meet targets

ChipRepair was set up six months ago by two school leavers with a passion for computers, especially taking them to bits! Andy and Kate decided during their A2 year that their business would specialise in fault finding, repair and servicing of home computers. They would travel to clients' houses as they could not afford their own premises. Limited market research had been undertaken, mainly questionnaires to the parents of school friends. They found out that, especially amongst the older generation, there was a lot of ignorance about computer problems, loading of new software and ways of updating existing hardware. The survey suggested that many people were prepared to pay for specialist computer help at home. This suggested a market opportunity!

In planning the business, the couple planned to aim for eight clients a week. They thought of charging £30 an hour, about £5 less than three competitors in their town. They estimated that each job would take two hours on average. So, the sales revenue target was £1,920 per month. Transport costs were difficult to predict – how far should they be prepared to travel for new business? Eventually, in the business plan they forecasted £200 per month each as the likely expenditure on travel. Promotion costs they estimated to be £100 a month – mainly on newspaper and magazine adverts. Finally, after considering other costs as well, they predicted that they would make a profit of around £500 per month.

After the first six months Andy and Kate had a reality check. Actual revenue was 50% less than target – new customers were harder to come by than predicted. As a result, they had travelled much further for new business than planned and this had increased transport costs. They had doubled their advertising limit to appeal to more potential customers. Over this period the couple only just broke even – they were so disappointed.

Discussion points

1. Why do you think Andy and Kate decided to set targets for income and spending for their new business?

2. Suggest several factors that could make these targets unreliable.

3. If you were advising Andy and Kate, how would you recommend them to make more reliable targets?

Key terms

Budgets: financial targets for the future covering revenue (income) and expenditure over a certain time period.

The importance of budgets

Perhaps, they did not realise it but Andy and Kate were setting **budgets** for their business. This is a very important part of financial planning and control.

What was the purpose of setting these financial targets? How did they help the two owners set up and control their business in its first few months of operation? There are a number of key benefits to a business – especially a new one such as ChipRepair – from planning future expenditure and income using budgets:

- **Expenditure budgets** (or cost budgets) set spending limits for a business and separate departments or individuals within a business. If every employee or **budget holder** was able to make sure that their own spending budget was not exceeded then the costs of the entire business should not get out of control.

- **Income budgets** (or revenue budgets) can be a motivating factor for those given the target. If these budgets are reasonable and realistic then employees will often want to do their best to ensure that they are achieved. By having a system of **delegated budgets**, most employees can be given some financial responsibility. A manager's performance can be measured by comparing targets with actual results.

- New businesses need budgets to be included in the business plan. With these it will be easier to judge whether the business idea is viable – and lenders can assess if it is worthwhile investing in the business.

- **Profit budgets** not only provide clear goals and targets that motivate people to perform well but also allow quick monitoring of performance against actual profits made.

💡 Setting budgets – how is it done?

- This is not an easy task as so many of a firm's budgets will depend on accurate sales forecasts.

- *Stage 1.* Set clear objectives for the firm for the coming year. For example, if the aim is to increase sales and/or market share then this must be reflected in the sales budget.

- *Stage 2.* Gather information, for example undertake market research to provide information to base sales on.

- *Stage 3.* Construct a sales budget showing target revenues from each product and region.

- *Stage 4.* Based on this sales budget, set budgets for major cost areas such as labour, material costs, energy costs, promotional spending.

- *Stage 5.* Set a profit target based on the sales and cost budgets already established.

Activity

When was the last time you did any budgeting? Perhaps when planning a summer holiday or just when trying to find out how you spend your money each month? Try to think about how much you are likely to spend and on what over the next four weeks.

Key terms

Expenditure budgets: a fixed sum of money to be spent in a given time period by a department.

Budget holder: a person who is accountable for seeing that a budget is kept to.

Income budget: the sales revenue target for a department or the whole business.

Delegated budgets: giving some control in the setting and spending of budgets to departments or individuals.

Profit budget: the target profit for the business over a given time period.

AQA Examiner's tip

A budget is not a forecast – it is a target. However targets such as the sales revenue budget, may be based on forecasts.

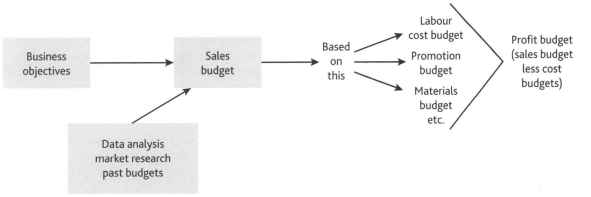

Fig. 14.1 *The budgeting process for the next financial year*

Setting budgets for new businesses

This is even more difficult because there is no past data to act as a guide – as Andy and Kate found out! Where did they go so wrong in setting their targets?

If they had followed a few basic rules or guidelines for entrepreneurs setting their first budgets they might have been more accurate with their targets.

1 Use spreadsheet software and keep updating records regularly – don't wait until the end of six months to be surprised by lack of progress!

2 Set budgets for at least 12 months as most new businesses will be expected to make a loss in the first few months. But is this loss still expected at the end of the first year?

3 Give great importance to monthly sales forecasts – this is the key factor, as explained above. Andy and Kate should have undertaken more detailed and extensive market research and sales forecasting.

4 Make sure ALL of the costs of operation involved in producing and delivering the product to customers are included in the budget.

5 Keep a cumulative, month by month total of profits or losses – this would have shown Andy and Kate the trends over the first six months and when the business actually broke even.

6 Monitor each major budget monthly and take corrective action as soon as possible. Perhaps ChipRepair could have seen the problem of transport costs much earlier.

💡 Monitoring budgets

Monitoring budgets is a vital part of the budgetary process. It attempts to make sure that:

- Money from each expenditure budget is being spent on the correct items and not being misallocated.
- All costs are being accounted for – an accurate record is being kept.
- Major cost 'excesses' are being reported to senior managers before the expenditure is agreed.
- Revenue and profits are meeting target levels – and senior managers informed if this is not the case.

■ Problems of setting budgets

Some of these must be making themselves clear already. The future can never be certain and no matter how much time and effort goes into forecasting and target setting, budgets can still turn out to be very different from the actual business performance. Apart from changes to the external environment which can make budgets inaccurate – such as an economic recession, technological change or inflation in raw material prices – numerous other factors can make the budgeting process less effective than it should be. This list gives an insight into just some of the main ones:

- Managers with delegated authority may try to persuade their bosses to set spending budgets higher than they really need to be. If they are successful, then these managers are much more likely to reach other targets set for them – such as a budgeted level of sales.
- Inaccurate budgets which may have been set by senior managers with no input from 'people on the ground' might be very demotivating for

---

AQA **Examiner's tip**

Unit 1 questions on setting budgets will focus on the benefits and potential problems of setting targets for planned businesses or recently formed ones.

■ Key terms

Monitoring budgets: keeping a check on progress towards achieving targets during the budget period.

■ Link

For more information on budgets, see Chapter 16 – Using budgets, page 102.

■ Activity

Put your own monthly expenditure budget on a spreadsheet and monitor actual spending, week by week, against your targets.

the manager and the department trying to keep to these inappropriate targets.

- Short-term decisions to keep to rigid budgets – e.g. using cheaper production materials, might damage the business's longer term reputation.

- Budgets that are too easy to achieve will not promote the motivational incentives that more challenging targets would.

- Most importantly though – and this applies to new businesses in particular – the key sales revenue budget is subject to so many constraints outside of the firm control that the process of planning for a certain sales level is very difficult indeed.

Despite all of these potential problems, virtually every business will undertake budget setting and will monitor performance against budget. As was stated at the beginning of the chapter setting budgets is a key part of financial planning.

Fig. 14.2 *London 2012 Olympic Logo. The original cost budgets for the Olympics were inaccurate. (www.london2012.com)*

Case study

ChipRepair: two years on

After their initial disappointment over the first six months trading, Andy and Kate set more realistic budgets for the next year based on the experience they had gained. The business proved to be increasingly successful. Two years from starting out, the owners had saved enough capital to allow them to plan for opening their own computer shop. This would not compete with the big multiple stores by selling mass market computers. It would focus on stocking specialist programs, upgrade equipment and peripherals that would appeal to computer 'buffs'. It would also offer on-site diagnosis and repair of computer problems.

The couple had found a suitable location – a former TV shop that had ceased trading. They were also lucky enough to recruit an ex-manager, Omar, from Dixons who wanted to work more independently and concentrate on computing rather than other electrical goods. He would run the ChipShop and the store's repair facilities. Andy and Kate would continue to expand the existing ChipRepair business.

The owners were keen to set clear monthly income and expenditure budgets for the shop and to monitor these carefully. They wanted to make sure that Omar was running the shop in the way they wanted. The targets for the first three months are given below.

Table 14.1

ChipShop budgets (£000)	April	May	June
Income: Sales revenue (sale of items from shop)	2	2	5
Repair revenue	1	2	2
Expenditure: Overheads	1	1	1
Labour costs (Omar's salary plus wage costs for an assistant)	2	2	3
Cost of items sold and materials used	1	1	2
Profit/(loss) budget	(1)	0	1

Activity

Analyse THREE problems that your school or college might have in setting subject department spending budgets for the next financial year.

The **actual** losses of the shop in the first three months totalled £4,000. The owners found that Omar had spent more on staffing than targeted – but less on advertising. He seemed not to be working in the shop himself but spending all day on dismantling customers' computers – his own real interest. Repair revenue was slightly higher than expected – but shop sales were much lower. They talked to Omar about this three monthly poor performance. His response was clear:

'If you had told me what the shop sales budget was I would have known how unrealistic this was. We need to staff the shop all day as I am busier than expected repairing computers. I can't do two things at once. Your budgets need to be discussed with me in future then we can monitor progress more accurately.'

Questions

1 What do you understand by the terms:
   a Income budget
   b Profit budget?

2 The actual results were used in setting the budget for July. Draw up a July budget, based on that for June, with:
   a Shop revenue down 20%, repair revenue up 20%;
   b All costs up 20%.

3 Analyse two problems of setting budgets for a new business, such as the ChipShop.

4 Discuss ways in which the two owners could set more realistic and useful budgets for the ChipShop.

☑ *In this chapter you will have learned to:*

■ understand what budgets are

■ explain how budgeting aids financial planning, especially for new businesses

■ differentiate between income, expenditure and profit budgets and explain how these can be set

■ understand why the monitoring of budgets is an important part of budgetary control

■ discuss the problems of setting budgets.

Assessing business start-ups

In this chapter you will learn to:

- compare different objectives for different start-ups

- assess the performance of business start-ups with original objectives

- analyse the strengths and weaknesses of a business idea and/or plan

- analyse the risks faced by new businesses

- evaluate the main causes of new business failures.

■ Setting the scene

A tale of three entrepreneurs

People start their own business for very different reasons. Robert Braithwaite established Sunseeker power boats in 1968 with a team of seven staff. It now employs 1,200 people and makes millions in profit each year. 'I was always a person with enormous ambition,' said Mr. Braithwaite after being awarded a prestigious prize for his entrepreneurship by Ernst and Young Accountants. He plans to increase sales and profits of Sunseeker each year and his aim is to make Sunseeker such a well-known brand that when people 'think power boats they will think Sunseeker'.

Chrissie Townsend heads an action group which has a clear objective: 'My aim is to break down social barriers on a crime ridden housing estate.' She set up a bus route which provided the first bus link to the estate and allowed people to have access to other areas.

Tony Cesay, a former boxer, uses sport and nutrition to build self-esteem in marginalised inner city kids. His enterprise is called 'Kid Gloves'. These are just two examples of entrepreneurs who have set up not-for-profit business ventures as a form of social enterprise. Tony said: 'The big problem with gaining finance is that councils and other bodies just do not understand if what you are proposing does not have profit as a clear objective.'

Business and social entrepreneurs have a lot in common. They build something out of nothing. They are ambitious to achieve. They set objectives – but not necessarily the same ones. They are creative and not afraid to make mistakes.

Discussion points

1. Do you think it is important for all entrepreneurs to have clear objectives for their enterprise? List as many advantages as you can for an entrepreneur having clear objectives.

2. Why will different entrepreneurs often have different objectives?

3. Is profit the only objective owners of new businesses should have and the only way to assess success?

Fig. 15.1 *Robert Braithwaite, founder of Sunseeker International*

💡 Objectives of business start-ups

No two entrepreneurs are the same. They may be from different social groups and have had different personal and employment experiences. Their reasons for starting their own business might be very different too. In a recent survey by accountants Coopers and Lybrand, entrepreneurs were asked for the main driving factors in setting up their own business:

- 65% said because of a sense of personal satisfaction from being independent.

Business objectives: clearly defined targets for a business to achieve over a certain time period.

Profit satisficing: making enough profit without risking too much stress or loss of control through employment of too many professional managers.

■ 43% liked the idea of doing things their way.

■ 37% said they were looking for profits and capital growth.

■ 16% said they wanted to pass something on to their children.

Different personal ambitions will lead to different **business objectives**. Here are just a few possible objectives that might be set for a new business:

Profit maximisation

Trying to earn as much profit as possible – but this might conflict with other objectives. For example, attempting to increase sales by cutting prices for long-term growth could damage short term profits.

A certain rate or level of profit

Most entrepreneurs need income and capital growth to lead to a desired lifestyle – but profit may not be a realistic short-term aim for some slow developing businesses. When this profit objective is just enough to give owners a 'comfortable' lifestyle without working too many hours or without danger of losing control it is often called **profit satisficing**.

Survival

This is likely to be a primary objective in the first few years of any new business. It may also become a primary objective for any business that enters a crisis stage in its development.

Sales growth

The owners try to make as many sales as possible. This may be because they believe that sheer size is the best chance of business survival. Larger businesses can also benefit from economies of scale.

Social objectives

In the case of social entrepreneurs, the main objective will be to correct one of society's problems but there may be a financial requirement to at least break-even too.

Why set objectives for a new business?

These are the key benefits from setting objectives:

■ Give direction and focus to the owners and the people who work in the business.

■ Create a well-defined target so the owners can make appropriate plans to achieve these targets.

■ Inform lenders and investors of the aims of the business.

■ Give a guideline for assessing the performance of the business over time.

The most effective objectives that a business might establish should meet the following criteria:

S

Specific – Clearly related to only that business, for example, a restaurant might aim to serve an average of 35 customers per night.

M

Measurable – Putting a value to an objective helps when assessing performance e.g. to achieve sales of £500 per month.

A

Agreed – By all of those involved in trying to achieve the objective. This will increase the motivational impact of the objective.

R

Realistic – Objectives should be challenging but not impossible! This would demotivate the staff involved.

T

Time specific – Objectives should have a time limit so that performance can be assessed effectively. Setting an aim of reaching profits of £10,000 has little meaning unless a time period is specified, e.g. in the first year of trading.

How to assess 'success' of a business idea

Just as business objectives can be very different so success or failure will be assessed in different ways. When judging the success of a new business it is essential to begin with the original objectives. If the main aim is sales growth then sales data must be referred to. Profit levels must be compared with the profit target if this was the primary initial objective. Business enterprises that have an initial objective of survival will be judged as failures if they do not exist 12 months after start-up!

There is little point in using an inappropriate measure of 'success'. In the 'setting the scene' case study, assessing the success of a social enterprise by means of profits or sales would be completely inappropriate. Instead social value indicators should be used, for example, how many poor children have been directly helped or how many unemployed have been taken on as workers. It is estimated that each social enterprise creates an average of five jobs and that £10,000 to train a social entrepreneur can lead to £100,000 of benefits to society. This benefit is not the same as 'business profits'.

What are the risks of business start-ups?

Entrepreneurs take risks – this is an unavoidable fact. Investing time and money into a new business idea can lead to failure for many reasons. Risks of business activity can be assessed and steps taken to reduce some of these but uncertainty will never be completely removed. What are the main risks that entrepreneurs face?

Lack of business and management skills

Many entrepreneurs, especially young ones, have no or few management skills and they may have little experience of business. This increases the chance of failure as lack of action when a crisis develops, due to inexperience, could lead to failure of the enterprise.

AQA Examiner's tip

Remember that the most effective objectives should be 'S.M.A.R.T.'

Activity

A Beauty Clinic has been operating for two years. It is owned and managed by a sole entrepreneur.

1. What evidence or data would you need to be able to assess the success of this clinic?

2. Why would it be important to know what the objectives of this entrepreneur were before assessing the success of the clinic?

Possible ways to reduce risk: Attend training courses in entrepreneurship; business advice from experienced consultants.

Lack of knowledge of legal requirements

The laws may be very detailed and complex for certain business ventures, such as those handling and selling food or when using machinery to make goods.

Possible ways to reduce risk: Training courses, specialist legal advice, take a partner with a legal background.

Competition

Unless the entrepreneur has come up with a really unique idea, there are likely to be close competitors who may have more experience and greater financial resources than a new start-up. Competitors may take actions to make it very difficult for the new business to survive.

Possible ways to reduce risk: Closely monitor the decisions and actions of key rivals, offer a better customer service than competitors.

Increased taxes or interest rates

As the finances for new businesses are often very limited at the best of times, any negative change in economic policy by the government could lead to increased outflows of cash from a small business with weak financial foundations.

Possible ways to reduce risk: Plan ahead as much as possible, cash flow forecasting essential.

Changes in consumer tastes

This is a potential risk for all businesses, not just new ones. The major difficulty for most business start-ups is that they tend to be focused on just one product – and if consumer demand switches away from this then the entrepreneur may have no other products to 'fall back on'.

Possible ways to reduce risks: Keep in close contact with customers – feedback from these would be very helpful.

Technology

New technology creates business opportunities AND risks for existing businesses. How many people now buy floppy disks or VHS tapes? Small businesses with creative entrepreneurs are often ahead of larger businesses in the application of new technological possibilities. 'Facebook' started as a single person operation. However, changes in IT can quickly wipe out a competitive advantage of a new business.

Possible ways to reduce risks: Training course, accept change positively and stay ahead of changes if possible.

◊ Why new businesses fail

Fail they certainly do. Statistics from the Small Business Association (2007) show that nearly 60 per cent of new start-ups fail within four years of being established. These are the most common reasons for new business failures:

Activity

A chef with years of experience in running large, busy kitchens invests her savings in her own specialist 'sushi' style restaurant.

1. What are the biggest risks that she could experience in setting up this business?

2. Explain how any two of these risks might be reduced.

3. Would the profit (or loss) made at the end of the first year be the best way to assess the success of this business? Explain your answer.

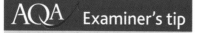

Examiner's tip

You will be expected to be able to discuss the chances of success or failure of new business start-ups operating in different markets/industries.

1 Insufficient capital

This is a common mistake – underestimating the amount of money needed both to start the business and keep it going during the first few years. This problem is often made worse by overestimating the income of the business in these crucial years. By assuming a low break-even point and a rapid payback of initial loans many entrepreneurs mislead themselves and when reality strikes, the shortage of capital forces the business into insolvency.

2 Poor management skills

By not having enough experience in the areas of finance, record keeping, purchasing, selling, hiring and managing employees, entrepreneurs are starting business life with a huge handicap. Sometimes sheer enthusiasm and energy will pull the business through but unless owners quickly recognise what they do not do well and seek help, the business may soon face disaster.

3 Poor location

This is a common problem for new business dealing directly or selling to the public. By not being able to afford prime sites, entrepreneurs have to be imaginative in the ways they use to attract potential customers. A good location can often allow a struggling business to survive – but a poor location may spell the end of even an effective new business idea and a well-organised owner.

4 Lack of planning

Failure to make realistic plans based on accurate, current information will often lead to the collapse of a business. Managing the business on a day by day basis – perhaps because the entrepreneur is so busy – does not allow for long-term decision making and planning for future problems. Planning should be a continuous feature of a start-up – and it will always require regular study of market research and customer data.

5 Over-expansion

New business owners often confuse success with how fast they can expand the business. However, rapid expansion requires injections of capital and management expertise. Trying to handle rapid growth with no assistance or with inadequate capital may lead to excess stress and insolvency.

6 External factors

Unexpected changes in demand, sharp increases in costs or the unavailability of essential supplies are all factors beyond a new business's control and they could all cause it to fail. Interest rate increases, oil price rises and the failure of a supplying business are events that are difficult to predict and plan for. The lack of finance and the high dependency on borrowed capital makes start-up businesses particularly vulnerable to these factors.

Activity

If you were planning to start up a business importing specialist food products from Europe, discuss **four** of the most important steps you might take to reduce the chances of failure.

Fig. 15.2 *Levi Roots, founder of Reggae Reggae Sauce*

■ Case study

The difference between success and failure

Music Zone collapsed in 2007 with the closure of over 100 branches. Started by entrepreneur Russ Grainger in 1984 with just one market stall, the business grew into the UK's third largest high street retailer of CDs and DVDs. He sold his stake in the business for £12 million in 2005. It was bought by a team of the existing managers. They had to borrow heavily to buy Russ out. The outlook for the business suddenly worsened in 2006. Interest rates started to rise, the business had over-expanded with borrowed capital and technological advances in downloading greatly reduced the demand for CDs and DVDs.

Levi Roots and his Reggae Reggae Sauce has been one of the great success stories of Dragons' Den. This BBC programme gave Levi the opportunity to gain £25,000 of funding from experienced entrepreneurs in exchange for giving up 20 per cent of his venture. He has now obtained huge orders from Sainsbury's and other supermarkets for his unique sauce based on his grandmother's recipe. One business consultant said: 'Levi had a clear sense of what he wanted to achieve – rapid sales growth. He obtained finance which was not borrowed and the support and advice of two experienced business managers. With Levi's skill in dealing with the media and marketing his unique product with his own music, I can't see how this new start-up can fail.'

www.reggae-reggae.co.uk

Questions

1. List three different objectives that an entrepreneur might set for a new business.

2. Outline two reasons why Music Zone failed.

3. Analyse two reasons for the initial success of Reggae Reggae Sauce.

4. Evaluate the chances of Levi's business continuing to be successful over the next five years.

5. Use the internet to research the reasons for the success or failure of any recently established business or well-known entrepreneur

☑ *In this chapter you will have learned to:*

- understand why new businesses need clear objectives

- analyse why different entrepreneurs will establish different objectives for their businesses

- assess the risks that business start-ups experience and the reasons why a high proportion fail.

i

Summary questions

Chapters 13–15

1   List three likely sources of cash inflows for a business selling petrol with
both cash and credit sales.   *(3 marks)*

2   **a)**   How would you attempt to forecast the cash inflows for an
entrepreneur setting up a wedding photography business?   *(4 marks)*

   b)   How could you forecast the cash outflows for the same business?   *(4 marks)*

3   Would you advise an entrepreneur, who is very busy in planning the setting
up of a new sports clothing shop, to spend time on creating a cash flow
forecast? Explain your reasons.   *(6 marks)*

4   Explain the difference between these two terms: Total monthly cash inflow
and monthly net cash flow.   *(4 marks)*

5   Explain why the cash inflows of a business selling goods on credit will be
more difficult to forecast than for a business just selling for cash payment. *(4 marks)*

6   **a)**   Explain to an entrepreneur setting up a hairdressing salon for both
men and women the importance of setting budgets for the business.   *(6 marks)*

   b)   Analyse three reasons why the income budget for this business
might not be achieved.   *(6 marks)*

   c)   What do you understand by the term 'monitoring budgets' and why
would this be important for the entrepreneur running this business?   *(4 marks)*

   d)   Explain why the sales budget is so vital in the overall budgeting
process of this hairdressing business.   *(4 marks)*

7   **a)**   If you were an entrepreneur about to start a business developing
computer games, what objectives might you set for this business,
and why?   *(4 marks)*

   b)   How would you assess whether, after two years, your business had
been successful?   *(4 marks)*

   c)   What are the risks in setting up a business developing computer games? *(4 marks)*

   d)   Explain three measures you could take to reduce the chances of this
business failing.   *(6 marks)*

Introduction

Chapters in this section:

i

HMV stores issue profit warning – what can managers do to improve profitability?

Setting up a business can be hard work and very risky. Once the firm is established and operating the hard work is not over! Entrepreneurs and managers need to continually monitor business performance, plan financial needs and take measures to improve cash flow and profitability.

The focus of this section is on improving the financial performance of **existing** businesses. This contrasts with Unit 1 which focused on planning for businesses yet to be established. All business enterprises whether they are recently established small firms or much larger, possibly famous enterprises that have been trading for many years, need to assess their financial performance regularly.

Decisions can then be taken to try to improve:

■ Performance compared to original budgets.
■ Cash flow to ensure adequate flows of cash are available to meet all likely future needs.
■ Profitability.

All three chapters in this section use financial measures to indicate how well a business is being managed. Each chapter also considers actions that managers and business owners can take to improve financial performance. Some calculations are included in this section as they will help to assess profitability and performance but each process is clearly explained and illustrated by examples.

This section builds on Financial planning in Unit 1 Section 2 so it is a good idea to re-read Chapters 11–15 to confirm your understanding of the concepts covered in this Unit.

Chapter 16: Using budgets This builds upon Chapter 14 – Setting budgets, page 100. It deals in detail with the comparison of budgeted and actual business performance. This information can then be used to inform decision making by managers.

Chapter 17: Improving cash flow Chapter 13 – Using cash flow forecasting, page 119, introduced the concept of cash flow forecasting. The ways in which a business can improve its cash flow – and the possible limitations of these ways – are considered in this section.

Chapter 18: Measuring and increasing profit The key importance of profit and how it was calculated was explained in Chapter 11 – Calculating costs, revenues and profits, page 75. Building upon this understanding Chapter 18 introduces the concept of net profit margin and return on capital as important measures of business efficiency. The methods managers can use to try to increase profitability are explained and evaluated.

16 Using budgets

Setting the scene

Missing the targets at XL Foods

'You are the only divisional manager who failed to meet their budgets over the last 12 months. I think you have some explaining to do.' Mick knew that the interview with the Chief Executive was going to be tough – but this was not a good start.

'I know the profit figures are below budget but this is only half the story,' began Mick in reply. 'Firstly, I argued for a higher budget for promotion spending for my frozen food division – but other managers got in first! This explains why sales are less than expected. Also, the unforeseen increase in petrol prices hit my division hardest as we have to transport goods the furthest – our biggest customer is in Eastern Europe. So our costs were higher than forecast. In all other cost areas I met the budget very closely so the differences are not that great.' Mick was relieved when the CE agreed after looking at the detailed figures Mick had prepared.

Discussion points

1. Can you identify one problem of setting budgets from this case?
2. Why is it important to compare 'budgets' with 'actual' figures?
3. How might the differences between budgets and actual figures be used by managers?

The benefits of using budgets

You will remember from Chapter 14 that budgets are financial plans. Why do firms use budgets and budgetary control?

1 Controlling finances

Expenditure budgets reduce the risk of a business over-spending. If every person in an organisation responsible for a budget – all budget holders – ensures that their own section or department does not exceed budget, the business will meet its overall expenditure plan.

A budgetary system allows more money to be allocated to 'problem' or under-performing departments or products. If a firm has one product that is failing to meet sales targets, then an increase in the promotional spending budget might be needed.

2 Improving staff performance

Many staff respond well to being given reasonable and agreed objectives to work towards. Budgets can be used as a financial objective for a department or section of a business. Employees can gain satisfaction from being given responsibility to meet a budget. Staff motivation may increase from being recognised as a responsible budget holder. This can encourage workers to keep within expenditure budgets and to try to exceed sales budgets.

The financial targets and workers ability to meet them can also be used as part of a staff appraisal system. This allows actual staff performance to be judged against the original budget.

The potential drawbacks of using budgets

1 Conflicts can arise in two main ways

First, departments may compete with each other for a larger slice of the expenditure funds available in the business. A strong manager or a skilled negotiator may gain a large budget for the department they are responsible for – at the expense of other sections which might actually have needed the resources more urgently.

Secondly, short-term budget cuts, for example in promotion, to meet strict targets might lead to long-term problems for the business if sales fall as a result. Those setting budgets should not just consider the immediate financial issues facing the business.

2 The motivating impact of budgets can fail to be achieved for two reasons

First, if very ambitious targets are set then these might be considered virtually impossible to achieve by the budget holder. These budgets will then fail to motivate and could instead disillusion those responsible for meeting them.

Secondly, target setting is likely to have most motivational effect when the people with the responsibility of meeting the targets are able to participate in the setting of them. If budgets are just 'handed down from higher management' with no input or discussion from budget holders then they will lose most of their potential for increasing motivation.

The calculation and interpretation of variances

We have identified that one of the main benefits of using budgets is to make comparisons between the original target and the actual figure. For example, comparing the budgeted sales figure set for a business 12 months ago with the actual sales value that was achieved. Any difference between these two figures is called a **variance**.

The purpose of **variance analysis** is to highlight and pinpoint areas of poor performance over a certain time period – as well as indicating areas where performance has been good.

There are two distinct types of variances – we will look first at **favourable variances**.

Favourable variances occur for two reasons. Either actual sales revenue was higher than budget or actual costs/expenditure levels were lower than budget.

Key terms

Variance: the difference between a budgeted figure and the actual figure achieved.

Variance analysis: is the comparison by an organisation of its actual performance with its expected budgeted performance over a certain time period.

Favourable variance: this is a change from a budgeted figure that leads to higher than expected profits.

Table 16.1

	Budget	Actual	Favourable variance
Sales revenue	£50,000	£60,000	£10,000
Fixed costs	£15,000	£13,000	£2,000
Labour costs	£20,000	£17,000	£3,000

Assuming these were the only costs and revenues for this business the actual profit is £15,000 greater than budgeted due to these favourable variances.

Key terms

Adverse variance: this is a change from a budgeted figure that leads to lower than expected profits.

AQA Examiner's tip

Do not assume that an adverse variance is always 'bad' – or a favourable one always 'good'! If costs are lower than budgeted due to cheaper materials being purchased this will cause a favourable variance – but could these cheaper materials lead to poorer quality and more wasted output?

The second type of variance is called an **adverse variance**.

Clearly, these arise either because sales revenue was *below* budget or actual costs/expenditure levels *exceeded* the budgeted figures.

Table 16.2

	Budget	Actual	Adverse variance
Sales revenue	£75,000	£71,000	£4,000
Fixed costs	£32,000	£33,000	£1,000
Labour costs	£18,000	£21,000	£3,000

Assuming these were the only costs and revenues for this business the actual profit is £8,000 less than budgeted due to these adverse variances.

In practice a business is likely to be faced with a combination of both favourable and adverse variances.

Case study

Table 16.3

	Budget	Actual	Variance
Sales revenue	£650,000	£645,000	V
Fixed costs	£46,000	£44,000	W
Labour costs	£230,000	£256,000	X
Material cost	£98,000	£94,000	Y
Profit	£276,000	U	£25,000 adverse

Questions

Copy out Table 16.3.

1. Calculate the actual profit and insert it in cell U.

2. Calculate all of the variances V–Y and indicate whether they are favourable or adverse.

3. Suggest two possible reasons for:

   a. the sales revenue variance and

   b. the labour cost variance.

AQA Examiner's tip

Do not confuse the terms favourable and adverse with positive and negative – as we have seen it is the impact on PROFIT that makes a variance either favourable or adverse NOT whether it is positive or negative.

💡 Using variance analysis to inform decision making

Managers can use variance information to improve decision making and planning for the future. This is most effectively done not just at the *end* of the budget period (often one year) but on a *monthly* basis. This will allow managers to take corrective action during the year and avoid the risk of a large adverse variance just at the end of it. To undertake variance analysis effectively, it is essential for managers to be able to identify the main possible *causes* of variances:

Possible causes of favourable variances:

■ Lower interest rates lead to a higher than expected increase in sales.

■ Bad publicity for a competitor's products boost sales above target levels.

- Unions agree to a wage settlement below the rate of inflation that was budgeted for.
- Higher £ exchange rate makes imported components cheaper than forecast.

Possible causes of adverse variances:

- Competitors offer special price deals that lead to lower sales for our business.
- Staff efficiency falls and this leads to higher wage costs for each unit produced or sold.
- Oil price increase raises energy costs.
- Rent increases forced through by property owner are higher than expected.

Having established the most likely causes of the variances, how will variance analysis affect managers' decisions? We will consider two examples.

1 One of the most frequent management problems highlighted by variance analysis is sales revenue falling below budget.

Table 16.4 *Adverse sales revenue variance*

Possible management decisions	Potential drawbacks of decision
1 Lower prices to increase sales and market competitiveness	Are consumers sensitive to price changes? Could this start a price war with rivals? Might perceived quality image be hit?
2 Increase promotional spending	This will affect the promotion budget Rivals might spend even more Will impact just be short-term?
3 Update the product range	How long will this take? Will new products be successful? New product development budget must be increased
4 Look for new markets, e.g. new segments or new countries	Market research costs will increase Will products need to be adapted to meet new market needs?

2 The second example concerns adverse production cost variances. If they were caused by higher production levels resulting from increased sales this would not be a problem. So, the first task of management would be to pinpoint the exact cause of these variances – were they caused by higher material costs, higher production levels or higher labour costs – or a combination of these?

Table 16.5 *Adverse production cost variance*

Possible management decisions	Potential drawbacks of decision
1 Obtain cheaper supplies of materials and components	Will quality and reliability be reduced? Will new suppliers be as reliable?
2 Cut wages	Impact on motivation levels? Could lead to disruptive industrial action
3 Increase labour productivity to reduce labour cost per unit	May need new machinery and staff training – adding to costs in the short term
4 Reduce waste levels	May need a change in working practices or a new recycling policy – short-term benefits may be limited

Case study

Variance analysis highlights problems at Highcroft

For the second month running, Highcroft Hotels had recorded lower profits than expected. The variance analysis is shown below:

Table 16.6

	Jan			Feb		
	Budget	Actual	Variance	Budget	Actual	Variance
Sales revenue	85	80	5 A	105	95	10 A
Food/drink costs	36	34	2 F	42	43	1 A
Labour costs	12	15	3 A	13	16	X
Fixed costs	16	18	2 A	16	15	Y
Profit	21	13	8 A			Z

The management of the hotel were particularly concerned about two of these variances. The sales revenue was substantially below budget – yet the number of guests staying at the hotel was almost exactly as they had originally forecast. Also, the adverse food and drink variance in February was a concern. With the guests spending less than budgeted, how had food and drink costs risen above budget?

The managing director of the hotel was relieved that these problems had been spotted early in the year. She was determined to take action which should solve these adverse variances in the months to come.

Questions

1 Calculate values for X, Y and Z and indicate whether the variances are adverse or favourable.

2 Explain the importance to the hotel of using monthly variance analysis – even though budgets are set for the whole year.

3 Analyse possible reasons for:
   a the sales revenue adverse variance and
   b the food and drink adverse variance in February.

4 Evaluate how the Managing Director of the hotel might overcome these adverse variances in the coming months of the year.

5 Research task: Access the BusinessLink government sponsored website, aimed at small businesses, to find out more about: 'Using your budget to measure business performance'.

💡✔ *In this chapter you will have learned to:*

- explain the benefits and drawbacks of using budgets
- calculate and interpret both favourable and adverse variances
- use the results of variance analysis to assist managers in taking decisions.

17   Improving cash flow

Setting the scene

Insolvency administrators take over company

About 200 jobs are under threat after Scott and Docherty, a Leeds based engineering firm set up in 1898, called in insolvency administrators. The company has, quite simply, run out of cash. Despite having record order books for its aircraft landing gear, the company has not been able to pay its suppliers for three months. The creditors called in administrators: either to run the business and make more cash from it or sell the assets to pay the bills.

How could an expanding business with an international reputation reach this position? Regular cash flow forecasts had been drawn up and they had suggested a cash flow problem for several months – but not a crisis like this.

Managers believe that the company was hit by a combination of factors that contributed to the cash flow problem. Prices of titanium and other specialist metals, the firm's main raw materials, have increased by 100 per cent in recent months, driven up by demand from China. An important computer-controlled machine broke down and was replaced by a much more expensive version – this had not been predicted in the cash flow forecasts. Finally, the company has expanded so quickly by trying to attract extra orders from Boeing and Airbus that the three monthly credit terms it offered for new orders could just not be afforded. The bank took fright at the ballooning overdraft and finally refused any more finance.

Discussion points

1. How useful had cash flow forecasts been to Scott and Docherty?

2. Explain how the company had 'quite simply run out of cash'.

3. How might the company have prevented this cash flow crisis and the collapse of the business?

What is a cash flow problem?

Just to say 'when there is not enough money' is too simplistic. Firstly, most of us could use more money most of the time! Secondly, it does not recognise the different degrees of 'problems' that can result from inadequate cash flow. The following two examples illustrate this.

Example 1

Firm A realises that its cash flow forecast was too optimistic. It assumed that debtors would pay after one month. In fact, they are taking two months to pay, on average. This is a problem as the firm has to increase its bank overdraft and this bears a high interest rate.

Expensive yes, but this problem does not threaten the survival of this business. After several weeks it is able to get debtors to pay more promptly and the business repays the overdraft.

This is a short-term cash flow problem.

Example 2

Firm B has reached its overdraft limit. It believes it can just survive until it receives cash from the sale of surplus land. Before this deal can be completed, a supplier suddenly insists on cash payment for all further deliveries. This cannot be afforded. Production stops, customers are disappointed and the cash inflows dry up. The firm is forced into insolvency by **creditors** who want all assets sold to be able to get back some of the money owed to them.

This is a long-term – and lethal – cash flow problem!

So, we can state that a cash flow problem occurs when a business is forced to take action that has negative short- or long-term effects because cash inflows are insufficient.

■ The causes of cash flow problems

Lack of planning

Chapter 13 – Using cash flow forecasting (page 94), covered how to construct cash flow forecasts and the importance of them. This form of financial planning can be used to predict potential cash flow problems so that business managers can take action to overcome it in plenty of time. A lack of such planning can make cash flow problems more likely.

Poor credit control

The credit control department of a business keeps a check on all customers' accounts, who has paid, who is keeping to agreed credit terms – and which customers are not paying on time. If this **credit control** is inefficient and badly managed then debtors will not be 'chased up' for payment and potential **bad debts** will not be identified.

Allowing customers too long to pay debts

In many trading situations businesses will have to offer trade credit to customers in order to be competitive. Assume a customer has a choice between two suppliers selling very similar products. If one insists on cash payment 'on delivery' and the other allows two months trade credit then customers will go for credit terms because it improves *their* cash flow. However, allowing customers too long to pay means reducing short-term cash inflows which could lead to cash flow difficulties.

Overtrading

Overtrading is when a business expands rapidly and has to pay for the expansion and for increased wages and materials months before it receives cash from additional sales. This can lead to serious cash flow shortages – even though the business is successful and expanding!

Unexpected events

A cash flow forecast can never be guaranteed to be 100 per cent accurate. Unforeseen increases in costs – a breakdown of a delivery van that needs to be replaced – or a dip in predicted sales income – a competitor lowers prices unexpectedly – could lead to negative net monthly cash flows.

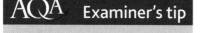

AQA Examiner's tip

Cash flow forecasts do not solve cash flow problems by themselves – but they are an essential part of financial planning which can help prevent cash flow problems from developing.

■ Key terms

Creditors: suppliers owed money by the business – purchases have been made on credit.

Credit control: the monitoring of debts to ensure that credit periods are not exceeded.

Bad debt: unpaid customer bills that are now very unlikely to ever be paid.

Overtrading: expanding a business rapidly without obtaining all of the necessary finance so that a cash flow shortage develops.

■ Activity

Using your knowledge of finance from Chapter 8 what sources of finance could a small business with ambitious expansion plans use to prevent cash flow problems arising?

Ways to improve cash flow

There are two main ways to improve net cash flow:

1 Increase cash inflows

2 Reduce cash outflows

Care needs to be taken here – the aim is to improve the cash position of the business *not* sales revenue or profits. These are different concepts. For example, a decision to advertise more in order to increase sales, which will eventually lead to increased cash flows, will *worsen* the short-term cash position as the advertising has to be paid for.

Activity

How would the following events affect the cash flow of a bus operating company:
- increase in oil prices
- increased unemployment
- lower train fares?

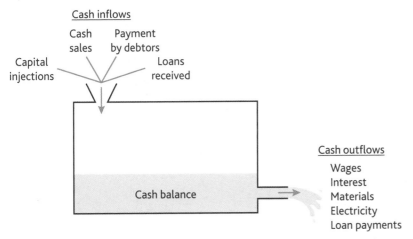

Fig. 17.1 *Symbolic drawing of cash flow 'tank' with leakages and injections of cash*

Table 17.1 *Increasing cash inflows*

Method	How it works	Possible drawbacks
Overdraft	Arranging a flexible loan on which the business can draw as necessary up to an agreed limit	High rates of interest. There may be an overdraft arrangement fee Can be withdrawn by the bank and this often causes insolvency
Short-term loan	Fixed amount borrowed for agreed length of time	Interest costs Must be repaid by the due date
Sale of assets	Cash receipts from selling off redundant assets will boost cash inflow	Selling assets quickly can result in low price The assets might be required at a later date for expansion The assets could have been used as collateral for future loans
Sale and leaseback	Selling an asset, e.g. to a finance company, but continuing to use the asset. An annual leasing charge is paid to the new owner	Leasing costs add to annual overheads Loss of potential profit if the asset rises in price The assets could have been used as collateral for future loans
Reduce credit terms to customers	Cash flow will be brought forward by reducing credit terms from, say two months to one month	Customers may purchase products from firms that offer extended credit terms
Debt factoring	Debt factoring companies buy the customer bills from a business and offer immediate cash. This reduces risk of bad debts too	Only about 90–95% of the debt will now be paid by the debt factoring company – reducing profit The customer has the debt collected by the finance company – does this suggest that your business is in trouble?

Table 17.2 *Reduce cash outflows*

Method	How it works	Possible drawbacks
Delay payments to suppliers (creditors)	Cash outflows will fall in the short term if bills are paid after, say three months instead of 2 months	Suppliers may reduce any discount offered with the purchase Suppliers can either insist on cash on delivery or refuse to supply at all if they believe the risk of never being paid is too great
Delay spending on capital equipment	By not buying equipment, vehicles, etc. cash will not have to be paid to suppliers	The efficiency of the business may fall if outdated and inefficient equipment is not replaced Expansion becomes very difficult
Use leasing not outright purchase of capital equipment	The leasing company owns the asset and no large cash outlay is required	The asset is not owned by the business Leasing charges include an interest cost and add to annual overheads
Cut overhead spending that does not directly affect output, e.g. promotion costs	These costs will not reduce production capacity and cash payments will be reduced	Future demand may be reduced by failing to promote the products effectively

AQA Examiner's tip

Remember: Just writing 'the firm should increase sales to improve cash flow' is NOT showing true understanding of the difference between sales revenue and cash flow!

If you suggest 'cutting staff and material purchases' this may reduce cash outflows but what will be the negative impact on output, sales and future cash inflows? This suggestion will nearly always be inappropriate for an examination question on improving cash flow.

Case study

It doesn't grow on trees

The violent storms in the autumn brought down thousands of trees and damaged millions of others. Some experts had estimated that it would take the 'tree surgery' industry several years to fell dangerous trees and trim others to make them safe. All councils and businesses were conscious of the huge liabilities they would face if one of their trees injured a member of the public. 'The good times have finally arrived,' said Damien to Gill, co-owners of Tree Trimmers Ltd.

Within days of the biggest storm, the company had been contacted by no fewer than 560 businesses and home owners concerned about the state of their trees. Damien ordered two new pick-up trucks, more chainsaws and employed two full time staff – who insisted on 50 per cent higher wages than was typical in 'normal' times in the industry. The company recruited a full time office administrator and took a mortgage out on a larger, more impressive office and yard.

Three months later, Damien and Gill were pleading with the bank manager for more time and a higher overdraft to save their business. 'I know we should have chased up our customers to pay on time and I am sorry about the bad debts, but this is still a growth industry,' pleaded Damien. 'How did we know the government was going to give grants to local councils to set up their own tree clearance teams?' explained Gill. 'Perhaps we could sell and lease back some of our new equipment'. 'You should probably have rented all of this extra equipment rather than buying it outright,' said the bank manager. 'We can offer our factoring service but with your bad debt collection record from customers, we could only offer around 80 per cent of invoice value.'

Business in action

Cosy Cottages

Cosy Cottages makes luxury playhouses for children. Graeme Bird, the owner, insists that all customer orders include a one third payment 'up front' so that 'if something goes wrong with the deal at least we won't be out of pocket for materials,' he said.

Questions

1 What do you understand by the term 'cash flow problem'?

2 Outline two reasons why Tree Trimmers Ltd had cash flow problems.

3 Analyse the consequences to Tree Trimmers of not taking urgent action to solve its cash flow problems.

4 Evaluate two ways, suggested in the case study, in which the business could reduce its cash flow problems.

5 Research how different firms approach the problems of late payment from customers.

In this chapter you will have learned to::

- explain what is meant by cash flow problems
- analyse the most likely causes of business cash flow problems
- evaluate the methods that businesses can use to overcome cash flow problems.

18 Measuring and increasing profit

In this chapter you will learn to:

- calculate and understand the net profit margin
- calculate and understand return on capital
- analyse different methods a business could use to increase its profits
- evaluate the possible impact of these different methods
- explain the difference between a firm's cash flow and its profit.

Setting the scene

Game profitability 'under threat'

Computer games developers are unlikely to make a profit on new titles until at least a year after launch. They are being trapped between rising development costs and increasing price competition. A report by media analyst Screen Digest said that the complexity of next generation games made it hard for publishers to cover production costs. Long development times and large production teams also affected profitability, the report found.

Games publishers which try to spread the appeal of their games across many different hardware platforms are also facing increasing price competition. With so many games to choose from, and rising numbers of publishers setting up in Asia, established producers are making less profit on each game sold.

Microsoft has adopted a different approach and is basing its strategy on exclusivity. It is encouraging some games publishers to produce games **only** for Xbox 360 which allows higher prices to be charged to Xbox users. It seems this strategy is beginning to pay off with the success of exclusive titles such as Epic's *Gears of War*.

Wii Nintendo is focusing on the strategy of game play innovation to attract a wide range of consumers willing to pay high prices. Some industry analysts think this is the best way to increase profitability. One said, 'This market is all about changing technology and games that reflect the latest technology will make the highest profits.'

Discussion points

1. Why is profitability so important for games developers?
2. Why is the profitability of some games developers likely to decline?
3. One strategy to increase profitability is to make technologically advanced, exclusive products. Would this be a good idea for games developers?
4. Suggest others ways a UK based games developer could try to increase profits.

Profit and profit margins

In Chapter 11 – Calculating costs, revenues and profits, page 70, the profit formula was given as:

$$Profit = Total\ revenue - Total\ costs$$

This formula gives the total level of profits made by a business in a given time period. It was also explained that total profits could be increased in two ways:

1. Increasing the number of units sold with the same price and cost per unit

If price = £10 and total cost per unit = £4, total profit = £6,000 if 1,000 units are sold. If sales rise to 1,200, total profit also increases, to £7,200.

2 Increasing the profit 'made on each unit'. This can be done by increasing price or reducing cost per unit or a combination of the two. See the next section for more detail.

If price is now increased to £11 and total cost per unit cut to £3, then if sales remain constant (a big IF perhaps?) then profit rises to £8,000 at the original sales level.

Using this second strategy increases the 'profit made per £ of sales'. This is called the **profit margin**. Profit margins are an important measure of business performance.

💡 Measuring profitability 1

Calculating and understanding the net profit margin

Do you recall the difference between fixed and variable costs that was explained in Chapter 11? This distinction is essential for understanding two different measures of profit: **gross profit** and **net profit**.

Gross profit = Sales revenue – Variable costs

Net profit = Sales revenue – Total costs

There is a clear link between these two profit measures. If a firm's gross profit increases AND there is no increase in fixed costs then net profit will increase too.

It is now possible to calculate the gross profit margin and net profit margin – these will provide an even clearer measure of the firm's performance.

$$\text{Gross profit margin (\%)} = \frac{\text{Gross profit}}{\text{Sales revenue}} \times 100$$

$$\text{Net profit margin (\%)} = \frac{\text{Net profit}}{\text{Sales revenue}} \times 100$$

Using these two formulae, we can work out the gross and net profit margins for T-Design:

Gross profit margin (%)

$$\frac{\text{Gross profit}}{\text{Sales revenue}} \times 100 = \frac{£150,000}{£250,000} \times 100 = 67\%$$

This means that on each £ of sales, T-Design makes 67 pence gross profit. Another way of putting it is that on each T-shirt sold, a gross profit of 67% is made.

Net profit margin (%)

$$\frac{\text{Net profit}}{\text{Sales revenue}} \times 100 = \frac{£70,000}{£250,000} \times 100 = 28\%$$

This means that on each £ of sales T-Design makes 28 pence net profit or, on each T-shirt sold, a net profit of 28% is made.

Key terms

Profit margin: the profit made as a proportion of sales revenue.

Gross profit: this is calculated by subtracting only variable costs from sales revenue, ignoring fixed costs.

Net profit: this is calculated by subtracting total costs from sales revenue.

Activity

A T-shirt retailer, T-Design, sells 50,000 units in 1 year at £5 each. Each T-shirt is purchased by the shop for £2.00 each. Annual fixed costs are £80,000.

Calculate:

a Gross profit and

b Net profit.

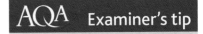 **Examiner's tip**

Although no questions will be set on the gross profit margin on AQA examination papers, it aids students understanding of why net profit margins may be rising or falling.

Net profit margin will always be less than gross profit margin as every business will have some fixed costs.

Activity

The following year the shop again sells 50,000 T-shirts for £5 each but gross profit increases to £160,000 and net profit to £90,000.

1 Calculate the new:
   a gross profit margin and
   b net profit margin.

2 Suggest two reasons for the improvement in the net profit margin.

Key terms

Return on capital: the proportion that the net profit is of the capital invested in the business or project.

Return on capital (%)

$$= \frac{\text{Net profit}}{\text{Capital invested}} \times 100$$

Activity

An entrepreneur plans to invest £12,000 in a new business. She has budgeted net profit of £3,000 for the first year of operation.

1 Calculate the expected return on capital.

2 Why should she be worried if another similar business is making a return on capital of 20 per cent each year?

AQA Examiner's tip

Many examination questions will ask for methods of increasing profitability of a business. If the question needs an evaluative answer it is very important that you consider at least ONE reason why your suggestion might not be effective.

Measuring profitability 2

Return on capital

Another way of measuring the profitability of a business or a new business project is to compare the profit made with the value of the capital invested. This gives the **return on capital**.

The higher the result of this ratio the more profitable the investment has been – and it could also indicate the efficiency of the management in managing the investment.

The result of this formula could be compared with other businesses in the same industry or other investment projects. The usefulness of the return on capital ratio is increased by making these comparisons. If a business needs to choose between two new projects it may choose the one with the higher return on capital. When rival companies are making a higher return on capital then this indicates that profitability is falling behind that of competitors.

The return on capital on a project or a new business proposal could be increased by either:

a Trying to increase profitability without investing any more capital.

b Attempting to make the same level of profit but with less capital expenditure.

Methods of increasing profit

Increasing profitability is the primary long-term objective of most businesses. There are four main methods businesses can use which might lead to an increase in profits:

1 Increase sales – without reducing the net profit margin.
2 Increase net profit margin by reducing variable costs per unit.
3 Increase net profit margin by increasing price.
4 Increase net profit margin by reducing fixed costs.

It sounds easy, doesn't it! But all four methods have potential **limitations** which can result in lower profitability in future or which have a negative impact on other objectives of the business. The following table explains how these four methods could be put into effect – and evaluates their possible impact.

The distinction between cash flow and profit

To many failed entrepreneurs there was no difference between cash and profit – which is why their new business collapsed so soon after start-up! All successful entrepreneurs, in contrast, understand that these two financial concepts do not have the same meaning or significance for a business – especially a newly formed one. It is very common for profitable businesses to run short of cash. On the other hand, loss-making businesses can have high cash inflows in the short term.

The essential difference between cash and profit can be explained with three business examples:

Table 18.1 *Methods of increasing profits*

Method of increasing profits	Examples	Possible limitations
1 Increase sales without reducing net profit margin	**1** Introducing new products, e.g. latest version of Sony Playstation **2** Increasing promotion of existing products, e.g. Nescafé TV adverts **3** Selling existing products in new markets, e.g. Tesco opening stores in Thailand	1 It's expensive to develop and launch new products, they are not always successful and it may take several years for sales to increase sufficiently to pay back costs 2 Adds to fixed costs so may reduce net profit margin, it may lead to competitors increasing their promotion too 3 Can be very expensive and fixed costs will increase. The culture and consumer tastes of new markets may be very different
2 Increase net profit margin by reducing variable costs	**1** Using cheaper materials, e.g. rubber not leather soles on shoes **2** Cutting labour costs, e.g. relocating production to low labour cost countries such as Dyson making cleaners in Malaysia **3** Cutting labour costs by increasing automation in production, e.g. the Mini production line uses some of the most labour saving robots in the world	1 Consumers' perception of quality may be damaged and this could hit the product's reputation. Consumers may expect lower prices – which may cut the net profit margin 2 Quality may be at risk, communication problems with distant factories 3 Purchasing machinery will increase fixed costs, remaining staff will need retraining – short-term profits may be cut due to these costs
3 Increase net profit margin by increasing price	Raising the price of the product with no significant increase in variable costs, e.g. BT raising the price of its broadband connections	Total profit could fall if too many consumers switch to competitors – this links to Chapter 32 and price elasticity Consumers may consider this to be a 'profiteering' decision and the long-term image of the business may be damaged
4 Increase net profit margin by reducing fixed costs	Cutting any fixed costs, such as rent, promotion costs or management costs but maintaining sales levels, e.g. moving to a cheaper head office location	1 Lower rental costs could mean moving to a cheaper area which could damage image, e.g. for a restaurant 2 Cutting promotion costs could cut sales by more than fixed costs 3 Fewer managers – or lower salaries – could reduce the efficient operation of the business

Example 1

Joe buys fresh fish from a market every day. He pays cash to the traders and gets a good deal because of this. He sells all of his stock on a High Street stall to shoppers who also pay him cash. In a typical week Joe buys fish costing £1,000 and sells it for £2,000.

Q: Ignoring all other costs, how much profit does he make in a typical week?
A: £1,000

Q: What was the difference between his cash inflows and outflows in a typical week?
A: £1,000 – as all purchases and sales were in cash.

In this very simplified example, CASH = PROFIT at the end of the week (but we have ignored other expenses too!)

THE HENLEY COLLEGE LIBRARY

■ Business in action

HMV

HMV's profits are continuing to fall as it faces increased competition from supermarkets and internet retailers. As part of a three year plan to increase profitability HMV plans to introduce a loyalty card, sell a wider range of portable digital products and completely revamp its website with a social networking facility.

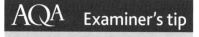

AQA Examiner's tip

When given the opportunity, emphasise the importance of a business having enough cash in the short term. Profit can wait – but cash payments are always being made.

■ Activity

In month 1, a business buys in 500 items for £5 each. It pays half the cost in cash and the other half is purchased on two months credit. The business sells all items for £10 each in month 1. Ignoring all other costs and payments:

1 How much profit did the business make on these 500 items?

2 What was its net cash flow in month 1?

Example 2

Shula owns Fine Foods, a specialist delicatessen. Last month she bought £500 of fresh goods from a supplier who offers one month's credit. The goods sold very slowly during the month and she was forced to cut her prices several times. Eventually she sold them all for only £300, paid in cash by her customers.

Q: What was her profit or loss, ignoring all other costs?
A: A loss of £200 – because even though she has not yet paid for the goods they are still recorded as a cost.

Q: What was the difference between her cash inflow and outflow?
A: A positive £300 – because she has not paid the supplier yet. So Shula has a positive cash flow from these goods this month even though she made a loss on them.

CASH was not the same as PROFIT for this business.

Example 3

Sanjit is concerned about competition for his jewellery shop. He buys most of his stock over the internet for cash – but has decided to increase the credit terms he gives to his customers to two months. Last month he bought some rings for £3,000 and paid in cash. He sold them all in the same month for £7,000– yet will not receive payment until two months time.

Q: How much profit did he make on these rings?
A: £4,000 – the rings have been sold and revenue recorded from the sale even though no cash payment has been made.

Q: What was Sanjit's cash flow position from these deals?
A: A negative outflow of £3,000 – he may be very short of cash until he receives payment from his customers.

CASH was not the same as PROFIT for this business – and there is a real danger that it could run out of cash to pay its everyday costs such as wages and rent.

So, profitable businesses can fail if they do not have sufficient cash to continue operations. The importance of cash flow forecasting, as explained in Chapters 13 and 17, is just as great for profitable businesses as those making a loss.

■ Case study

Tesco and Sainsbury's – which supermarket is more profitable?

Bitter rivals for many decades, these two giant retailers have both made big profits in recent years. However, Tesco has grown much more rapidly and now has total sales twice that of Sainsbury's. By looking at the published accounts of both companies the following sales revenue figures can be compared:

Table 18.2

Sales revenue (all figs in £m)	2006	2007
Tesco	39,454	42,641
Sainsbury's	16,987	17,151

Sales are important, of course, but which of these two rivals is more profitable? We will now compare net profit:

Table 18.3

Net profit (all figs in £m)	2006	2007
Tesco	2,280	2,648
Sainsbury's	229	520

Fig. 18.1 *Total sales revenue for Tesco was more than double that of Sainsbury's in 2007*

Sainsbury's has made lower profits in each of the years being considered. But, is this just because its sales are lower? Or could it be that the business is less profitable than Tesco because it also has lower net profit margins?

Questions

1 Explain the term 'net profit margin'.

2 Calculate the net profit margin for both companies for 2006 and 2007.

3 Analyse two possible reasons for Sainsbury's lower net profit margin.

4 Evaluate any two decisions the management of Sainsbury's could take to increase the profitability of the business.

5 Research task: Use the internet or copies of these two companies' published accounts to discover the following data for the latest year possible: Sales revenue; gross profit; net profit. Calculate net profit margins for both companies and compare with your previous results. Which company has improved profitability most?

✔ *In this chapter you will have learned to:*

■ explain the difference between gross and net profit

■ calculate and understand the importance of net profit margin

■ calculate and understand the importance of return on capital

■ analyse different methods businesses can use to increase profits and profitability

■ evaluate the impact of these methods on business

■ differentiate between cash flow and profit.

i

Summary questions

Chapters 16–18

1 Explain two advantages to a furniture manufacturing business from using a budget system. *(4 marks)*

2 Explain two problems this business might face when setting budgets. *(4 marks)*

3 Distinguish, with the aid of examples, between 'favourable cost variances' and 'adverse cost variances'. *(6 marks)*

4 Distinguish, with the aid of examples, the difference between a 'favourable revenue variance' and an 'adverse revenue variance'. *(4 marks)*

5 The following variance data has been produced for 'Value Furniture Ltd.'

Item	Budget (£)	Actual (£)	Variance
Sales revenue	960,000	1,200,000	Favourable £240,000
Labour costs	275,000	360,000	X
Rent and business rates	190,000	170,000	Y
Raw materials	230,000	320,000	Z

    a)   Calculate the variances X, Y and Z and indicate whether they are favourable or adverse. *(6 marks)*

    b)   Identify and explain the possible causes of the sales revenue and labour cost variances. *(6 marks)*

    c)   Assess the value of variance analysis to this business. *(8 marks)*

6 Outline two possible actions a business might take in response to an adverse sales revenue budget. *(6 marks)*

7 Outline two factors that might lead to a car retailing business experiencing cash flow problems. *(6 marks)*

8 Explain two ways that an entrepreneur might use to try to avoid cash flow problems. *(4 marks)*

9 A TV retailing business is experiencing a cash flow crisis. Explain and evaluate two ways in which the business might overcome this cash flow problem. *(8 marks)*

10 Explain, with a worked example, the meaning of the net profit margin. *(6 marks)*

11 Explain how a firm might be experiencing an increase in gross profit but a fall in its net profit. *(3 marks)*

12   A clothing manufacturer, Barca Designs, produces most of its products in
Spain. It sells to European retailers which operate in a competitive market
segment for smart, high priced clothing. Consumer incomes have been rising
in recent months and sales of up-market clothing retailers have been reported
as reaching record levels. Many of these firms sell very up to date fashions and
are increasingly importing their clothing from manufacturers in low wage
countries.

Profit, sales and capital invested data over the last two years for Barca Designs
is shown in the following table:

	2007 (£m)	2008 (£m)
Sales revenue	35	42
Gross profit	7	8
Net profit	4	3
Capital invested	25	25

a)   Calculate the following ratios for both years:

  i)   Net profit margin   *(2 marks)*

  ii) Return on capital   *(2 marks)*

b)   Analyse possible reasons for the trend in the net profit margin ratio.   *(8 marks)*

c)   Explain why the return on capital result is important to this business.   *(3 marks)*

d)   The business has an opportunity to invest capital in a new Spanish
factory project costing £5m. The expected annual net profit from the
project is £2m. Explain, with calculations, whether this project would
improve the company's overall return on capital.   *(6 marks)*

e)   Evaluate TWO further ways that this business might use to
attempt to increase its profitability.   *(8 marks)*

People in business

Introduction

Chapters in this section:

This section continues to develop the theme of improving the effectiveness of a business. The growth of many small firms happens in a very haphazard and unstructured way and this can lead to unnecessary inefficiency. At some point the manager must face the issues that are bound to emerge as the workforce increases in size and complexity.

Entrepreneurs generally start by doing all the important jobs in the business themselves, and it is difficult for them to let go of some of the responsibility for tactical decision-making, and pass it on to other members of the workforce. This process can influence how the structure of the organisation evolves. If the founder(s) want to retain as much control as possible, the decision-making will be contained within a small group of powerful people at the centre of the organisation. However, while this approach may be very successful when the business is small, it is not an efficient way to run a larger business, and at some point decisions must be taken as to the best ways to improve the organisational structure.

In Chapter 10 we saw that small businesses employ a range of workers and make use of specialist advisors and consultants. As firms grow, the need for such specialist skills, and for a stable workforce increase. This may mean that instead of using outside agencies, the firm needs to recruit specialists to work within the business full time. This section looks at the options available to businesses so that they can develop an effective workforce to meet the needs of the market. This includes the recruitment and selection process and a life-long learning approach to developing existing employees who may need to be retrained due to new technology, products and customer demands.

Once an effective workforce has been recruited and trained, how can it been retained? There is always the possibility that a rival business will tempt the best employees away with attractive financial rewards and the promise of better promotion prospects. For growing businesses, there is a need to ensure that the money spent on recruiting and training the workforce is not wasted. This section looks at the range of motivational techniques that can be used to ensure that the effectiveness of the workforce is not diminished by rising absenteeism and falling productivity.

This section is divided into four chapters. The key issues covered by each chapter are:

Chapter 19: Improving organisational structure What are the key elements of organisational structures? How important are the issues of levels of hierarchy/spans of control, work loads, job allocation and delegation? What are the workforce roles within a business, and how can organisational structure affect business performance? To what extent does the quality of internal business communication impact on the effectiveness of businesses?

Chapter 20: Measuring the effectiveness of the workforce This chapter looks at how those involved in decision making can make better judgements about the contribution made by employees to the success of the business. What is labour productivity and how is it calculated? What is the calculation for labour turnover? Is absenteeism from work a serious problem for businesses and how does a firm know what the rate of absenteeism is?

Chapter 21: Developing an effective workforce: recruitment, selection and training Here we investigate the process of creating the best possible workforce. What types of recruitment are there? What are the stages in the recruitment process from identifying the vacancy to receipt of applications? Which method of selection is most appropriate for choosing the best employees? How can recruitment and selection improve the workforce? What methods of training are available to small to medium-sized businesses?

Chapter 22: Developing and retaining an effective workforce: motivating employees This chapter looks at the options available to businesses to ensure that they get the very best out of their most important asset – their employees. Which financial methods can be used to motivate? How can improving job design motivate workers? Is empowering employees effective and can team working be used in small businesses? What are the main motivational theories? What is the link between the organisational structure and the motivational techniques available to managers? How would you select the best candidate for this job?

In this chapter you will learn to:

- explain the different ways in which organisations can be structured

- apply effective organisational structures to different scenarios

- explain workforce roles within a business

- analyse how organisational structure affects business performance

- analyse the importance of issues such as levels of hierarchy/spans of control, work loads, job allocation and delegation

- evaluate the extent to which the quality of internal business communication can impact on the effectiveness of businesses.

Fig. 19.1 *YogaBugs Logo (www.yogabugs.com/uk)*

Key terms

Organisational structure: the way the jobs, responsibilities and power within a business are organised.

Setting the scene

Family business

It surprises a lot of people that 75 per cent of businesses in the UK are family run: most people cannot imagine anything worse! YogaBugs Ltd, the brainchild of Fenella Lindsell and her sister-in-law Lara Goodbody, was launched in 2003. 'I should say I can see problems with working with family but I can't,' Lindsell says. 'I feel very privileged to work with Lara. We have different strengths – she's a figures girl, better at all the accounting and she gets things done very quickly, but I think I'm better at writing and taking care of the intellectual property.'

Bringing your work home can even have its advantages: 'We have a hell of a time. My husband is in brand licensing, and my brother works for a marketing agency and they're always happy to help. No money changes hands; they come up with ideas then we all talk about them. There are lots of conversations in the kitchen and in the car; we even go on holiday together!'

YogaBugs' initial aim, tapping into the government initiative to get children more active, was to train people to teach children yoga. Soon demand for their teachers outstripped supply and they started franchising. As the business has expanded, they have taken on other members of staff. Is there friction between outsiders and those in the family? 'We've got two other people on staff who are fabulous, so luckily there is no conflict. We all work hard, and keep everything professional, but I think we strike a good balance.'

Guardian Sept 2006/She Oct 2007

Discussion points

1. Given their personal strengths, how might Fenella and Lara have organised YogaBugs when they first launched the company?

2. Fenella and Lara decided to franchise their business idea (see Chapter 2 – Generating and Protecting Business Ideas, page 9) and have appointed an Operations Manager to support this method of expansion. Will it be easy for them to trust someone outside the family with such an important job?

3. 'The quality of internal communication can be vital to the success of a small business as it expands.' To what extent do you think this is true of YogaBugs?

Organisational structure

In any organisation, the allocation of jobs is necessary to ensure that the business operates as efficiently as possible. In its simplest form, an **organisational structure** may only involve two or three people; however, as the firm becomes more successful and employs more staff, the need to make individual roles and responsibilities clear becomes ever more important. An **organisational chart** can be used to illustrate the structure in place or proposed, and should include the following features:

- Where the responsibility and authority for decision making lies within the business.
- The job titles and roles of positions in the business (and the name of the person currently holding that position).
- The lines of authority which show who each employee is accountable to and who they are responsible for.
- The lines of communication through the business.

Small and medium-sized businesses, especially those that are growing quickly are likely to change the organisational structure quite regularly. In the early stages of any firm's life, the entrepreneur is likely to take a very 'hands-on' approach, but this becomes less practical as the business becomes bigger, and gradually many of the day-to-day decisions are passed on to other trusted members of the team. (The way in which the organisational structure is developed by a business's owners may take into account a number of factors:)

- The business environment – is the market very competitive and does the business need to keep costs low and be as up-to-date as possible?
- The skills of the employees – if the business is made up of a small number of highly trained professionals, the organisational structure may be very different to a firm employing a larger number of unskilled or semi-skilled workers.
- The culture of the organisation – if the business has gained its market share based on originality, cutting-edge design and flair, the organisational structure must not restrict creativity. However, the firm may have developed its place in the market because of an emphasis on traditional values, with consistency being very important. In this case, the structure is likely to be formal and each position within the organisation clearly defined.

Key elements of an organisational structure

When deciding on how to develop the most effective structure in a small or growing business, there are several key elements that the entrepreneur should consider.

Key terms

Organisational chart: a diagram showing job titles, lines of communication and responsibility within a business.

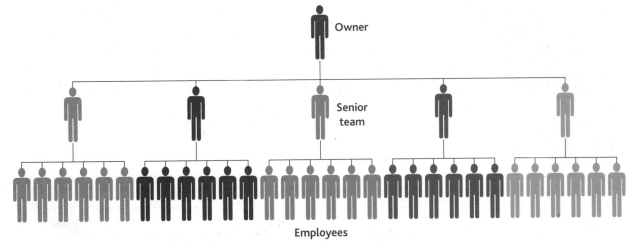

Fig. 19.2 *Diagram showing three levels of hierarchy*

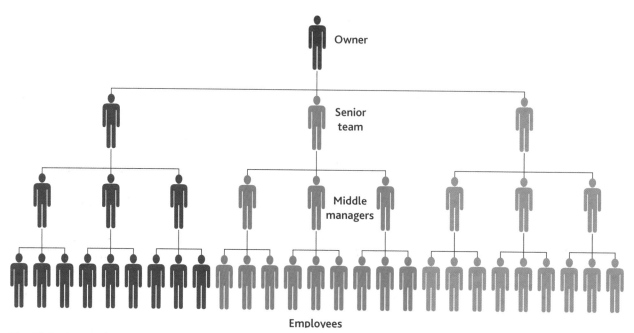

Fig. 19.3 *Diagram showing four levels of hierarchy*

Levels of hierarchy

Levels of hierarchy refer to the number of layers within an organisation, with each layer representing a level of authority. All employees have a clearly defined role and their relationship with every other post holder in the business is established. This approach is usually based on departments, and is a formal approach to organisational structure, favoured by more traditional businesses. The more layers that exist in the hierarchy, the longer the **chain of command** from those at the top to those at the bottom of the organisation. This structure can lead to communication problems because the **lines of communication** are stretched, which can slow down the movement of important information. This can cause particular difficulties for smaller businesses that have to stay in touch with market conditions if they are to maintain their market share.

As you can see, in Figures 19.2 and 19.3, these two firms are run by the owner. The structure of the organisation is very different, with the second business having one more level in the hierarchy.

Span of control

This is also illustrated in Figures 19.2 and 19.3. In Figure 19.2, each member of the senior team has a wide **span of control** because he/she is responsible for six members of their department. In Figure 19.3, the span of control is much narrower: each manager is responsible for three people. A narrow span of control allows for close supervision of the work of employees, whereas a wider span gives subordinates the chance for more independence.

Work load and job allocation

As small businesses grow, one of the reasons why a structure emerges is because the **work load** for individual employees becomes too great, and some of their tasks are passed to other, probably new workers. When a structure is being designed and improved, the question of work load must be considered. In Figures 19.2 and 19.3, the work load of the managers in the first organisation is likely to be greater than that for the managers and supervisors in the second, because they have a wider span of control, that is they are responsible for more subordinates. The importance of

■ Key terms

Levels of hierarchy: the number of layers of management and supervision existing in an organisation.

Chain of command: the lines of authority within the business.

Lines of communication: how information is passed up, down and across an organisation.

Span of control: the number of subordinates, one job/post holder is responsible for.

Work load: how much work one employee, department or team have to complete in a given period of time.

work load should not be underestimated, because an employee feeling that they have too much work to do is likely to be unhappy and this can cause problems for the business (Chapters 20 and 22 – Measuring the effectiveness of the workforce and Developing and retaining an effective workforce, pages 143 and 160).

The way in which **job roles** are allocated within a business can also have an impact on the structure which develops. In traditional organisations, jobs are grouped by function, for example marketing, finance, human resources and operations. However, in many small firms, a task-based approach is taken where jobs are grouped around the completion of a particular task or project, for example opening a new office or completing a contract for a specific client.

Delegation

The founders of successful firms can easily find themselves overwhelmed by work and need to appoint more staff in managerial or supervisory/ team leader roles, so that they can delegate tactical decision making. This leaves them free to concentrate on making longer-term plans for the development of the business. The **delegation** of decision making is one of the most difficult things for the entrepreneur to do, yet if the recruitment and selection of new employees (Chapter 21, page 149) is effective, there is no reason to assume that subordinates are not capable of making good decisions. Delegation may also have a very positive impact on motivation (Chapter 22, page 160) which is a very important factor in the development of an effective organisation.

Communication flows

The structure of any organisation indicates the lines of communication. This shows how simple or complicated it may be for information to be passed around a business. In a small firm it should be possible for the **communication flows** to be very quick and accurate: the chances are that most of the communication will be face-to-face, unless it is a legal document such as a contract of employment. As a business grows, it is important that these communication flows are maintained, particularly if the firm becomes split geographically. For example, if a family-run removals business based in Cumbria, opens a second office in Northampton, the directors must be sure that the lines of communication between the new site and the head office are efficient and that employees in Northampton do not feel too remote from the day-to-day running of the firm. Good communication flows, using available technology are an important part of the successful expansion of a small business. There are always issues of cost to consider, and you should not assume that small and medium-sized firms can afford to invest in the latest high-tech equipment. For many businesses, the option to buy-in expertise is more cost-effective than trying to improve communications in-house.

Why are good internal communications important?

Whatever the media, it is important for new and growing businesses to have efficient internal communications.

■ Everyone in the firm knows what the company is aiming for, and can use this as the basis for tactical decision-making. If the directors want to expand the range of services offered, the human resources department can organise a training programme so staff can acquire the necessary skills.

■ Customer needs can be met: market research, after-sales service and increasingly business 'blogs' are used to gather information about customer satisfaction, which must be communicated to the appropriate department so changes can be made.

■ Key terms

Job role: the tasks involved in a particular job.

Delegation: passing the authority to make specific decisions to somebody further down the organisational hierarchy.

Communication flows: how information is passed around an organisation including downwards, upwards, sideways and through the grapevine or gossip network.

■ Link

For more information on Human Resources training see Chapter 21 – Developing an effective workforce: recruitment, selection, training, page 156.

■ Business in action

Yellowcom.com

Yellowcom.com is a small internal communications agency that works with other organisations to improve their internal communications. The team, based in Manchester, use all sorts of media including the traditional printed page, DVD, TV, mobile devices and the intranet to meet the needs of its clients. In 2006, for example, they created a regional launch event for employees at the Co-op Bank, to support its Bank Transformation Project. (Visit www.yellowcom.com for more examples of their work).

Fig. 19.4 *Hierarchical structure*

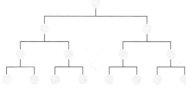

Fig. 19.5 *Matrix structure*

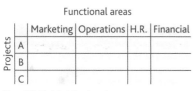

Fig. 19.6 *Entrepreneurial structure*

■ Decision-makers are aware of ideas and improvements for the business: in a competitive market, this could mean the difference between success and failure for a small or growing firm. Listening to the opinions of employees can be a cheap and effective way to improve the quality of goods and services provided.

■ Decision-makers are aware promptly of changes in the business environment: this could be a new competitor entering the local market or a change in tastes and fashion. As a business grows, how can the entrepreneur ensure that he/she does not lose touch with the dynamics of the market? The answer is to ensure that up-to-date information is available to the tactical decision-makers. Communications should flow in all directions, not just downwards. However, the lines of communication need to be organised rather than chaotic and haphazard.

■ Types of organisational structures

There are a variety of structures that small and growing businesses can use, which may depend on the personality of the founder of the organisation as much as any other factor such as the business environment and the skills of the employees.

Hierarchical structures

Hierarchical structures, such as those illustrated in Figures 19.2, 19.3 and 19.4, allow specialist functional job roles to develop in a business, which can be very useful for employees who can see the promotional opportunities available within their area. The work load for managers and supervisors may be determined by their span of control: a narrow span reducing the work-load, and a wider span of control having the opposite affect. A possible disadvantage of an increasingly hierarchical structure is that communication can slow down, and this may hamper decision-making.

Matrix structures

Matrix structures are based around tasks or projects and involve the creation of teams that include all the necessary functional specialists. Employees are encouraged to use their individual talents and skills and their job roles are likely to be much more varied. Teamworking in a matrix structure can be very motivating. However, the work load may be unevenly spread amongst the members of the team, which can cause resentment. Each team member may have loyalties to both the team and his/her department.

Entrepreneurial structures

Entrepreneurial structures are usually found in small businesses in very competitive markets, where quick decision-making is important to maintain and increase market share. A core team of decision-makers, the founder(s) and a small number of trusted colleagues with or without specific job roles are supported by a number of general employees with little or no decision-making power. This approach can only really work in a small business situation, because as an organisation grows, the increasing work load makes it impossible for such a small number of employees to be effective.

Informal structures

These exist where there is no obvious need for any formal structure. In a firm of professional specialists such as doctors or solicitors, everyone works as part of one team, with perhaps centralised administrative support. If a business decision needs to be taken, a meeting of all members of staff will be arranged.

■ Workforce roles

There are some key **workforce roles** within any organisation. The people in the following positions can have a direct impact on the motivation of employees and the efficiency of communication flows throughout the firm.

Supervisors

People who are directly responsible for one or more subordinate, depending on whether the organisational structure is tall (narrow span of control) or flat (wide span of control). All the employees within their area of responsibility will have a work load to fulfil and the amount of delegation will depend on the management style adopted by the supervisor (see Chapter 22, page 160). Essentially, the role of the supervisor is to allocate jobs to subordinates and ensure that tasks are carried out to a satisfactory standard.

Team leaders

Employees who facilitate the functioning of a group of employees within the organisation. This role fits best with a matrix structure, but a team approach to working can function within a hierarchical structure as well. Rather than allocating jobs, the team leader ensures that the work load is spread fairly between team members, that the resources required by the team are available, and that deadlines are met.

Managers

Employees who oversee the operation of a specific area of a business. This involves not only the staff within their area, but also resources such as stock, materials and equipment. Managers will delegate to subordinates such as supervisors and team leaders, if that is their style. However, they retain responsibility for decisions made and need to have confidence in their team/department.

Directors

Appointed by the shareholders to oversee the running of the business. They usually take responsibility for a particular function/area of the organisation. However they do not generally get involved in the day-to-day running of larger organisations, but are likely to be very hands-on in new and small to medium-sized businesses.

■ Can improving the organisational structure enhance business performance?

There is no structure which suits all businesses and every set of circumstances and you will need to consider which structure might be the most effective for a firm facing a range of scenarios.

Financial problems

A firm is facing increased price competition and needs to reduce overhead costs. In this case it might be that a level in the hierarchy is removed. This may significantly reduce fixed costs, but it will increase the span

Key terms

Workforce role: the tasks involved in a particular level or grade of job within an organisation.

Link

For more on team working see Chapter 22 – Developing and retaining an effective workforce: motivating employees, page 160.

Link

For more information on reducing costs see Chapter 11 – Calculating costs, revenues and profits, page 75.

Activity

1. Construct an argument to support using supervisors in medium-sized clothes retailing business rather than team leaders.

2. Prepare the counter-argument that suggests team-leaders would be better.

3. Finally, make a judgement about which argument is stronger in this scenario incorporating the phrase 'it depends on'.

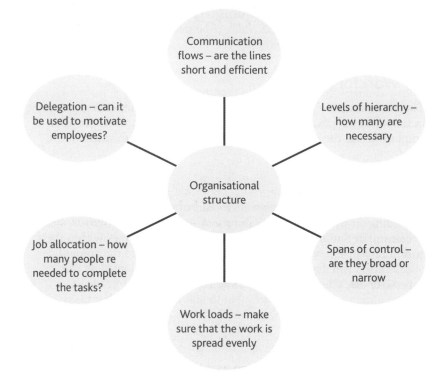

Fig. 19.7 *Diagram to show the influences on an effective organisational structure*

of control of the remaining managers. Care must be taken otherwise the additional work load could be de-motivating. However, the lines of communication will be shortened, which should be an advantage to the firm.

The Human Resources manager is unhappy

She complains that her work load has increased as the business has grown. The solution might be that the structure becomes more hierarchical and her job role is divided between two managers each with a particular specialism. Again, it is important to consider the implications of this in terms of motivation and communication. Don't forget, there will be disadvantages as well as advantages.

■ Adjusting the organisational structure

Remember, an organisational structure is not static; it should evolve over time as changes occur.

The growth of the business

If the firm has grown in an informal, haphazard way, does the structure need to become more formal, and roles more clearly defined? How will this affect the communication flow and the motivation of employees? By making adjustments to the structure, the business can operate more efficiently, perhaps changing from an entrepreneurial structure to a hierarchical structure with a few levels in the hierarchy.

Market conditions

Have new competitors entered the market, forcing prices down and increasing the need for financial efficiency? Can changes in the organisation of the business, such as creating a flatter, less hierarchical structure help to achieve this? With shorter lines of communication the business may be more responsive to changes in the market which could give it an edge over more bureaucratic rivals.

Ownership

Does a change from sole trader to partnership or to private limited company (Chapter 7, pages 44–8) present an opportunity to improve the business's organisational structure? What workforce roles can be created and how involved are the new partners or shareholders going to be?

Customer's needs

Are the requirements of individual clients so specific that introducing an organisational matrix structure would be best, or should a project-based approach be confined to the operations and sales departments? An alternative might be to organise the structure of the business into customer types rather than functional areas.

The entrepreneurial culture within the company

Are creativity and risks-taking being stifled by the formal organisational structure that has developed? How could a change in the way the business is organised ensure that an entrepreneurial culture is retained? The business could be organised into product areas which could encourage specialist teams. On the other hand, is it time for the firm to create a more stable, formal structure because the potential costs of failure have become too great, and new ideas need more careful consideration?

Factors such as these can be the basis for an evaluation of proposed changes to an organisational structure. Use your judgement to assess the extent to which improving the structure might increase the effectiveness of the organisation.

> ### AQA Examiner's tip
>
> Most organisations use some sort of hierarchical structure because this identifies job roles and responsibilities within the business. However this does not mean that they do not use a matrix structure within the organisation: a project-based approach may be the most appropriate for research and development, IT and marketing.

Case study

Bighams

Bighams is a private limited company creating hand-made food using fresh ingredients every day. The business, started 10 years ago by Charlie Bigham, has recently moved to a new location and now employs 300 staff. There are very few levels of hierarchy in the firm, Charlie takes a hands-on approach to running the business and is directly involved in the decision making: new products, finances, location, etc. However, he has delegated some responsibility to specialists who run various functional areas within the business including: sales, marketing, finance, operations, packing, purchasing, health and safety and human resources. Each of these managers is responsible for all employees working in that area and most have quite a wide span of control.

Bighams are very keen that customers give their opinions about products. They encourage people to give feedback either by email, telephone, in writing or by visiting the premises in London. They also organise masterclasses for employees, where one of the chefs instructs other members of the team on how to cook a variety of regional dishes. The recipes can then be downloaded from the Bighams website, and employees are encouraged to try out their new skills on friends and family.

www.bighams.com

Questions

1 Explain the following terms in the context of Bighams:

a levels of hierarchy

b span of control.

2 Why has Charlie had to delegate some decision making to experts in different functional areas of the business?

3 The masterclasses increase the work load of the chefs at Bighams. What are the advantages and disadvantages of this approach in terms of the overall performance of the business?

4 To what extent will the quality of internal communications impact upon the continued success of Bighams?

5 Go onto the Bighams website to look in more detail at the organisational structure and job roles of people in the organisation.

💡✔ *In this chapter you will have learned to:*

■ explain the different ways in which organisations can be structured as they grow in size

■ describe important workforce roles: supervisors, team leaders, managers and directors

■ analyse the importance of issues such as levels of hierarchy/spans of control, work loads, job allocation and delegation

■ discuss the impact the key elements of organisational structure can have on the effectiveness of a business

■ discuss the extent to which the quality of internal business communication can impact on the effectiveness of businesses.

Measuring the effectiveness of the workforce

Setting the scene

Productivity

British productivity, or output per worker, enjoyed its fastest growth in almost three years in the first quarter of 2007. In figures that will make good reading for the new Chancellor, Alistair Darling, labour productivity grew 2.7 per cent year-on-year in the first three months of 2007. Growth in output per hour climbed to 2.8 per cent from 2.7 per cent in the fourth quarter of 2006. Output growth per hour was up by a hefty 3.6 per cent year-on-year in the manufacturing sector. Manufacturing output per hour worked expanded by 2.2 per cent in the first quarter. Manufacturers had been holding up their productivity through last year by cutting jobs at a time when output was increasing solidly. Service sector output per hour rose to an annual 3.5 per cent. For the first time in years it has been stronger than manufacturing, reflecting strong service sector growth.

Ashley Seager, Guardian, 2 July 2007

Measured by output per hour, the UK lags behind its main competitors. Recent figures show that in 2004 American workers added 34 per cent more value per hour than their UK counterparts, Germans 11 per cent more, and the French 25 per cent more.

Simon Caulkin, Observer, 22 July 2007

Discussion points

1. What does labour productivity measure?

2. Why should British businesses be concerned if the labour productivity in the UK is less than in other industrialised countries?

3. Can all businesses measure labour productivity?

4. How else might the performance of the workforce be measured?

Measuring the efficiency of an organisation

The question of the efficient use of resources is considered in the Operations Management section of this book. In the same way that machinery and vehicles must be used rather than standing idle, it is possible to measure the **workforce performance**, and make a judgement about whether or not it is efficient. The aim is to reduce unnecessary costs to the business thereby improving efficiency.

Labour turnover

This refers to the number of employees who leave and join an organisation over a specified time period, for example one year. **Labour turnover** can be classified into two types:

- **Voluntary** – when the employee leaves for their own reasons. This is usually unplanned as far as the organisation is concerned, and is most likely to happen in the first few months of employment.

Key terms

Workforce performance: methods of measuring the effectiveness of employees including labour productivity, staff turnover and absenteeism.

Labour turnover: percentage of the total workforce who leave in any given time period (e.g. one year).

■ **Involuntary** – refers to dismissal or redundancy.

Normally voluntary turnover is much higher than involuntary and is calculated using the following formula:

$$\text{Labour turnover} = \frac{\text{Number of leavers per year}}{\text{Average number of employees per year}} \times 100$$

In the UK the average is currently between 16 and 18 per cent.

Why should labour turnover be calculated?

Obviously a lot will depend on the type of business, and a low percentage can cause problems such as stagnation with a lack of new ideas coming into the firm. However, most businesses would be concerned if the rate of labour turnover was rising, because that would suggest that a growing number of employees were dissatisfied with their current position. According to the Human Resource Management Guide, the cost of labour turnover is about £8,200 per employee, which rises to £12,000 for professionals and managers. The calculation of labour turnover may encourage employers to investigate the causes and find solutions which will save money and may have a longer-term benefit in terms of improved recruitment, selection and training (Chapter 21, page 149) and the motivation of employees (Chapter 22, page 160).

Link

For more information on recruitment, selection and training of employees, see Chapter 21 – Developing an effective workforce, page 149.

Theories of motivation are discussed in detail in Chapter 22 – Developing and retaining an effective workforce, page 160.

■ Case study

Calculating labour turnover

Here are the details of a medium-sized double glazing company which operates throughout Scotland. A new training programme and bonus scheme was introduced in Year 2.

Table 20.1

	Year 1	Year 2	Year 3	Year 4
Average number of employees	42	41	42	43
Number of leavers	3	6	2	2

Questions

1. Calculate the labour turnover rate for each year.

   a Year 1: $3/42 \times 100 = 7.14\%$

   b Year 2: $6/41 \times 100 = 14.63\%$

   c Year 3: $2/42 \times 100 = 4.76\%$

   d Year 4: $2/43 \times 100 = 4.65\%$

2. What do the figures suggest about the introduction of the new training programme and bonus scheme?

3. Make a list of what the costs of labour turnover might be?

Key terms

Labour productivity: the contribution made by employees to the output of a business.

Labour productivity

Labour productivity can be measured in three ways:

1 Output per employee

In some companies this may be quite straight forward, for example the number of zips sewn into pairs of jeans per hour. But where jobs are more complex, a better measure is the total output generated by the employees of the business which can then be turned into an average as follows:

$$\frac{\text{Total value of output}}{\text{Total number of employees}}$$

2 Labour cost per unit of output

Focus on production costs is preferred by many businesses:

$$\frac{\text{Total labour costs}}{\text{Total output}} \times 100$$

An increase in labour productivity will reduce labour cost per unit of output and will improve competitiveness.

3 UK productivity

This is the preferred option of the government to compare with international rivals using a measure of total output per hour worked. By this measure, the UK falls behind France, Germany and the US:

$$\frac{\text{Total UK output}}{\text{Total UK hours worked}}$$

Case study

Calculating labour productivity

Here are more details of the medium-sized double glazing company which operates throughout Scotland. A new training programme and bonus scheme was introduced in Year 2.

Table 20.2

	Year 1	Year 2	Year 3	Year 4
Average number of employees per year	42	41	42	43
Number of leavers	3	6	2	2
Value of output (£)	1,500,000	1,300,000	1,600,000	1,800,000
Total labour costs	948,600	951,200	948,600	962,400

Questions

1 Calculate the labour productivity per year using the output per employee formula.

   a Year 1: 1,500,000/42 = £35,714.28
       Year 2: 1,300,000/41 = £31,707.32

   b Year 3: 1,600,000/42 = £38,095.24
       Year 4: 1,800,000/43 = £41,860.46

2 Calculate the labour productivity using the labour costs per unit of output method.

   a Year 1: (948,600/1,500,000) = 63p
       Year 2: (951,200/1,300,000) = 73p

   b Year 3: (948,600/1,600,000) = 59p
       Year 4: (962,400/1,800,000) = 53p

3 What do these figures suggest about the effectiveness of the workforce?

4 What other information might be needed to explain the changes identified?

Why should labour productivity be calculated?

In a competitive market, any business needs to be sure that it is using its resources efficiently. If the output per employee is falling, this suggests that there is room to improve efficiency. Again, the figures do not provide a solution to any underlying problem, but can be the basis for an investigation into possible causes within the business which can then be remedied. It could be that employees need specific training, or that the payment system needs to be revised in order to improve motivation (Chapter 21, page 160).

Absenteeism

Absenteeism is seen as a good indicator of satisfaction at work and can be calculated using the following formula:

$$\frac{\text{Average number of staff absent on one day}}{\text{Total number of staff}} \times 100$$

Case study

Calculating absenteeism

Here are even more details of the medium-sized double glazing company which operates throughout Scotland. A new training programme and bonus scheme was introduced in Year 2.

Table 20.3

	Year 1	Year 2	Year 3	Year 4
Average number of employees per year	42	41	42	43
Number of leavers	3	6	2	2
Turnover/value of output (£)	1,500,000	1,300,000	1,600,000	1,800,000
Total labour costs	948,600	951,200	948,600	962,400
Average number of staff absent on one day	5	6	2	1

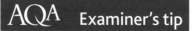

Questions

1. Calculate the percentage absenteeism rate for years 1–4:

   a Year 1: 5/42 × 100 = 11.9%

   b Year 2: 6/41 × 100 = 14.6%

   c Year 3: 2/42 × 100 = 4.8%

   d Year 4: 1/43 × 100 = 2.3%

2. Describe the trend you observe from the answers above. How might you explain this?

Absenteeism costs the UK £11.6bn a year according to the Confederation of British Industry (CBI). This organisation believes that high absenteeism levels are the main reason why UK productivity is much lower than the US and some other parts of Europe. On average, absenteeism costs UK industry 2.9% of total costs but for British Airways it is 15%.

Key terms

Absenteeism: The number of working days lost as a result of an employee's deliberate or habitual absence from work.

Activity

What are the costs of absenteeism to a business?

AQA Examiner's tip

You should memorise the formulas for labour turnover and productivity. Remember that all the information you need will be provided, even if you have to do some work to find it! Start your calculations by writing down the formula – it will help you to focus on the information you need – and get you marks for knowledge.

Business in action

Invesco

For most adults at work having one day off sick is not a crime, but it is a major headache for UK industry. According to healthcare consultancy IHC, 40 million days are lost each year in the UK to workplace absenteeism.

93 per cent of employees blame absence on flu; however IHC says that at least 50 per cent of absence is not about health, it is because of bullying at work, family responsibility, job demotivation, low pay, or a hangover.

Ill health can still be caused by someone's job: IHC estimates that 13.4 million working days a year are lost to stress, anxiety and depression, and 12.3 million to back and upper limb problems. This costs UK industry £11.5bn in wages to absent employees, additional overtime and payments to temporary staff.

One firm that decided to tackle the problem is investment management company Invesco, where they calculated that absenteeism cost about £38,000 a year. Invesco overhauled its staff's health provision offering their staff a private GP, physiotherapist, workstation assessments, free health tests, counselling and a non-contributory private medical insurance scheme. One-day sickness absences fell by 6%, saving 60 working days per year. 'It has helped us raise staff morale and increase general health, while reducing down-time in the office and improve productivity' said a spokeswoman.

Why should absenteeism be calculated?

As with the other measures of workforce effectiveness, high or rising absenteeism represents a cost to the business, and as such should be investigated. Some firms take a very heavy-handed approach to this issue, implying that employees are faking illness. However, it might be more appropriate to look in more depth at the possible causes, and find a solution which suits everyone within the firm. That way motivation might increase which may have a positive impact on the quality and quantity of output.

The importance of workforce measures

For any organisation it is important to monitor changes over time so that efficiency and effectiveness can be evaluated. The information gathered about employees can be compared to data from previous years and other businesses or sectors to judge whether or not policies and procedures are working. The questions posed throughout this chapter make it clear that the calculations may not provide the answers to problems within a business however they can highlight issues which should be addressed. Chapters 21 and 22 – Developing an effective workforce: recruitment, selection, training and Developing and retaining an effective workforce: motivating employees, pages 149 and 160, contain details of some of the possible solutions available to firms who find that their workforce is becoming less effective.

Case study

The White Hart Hotel

The White Hart Hotel is a great success as it has an excellent reputation and is very profitable. The hotel is well known for great comfort, fine service and exceptional food. Gill and Savan bought the property in the south-west of England six years ago after studying hotel management and catering in Switzerland. Gill manages the staff fairly but firmly. She believes that there is little scope for employee participation in this industry. Until recently, she has been rewarded with excellent employee performance but the latest data suggested some staff discontent (Table 20.4). One employee was overheard to say: 'This hotel is making so much money, why shouldn't we be offered a share of the profits as well as our wages?'

Table 20.4 *Summary of employee performance at the White Hart Hotel*

	6 months ending 31 December 2006	6 months ending 30 June 2006
Average staff employed (full-time equivalent)	42	40
Staff leaving	7	4
Reason most often given for leaving	'Lack of promotion prospects'	'No opportunity for participation'
Absenteeism rate	8%	6%
Serious customer complaints	155	40
Number of customer nights spent in hotel	12,500	11,500

Questions

1. Calculate the difference in the rate of labour turnover between the two six-monthly periods referred to in Table 20.4.

2. Explain what the term 'absenteeism rate' means, and why it is calculated

3. Use the information provided and your own knowledge to analyse the strengths and weaknesses of Gill's approach to her staff.

4. To what extent is high labour turnover and above average absenteeism inevitable in the hotel industry?

5. Although it is difficult to get exact figures for particular industries, there is a lot of information about general trends on the government's National Statistics website . Make sure that you are familiar with the current situation with regard to UK labour efficiency.

✓ *In this chapter you will have learned to:*

- calculate methods of measuring workforce performance including labour turnover, labour productivity and absenteeism

- discuss measures of workforce performance such as the costs to the business of high labour turnover and absenteeism, and the benefits of improved labour productivity.

Developing an effective workforce: recruitment, selection and training

Setting the scene

Gilds Associates

Gilds Associates provides temporary and permanent catering staff to businesses in Manchester. Their clients include Manchester United and Manchester City football clubs.

They ran a successful in-house training programme which equipped recruits with all the vocational skills they needed. However, many candidates lacked basic maths and English skills. Gilds firmly believed that these people had a lot to offer as employees if only they had the relevant skills.

The solution came through the Learning and Skills Council who introduced them to the Train to Gain service. A Skills for Life training provider, WEA North West, came in and shadowed Gilds' own training and assessed how to embed the new programme as effectively as possible. They then ran the training at the Gilds' on-site learning centre. Initially the programme was piloted with 6–12 learners, but the plan is to make it available to any employee who needs it.

As a result Gilds Associates are now able to offer a greater range of services to their clients, which makes the business, as well as their employees, more effective.

Discussion points

1 Why does Gilds need to train its employees?

2 Gilds now claims to offer its employees more challenging opportunities which helps them realise their true potential. How is Gilds benefiting from this development?

3 Releasing staff for training is a cost to Gilds. Are there any other solutions to the recruitment problem they faced?

Key terms

Recruitment and selection process: how a business chooses the best candidate for a vacancy it has identified.

💡🗂 The recruitment process

When a vacancy is identified in an established small to medium-sized business, the **recruitment and selection process** provides an opportunity for the firm to develop a more effective workforce, that is, make the best use of the people it has employed. The recruitment process begins with an analysis of the job itself. It would be a mistake to assume, for instance, that when an employee leaves, the replacement has to have exactly the same job. It could be that the business has grown and the role has changed. For those involved in the recruitment process, the first question should be 'what do we want the new employee to do?' This can lead to improvements in the organisational structure by clarifying job roles and work loads. Similarly, with a completely new role, created by the expansion of the business, the opportunity to reconsider levels of hierarchy, spans of control and work loads within the firm should not be missed.

Identify the vacancy

↓

Write a job description and person specification

↓

Advertise the position internally and/or externally

↓

Receive and process applications

Figure 21.1 *The steps in the recruitment process*

■ **Key terms**

Job description: a summary of the main duties and responsibilities associated with an identified job.

Person specification: identifies the skills, knowledge and experience a successful applicant is likely to have.

Internal recruitment: candidates from inside the organisation.

External recruitment: candidates from outside the organisation.

■ **Link**

For more information on levels of hierarchy, see Chapter 19 – Improving organisational structures, page 134.

■ **Activity**

At Gilds Associates did they seem more interested in the Job description or the Person Specification when recruiting new employees?

Fig. 21.2 *Using personal networks is one way of recruiting employees*
www.gilds.co.uk

Once the role is clear, a **job description** can be written. This should include:

■ the job title
■ the position in the business including the job title of the person the employee reports to and of those who report to them, if any
■ the location of the job
■ a summary of the general nature and objectives of the job
■ a list of the main duties or tasks of the employee

From this description, a **person specification** can be drawn up. This should include the qualities required in a person likely to fill the vacancy.

■ Knowledge: the level of education and/or of a more job-specific nature.
■ Experience of the type of work involved.
■ Skills: practical, interpersonal, managerial, etc.

These can be separated into those which are essential for the job and those which are not essential, but would be helpful.

Why might job vacancies occur in a business?

1 Promotion – the post-holder gets a job higher up the organisational structure (**internal recruitment**) or with another organisation (**external recruitment**).

2 Expansion – creating new jobs which did not exist before.

3 Natural wastage – the post-holder might retire, move away or retrain for another career.

How might a business recruit the best employee for a job vacancy?

Job vacancies may be filled internally or externally, and the choice may be influenced by factors such as available finance and time constraints.

Internal recruitment

1 Promotion/transfer

Somebody who already works for the organisation and has the potential to do a different, or more demanding job. This may come out of a performance management interview.

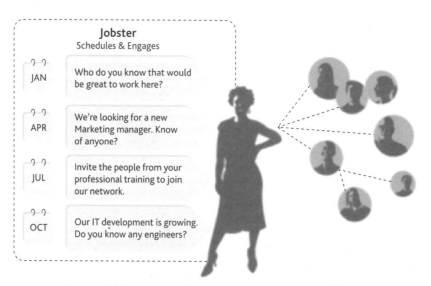

Table 21.1 *The benefits and drawbacks of internal and external recruitment*

Internal recruitment	External recruitment
Benefits	**Benefits**
■ Cheapest option: very low advertising cost, and limited time taken to complete the process ■ Promotion/varied job opportunities can be used to motivate employees (see Chapter 22)	■ A bigger choice of alternative candidates, making it more likely that the best person will be selected to meet the specifications of the post ■ New ideas and perspectives may be brought to the business
Drawbacks	**Drawbacks**
■ Another vacancy may be created as a result which may then require external recruitment ■ Ideas generation may stagnate due to lack of 'new blood' in the organisation. Employees staying too long can be as much of a problem as staff leaving too quickly	■ Can be a very expensive and time-consuming process, particularly for a small business. The use of recruitment consultants is very expensive ■ Induction training will be needed for employees new to the company which is an additional cost

2 Internal advertisement

Job vacancies can be advertised in the organisation's newsletter, magazine, on notice boards or via the company intranet.

3 Personal recommendation

Managers, team leaders and supervisors may see potential in a member of their team or department and suggest their suitability for a different post.

External recruitment

1 Job advertisements

Local and national newspapers, recruitment fairs, notice boards at the place of work and increasingly, the internet: both the company website and specific job vacancy websites.

2 Recruitment agencies

Act on behalf of the employer in the process and for a fee will find a candidate with the most appropriate qualifications. They often specialise in particular areas of employment, for example medical, financial, IT.

AQA Examiner's tip

It is essential that the method of selection chosen fits the budget, timescale and specialist skills available to the organisation. It should also be appropriate to the vacancy. Do you ever see job advertisements on prime time television? Then don't suggest it as a method of recruitment!

Business in action

Online recruitment

Although a study found that many organisations were trying to save money by shifting the bulk of their recruitment activity from printed material to online media, substantial numbers have been spurred on by budget pressures to review the whole of their hiring process. The report found that moves to make greater use of online recruitment were both the most widespread change, introduced by 44 per cent of organisations, as well as being the most effective. Two other changes that had been widely adopted were the appointment of a dedicated recruitment manager or recruitment team (used by 42 per cent of organisations) and a greater use of internal recruitment (used by 44 per cent of employers). One in four organisations (25 per cent) that took part in the survey had also introduced a bonus scheme for employees who referred successful candidates to the company.

3 Personal recommendation

Friend or family of an existing employee. This is becoming increasingly popular in small-scale businesses. Employees may be given financial rewards if the person they recommend stays with the company and

Most effective changes in online recruitment

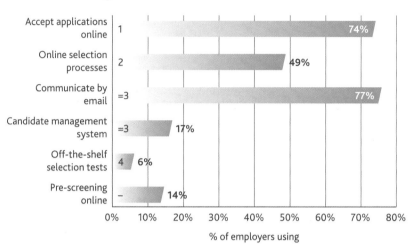

Fig. 21.3 *Using technology to cut their recruitment costs adapted from www.personneltoday.com*

Activity

Which methods of recruitment do you think would be most effective for Gilds Associates to use and why?

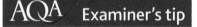

AQA Examiner's tip

Many students don't apply their knowledge of recruitment to the scenario given and just write a general answer about the options available to all businesses. It is very important to think from the point of view of the organisation in the case study: try to imagine that you are the person actually making the decision, it is your business!

Key terms

Methods of selection: ways in which businesses recruit the best candidate for an identified vacancy. These can be internal or external to the organisation and will depend upon the time available, the budget available and the specialist skills available in the organisation.

proves to be a valuable addition to the workforce. An assessment of the applicant's capabilities will still be required of course.

4 Job centres

Designed to get the unemployed into work by advertising vacancies.

Which method is best?

The decision about which method(s) of recruitment to choose will be different for every business. The best alternative may be influenced by circumstances such as the available budget, or the location of the firm. If there is very little money available, because the business is new or expanding, then the cost of each option becomes very important. The availability of a suitable workforce in the local area, perhaps as a result of the closure of a large company nearby, will probably result in a different choice from that where there is a skill shortage and full employment in the region.

The selection process

Once applications have been received for a job, the process of selecting the best candidate can begin. Again, this represents an opportunity for the organisation to improve the workforce by choosing the most appropriate **method of selection**, so that the successful candidate meets the needs of the business. The quality of the job description and person specification will have a significant impact on the success of the selection process. If these documents are vague and general, then it is more difficult to prepare appropriate interview questions, or select the best methods of testing, to discover the most suitable candidate.

Methods of selection

There are a number of ways in which candidates can be selected from those who apply. Some businesses may only use one option, but increasingly a range of methods of selection are employed. Selection can be carried out within the business, but for many small and medium-sized firms, the specialist skills required mean that this work may be sub-contracted out to a specialist recruitment agency.

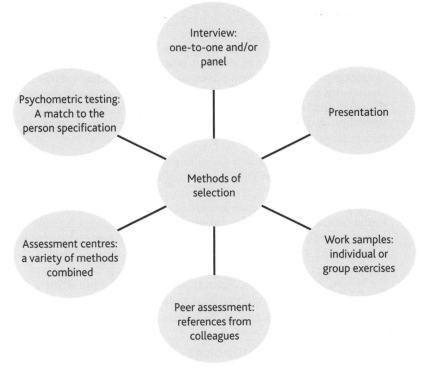

Fig. 21.4 *The main methods of selection*

Interview

The most common method of selection which can range from an informal chat over lunch, to a telephone interview or a formal panel interview. The principle is to ask all candidates the same questions and make a judgement about suitability for a job based on their responses.

Presentations

Candidates are given a subject related to the job or career and are asked to prepare and give a presentation of between five and fifteen minutes to an audience of one or more people.

Work samples

Involve an individual or group of candidates completing exercises that they would be required to undertake as part of the job they have applied for.

Peer assessment

A candidate's colleagues predict how the candidate will respond if placed in a particular work situation or role. This may take the form of a questionnaire sent to current co-workers.

Assessment centres

Assessment centres are used mostly for large-scale recruitment because they are complicated and costly to organise and run. A typical assessment may take two days and could include interviews, written tests, group exercises and individual tasks. Trained assessors collect evidence and present a final collective decision.

Psychometric tests

These are administered by trained professionals and can be used at all levels in an organisation to indicate candidates whose characteristics match those required for a particular job, as described in the Person Specification.

Activity

Use the internet to complete a variety of online application forms for jobs in your area. You don't need to press the send button. The aim is to note the similarities and differences between the recruitment processes used by a range of businesses.

Activity

Explain why the most effective recruitment and selection process for Gilds Associates is likely to be different to that of a solicitors' firm.

Business in action

Recruitment in practice

The Cooperative Group assessment centre consists of a number of exercises, which include a presentation, an individual exercise, group work and an interview. The exercises are designed to measure the skills and behaviours required to be successful, including flexibility, challenge, customer focus, cooperative commitment and results focus.

Team Insight, a recruitment consultancy, helped with the selection of a new Head of Town Planning in local government. The Person Specification was very specific: honesty, integrity, leadership skills, strategic thinking, influencing skills as well as superior number and verbal reasoning skills. Team Insight gave each candidate a range of psychometric tests including a Verbal Analysis Test and a survey of Interpersonal Values. Following a feedback session with each candidate and a formal interview alongside two representatives of the Personnel Department, Team Insight produced a full written report on each candidate to assist the selection process.

Activity

Which factors do you think Gilds Associates may consider to be the most important?

Which method of selection is best?

As you will have gathered by now, there is no method of selection which is suitable for all types of job. There is evidence that firms are moving away from the traditional one-to-one interview, but for small or medium-sized businesses the issue may be that there is nobody within the organisation with the skills to carry out other types of selection. This means that the process could be external to the business – sub-contracted to a specialist consultancy firm. This is likely to be a very expensive option in the short term, but if the best candidate is selected, will save money in the longer term because the employee is more likely to be happy. This should mean a better standard of work, and they are less likely to leave or take days off for stress at work.

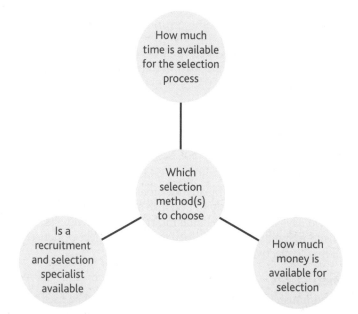

Fig. 21.5 *Factors to take into consideration when deciding which method(s) of selection to use*

How recruitment and selection can improve the workforce

It should be clear by now, that the recruitment and selection process can be used to improve the quality of the workforce. The starting point must be an assessment of the future needs of the business by answering the following questions:

- What quantity of labour, with which skills are needed in the near future? (Discovered from sales forecasts).
- What is the labour turnover rate for the business?
- Trends in wage increases – is the cost of labour rising rapidly or is it stable?
- Are current training programmes likely to lead to increases in productivity?
- Will changes in technology alter the skills needed by employees in the future?

This assessment can then be developed further by an audit of the skills of the existing workforce to identify the abilities of current employees. This process may inform the decision as to whether to recruit internally or externally. When all these questions have been answered, a plan to improve the performance of the workforce, by recruiting people with the required skills from outside the organisation, and training existing employees can be put into action.

An essential element of putting the plan into action is the drawing up of accurate job descriptions and person specifications. If these documents are thought through very carefully, then it should be possible to identify the best candidate for a job. If either one is vague or misleading, the job may turn out to be very different to what the candidate was expecting, which could lead to dissatisfaction and frustration for the employer and employee.

Training

Once a new recruit has been appointed to the business, it is important that they become part of the team as quickly as possible. Furthermore, no firm stays the same for ever, and organisations should try to keep up with developments that affect their industry. This means that **training** should be an on-going process. The skills and qualifications that a new employee brings to the business may not be what are required in one or two years time, so successful firms, and their workforce, will see training as a process of lifelong learning.

Induction training

Good **induction training** means that new starters settle in quickly and happily to a productive role within an organisation and are less likely to leave after the first week! It is the first impression a new employee gets of the business and it needs to be organised and professional. A good induction programme helps with questions about routines, lunch facilities, parking and all the other things that most employees take for granted. It also provides a perfect opportunity for the values and expectations of the business to be made clear to the new employee. Legally, there is also a requirement on employers to ensure that new starters are aware of all issues relating to Health and Safety at work.

The success of any business will depend upon its employees. There are very few firms that do not exist in a competitive environment. Whether it

Link

For more information on the labour turnover rate and productivity, see Chapter 20 – Measuring the effectiveness of the workforce, page 143.

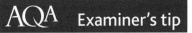 **Examiner's tip**

To make a judgement about how well the recruitment and selection process is being used to improve the workforce, think about what the firm is trying to achieve by the process, for example more highly skilled employees. You can then decide whether or not they are likely to achieve this outcome and why.

Key terms

Training: giving employees the knowledge, skills and techniques necessary to fulfil the requirements of a job.

Induction training: is given as an initial preparation upon taking up a post. Its goal is to help new employees reach the level of performance expected from an experienced worker.

Activities

1 Ask family and friends who have a job of any kind about the induction process they experienced. Find out as much as you can about the programme content, how long the training lasted and how useful it was.

2 Why is a good induction programme important to a firm like Guilds Associates?

Key terms

Off-the-job training: away from the place of work e.g. at a training centre or college.

Activity

Why might Gilds Associates use off-the-job training for their employees?

Key terms

On-the-job training: learning by doing the job, under the guidance of an experienced member of staff or external trainer.

is the level of skill employees have or the professional way in which they work, the training provided can make all the difference to the on-going success of a business.

Business in action

Center Parcs

Center Parcs, with its head office in Newark, Nottinghamshire, operates four holiday villages in the UK. Each is set in a forest environment offering sports and leisure facilities plus numerous restaurants, bars and retail outlets. All new employees have the opportunity to find out more about Center Parcs either through its newly launched training website or are invited to spend a day in a Village and experience life as a guest. This is followed by a 'Welcome Workshop' which is an induction to the company and guest care training.

Types of training

There are two types of training available to businesses:

Off-the-job training

Off-the-job training takes place away from the workplace. This could be at the firm's training centre, as is the case with Gilds Associates. Other firms encourage employees to complete courses provided by local colleges on a day-release scheme or distance learning/evening classes. Another alternative is to take advantage of courses provided by specialist firms including management training, financial management and marketing.

There are several advantages to off-the-job training:

- The use of specialist trainers and accommodation. This would not be financially viable for smaller businesses to provide in-house.
- Employees can focus on the training and not be distracted by work. This is particularly true at management or supervisory level, where the temptation to check on how things are going without you, might be too much for some.
- Opportunity to mix with employees from other businesses can be a great support for those who might have sole responsibility for a particular area in their place of work.

There are also disadvantages to off-the-job training:

- Employee needs to be motivated to learn, particularly if the training is undertaken in their own time.
- It may not be directly relevant to the employee's job because the training may have to cover a wide range of jobs – it may be too general.
- Costs (transport, course fees, examination fees, materials, accommodation) can make off-the-job training beyond the financial resources of smaller businesses.

On-the-job training

On-the-job training is given in-house by an experienced member of staff or external trainer to an employee as they are doing their work. It is based on the principle of learning by doing. Ideally, a structured approach should include learning and procedures guides, a form of assessment (formal or informal), and be integrated into the organisation's induction, probation and performance programme. On-the-job training should be monitored by an appropriate supervisor who shows a good example of the processes and procedures being learnt. Trainees should have a learning plan that details the what, how, when and where of the structured training programme. This learning plan should have a checklist or diary in which the activities to be learnt are listed and may be endorsed when each step is mastered. This gives a sense of achievement to trainees and also provides evidence to managers and supervisors that trainees have mastered their work.

There are advantages to on-the-job training:

- Training an employee in their own working environment, with equipment they are familiar with and people they know can help them gain direct experience to a standard approved by the employer.
- Employees may find that they have more confidence to use the equipment if they are supervised and guided as they feel they are doing the job right.
- Employees may feel more at ease being taught or supervised by people they know rather than complete strangers.
- Managers or supervisors can assess improvement and progress over a period of time and this makes it easier to identify a problem, to intervene and resolve problems quickly.
- This type of training is also productive, as the employee is still working as they are learning.
- As training progresses and the employee begins to feel more confident, this confidence would allow them to work at a higher standard and ultimately be more productive.
- Training 'on-the-job' would also prove an opportunity to get to know staff they might not normally talk to.
- It can be much more cost effective than off-the-job training because it is very specific to the requirements of one job.

There are also disadvantages to on-the-job training:

- Training a person requires skill and knowledge, without which the training may not be done to a sufficient standard.

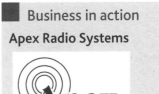

Business in action

Apex Radio Systems

Fig. 21.6
www.apexradio.co.uk/

Apex Radio Systems is based in Newcastle upon Tyne and specialises in the hire and sale of two-way communications equipment to the retail, leisure and construction industries. It is a fairly small company and employs just ten people. Three of these have recently completed *NVQ level 2 in Information Technology*, delivered by Newcastle College, through the Train to Gain scheme.

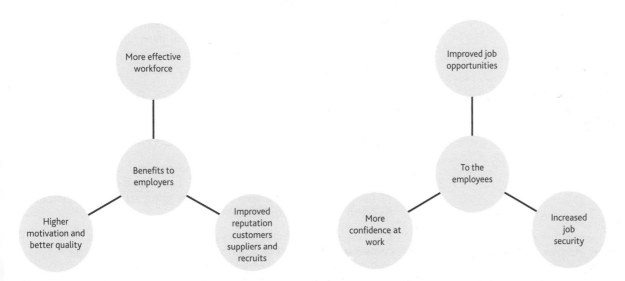

Fig. 21.7 *Benefits of training to employers*

Fig. 21.8 *Benefits of training to employees*

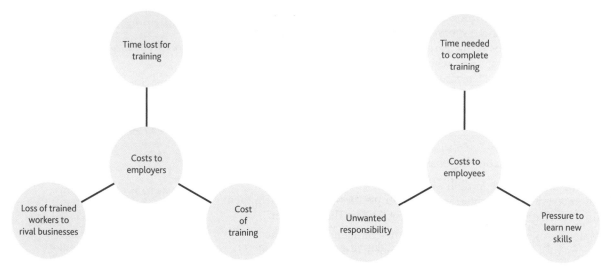

Fig. 21.9 *Costs of training to employers*   **Fig. 21.10** *Costs of training to employees*

AQA Examiner's tip

The basis for evaluation of the most appropriate training method could be the size of the organisation, the budget available, the nature of the job and the training required.

■ The trainer may not be given the time to spend with the employee to teach them properly, which may lead to substandard training.

■ The trainers may possess bad habits and pass these on to the employee being trained.

■ If a trainer has been brought into the company externally they might not be familiar with the equipment, or layout of the firm, and this could waste time.

Is training important?

Training is often seen by businesses as a luxury, and this is particularly true in smaller firms where the costs involved outweigh the perceived benefits. This is partly because it can be difficult to measure the outcome of training and its impact on the effectiveness of the workforce. It could also be that the directors of the firm think that once trained, their employees will leave to work for a rival business, or to set up in competition with their current employers. Furthermore, many employers may not be familiar with the latest qualifications on offer at local colleges. That is one of the reasons why the Train to Gain scheme was set up to encourage businesses of all sizes, but particularly smaller firms, to see the competitive advantages of training employees throughout their working life.

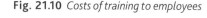

■ Case study

Peters Cathedral Bakery

Peters Cathedral Bakery, the largest independent craft bakery business in the north-east of England, has a head office in Durham, 71 branches, 560 employees and a reputation across the region for its bread, savouries and cakes.

It is very successful, but knows that to stay ahead of the competition it must continually train and develop its staff.

The hygiene operatives play a key role in keeping the bakery scrupulously clean and need to keep up-to-date with changing legislation and health and safety issues.

The newly-built state-of-the-art bakery means that they now use a very high-tech approach to everything they do and so staff need to have highly developed skills to match.

All staff should see how their job role fits into the overall success of the business and understand the company's procedures in more depth.

Options:

1 Hygiene Operatives to attend Bishop Auckland College on a day-release basis (it will take several years for them all to achieve Level 2 NVQ in Cleaning and Support Services).

2 Hygiene Operatives to be trained in the evenings by Bishop Auckland College Distance Learning Department to achieve Level 2 NVQ in Cleaning and Support services.

3 Two days off-the-job training for all department supervisors on new technology used at the bakery.

4 On-the-job training for all operatives (this can be completed over a one month period).

5 Closing the bakery for one week's intensive training for all staff to update skills required.

www.peters.co.uk

Questions

1 Use an example from the case study to explain the term 'off-the-job training'.

2 Explain two reasons why Peters Cathedral Bakery needs to train its staff?

3 Analyse the arguments for and against closing the bakers for one week to update the skills of the staff at Peters Cathedral Bakery.

4 To what extent can Peters Cathedral Bakery use recruitment, selection and training to help in the development of an effective workforce?

5 Investigate a local employer in your area (try not to use a national organisation). Find out how they recruit and select employees at two different levels of entry. Do they offer training and if so, what is it?

☑ *In this chapter you will have learned to:*

- describe the stages of the recruitment and selection process
- discuss the benefits and drawbacks of internal and external recruitment
- consider the factors affecting the method(s) of selection chosen by a business
- discuss meaning and importance of induction training
- explain the purpose of training, and the training methods available to a business
- analyse the benefits and drawbacks of off-the-job and on-the job training to businesses
- evaluate the extent to which recruitment, selection and training can help with the development of an effective workforce.

22 Developing and retaining an effective workforce: motivating employees

In this chapter you will learn to:

- describe the range of financial and non-financial methods used to motivate employees

- analyse the benefits and drawbacks of working in teams to improve the effectiveness of a workforce

- discuss how the motivational techniques used are linked to the structure/design of the organisation and employee's roles within it

- evaluate the extent to which empowering employees can benefit a business.

Key terms

Motivation: the factors that inspire an employee to complete a task at work.

Link

For more information on calculating output and productivity, see Chapter 20 – Measuring the effectiveness of the workforce, page 144.

Setting the scene

Wollaton Dental Care

Fig. 22.1 *Wollaton Dental Care*
www.woolatondentalcare.co.uk

Wollaton Dental Care is located in a Nottingham suburb. There are five dentists working part time and full time, three receptionists, three dental nurses and a hygienist. The environment at the surgery is happy, although there have been a lot of changes to working practices over the last few years. Some of this has been due to government legislation, and some due to changes in the needs of individuals and clients, for example longer opening hours.

Discussion points

1. What are the factors/needs that motivate the employees at Wollaton Dental Care?

2. Do you think that everybody is happier at Wollaton Dental Care since the changes were introduced at the surgery?

3. Could you suggest any further changes which would make the receptionists/dentists/support staff's job more rewarding?

The meaning and importance of motivation

Motivation is what makes a person do something. Motivation at work is employees performing their tasks to the best of their ability. In business, every employee, whatever their status in the organisation is motivated by their own personal needs and it would be a mistake to assume that there is any one method of increasing motivation which will work for everybody. Motivation is not static: people's lives and priorities change, so do their needs and their motivation. What motivates somebody when they join a firm may not be the same two, five or ten years later.

Motivation is important because it affects the efficiency of a business both in terms of quantity and quality.

Quantity

This refers to the productivity of an employee – output per person. If each employee produces more items for the same level of pay, the labour costs per unit go down, which means that the business is using its resources more efficiently. The Government prefer to use the calculation of UK productivity as a measure of business efficiency. This shows the total output achieved by the UK divided by the total number of hours worked. If the same level of output can be achieved in less time then productivity has increased. Many employees do not produce easily quantifiable output, but the calculation can still be made using turnover and workforce figures. The question for any business is 'how can we achieve greater employee productivity?'

Quality

This refers to how well the work is done. If there are a lot of complaints, repeat business is low, or wastage rates are high or rising, then this suggests that the quality of work is not of an acceptable standard. In a competitive market, customers will judge a firm on the value for money they receive, which is largely based on product quality (see Chapter 24) and customer service (Chapter 25). Motivated employees are more likely to care about the impact of their work on the success of the business.

💡🗂 Financial methods of motivation: payment systems, bonus systems

Using monetary reward to motivate employees can have significant short-term benefits particularly when the quantity of output or sales is important. The use of these techniques will depend upon particular circumstances. For example, if a business needs to employ additional workers to meet a seasonal increase in demand, they may well use a high rate of pay to attract enough people. Similarly, firms who employ temporary staff to cover for absent employees (holiday, illness, maternity leave) may offer a higher hourly rate than that given to those on a full time permanent contract. However, they won't have the same terms of employment such as paid holidays or sick pay.

■ Business in action

John Lewis

John Lewis employees received a whopping 18 per cent of their salary as a bonus this year, equivalent to nine week's pay. The company has enjoyed such a good year that it could afford to pay out £155 million in bonuses alone. Follow-up media coverage asked how much of John Lewis Partnership's success was down to the buy-in of the workforce, who have an even stronger vested interest in going the extra mile than staff in more conventional relationships with their employers.

www.guardian.co.uk

■ Activity

Is the quality of service more important than the quantity of clients treated at Wollaton Dental Care?

Fig. 22.2 *John Lewis*

Table 22.1 *Advantages and disadvantages of payment systems and bonus schemes*

Method	Advantage to the business	Disadvantage to the business
Piece rate: paying employees based on the number of units they produce	Increase in output per person. Particularly useful when production is running below the required level	Quality may drop which can have a knock-on effect on future orders or the price that can be charged for the product
Commission: payment based on the number of units sold	Increased sales and therefore revenue	Employees may be tempted to use unethical techniques which could lead to customer-relations problems
Fringe benefits: options include a company car, private medical insurance or a subsidised canteen	Often valued more highly than increased wages by employees and cheaper to provide	Represent a long-term commitment by the company so reduce flexibility
Profit-sharing scheme: a percentage of the company's profits are distributed to employees	Individual employees see that their effort can make a difference: encourages team working	Divisive if some members of the team do not work as hard as others, but get the same reward
Quality-related bonus schemes: salary is reviewed based on the contribution made in terms of the standards achieved	Employees are motivated to work to the highest possible standard to gain an increase in pay	Difficult to judge quality objectively in the service sector. which can lead to discontent

■ Activity

Which financial and non-financial methods of motivation do you think would be most effective for these groups of people at Wollaton Dental Care:

1. Dentists
2. Administrative staff

■ Non-financial methods of motivation: improving job design

There is a lot of research to suggest that people perform better at work if their job is more interesting and rewarding. A person who carries out exactly the same tasks, every day, with no variation, is likely to lose interest in their work, and the quality may fall. Motivational theorists suggest that changing the job may increase motivation, or at least reduce boredom and dissatisfaction at work. **Job design** is about looking at the tasks involved in a person's role and trying to make them more interesting and rewarding.

Table 22.2 *Methods of improving job design – advantages and disadvantages*

Method of improving job design	Advantage to the business	Disadvantage to the business
Job enlargement: including a wider variety of tasks within a job description. This is sometimes called horizontal loading and involves giving people more jobs to do that require the same level of skill	Fewer problems with boredom, so mistakes are less likely, which reduces costs	There will be training costs involved and employees may expect more pay
Job rotation: movement between different jobs. Leads to multi-skilling. The ability to carry out several different jobs	Multi-skilling benefits the employer because staff shortages can be covered more easily	This system can be very complicated to organise, and the skill level achieved by an employee may not be the same for each job, causing variations in quality
Job enrichment: increasing the depth of the job by increasing the amount of discretion and authority for decision-making the job holder has	It allows employees to test and develop their managerial skills, which can lead to an increase in internal recruitment opportunities	High training costs: it may be difficult for the employee to balance new responsibilities with their existing work load

■ Key terms

Job design: changing the nature of a job role in order to increase motivation or reduce dissatisfaction at work.

Empowerment: giving employees the *power* to do their job: trusting them, giving them the *authority* to make decisions and encouraging feedback from them.

Job rotation: varying an employee's job on a regular basis.

Job enlargement: expanding the number of tasks completed by an employee.

■ Organisational design and methods of motivation

One of the principles behind many of the non-financial motivation methods is **empowerment.** This is based on the observations of theorists who came to the conclusion that employees work best when they have some control over their jobs, rather than simply following a detailed set of instructions, and being closely supervised. With the introduction of any new system to a business, the design of the organisation can have a big impact on the likelihood of success. Human nature tends to lead people to want to protect their position and one way to do this is to retain as much control and power as possible, making employee empowerment difficult to achieve in practice.

Motivational techniques

In a small business the entrepreneur may try to retain control over all aspects of the business, thus making it difficult to use a wide range of methods of motivation.

In Figure 22.3, all the decisions are taken by the Entrepreneur who communicates in one way (downward) with the employees (see Chapter 19). This may be a good way to start a business so that everybody involved is clear about the aims of the business. The methods of motivation available in such circumstances are likely to be financial: saying 'thank you' for increasing output or sales, or benevolent: showing how valued employees are by giving fringe benefits. Non-financial methods of motivation are likely to be limited to **job rotation** and **job enlargement** because there is no loss of control for the entrepreneur. Although this approach can be very successful, because decision-making is not delegated by the entrepreneur, the employees are not empowered. It will become frustrating for staff after a while, and can lead to inefficiency, particularly as the business starts to grow and the quantity of decisions to be taken, increases.

Fig. 22.3 *A basic top-down organisation structure*

Delegation and empowerment

An alternative structure which encourages delegation and empowerment might look like this.

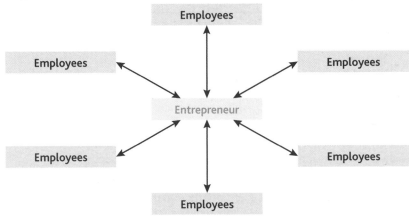

Fig. 22.4 *Organisational structure encouraging delegation and empowerment*

Here the lines of communication are two-way and the employees will be able to contribute to the decision-making. In these circumstances, both financial and non-financial methods of motivation are available to the entrepreneur, including **job enrichment** which empowers employees.

Delegating authority to subordinates can be seen as threatening at any level in the organisation, and as a business grows many managers, having been given authority to make decisions, may resist further empowerment of subordinates – they have responsibility for the decision made after all. This is most likely in a traditional hierarchical organisational structure, where job roles are clearly defined and therefore delegation is limited.

■ Key terms

Job enrichment: increase the level of responsibility within a job to make work more challenging and rewarding.

Functional structures

A business may develop a functional structure as it grows, as in Figure 22.5, with a clear distinction between marketing, operations, finance and human resources. In this case, all types of motivation are available, although methods such as piece rate are only appropriate for jobs where output per person can be measured. In reality, this traditional approach to organisational design may not encourage empowerment, particularly if the structure becomes increasingly hierarchical as the business expands. Narrow spans of control and long lines of communication do not encourage delegation (Chapter 19).

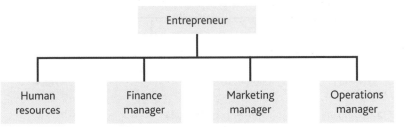

Fig. 22.5 *Organisational structure based on functional areas*

Divisional structures

However, an alternative model is based on the observation that most of the important decisions in a growing business are likely to be about products or customers. By organising the firm into divisions, it is possible to empower more employees which may have a positive impact on

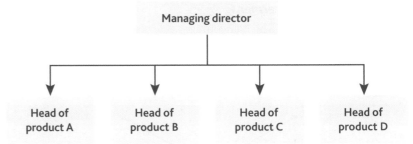

Fig. 22.6 *Divisional organisational structure*

motivation. Within each division, there is marketing, production, finance and other specialist staff who work together, and they will all have to make a contribution to decisions taken about their product.

In Figure 22.6, the entrepreneur runs a business with four different products, each one having a team of functional experts. Each division can set targets and employees are likely to feel a strong sense of belonging to the team, because their contribution can be clearly identified. Financial motivators are likely to be profit-sharing, and fringe benefits because others that reward the output of individuals rather than the group would work against this structure. Non-financial methods can include job enlargement and job enrichment.

Structure by customer type

In Figure 22.7, the business has designed its organisation by dividing its customers into different types, for example, commercial local, commercial national, private local and private national. The firm does not have to be very large, but the employees working in each section have very clear responsibilities, and their success can be measured quite easily. Again the emphasis is on the team sharing responsibility and specialist skills can be developed to suit the needs of the customers. Financial motivators can reward those who increase sales such as commission, profit-sharing, and quality-related bonuses, however, care needs to be taken to ensure that the scheme is not divisive, with individual members of a team competing against each other. Non-financial motivators may include all types of job design including job enrichment, which means that employees throughout the organisation can be empowered.

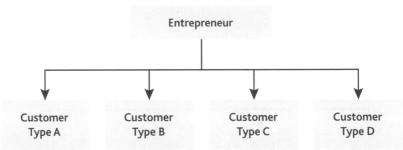

Fig. 22.7 *Organisational structure by customer type*

Does empowering employees benefit a business?

For empowerment to be effective in any business, it needs the support of the most senior staff. Secondly, the objectives of the organisation should be very clear to all employees, so they have a reference point for decision making. Neither of these prerequisites should be difficult to achieve in a small to medium-sized business.

Advantages of empowerment can be:

- It enhances motivation.
- It increases employee commitment, thereby reducing labour turnover and absenteeism.
- It increases team spirit and a goal-orientated approach to working.
- It frees the time of senior management so they can focus on more strategic decisions.

Disadvantages of empowerment can be:

- Employees may need to be trained and educated in decision making, which can take time and money.
- Processes cannot be standardised so there may be wide variations in the effectiveness of individual employees and how they respond to empowerment.
- The role of the manager becomes less clear which can lead to different motivational problems.

For empowerment to be successful within a business there needs to be a balance between the role of the individual employee and a more traditional managerial approach to running an organisation. It certainly fits into a flat organisational structure with a wide span of control, rather than a tall hierarchical structure.

Working in teams

The use of teams is common in business, and can be applied to most organisational structures. As shown in Chapter 19 – Improving organisational structures, page 138, a matrix structure supports a project team approach, which can operate very successfully in small businesses. However, there are other examples which fit into a hierarchical structure: organisation by product or by customer for example. There are also opportunities for team-working within firms, based around company-wide concerns such as health and safety or the introduction of new technology. Short-term issues such as relocation to a new site, the Christmas party, fire damage or a security threat, also lend themselves to team-working.

What are the benefits and drawbacks of team working?

Team working is designed to unite employees towards a common organisational goal.

Advantages include:

- A feeling of personal responsibility to one's team mates, encouraging the least effective employees to meet team and company standards.
- Higher levels of satisfaction about completing a job.
- Productivity is usually higher.
- Employees are able to learn different skills from others.
- Problem solving is easier in teams.
- Theory suggest that all these factors improve motivation and ensure that each employee is not only efficient, but an effective member of the workforce, because everyone is directly involved in the decision-making process. As a result the quantity and quality of work should increase.

However, there are disadvantages as well as benefits to this approach, which need to be considered when looking at organisational design and motivation.

Disadvantages include:

- Productivity may fall to the level of the weakest worker.
- Too many meetings and discussions on what action to take may waste time and slow down the decision-making process.
- Individual self-worth is diminished.
- Individual team contribution may be hidden, and those with real potential overlooked.
- It may cause difficulties when developing performance measures which are fair.
- Organisational flexibility may be undermined. Cohesive and high-performance teams may be unwilling to change: the success of the team becomes more important than the success of the business.

Business in action

Business Link and True North

Business Link Berkshire and Wiltshire provide advice and support to start-ups and established businesses in the Berkshire and Wiltshire area. Business Link Wiltshire and Swindon had recently acquired Business Link Berkshire and the two businesses needed to integrate efficiently. The aims were:

- to develop a more coordinated operations team
- to raise the profile and the perception of the value of the operations team within the company
- to develop the project management capabilities of the team to be better able to provide skills and resource for projects companywide.

True North, a learning and development consultancy, designed a programme of workshops to develop a better understanding of preferred working styles, team dynamics, team performance and project management techniques. This programme was implemented over multiple sessions, allowing time for the application of new ideas, the review of that application at each subsequent session and gaining commitment to specific changes by individual team members and the team as a whole.

As a result, the team has become more efficient in the way it operates and has been able to support the growth of the company without increasing head count. Morale in the team is now buoyant, with members challenging each other in a positive and constructive manner.

www.truenorthgb.com

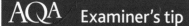

Examiner's tip

You will not be asked direct questions about specific motivation theories by examiners, but it is useful that you appreciate how they have been used by businesses to motivate their employees.

Theories of motivation

Motivation has been studied for many years, and there are a number of popular theorists whose work forms the basis of practical motivational techniques.

Frederick Taylor

Taylor was one of the first to look at employee motivation in a mass production setting. His theory was based on an assumption that the only motivator was money. He discovered, through observation, the most efficient way to carry out a task. Taylor believed that any pay scheme should reward those who produced the most, that is, piece rate. He also advocated the close supervision of workers.

Elton Mayo

Mayo looked at how changing physical factors such a light and heat, improved worker's performance. He found out that it wasn't the physical conditions being changed that made people work harder but instead performance increased because social interaction was important, and people worked well if they felt valued. Mayo's work led to the Human Relations School of Motivation, and is the basis for much of the motivational theory that followed.

Abraham Maslow

Maslow's 'hierarchy of needs' is probably the most famous motivation theory. He suggested that within each person there is a hierarchy of needs and the individual must satisfy each level before they move onto the next. There are five hierarchical levels. These are:

Physiological needs, Safety needs, Social Needs, Esteem needs and Self fulfilment.

Maslow suggested that to motivate an individual an employer needed to know where they believe they were within the hierarchy. Figure 22.8 shows how an organisation might use Maslow's theory.

Maslow's level	What the organisation could do
Self actualisation	Allocating more challenging and stimulating work, delegating responsibility, training, opportunities for promotion
Esteem	Feedback via appraisal, praise, recognition of success
Social	Work social events, team working
Safety	Safe working conditions, induction training, permanent contracts
Physiological	Competitive salary

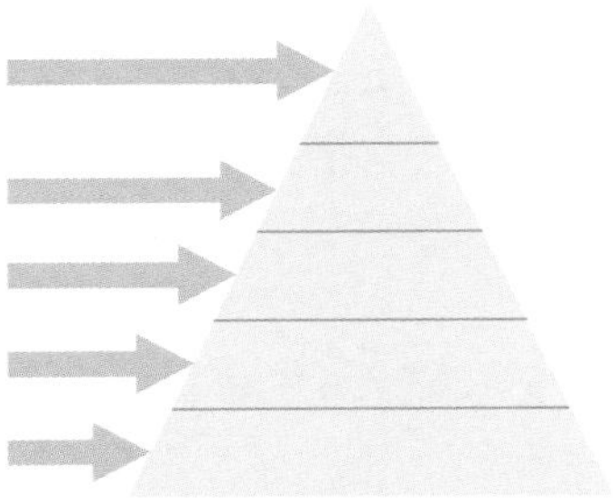

Fig 22.8 *Application of Maslow's hierarchy of human needs*

Frederick Herzberg

Herzberg explored the question 'What do people want from their jobs?'. He found evidence to suggest that there were two types of factor affecting how people felt about work. The first type could lead to job dissatisfaction, for example, how the business was run, too much supervision, working conditions and pay: these he called hygiene factors. A second set of factors lead to motivation and these included a sense of achievement, recognition for work well done, the nature of the job role, and the level of responsibility: Herzberg called these motivators. There was some cross-over between the two sets of factors: pay for instance could cause dissatisfaction if it was believed to be too low and motivation if it increased significantly. However, Herzberg believed that the factors which motivate people are not the opposite of those which cause dissatisfaction.

Activity

Look back at the financial and non-financial methods of motivation discussed earlier in this chapter. See if you can link the theories outlined above with the practical techniques used by businesses.

Case study

Foster Yeoman and True North

Foster Yeoman, a family-owned quarrying business with over 700 employees, produces 10 million tonnes of dry-stone aggregate per year. When the company went through a period of significant change it found that several areas of the organisation needed to be improved:

■ The management team needed to be able to undertake and cope with change and use their influence to ensure that new skills were filtered through the organisation.

■ Management skills needed to be developed at lower levels of the hierarchy so that internal promotion into management roles became more realistic and the company could be confident of retaining the experience of its many long serving employees.

■ A reduction in the cost of staff turnover was needed, particularly in the first two years of employment.

The company brought in True North management consultants who analysed the needs of the company and designed and created two distinct programmes for management development.

A programme of empowerment for quarry managers designed to build confidence in core management skills such as delegation, time management, planning, communication, performance management, decision making and motivation.

A programme for senior managers and directors, which was focused on self-confidence, self-awareness, relationship-building and communication.

The results are that Foster Yeoman has significantly improved internal promotion opportunities and staff are able to deal with and promote change in the organisation. Quarry managers are confident to delegate to others who relish taking on more responsibility. They are working more effectively as a team and as team leaders. The company is more confident of retaining the existing experience, knowledge and family culture which is core to its future success. Many managers and directors have changed their attitude towards personal development and are now actively promoting its value.

www.truenorthgb.com

Questions

1 Explain the term empowerment, using Foster Yeoman as an illustration.

2 Explain why the development of managerial skills at lower levels of the organisational hierarchy might help to reduce staff turnover.

3 Analyse the benefits and drawbacks to Foster Yeoman of using financial methods to motivate their employees.

4 To what extent will changes to the attitudes and training of managers and directors at Foster Yeoman lead to improved motivation of all employees?

5 Look at the case studies and testimonials of a range of UK business consultants to discover how changes in employee motivation have been achieved.

☑ *In this chapter you will have learned to:*

■ discuss financial and non-financial methods of motivating employees

■ examine the links between the structure/design of the organisation and the motivational techniques used by businesses

■ evaluate the extent to which empowering employees can benefit a business

■ analyse the benefits and drawbacks of working in teams to improve the effectiveness of a workforce

■ explain the importance of motivation and motivational theories

Summary questions

Chapters 19–22

1   What do you understand by the term 'organisational structure'?   *(3 marks)*

2   List three features of a tall organisational structure.   *(3 marks)*

3   Explain briefly two benefits to a business of a flat organisational structure.   *(3 marks)*

4   Explain why a growing business might benefit from the delegation of tactical decision-making.   *(4 marks)*

5   Describe the main features of the following job roles:
    a)   Supervisor
    b)   Team-leader
    c)   Manager
    d)   Director
              (8 marks)

6   Explain three factors that have an influence on effective organisational design.   *(6 marks)*

7   Organic Lunches was set up by two friends in Cardiff who wanted to provide good food to workers on a large industrial estate on the edge of the city. The business was very successful and a retail outlet was opened in the city centre to meet rising demand from office workers for healthier lunches.
    a)   Describe and explain an effective organisational structure for this business.   *(4 marks)*
    b)   Analyse which job roles may be key to the success of Organic Lunches.   *(8 marks)*
    c)   Evaluate the importance of good internal communications to Organic Lunches.   *(11 marks)*

8   Indicate whether each of the following statements are TRUE or FALSE. Briefly explain your decision.
    a)   Voluntary labour turnover is normally lower than involuntary labour turnover.
    b)   The Government prefers to measure UK productivity rather than output per employee.
    c)   If output per employee is falling then efficiency is increasing.
    d)   The CBI believes that high absenteeism is the reason why productivity in the UK is lower than in the USA.
              (3 marks each)

9   Explain why calculating workforce performance is important to businesses.   *(3 marks)*

10   Describe the stages in the recruitment process.   *(6 marks)*

11   Is external recruitment always necessary? Explain your answer.   *(3 marks)*

12   What do you understand by the term 'assessment centre'?   *(2 marks)*

13   Explain three factors that might affect a restaurant's method of selection.   *(6 marks)*

14   To what extent can recruitment and selection improve the workforce
of a soft toy manufacturing firm where labour turnover is rising and product
quality is falling.   *(12 marks)*

15   Briefly describe three financial methods of employee motivation.   *(6 marks)*

16   Why might directors of a construction firm be against the introduction of
non-financial methods of motivating their construction workers such as job
enrichment and job enlargement.   *(8 marks)*

17   To what extent does organisational design help to motivate employees?   *(10 marks)*

18   Shipley Sheds design and build wooden constructions for gardens, ranging
from tool sheds to summer houses. The directors have decided to introduce
team-working in an attempt to stop their trained carpenters leaving to work
for rival business The World of Wood. They are optimistic that empowering
their employees will increase motivation and have organised appropriate
off-the-job training at a local college so that all members of staff will feel
confident to be involved in decision-making.

    a)   Explain the difference between 'on-the-job' and 'off-the-job' training.   *(4 marks)*

    b)   Analyse the possible drawbacks of introducing team-working to the
business.   *(8 marks)*

    c)   Evaluate the extent to which empowering employees will benefit
Shipley Sheds.   *(10 marks)*

Introduction

Toyota is one of the world's largest and most successful car manufacturers – the effectiveness of its operational management has been a major reason for its success.

Think about what you had for breakfast this morning. Unless you live on a farm and you produced the ingredients yourself, the eggs, cereals, bread, milk and jam you may have consumed all passed through a number of different processing stages between the farmer and your table. These processing steps were probably handled by a number of different organisations. The study of operations management looks at how the goods and services that we buy and consume are produced and delivered to us as efficiently as possible using key resources of land, labour and machines.

One definition of Operations Management is 'managing the activities needed to create and deliver an organisation's goods and services'. Some people argue that this definition is too broad and they prefer this alternative:

'Operations management is about producing the right amount of a good or service, at the right time, of the right quality and at the right cost to meet customer expectations.'

Operations managers, then, are responsible for managing activities that are essential for the production of goods and services. These managers will be responsible for a wide variety of different decisions. These are some of the most important areas of an operations manager's decision-making responsibilities:

- Which production methods to use?
- Which new products should be developed and designed – linking closely with the marketing department?

■ Which quality standards are necessary to meet customer expectations?

■ What production capacity is needed by the business – and how best to increase it if necessary?

■ What stock levels of materials are needed to produce goods and services?

In order to take these important decisions Operations Managers will need to control and oversee:

■ Important business assets such as buildings, equipment and stock.

■ Cost levels to ensure that production is carried out efficiently whilst maintaining acceptable quality levels.

■ Human resource effectiveness to achieve productivity and quality of acceptable levels – linking closely with the Human Resources department.

This brief introduction emphasises both the importance of and the wide ranging nature of an Operations Manager's responsibilities. If one term sums up these tasks it is 'productive efficiency'. Transforming resources into quality goods and services more efficiently than rival firms is a major competitive advantage. Most industries are now dominated by the most efficient businesses in their fields. This means that they have high 'productive efficiency'. In simple terms this means reducing the cost per unit, in terms of the resources used to produce it, to the lowest possible level. Failure to match the production effectiveness of major competitors is, in most cases, likely to lead to eventual business failure.

The range of activities that make up the responsibilities of operations managers are reflected in the chapter headings for this section:

Chapter 23: Making operational decisions This chapter studies the importance of setting operational targets. Also, making sure that the business has the capacity to meet expected demand requires important operations decisions to be made. This should mean that the Operations Manager is able to match output to demand.

Chapter 24: Developing effective operations: quality This chapter sets out to define quality – and it does not always mean 'the best possible'. The importance of quality control and quality assurance is examined and the benefits of meeting quality standards are assessed.

Chapter 25: Developing effective operations: customer service This chapter explains that Operations Management is not just about the product or service being offered – it includes the way in which customers are treated at all stages of the 'buying experience'. Customer service is becoming increasingly important in competitive markets where products are often of similar design and quality levels. Making customers feel special can deliver a real 'USP'.

Chapter 26: Working with suppliers Effective operations cannot take place without reliable suppliers delivering goods and services at the right time and at the right price. This chapter examines the importance of close coordination with suppliers. This can help a business become more flexible to customer demand and more efficient in delivering quality products 'right first time'.

Chapter 27: Using technology in operations IT has had a huge impact on every aspect of business activity. This is certainly true in the area of Operations Management. This chapter examines the advances in automation, computer aided design programs, stock control programs and retail management IT applications and the effect they are having of improving flexibility and efficiency of operations – but at a cost.

23 Making operational decisions

Setting the scene

How could we increase efficiency?

Plasma Designs Ltd (PDL) is a relatively small manufacturer of very large plasma TV screens for executive offices and trade shows. It has a good reputation in this specialist field, but like much of UK manufacturing, is now experiencing much competition from imports. This is forcing the business to find new ways of increasing competitiveness. It has a target of introducing at least three new models each year and this helps to maintain customer interest. In fact, demand for the latest models has exceeded expectations and the company's target of meeting all orders within three months is not being met.

There are disagreements amongst the directors as to how this shortage of production capacity should be handled. One wants to see a new workshop built on a larger site which would permanently increase the number of units that could be made. Another option supported by other directors is to ask other local electronic companies to produce goods under PDL's name. Finally, the Human Resources Director prefers the option of hiring part time staff to work an evening shift in the existing workshop.

Discussion points

1. Why is the company unable to meet its delivery target?
2. How useful is it for a business to have targets for delivery dates, quality levels and new product launches?
3. Which of the three options for expanding output do you think the company should go-ahead with? You should also consider the other information that you would find useful in making your decision.

Operational targets – what are they?

This diagram indicates the range of different activities involved in a typical operations management department:

These operational activities are interlinked. For example: a) The quality of a product should be related to its reliability. b) The design of a product will influence the cost of making it. Each of these activities will have **operational targets** set for them – and these targets need to be interlinked too.

In the case of a breakfast cereal manufacturer, some of these targets might be:

- Cost – to reduce variable costs of production by 5% annually for the next three years.
- New products – to develop and launch one new breakfast cereal range each year.
- Quality – to keep wastage caused by faulty batches of cereals to below 3% of output.

Key terms

Operational targets: these are specific and usually measurable objectives set for each operations activity of a business.

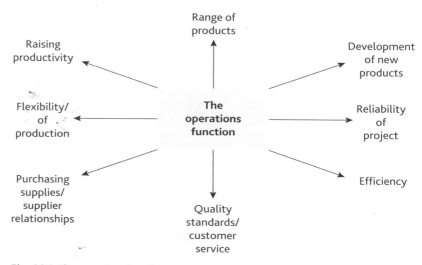

Fig. 23.1 *The operations function*

- ■ Delivery times – to meet supermarket orders within two days of receiving the order.
- ■ Productivity – to increase output per worker by 5% each year.
- ■ Capacity utilisation – to maintain a high level of output compared to total capacity.

These examples of operational targets are taken from the secondary sector. However, all organisations – private sector or public sector, primary or tertiary sector – need to set operational targets that, taken together, should improve productive efficiency. Here are some examples from the primary sector:

- ■ Dairy farm – milk yield per cow
- ■ Forest managed for timber – number of replacement trees planted per month.

For the tertiary sector, operational targets could include:

- ■ Insurance company – number of insurance renewals from existing customers achieved
- ■ Credit card provider – percentage of 'cold telephone calls' converted into eventual new customers
- ■ Hospital – number of patients on waiting lists; number of operations per week.

Why set these operational targets?

The purpose of these targets is to improve operational efficiency. The aim may be to achieve efficiency equal to the best in the industry. Unless targets are set and agreed with operations staff there is likely to be no improvement from one year to the next in the ability of the organisation to convert resources into output efficiently.

■ Capacity utilisation

All firms have a maximum **capacity** output.

Sandwich bars, hospitals, car factories – they all have a maximum number of units of output or customers they can serve in a certain period of time. Most businesses do not work at full capacity all the time. There are often real disadvantages to doing this. For example, there will be no time for repair and maintenance of equipment and the staff

Key terms

Capacity: the maximum output that a firm can produce with existing resources.

will have little time to discuss problems or new ideas for production improvements.

It is useful to measure the proportion of maximum capacity that is being achieved. This is called the rate of **capacity utilisation**.

For example, if a factory produced 300 units last year yet it had the capacity to produce 500, it operated at 60% of capacity.

$$300/500 \times 100 = 60\%$$

Apart from the limitations of always operating at 100 per cent of capacity referred to above, why would it be an advantage to a business to operate at, say, 90 per cent of capacity rather than 50 per cent of capacity? The main benefit is the greater use it makes of the company's fixed assets. This means that the fixed costs are 'spread out' over a higher level of output. It helps to reduce **unit costs** (or average costs).

Example

If total costs of production are £12,000 and output is 5,000 then unit cost is £2.40.

Key terms

Capacity utilisation: this is the proportion that current output is of full capacity output. It is calculated by the formula:

$$\frac{\text{Current output}}{\text{Maximum output}} \times 100$$

Unit cost: is average cost per unit of output. It is calculated by the formula:

$$\text{Unit cost} = \frac{\text{Total costs}}{\text{Output}}$$

Activity

Calculate the rate of capacity utilisation in all of the following cases:

Table 23.1

Business	Current output	Maximum annual output	Capacity utilisation %
A	3,500	7,000	
B	26,000	48,000	
C	36	42	
D	550,000	600,000	

Unit cost is of great significance to the competitiveness of any business. If operations managers can reduce this cost to levels equal to or below that of the firm's main rivals and maintain an appropriate level of quality then the profitability of the business will be much higher and its future should be secure. This fact just reinforces the great importance of operational issues and operations managers to the long term success of any organisation.

Activity

Copy out this table. Calculate the unit cost at different levels of output:

Table 23.2

Output	Total costs (£)	Unit cost (£)
100	12,000	
200	20,000	
300	26,000	
400	30,000	
500	33,000	
600	35,000	

■ Other operational issues

Non-standard orders

These are orders for products that the business does not normally produce. Here are some examples:

- Morgan Cars – special colour scheme for a customer's car
- An envelope company – supply a million non-standard sized envelopes
- An insurance company – insure a new design of space satellite
- A restaurant – prepare a complex, special menu for a large group.

Management have to take two important decisions:

Do we accept the order?

This will depend on:

- Revenue gained from the order compared to the cost of producing the non standard order
- Whether further orders are likely to be received
- The importance of the customer to the supplier
- Whether other potential customers exist for this product.

If so, how do we cope with the operational problems involved?

- Sub-contracting or outsourcing – see Table 22.3. The restaurant in the case above could outsource some parts of the menu to another catering firm
- Hire machines and temporarily employ specialists to operate them
- Job production – meeting special customer demands by producing each product as a separate item. Morgan Cars would find this easier than Ford.

Matching production to consumer demand

This is one of the biggest problems that Operations Managers have to solve. If customer demand is constant or easy to predict accurately then this problem is much reduced. For many businesses though, periods of slack demand and excess capacity, followed by high demand and full capacity working create special operational difficulties. Causes of demand fluctuations include seasonal demand patterns and economic factors such as growth or recession in the economy.

The production capacity of the business can be revised, over time, to match demand. In practice, the methods used to match output and demand can have limitations for the business.

Uncertainty does not just exist with customer demand. Machine breakdowns, staff absences and factory fires could all reduce a firm's production capacity to such an extent that it cannot match output to demand.

■ Ways of matching production with demand

These are the main methods that an organisation could use to try to ensure that output meets demand and customers are not left waiting – or assets are not left lying idle if there is **excess capacity**.

Activity

Explain why demand is likely to vary frequently, and sometimes unpredictably, for the following goods or services:

- Hospital accident and emergency services
- Barbecue charcoal
- Textbooks
- Luxury cars
- Restaurant meals

Key terms

Excess capacity: when a business has greater production capacity than is likely to be used in the foreseeable future.

Overtime: staff working beyond their contracted hours in exchange for a higher hourly wage.

Temporary staff: workers employed for a fixed period of time after which the employment contract may not be renewed.

Method – and how it operates	Main limitations
Overtime: This will increase output as staff are available for more hours, using the existing resources of the business.	Staff will be paid a higher hourly wage rate and this will increase unit costs. Workers may 'slow down' production to ensure that overtime is worked.
Temporary staff: They will be employed to cope with higher demand but released when demand falls back.	Temporary staff will still need to be recruited and trained and this may be expensive. These workers may lack the loyalty and commitment of permanent staff
Part-time staff: They will be called in to work at peak periods and will not be needed – or paid – at other times. These may be permanent or temporary contracts.	If these workers have other jobs too, they may not have the loyalty or commitment of full time staff.
Sub-contracting: A supplier will provide all or some of the goods or service that the contracting business produces. This may be for a temporary period only. If the business is a specialist it may provide permanent services that the contracting firm cannot provide itself. Also known as out-sourcing.	This may be more expensive than producing the goods or services 'in-house' as the sub-contractor will add on a profit margin to the cost of the work. Quality assurance becomes more difficult as the sub-contractor will have to agree to meet the same quality standards as the contracting business.
Managing stocks efficiently: Stocks can act as a 'buffer' between production and customer demand. Stocks of both materials and finished goods may be held.	Stock holding is expensive and carries an opportunity cost. Goods can become out of date or may be perishable. Services cannot be stored – they must be produced when the customer is present. Waiting lists and customer queues are a form of 'buffer' for providing services.
Rationalisation: All of the other methods assume that demand exceeds production – rationalisation is often concerned with cutting back on production capacity to match lower demand levels. This is likely to reduce both fixed and variable production costs.	If staff are made redundant then this may reduce job security and motivation of staff remaining. If capacity is cut permanently then if demand increases in the future, capacity shortages will again occur. Cutting costs may mean redesigning peoples' jobs and this can cause uncertainty amongst the staff.

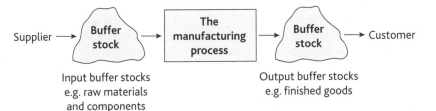

Input buffer stocks
e.g. raw materials
and components

Output buffer stocks
e.g. finished goods

Fig. 23.2 *Holding stocks helps to match output to production*

Case study

Can we match Swatch?

The last UK based manufacturer of watches, Trutime, was heading towards closure. All of the other UK watchmakers of any size have already been swamped by cheap but often high quality products from Far Eastern makers. But Trutime's Chief Executive, Amir Khan, was determined to have one last go at matching the productive efficiency of the best in the industry.

Key terms

Part-time staff: workers employed on a less than full weekly hours contract e.g. 15 hours per week.

Sub-contracting: using a supplier to manufacture part or all of a firm's product or service.

Stocks: materials or finished goods held by a firm as needed to supply customers demand.

Rationalisation: reorganising resources to cut costs – often leading to a cut back in capacity.

Fig. 23.3 *Holding stocks of unsold cars is an expensive way of trying to match supply with changing customer demand.*

■ Link

If the mismatch of production and customer demand remains a problem in the long term then the business will need to think carefully about its scale of production. For more information, see *AQA Business Studies for A2*.

'If we use Swatch as an example, we might be able to rescue our business' he told a recent Board meeting. 'Since the 1980s this company has been able to double the market share of Swiss watches by taking fantastic operational decisions'.

He then listed some of these:

■ Plastic cased watch with hundreds of different designs

■ Quartz mechanism built directly into the watch using half the components of other watches

■ Fully automated manufacture – unit costs are competitive with Asian watches even though Swiss wages are up to 50 times greater

■ Variable labour cost has been kept below Swatch's target of 7% of total unit production cost.

'I estimate the unit cost of a typical Swatch to be £5. In contrast, last year we produced 350,000 watches at a total cost of £2.8 million at a capacity utilisation of 55 per cent. Low cost, high quality in terms of reliability and time keeping and constantly changing fashionable designs – that must be the way forward for us', he concluded.

As if to confirm Amir's views, the business news that day carried a story that the demand for Swiss watches exceeded production. Swatch is considering plans to avoid this mismatch between production and customer demand. Should they sub-contract to Asian manufacturers with spare capacity or employ temporary staff to increase production?

Questions

1 Explain what is meant by the term 'productive efficiency'.

2 Calculate Trutime's unit cost of production last year.

3 Explain one benefit to the business, with a simple numerical example, of operating at a higher rate of capacity utilisation.

4 Outline two operational targets that Trutime might set if it started production of a watch to compete with Swatch.

5 Evaluate two of the ways in which a watch manufacturer such as Swatch might deal with a period of demand exceeding production capacity.

💡✔ *In this chapter you will have learned to:*

■ appreciate the huge scope of operational issues

■ understand what operational targets are and why they are set

■ calculate capacity utilisation and unit costs

■ evaluate different ways a business might be able to match production to demand.

24 Developing effective operations: quality

Key terms

Quality product: a product or service that meets customers' expectations and is therefore 'fit for purpose'.

Quality standards: the expectations of customers expressed in terms of the minimum acceptable production or service standards.

Fig. 24.1 *Rolls Royce aircraft engine. Customer expectations of quality lead to these being constructed to the highest possible standards*

🗁 Setting the scene

Swift Shoes

The Operations Manager at Swift Shoes was proud of the quality standards his business achieved. 'Our sports shoes sell for a retail price of £25 so they are not the best or most stylish on the market. However, only four customers returned shoes because of serious problems over the last year when we sold 50,000 pairs. We always inspect a sample of finished shoes before they are despatched to shops. Of course there are better shoes available, but our customers know what they are getting.'

The Customer Service manager at Exclusive Footwear was about to return a pair of 'hand made leather fashion shoes' to Ital Fashion Shoe producers. 'We retail these for £400 a pair and customers paying such high prices expect, reasonably in my view, a near perfect product. Even the smallest scratch or imperfection means the customers reject them. Even though Ital check every shoe made at each stage of production a few very minor blemishes are sometimes missed.'

Discussion points

1. The consumers of these different types of shoes seem to have different requirements. Why is this the case, do you think?

2. Using just this case study, how would you attempt to explain what 'quality' means?

3. Briefly explain how the two different methods used for achieving quality seem to operate.

💡 What is meant by 'quality'?

A **quality product** does not necessarily have to be the 'best possible'.

As the case study above showed, these consumer expectations will be very different for goods and services sold at different prices. So, we have to make clear from the outset that a quality product does not have to be made with the highest quality materials to the most exacting standards – but it must meet consumer requirements for it.

In certain cases, a product must meet the highest **quality standards** and the high cost of it becomes almost insignificant. Internal parts for a jet engine used on a passenger plane will be expected to have a failure rate of less than 1 in 1 million. However, if fashion clothing was made to the same exacting standards with regards to stitching, buttons, zips and so on – how much would a pair of jeans cost then?! Designing too much quality into a product that consumers do not expect to last for many years can make the product very expensive and uncompetitive.

A quality product does not have to be expensive. If low cost light bulbs and clothes pegs last for several years in normal use then they have still met consumer expectations and have been of the required quality.

■ Activity

Why might a restaurant that buys in the best food ingredients still fail to meet its customers' expectations of quality?

AQA Examiner's tip

Quality is often viewed by students as an absolute concept and not a relative one. Quality must be explained in reference to the expectations of the target market consumers. The level of quality selected by any business must be based on the resources available to it, the needs of the target market and the quality standards of competitors.

■ Key terms

Quality control: this is based on inspection of the product or a sample of products.

Quality assurance: this is a system of agreeing and meeting quality standards at each stage of production to ensure consumer satisfaction.

■ Business in action

Achieving quality

Pre-determined quality standards are set and checked on at each stage of the assembly of Nissan cars at the company's Sunderland factory.

First Direct operates its telephone banking system by setting limits on waiting times for calls to be answered, average time taken to fulfil every customer request and assurance standards to monitor that customer requests have been acted on correctly.

So a highly price good may still be of low quality if it fails to come up to consumer requirements. A cheap product can be considered of good quality if it performs as expected. It should now be clear that quality is a relative concept and not an absolute one – it depends on the product's price and the expectations of consumers.

How can consumer 'expectations' or 'requirements' be established by a business? The most common methods would be using market research and by analysing results of consumer feedback data. This research can establish the quality standards that customers expect.

It is easy to think of quality standards in terms of manufactured goods – the reliability of cars or the wear rate of clothes, for example. However, quality is a crucial issue for *service providers* too. For example, the quality of service offered by UK banks is claimed to be inferior to those in other countries in terms of:

■ Speed taken to answer the telephone.

■ No indication of waiting time on the telephone.

■ Queuing time in branches.

■ Contact with the same person on each occasion.

■ Number of accounts errors made.

■ Quality of financial advice given.

■ What are the differences between quality control and quality assurance?

These two terms are used to classify two very different approaches to managing and achieving quality in any business.

Quality control is based on inspection or checking, usually of the completed product or of the service as it is being provided to a consumer.

For example:

An iPod player being tested at the end of the production line for battery charging capability.

A telephone banking adviser having a call to a customer listened to and recorded.

Quality assurance is based on setting agreed quality standards at ALL stages in the production of a product or service in order to ensure that customers' satisfaction is achieved. It does not just focus on the finished product. This approach often involves self-checking by workers of their own output against these agreed quality standards. The key differences between the two methods are that quality assurance:

■ Puts much more emphasis on prevention of poor quality rather than inspecting for poor quality products – 'getting it right first time'.

■ Stresses the need for workers to get it right first time and reduces the chances of faulty products occurring or expensive reworking of faulty goods.

■ Establishes quality standards and targets for each stage of the production process – for both goods and services.

■ Components, materials and services bought into the business are checked at the point of arrival or delivery – not at the end of the production process by which stage much time and many resources may have been wasted.

Quality assurance has the following claimed advantages over quality control systems based on final inspection:

- It makes everyone responsible for quality. This can be a form of job enrichment.
- Self-checking and making efforts to improve quality increases motivation.
- The system can be used to 'trace back' quality problems to the stage of the production process where a problem might have been occurring.
- It reduces the need for expensive final inspection and correction or reworking of faulty products.

Why is it important for businesses to establish quality assurance systems?

There are several reasons for this:

- To involve all staff and this can promote teamwork and a sense of belonging which aids motivation.
- To set quality standards for all stages of production so that all materials and all production phases are checked before it is 'too late' and the whole product has been completed.
- To reduce costs of final inspection as this should become less necessary as all stages and sub-sections of the process have been judged against quality standards.
- To reduce total quality costs. By instilling in the whole organisation a culture of quality, it is possible for quality assurance to lead to reduced costs of wastage and faulty products.
- To gain accreditation for quality awards. These can give a business real status or kudos. The most widely recognised quality award within the European Union is **ISO 9000**.

ISO 9000

This award is given to firms that can demonstrate that they have a quality assurance system in place which allows for quality to be regularly measured and for corrective action to be taken if quality falls below these levels. This award does not prove that every product produced or service provided by the business is of good quality. It is an indication that a business has a system of quality in place that has relevant targets set and activities ready to deal with a quality problem.

To achieve ISO 9000 a business must:

- Have clear and appropriate quality targets.
- Have a system in place to assure that targets are being met.
- A measuring system to record actual results and resources available to correct the problem should one arise.

Total Quality Management

This approach to quality requires the involvement of all employees in an organisation. It is based on the principle that **everyone** within a business has a contribution to make to the overall quality of the finished product or service.

Total Quality Management (TQM) often involves a significant change in the culture of an organisation. Employees can no longer think that quality is someone else's responsibility – instead, the search for quality

Fig. 24.2 *Quality is important in service industries too – failure to meet customer expectations for speed of phone answering and clarity of information given will reduce a firm's competitiveness*

 Link

For more information on job enrichment and human resources, see Chapter 22 – Developing and retaining an effective workforce: motivating employees, page 160.

AQA Examiner's tip

Quality is not just an issue for large businesses. Small and medium-sized firms also need to give consideration to this vital operations management area. They must ensure that the quality level selected and the quality assurance methods used are within their resources. In fact, by using quality assurance with the emphasis on reducing wasted faulty products and on staff self-checking quality levels, these businesses can save money in the long term.

Key terms

ISO 9000: this is an internationally recognised certificate that acknowledges the existence of a quality procedure that meets certain conditions.

Total Quality Management (TQM): an approach to quality that aims to involve all employees in the quality improvement process.

■ Key terms

Internal customers: people within the organisation who depend upon the quality of work being done by others.

must affect the attitudes and actions of every employee. When adopting this concept, every worker should think about the quality of the work they are performing because another employee is, in effect, their **internal customer**. Consider these examples:

■ A truck driver who drops off supplies to retailers is the internal customer of the team loading the vehicle – goods must be handled carefully and loaded in the right order. The truck driver has to face the retailer if goods are damaged or the wrong ones delivered.

■ A computer assembly team is the internal customer of the teams producing the individual components – a fault with any of these means the assembled computer will not meet quality standards.

The TQM concept has revolutionised the way all workers are asked to consider quality. To be effective the concept must be fully explained and training given to all staff in its scope and the techniques used to put it into effect.

AQA Examiner's tip

ISO 9000 is not a guarantee of good quality.

Fig. 24.3 *Jaguar use quality assurance systems and they now have one of the highest USA customer satisfaction ratings of any car maker*

What are the costs and benefits of introducing and managing quality systems?

All quality checks and quality assurance systems involve incurring costs. In a business that is effectively managed these costs will be covered by the expected revenue gains from producing products of the expected quality. In addition, other costs may be reduced, such as wastage costs and promotion costs to overcome a poor quality image.

How can the competitiveness of a business be improved by managing quality effectively?

1 Most markets are now more open to competition than ever before. Globalisation has increased this trend and so has consumer access to the internet. Lowering prices is not the only method of increasing competitiveness and, indeed, it may not be the wisest way, if a

Table 24.1 *The costs and benefits of quality systems*

The potential costs of quality systems	The potential benefits of quality systems
Market research to establish expected customer requirements.	Consumer satisfaction and repeat custom as there is nothing like a good experience with the quality of a product to encourage consumers to buy more – and to tell their friends about it!
Staff training costs to ensure that standards are understood and the operations needed to check them can be undertaken. This will be especially important with TQM.	Good publicity, e.g. from consumer pressure groups and consumer oriented articles in the media.
Material costs – rejecting below standard materials and components before they are used in the production process. This will almost certainly lead to higher expectations from suppliers.	Reputation for quality encourages retailers to stock the firm's products so this will increase the distribution outlets for a product.
Equipment costs for checking standards at each stage, e.g. laser measuring machines for accuracy of panel fit on a vehicle.	Easier to establish new products in the market as consumers will associate the business' good reputation with the new product.
Inspection and checking costs.	Allows the brand to be built around a quality image and branding is an important form of non-price differentiation for businesses.
Reworking of faulty products or rejection wastage costs – the aim of quality assurance is to reduce these to an absolute minimum – 'right first time'.	It may allow a price premium to be charged over other similar products in that market segment. Quality can be used as a 'USP' or unique selling point. This would be a clear demonstration that 'quality pays' as the extra revenue gained should cover the quality costs explained above.
Stopping production to trace and correct quality problems will disrupt output.	

business is unable to reduce its costs at the same rate. Achieving consistent quality is often a more effective method of competing in both domestic and international markets.

2   Consistent high quality can lead to such a well known brand image that higher prices can be justified for this USP.

3   As consumer incomes rise with world economic growth the average consumer buying decision will become more influenced by quality and fitness for purpose. Excess capacity exists in most of the world's manufacturing industries. It is increasingly vital for businesses to differentiate themselves with a quality brand image and, remember, this does not mean 'quality at any price' but regularly and consistently meeting consumers (rising) expectations. Cost factors involved in improving quality must always be weighed up against the expected gains in competitiveness.

AQA   Examiner's tip

The costs of quality are often obvious yet the benefits can be long-term and difficult to measure or quantify. This does not mean that they do not exist – in fact long-term survival in competitive markets can be based upon a good quality image.

Case study

Quality assurance in practice

The Croydon branch of FatBoyTrims had come bottom of all of the company's branches for customer satisfaction. The number of complaints received at Head Office about this branch and the quality of its haircutting and styling services had been much greater than for any other location. Revenue had fallen in recent months and the number of repeat customers had fallen to 15 per cent of total custom. A competing business nearby, that charged at least 30 per cent more, was always full. As a consequence, this FatBoyTrims branch had spent more on advertising for new business than any other. The revenue per customer was also low as high value services – such as colouring and tinting – were avoided by customers. A new manager had just been appointed to the branch and she immediately set about establishing quality targets for each stage of the 'customer experience'. These included:

- ▨ maximum time for phone to ring
- ▨ maximum waiting time for appointment time
- ▨ maximum times between hairwash and cutting begins
- ▨ all customers to be offered refreshments
- ▨ minimum time spent by stylists with each customer
- ▨ feedback forms to be filled in by 20% of clients and stylists responsible for each client to discuss answers with client.

Each member of staff was given responsibility for at least one of these targets. A record had to be kept of the branch's success at meeting these targets. At first, branch costs increased as an additional staff member had to be recruited to help meet the quality standards. After two months, the number of repeat clients had reached 36 per cent and the branch reduced its advertising expenditure. After four months, revenue had climbed by 38 per cent and the branch had reached third place in the company league table for customer satisfaction. The competing business had reduced many of its prices by 15 per cent.

Questions

1 What do you understand by the terms:

a quality

b quality assurance?

2 Outline two drawbacks to this business of not meeting customer expectations.

3 Analyse the benefits to this service business of improving quality.

4 Do you think the manager was right to introduce the changes she did? Assess the costs and benefits of introducing and managing a quality system in your answer.

5 Access the web pages of any two UK supermarkets. Discover as much as you can about the approaches to quality of these two businesses. Write a brief report explaining why quality is so important in this industry and how firms try to achieve it.

☑ *In this chapter you will have learned to:*

- ▪ explain what quality means and the significance of establishing what customer expectations are
- ▪ differentiate between quality control and quality assurance
- ▪ analyse the importance of quality to successful businesses
- ▪ evaluate the costs of quality control and assurance systems against the benefits to be gained from high quality.

Developing effective operations: customer service

In this chapter you will learn to:

■ define 'customer service'

■ apply methods of meeting customer expectations to different business situations

■ analyse ways of monitoring and improving customer service

■ evaluate the benefits of high levels of customer service.

Fig. 25.1 *Demand for glass conservatories and house extensions has increased significantly in recent years*

Setting the scene

Customer complaints at BriteGlass

BriteGlass was set up in Reigate seven years ago. The business designs and builds glass conservatories and house extensions. Customer demand has increased significantly in recent years. This is due to increasing incomes and rising house prices. People can afford to spend more on their houses and can justify the cost of extensions with a higher selling price.

The business has struggled to cope in recent months. The owner, Bill Smart, has given big incentives to sales staff to get more orders and he has kept prices very competitive. However, the capacity of the firm to meet orders has not increased sufficiently and more errors in design and construction are being reported. One letter of complaint is typical: 'Not only did your workmen not turn up when promised, when they did finally arrive most of the glass sections were the wrong size. Now it is completed, the roof leaks and the tiles on the floor are cracked. I have tried to contact you on the telephone and through your website but have received no reply. I will not pay the final payment unless these errors are rectified'.

Bill took some time to reply as he was busy signing up new customer orders. He offered a 20% price reduction to the customer who complained. He was taken aback when they refused his offer saying 'I am prepared to pay a reasonable price for a good job – you need to do a good job first. You have failed to deliver on all of your so-called quality standards'.

Discussion points

1 List as many examples as you can of what you consider to be poor customer service in this case.

2 Should Bill have been surprised that the customer refused the offer of a discount and demanded the job be completed to a high standard instead?

3 What quality standards of customer service do you think Bill might have originally promised?

4 What do you think will be the future problems for BriteGlass if it does not improve its customer service?

Key terms

Customer service: the provision of service to customers before, during and after purchase to the standard that meets customer expectations.

Customer service – what does it mean?

In a world of competitive markets the idea of offering customers services that meet – and possibly exceed their expectations – is becoming increasingly important. The significance of **customer service** and the levels of it expected by customers will vary by product, industry and customer. For example, an expert customer of IT equipment may need less pre-sales advice than a 'novice'. In the case of a customer purchasing a computer for the first time in a specialist IT retailer, these are the likely expectations of the level of service needed:

■ Pre-sales service: Advice on the range of options available, the advantages and disadvantages of different models and brands, explanation of key terms.

■ Service at time of purchase: Final assessment that product meets customers expectations, explanation of different purchasing methods, ensuring customer is aware of operation of computer and how to set it up.

■ After-sales service: Help line or web service to answer important queries about set up or operation; advice on future upgrades, repair and maintenance.

Offering good customer service is an essential part of the modern concept of 'customer relationship marketing' (CRM) which focuses attention on the importance and profit gains to be made from **keeping** existing customers rather than spending money on attracting **new** customers.

■ Methods of meeting customer expectations

Market research

The most important first step in meeting customer expectations is to find out what customers expect! Unless a business understands customer needs and expectations then it can never hope to fulfil them. This means communication with customers or potential customers and analysis of results to questions such as: 'How quickly do you expect to be served?' and 'What would make you most want to buy from our business again?'

Put customer service as number one priority

Another starting point for achieving good customer service is making it a major business priority. The following research findings make an interesting comparison between the replies from hundreds of management questionnaires in the UK and France:

Table 25.1 *Which of the following is the most important to your company?*

	UK	France
Customer service	46%	22%
Profit	12%	16%
Social responsibility	9%	13%
Environment	10%	7%
Market share	4%	8%
Reputation	12%	20%
Shareholders	3%	5%
Other	4%	9%

Training

This is crucial because no matter how good the market research and no matter how effective quality assurance is, unless staff know what is expected of them, one day they will let the business down with poor customer service. Staff need to know what good customer service means in their industry and what the firm's customer service standards are.

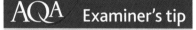
AQA Examiner's tip

Do not confuse 'customer service' with low discounted prices. Many firms that offer rock bottom prices can only do so by offering poor service.

■ Activity

Think about the levels of customer service expected by customers in the following situations:

1. Buying a holiday in
   a a travel agent, and
   b over the internet.

2. Buying a few groceries at a discount supermarket.

3. A disabled person wanting to deposit money into a bank.

4. A qualified IT engineer purchasing a new mobile phone.

Every member of staff who comes into contact with customers needs enough information and delegated power to make small, customer pleasing decisions without always having to say 'I am not sure so I will have to check with . . .'

Activity

How might staff training have prevented these 'gaffs' made by staff? Suggest alternative statements that reflect good customer service. These are published on the Microsoft support site for small businesses:

1 'Are you sure you can afford that?' – this questioned a customer's ability to pay for a new car.

2 'I only work here' – in four wretched words a waitress delivering the wrong meal conveys complete lack of enthusiasm and involvement.

3 'We don't have it' – this sounds as if the customer is unreasonable to ask for it.

4 'Why are you doing that for him' – surprise expressed by another employee when a shop assistant offered to put batteries in a radio for an elderly customer.

Use of quality assurance and quality control

The distinction between these concepts has already been covered in Chapter 24. The maintenance of quality standards throughout the production process (for both goods and services) is an important feature of achieving satisfied customers. The key purpose of quality assurance – 'getting it right first time with zero defects' – should be reflected in the quality standards that a business sets for customer service.

Quality standards

Customers need to know what to expect from the organisation they are purchasing a product from. This allows them to:

■ Make comparisons between quality standards of competing firms.
■ Make complaints when the publicised quality standards have not been met.

The quality standards set by Fine Games are typical. The consumer knows what to expect and can compare this service level with that offered by rival firms. You could walk into most high street stores and either see similar 'promises of quality' or ask to see the shops customer charter. Another key benefit from clearly stating these quality standards is that staff know precisely what is expected of them and what failings will make customers complain.

📂 Monitoring and improving customer service

Monitoring customer service

These are some of the most used methods of communicating with customers to monitor customer service:

Satisfaction level surveys

These provide detailed feedback which can be stored on a database and analysed for a number of uses. For example, First Choice holidays gather data from as many returning holiday makers as possible. These results are quickly analysed and results sent back to hotel owners and tour representatives so that feedback may be acted on.

Business in action

Fine Games

Fine Games sells strategy games on the internet. It promises consumers the following quality standards:

We will always inform you of what is available, the current price and any shipping costs, the dispatch and delivery dates.

We will always deliver the right goods in perfect condition.

We will respond to all queries and communications on the same day.

We will offer a clear complaints procedure should complaints arise.

www.finegames.com

AQA Examiner's tip

Try to link the Human Resource function of recruiting and training staff with the objective of giving good customer service. If the wrong people are recruited and then poorly trained – what hope is there for customer service?

CUSTOMER SATISFACTION SURVEY

The ACME Department Store Group is committed to customer satisfaction and would like to know how well we're doing. Your answers will help us to identify areas needing improvement. If you have questions about this survey, please contact Jayne Wyman (038562189). Thank you for your time and comments.

Which store did you visit?

Please indicate your level of agreement or disagreement with each of these statements regarding the store you visited

	Strongly agree	Agree	Neutral	Disagree	Strongly disagree
	○	○	○	○	○
Store hours are convenient for my shopping needs	○	○	○	○	○
Store atmosphere and decor are appealing	○	○	○	○	○
A good selection of products was present	○	○	○	○	○
Store has the most knowledgeable staff in the area	○	○	○	○	○
Merchandise sold is of the highest quality	○	○	○	○	○
The merchandise sold is good value for the money	○	○	○	○	○
Staff are friendly and helpful	○	○	○	○	○
Any complaints I had were dealt with efficiently	○	○	○	○	○

Overall, how satisfied or dissatisfied are you with the level of customer service you received today?

○ Very satisfied
○ Satisfied
○ Neither satisfied nor dissatisfied
○ Dissatisfied
○ Very dissatisfied

How satisfied or dissatisfied are you with the *quality* of the merchandise?

○ Very satisfied
○ Satisfied
○ Neither satisfied nor dissatisfied
○ Dissatisfied
○ Very dissatisfied

Please tell use something we could do to improve our customer service

Thank you for completing this survey!

Fig. 25.2 *A typical customer satisfaction survey form used by a chain of department stores*

Focus groups

These provide useful insights into customers' views and experiences. Each member of the group hears the reactions of the rest of the group and this can lead to more detailed research findings than a simple survey. The web can now be used to host focus groups where customers join an open forum to discuss views. First Direct bank has extended this concept. They sent out 30,000 e-mails, received over 1,000 replies and subsequently interviewed and filmed 14 respondents. These customer comments then formed part of the bank's advertisements.

Tracking surveys

These are customer satisfaction surveys that are carried out over time with the same customers/groups of customers to see how the company's performance is changing. Tracking surveys can also be undertaken with different groups of customers, for example, in different regions of the country, to see if they experience different levels of customer service – and why.

Encouraging instant feedback e.g. by the use of IT

As well as making available a wide range of customer service tools, such as support websites, technology has also created new communication channels to allow customer feedback.

Business in action

Blogging customer feedback

Ewan MacLeod was angry. He had been charged for sending an e-mail from a mobile phone via a package that claimed to offer free, unlimited data usage. He wrote about his experiences on his blog. He was surprised to receive a call from the mobile phone company, 3, inviting him to meet chief finance officer, Frank Sixt. Apparently, someone had posted his comments on the company's blog, set to promote the free service!

'Any big business is a faceless wonder, but a blog gives you the power to let the company and others know how you feel,' said Mr. MacLeod. 'I had a call saying Frank would like to meet me. I was proved correct and was refunded. I was entirely satisfied with the result.' The company then invited Mr. MacLeod to post another blog, a positive one this time, on the company's website.

The 'Business in Action' above highlights both the tremendous power of IT in providing companies with feedback and also the problems firms have in monitoring the huge amount of feedback being published about them. Blogs, forums, wikis, and even homemade TV clips posted on websites such as YouTube have given everyone the power to publish reports of bad – or good – customer service. National Express, the UK coach company, invites passengers to send text messages of their feedback while riding on the bus! Firms need to respond rapidly and positively to what is being said about them.

Improving customer service

What can any business do – large or small – to improve its levels of customer service? The UK-based Institute of Customer Service (ICS) undertakes regular surveys of large representative samples of UK adult consumers. ICS research found that the top ten priorities for customer service are:

1 Overall quality of the product or service
2 Being treated as a valued customer
3 Speed of service
4 Friendliness of staff
5 Efficient handling of complaints

Activities

1 Dell, the computer manufacturer, was criticised when it was accused of closing its customer support forums in an attempt to silence negative feedback. How would you advise a business to use new technologies to its advantage when attempting to improve customer service?

2 Some expensive restaurants can charge £50 for a three course meal. The actual food ingredients might only cost £5. Discuss the significance of the priorities indentified by the ICS for such a restaurant. How might the restaurant owner try to make sure that these customer expectations are met?

Activity

Using the list of priorities from the ICS to help you, discuss how the level of customer service in a large department store could be improved.

6 Accurate information provided in response to enquiries
7 Competence of staff
8 Ease of doing business
9 Being kept informed
10 Helpfulness of staff.

Some business consultants believe that there is a basic set of rules for improving customer service:

1 Answer the telephone quickly – going through a series of recorded keypad instructions loses customers.

2 Don't make promises that are unlikely to be kept – not delivering goods when customers have arranged to stay at home is guaranteed to cause offence.

3 Listen to customers – feedback can always be used to improve services for others.

4 Deal with complaints efficiently – perhaps these should be handled by more senior staff.

5 Be helpful even if there is no immediate profit to be made – should a regular customer be charged for a five minute adjustment job on a car's wiper blades?

6 Recruit staff with the right attitude and train staff in customer service.

7 Go the 'extra mile' – if a customer cannot find an item in a large store do not direct them to the correct aisle but take them there and see if he/she has any further requests.

8 Add in something extra – perhaps an expensive dress could be lengthened, if required, free of charge?

The benefits of high levels of customer service

■ Better customer service than competitors can give competitive advantage and lead to higher profits.

■ Good customer service may help to clearly differentiate the business from the other firms in the market.

■ Slashed prices and special promotions may bring in NEW customers once but unless some of these customers return because of the service they were offered, then the business is unlikely to be profitable for long.

■ Good customer service is all about sending customers away happy – as this will bring them back. Happy customers will pass on positive feedback about the business to others who may then try the product for themselves.

■ A good customer service reputation can become a unique selling proposition which might allow the business to successfully justify higher than average prices.

Business in action

Pan Book Shop

This is one of the few remaining independent book shops. The market has become increasingly dominated by price discounting internet stores, large book shop chains such as Waterstones and even supermarkets such as Tesco. Even though books are sold for their full cover price, Pan Books survives and thrives because of the personal service it offers. The owner, Robert Topping puts this down to four main factors:

■ Wide range of books

■ Getting in new titles quickly in response to customer feedback

■ Knowledgeable staff with an enthusiasm for books

■ Customer friendly ambience and long opening hours to suit them

■ Regular special author signings and other events.

www.thepanbookshop.blogspot.com

Business in action

Ritz Carlton Hotels

This international chain of hotels consistently scores one of the industry's highest guest satisfaction ratings – 92 per cent compared to an industry average of 75 per cent. The benefits are obvious. The chain also enjoys one of the highest levels of room occupancy and profitability in the industry.

Customer service and profits are linked. How can this level of customer service be consistently achieved across 50 international hotels with 19,000 employees? The Director of Training has four simple answers:

1   Recruit the right people. The interview process includes a couple of existing employees so they can judge if the new applicant will be a good team member.

2   Each staff member carries a card with 20 rules of customer service and the mantra 'we are ladies and gentlemen serving ladies and gentlemen'.

3   300 hours of structured formal training for new recruits.

4   Daily team briefings to discuss issues of improving customer service.

Case study

Pret a Manger – a cut above the rest?

Companies do not give good customer service, people do. If this view is actually true then Pret a Manger, the sandwich and coffee store, do their best to put it into practice. One shop manager, Anson Read summed up his approach: 'At the end of the day all we do is sell sandwiches. What really matters is the service. People can see through promotional hype – they judge us by what we do.' The firm operates a 'mystery shopper' scheme. An anonymous representative from head office descends on a shop to test customer service. They check to see if the customer charter is actually carried out in practice:

- Are customers greeted in a friendly way?
- Is there a good range of sandwiches available and are they all 'picture perfect'?
- Is coffee served of the correct strength and volume?
- Is each customer served within 60 seconds of giving their order?

If the shop scores well in a mystery shopper report then all the staff receive a £30 bonus. The culture of frequent and objective feedback is very strong. Customers are encouraged to fill in report cards and shops are regularly audited for health and safety, food hygiene and food quality. Some customers report that they become so well known to staff members that coffees are made for them as they arrive without asking and first names are used. Staff work as a close knit team. Staff turnover in this industry averages an astonishing 270% per year but at Pret a Manger it is one third of that. People want to work for a business that receives good customer feedback. Ewan Stickley, the Head of Training, recalls that the best thing he heard a customer say was 'I like coming to Pret because I get served by human beings.'

Compare that with your local fast-food joint!

www.pretamanger.co.uk

★ PRET A MANGER ★

Fig. 25.3 *Pret a Manger: effective staff selection, training and clear customer service standards have contributed to the success of this business*

Questions

1 What do you understand by the term 'customer service'?

2 Outline four service expectations that a typical customer at Pret a Manger would have.

3 Analyse two of the long-term benefits to Pret a Manger of developing a good reputation for customer service.

4 To what extent do you agree with the statement that 'companies do not give good customer service, people do'?

5 Look up the Institute of Customer Service website (www.ukcsi.com) and find out how they gather information for companies on levels of customer service.

In this chapter you will have learned to:

- understand the concept of customer service – meeting customers' expectations

- analyse the different methods of meeting customer expectations in different business situations

- explain how customer service can be monitored and improved

- evaluate the benefits of high levels of customer service in a range of different industry settings.

Summary questions

Chapters 23–25

1   What do you understand by the term 'Operations management'? *(3 marks)*

2   List three operational targets that a business manufacturing personal computers might establish. *(3 marks)*

3   Explain briefly the benefits to a business of setting operational targets. *(3 marks)*

4   Explain why a bank branch with four cashiers might not plan to operate its service at full capacity all day and every day. *(4 marks)*

5   Explain how unit costs are calculated. *(2 marks)*

6   Write out this table and fill in the missing data:

	Current output	Maximum capacity	Rate of capacity utilisation	Total costs at current output (£)	Unit cost at current output	Total costs at maximum capacity	Unit cost at maximum capacity
Firm A	100	200		1,000		1,500	
Firm B	5,000	6,000		150,000		160,000	
Firm C	880	980		4,400		4,704	

7   'Food Direct' specialise in packaging and supplying food hampers containing expensive foods and wines. The demand is very seasonal. Many retailers order these in the summer as consumers buy them as ready made picnics. October to December is also very busy due to the demand for Christmas hampers.

    a)   Explain TWO operations problems this seasonal demand pattern causes for Food Direct. *(4 marks)*

    b)   Explain why it is important to this business to attempt to match output to order levels. *(6 marks)*

    c)   Evaluate TWO ways in which Food Direct could try to match output to seasonal demand patterns. *(8 marks)*

8   Indicate each statement as TRUE or FALSE. Briefly explain your decision. *(3 marks each)*

    a)   An expensive product is always of higher quality than a cheaper one.

    b)   Insisting on higher quality standards always costs a business more.

    c)   ISO 9000 ensures products are of a high quality.

    d)   Quality assurance systems can result in lower total costs for a business.

9   Explain why improving quality is important in an increasingly competitive market. *(3 marks)*

10   Differentiate clearly between quality control and quality assurance. Use the example of a small manufacturer of fashion clothing to illustrate your answer. *(6 marks)*

11   Is 'quality' a relative or an absolute concept? Explain your answer.   *(3 marks)*

12   What do you understand by the term 'customer service'?   *(2 marks)*

13   Explain THREE ways in which a small car repair garage could monitor its customer service.   *(6 marks)*

14   Explain why it might be cheaper for a restaurant business to increase its loyalty levels amongst existing customers than to attempt to gain new customers.   *(4 marks)*

15   Analyse TWO ways in which a hairdressing salon could try to improve the levels of customer service it offers.   *(4 marks)*

16   Why is market research important before establishing the customer service levels for a new fast food take-away café?   *(4 marks)*

17   Analyse TWO long term advantages to the café in Q16 of establishing and maintaining very high levels of customer service.   *(6 marks)*

18   Bill Ahmed has just bought out a small regional car hire business called 'Kool Kars'. He did not realise until he started talking to customers that the reputation of the business was so poor. Even though car hire charges were the lowest in the area, only 20 per cent of customers returned to hire cars for a second or further occasion. This compares to big national firms who claim 85 per cent customer loyalty. Bill found out that staff had received no training in dealing with customers politely and over 35 per cent of car hire bills were inaccurate too. Kool Kars vehicles had an average age of two years – 18 months older than bigger firms.

    a)   Explain TWO ways in which Bill could monitor customer service in future.   *(4 marks)*

    b)   Analyse TWO ways in which he could try to improve customer service.

    c)   Evaluate the importance of improving customer service compared to keeping low prices for this car hire business.   *(10 marks)*

26 Working with suppliers

In this chapter you will learn to:

■ analyse the importance of good relationships with suppliers

■ evaluate the importance of the factors that should be considered when choosing suppliers

■ assess the operational benefits of good supplier relationships.

Setting the scene

Cheapest not best for Design Light Co.

'I used Yellow Pages to ring around all of the local firms who supply electrical components and they were the cheapest by far.' Clare, the purchasing manager, was explaining to the company Managing Director how SparksBitz had been chosen as the main supplier to the business of the electrical components. The Design Light Co. needed a wide range of parts to assemble the lighting and heating units it produced. The company's products were designed to meet customers' special 'one-off' requirements. SparksBitz had, it is true, kept its prices very low but it had also failed to deliver key components on several occasions. There were also two legal cases the customers had started against the Design Light Co. for supplying dangerous lights that had exploded after just a few hours use. A faulty part had been traced back to SparksBitz who had obtained them from an unnamed East Asian supplier who had now gone out of business. Replacements could not now be obtained. SparksBitz was now also demanding cash on delivery of any future small orders – its last communication with Design Light Co. had stated that 'we prefer to deal with customers who order large quantities of standard items. Your company's orders are for a few special items that we often have trouble getting hold of.'

Discussion points

1. Was price the key factor in choosing a supplier for Design Light Co.?

2. What factors would you look for in a good supplier if you were purchasing manager of Design Light Co.?

3. What competitive advantages would having good suppliers offer to Design Light Co.?

■ Why are suppliers important?

Customers provide sales that generate cash and profit so customer relationships are vital for long-term success. Surely business managers should devote all available time and energy into establishing effective links with customers and building their loyalty? This is too simple a view of business activity. To meet customers' expectations consistently it is essential to have reliable suppliers of materials, components and business services. A pizza delivery business might pride itself on a rapid response to all telephoned orders – yet if it fails to meet its promises to customers because it has not received a delivery of important ingredients it will face several problems:

■ High labour costs as idle staff wait for ingredients

■ Limited choice of products when customers ring up

■ Disappointed customers who are left waiting for pizzas.

Key terms

Supplier relationships: these are links with the companies that supply a business with goods and services.

It pays any business to invest time in choosing the right suppliers and then building good long-term **supplier relationships** with them. The main operational benefits are explained in more detail at the end of this chapter.

💡 Choosing effective suppliers

The most important factors

A lot of companies, especially newly formed ones, focus on just one factor when choosing suppliers – price. Just like the Design Light Co., above. Obviously prices of goods and services are important when operating in a very competitive and cost conscious market – but is it always the most important factor?

Good suppliers should have these qualities:

- Quality of product as this will increase the chances of the final product being of high quality.
- Flexibility to meet special requirements will be important for providers of one-off or unusual goods and services.
- Reliability of delivery – and this may be linked to location. Offering customers 'next day delivery' will be very risky if the suppliers cannot be relied upon. Sometimes, the biggest suppliers can be the most reliable as they have the resources to devote to good transport links and back-up systems. They may lack flexibility when dealing with smaller, specialist business customers, however.
- Value for money – this does not necessarily mean the cheapest. Insisting on the cheapest supplier may lead to poor quality service and goods of dubious quality.
- Good communication links so that frequent contact can be made.
- Operate the same computer software as the purchasing firm to allow immediate orders and requests to be processed.
- Be financially secure – going into liquidation will mean another supplier has to be found quickly.

Although all of these qualities are important, the first step in choosing a supplier is for a business to identify the two most important factors in their particular situation.

1. The most significant strategic goods or services. These can then be differentiated from commodities they also need. Strategic goods are crucial to the success of a business. Commodities are of less importance and can be obtained from many suppliers of equal quality.

Example 1

A business manufacturing quality furniture will have strategic suppliers of wood and leather. The commodities it needs will include nails and screws and stationery for the administration department.

Example 2

A car hire company taking bookings exclusively over the internet will have strategic suppliers of both vehicles and IT software. Commodity needs will include petrol and oil for the cars.

Clearly, businesses will devote more time and effort to developing close relationships with suppliers of strategic goods and service than commodities.

2. The most important factor in choosing a supplier. This could be reliability, quality, value for money or speed. The crucial factor will depend greatly on the nature of the business.

Example 1

Medical product manufacturer – will need high quality suppliers with the highest standards of cleanliness.

Example 2

Insurance company – will require suppliers of legal services with an excellent record of accurate advice.

Example 3

'Value for a £' retailer – empty shelves occasionally will be much less important than low, low prices from suppliers.

How to choose: the supplier selection process

These are the major steps that should be taken in choosing a firm's main suppliers:

1   Make a list of potential suppliers. Details of potential suppliers can be obtained from trade shows, business directories and the internet.

2   Meet them and see how they operate. This may not be possible if they are thousands of miles away. For some businesses it is vital, however. Purchasing managers from Marks and Spencer visit their food suppliers several times a year to check on standards.

3   Discuss reliability and flexibility. These criteria may need to be built into the **service level agreement** – see point 9 below.

4   Payment terms. For small business customers, these may be strictly cash on delivery or one month credit at most. The more flexible the payment terms offered by suppliers the greater the benefit to the purchasing firm's cash flow position.

5   Prices – value for money has already been referred to. As well as 'list prices' from suppliers, additional costs such as delivery and insurance during transit may need to be added. Comparisons between suppliers need to be on a 'like for like' basis. Reducing costs of obtaining important supplies can increase a firm's profitability.

6   Capacity. This is the ability of the supplier to meet increased orders in the future. It may be disruptive to a rapidly expanding business to have to find a new strategic supplier because the original one does not have the capacity to meet increasingly large orders.

7   Quality. This is increasingly important in a world of greater competitiveness and one in which final consumers have higher and higher expectations. Does the supplier have a verified quality assurance system? Can the supplier meet the quality standards expected? Are they so reliable that there will be no further need for quality control checks once supplies arrive at the customer businesses location? This would help to save time and costs.

8   Reliability of deliveries. When a vendor's deliveries start arriving consistently late, incomplete, damaged or otherwise incorrect, it's time to choose another one. On the other hand all firms can have occasional problems and the cause of any one delivery failure may need to be investigated. The need for speedy and utterly reliable deliveries has increased with the trend towards lean production.

THE HENLEY COLLEGE LIBRARY

> **Activity**
>
> Discuss what you think will be the most important factors to be considered when choosing suppliers by these firms:
>
> - Pizza take-away
> - School book shop
> - Specialist car manufacturer
> - Fashion clothing store.

> **Key terms**
>
> **Service level agreement:** agreements or contracts with suppliers that clearly lay down the service that they must provide.

■ **Business in action**

Abel and Cole

Abel and Cole operate an organic food box delivery service. It insists that all suppliers are registered with the Soil Association as being organic providers of food. Suppliers must use the absolute minimum of packaging, which must all be recyclable or biodegradable, and must be as local as possible to reduce transport carbon emissions. A food retailing consultant remarked that 'Any bad publicity about any of its suppliers and the methods they use to grow food would be very serious for ethical retailers such as Abel and Cole. Supplier service agreements must be water tight and strictly monitored'.

9 Establish a service level agreement. These contracts will indicate to the supplier:

■ The standards of service to be provided
■ The delivery timetable
■ Payment terms
■ Quality levels
■ Sources of supplies, e.g. ethically sourced coffee or sustainable supplies of timber
■ IT systems to be used to achieve compatibility with the IT system of the purchasing company
■ Termination of contract details
■ How disputes are to be settled.

These service level agreements are becoming increasingly important in cementing the long-term relationships between a business and its major suppliers. They offer the supplier some confidence that the orders will keep on flowing IF they meet all of the conditions that the agreements contain.

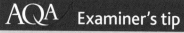

Operational benefits of good suppliers

These benefits should already have started to become clear. These are the most significant ones:

1 **Better customer service**. Choosing suppliers who can deliver on time allows promises to be made to customers with an excellent chance of being able to keep them.

2 **Fewer production delays**. Rapid, reliable supplies of parts and components will allow for continuous production and prevent resources lying idle. This is particularly important if a business operates 'lean production' and 'just in time' stock control methods.

3 **Lower costs**. Yes, cost is an important factor – even if it is not always the most important one. Lower supplier costs will allow a business to gain competitive advantage over rivals.

4 **More consistent quality**. Suppliers who can reach and maintain the quality level being aimed at by the purchasing business will mean that there will be far fewer disappointed final consumers of the product or service.

5 **More flexibility to cope with unusual customer requirements**. This will mean that the purchasing business can offer a wider range of products to the final customer.

6 **Improved communications as a result of similar IT systems**. Collaborative software will mean that 'supplier relationship management' (SRM) can be undertaken speedily and accurately. This will allow for automated ordering processes as the computer system at the purchasing firm alerts the suppliers IT system that new supplies are needed.

AQA Examiner's tip

If a question refers to 'operational benefits' don't forget that there could be many of these, not just lower costs of production.

■ **Case study**

Treat your suppliers like kings

When Mark Balla, Managing Director of MultipliCD Duplication Services recently organised a dinner for his staff he invited a few of his best suppliers along. 'It seemed like a natural thing to do, they are part of the team and the staff know them well,' Mark says. The company's suppliers have helped his business develop in many ways. One Taiwanese supplier offered £25,000 of credit which allowed Mark to spend more on advertising which helped increase sales. Another supplier fulfilled an order for disks in 14 hours when it would normally take 4–5 days – because one of Mark's own customers was pushing for immediate delivery. Meeting his suppliers face-to-face has also led to Mark being offered low prices that would usually only be offered to much larger businesses.

T.G.I. Friday's strategic sourcing director, Roland Ornleas, emphasises the importance of innovative products and good communication as being the key advantages of long-term supplier relationships. 'When we recently added shareable starters to our menus our suppliers came up with really good suggestions. They helped us develop this new product. Also, we are constantly kept informed of price changes in food products and suppliers will come up with new ingredients that help to maintain food flavour but at lower cost'.

Questions

1. What do you understand by the term 'a good supplier relationship'?

2. Outline two benefits to MultipliCD of good supplier relationships.

3. Analyse the most important factors that a business such as T.G.I. Friday's would consider in selecting its suppliers.

4. Evaluate the importance of good long-term supplier relationships to the success either of a car manufacturer or a food retailing business.

5. Research task: Use the www.businesslink.gov.uk website to find out more about:

   a Service level agreements, and

   b Supplier relationship management.

Fig. 26.1 *T.G.I. Friday's depend on reliable suppliers for quality food and menu suggestions*

In this chapter you will have learned to:

- understand the importance of working with suppliers

- analyse the most important factors that determine which suppliers a business will choose

- evaluate the impact on effective operations of working closely with suppliers.

Using technology in operations

Setting the scene

Using IT helped us improve customer service

The Hi-Technology Group, based in the south east of England, uses IT in many aspects of its business. It offers a total design and specialist manufacturing service. It recently introduced a computerised system to keep in closer contact with both suppliers and customers. This is called supply chain management. 'It allows us to monitor and integrate each customer quote for new contracts, the orders that come in, the purchase of raw materials, scheduling of jobs in our workshop through to transport of the finished goods and sending the bill to the customer. We can keep a check on the progress of everything by using our computers', explained Project Manager Chris Moore.

Hi-Technology Group believes that this use of IT has speeded up customer service and reduced wasted time and resources. Introducing this new IT was not a quick process, however. 'We needed to gain support across the whole business first, from the boardroom to the shop floor', said Chris.

'We set up a project team and involved department heads by asking what they would like to see the new IT software achieve. The installation and testing took several months. Part of the plan included extensive staff training and demonstrations. Everyone knew what to expect when the system was introduced. It was worth taking the time to get it right.'

Discussion points

1. What benefits does the Hi-Technology Group seem to gain from the use of IT?

2. Using supermarkets as an example of a service sector industry, what IT applications do you think these businesses use?

3. Why do you think it was important to Chris and his project team to plan the introduction of the new IT carefully?

Technology – what does it mean?

In its simplest form, technology means the use of tools, machines and science in an industrial context. This chapter is not concerned with the business use of 'low technology' tools and machines such as drills and lathes. Many of these have been in use for hundreds of years. Instead this chapter will analyse the impact on businesses of the introduction of high technology machines and processes that are based on **information technology**. This is a much more recent development.

Key terms

Information technology: the use of electronic technology to gather, store, process and communicate information.

💡 Types of technology in operations management

Robots

Once the preserve of science fiction films, **robots** are now widely used in nearly all manufacturing industries. Using robots for this purpose is called computer-aided manufacturing (CAM).

Manufacturing robots are known for their speed, accuracy and efficiency. When correctly programmed, they increase product quality compared to manual production methods. They are more exact and thorough and they do not take breaks! They are most frequently used for repetitive, hazardous and boring tasks such as spot welding, metal cutting and shaping and circuit board assembly. They free workers to take up more rewarding and challenging work. As they are more accurate than workers, they reduce waste and reject rates – and this has a benefit for the firm's environmental record.

Key terms

Robot: computer controlled machine able to perform a physical task.

Fig. 27.1 *Robots increase productivity by performing repetitive tasks quickly and accurately*

Business in action

Land Rover

Land Rover uses advanced robots that can be rapidly adapted to make more than one model on each production line and also allows different features and extras to be added. This allows replacement of the typical 'standardised' product usually associated with production lines with a 'customised' product that meets individual customer's preferences.

A washing machine manufacturer reported a 25 per cent rise in output with no increase in staffing when robots were first used on the production line. Defective products fell from 3 per cent to 0.5 per cent of output. Outline three long-term benefits to the business of these improvements.

Automated stock control programs

Computerised stock control systems run on the same principles as manual ones but they are more flexible and information is easier to retrieve. These are very widely used in service and manufacturing businesses. These IT programs can be used to answer these common key questions:

- How much is there in stock?
- What is the current value of stock held?
- How old is this stock?
- Which are the fastest moving items of stock and which are the slowest?

Not only will computerised systems allow quick answers to these questions, they will give the following benefits:

- Automatic stock monitoring, triggering orders when the re-order stock level is reached;
- Identifying the cheapest and fastest suppliers;
- Bar coding systems which speed up processing, recording of stock and customer check-outs;

■ Radio Frequency Identification (RFID) can now be used which enables individual products or components to be tracked throughout the supply chain.

Supply chain management programmes

Supply chain management (SCM) is becoming an increasingly significant application of IT. Operations Managers can use SCM programs to improve customer service and gain competitive advantage.

The five main stages of SCM for one customer's large order can all be made more effective by using IT software known as Enterprise Resource Planning (ERP):

■ Plan: Deciding which resources are needed for this order and how many.

■ Suppliers: Choosing the best and most cost effective suppliers of the components needed and ordering them to arrive just in time.

■ Manufacture: Check the quality and monitor the rate of progress of the customer's order.

■ Deliver: Pick transport systems that can deliver goods on time, safely and cost effectively.

■ Returns: If there is a problem with the product it will have to be taken back from customers and other items made or the cost reimbursed.

ERP software will monitor all of these stages AND by using the internet, allows the supply chain of a business to be linked into the supply chains of customers and suppliers in a single overall network. This is often referred to as B2B – business to business communication. The following benefits can be gained from ERP software:

■ Supply only according to demand – lean production which avoids waste and helps move the business towards achieving **sustainability** in its operations.

■ Just in time ordering of stocks.

■ Reduces costs at all stages of the supply chain – materials and products are electronically tracked at all stages.

■ Improved delivery times and better customer service.

Key terms

Supply chain: All of the stages in the production process from obtaining raw materials to selling to the consumer – from point of origin to point of consumption.

AQA **Examiner's tip**

Application is a very important skill to demonstrate when discussing uses of IT. Different types of businesses will find some software applications much more useful than others.

Key terms

Sustainability: production systems that prevent waste by using the minimum of non-renewable resources so that levels of production can be sustained in the future.

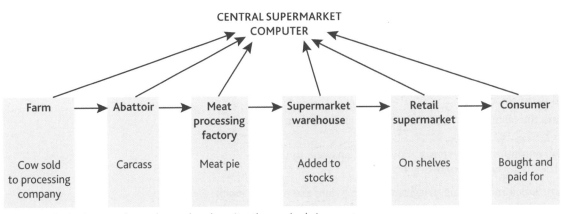

Fig. 27.2 *Technology can be used to track and monitor the supply chain*

Communications technology

Virtually every business will have access to the internet and e-mail. These can be used for external communication with suppliers and customers. An intranet system will allow rapid, cheap and frequent internal communication within the organisation. This can be used to improve the accuracy and speed of passing information between the Operations Management department and other departments of the business. Inter-departmental communication is essential to ensure integrated and consistent policies are adopted and strategies followed. However, too much dependence on IT for communication can have problems too.

Design technology

Computer-aided design (CAD) is the use of a wide range of computer-based tools that assist engineers, architects and other design professionals in their design work. CAD enables designers to lay out and develop their work on screen, print it out in 2-D or 3-D images and save it for future editing. This saves a great deal of time. Due to this greater speed, it takes much less time to develop new products than it used to when designers used manual drawings. This could give a business a real competitive advantage over businesses that do not apply CAD to the same extent. By reducing the product design cycle, updated, revised or completely new products can be launched before those of competitors.

Other benefits of modern CAD systems include:

- Simulation of designs without building a physical prototype – reducing the use of scarce resources
- Passing design data directly to computer controlled machines for production – reducing the risk of errors and wastage – improving the firm's environmental image
- Ability to design a large number of different versions of a standard product – improving the firm's ability to focus on different target markets.

Business in action

No e-mail day

Due to the growing problem of 'information overload' with office workers sending an average of 47 work-related messages each day, Intel has become the latest in a long line of companies to launch a so-called 'no e-mail day'. Instead, engineers are encouraged to talk to each other face-to-face or pick up the phone.

Activity

Think of three ways in which the efficient operation of your school or college is assisted by communication technology.

Fig. 27.3 *CAD allows quick changes to designs to be made and different variations of the same basic design to be developed*

Overall benefits of using new technology

These can now be summed up as being:

- Lower unit costs of production as technology replaces labour intensive methods increases labour productivity
- Better communications and management information systems
- Quicker and more flexible operations
- Better customer service e.g. through internet purchasing.
- Improves quality and reduces wastage.

Introducing and updating technology

IT is a part of almost all businesses' everyday life. The software applications above illustrate how businesses can work more effectively and take advantage of new opportunities. However, it is almost too easy for businesses, including start-ups, to spend capital on IT 'solutions' without giving sufficient thought to what the problem is that needs solving. Just purchasing IT applications is not enough – it is very important that the application used is a cost effective solution to a clearly defined business problem. Apart from cost these are other potential problems from introducing and using technology:

- *Staff resistance to change*

  Some workers may be fearful of rapid technological change. Will they be able to cope with the new techniques they will have to learn? Will their jobs be put at risk?

- *Training costs*

  New technology often replaces relatively low skilled jobs – but the programming and maintenance of the software and hardware will require considerable investments in training.

- *Maintenance and updating costs*

  Purchasing or leasing new technology is not the end of capital expenditure – the increasing pace of obsolescence will lead to frequent updating and replacement costs.

- *Breakdown costs and disruption caused by systems not working*

  Dependence on technology has its drawbacks too and customer service can be put at risk by, for example, unreliable computer systems.

- *IT-based communication systems can create information overload*

  E-mailing has generated an explosion of messages and these can prevent key information being lost in the sheer volume of communications. Much staff time is spent in sending and reading e-mails.

To minimise these costs and potential limitations, these are the important stages a business should go through when introducing or updating technology:

- *Analyse* the potential use of IT and the ways in which it can make the business more effective.
- *Involve* managers and other staff in assessing the potential benefits and pitfalls of introducing it – better ideas often come from those who will use the system than those responsible for purchasing it.

Evaluate the different systems and programs available – compare the cost and the expected efficiency and productivity gains. Consider the budget available for this system.

Plan for the introduction of the new system including extensive training for staff and demonstrations to all users.

Monitor the introduction and effectiveness of the system – is it giving the expected benefits and if not, what can be done to improve performance?

Case study

More chips at the supermarket?

The major UK supermarkets have been putting Information Technology at the forefront of their drive for lower costs, improved customer service and more information about their customers. Bar codes, check out scanners, automatic product re-ordering systems, automated stock control programs, robot controlled transport systems in warehouses, chip and pin machines for payment, loyalty cards that record each individual shopper's purchases and internet shopping for customers –the list of IT applications employed by the large supermarkets is almost endless.

Some of these systems have been controversial. For example, centralised ordering and delivery of products reduced the independence and control of individual store managers. The rapid growth of internet shopping left some companies with a shortage of stock and delivery vehicles which led to poor service. Some smaller suppliers who have been unable to cope with the cost of introducing compatible IT systems to take orders from the huge retailers have been dropped.

And now the latest development is causing further controversy. Radio Frequency ID tagging (RFID) involves putting a small chip and coiled antenna, at the initial point of production, into EVERY item sold through the supermarkets. Unlike bar codes that have to be manually scanned, the RFID simply broadcasts its presence and data, such as sell by date, to electronic receivers or readers.

German supermarket chain Metro already use RFID and claims that food can be easily traced back to the farm where it is produced, queues at tills no longer exist as customer's bills are calculated instantly as they pass by a receiver and all products are tracked at each stage of the supply chain – 'we know where everything is!'

There are some concerns however. Consumer groups suggest that shoppers will be tracked and traceable too – not just the goods they have bought. Isn't this an invasion of privacy? Unions are opposed to it as it could lead to many redundancies due to its non-manual operation. Some supermarket managers fear yet another IT initiative that will mean even more central control over them and they fear breakdowns in the system and lack of training in dealing with problems.

AQA Examiner's tip

Be prepared to evaluate a firm's use of IT and how it introduced the systems. Using IT is NOT the best solution to all problems – and by introducing it badly it can create more problems than it solves.

Questions

1. What do you understand by the term 'Information Technology'?

2. Outline how any two of the IT systems mentioned in the passage are likely to benefit customers.

3. Analyse the likely benefits of supermarkets using RFID to trace and collect data from every product they sell.

4. Discuss how a supermarket business should effectively introduce the new RFID technology.

5. Use the internet to research one of the following and write a brief report explaining the potential benefits to any one well known business: CAD; CAM; RFID.

In this chapter you will have learned to:

■ explain what information technology means

■ analyse the different business applications of technology

■ assess the problems of introducing and updating IT applications – and how these might be overcome.

Summary questions

Chapters 26 & 27

1   List THREE of the suppliers that an internet café will need to deal with.   *(3 marks)*

2   Explain THREE factors that the manager of the internet café should consider when selecting any ONE of the suppliers you listed in Q1.   *(6 marks)*

3   List TWO ways in which the manager of the internet café could discover a list of suitable suppliers for any one product or service required by the café.   *(2 marks)*

4   Using a business example, analyse the importance of price and payment terms offered by suppliers to this business.   *(6 marks)*

5   Why is the supplier's production capacity a factor to be considered when selecting a supplier for a fast expanding manufacturer of central heating boilers?   *(4 marks)*

6   A medium-sized supermarket chain that has most of its branches in the north-east is planning to expand operations to the south-east. This will involve a possible 30 per cent increase in sales over three years. It will stretch the cash flow of the business to the limit. It has a good reputation for good customer service and never running out of stock of major items. The Operations Manager is keen to establish supplier relationships with food and drink manufacturers in the south east. She realises that the choice of suppliers will have an important impact on the success of these new stores.

    a)   Define what is meant by 'supplier relationship'.   *(2 marks)*

    b)   Explain two benefits to this business of establishing good links with suppliers.   *(6 marks)*

    c)   Analyse two factors that the Operations Manager should consider when selecting new suppliers for the shops in the south-east.   *(8 marks)*

    d)   Evaluate the role that its relationship with suppliers will have on the success of this expansion plan.   *(10 marks)*

7   What do you understand by the term 'Information technology'?   *(2 marks)*

8   List FOUR possible uses of modern technology that a food retailing business might use.   *(4 marks)*

9   Differentiate between 'CAD' and 'CAM' technologies.   *(3 marks)*

10   Explain what type of business might find CAD useful and why.   *(4 marks)*

11   Explain the benefits of using CAM to a motor manufacturer.   *(6 marks)*

12   Analyse the possible reasons why a manufacturer of specialist chocolates might keep uses of technology to a minimum.   *(6 marks)*

13 'By using the latest computer controlled machinery we were able to increase productivity,' said the manager of a large dry cleaning business. Explain what she meant by this.   *(4 marks)*

14 Sarah Cahill owns a business that designs and makes fabrics for curtains and upholstery. The market is very 'design conscious'. Low prices are less important than original design and responding quickly to customers requests for new materials. The business employs 35 specialist designers, weavers and dyers. The processes used are very labour intensive. Total sales and market share are falling significantly due to foreign competition that can respond very rapidly with new fabrics to the latest changes in colour and design trends. Sarah's business has quite limited finances but she has asked a business consultant to advise her. He suggested a complete change of design and manufacturing systems that used technology in place of most of the skilled employees currently working for the business.

    a)   Define the term 'Information Technology'.   *(2 marks)*

    b)   Outline two possible IT applications that Sarah could employ within her business.   *(6 marks)*

    c)   Analyse the problems that Sarah might experience when introducing new technology into her business.   *(8 marks)*

    d)   To what extent might further application of technology reverse the fortunes of this business?   *(10 marks)*

Marketing and the competitive environment

Introduction

The next seven chapters build on ideas developed in the first section 'Starting a Business'. In particular, Chapter 5 – Conducting start-up market research, Chapter 6 – Understanding markets and Chapter 25 – Developing effective operations: customer service would be worth re-reading before going any further. Reference to other parts of this book are made throughout this section, which should help you to see how all the elements of a business should be integrated and not seen as distinct from each other. All functional areas rely on each other in a successful business and work together to achieve the goals of the organisation, no matter what its size.

The major issue discussed throughout this section is the competitiveness of a business and the need for any firm to be aware of who their rivals are and what they are doing. This should enable the business to create a competitive advantage through its chosen marketing mix. There are lots of examples of success in highly competitive markets, but it is worth bearing in mind that there are a lot more failures. The aim is to use the marketing mix to ensure success for any size of business.

In this section of the book you should gain an understanding of the importance of marketing to businesses and the huge variety of options available to firms when developing their marketing mix. The results of market research, both primary and secondary, form the basis of developing an appropriate and integrated marketing mix covering the four basic elements of product, price, place and promotion. Firms need to have a very clear understanding of the need of their customers, because mistakes can be very expensive.

Another theme running through this section is the impact of technology on marketing. Developments such as e-commerce are considered in terms of how this has revolutionised the way final consumers and businesses as consumers purchase goods and services to meet their needs.

Chapter 28: Effective marketing This chapter looks at the purpose of marketing and how it can be most effective. What are the benefits and drawbacks of niche and mass marketing? Is there a difference between the *business to business* and *business to consumer* markets?

Chapter 29: Designing an effective marketing mix Here we investigate the influences on the marketing mix which include finance, technology and market research. How important is an integrated marketing mix to the success of a business?

Chapter 30: Using the marketing mix: product This chapter looks in detail at the product element of the marketing mix. What are the influences on the development of new goods and services? The possibilities include technology, competitors' actions and the entrepreneurial skills of managers and owners. What are the advantages to a business of creating a unique selling point, and are there any other ways to differentiate one product from another? In answering these questions you will be introduced to product portfolio analysis and will learn how to use the Boston Matrix and interpret the Product Life Cycle diagram.

Chapter 31: Using the marketing mix: promotion This covers the second element of the marketing mix: promotion. What are the elements of the promotional mix? How important are factors such as branding, merchandising, sales promotions, direct selling and advertising? Why do businesses get involved in public relations? What are the influences on the promotional mix chosen by a firm, apart from the finances available?

Chapter 32: Using the marketing mix: pricing Pricing strategies are discussed in this chapter. What is the difference between price skimming and penetration pricing? Is a strategy the same as a tactic? What is psychological pricing? How does a firm decide on the price to charge for its goods and services? The concept of elasticity of demand is introduced. Why does a change in price benefit some firms/products and not others?

Chapter 33: Using the marketing mix: place This chapter covers the fourth main element of the marketing mix: place. The impact of technology is particularly evident here because the internet has changed the balance of distribution for many smaller businesses, away from traditional routes. What types of distribution channels are available to businesses? Which are the most appropriate outlets or distributors for a firm?

Chapter 34: Marketing and competitiveness This section is brought to a close by considering the relationship between marketing and competitiveness. You will look at the range of market conditions facing firms from those where a small number of businesses dominate to others where there are lots of similar, small firms. How do market conditions influence the design of the marketing mix? What is competitiveness and how can it be improved?

28　Effective marketing

Setting the scene

Spring research

Many business start-ups rely on 'gut instinct' that their product will sell, because they don't think they can pay for research into their potential market. Interviewed on Smallbizpod, Steve Phillips of Spring Research disagrees. He discussed the problems facing business start-ups with no money ('bootstrappers') and suggested that competitor research was essential. The internet has made it easy to discover products on offer, customer profiles and prices. However, talking to as many potential customers as possible is also very important. Chatting about the proposal with family and friends could lead to biased responses, so again the internet can be used: a MySpace page, a blog or pod cast can all lead to very honest feedback. If some money is available, there are sites such as Surveymonkey, or a question can be bought for about £350 on an omnibus survey run by a big market research company, which will give a much larger sample size.

www.smalbizpod.co.uk

Discussion points

1　Why should market research be the starting point for any marketing plan?

2　Is marketing important?

Key terms

Marketing: identifying and meeting customer needs.

Niche marketing: meeting the needs of a relatively small number of potential customers.

Market: anyone willing and with the financial ability to buy a product or service.

💡 The purpose of marketing

Many new businesses do not succeed because they have not clearly identified their customers. This starts with good market research, (Chapter 5 – Conducting start-up market research) which must then be translated into an effective **marketing** mix. Many new firms also underestimate the competition they will face when they enter the market. To be successful, any new business must quickly establish a competitive advantage which will persuade potential customers to choose them rather than their existing supplier, or the nearest rival offering a similar product or service. Customers will always have at least one choice: to buy or not to buy. The purpose of marketing is to ensure that the customer picks the first option rather than the second.

There are two main strands to successful marketing:

- Identifying customer needs: in other words finding out what the customers want that is not already being provided to a sufficiently high standard (Chapter 5)

- Meeting customer needs: making sure that your product or service is exactly what customers are looking for (Chapters 29–34).

Niche and mass marketing

Niche marketing

This involves meeting the needs of a small **market**. Small firms often use this approach because they can concentrate on establishing a strong position in the market. Niche markets are usually too small to attract the interest of larger businesses. Delicious Alchemy (see the Business in Action case study below) is a good example of such a business because it is aimed at people who suffer from food allergies.

Advantages of niche marketing:

- ■ The ability to focus on the needs of individual customers and respond quickly to changes in these needs
- ■ The return on marketing expenditure is often high because it can be so well targeted
- ■ There is little competition which makes it easy to gain market share
- ■ It may be possible to charge premium prices because of the lack of direct competition. This will lead to increased profitability.
- ■ In a new market, it may be possible to achieve first mover advantage. For a completely new product, where the potential market is unknown or very difficult to estimate, it may be possible for a small business to gain a significant market share and a strong brand image before larger firms get involved. This is even more likely if the innovation is protected by a patent.

Disadvantages of niche marketing:

- ■ The degree of specialisation makes niche markets vulnerable to changes in market conditions, which could make their lifespan relatively short-term
- ■ A successful niche may attract the interest of large, multi-national companies. Once such organisations enter the market, small firms will find it difficult to compete
- ■ Sales levels may be relatively low which could cause problems if costs rise unexpectedly, and profit margins are squeezed. This is one of the reasons why many businesses operating in niche markets have found greater success through the internet and e-commerce: running costs are much lower, therefore giving higher profit margins.

Activity

Can you identify the needs being met by the three businesses described in the *Customer needs* Business in Action?

Fig. 28.1 *facebook.com*

Business in action

Customer needs

facebook.com, the social networking website was started in 2004 as a small project for Harvard students in the US. It has now grown into a world-wide phenomenon. It is the fact that you can control who sees your profile that currently gives Facebook the edge over its rivals.

Celebrity Castoffs is an internet auction site where celebrities donate their high-profile clothes, which are so unique that they cannot be worn more than once. The additional incentive of donating 70% of the proceeds to charity made the proposition even more attractive. It is the brainchild of Hayley Smith, who came up with the idea whilst reading a celebrity magazine. Her first move was to register the domain name, and she didn't launch the business until she had researched the idea thoroughly.

Delicious Alchemy is a business selling wheat, gluten and lactose-free foods. It was founded by Emma Killies after she was diagnosed with having severe wheat intolerance. She decided to specialise in baking allergen-free food for hotels and restaurants, and started by exhibiting some of her range at a food show in Yorkshire. Emma sub-contracts work to a baker who produces food such as mocha-syrup sponges and ginger mini-loaves on a commercial scale.

Mass marketing

Many businesses start life with niche market products, but as they grow their goal becomes the mass market. The Body Shop started by Anita Roddick as a firm which targeted a small group of consumers for whom ethical trading was important. However, the perceptions of the general public changed, in no small part due to the efforts of the Body Shop's founder: the values she championed, for example ingredients not tested on animals, were what most consumers came to expect when buying cosmetics and toiletries.

Other firms have always aimed at the mass market, although they may have begun by concentrating on a particular geographical area. Wilkinson's started with one hardware store in Leicester in 1930, and now has 285 shops nationwide.

Advantages of mass marketing:

- High sales, at low prices, mean that costs are spread over a greater number of units. This may mean for example, that a firm in the mass market can afford expensive advertising. Profit margins may be low, but actual profits can still be very high due to the high volume sold

- As products are aimed at a large range of potential customers, it is likely that revenue will be regular, and cash flow problems are less likely.

Disadvantages of mass marketing:

- High profits will attract a lot of competitors into the market which can drive down prices and reduce profit margins

- It may be very difficult to spot changes in consumer needs because the market is so large, which could lead to a loss of market share

- It is very difficult for small or medium-sized businesses to compete with the small number of very large organisations operating in many mass markets.

Which is best – niche or mass?

As you probably realise, there is no right or wrong answer to this question. The decision will depend on the individual business context. However, there is a growing body of evidence to suggest that due to the growth of e-commerce, it is now possible for niche businesses to operate in the global market. Therefore, there might not be the same need to enter the mass market in order to grow. You will also have noticed that many of the advantages of the niche market are disadvantages of the mass market and vice versa. The question you will need to ask is whether the potential for growth in the market is really limited, and what the aspirations of the directors of the firm really are.

Consumer marketing and business to business marketing

We are all consumers and it is easy to forget that many firms do not do business with the public, but meet the needs of other organisations. Do they still need to do marketing? Yes of course they do. The environment in which most firms operate is still competitive.

Consumer marketing is aimed at the general public who are the final users of the product. In other words, the product is not being bought to be resold, but to meet the personal needs of the buyer. Consumer markets typically have a large number of potential buyers and purchasing alternatives. Consumer markets may contain millions of individual consumers. It is very difficult to predict or forecast changes in consumer

Key terms

Mass marketing: meeting the needs of a very large number of potential customers.

Business in action

Torchshop

Torchshop sells only Mag-lite flashlights and accessories, via its website, and offers a very high level of customer service to the people who are interested in their products. Another example from the US is Buymybrokenipod, which offers consumers a very simple way to sell their broken or unused iPods, again via the internet.

Link

For more information on revenue and cash flow, see Chapter 17 – Improving cash flow.

Activity

Prepare a marketing proposal for a niche product or service aimed at the 16–25 year old market in your area. Try to give your product some element that differentiates it from the competition it may face.

Key terms

Consumer marketing: creating and delivering products to solve consumer's needs.

■ Key terms

Business marketing: serving the needs of a business or businesses within one or more industries.

$\mathbb{AQA}$ Examiner's tip

Don't assume that all businesses want to grow into multinational corporations. Many entrepreneurs are only interested in a niche market existence, and can achieve high profits by operating efficiently in their chosen specialist area.

■ Business in action

Lapel Men's Hire

Lapel Men's Hire trade through the hire and retail of menswear for special occasions, weddings and black tie events. They market themselves through Yellow Pages, advertising and weddings shows, and most recently via a website.

■ Business in action

Venom

Venom RIBs (Rigid Inflatable Boats) is a business targeting the professional RIB user: sailors and sailing instructors. This means that their marketing needs to be tailored to meet the specific needs of their customers. Their website includes a lot of technical data which is very important to potential clients

tastes or consumer behaviour. Consumer marketing must rely on the statistics gained from a larger population to predict this behaviour.

Business marketing is concerned with one company identifying the needs of a potential customer who is buying the product as part of their own business process. Business to business markets (B2B) typically contain significantly fewer possible purchasing alternatives than consumer markets. It may be possible to identify all possible buying organisations in a particular niche business market, gather information about each of them and approach them individually.

■ Is marketing important?

It does not matter whether a business is small or growing, in the consumer or the business market, effective marketing is always important. Any business must ensure that potential consumers are aware of the goods and/or services on offer, or they will not survive. Marketing is effective if it achieves the goal of increasing customer awareness to the extent that they choose to become a customer of your business.

■ Case study

Jack's of London has been developed by Sue Whitehead who ran a successful unisex hairdressing salon in Wimbledon. She noticed that she didn't have many male clients and conducted a lot of market research to discover that men really wanted:

■ their hair cut in a male environment
■ to be able to walk in and get a haircut
■ their hair cut before or after work.

Sue created a business with a different feel to a regular barbers shop: there are plasma screens, internet access, free beer and the right magazines. There is a webcam so customers can see if there is a queue, and the salon opens for 12 hours a day, 7 days a week.

This is a niche market with a lot of potential for growth by franchising the business concept. Prices are mid-range and the business exploits the huge growth in the men's grooming market. The marketing mix is built around a strong brand image. The internet, the innovative queue webcam system, on-line style guide and product sales, and an in-house magazine 'Evolve' featuring competitions, gadgets, latest style collections and grooming tips all support the brand and increase awareness. Most recently, Jack's of London has been nominated for the finals of the annual British Hairdressing Awards.

Questions

1. Use the case study to explain the term 'niche market'.
2. Describe Jack's of London's place in the consumer and business market.
3. What are the advantages to Jack's of London of niche marketing?
4. To what extent has the effective marketing of Jack's of London been the cause of the firm's success?
5. Use the company website to investigate further the story of the business and what plans the owners have for the future.

☑ *In this chapter you will have learned to:*

- explain the purpose of marketing
- discuss the benefits and drawbacks of niche and mass marketing
- discuss the difference between *business to business* and *business to consumer* marketing
- evaluate the importance of effective marketing for small and medium-sized businesses.

Designing an effective marketing mix

Fig. 29.1 *Coco Ribbon are a luxury company*

Setting the scene

Coco Ribbon

Coco Ribbon is the ultimate in luxury – a shop for people with an almost unlimited budget. Sophie and Alison set it up in 2002 and the long list of celebrity customers includes Jamie Oliver, Jennifer Love Hewitt, Elizabeth Jagger and Minnie Driver. It sells a carefully selected range of products from perfume to clothes to homeware which must have the 'wow!' factor. The shop is located in the coolest part of London – Notting Hill – and it has had lots of attention from upmarket magazines. There are hundreds of shops selling perfume, clothes and homeware but Sophie and Alison seem to have found something different – Coco Ribbon has gone for a niche.

Sophie and Alison have to be very careful about what they sell in the shop so customers continue to feel that it is special. They buy 'wide but shallow' – not too much of any one thing because it's better to run out than have stock left over. It makes every item feel even more exclusive. Nothing is cheap at Coco Ribbon but getting the price right can be tricky. Sophie and Alison need to know what customers are prepared to pay before they set the price. This means looking carefully at the competition. If they set the price too low, customers won't buy because they think the product isn't good enough. If it's too high, they won't buy either.

Discussion points

1. Sophie and Alison seem to have done something right. What do you think it is?

2. Why do you think Coco Ribbon has a different pricing strategy from Ikea, Gap or Tesco?

3. Why was Notting Hill a good place for this small business to start?

4. How have Sophie and Alison promoted their shop?

5. Running out of stock annoys Marks & Spencer's customers but has its benefits for Coco Ribbon. Why?

Key terms

Marketing mix: the integration of product, place, promotion and pricing designed to achieve the marketing objectives of the business.

💡🗂 The marketing mix

The **marketing mix** refers to all those elements of marketing which help to meet identified customer needs. These elements are generally referred to as the 4Ps, although there have been additions to the original list, for example packaging and people.

1. Product

Product refers to the features and functions of the product or service being offered. If a product has a unique selling point/proposition, it

Fig. 29.2 *Diagram to show the marketing mix available to businesses*

means that one of these features or functions is not available anywhere else. The development of new and existing products should be based on market research which has identified the needs of consumers in the market.

2. Promotion

Promotion concerns communication with the consumers. A new product could meet all the needs of customers, as identified in primary market research (Chapter 5 – Conducting start-up market research, page 27), but unless they are aware of its existence, the product or service will not be bought. Promotion is not just about advertising: it covers all opportunities to inform the market about a firm's products from trade fairs to an item on the local radio.

3. Place

Place is where the purchase can be made by the consumer. Traditionally many products were purchased through retail outlets or catalogues. Today, the growth of e-commerce is such that an increasing amount of purchasing is via the internet. This development applies to both the consumer and business markets (Chapter 28 – Effective marketing, page 213).

4. Price

Price refers to how much the consumer is expected to pay for the product or service. The price should give an indication of the value of the product, and can be altered as demand for the product changes. New, innovative products are usually given a very high price to reflect their unique qualities, whereas new products launched into a very crowded and competitive market such as biscuits or music CDs could have a low price to attract the attention of consumers.

Business in action

Divine Chocolate

Divine Chocolate, the leading UK fair trade chocolate business, was founded in 1997. In February 2007 the company launched a new US firm in Washington, with a news event and chocolate tasting at the Old Ebbitt Grill, the capital city's oldest restaurant, where Ghanaian-born chef Marion Pitcher created the 'Divine Double chocolate Torte'. The product will be sold in independent retail locations and natural food stores, but the hope is to expand to major supermarket chains later in the year, to gain a share of the $13 billion US chocolate market. The price will be set in line with other high quality chocolate bars.

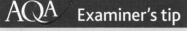

Examiner's tip

It is more important to be able to apply your knowledge of the marketing mix, than to be able to regurgitate definitions learnt by heart.

Activity

Write a short news item outlining the launch of a new live music venue in your area. You should describe an integrated marketing mix which supports a clear message to the target audience.

Packaging and people

Packaging and people are often identified as other important elements of any marketing mix because both can play such an important role in the buying decision. Huge amounts of money are spent every year by businesses to ensure that their product looks appealing to consumers. The importance of people in marketing relates to the principles of TQM (Chapter 24 – Developing effective operations: quality, page 181) which suggests that every employee is part of the marketing of a business.

💡🗞 An integrated marketing mix

A detailed analysis of the marketing mix will be considered in Chapters 30–33. However, it is important at this stage to understand that the elements outlined above must be used effectively and coherently, and do not contradict each other. There is no point spending millions of pounds on advertising a product if it is not available to purchase for another six months; the price charged should reflect the quality of the product nobody would expect to pay £350 for a pair of shoes sold in a supermarket. In the same way, if you buy a watch for £5, you would not expect it to be gift-wrapped, offered with a life-time guarantee and a free pair of diamond studs. Making mistakes with the co-ordination of the mix can be very costly to businesses both large and small.

Divine Chocolate (page 217) illustrates the importance of an integrated marketing mix. All the elements of the marketing mix work well together to ensure that the message is clear. The product has the fair trade unique selling point and is made using the highest quality cocoa beans, which is reflected in the above average prices that Divine charge. They are targeting people who don't make their decisions based on the price of the chocolate, but on the quality of the product. Products are placed at independent retailers and health food stores where consumers would expect to find Divine Chocolate. Finally, the promotion was very exclusive: the oldest restaurant in the capital city of the USA! Note also that the launch promotion does not include an expensive advertising campaign, but uses free news coverage.

Influences on the marketing mix

There are many factors which could influence the composition of the marketing mix.

Finance

How much money does a firm need to spend on marketing? Multinational organisations such as Unilever, Coca Cola and Colgate, spend billions of pounds on marketing, whereas small businesses may have a marketing budget of £500 per year. This does not mean that small business marketing is not going to be effective, if the elements of the mix are used in an integrated and creative way, the impact on customers can be just as positive.

The needs of the market/market research

The marketing mix should be based on the identified needs of customers which in turn should come from market research (Chapter 5 – Conducting start-up market research, page 27). It is also important for firms to continue carrying out market research as their business grows. The needs of customers change over time and the marketing mix may have to be adapted to take this into account.

Business in action

Marketing on a Shoestring

Marketing on a Shoestring is an agency for small businesses, with limited budgets. One of their clients, Silverwell Dental Surgery is a successful and busy surgery in the town centre of Bolton. The dental partners wanted to encourage their current patients to think more broadly about their dental health and appearance and also to generate greater levels of referrals for dental implant treatments from other local dentists. Marketing on a Shoestring conducted market research, developed a range of printed items, a direct mail pack and a website to meet the specific needs of the dental surgery. The dental partners were very happy with the results of the new approach to marketing and the increased take-up of the services they offered.

Competitor actions

Any marketing mix should be seen as ever-evolving rather than something fixed and permanent. It can be used as the basis of a response to the actions of competitors in the market. For example, if a major competitor brings out a new product or lowers prices, other firms in the market must react to safeguard their position and retain their market share. This may involve taking similar action such as introducing a rival product, or matching the new prices, but there are other options available to businesses that are prepared to use the whole marketing mix in a creative way.

Technology

There have been big changes in recent years which have affected the marketing mix. The most obvious area is the 'place' where goods are bought and sold, with the internet becoming a major source of business. This has been particularly useful for small businesses as the costs are so low. However pricing strategies should also reflect technological change, for example charging less for buying and booking online. Marketing by mobile phone has also increased rapidly, with the technology becoming available to almost all consumers.

Business in action

Harry Tuffins

Paul Delves is managing director of Harry Tuffins, a small chain of five independent supermarkets, all within 25 miles of each other around the border between Shropshire and Wales. Before the opening of the firm's sixth store, builders had been hard at work behind a large advertising boarding on the A49 in Ludlow. As Mr Delves worked to make sure everything was on track for the store opening, it appears local rival Tesco had been keeping a watchful eye. Britain's largest retailer sent a mail shot to shoppers within 10 miles of Ludlow offering them two vouchers for its local store. The offer gave customers £10 off any shopping over £30, with the first voucher redeemable a fortnight before the Tuffins store opened and the second valid for the fortnight after. 'This is the first example I have seen of predatory pricing,' Mr Delves said. What appears to have triggered Tesco's Ludlow voucher campaign is Tuffins' opening

Activity

If you were in charge of Harry Tuffins' marketing mix, what would you do in response to the Tesco campaign?

promotion offer of 10p off a litre of petrol for any customer spending more than £60. Mr Delves described the response as a 'David and Goliath action'.

Guardian, 24 January 2007

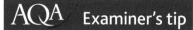

Examiner's tip

A successful marketing mix will reflect the marketing objectives of the business. Make sure you understand what it is that the firm is trying to achieve.

■ Case study

Alara

Alara is a specialist muesli manufacturer. It has been trading since 1975 and has a history of growth and change. The firm currently has 50 per cent of the organic muesli market and exports 20 per cent of its products. The factory is located in Kings Cross, in the heart of London where the firm plays an active part in a diverse and vibrant local community. Operating from a modern unit, production is done in adherence to British Retail Consortium higher-level quality standards. The product is the centre-piece of the business's marketing mix: they provide very high quality products to meet specific requirements including organic, gluten free, kosher, fair trade and small production runs of customer specified blends using a unique database control solution they have developed. At the moment there are 250 different kinds of muesli for sale online, and a smaller choice is also available through health food shops. Tesco, Asda and the Co-op all stock Alara gluten-free muesli. Prices online range from £1.85 for a 500g box of Organic Rich to £3.85 for 750g of Goji and Yacon. In 2006 Alara won two prestigious awards: the Gold Great Taste Award from the Guild of Fine Food Retailers and the Best Food and Drink Product at the Natural Trade Show in Harrogate. 2007 saw the launch of the firm's first major promotional campaign which included consumer media relations, sampling activities and advertising.

Questions

1. What are the main elements of Alara's marketing mix?

2. How might the actions of a major manufacturer like Nestle affect the components of the marketing mix for Alara?

3. What are the advantages and disadvantages to Alara of making the product the centre-piece of its marketing mix?

4. Should Alara aim to increase sales in the major supermarkets in the UK, or continue to expand its overseas business?

5. Use the Yellow Pages or a similar phone book to select a local business to study. Try to identify its marketing mix, and the factor(s) most likely to influence this mix in the future.

✓ *In this chapter you will have learned to:*

- discuss the components of the marketing mix

- analyse the importance of an integrated marketing mix

- discuss the relative importance of the factors influencing the marketing mix.

30   Using the marketing mix: product

In this chapter you will learn to:

- explain the meaning and importance of the development of goods and services
- explain the importance of a unique selling point to a business
- discuss the factors influencing the development of new goods and services
- explain the meaning of a product portfolio
- use the Boston Matrix to assess the suitability of a businesses product portfolio
- explain the meaning and significance of the product life cycle.

Key terms

Product development: changing aspects of goods and services to meet the changing needs of existing customers or to target a different market.

Product line: a set of related goods or services.

Product mix: the full range of products offered by a business, also known as product portfolio.

Setting the scene

Space-pod – hotdesking!

There are many problems with offices, and all too often workers have to 'hotdesk' (share their desk and computer with colleagues). Space-pod has created a mobile workstation which is a fully integrated, self-contained office space that folds out from a very small unit and is completely mobile. The Macro-pod contains a computer, printer, phone, chair and filing. Pods can be joined together to create a team environment and there is a Macroscreen for team meetings and one-to-one interviews. Customers include media centres, local authorities, banks, airports and hospitals as well as the target market of blue chip corporate giants.

Discussion points

1. Why has the business changed the appearance and function of the office?

2. Why is product possibly the most important element of the marketing mix for the Space-pod?

What does product development mean and why is it so important?

Product development involves looking at the market for a product or service and identifying how customer needs have changed and can be met better. By modifying aspects of a product, by adding to an existing **product line**, or extending the **product mix**, a business can meet a wider range of customer needs and/or aim the product at a different target market. For example, an independent health food store may offer fair trade as well as organic food and drink, essential oils in a larger variety of sizes and a new range of locally produced jewellery. Product development is very important to small and growing businesses because it comes from identifying the needs of customers who should always be the focus of an organisation. Product development is also important because no market stands still forever. Although the rate of change will vary, it would be dangerous for any business to assume that a successful product will be just as popular in a year's time!

The product development process

A product development process is needed in a business of any size, because it helps to control the costs and the time taken to develop a new good or service. Successful firms divide development up into a number of identifiable stages which can be applied to goods and services, to product differentiation, to the extension of an existing product line, and the expansion of an organisation's product mix.

1. Creativity: coming up with new ideas to meet consumer needs.
2. Defining the concept: turning an idea into a real business opportunity.

AQA Examiner's tip

Products include services as well as goods!

■ Key terms

Unique selling point (USP): a feature or function of a product that makes it different to any other on the market.

Product differentiation: creating a perceived difference for a product in a competitive market.

■ Activity

Does the Space-pod *Macro-pod* have a USP, and if so what is it?

■ Business in action

ScooterMAN

ScooterMAN is a business which offers a positive solution to drink driving and is a very different take on the concept of chauffeuring. If you have gone for a drink with friends and have your car with you, call ScooterMAN, and a professional, fully-insured chauffeur arrives on a folding scooter, which is packed into the boot of your car, and you are then driven home.

Fig. 30.2 *ScooterMAN is a novel solution to avoiding drinking and driving* www.scooterman.co.uk

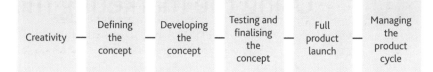

Fig. 30.1 *The product development process*

3 Developing the concept: defining the customer requirements, creating a prototype or pilot service.

4 Testing and finalising the concept: controlled release to test the market.

5 Full product launch: employing all elements of the marketing mix.

6 Managing the product life cycle: monitoring sales and improving features to increase longevity (see page 226).

The unique selling point/proposition

Product development is also important because it can create a **unique selling point (USP)**. If there is something about the design of the product or what it can do, which makes it identifiably different to others on the market; the business can use this as the basis for their marketing mix.

Even if it is not possible to create and maintain a USP, businesses will try to achieve **product differentiation** by making their product different in some way from others on the market. This will make it easier to apply the other elements of the marketing mix, because there is something specific to identify the product or service. It could be as simple as saying that a plumbing company has been established for 40 years, or that a shampoo has just won 'Product of the Year', or offering a 24/7 service. However it is achieved, product differentiation is very useful in a competitive market, because it is a way of distinguishing one business from another, and gives customers a reason to select one firm rather than any other. This can lead to benefits such as repeat business and personal recommendation. In other words, the business that achieves product differentiation is more likely to be successful.

■ What factors influence product development?

The product mix offered by a firm should not stay exactly the same over time. As you have already seen, customer needs will change and businesses must respond positively to retain their share of the market.

However, there are other influences on the market which might appear to pose a threat to a business, but which can also provide opportunities to be exploited by those with a strong entrepreneurial drive.

Advances in technology

Technology has led to significant changes in most areas of business. Technology such as robotics and automated stock control (Chapter 27 – Using technology in operations, page 201) may be beyond the budget of many small businesses, and this could lead to fears that such firms cannot compete against organisations able to achieve lower costs and improved product quality. However, by searching out niche markets, and developing their product lines and product mix, small businesses may still be able to offer clients a product to meet their specific requirements, which larger organisations aiming at the mass market may not be willing or able to supply. At the same time, advances in communication technology have created opportunities to enter new markets. Small businesses can now trade in the global market place via the internet. However, this in itself can be a threat, as the number of competitors in the market has also increased.

The actions of competitors

Competitors may threaten market share, and lead to the necessity of new product development. A large company, with a reputation for high quality products at low prices, may decide to move into a new market. Existing firms in that market, particularly the smaller ones, may not be able to compete on price, so what should they do? One solution may be to extend their product mix to meet the needs of a wider range of consumers, or develop their existing product lines to provide a greater range of options. A more high risk option may be to develop completely new products.

The entrepreneurial skills of managers and owners

Managers and owners, through their creative thinking and risk-taking, move products/brands in new directions. Examples include Richard Branson and his use of the Virgin brand and Stelios and the growth of Stelio's Easy.com to incorporate 15 diverse product ranges from easyJet to easyPizza! It also includes hairdressers such as Trevor Sorbie who have taken their talent from the salon onto the high street. It is the ability to see an opportunity and develop the product to exploit it that can make the difference between a successful small business, that survives in a competitive market and increases its share of the market, and a firm that joins the large percentage of new businesses that fail within the first three years.

Link

For more information on entrepreneurs, see Chapters 1 and 2.

Business in action

Hair today

The hairdressing salon, Hair Today, discovered that a new salon, part of a national chain which also offered self-tanning facilities, was opening close by. Many regular customers made it clear that they would be trying out the new alternative as soon as it opened. In response, the owner of Hair Today, Stacey Smith commissioned some primary market research in the area and discovered that 40 per cent of customers would prefer the additional of a nail care service: gel nail enhancements, natural nail overlays, French manicure, and a range of nail art. Stacey recruited a nail technician and reorganised the salon to cater for this extra service. As a result, she gained new customers as well as keeping most of her existing clients and increased her share of the market.

Business in action

Today is boring

The development of DVDs, hiring online and digital television has seen the decline of the local video shop. However one business which has developed this generic product in its own way is Today is Boring, a video shop with a difference in Shoreditch, London. The selection of 2,500 titles comes from the interests and preferences of the local residents and community. Special offers include money off pizza from the local food shop 'The Grocery' when you hire a film.

Product portfolio analysis

All businesses, no matter how small, should regularly assess their marketing performance: how well each of the products in its product portfolio is doing. This process should ensure that the money allocated to the marketing budget is used effectively. **Product portfolio analysis** is a technique used to identify the position of every product in a firm's portfolio within its market.

Key terms

Product portfolio analysis: analysing the existing product mix to help develop a balanced range of goods and services.

■ **Key terms**

Boston Matrix: a method of analysing the products in a firm's portfolio based on relative market share and market growth.

■ **Activity**

Returning to the initial case study on page 221, which factors influenced the development of the Space-pod *Macro-pod*?

The Boston Matrix

The **Boston Matrix** is a model which analyses the goods or services offered by a business in terms of their share of the market, and whether the market itself is growing. Using this method, a firm can quickly assess the position of all their products in their relative markets. From this assessment, decisions can be made about how each product should be treated in the future. The descriptions of each quadrant are deliberately humorous: to help you remember them!

The Question Mark/Problem Child

A new product with a small share of a growing market; high maintenance: needing relatively high levels of investment to become well established in the market; high failure rate but potential for future success.

The Rising Star

High share of a growing market; high maintenance: marketing resources and effort should be concentrated on this type of product so that market share is maintained; fierce competition is likely.

The Cash Cow

High share in a low growth market; any increase in sales will be at the expense of a competitor; low maintenance; little marketing expenditure needed; relatively high profits.

The Dog

Low share of a declining market; may be kept going because they complete a product line; can possibly be revived.

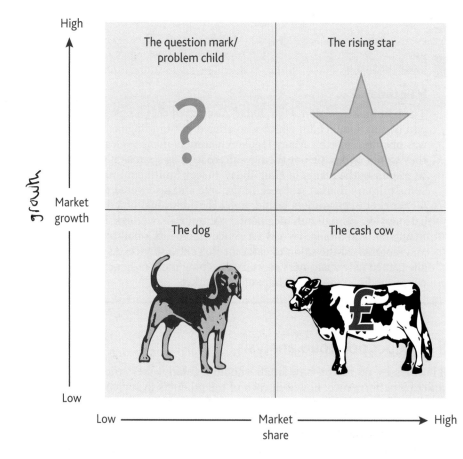

Fig. 30.3 *The Boston Matrix*

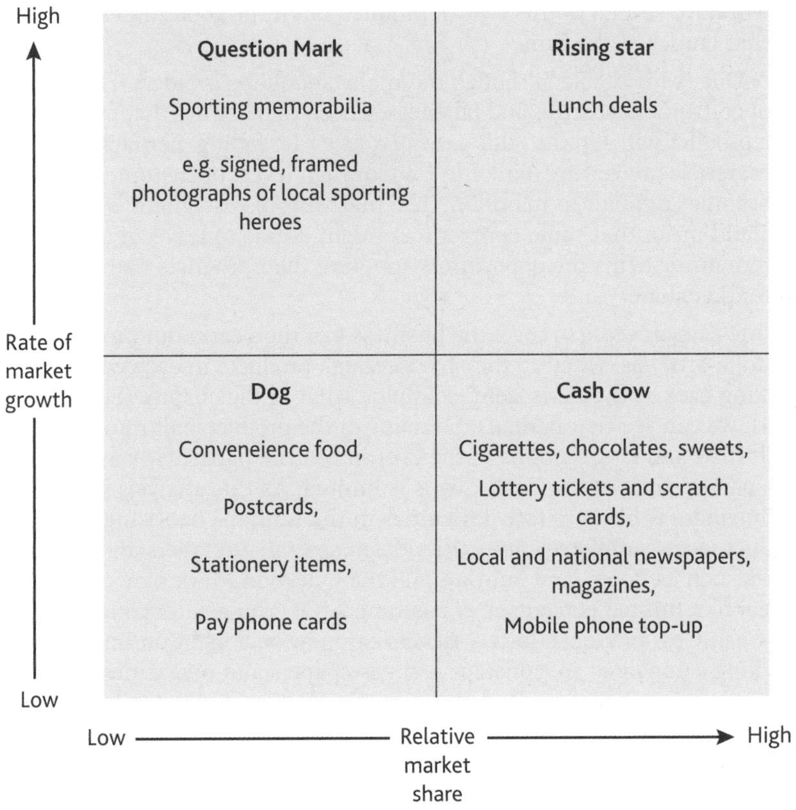

Question Mark Sporting memorabilia e.g. signed, framed photographs of local sporting heroes	**Rising star** Lunch deals
Dog Conveneience food, Postcards, Stationery items, Pay phone cards	**Cash cow** Cigarettes, chocolates, sweets, Lottery tickets and scratch cards, Local and national newspapers, magazines, Mobile phone top-up

High → Rate of market growth → Low

Low ——— Relative market share ——→ High

Fig. 30.4 *Boston Matrix for an independent newsagent*

Figure 30.4 shows an example of how the Boston Matrix can be used to classify the range of products offered by an independent newsagent. The business sells the following items: national and local newspapers, sweets and chocolate snacks, lunch deals comprising a sandwich, drink and snack; convenience food such as bread and milk; postcards of local views; stationary items such as envelopes; pay phone cards; cigarettes, National Lottery tickets and scratch cards, specialist magazines and mobile phone top ups.

How can a business use the Boston Matrix to analyse the suitability of their product portfolio?

Any business, not matter how big or small should ideally have a balance between the four types of products shown in the Boston Matrix. The profits from Cash Cows can be used to help finance the Rising Stars and any investment in the Question Marks. Having decided which categories the product portfolio falls into the following analysis is useful:

1 A **Question Mark/Problem Child** helps to ensure that the business is meeting the needs of customers in the market; it is a Star of the future. Without new product development the firm could miss opportunities and lose market share.

2 A **Rising Star** is potentially the real revenue-earner. It brings new customers to the business, who may well become loyal to the brand and buy other products within the portfolio, including Question Marks and Cash Cows. However, it may still need a great deal of cash investment to remain competitive in the face of fierce competition.

3 A **Cash Cow** can be 'milked' to provide the finance needed to pay for the marketing of Question Marks and Rising Stars. Most businesses

> **Activity**
>
> Use the Boston Matrix to categorise the goods or services offered by a small and medium firm you are familiar with. Present your findings in diagrammatical form.

will have several of this type of product, often the goods and services that launched the firm.

4 A **Dog** is inevitable, although too many should be avoided. The needs of consumers change, and businesses need to be aware that eventually a product will slip into this category: sales are falling, perhaps materials are getting harder to find, or high levels of customer support becomes difficult to maintain. The market is also stagnant which could mean that some competitors might decide to leave, giving the remaining firms the opportunity to revive their products and increase market share.

Having categorised its range, the business can then carry out product portfolio analysis; whether they have enough products in each category. Looking back at the newsagent example earlier in the chapter (Figure 30.4), we can see that perhaps too many of the products fall into the Cash Cow and Dog sections of the Boston Matrix, particularly as the life-span of some of the Cash Cow's is limited. As this analysis shows, the business is likely to face difficulties in the future. The Rising Star product faces very fierce competition from specialist retailers and large stores such as Boots, and Subway, and the Question Mark may only appeal to a limited percentage of customers. Of even greater concern are the Cash Cow products: lottery tickets can now be bought on line, anti-smoking campaigns are constant and newspapers and magazines can all be purchased in supermarkets or delivered. The owners of this business need to consider very carefully how to attract more customers and what products they should supply to their market.

Are there any drawbacks to using the Boston Matrix?

As an aid to decision-making, when deciding on product development, the Boston Matrix is a quick and easy way to make general decisions. However, it is based on two assumptions which are flawed:

1 Market share is the best way to measure the success of a product: a great deal will depend on the type of market and the overall market size. If a firm is trading in a very competitive market, with many other businesses, then a relatively small market share is perfectly acceptable. If the product is competing in a very large, global market, however, a small market share could be seen as successful.

2 A fast growing market is the most important quadrant to be in. This may be true for an entrepreneurial business that thrives on risk-taking and cutting-edge innovation, but there is plenty of scope for success for businesses involved in a slow moving market as well.

As with many business models you will come across, the Boston Matrix should be treated with caution, and certainly not taken too literally. It can be used best as an analysis of the current product portfolio of a business and as the starting point for discussions about future product development and maintaining share of a particular market.

What is the product life cycle?

Figure 30.5 illustrates the path of a product from its development to its disappearance from a business's portfolio (**the product life cycle**). The time scale will vary – some products only last a few months (think World Cup T-shirts) while others seem to go on forever (think chocolate biscuits). During the introduction or launch stage, sales will grow slowly. This is often followed by a sharp rise in sales as the product becomes

AQA Examiner's tip

Products don't go backwards through the Boston Matrix! It follows a logical progression from Question Mark through to Dog. It applies to the products of one business and is not used to make comparisons with products offered by competitors. It is not necessary to draw the matrix or describe the four elements in detail.

Key terms

The product life cycle: the path of a product from its introduction onto the market, to its eventual disappearance from that market.

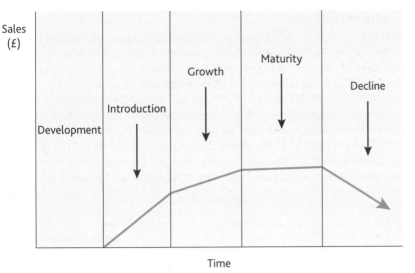

Fig. 30.5 *Product life cycle*

better known. At some point, sales stabilise into the maturity phase, before being overtaken by new product developments or changes in consumer needs, causing a decline in sales.

Why is the product life cycle significant?

■ At the **development stage** the product is being researched and prepared for introduction to the market. No sales are made during this phase.

■ At the **introduction stage** the product is being launched onto the market. There will be a lot of money spent on product development and sales promotion, and because sales are low at this stage, cash inflows are likely to be less than cash outflows. The firm needs to have sufficient finance available to support the new product, and should use techniques such as budgeting and cash flow forecasting to make sure that this stage of the product life cycle does not lead the firm into financial difficulties.

■ The **growth stage** should see sales increase significantly, and the product should achieve break-even. The issues at this stage will be about maintaining the expansion of sales and operational decisions will be very important.

■ The **maturity stage** occurs when sales level off and revenue generated by the product stabilises. Customer loyalty has been achieved and less needs to be spent on promotion. Expenditure on the product can be reduced and possibly transferred to others in the introduction and growth stages.

■ **Decline** starts when sales begin to decline, and is perhaps the most difficult stage to spot. Fluctuations in the level of sales can occur for any number of reasons, but is it the start of a long-term decline in the popularity of the product? Businesses can take one of two options at this stage: they can consider extension strategies where modifications are made to the product or service to meet the changing needs of customers (think mobile phones and electronic gaming products); or the product can be allowed to decline with little on-going expenditure by the business (think chocolate bars that you remember from your childhood that no longer exist).

Extension strategies

In terms of product development, the maturity stage of the product life cycle is particularly significant. The aim of marketing will be to maintain this level of sales for as long as possible, perhaps even increasing sales through product development. This is when modifications can be introduced to extend the life of the product. Consider mobile phones or electronic gaming products where updated versions are launched on a regular basis. Businesses must prepare for this stage, and make sure that the revised version is ready when needed and (as ever) meets the needs of the customers. It is important to note that any element of the marketing mix can be changed to maintain or increase sales (see Chapters 31–33).

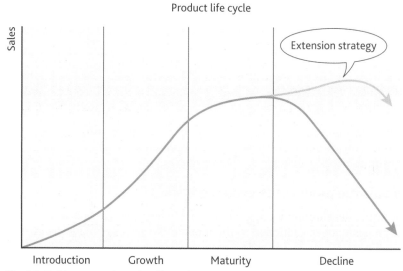

Fig. 30.6 *Diagram to show the effect of an extension strategy on sales*

How useful is the product life cycle?

As with the Boston Matrix, the product life cycle should be treated with caution. It is useful for analysing past sales figures, but it is very difficult to say with any certainty where exactly a product is on the graph at any particular time. There is also a danger that firms may anticipate stages in the product life cycle and react too quickly to variations in sales: reducing marketing activities because they believe that a product has gone into decline, rather than looking for any other explanation for a dip in sales. In fact, there are a range of factors that affect sales, such as the activities of competitors and changes in tastes and fashion, and a product's declining sales may be due to an inappropriate marketing mix rather than any intrinsic problem with the product. There are goods and services that have been on the market for a very long time, such as Monopoly, which prove that with product development, new packaging, new designs and new distribution channels, the maturity stage might never end.

■ **Activity**

How does the product life cycle relate to the Boston Matrix?

■ Case study

G.B. Kent & Sons

G.B. Kent & Sons Ltd, manufacturers of brushes since the eighteenth century, is one of the oldest established companies in Great Britain.

Kent Brushes was founded in 1777 by William Kent in the reign of George III. The Kent family continued to run the company for six generations until 1932 when Mr Eric L.H. Cosby, owner of Cosby

Brushes Ltd, entered into an association with G.B. Kent & Sons, and since that time the company has been under the creative and dynamic direction of the Cosby family.

The company continues to retain the craftsmanship and unprecedented quality that is Kent's reputation. Even in today's fast moving, mass-produced assembly, Kent are proud to still be manufacturing many of their original brushes by hand, which gives them a product life cycle of at least 230 years!

Nevertheless, Kent Brushes is committed to developing and enhancing its products, using the latest hi-tech manufacturing processes, whilst building on the time-honoured traditional methods to create the world's finest example of each and every brush that leaves their factory.

Kent Brushes currently manufacture an exceptional choice of products, with ranges for hair, body, clothes, make-up, teeth and shaving. Part of Kent Brushes' success with major retailers has been built on their reputation for efficiency and quality. Kent have been supplying stores such as John Lewis, Selfridges, Harrods, Fortnum and Mason along with leading chemists in the UK for over 200 years. They also distribute to over 50 countries worldwide, including USA, Hong Kong, Canada, Australia, Japan, Europe, Scandinavia and the Middle East.

Kent's range is now so vast, that it has a selection of over 250 brushes to choose from. The most comprehensive of these is the hairbrush range, providing brushes for use on any hair type, style and length and for every budget. With a selection of styling brushes, radials, ceramics, vents, ionic, paddle, volumising and pure bristle, Kent are now the perfect choice for salon use and retail.

Questions

1. Use examples from Kent Ltd to explain the meaning of the term 'the product life cycle'?

2. Why might Kent Ltd have changed the functions offered by its brushes in the last 230 years?

3. Are long product life cycles an advantage to Kent Ltd?

4. To what extent should Kent Ltd use the Boston Matrix to analyse it's product portfolio?

✅ *In this chapter you will have learned to:*

- explain why the development of goods and services is important
- explain why a USP and product differentiation are important to a business
- discuss factors influencing the development of new goods and services
- explain the meaning of a product portfolio
- discuss the meaning and significance of the product life cycle
- evaluate the value of the Boston Matrix and the product life cycle for marketing decision-making.

Summary questions

Chapters 28–30

1   Explain the purpose of marketing.   *(2 marks)*

2   Explain the difference between a niche and a mass market.   *(2 marks)*

3   What is the difference between a consumer market and a business market?   *(2 marks)*

4   Ferrets UK is a niche market business which sells everything to do with this increasingly popular pet. The owner Karen Parker operates her business via the internet and has customers from all over the world. Before launching the website and trade-marking the name, Karen conducted a lot of internet market research to ensure that her idea was commercially viable.

    a)   Explain two advantages of operating in a niche market.   *(4 marks)*

    b)   Karen is hoping to get into the mass market with a series of children's stories called Ferret Tales. Analyse the advantages and drawbacks of this plan.   *(8 marks)*

    c)   Evaluate the importance of good market research to the successful marketing of Ferrets UK.   *(10 marks)*

5   Identify and explain the main components of the marketing mix.   *(6 marks)*

6   Explain the importance of an integrated marketing mix to the success of a business.   *(6 marks)*

7   ABC Cabs is a family run taxi business which is facing strong competition from a new business that has just opened in the same town, offering lower fares and quicker response times. Jerry Smith, the marketing director for ABC Cabs has decided to revamp the existing marketing mix in response to this development in the market.

    a)   Identify the four main influences on the marketing mix of a business.   *(4 marks)*

    b)   Jerry thought that customers were most interested in clean vehicles and a reliable service. Explain why ABC Cabs needs to keep in touch with the changing needs of consumers.   *(4 marks)*

    c)   One of the drivers for ABC Cabs suggested that an on line booking service might help to increase market share. To what extent should changes in technology influence the marketing mix for this business?   *(10 marks)*

8   What do you understand by the term 'product development'?   *(2 marks)*

9   Explain the stages in the process of product development.   *(4 marks)*

10   Explain the difference between product differentiation and a unique selling point.

11   Explain how developments in technology can effect product development.   *(3 marks)*

12   Explain the term 'product portfolio analysis'.   *(2 marks)*

13   The owners of Johnson's, an independent grocery and flower shop, used the Boston Matrix to analyse its product range: potted plants, cut flowers, dried flowers, imitation flowers, traditional fruit and vegetables, organic, locally grown fruit and vegetables.

     a)   What is the Boston Matrix?   *(2 marks)*

     b)   Analyse the benefits to Johnson's of using the Boston Matrix to assess the suitability of their product portfolio.   *(8 marks)*

14   What is the product life cycle?   *(2 marks)*

15   Should Johnson's use the product life cycle, as well as the Boston Matrix to analyse their product portfolio?   *(10 marks)*

31 Using the marketing mix: promotion

In this chapter you will learn to:

- explain the aims of promotion

- discuss the range of promotional activities available to a business

- explain the meaning of a promotional mix

- discuss factors that might be considered when choosing the promotional mix

- evaluate the final choice of the activities included within a promotional mix.

Setting the scene

Marketing supports flood recovery

Advantage West Midlands (a promotional campaign to help the rural areas of Shropshire, Herefordshire, Worcestershire, Gloucestershire, Warwickshire and Staffordshire recover from the floods and bad weather) was launched at the end of July 2007. The aim was to encourage more visitors to the region's attractions and included a print and broadcasting advertising campaign, a new website with details of attractions, restaurants and accommodation providers, special offers to attract visitors, and a leaflet drop to over 500,000 homes, with more special offers.

Advantage West Midlands

Discussion points

1. What types of promotional activities do businesses use when communicating with their customers?

2. Why might a business need to use a range of promotional activities?

3. What factors might influence the choice of promotional activities used by a business?

The aims of promotion

Promotion is the element of the marketing mix concerned with ensuring that customers and potential customers are aware of current and new products in a firm's range. As a result of this awareness, the business hopes to increase sales to existing and new customers.

There are also a number of secondary purposes of promotion which may apply to a particular business:

- To persuade customers that one product is better than others on the market, thereby encouraging people to change their buying habits

- To increase awareness among a greater number of potential customers e.g. those spread over a large geographical area

- To remind consumers about a product e.g. during the maturity stage in the product life cycle when marketing expenditure may be reduced (Chapter 30). This can encourage repeat purchasing and may attract new customers

- To establish an identity for a business rather than a specific product.

The range of promotional activities available to a business

Sales promotions

These are offers designed to increase short-term sales by giving consumers incentives to purchase one product or service rather than another. **Sales promotions** and **promotional activities** will hopefully lead to longer-term loyalty.

Key terms

Promotion: bringing a product or range of products to the attention of existing and potential customers.

Sales promotion: offers designed to increase sales.

Promotional activities: the ways in which a business can communicate with its potential and existing customers with the aim of increasing sales.

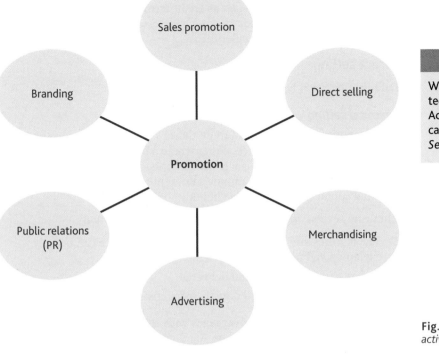

Activity

What sort of sales promotion techniques do you think the Advantage West Midlands campaign could have used (see *Setting the scene* on page 232)?

Fig. 31.1 *The range of promotional activities available to businesses*

Business in action

Nando's

Nando's Chicken Restaurant in Manchester wanted to:

■ increase sales in its Manchester branch by 10% on the average weekly sales (calculated over the four weeks before the campaign).

■ increase sales over the lunch period by £1,000 per week.

■ Introduce new customers to the store.

The sales promotion chosen was to send a lunch box with a typical sandwich pack and free lunch vouchers worth £4 to offices in the local area. The vouchers were redeemable between 12 noon and 3pm Monday to Friday and customers were invited to telephone their final orders in advance. On redemption of the vouchers they received a 'bounce back' offer for a return visit (buy one get one free). As a result weekly sales increased by 19 per cent, total vouchers redeemed was 17 per cent and sales per week over the lunch period increased by over £1,500. The tick box on the voucher revealed that the sales promotion had attracted over 40 per cent new customers.

Options available to businesses include:

■ Money-off vouchers; discounts; loyalty cards; buy-one-get-one Freef. These techniques are commonly used by large high street retailers, but smaller firms can also use them just as successfully

■ Competitions with prizes to encourage people to make a purchase

■ Endorsements from respected personalities. Again, although major brand endorsements are very familiar, small, local firms can also use this technique quite successfully;

- Free gifts offers when a purchase is made
- There are other options such as credit terms and product placement, which may be possible for growing businesses, but could prove to be too costly or risky for smaller firms.

Direct selling

Direct selling can be split into two parts:

Personal selling

This accounts for total sales of more than £2 billion per year in the UK. It is usually made face-to-face; either where a product is demonstrated in the home or a catalogue is left with the customer. In the business to business market, firms will employ sales representatives who make direct personal contact with potential clients.

There are several **advantages** of this method of promotion:

- The features and functions of the product or service can be fully explained and questions answered.
- Orders can be collected and delivered.
- Feedback can be gathered directly form customers.

However, there are also **disadvantages** with this option:

- It can be expensive to maintain a sales team.
- Some customers dislike 'cold callers'.
- There are legal issues to protect consumers from being intimidated by forceful sales people, which may be difficult to monitor, and may require expensive induction training.

Direct mailing

Direct mailing involves sending information about a product to potential customers through the post. This may be seen as 'junk mail' by some consumers, but this form of promotion can be very successful, particularly for small and new businesses who want to get a foothold in a market.

■ **Business in action**

Twinings

Twinings speciality teas provide merchandising support for their products including cards and signs, display stands and boxes, guides and leaflets. The company believes that their merchandising projects a quality image which is the basis for all their marketing. Because their products are sold in such a wide range of outlets, supplying the merchandising material helps Twinings to control its brand image.

Merchandising

Merchandising is about the visual presentation of a product to the consumer at the point of sale. Merchandising attracts the customers to buy a particular product in a shop, and is often targeted at impulse buyers, and takes advantage of pester power – children trying to persuade parents to buy them a gift. The features of good merchandising include high quality display material, full shelves and the layout of products

■ Key terms

Direct selling: a way of selling directly to the final consumer without another intermediary. ✓

■ Key terms

Merchandising: the visual presentation of a product to the consumer at the point of sale.

within a store being well planned: putting very popular items at the back of the store so shoppers have to pass all the other items first for example. Appealing to people's senses is also a successful technique: clever lighting and enticing aromas can attract people into a store.

Advertising

This is probably the most familiar method of promotion and involves the use of media such as billboards, newspapers, trade and technical press, TV, radio, directories, internet and cinema, to communicate with consumers. It can be local or national, relatively cheap or incredibly expensive! **Advertising** is known as 'above the line' promotion, whereas all other types of promotion are called 'below the line'. It is generally a longer-term option compared to some of the other promotional techniques, and advertising is categorised into two main types, each with a different objective:

- **Persuasive**: trying to convince consumers to buy a product. This can be the most controversial type of advertising and has lead to controls being placed on advertisers, e.g. the Trades Descriptions Act 1968 and the Advertising Standards Authority which regulates the content of advertisements, sales promotions and direct marketing in the UK has outlawed Pester Power. Advertisements should not actively encourage children to make a nuisance of themselves to parents or others.

- **Informative**: increasing consumer awareness of a product, by providing details of its features. This sort of advertising is less controversial and, it is argued, enables the consumer to make a rational choice about which product or service to buy.

There are advantages and disadvantages to every type of advertising, and not all of them are appropriate for smaller businesses. In general terms, firms need to consider the following factors when deciding between advertising media:

- Cost – most small organisations will have to think about which media they can afford to use.

- The audience reached by the media – it is better to concentrate on the target audience only e.g. through specialist magazines to maximise impact.

- Competitors' advertising, if successful, will indicate the best media for a business to use.

- The law may have an impact on how and where a firm can advertise.

Public relations

The aim is to increase sales by enhancing the reputation of the business. **Public relations** is a planned and sustained effort to make sure that customers have a good opinion of the organisation. Options include press releases, launch parties, editorial features, media events, charity support, sponsorship and competitions.

Branding

Branding is a means of identification for consumers of a business or one or more of its products. Successful **branding** promotes the strengths, and increasingly, the values of the business. Although the concept of branding is most familiar with household names such as Coca-Cola and Pepsi, where millions of customers are loyal to one brand and will not buy another, smaller firms can create brand loyalty. This could be a family-run business that gains such a good reputation for excellent quality and

Key terms

Advertising: the use of media to communicate with consumers.

Activity

What might have been the benefits and drawbacks of including an advertising campaign in the Advantage West Midlands promotional campaign?

Key terms

Public relations: communicating with the media and other interested parties to enhance the image of the business and its products, and thereby increase sales.

Branding: creating an identity for a business and its products to differentiate it from rivals in the market.

customer service, that when a new range of products is launched, the loyalty of previous customers to the brand ensures a steady stream of business. For many firms, the aim of branding is to become the brand leader in their particular market. The most successful branding occurs where the generic name for the product is replaced by the name of the brand – when you talk about a MacDonald's rather than a burger for instance. Obviously, if a small business is competing in the mass market it will be very difficult to have the most well known brand, but for firms operating in niche markets the opportunity to develop the leading brand is always a possibility.

Business in action

Attenborough Saffron and Blue Dragon

Attenborough Saffron is a Public Relations company with a wide range of clients including Blue Dragon, importers and manufacturers of oriental speciality food. To reinforce and support Blue Dragon's authentic marketing, Attenborough Saffron organised sponsorship of the Chinese State Circus tour to the UK, negotiated extensive on-site product placement e.g. in the programme and banners in the 'big-top', set up regional press competitions to win tickets to local performances and offered tickets to VIPs within the trade media and for sales force use.

Business in action

Apple

Apple is a particularly interesting brand. The company only has a global market share of about 3 per cent and almost went out of business in the 1990s. The Apple brand is successful because it is based on emotional rather than functional values. It is synonymous with creativity, the choice for designers everywhere and has communicated itself as funky, quirky and colourful – a vibrant alternative to its drab and business-like competitors. Their products such as the iPod and iMac support this brand image.

www.cim.co.uk

Fig. 31.2 *The iPhone supports Apple's image-conscious brand*

Key terms

Promotional mix: the combination of promotional activities which make up a campaign to communicate with a target market.

💡 The promotional mix

All businesses will use a combination of these methods to make up the promotional element of the marketing mix. This is called the **promotional mix** and the combination chosen will depend on a number of factors, which could include the following.

Costs

For many small and growing businesses, the marketing budget is not likely to be very large, and so the choice of promotional mix may not include high cost options such as television advertising, high-profile endorsements and expensive competition prizes.

Competitors

The promotional mix of rival companies can have an impact on activities selected by a business: do you match their sales promotions for instance, or offer something better? What is important is that an organisation is aware of what competitors are doing in terms of promotion, so that they are not caught out and lose valuable customers.

Target market

Any business should have a clear idea about which consumer group they are aiming a particular promotional campaign at. In all the examples given in this chapter it is quite easy to identify the target market.

The product

If it is a new product or service, being launched onto the market, the emphasis will be on product awareness, and the promotional mix should reflect this, with more emphasis on advertising and sales promotion. Later, when the product has become established in the market, the focus could change to developing brand loyalty and a comprehensive merchandising package.

The market

If the business is operating in the consumer market, the target for advertising and branding will be the end consumer. In the business to business market, personal selling may be much more important than any other elements of the promotional mix.

The other elements of the marketing mix

In any decision about which mix of promotional activities to select, the point of reference should be full integration with the other elements of the marketing mix, which in itself comes from an understanding of what the business is trying to achieve. Only if there is full integration between all parts of the marketing mix will sales success be maximised.

Case study

Irish Tourism gets £40m promotional boost

A campaign was launched in 2006 which aimed to target 200 million people from around the world. It was a joint venture between Tourism Ireland and the Northern Ireland Tourist Board. Part of the campaign was tied in with the launch of the film *The Lion, the Witch and the Wardrobe*, based on the book by Belfast-born C.S. Lewis. An advert 'Discover the Land that Inspired Narnia' was shown in more than 600 British cinemas. The wider campaign's theme was 'Discover Your Very Own Ireland' and promotional activities ran across TV, radio, print, online and in cinemas. The campaign reflected the core strengths of Ireland: the beautiful scenery, the warmth of the people, and the living and historic culture. It provided information about the wide range of holiday choices and activities available.

In Northern Ireland alone, tourism generated £439m in 2004, which was a growth of 10 per cent. However, this is a very competitive market and the tourism officials hoped to ensure continued growth of overseas visitors, by targeting new markets such as China and expanding the existing markets of Western Europe, the USA and Canada.

Activity

Promotion is communication, so it is very important to understand the behaviour of the target market. Avon failed to anticipate the size of the response to a campaign offering a free Orange mobile phone to customers who spent £15 or more on skincare products. Many customers were disappointed and this caused negative publicity for the business.

How can firms avoid this type of mistake?

Business in action

Media Communications

Media Communications have Chartered Institute of Marketing qualified staff and therefore are able to fully understand the client's needs before producing design work. They ask questions, sometimes difficult ones, so they can understand the purpose of a firm's marketing literature and therefore ensure it is targeted correctly at the clients. 'With advertising, the approach should always be targeted, never random.'

AQA Examiner's tip

Promotion is more than advertising and the budget available will affect promotion possibilities.

Questions

1. What is meant by the phrase 'promotional activities'?

2. Identify and explain two promotional activities which could be used by the Northern Ireland Tourist Board.

3. What are the advantages and disadvantages of linking a promotional campaign to the release of a major film?

4. Is the campaign likely to attract consumers from new target markets such as China?

5. Investigate a promotional campaign intended to increase tourism to the area you live in, or an area you particularly like in the UK or abroad. Assess the strengths and weaknesses of the campaign.

☑ *In this chapter you will have learned to:*

- explain the aims of promotion
- describe the range of promotional activities available to a business
- discuss the creation of a promotional mix
- analyse factors that might be considered when choosing the promotional mix
- discuss the final choice of the activities included within a promotional mix.

32　Using the marketing mix: pricing

In this chapter you will learn to:

- explain pricing strategies used by businesses
- explain pricing tactics used by businesses
- analyse the importance of price within the marketing mix
- discuss the factors influencing the price decision
- explain the significance, determinants and the problems of measurement of price elasticity
- use the price elasticity coefficient to show the effects of price changes on total revenue.

Key terms

Pricing strategies: long-term pricing plans which take into account the objectives of the business and the value associated with the product.

Price skimming: entering a market with a high price to attract early adopters and recoup high development costs.

Penetration pricing: below market pricing to gain a foothold in an established and competitive market.

Setting the scene

Kate Moss @ TopShop

TopShop launched the Kate Moss range of clothing in its 225 shops across the UK on 1 May 2007. Fashion fans were allowed to buy just five pieces per person to prevent the clothes being sold off on Ebay. The clothes were competitively priced and sold out in record time because the target market of young female shoppers wanted to buy into the Kate Moss look. The most popular item was a £45 floral print dress. When the range was launched in Barneys in the USA, it reportedly sold out within one hour!

Discussion points

1. Is price important?
2. What factors might have influenced the pricing decisions taken by Top Shop when launching the Kate Moss collection?
3. Do you think the attempt to stop the clothes being sold on Ebay worked?

Pricing strategies

When a new product is launched onto the market, the firm must decide how much to charge. If the price is too high or too low for the market, it can at best limit the growth of the business and at worst cause sales and cash flow problems. At a basic level, a firm needs to know approximately how much it costs to provide a product or service, and then make sure that the price charged is above that figure. The **pricing strategy** should reflect the perceived value of the benefits a product provides for customers, always bearing in mind what competitors are charging of course!

Pricing strategies for new products

Price skimming

Price skimming is used for the launch of a new product which faces little initial direct competition, for example the product has a unique selling point/proposition. The launch price is high so the product is bought by a small number of consumers, known as 'early adopters', who are not very concerned about the price. The profit margin is high, but this is often necessary to recover very large research and development costs. At some point the price is lowered. This is either because competitors have launched a rival product or because the objective of the business is now to sell the product in large numbers.

Penetration pricing

Penetration pricing is the opposite approach to skimming, although it is also used for the launch of a new product. The aim is not to sell to an exclusive segment of the market, but to capture a large share of the market as quickly as possible. It is a strategy used mostly in a very competitive market where there is little real product differentiation. The pricing policy will be supported by other elements of the marketing mix such as promotion to try and establish brand loyalty. If this can be achieved, then the price can be gradually increased. The legend 'introductory offer' suggests penetration pricing.

■ Link

For more information on pricing and costs, see Chapter 11 – Calculating costs, revenues and profits, page 76.

■ **Business in action**

Skimming in action

The Apple iPod, Playstations 1–3, Panasonic plasma screen TVs and Sky Sports have all been launched using this strategy.

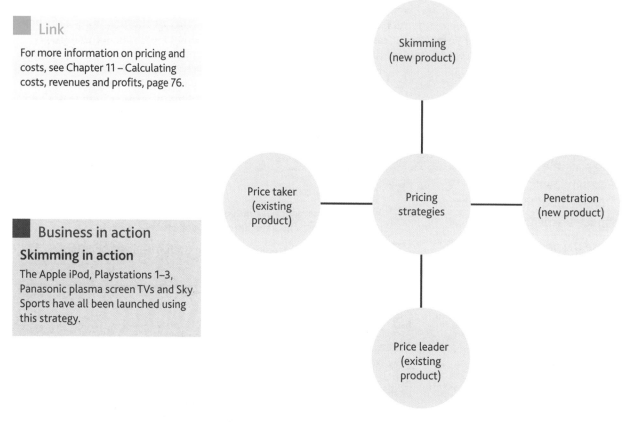

Fig. 32.1 *The main pricing strategies available to businesses*

Pricing strategies for existing products

Price leaders

These are businesses that dominate a market and can set the price for certain products. Every other business in the market has to follow their lead. This **price leader** strategy can be used when one business has a very strong brand image, and the product differentiation is minimal.

For smaller businesses it may be possible to dominate a local market with a very strong brand, for example a taxi service, and operate as a price leader.

Price takers

These are firms that have no option but to charge the market price for their products. This applies when there are many small businesses, with very little difference, as far as consumers are concerned, between one product on the market and another, or where one or a few companies dominate a market which also has many small firms. Businesses that are **price takers** will use other elements of the marketing mix to try and establish product differentiation, which may give them more freedom when it comes to price setting.

■ Key terms

Price leader: a product that has significant market share and can influence the market price.

Price taker: a firm which sets its prices at the same or similar level to those of the dominant firm in the industry.

Pricing tactics

Pricing tactics are short-term pricing plans designed to achieve a particular business objective such as increasing market share or to increase the sales of a product range.

Loss leaders

Loss leaders are products sold for less than it costs to make or buy from the manufacturer/wholesaler. The aim is to create interest and encourage customers to visit the shop, website, or catalogue. Once the consumer is 'captured' they are likely to buy other products in the firm's range, therefore increasing the total value of sales.

Psychological pricing

This is the use of prices that seem to be significantly lower than other very similar prices and so appear to the consumer to offer better value for money, for example £5.99 rather than £6.00. **Psychological pricing** is also known as odd value pricing and only really works if price is an essential part of the consumer's buying decision, that is when there are lots of very similar products at around the same price.

Business in action

Harry Potter

The final Harry Potter book *Harry Potter and the Deathly Hallows* was distributed wholesale for £10.74, and had a Recommended Retail Price of £17.99. However, Waterstones, WH Smith and Amazon priced it at just £8.99 and Asda and Tesco sold it for even less. When questioned about this tactic, Waterstones, for example, were confident that once the Potter fans were in the store they would buy other titles, thereby increasing total sales.

Activity

Amazon may offer a DVD for £10.98, Play.com for £9.99.

1. Which DVD supplier would you choose?
2. Would your decision change if you knew that Amazon would deliver the product to you in two days, whilst Play.com would take one week?
3. Is there any length of time at which your purchasing decision would change?

Influences on pricing decisions

When a company decides on its pricing structure, there are several factors that must be taken into consideration.

Costs

Even if a business elects to use a loss leader pricing tactic, this can only operate in the short term, unless there are other products to cover the losses made (see Cash Cow, Chapter 30). One of the main reasons for new business failure is poor planning, and this includes understanding costs, profit and margins. If the price charged is wrong and costs are not

Key terms

Pricing tactics: the manipulation of price to achieve a specific short-term objective.

Loss leaders: products sold at less than cost to attract customers to a product range.

Psychological pricing: the use of odd number pricing to increase the value-for-money appeal of a product.

Activity

Why was the final Harry Potter book sold as a loss leader by the supermarket chains Asda and Tesco?

Link

For more information on the using marketing mix, see Chapter 30 – Using the marketing mix: product.

Business in action

Boots as price takers

Independent chemists and even large businesses like Boots are price takers in a market now dominated by the large supermarkets. They emphasise high quality customer service and promotional techniques to attract consumers instead. Other examples will include independent garages offering vehicle repair and maintenance and sandwich shops.

Fig. 32.2 *Influences on pricing decisions*

AQA Examiner's tip

Cost is not the same as price. Make
sure that you always use the terms
correctly, otherwise your answer
may appear confused. The cost of
a product is what a business *incurs*
when it pays its suppliers; the price is
what the firm *charges* its customers).

Activity

Under what market conditions
might rival companies enter a price
war, and when might competitors
not respond by changing price?

Business in action

Somerfield

Somerfield introduced an advertising
campaign in the autumn of 2007
which announced that 100 of its
most popular lines were the same
price as Tesco.

covered, the business will have cash flow problems and is unlikely to
survive (see Chapter 17 – Improving cash flow, page 119).

Competitors

Competitors will have a big impact on pricing decisions. The price that
rivals in a market charge will be very important if the product being
sold is perceived as very similar by consumers. If one firm in the market
decides to drop its price in an attempt to increase market share, others
will have to decide whether or not to follow suit. If rivals decide to match
the lower price, a price war may begin which will reduce the profit margin
for all businesses in the market and can lead to shortages and restriction
on consumer purchases. The nature of the product is also important, and
businesses will use the marketing mix to try and persuade consumers
that their product is in some way superior to that of competitors, thereby
justifying a higher price.

The market

The market itself has a significant influence on pricing decisions. The
fast rate of change in one market may lead firms to believe that their
product has a relatively short life cycle. The decision may be made to try
and exploit the 'early adopter' consumers with a price skimming strategy.
If the market is not growing very quickly and products have reached the
maturity stage of the product life cycle, a change in price may be used as
a way of regenerating interest in a product to extend its life.

The target market

This will have an impact on the pricing decisions made by a business. There is no point putting a very high price on a product when the target consumer group is low to middle income earners. This has certainly been an issue facing drugs companies producing chronic disease medication such as drugs to treat HIV/AIDS. Should they operate a differentiated pricing structure based on socioeconomic indicators to make them equally affordable to people and countries with different incomes and disease burdens, or skim the market to recover the very high research and development costs?

The objectives of the business

Business objectives will also be important in the decision-making process. If the organisation wants to maximise profits in the short term, then the price should reflect that. On the other hand, if the firm wants to increase its share of the market, then a lower price and reduced profit margins may be more appropriate.

The other elements of the marketing mix

The rest of the marketing mix will influence the price, because the elements must be fully integrated for the mix to be effective. If the product is sold on line as well as in retail outlets, there may need to be different prices for each market. In the same way, a product which is differentiated from others on the market may enable the business to charge a higher price.

Sensitivity of demand to price changes

The relationship between demand and price is called **price elasticity of demand** and is particularly important for a business considering price changes. For most products it is safe to suggest that if the price increases, demand for the product will fall and vice versa. However, by how much will the demand change? Price elasticity of demand theory attempts to predict the impact a change in price will have on demand and therefore total revenue and profit.

Price elasticity of demand (PED)

If Apple cut the price of its iPod players by 10% but demand only increased by 5%, would this have been a good decision? It seems that demand is not very responsive to this price cut – so the total sales revenue (i.e. price × quantity) will actually fall.

Our answer to this question: 'Is it a good decision?' would be helped by calculating the price elasticity of demand. The following formula is used:

$$\text{Price elasticity of demand} = \frac{\text{\% change in demand}}{\text{\% change in price}}$$

Using the iPod data above, the PED will be:

$$\text{PED} = \frac{5\%}{10\%} = -0.5$$

This result means that, for every 1% change in price, demand only changes by 0.5% but in the opposite direction! So if the price rises, demand falls and vice versa. This is what we would expect. This simple relationship between the price of a product and the demand for it will mean that the PED results will be *negative*.

Key terms

Price elasticity of demand: the responsiveness of demand for a product to a change in its price.

Link

For more information on price, revenue and demand, see Chapter 11 – Calculating costs, revenues and profits, page 75.

Activity

Prove to yourself (by using the formula above) that if the price of Polo mints increased by 4% but demand for them *fell* by 8%, then the PED result will be –2.

When the demand for a product is *very responsive* to a change in prices, PED is said to be *elastic* and the result will be a number greater than -1. When the demand for a product is *very unresponsive* to a price change, PED is said to be *inelastic* with a number less than -1.

So, the PED calculation results in a number which is either greater or less than -1. This PED result indicates to a business whether a change in prices will have a positive or a negative effect on total sales revenue. Marketing managers will want to take price decisions that increase total sales revenue. How can knowing PED help them take the right price decision? By working through the following two examples we will be able to make some simple statements about how the PED result can influence pricing decisions:

Example 1: Car tyres

a   A car tyre business sells 500 tyres per week. The average selling price is £50.

Total weekly sales revenue = 500 × £50 = £25,000

b   The manager estimates the PED for car tyres sold by his garage is -2 (i.e. it is elastic).

c   One week, he reduces tyre prices by 10% to £45.

d   Using the PED coefficient of -2 and the % change in price of 10%, the manager can now calculate the % change in demand:

$$-2 = \frac{\text{change in demand}}{10\%}$$

Therefore the change in demand is 20%

$$-2 = \frac{20\%}{10\%}$$

e   Demand was 500 and has now increased by 20%

$$500 \times 0.20 = 100$$

Therefore new demand = 500 + 100 = 600 tyres

f   Total weekly sales revenue = 600 × £45 = £27,000 (*more* than it was originally)

This shows that total sales revenue will *increase* if prices are reduced when PED is *elastic*.

Activity

Calculate the total weekly sales revenue if the tyre business increased tyre prices by 5% from £50 to £52.50.

Example 2: Florist

a   A flower shop sells 300 bunches of flowers each week for an average of £10.

Total weekly sales revenue = 300 × £10 = £3,000

b   The manager estimates that PED for flowers sold from her shop is -0.5 (i.e. it is inelastic)

c   One week, she reduces prices by 10% to £9.

d   Using the PED coefficient of -0.5 and the % change in price of 10%, the manager can now calculate the % change in demand:

$$-0.5 = \frac{\text{change in demand}}{10\%}$$

Therefore the change in demand is 5%

$$-0.5 = \frac{5\%}{10\%}$$

e Demand was 300 and has now increased by 5%

$$300 \times 0.05 = 15$$

Therefore new demand is 300 + 15 = 315 bunches

f Total weekly sales revenue = 315 × £9 = £2,835 (*less* than it was originally)

This shows that total sales revenue will *fall* if prices are reduced when PED is *inelastic*.

The following table should now help to make clear the impact of elasticity on sales revenue following price changes:

Table 32.1 *Price elasticity of demand and the impact on total revenue*

PED result	Price change	Demand change	Impact on total revenue
0 to −1 (inelastic e.g. −0.5)	Rise	Fall (but by a smaller proportion)	Increase
	Fall	Rise (but by a smaller proportion)	Decrease
> −1 (elastic e.g. −2.5)	Rise	Fall (but by a greater proportion)	Decrease
	Fall	Rise (but by a greater proportion)	Increase

Activity

Calculate the weekly sales revenue if the flower shop manager increased prices by 10% from £10 to £11.

Case study

PED of Pizza

Jane and Ashif run a pizza takeaway business. Based on their past experience, they estimate that their products have a price elasticity of demand of −0.6. The average price per pizza is £6.50 and they sell 200 per week. Total weekly revenue is 200 × £6.50 = £1,300.

Their landlord has recently increased the rent on the shop. Jane and Ashif have reluctantly decided to increase the prices of their pizzas by 20% to £7.80. They were relieved to find that sales only fell to 176 per week because the PED estimate was correct. Sales fell by 24 pizzas which is 12% of the original 200.

$$\text{PED} = \frac{-12\%}{20\%} = -0.6$$

Total weekly sales rose to £1,372.80.

Total weekly sales revenue = 176 × £7.80 = £1,372.80

Three months after the price increase another takeaway business opened up in the same street. This charged lower prices than Jane and Ashif's business. They realised that demand for their pizzas would now be more elastic than before. For one week only, they lowered the prices of the largest pizzas from £10 to £8 (−20%). Sales shot up by 30% from 50 to 65 during this week.

Business in action

In the first three months of 2008, Cadbury was forced to increase confectionery prices due to rising raw material costs. Total sales revenue from its confectionery increased over the same period. Does this suggest the PED for Cadbury's sweets was elastic or inelastic?

Questions

1 Calculate the total sales revenue from the large pizzas
   a before the price reduction
   b after the price reduction

2 Do your results mean that the demand for these pizzas was elastic or inelastic?

3 Explain why new competition has made the demand for pizzas more elastic.

What determines a product's price elasticity of demand?

The number of similar products available to consumers

If there are lots of competing products PED is likely to be elastic because a rise or fall in price will cause customers to switch from one supplier to another. Don't forget though, that if a business can achieve strong customer loyalty, they can reduce the PED.

AQA Examiner's tip

You will not have to calculate the coefficient of price elasticity, but you will be expected to use it! Remember, the sign will always be negative because an increase (+) in price will always lead to a fall (-) in demand, and a decrease in price (-) will always lead to a rise (+) in demand.

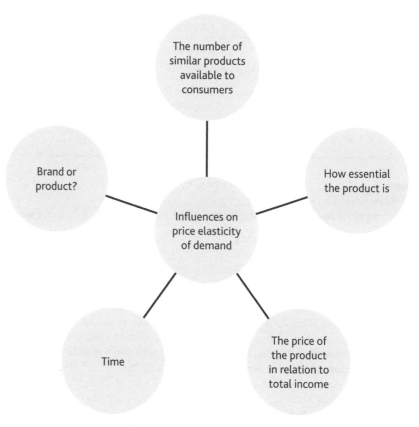

Fig. 32.3 *Influences on price elasticity of demand*

Key terms

Price inelastic demand: the demand for a product changes relatively less than the change in price.

How essential is the product?

This will also affect consumers' reactions to changes in price. If the product is a necessity, or very addictive, customers will continue to buy the same quantity even though the price changes. This suggests that essential and very addictive products are **price inelastic**.

The price of the product in relation to the total income of the consumer

This may also be significant because price becomes a more important consideration. This would suggest that when the product is expensive (a large percentage of disposable income e.g. a car, a house, a holiday) the product will be **price elastic**, whereas a cheap product, for example a packet of crisps is likely to be price inelastic. Note that this refers to product groups rather than individual brands or makes.

Time will affect price elasticity

In the short term consumers are often loyal to their chosen brand and won't change their buying habits even if the price changes. This makes products more price inelastic in the short term. In the longer term they may look for alternatives, particularly if satisfaction in the brand decreases, making demand more price elastic.

Brand or product?

The demand for petrol is likely to be price inelastic due to the essential nature of the product. However, the demand for any one *brand* of petrol could be elastic if only one company, Shell for example, increased their prices. Car owners would quickly switch to Esso and other retailers.

In some markets, though, brand loyalty is very strong, helped by promotion and brand image. So if the price of Jimmy Choo shoes increased, for instance, the sales of them might not be much affected, as demand is inelastic.

Are there any problems with measuring price elasticity?

The main difficulty is getting accurate information about consumer demand at different prices. This requires market research which can be time-consuming and expensive if it is to be reliable. In addition, price elasticity does not stay the same at every price and the reaction of consumers to a very small change in price may be different to their buying behaviour if price change is significant in their eyes. Finally, it is not always possible to attribute changes in demand for a product directly to a change in price. As we have already seen there are other elements of the marketing mix, and external factors such as competitor's actions to consider.

> ### Key terms
>
> **Price elastic demand:** the demand for a product changes relatively more than the change in price.

Case study

Levi's sustainable denim

Levi's launched what it claimed to be the first fully sustainable denims from a major brand in November 2006. The jeans, made with completely organic material went on sale at 20 Levi's stores in the UK. A spokesperson for the company said that market research showed customers were becoming interested in clothes made using sustainable production methods, but still wanted style and quality. Levi's produced 30,000 pairs of jeans for the launch across Europe and initially stocked them in just 2 per cent of stores. This was partly due to the limited availability of organic cotton. The price tag was £80 which suggested that demand is price inelastic: a small number of consumers wanting to buy organic products. Interestingly, the jeans were only available in Europe: Levi's claimed that European consumers were more interested in products that have been made in a sustainable way than customers in the USA and Asia. (Source: Guardian November 2006).

Questions

1 What is meant by the phrase demand is price inelastic?

2 Calculate the total revenue the company would achieve if it sold all 30,000 pairs of organic jeans.

3 If the price elasticity coefficient for organic Levi jeans was -0.5, what would be the new total revenue if they raised the price of the jeans by 5%?

4 Why couldn't Levi's use penetration pricing to launch this product into the competitive jeans market?

5 Why might the premium price be justified in Levi's overall marketing strategy?

6 To what extent is cost a determining factor in the £80 price tag on Levi's 'green' jeans?

7 Investigate the pricing strategies used for the launch of fair trade and organic products in the UK.

💡✔ *In this chapter you will have learned to:*

- describe the pricing strategies used by businesses

- describe the pricing tactics used by businesses

- discuss the importance of price within the marketing mix and how it can be used to deal with competition and meet the needs of the target market

- analyse the factors influencing the price decision

- discuss the significance, determinants and the problems of measurement of price elasticity

- use the price elasticity coefficient to show the effects of price changes on total revenue.

33 Using the marketing mix: place

Setting the scene

Old Oak Insurance

Old Oak Insurance was established in 1938 by Peter Evans and Hugh Williams, who have invested considerable time and resources growing the company to its current size. They have three different offices in West Wales and service their clients with ten different types of cover including home, marine, farm, travel, taxi, church and pet insurance. Although they can be contacted via email, and have a comprehensive website, they encourage clients to 'talk to us to find out how we can help you with your insurance.'

However, the number of people searching for and arranging insurance online, rather than through a broker, doubled between 2003 and 2005. Insurance-related searches for motor, household and travel cover was over 7.6 million in one month in 2005. Firms such as eSure aim to transact 90 per cent of business via the Internet, and the growth of aggregator sites such as Confused.com allow consumers to quickly compare quotes. Only three brands, Tesco, Norwich Union and Direct Line are sought out by customers directly on the internet.

Discussion points

1. Does it matter where a business decides to sell its products?

2. What factors might influence a business's choice of retail outlet or distributor for its products?

3. 'Insurers need to improve their visibility on both search engines and aggregator sites.' (Source: e-consultancy.com) Do you agree?

4. How can Old Oak Insurance Brokers try to compete with Confused.com?

What is 'place'?

This element of the marketing mix is concerned with the distribution of the product to the purchaser, whether it is another business or the final consumer. The aim is to ensure that the product gets to the right place at the right time. A fantastic product can be priced correctly and promoted cleverly, but if it is not available to buy, it will not be really successful.

Distribution channels

Companies can be involved in consumer marketing and business to business marketing, which may be significant when considering how customers gain access to a firm's products. There are a wide range of **distribution channels** used by businesses selling to final consumers and other companies, some are the same, but others are more specific to one or other type of market.

Key terms

Distribution channel: method by which a product is sold to the customer.

Key terms

Direct sale: where no intermediaries are used.

Intermediaries: organisations involved in the distribution of goods and services on behalf of other businesses.

Activity

When selecting the distribution channel a business will always have to take into account the risks involved. There will always be a trade-off between higher profit margins achieved by using a low cost option, and guaranteed sales which may come at a higher cost. A lot will depend on whether the business has the financial resources to take a short term risk for possible longer term gains.

Does the nature of the product have to dictate the channel of distribution?

Direct distribution

A **direct sale** is where the product or service is sold by the supplier to the final consumer without the intervention of any **intermediaries**. The development of e-commerce has made the direct sale an increasingly realistic option for many smaller firms because it can keep the price that the final consumer pays to a minimum. Examples include farmer's markets, hand-made furniture makers and chiropodists.

Fig. 33.1 *Direct channel of distribution*

Traditional distribution

For many firms, whose customers are geographically dispersed or who need to reduce the quantity sold into smaller units, intermediaries such as wholesalers, retailers and agents are used. Examples include soft toy manufacturers who use regional wholesalers to distribute their products to local retailers; market gardeners who distribute their produce directly to retailers and educational book publishers who use agents to distribute their products to schools and colleges.

Business to consumer markets

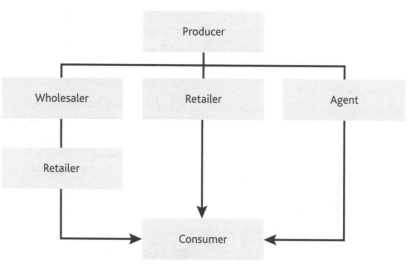

Fig. 33.2 *Traditional channels of distribution*

Retail

This covers everything from a market stall to a hypermarket. There have been trends away from high street retailing over the past 20 years, but there is growing pressure for urban renewal and incentives are available to attract businesses back to town centres. This is an expensive form of distribution because the costs for premises and staff are higher than other alternatives.

Mail order

Catalogues can give access to a greater number of potential customers or can be used to target a particular consumer group. Costs are lower than for retailing.

Direct selling

The producer sells straight to the final consumer of the product or service, without intermediaries such as wholesalers or retailers. It includes door to door selling, telephone sales and product parties. It is particularly successful for high-value and complex products such as building work, double-glazing and life insurance.

Internet/e-commerce

Selling goods and services via a website, using search engines, web links and pop-ups. It has grown to become a very important method of distribution, particularly for small, start-up businesses because of the low initial cost. The development of secure methods of payment has increased the use of this option by consumers.

Multi-channel

Businesses using more than one channel of distribution. The coordination of these different options has been made possible by related developments in technology.

Business to business markets

Wholesaling is used by many small and medium-sized businesses. It provides a link between manufacturers and retailers and allows for goods to be bought in manageable quantities.

Direct sales

Without the use of any intermediaries, direct sales are very important in the **business to business market** because many products or services are high-value and complex. For example, expensive machine tools will be sold directly from the manufacturers to the factory planning to use them.

E-commerce

This is of growing importance in this market, particularly for small businesses wanting to sell goods and services, for example website design services, via the internet. There are a growing number of intermediary sites that facilitate the distribution process on the web. Businesses can display examples of work and include testimonials and case study examples from existing clients.

Mail order/catalogue

This method of selling is used in particular by businesses that have a wide range of product options for clients to choose from. It can be used to display examples of previous work. Many offices still purchase stationery and supplies from mail order catalogues.

Multi-channel distribution

This is also growing in importance in the business to business market.

Intermediaries

In both markets, the role of intermediaries can be very important. These individuals or organisations act on behalf of the business, but are not employed by them. In many case, intermediaries in the chain of distribution will act on behalf of many different businesses such as wholesale businesses.

In the **business to consumer market** many insurance businesses use brokers rather than dealing directly with customers, and holiday

Business in action

Freshline Ltd

Freshline Ltd specialise in creating e-commerce solutions specifically for the needs of their customers. They provide web design, web hosting and multi-media design for business clients.

Activity

1. Select a product or service. What are the advantages and disadvantages of each method of distribution for this good or service?

2. Why are an increasing number of businesses using multi-channel distribution?

Key terms

Business to business markets: companies meeting the needs of other businesses in the market place.

Business to consumer markets: companies meeting the needs of final consumers of goods and services.

Business in action

B2B

(b2b) index

Fig. 33.3 *B2B index*

The B2B index provides a business to business directory that enables firms to see all the leading companies in one place, fill in their requirements and send them to multiple suppliers. This makes it easy to compare suppliers because all the relevant information is available in one place.

companies use travel agents, and cosmetics and toiletry manufacturers use high street retailers and supermarkets.

In the business to business market, agents are also commonplace, particularly when a company is new to the market and needs their expertise.

📎 Choosing appropriate outlets or distributors

Businesses will take several factors into consideration when selecting the best outlets or distributors for their products.

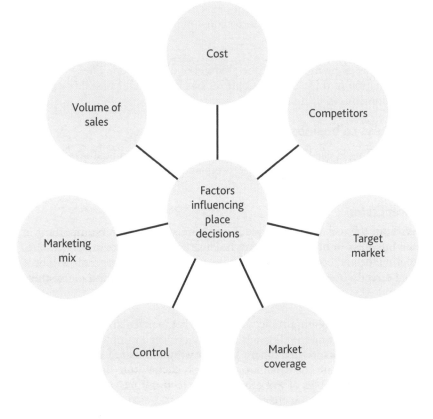

Fig. 33.4 *Factors influencing the choice of outlets/distributors*

■ **Business in action**

Glasgow Radiators

Glasgow Radiators supply and repair automotive, industrial and commercial radiators. Although they can be visited at their Glasgow premises, they can also be contacted via multiple channels – their website, by telephone or fax, and they have an on line catalogue.

Cost

Cost will be important. In both the business to consumer and business to business markets, fixed and variable costs need to be calculated and comparisons made. Many small businesses now distribute their products via the internet because the start-up and running costs are much lower.

Competitors

The competition should also be taken into consideration. If most suppliers of a particular product or service use one channel of distribution, one company might increase market share by using a different one. However, if customers expect to buy through an established route, this strategy could be risky. For example, it took Amazon many years to become profitable when it introduced internet shopping for products normally bought through retail outlets.

The target market

The target market should always be considered when selecting appropriate outlets. For example, locating a fashion clothing store with a target market of teenage girls, at an out-of-town retail park, may not be as successful as a city/town centre location.

Market coverage

Consider the need of suppliers to reach a large number of potential consumers. This may not be possible for the producer without the help of intermediaries who can spread the coverage over a wider geographical area.

Control

Control over the distribution process is also very important, and the more intermediaries a business uses, the less influence the original supplier may have.

The marketing mix

The other elements of the marketing mix will also have an impact on the choice of distributor and outlets. As we have seen before, the mix must be integrated, and the place element is no exception.

Volume of sales

Sales volume will be an important consideration. If the business needs high volume to cover costs and achieve profit, there must be an appropriate distribution network in place. If the firm is aiming for exclusivity this should be reflected in the quality and quantity of chosen outlets.

■ Case study

It is claimed that in the business to business world, the best channel of distribution, offering the highest return on investment, is the exhibition. They offer suppliers the opportunity to demonstrate products, answer questions, overcome objections and build relationships. According to the latest research, exhibitions are seen as the best marketing channel for building relationships with customers, above direct selling, PR, advertising and the internet. Visitors are already expressing an interest and are pre-qualified, so there are few time-wasters. Firms can be sure that those people are worth talking to. It is the best chance to have face-to-face contact, and it is most likely to lead to a fruitful business relationship. The advantage for the smaller business is you are getting the same access to prospects as the larger companies. If you do your pre- and post-marketing, then there is no reason why you can't compete with your larger competitors.

Exhibitions are not only about sales, there are a host of other objectives that can be met successfully at the show, such as educating the market or raising brand awareness.

Exhibitions also make good platforms when you need to re-position the company or launch a new range.

They offer a cost-effective opportunity to encourage trial of your product and give out samples. And that's not all. You can use a show to build a database or to conduct market research or even test the market for a new product. Many companies find exhibitions are also the best place to secure new dealers and distributors as well as being the ideal forum for finding new personnel. Do your preparation, chase the leads and remember you are only as good as your follow-up.

www.weddingextravaganza.co.uk

Questions

1. What is direct selling?

2. Why might an exhibition be particularly useful in the wedding market?

3. Analyse the advantages and disadvantages to a wedding stationary supplier of paying for a stand at a Wedding Extravaganza exhibition.

4. Should businesses always sell directly to their final customers?

5. Conduct research into the claim that within 10 years the internet will have replaced the traditional role of the estate agent in the property market.

In this chapter you will have learned to:

- explain the various distribution channels used by businesses in the consumer and business to business markets

- analyse the factors influencing the choice of suitable distributors/outlets.

34 Marketing and competitiveness

In this chapter you will learn to:

- explain a range of markets with differing numbers of businesses and degrees of competition

- discuss the possible impacts of market conditions on the marketing mix

- analyse the determinants of competitiveness

- discuss how businesses use marketing and non-marketing methods to improve competitiveness.

Fig. 34.1 *The pricing of the final Harry Potter book was very competitive*

Key terms

Degree of competition: the number and size of businesses operating in a given market, be it local, regional, national or international.

Setting the scene

The World of Harry Potter

In July 2007, Waterstones and WH Smith expected to lose money on the final Harry Potter novel as they tried to match the aggressive pricing of Tesco, Asda and Amazon. They hoped that through publicity stunts and midnight openings the book would act as a loss leader, encouraging other book purchases from customers once inside the store. Independent book retailers didn't even try to compete in the price war.

Market conditions have changed and increasingly a small number of blockbuster titles are sold at a heavy discount through supermarkets and over the net. High street retailers are struggling: Waterstones bought Ottakar's in 2006 which reduced the direct competition. There are fewer independent book shops and competition for the best sellers is now concentrated amongst a small number of very large retailers who buy the top 200 titles in such quantities that they can sell them on at prices which independent book shops and book shop chains cannot match. Retailers have to respond by looking to other elements of the marketing mix: promotional offers, a bright appealing environment and almost instant delivery.

Discussion points

1. How could the market for books be segmented by retailers?

2. Why are book retailers likely to continue to struggle against the supermarket giants and internet businesses?

3. Why might consumers prefer to browse in a bookshop rather than buy books off the internet or with their weekly shop?

Market conditions: do all businesses face the same amount of competition?

It is very unusual for a business in the UK to have no competitors. In the past, when there was a public sector (owned by the State), which included gas and electricity supplies, telephone services, postal delivery, and steel and coal production, there was only one supplier. Now all these markets are competitive to a certain extent: even the Royal Mail does not control 100 per cent of letter-post deliveries and faces a high **degree of competition** in the parcel delivery market.

Classification of markets

The number and size of firms operating in a market can be a useful way of describing the conditions facing a firm.

- A highly competitive market will exist where there are many firms all offering a very similar product or service. Firms will be price takers and to ensure survival, will have to keep costs low by using all their

AQA Examiner's tip

If more businesses enter a market, it does not necessarily mean that the market grows in size. Market size measures the value or volume of sales, not the number of businesses doing the selling. If the number of firms in the market increases, that does mean more competition however.

resources efficiently. Businesses start-up and close down/change ownership regularly and it is not difficult to achieve a share of the market. The promotional element of the marketing mix is very important for a firm in this market, because it can be used to attract the attention of potential consumers. Examples include hairdressers, fish and chip shops and car mechanics.

■ Some markets are dominated by a few large firms that tend to compete through the non-price elements of the marketing mix: place, promotion and product. The actions and reactions of competitors is a very important consideration when choosing the marketing mix. Firms try not to compete on price for any length of time, because they fear a price war (Chapter 32). Examples of this type of market in the UK include supermarkets, breakfast cereal manufacturers, bus companies and banks.

■ In a few cases, there is only one business that operates in the market, or controls a significant share of that market. This tends to be where there are very high barriers to entry (e.g. start-up costs) or the business has built up their position over many years. Examples include East Midlands Trains and Airbus.

	Great competition		Less competition
	Many small firms (e.g. hairdressing)	A few large firms dominate industry (e.g. supermarkets)	One dominant firm-monopoly (e.g. London Underground)
Key features	Similar product – but try to differentiate	Try to differentiate products or service – may be difficult	Little consumer choice – may lead to inefficiency
	Price takers – may not be abe to charge proces different to competitors	Price competition could lead to price wars	Price maker
	Competition will force firms to be cost efficient	High marketing and promotional spending	May not have incentive to develop new products or services

Fig. 34.2 *Market classification based on competition*

How do market conditions impact on the marketing mix?

Markets are not always this simple to categorise in reality, but the features of each example can be a useful reference point when making decisions about how to develop a successful marketing mix. A lot will depend on whether or not the market is local, national or international: does the business want to attract customers from anywhere in the UK to buy their products, or do consumers in a specific area form the target market? Although a small firm may be one of many thousands of providers of a product or service nationally, there is a possibility in a local area for a firm to be in a situation where it dominates the market. It is also important to remember that firms in the business to business market will have a marketing mix in just the same way as a business in the consumer market.

■ Key terms

Market conditions: the nature of the product, the needs of consumers, the number of firms and the ease of entry to the market.

■ Activity

Select one product from each of the primary (e.g. farming, fishing, forestry, mineral/oil extraction), secondary (e.g. manufacturing, construction, processing, refining) and tertiary (services to business and/or consumers) sectors and write a brief assessment of the market conditions facing one business.

Try to include at least one business to business market.

Table 34.1 *Examples of the impact that market conditions may have on the marketing mix*

Marketing mix	Market conditions: very competitive with many small to medium-sized firms	Market conditions: a few firms dominate	Market conditions: one firm controls the market
Product	All products are very similar and firms must try to develop and differentiate their goods and services to meet the needs of their particular customers e.g. offering a higher level customer service	New product development, USPs and extension strategies enable firms to compete. Smaller firms may find a niche in the market and offer a narrower range of specialist products	There is no pressure on the business to improve their products or innovate, unless there is another market that acts as competition, e.g. train travel, short haul air travel.
Promotion	Cost is an important factor in the choice of promotional mix. Businesses need to find out the best way to reach their customers and how to attract their attention. Word-of-mouth promotion is particularly cost-effective	Branding is very important, and firms will compete by trying to establish brand loyalty. High cost advertising such as television, is popular	The promotional mix is likely to concentrate information advertising to consumers and Public Relations
Pricing	Firms are price takers, and do not usually use pricing as a way of competing with rivals	Pricing can be very competitive, particularly where the market is not growing very quickly and one firm tries to take market share off its rivals. The largest of the dominant firms may become the price leader. However there is a reluctance to compete too heavily on price because of the possibility of a price war	Pricing is not competitive although it may be regulated by a government agency
Place	Cost is an important consideration so that efficiency is maximised. Direct selling is becoming an increasingly popular channel of distribution: using the internet rather than traditional channels	Technology will be used to great effect by large businesses with the resources to pay for the latest expertise. All possible channels of distribution will be exploited to gain a competitive advantage	The channels of distribution will depend on the market, but need to be convenient rather than competitive

Competitiveness

Competitiveness will enable a business to survive and grow in a market: consumers will be attracted to buy the product because it meets their needs. The marketing mix, when used successfully, differentiates one firm sufficiently from its rivals and therefore gives that business a **competitive advantage**.

Methods of improving competitiveness

A firm facing any market conditions has the choice of whether to take action to increase its competitiveness, or to react to the actions taken by rivals in the market. In markets dominated by a small number of larger businesses, smaller firms may tend to be reactive rather than proactive. However, that need not be the case, because larger firms may not be as aware of changes in consumer wants and needs. Smaller firms may be able to make short terms gains because they take action to increase their competitiveness.

In more competitive markets, with many small and medium-sized firms, those businesses that take action may be able to gain a long-term competitive advantage over rivals of a similar size.

> **Key terms**
>
> **Competitiveness**: characteristics that permit a firm to compete effectively with other businesses.
>
> **Competitive advantage**: discovering and using methods of competing which are distinct and offer consumers greater perceived value, than those of rivals in the market.

■ **Business in action**

Leggetts Transport

Road haulage in the UK is dominated by seven large businesses including Christian Salvesen, Stobart Group and Exel. However, there are at least 13,000 haulage firms in the UK. Many of the smaller, family-run firms specialise in a segment of the market such as frozen food transporting, or cover a geographical region. For example, Leggetts Transport is a family-run regional haulage business based at Woolpit, Suffolk. This business does not compete with the major businesses, but with local rivals. They differentiate their product by offering a wider range of services including storage and distribution as well as haulage. Leggetts competes in the upper/middle market for the regional hauliers where required service levels are beyond that of smaller companies. Overall service levels comprising complete service, time keeping, driver politeness and smartness, efficient administration, communication of problems when they arise, adaptability, meeting delivery windows, rapid response to questions and security are the cornerstones of the business.

Marketing methods

As we have seen, marketing can be used to improve the competitiveness of a business in many ways.

Market research

This should be a significant influence on the marketing mix because it will identify the needs of consumers which can be met by the business through an effective integration of the main elements. Markets are not static, and the firm that is aware of the changing needs of consumers and reacts to those changes can gain a competitive advantage over rivals.

Product

Product developments can be made to existing products during the product life cycle, and new products can be launched onto the market, possibly with a USP or at least clear differentiation.

Promotion

By using the full range of options available, a firm can create a promotional mix that will attract the attention of consumers and encourage them to choose one business over others in the market. This does not have to be expensive: word of mouth is one of the most effective ways of increasing market share, and it costs nothing! As with the marketing mix as a whole the promotional mix must be integrated to achieve maximum impact. Small businesses need to be very clear about what they hope to achieve from promotional activities so that the outcomes can be evaluated.

Pricing

Pricing is a difficult element for smaller firms to use, because they are not free to choose the prices they charge. Instead they must select the best tactics to make short-term gains such as loss leaders to increase overall sales. The importance of elasticity of demand should not be underestimated. A very small short term drop in price can have a positive impact on total revenue, particularly in a competitive market.

Activity

Since the patent for the Dyson vacuum cleaner ended, how has the company used the marketing mix to maintain its share of this market?

 Examiner's tip

Competitive advantage is more than a USP!

'Place'

Place is the area of the marketing mix that has seen most change for smaller businesses, because the internet has opened up a new channel of distribution that potentially has lower costs than other alternatives, particularly in the retailing sector. By keeping up with e-commerce developments, one business can gain a significant cost advantage over rivals. Using the most appropriate outlets and distributors can certainly help to create a competitive advantage.

Non-marketing methods

As well as using the marketing mix to increase competitiveness, non-marketing methods can also be effective.

Reducing costs

If labour costs can be reduced, cheaper sources for raw materials found, or indirect costs cut, then a business has the option to reduce price and still maintain its profit margin. This is particularly important in a competitive market and can enable a firm to make use of more elements in the marketing mix.

Quality

Product is one of the elements of the marketing mix, so improvements in quality can be integrated with the promotional mix and help to achieve a competitive advantage. In the same way, we have seen throughout this section that small firms use the quality of service they offer to customers as their method of product differentiation. This highlights the need for an integrated approach, involving all parts of the business to achieve increased competitiveness.

Staff training

There are many examples of small businesses that have found that when employees are better trained, sales increase. It might be that a wider range of services can be offered, or that costs are reduced because labour turnover falls.

Link

Chapter 24 – Developing effective operations: quality, page 179, and Chapter 25 – Developing effective operations: customer service, page 185, look at how the quality of products and customer service can be improved.

Case study

Petrol retailing

It would appear that the marketing strategies of the major petrol retailers have driven smaller retailers out of business. There has been a dramatic decline in the number of filling stations from about 18,000 in 1990 to 9,382 at the end of 2006. Petrol retailing is a high volume low margin business and increased competition, particularly from supermarkets, has squeezed profit margins. Coupled with the higher standards that customers expect on the forecourt and stricter environmental legislation, a lot of sites just could not justify the investment needed to keep up with modern standards. Inevitably many of these were smaller independent sites but the major companies have closed many of their own forecourts. However, there are few barriers to entry into the petrol retailing market and although there are only nine refineries in the UK, commercial arrangements promote local competition and prevent the owner of a refinery developing a dominant local position.

www.ukpia.com

Questions

1. How has competition in the market for petrol retailing changed over the last 16 years?

2. How can independent businesses compete with the major companies in the petrol retail market?

3. Why would petrol retailing appeal to the major supermarkets?

4. Would market conditions prevent a new business entering the petrol retail market?

In this chapter you will have learned to:

- describe a range of market conditions facing businesses
- analyse the possible impacts of market conditions on the marketing mix
- explain competitiveness
- evaluate the extent to which businesses can use marketing and non-marketing methods to improve competitiveness.

Summary questions

Chapters 31–34

1   What do you understand by the term 'promotion'?

2   Explain three aims of promotion.   *(6 marks)*

3   Describe and briefly explain four types of sales promotion available to
    businesses.   *(8 marks)*

4   Explain the difference between direct selling and direct mailing.   *(2 marks)*

5   Merchandising: Eye Level is Buy Level – When you go to a supermarket
    you can notice that the high profit earning products are always placed on
    the upper shelves, because retailers know customers don't readily view the
    lower shelves.
    a)   What is merchandising?   *(2 marks)*
    b)   Explain two features of successful merchandising.   *(4 marks)*
    c)   Analyse the benefits to a producer of getting their products on
          the eye level shelves in supermarkets.   *(6 marks)*

6   Analyse the factors which might affect the choice of promotional mix for a
    regional supplier of organic fruit and vegetables?   *(8 marks)*

7   What is the difference between a pricing strategy and a pricing tactic?   *(2 marks)*

8   Explain two pricing strategies available for the launch of new products.   *(4 marks)*

9   Explain the difference between a price leader and a price taker.   *(2 marks)*

10 Between 2008 and 2012 television services in the UK will go completely
    digital. Viewers will need to convert or upgrade their TV equipment to
    receive digital signals, through their aerial, by satellite, cable or broadband.
    C & G Television Services is preparing for the changeover by looking at future
    pricing.
    a)   If price elasticity of demand for digital equipment is -0.25 and a local
          television aerial fitting business decides to raise its prices by 10%,
          explain the impact on total revenue?   *(4 marks)*
    b)   What other factors might influence the pricing decisions of C & G
          Television Services?   *(8 marks)*
    To what extent will the actions of competitors in the market influence the
    pricing decisions of C & G Television Services?   *(12 marks)*

11 Evaluate the advantages and drawbacks of using price elasticity of demand
    to make pricing decisions.   *(10 marks)*

understand by the term 'place' in the marketing mix? *(2 marks)*

ain the difference between direct distribution and traditional distribution. *(4 marks)*

Analyse the factors that might influence the channels of distribution decisions made by a business selling hand-made hats and scarves. *(8 marks)*

15   Three years ago Wilfred Emmanuel-Jones launched his food brand 'The Black Farmer', daring to take on the big stores and their own labels dominating the market at the time. Based in Devon, his range of sausages, burgers and barbeque products is now stocked in major supermarkets across the UK.

    a)   The Black Farmer is operating in the business to business market. Explain three channels of distribution that he could use for his products. *(6 marks)*

    b)   What type of market is the Black Farmer competing in? *(4 marks)*

    c)   Analyse the impact that market conditions might have on the Black Farmer's marketing mix. *(8 marks)*

    d)   To what extent can The Black Farmer use marketing and non-marketing methods to improve his competitiveness? *(12 marks)*

35 Examination skills

The AQA AS Business Studies Examinations

There are two examination papers that make up the AQA AS Business Studies qualification.

Unit 1 BUSS1 – Planning and Financing a Business

- This is worth 40% of the final AS level grade (20% of the A level grade).
- The examination is 1 hour 15 minutes long.
- The total marks awarded to all questions is 60.
- There are **two** compulsory structured questions both based on a mini business case study.
- Question 1 will contain short answer questions including calculations.
- Question 2 will contain questions requiring longer written answers.

All questions will be based on the Unit 1 section of the specification and this book:

1 Starting a Business – introduction to Business Studies and an overview of activities involved in setting up a small business.

2 Financial Planning – essential financial concepts and the basic relationships between finance and other business functions.

Unit 2 BUSS2 – Managing a Business

- This is worth 60% of the final AS level grade (30% of the A level grade).
- The examination is 1 hour 30 minutes long.
- The total marks awarded to all questions is 80.
- There are two compulsory multi- part data response questions. There will be questions requiring calculations and questions requiring extended written answers.

All questions will be based on the Unit 2 section of the specification and this book:

1 Finance – using budgets, improving cash flow and profits

2 People in Business – organisational design, recruitment, selection, training, motivation.

3 Operations Management – operational decisions, quality, customer service, suppliers, technology.

4 Marketing and the Competitive Environment – designing and using an effective marketing mix, market conditions and competitiveness.

Examination entries

Both Units 1 and 2 will be offered in January and June each year. Depending on the policy that operates in your school or college you may be entered for these in a number of different ways. The most common ones are likely to be:

Table 35.1 *Methods for examination only*

	January AS year	June AS year
Method one		
Unit 1	1st attempt	Retake (if necessary)
Unit 2		1st attempt
Method two		
Unit 1	—	1st attempt
Unit 2	—	1st attempt

Other entry combinations are possible. For example, Unit 2 could be taken in January of the AS year but this would be most unlikely given the progression of the syllabus content built into the first year's programme.

In addition to the examination entries outlined above, it will also be possible to retake Units 1 and 2 in the SECOND year of the course – the A2 year, in order to try to gain an improved result. Your best result in any one Unit will always count towards your final grade.

The main aim of the remainder of this chapter is to help you prepare for these Unit examinations so thoroughly that you don't have to retake these Units at all!

■ What examiners are looking for – the assessment objectives

'Assessment objectives' is a technical term for 'examination skills'. These are the particular abilities that you will be expected to demonstrate in your examination answers. They are the skills that examiners will be awarding marks for as they assess your exam. paper. So, it is very important that you:

■ Understand what these examination skills – or assessment objectives – are.

■ Know how you can demonstrate them in your answers.

■ Understand how examiners will award marks for them.

There are four assessment objectives. This is what the specification says about them:

Table 35.2

AO1 – Assessment Objective 1	Knowledge	Demonstrating knowledge and understanding of the specified subject content
AO2 – Assessment Objective 2	Application	Apply knowledge and understanding to problems and issues arising from both familiar and unfamiliar situations
AO3 – Assessment Objective 3	Analysis	Analyse problems, issues and situations
AO4 – Assessment Objective 4	Evaluation	Evaluate, distinguish between and assess appropriateness of fact and opinion, and judge information from a variety of sources

Assessment Objective 1 – 'Knowledge'

Table 35.3 *Achieving AO1 (Knowledge)*

What the examiner is looking for	Checklist of how to show the skill
■ Evidence that you have relevant knowledge and understanding of Business Studies terms ■ Evidence that you have responded to the demand in the question for 'Two factors' or 'Two items' by identifying relevant points ■ Evidence that you remember basic formulae or calculation methods e.g. profit	■ Identify the key Business Studies terms referred to in the question ■ Define terms or 'explain what is meant by it'. ■ Identify what else you are asked to do e.g. 'List two factors'. ■ Use your knowledge and the case study to help you list the points you have been asked for.

Command words that test only 'Knowledge'

There will be surprisingly few questions that only test knowledge. These will appear in Unit 1 Question 1. **All other** questions will carry knowledge marks – but will also test other skills. We will look at some of the 'command words' that are used in these questions later. For now you just need to know that when the following command words are used only knowledge is being examined:

Table 35.4 *Examples of command words testing only AO1 (Knowledge)*

Command words/terms	Examples
Define . . .	Define 'budget'. Define 'market growth'. Define ' adding value'.
What is meant by . . .?	What is meant by 'entrepreneurs'? What is meant by 'opportunity cost'? What is meant by 'fixed costs'?
List . . .	List two factors that are included in a cash flow forecast. List two types of employees used in small businesses. List two factors that influence the choice of sampling method.
State . . .	State two methods of market research data. State two sources of new business ideas. State two factors influencing start-up locations.

Questions that are expecting *only* knowledge to be shown will usually be worth *just* two marks:

■ 1 mark for 'some understanding of the term', or
■ 2 marks for 'good understanding of the term'.

Examination examples

All of the points that have been made about the examination skill of knowledge can now be illustrated by looking at an example Unit 1 Paper and the THREE 'knowledge only' questions that are based upon it:

Unit 1

Decoplates Ltd

The idea for Decoplates came to Ian after his young son told him about a game played at a party he had been invited to. This was a competition to decorate a plate with paints. These were then sent away to be 'glazed and fired' in a kiln so everyone had a permanent record of the party. This was incredibly messy but great fun! Ian's own career as a designer was in a rut and he was looking for a fresh challenge offering independence. Why not open a studio to allow people of all ages to decorate plates, vases and other pottery pieces? The studio could also offer fully decorated plates as souvenirs of important events such as birthdays, weddings and anniversaries.

He discussed his idea with a neighbour, Kate, who had experience in running a clothing shop. She was enthusiastic but warned Ian that being an entrepreneur offered great independence but involved considerable risks too. She offered to invest £5,000 in the venture if he would match this, which he did. Over the next few weeks they decided to form a private limited company called Decoplate Ltd., and started to draw up a business plan.

Market research proved to be a problem. They had little experience of gathering primary data but the feedback from friends and relatives about the idea was positive. Ian tried to collect secondary data about the market for 'pottery shops' but none was available. He did find that the total market for 'Art and creative products' grew from £4.5m in 2005 to £8m in 2007.

They realised that £10,000 would not be enough to finance the business start-up. A bank loan would be necessary. They were disappointed that the local bank initially rejected their business plan. 'We need to see some figures. The basic ideas are fine and the location you suggest has potential – but financial forecasts are essential before we can agree a loan,' explained the Small Business Adviser of the bank.

The revised Business Plan contained much more financial information including the following cost, price and customer forecasts:

Decoplate Ltd: first year: forecasted cost, price and customer numbers	
Variable cost per customer	£2
Annual fixed costs	£27,500
Average price per customer	£7.50
Annual customers	8,000

A cash flow forecast for the first year's trading was included and this indicated that a loan of £20,000 would be needed. The interest on this would add to the fixed costs of the business. Kate had wondered if another shareholder should be accepted into the business or if venture capitalists should be approached but the couple agreed that they wanted to keep full control.

In the first year of trading, the profits of the business exceeded budget. Interest in the original product being offered had been much greater than expected and customers were spending more, on average, than forecast in the Business Plan. Farah, a parent of one of the younger customers was so taken by the business idea that she proposed to Kate and Ian that she could open a similar shop in a nearby town. She wanted to be allowed to operate the business as a franchise operation, using the name and same suppliers as Decoplate Ltd. She owned a shop in the town which had recently traded as a hairdressing salon but had closed. It seemed to be well located on the High Street. Kate and Ian were keen on the idea but they explained that the market in the local town needed to be researched. They were not sure if the same marketing mix would be successful in this town. In addition, they had been very lucky in employing some part-time staff who were really hard working and enthusiastic. Would Farah be this lucky?

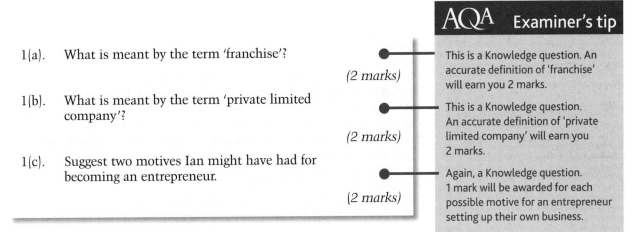

1(a). What is meant by the term 'franchise'?

(2 marks)

This is a Knowledge question. An accurate definition of 'franchise' will earn you 2 marks.

1(b). What is meant by the term 'private limited company'?

(2 marks)

This is a Knowledge question. An accurate definition of 'private limited company' will earn you 2 marks.

1(c). Suggest two motives Ian might have had for becoming an entrepreneur.

(2 marks)

Again, a Knowledge question. 1 mark will be awarded for each possible motive for an entrepreneur setting up their own business.

Assessment Objective 2 – 'Application'

Table 35.5 *Achieving AO2 (Application)*

What the examiner is looking for	Checklist of how to show the skill
■ Evidence that you have read and understood the case study and realise how it can be used to support your answers.	■ Read the case study before answering any questions! Never assume that questions can be answered without understanding what the case is about.
■ Evidence that you can use the case study and the issues it covers to illustrate the knowledge point that you are making.	■ Identify sections of the case study that are relevant to each question.
■ Evidence that you can accurately extract relevant figures and complete the calculation asked for.	■ Use quotes and phrases from the passage in your answer that illustrate or support the point being made.
■ Evidence that you can answer the questions in the context of the business study	■ Be careful to use the right figures from the case if a calculation is asked for.
	■ Think about how the question affects the business study in order to demonstrate application

Command words that test only 'Knowledge' and 'Application'

It is very important to remember that there will be NO marks given for copying out parts of the case study in an answer if no relevant subject knowledge has been demonstrated. In fact, we can go further than this, without SOME relevant subject content (knowledge and understanding) in all of your answers then they will not gain any marks at all! Demonstrating relevant subject knowledge in each and every answer is essential for any marks to be gained for the other assessment objectives too. So, there is no such thing as 'a well applied or analysed answer with no appropriate subject knowledge'!

Table 35.6 *Examples of command words testing AO2 (Application)*

Command words/terms	Examples
Explain with an example what is meant by . . .	Explain, with a numerical example, what is meant by the phrase 'falling net profit margin'.
	Explain, with an example from the case, what is meant by 'the legal structure of business'.
Explain why . . .	Explain one reason why the owners might have decided to use primary market research.
	Explain one factor that might have influenced the owners' decision to locate in the town centre.
Outline . . .	Outline one benefit to this business of using a business consultant.
	Outline one disadvantage to this business of using niche marketing.
Calculate . . .	Using the information in the table, calculate the net profit margin for this business.
	Calculate the company's profit variance for May.

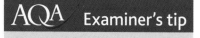

AQA Examiner's tip

This question carries 2 knowledge marks. These will both be awarded for an answer that demonstrates a good understanding of what a cash flow is and/or one reason why it is important to include it in a business plan. The question also carries 2 marks for APPLICATION of the answer to the case study.

Examination examples

These questions are based on the Unit 1 paper 'Decoplates Ltd' (see page 264).

(d). Explain ONE reason why the bank insisted on a cash flow forecast in the Business Plan.

(4 marks)

(e). Use the information in Table 5 to calculate:

i) The number of customers required to break-even.

(3 marks)

ii) The total forecasted profit in the first year.

(3 marks)

(f). Calculate the percentage growth in the UK market for 'Art and creative materials' from 2005 to 2007.

(4 marks)

Assessment Objective 3 – 'Analysis'

Table 35.7 *Achieving AO3 (Analysis)*

What the examiner is looking for	Checklist of how to show the skill
■ Evidence that you can explain an answer using logical and reasoned arguments e.g. X leads to Y which may cause Z! ■ Evidence that you can explain points made with supporting use of Business Studies theory and ideas. ■ Evidence of appropriate use and understanding of numerical and non numerical techniques.	■ Most importantly, you should firstly establish that the question is asking for detailed explanations. If the question uses the command words referred to below then time will be wasted analysing your answer in detail – time that should be spent on those questions that need this development. ■ Identify the Business Studies techniques and ideas that could be used to support the points made e.g. price elasticity when analysing the impact of a proposed price change. ■ Build up an argument showing, for example, how a business decision might have either a positive or negative impact on it. ■ **Only** if asked to, build up arguments both for and against the point made in the question.

Command words that test 'Analysis'

There will be three main ways in which examiners will ask for this skill to be shown. Don't forget, though, that your answer must contain appropriate knowledge and this will often be best demonstrated by defining the business term in the question. Questions which demand analysis will always also carry application marks – so your answer should be based on case study evidence too!

You will notice that 'Explain how' is included in this list. To answer this type of question effectively it is necessary to use powers of analysis. Compare this with 'Explain why' in Assessment Objective 2 which only requires an applied use of knowledge – not analysis.

Table 35.8 *Examples of command words testing AO3 (Analysis)*

Command words/terms	Examples
Analyse . . .	Analyse the importance of monitoring quality to . . .
	Analyse TWO advantages to the business of using internal recruitment in this case.
Examine . . .	Examine TWO possible reasons why the net profit margin has fallen.
	Examine TWO ways in which the business might increase sales of this product.
Explain how . . . might . . .	Explain how . . . might develop a more effective workforce.
	Explain how . . . might improve customer service.

Examination examples

These examples are based on the Unit 1 paper 'Decoplates Ltd'
(see page 264)

2(a). Examine the possible reasons for the profit target being exceeded.

(10 marks)

2(b). Analyse TWO benefits to Kate and Ian of producing the more detailed Business Plan.

(8 marks)

AQA Examiner's tip

Don't forget that although these questions carry 4 Analysis marks each, you must show relevant subject understanding to gain Knowledge marks and your answer must use case study evidence too.

Assessment Objective 4 – 'Evaluation'

Table 35.9 *Achieving AO4 (Evaluation)*

What the examiner is looking for	Checklist of how to show the skill
■ Evidence that a judgement has been made in the answer or the conclusion to the answer.	■ Check that the question requires judgement – this depends on the command word. So much time is wasted by students making judgements or coming to conclusions when none was asked for!
■ Evidence that the arguments used have been weighed up and the most important one(s) identified.	
■ Evidence that a recommendation has been given, if asked for, which is supported by the arguments used.	■ Decide on what matters most in this case – and support your judgement.
■ Evidence that the case study business and the issues it faces have been built into the judgement and that evaluation is not just made up of pre-learned phrases such as 'on the other hand . . .'	■ Compare and contrast 'arguments for ' and arguments 'against' an issue.
	■ Conclude the answer with a clear conclusion and/or recommendation which is based on the arguments used.

Table 35.10 *Examples of command words testing AO4 (Evaluation)*

Command words/terms	Examples
Evaluate . . .	Evaluate the actions that CP Crisps might take to improve its profitability.
Discuss . . .	Discuss the case for this business introducing a system of quality assurance.
To what extent . . .	To what extent do you agree with Paul's view that drawing up cash flow forecasts is vital for the company's long run success?
Recommend . . . Justify your answer.	Recommend appropriate financial methods of motivation in this case. Justify your answer.

Examination examples

This example is taken from the Unit 1 paper 'Decoplates Ltd' (see page 264).

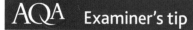

Examiner's tip

To gain access to high marks your answers to these questions must include judgement. This should balance the arguments for and against the point of the question and you must give a reasoned conclusion.

3(a). If you had been advising Ian and Kate, would you have recommended raising the extra £20,000 from other shareholders rather than a bank loan? Explain your answer.

15 marks

3(b). To what extent might the new studio's location determine the future success of the franchised outlet?

15 marks

Unit 2

These further examples are taken from this Unit 2 case study question. See if you can now identify which assessment objectives are being examined in each of the questions that follows.

Gardiner Stores plc

Gardiner Stores plc is one of the UK's smaller supermarket chains. The company operates 50 supermarkets mainly in the Midlands and the South East of England. It was founded in Birmingham and still owns undeveloped land in the city. The company sells only groceries and it aims to supply quality products and to provide excellent customer service. Gardiner Stores plc charges premium prices and expects each sale to make a contribution towards overheads.

The company's financial position is improving slowly. It has made small but rising profits over recent years, and its share price on the Stock Exchange has increased. The company gives the managers of each supermarket responsibility for setting and monitoring budgets for their stores. Gardiner Stores plc has pursued a policy of steady expansion, opening two or three stores every two years, and this has led to occasional cash flow problems.

In 2006, Gardiner Stores plc opened a new supermarket in Oxfordshire. The forecast and actual figures for the first two months of trading for this supermarket are shown in Table 10 below:

Table 15 *Actual and budgeted sales, costs and profits for Oxfordshire store*

	April		May	
	Budget £000s	Actual £000s	Budget £000s	Actual £000s
Sales revenue	966	y	957	967
Purchases of stock	606	630	611	615

Wages/salaries	241	250	245	249
Other costs	98	96	97	97
Total costs	x	976	953	961
Profit/(Loss)	21	(79)	4	z

Gardiner Stores plc is planning further expansion. Two new stores are planned in Surrey, a county with many wealthy consumers. The Human Resources director plans to recruit the new store managers and departmental managers internally from within other company stores. The Operations Director is determined to apply the latest I.T. to these new stores. He is planning to trial a Radio Frequency ID tagging system for all groceries. He is convinced that this will be the key factor in the company maintaining its reputation for excellent customer service. He told his staff that 'Buying the latest I.T. equipment is the most important operational issue for Gardiner Stores plc'.

1(a). i) Calculate the value of Gardiner Stores plc's BUDGETED total costs and ACTUAL sales revenue for April 2008.

(2 marks)

ii) Calculate the company's total profit variance for the Oxfordshire store for the two month period, April–May 2008. Show your workings. State whether this variance is adverse or favourable.

(6 marks)

AQA Examiner's tip

Examiner's mark scheme: 1 mark for each correct answer (*budgeted* and *actual*).

Examiner's mark scheme: 2 marks for Knowledge; 4 marks for Application if calculation is correct plus correct adverse/favourable statement.

2(b). Analyse TWO advantages to Gardiner Stores plc of using internal recruitment to appoint new store managers.

(8 marks)

AQA Examiner's tip

Examiner's mark scheme: 1 mark for Knowledge; 1 mark for Application; 2 marks for Analysis – for explaining EACH advantage.

2(c). To what extent do you agree with Chris that, 'Buying the latest I.T. equipment is the most important operational issue . . .' for this business?

(13 marks)

2(d). Evaluate the actions that Gardiner Stores plc might take to improve its profitability.

(13 marks)

AQA Examiner's tip

Examiner's mark scheme for c) and d): 3 marks for Knowledge; 2 marks for Application; 3 marks for Analysis; 5 marks for Evaluation.

Examination skills – final advice

1 Read the case study carefully.

2 Identify the key command word in each question.

3 Define/explain the key business term in each question no matter what the command word – knowledge marks are awarded for this in all questions.

4 Allocate time carefully between each question – after reading the case study material you will have around '1 minute per mark' to spend on each question.

5 Do not waste time on unnecessary analysis or evaluation if the command words do not require these skills.

6 Write in full sentences.

7 Use separate paragraphs for each separate point being made.

8 Show all numerical working and lay this out as clearly as you can – marks can still be awarded for incorrect results if the working has some logic to it.

Index